The Study of Religion

This collection illustrates the spectrum of ideas that people throughout history have had when considering how to understand and study religion. The editors present a selection of key writings that reflect a broad range of voices on the nature and practice of the discipline. Religious studies draws on work by anthropologists, sociologists, philosophers, theologians, and others, and this has had a notable impact on our understanding of the concept of religion, of particular religious ideas, and on how religion should be studied. *The Study of Religion: A Reader* contains both classic and contemporary perspectives, including material from non-Western traditions. It provides students of religion with an understanding of how the discipline developed, some of the current issues and lines of thought, as well as future prospects.

John S. Harding received his PhD in Religious Studies from the University of Pennsylvania. He is Associate Professor and Chair of the Religious Studies Department at the University of Lethbridge in Alberta, Canada. His books include *Introduction to the Study of Religion* with Hillary P. Rodrigues (2008), *Wild Geese: Buddhism in Canada* with Victor Sogen Hori and Alexander Soucy (2010), and *Studying Buddhism in Practice* (2011).

Hillary P. Rodrigues received his PhD in Religious Studies from McMaster University. He is Professor of Religious Studies at the University of Lethbridge in Alberta, Canada, where he has been honored with a Distinguished Teaching Award. His books include *Introducing Hinduism* (2006), *Introduction to the Study of Religion* with John S. Harding (2008), and *Studying Hinduism in Practice* (2011).

To scholars of religious studies, our own teachers and colleagues.

The Study of Religion

A Reader

Edited by
John S. Harding and Hillary P. Rodrigues

LONDON AND NEW YORK

First published in 2014
by Routledge
2 Park Square, Milton Park, Abingdon, Oxon OX14 4RN

Simultaneously published in the USA and Canada
by Routledge
711 Third Avenue, New York, NY 10017

Routledge is an imprint of the Taylor & Francis Group, an informa business

British Library Cataloguing in Publication Data
A catalogue record for this book is available from the British Library

Library of Congress Cataloging in Publication Data
The study of religion : a reader / edited by John S. Harding and Hillary P. Rodrigues.
pages cm
Includes index.
1. Religion. 2. Religions. I. Harding, John S., 1971-, editor of compilation.
BL41.S785 2013
200--dc23
2013007888

ISBN: 978-0-415-49586-8 (hbk)
ISBN: 978-0-415-49587-5 (pbk)

Typeset in Baskerville
By Taylor & Francis Books

Contents

B. Contemporary Social Scientific Perspectives (Sociological and Anthropological)

Perspectives on Myth and Ritual

Perspectives on Symbol and Cultural Construction of Religion

Analysis of Symbols

C. Contemporary Phenomenological and Psychological Perspectives

PART 4
The Discipline: Contemporary Practices and Positions   337

A. Critical Stance for Secular Study of Religion

B. Positions and Practices in the Discipline

PART 5
Religious Studies: Prescriptions and Prospects   441

A. Disciplinary Boundaries

B. Religious Studies in the Academy

Acknowledgements

We would like to express our appreciation for the contributions of many people who have shaped, encouraged, and constructively critiqued this edited volume. We appreciate the scholars whose work appears among the selections in this volume and the scholars who have shaped the field and expressed enthusiasm for this project but do not have selections in the final configuration of our anthology. We extend special gratitude to Robert Bellah, Sam Gill, Wendy Doniger, Judith Plaskow, John Hick, Seyyed Nasr, P. Pratap Kumar, John Makransky, Talal Asad, Justin Barrett, Daniel Dennett, Jacques Berlinerblau, Huston Smith, Thomas Tweed, Rodney Stark, William Paden, Leila Ahmed, Rita Gross, Donald Wiebe, Frank Reynolds, Gregory Alles, and J. Z. Smith for their communications and permissions to include their specific selections. In many cases these articles represent their thought at particular phases in their careers, or were produced in particular contexts, and by no means represent the full compass of their work or ideas on the notion of religion or its academic study.

We owe a debt of thanks to the anonymous reviewers, who read drafts of the manuscript and improved it through their discerning comments. In addition to encouragement and suggestions from anonymous reviewers, we have received constructive comments from various scholars and students including Michel Desjardins at Wilfrid Laurier University and the students in his 2009 comprehensive seminar (RE 693), who provided gratifyingly positive reviews of our *Introduction to the Study of Religion* and encouraged our plans to follow that manuscript with this edited anthology. Similarly, students in our Fall 2010 and 2012 Concepts and Methods capstone seminars at the University of Lethbridge engaged with all these entries in draft form and provided comments. Additionally, our colleagues in the Department of Religious Studies, Jim Linville, Atif Khalil and Tom Robinson, suggested selections to enrich and diversify this volume.

The development of religious studies, and our understanding of it, have benefited from seminal figures and schools of thought. We especially wish to thank faculty members with whom we did our graduate studies at McMaster University and the University of Pennsylvania. Although our PhD supervisors taught in different countries, each had studied under Eliade and his colleagues at the University of Chicago. However, as graduate students we were also mentored in theory and method by scholars from Harvard, Princeton, Yale, Münster, Columbia, Berkeley, and other institutions that have played key roles in shaping the discipline. We have had the good fortune of intellectually stimulating interactions with various figures, now deceased, such as John Hick and Ninian Smart, and a number of the other contributors in this reader. We want to acknowledge explicitly the aforementioned rich source of influences, and express our appreciation for the wide range of contributions these figures and schools have made to the discipline. We have tried to present accurately the diverse movements they represent, and modestly advance the legacy of earlier figures and schools without attempting to hold too closely to any one in particular.

This reader, like our *Introduction to the Study of Religion*, originated in conversations with Lesley Riddle, the acquisitions editor for Religion and Anthropology, at the 2005 International Association for the History of Religion meeting in Tokyo. Lesley's enthusiastic support – and patience – for this project were much appreciated. We extend our thanks to Katherine Ong as well, who patiently assisted this project in an ascending succession of roles. We also appreciated the work of others on and beyond the production staff at Routledge, including Ruth Berry, the production editor at Routledge; Tony Hirst, for his much appreciated copy editing contributions; and Bev Garnett, for her assistance tracking permissions and helping on many other fronts throughout the long duration of this project.

Every effort has been made to trace copyright holders and obtain permission to reproduce material. Any errors or omissions brought to the attention of the publisher will be remedied in future editions.

1. Sharpe, Eric J. "The Study of Religion in Historical Perspective" in *The Routledge Companion to the Study of Religion, second edition*, edited by John Hinnells. Abingdon: Routledge, 2009, pp. 1–38.
2. Smith, Wilfred Cantwell. "Methodology and the Study of Religion: Some Misgivings" in *Methodological Issues in Religious Studies*, edited by Robert D. Baird. Chico, CA: New Horizons Press, 1975, pp. 1–30. Courtesy of the University of Iowa.
3. Rodrigues, Hillary P. "Premises Concerning Religious Studies."
4. Plato. "Allegory of the Cave." From Book VII of *The Republic*, translated by Benjamin Jowett, 1871.
5. Kūkai. "The Difference between Exoteric and Esoteric Buddhism." From *Major Works of Kukai*, translated by Yoshita S. Hakeda. NY: Columbia University Press, 1972, pp. 151–57.
6. Paley, William. Extracts from *Natural Theology: or, Evidences of the Existence and Attributes of the Deity*. 12th edition. London: J. Faulder, 1809.
7. Feuerbach, Ludwig. Extracts from *The Essence of Christianity*, translated by Marian Evans. London: John Chapman, 1854.
8. Daly, Mary. "After the Death of God the Father." *Commonweal*. XCIV (March 12, 1971), pp. 7–11. Courtesy of Commonweal Foundation (www.commonwealmagazine.org).
9. Plaskow, Judith. "The Coming of Lilith: Towards a Feminist Theology." From *Womanspirit Rising: A Feminist Reader in Religion*, edited by Carol P. Christ and Judith Plaskow. New York: HarperCollins, 1979, pp. 198–209.
10. Malinowski, Bronislaw. "The Art of Magic and the Power of Faith." From *Magic, Science, and Religion and Other Essays*. Glencoe, IL: The Free Press, 1948, pp. 69–92.
11. Durkheim, Émile. "Definition of Religious Phenomena and of Religion." From *The Elementary Forms of the Religious Life*, translated by Joseph Ward Swain. London: George Allen & Unwin Ltd., 1915, pp. 23–47.
12. Weber, Max. "Asceticism and the Spirit of Capitalism." From *The Protestant Ethic and the Spirit of Capitalism*, translated by Talcott Parsons. London: George Allen & Unwin Ltd., 1930, pp. 102–25.
13. James, William. "Mysticism." Lectures XVI and XVII in *The Varieties of Religious Experience: A Study in Human Nature*. New York: Longmans, Green & Co., 1902, pp. 370–420.

14. Freud, Sigmund. *The Future of an Illusion*, translated by Gregory C. Richter. Calgary: Broadview Press, 2012. Extracts from pp. 80–95, 109–13.

15. Otto, Rudolph. "The Analysis of 'Mysterium'." From *The Idea of the Holy*, translated by John W. Harvey. London: Oxford University Press, 1923, pp. 25–30.

16. Eliade, Mircea. "Approximations: The Structure and Morphology of the Sacred." From *Patterns of Comparative Religion*, translated by Rosemary Sheed. Lincoln, NE: University of Nebraska Press, 1996. Extracts from pp. 1–37.

17. Hick, John. "On Doing Philosophy of Religion." 2001. Courtesy of John Hick.

18. Nasr, Seyyed Hossein. "Islam and the Encounter of Religions." From *Sufi Essays*. London: George Allen & Unwin Ltd., 1972, pp. 123–51. Courtesy of Seyyed Hossein Nasr.

19. Kumar, Pratap P. "Insiders and Outsiders: Studying Hinduism Non-Religiously?" in *Introducing Religion: Essays in Honor of Jonathan Z. Smith*, edited by Willi Braun and Russell T. McCutcheon. London: Equinox, 2008, pp. 192–207.

20. Makransky, John. "Contemporary Academic Buddhist Theology: Its Emergence and Rationale" in *Buddhist Theology: Critical Reflections by Contemporary Buddhist Scholars*, edited by Roger R. Jackson and John J. Makransky. London: RoutledgeCurzon, 2000, pp. 14–21.

21. Doniger O'Flaherty, Wendy. "Other Scholars' Myths: The Hunter and the Sage." From *Other People's Myths: The Cave of Echoes*. New York: Macmillan, 1988, pp. 7–24. Courtesy of Wendy Doniger.

22. Turner, Victor W. "Liminality and Communitas." From *The Ritual Process: Structure and Anti-Structure*. New York: Aldine de Gruyter, 1969. Extracts from pp. 94–139. Courtesy of Transaction Publishers.

23. Bell, Catherine. "Ritual Reification." From *Ritual Perspectives and Dimensions*. Oxford: Oxford University Press, 1997, pp. 253–68.

24. Asad, Talal. "The Construction of Religion as an Anthropological Category." From *Genealogies of Religion: Discipline and Reasons of Power in Christianity and Islam*. Baltimore, MD: Johns Hopkins University Press, 1993. Extracts from pp. 27–54.

25. Bellah, Robert N. "Civil Religion in America." *Daedalus* (Journal of the American Academy of Arts and Sciences). 96:1 (Winter 1967), pp. 1–21. Courtesy of MIT Press Journals.

26. Douglas, Mary. "The Abominations of Leviticus." From *Purity and Danger: An Analysis of the Concepts of Pollution and Taboo*. London: Routledge and Kegan Paul, 1966, pp. 41–57.

27. Gill, Sam. "Beauty and the Drainpipe: Art and Symbolism in Religion." From *Beyond 'The Primitive': The Religions of Nonliterate Peoples*. Englewood Cliffs, NJ: Prentice Hall, 1982, pp. 28–37. Courtesy of Pearson Education.

28. Smart, Ninian. "The Principles and Meaning of the Study of Religion." From *Concept and Empathy: Essays in the Study of Religion*, edited by Donald Wiebe. New York: New York University Press, 1986, pp. 195–206.

29. Barrett, Justin L. "Cognitive Science of Religion: What Is It and Why Is It?" *Religion Compass*. 1: 6 (Nov. 2007), pp. 768–86. Courtesy of Wiley-Blackwell.

30. Dennett, Daniel C. "Breaking Which Spell?" From *Breaking the Spell: Religion as a Natural Phenomenon*. New York: Penguin Books, 2007, pp. 3–28.

31. Berlinerblau, Jacques. "Introduction: Secularists and the Not Godless World." From *The Secular Bible: Why Nonbelievers Must Take Religion Seriously*. New York: Cambridge University Press, 2005, pp. 1–13.

32. Smith, Huston. "Who's Right about Reality: Traditionalists, Modernists, or the Postmoderns?" From *Why Religion Matters*. New York: HarperCollins, 2001, pp. 11–22.

33. Tweed, Thomas A. "Who Is a Buddhist? Night-Stand Buddhists and Other Creatures" in *Westward Dharma: Buddhism Beyond Asia*, edited by Charles S. Prebish and Martin Baumann. Berkeley, CA: University of California Press, 2002, pp. 17–33.

34. Stark, Rodney. "Rationality" in *Guide to the Study of Religion*, edited by Willi Braun and Russell T. McCutcheon. London: Continuum, 2000, pp. 239–58.

35. Paden, William E. "World" in *Guide to the Study of Religion*, edited by Willi Braun and Russell T. McCutcheon. London: Continuum, 2000, pp. 334–49.

36. Ahmed, Leila. "Conclusion." From *Women and Gender in Islam: Historical Roots of a Modern Debate*. New Haven, CT: Yale University Press, 1992, pp. 235–48.

37. Gross, Rita M. "Defining Feminism, Religion, and the Study of Religion." From *Feminism and Religion: An Introduction*. Boston: Beacon Press, 1996. Extracts from pp. 5–28.

38. Wiebe, Donald. "The Failure of Nerve in the Academic Study of Religion". From *The Politics of Religious Studies: The Continuing Conflict with Theology in the Academy*. New York: St. Martins Press, 1999, pp. 141–62. Courtesy of Palgrave Macmillan.

39. Smith, Jonathan Z. "'Religion' and 'Religious Studies': No Difference at All." *Soundings: An Interdisciplinary Journal*. LXXI (1988), pp. 231–44. Courtesy of Pennsylvania State University Press.

40. Reynolds, Frank E. "Teaching Buddhism in the Postmodern University: Understanding, Critique, Evaluation" in *Teaching Buddhism in the West: From the Wheel to the Web*, edited by Victor Sōgen Hori, Richard P. Hayes and J. Mark Shields. London: RoutledgeCurzon, 2002, pp. 3–16.

41. Alles, Gregory D. "Afterword: Toward a Global Vision of Religious Studies" in *Religious Studies: A Global View*, edited by Gregory D. Alles. Abingdon: Routledge, 2008, pp. 301–22.

Introduction

This book is a collection of articles or excerpts from longer writings that illustrate the spectrum of ideas that people throughout history have had when reflecting upon religion and how it should be understood and studied. The selections are not primarily about specific religious traditions, such as Christianity or Buddhism, but about religion in general. People have likely speculated on the nature of their beliefs and activities – including those we now designate as religious ones – since human beings began ruminating on what they think and do. Most people have opinions about religion, often based on a relatively narrow and superficial understanding of what it is, generally drawn from the experience of the faiths they might personally profess. That, too, is likely an enduring tendency. However, the attempt to understand religion broadly, systematically, and methodically is a relatively recent phenomenon, developing primarily in the post-Enlightenment period.

Nowadays, this work is most formally conducted within the purview of the discipline of religious studies, which developed less than a century ago. Of course, theories about the origin of religion, why it appeals to human beings, how it functions in society, and so on, as well as prescribed methods for how it should best be studied, derive from a wide assortment of disciplines. Many of these are older than the discipline of religious studies and are characterized by their specific methodologies or objects of study. Thus anthropologists, sociologists, psychologists, and historians are among those who have contributed to our understanding. Some people argue that religious studies should not be called a discipline, because it does not have a distinctive methodology. The distinctive methodology for anthropologists is participant observation while conducting fieldwork, and sociologists often use the quantitative statistical analysis of surveys. Religious studies scholars, however, draw on a variety of methods, employing whichever is regarded as well-suited to the particular feature of religion under examination. Thus textual analytic techniques are appropriate when examining scripture, whereas participant observation and fieldwork seem useful when studying rituals.

Religion continues to be a somewhat enigmatic category despite the variety of writings produced in the last century and a half directed at explaining its nature. There is no universally acceptable definition for what it is, and almost all of the selections in this volume provide only partial insights into the phenomenon. Some writings are highly critical of religion, while others see it as a valuable dimension of the human condition. Along with the discerning perspectives that each selection provides, many have been criticized for what they have ignored or misunderstood about religion. Our choices for inclusion in this volume, then, are not based on each selection being perfectly correct and complete. Were we to use such criteria, we would have had no selections. On the contrary, the tracts we include represent strong strands of discourse, vibrant streams in the history of ideas about religion that have existed or continue to exist. We assert that a better understanding of religion can be attained by reading widely, with an alert and critical faculty analyzing what influential thinkers have had to say about religion. From this broad-based exposure to ideas, one will be better equipped to understand the human religious response in its many forms and facets.

There are excellent resources that illustrate and promote reflection about religion. However, articles by scholars for other scholars and advanced graduate students are better represented in this literature than texts that can help launch one's entry into this academic exploration of the nature of religion. The idea of compiling a reader in religious studies sprang up at the same time that we envisioned writing an introductory text on theory and practice in the discipline. Over the decades that we had collectively taught courses on concepts and method in religious studies, we had experimented with many of the books that were then currently available and found them all to be lacking in certain crucial ways. In particular, they often assumed too much background theoretical knowledge on the part of students. In addition, readers contained too many pieces that were beyond the ready grasp of our students. In some cases, this was due to theoretical orientations that assumed command of theorists and ideas unfamiliar to many undergraduates as well as specialized vocabulary ranging from unnecessary jargon to quite useful terms worth students' efforts to gain mastery. When we completed the first edition of *Introduction to the Study of Religion* (Routledge, 2009), we recognized that we had managed to write a textbook that came closest to our needs and those of our students. Naturally, we have been delighted to hear that the book has been appreciated by colleagues who have adopted it for use in their courses. With the feedback that we have received and continue to receive from them we hope to refine that book, so that the second edition is even better suited to the needs of instructors and students. It is in the same spirit that we have put together *The Study of Religion: A Reader*.

Of course, when we began this project, our ambitions were lofty. We imagined compiling a text that contained selections from the great religious traditions as well as intellectual ruminations on them. We wanted to include something by virtually all of the figures who have had something influential to say about religion. We quickly comprehended how some readers grow voluminous in size, hefty in price, and go half unused by students and instructors. Fortunately, budgetary constraints and concerns about volume size forced us to rein ourselves in and winnow our wishlist to something close to its present configuration. We make no pretensions to have exhaustively covered all of the pertinent thinkers or issues in the discipline of religious studies, and quite frankly would have liked to include a seminal piece or two by a few more thinkers. However, we can assert from experience that this collection may be effectively used in its entirety (even with some supplementary readings) in an upper-level seminar on theory and method in religious studies, along with a suitable introductory textbook on the subject, such as our own.

The *Reader* could complement most of the available introductory textbooks on the subject; it is not designed as a substitute for a textbook and the labors of a competent instructor. We have ensured that our anthology does not rely on familiarity with our introductory textbook, although it is particularly suitable in content, approach, and structure. Our *Introduction to the Study of Religion* contains useful information on the history of the discipline, summarizes the contributions by seminal thinkers within various approaches, and includes other helpful features, such as an extensive time-line and a glossary of common religious studies terminology. Moreover, this reader is structured in some measure along the lines of our introductory text. In part, this is because we had put some effort into thinking about complementary categories to group together when writing that book. As a result, the *Reader* is an effective companion to *Introduction to the Study of Religion*, but it also complements other religious studies theory and methods texts, which almost certainly will reference many of the selections contained in this anthology. The selections here in the *Reader* are not prefaced with lengthy introductions, which would only reiterate what we have already said in the introductory text and other texts likely will have covered as well. Rather, our method is to present the article after a terse introduction, so that the reader may engage with the piece on its own terms. We then append some questions to aid in reviewing major themes within the article, and others as springboards for discussion.

We imagine that the *Reader* may also be used in tandem with more advanced texts than our primer or other introductory textbooks mentioned above. This is because many of the selections contained here are seminal contributions by influential authors, whose ideas may be plumbed in far greater depth than we intended in our introductory text. We envision *The Study of Religion: A Reader* as something that novice students might purchase along with *Introduction to the Study of Religion* in an early religious studies course. However, although one should probably hang onto both texts through the whole of one's formal education in religious studies, the *Reader* in particular is likely to continue to be useful near the end of one's undergraduate studies, as well as within a graduate milieu. For while advanced students may have already absorbed what we had to say in our few pages on William James or Émile Durkheim's views on religion in the *Introduction to the Study of Religion* text, one may nevertheless continue to profitably reread the selections by those authors contained in the *Reader* well into graduate school and beyond. If one continues beyond an initial religious studies theory and method course at the undergraduate level, the introductory text may then serve primarily as a handy reference and supplement to a more substantial text about theoretical approaches. However, in our experience, both the *Introduction* and the *Reader* work well at all levels of undergraduate study, and may continue to be mined effectively throughout one's formal education.

This reader is distinctive, differentiating itself from other such anthologies in notable ways. As previously mentioned, it does not suffer from a surfeit of readings, and may be used in its entirety in a single semester. While some readers tend to focus on classical writings on religion, and others mostly on essays by contemporary scholars, this reader contains both types of selections, although the emphasis is upon the latter. Contemporary theorists tend to write for their peers, namely religious studies scholars, with the reasonable assumption that their audience members have already read foundational theorists such as Max Weber or Mircea Eliade. However, our experience revealed that such articles by contemporary scholars were often difficult for our students, who, unlike mature scholars, typically had not been exposed to the actual writings of the foundational theorists. We feel it is essential to expose students first hand to some of those significant foundational theorists or theories, so that they may make their own appraisals of those figures and their thoughts, before going on to read current thinkers and their critical analyses. There is much of value in the older strata of writings, which should not simply be ignored because they had demonstrable shortcomings. Moreover, contemporary theorizing is made more accessible when one has read classical thought, because there are frequent references to the works of predecessors, which are often the subjects of critique.

Another distinctive feature of this collection is that it strives to move beyond an overly Western-centric theoretical framework. It does not do so by artificially attempting to equalize East–West contributions, because the bulk of theorizing within the discipline of religious studies has historically emerged from the West. However, where possible, we have attempted to include writings by thinkers from non-Western religious traditions (e.g., Kūkai), or include examples of theorizing that utilize non-Western traditions as their sources. Malinowski, Durkheim, and Gill, for example, derive their ideas from aboriginal religious beliefs and practices. Kumar and Doniger use Hinduism as a springboard, while Makransky, Tweed, and Reynolds utilize Buddhism. The diversity of religious traditions in this collection extends to included essays with Islamic themes (e.g., Nasr and Ahmed), as well as those focused on themes from the Judeo-Christian tradition (e.g., Paley, Feuerbach, Daly, Asad, Douglas, and Berlinerblau) and essays that promote the merit of comparative approaches (e.g., James, Otto, Eliade, and Smart).

While a succinct articulation of one of the authors' desiderata concerning the practice of religious studies is found in the contribution by Hillary Rodrigues, this collection includes a broad spectrum of disparate voices on the nature and practice of the discipline. We demonstrate a post-modern orientation in the compilation of the *Reader*, implicitly holding that exposure to a wide variety of lenses through which religion has been viewed might provide readers with a superior understanding of the contours of the subject matter. And while the views expressed in these selections may sound prescriptive and perhaps convincing, their authoritative tone only illustrates the mode in which they were written. They do not embody definitive and "correct" views about what religion is and how it should be studied. Put differently, they were not included in the *Reader* because they encapsulate the "proper way" in which religion should be understood and studied. Instead they offer the student fodder for analysis. They need to be intellectually dissected, scrutinized, appraised, and evaluated. Working through the readings contained in this anthology, and applying one's own critical analytic faculties to their content, is a crucial feature of what the discipline of religious studies actually entails. The academic study of religion is not merely grounded on learning about the history, beliefs, and practices of various people within specific religious traditions. One does not only study about Christianity, Hinduism, Daoism, and so on. Religious studies involves thinking about the ideas found within diverse traditions synthetically and thematically, discerning patterns and processes that transcend individual traditions, and then speculating on the nature of religion as a whole. However, rather than reinvent the wheel, it is advantageous to examine what our predecessors and contemporaries have had to say, and ascertain what we can extract from their thoughts that might further our own understanding.

The *Reader* begins with some selections orienting one to general issues in religious studies. While these selections could easily have been placed at the end, where contemporary voices reflecting the most nuanced or comprehensive perspectives are found, we chose to place these at the very beginning. They immediately oblige one to recognize that each selection that is to follow in the anthology represents a particular perspective – either articulating a view that was already in wide circulation, or spearheading an influential line of thought or interpretive orientation. Each of these contributions derives from a specific period of history with its own cultural and social orientations; each communicates a certain disciplinary focus and often assigns to religion a particular value. In other words, each of the contributions in this anthology is bound by the historical, social, cultural, and other contexts within which it was produced. It is crucial that one attempt to recognize these contextual factors, and then ascertain to what extent the perspective or viewpoint that is expressed is informative and useful in furthering one's own understanding of religion.

Part 1 of the *Reader* offers introductory selections, namely, the historical overview by Eric Sharpe, the critique of methodology by W. C. Smith, and some key disciplinary prescriptions by Hillary Rodrigues. It is followed by **Part 2**, which contains classic theorists or foundational writings. The Greek philosophical tradition is represented by Plato's "Allegory of the

Cave," which addresses the notion of revelatory experience, while Kūkai's differentiation between exoteric and esoteric Buddhism(s) serves as an example of Eastern ruminations on distinctions within religious traditions. It was only after the Age of Enlightenment that the academic study of religion began to take root, and early philosophical voices from the nineteenth century are represented in the selections by William Paley and Ludwig Feuerbach. Paley's is the classic argument from design for the existence of God, while Feuerbach uses rationality to critique the human religious impulse as naïve projection.

One might be surprised to see selections by Mary Daly and Judith Plaskow in this section, especially since Plaskow is still writing, but both are matriarchs within feminist studies of religion. Both pieces are theological in nature. They are included here because – and this is a crucial point – the *Reader* does not only contain works that demonstrate the ideal exercise of the academic study of religion or the authors' most recent work. Rather, the *Reader* includes works that blur the distinctions between philosophy, theology, the secular academic study of religion, and other related disciplines. By reading at the margins, or even in areas well beyond the margins, we hope that readers will learn to discern and appreciate the differences between these areas of study. The selection by Daly is culled from one of her earlier contributions, and lacks the radical tone and linguistic tropes (Daly-isms) that characterized her later work. Plaskow's piece, by contrast, is radical feminist theology, illustrating an attempt to mold religious thought through myth-making, for instance, to serve a particular agenda. Plaskow's subsequent work is more balanced in nature, and more closely aligned with the religious studies approach than is evident in this early work.

Scientifically aligned approaches to the study of religion that strove for objectivity emerged in the works of social scientists. We include selections from Malinowski, Durkheim, and Weber in this category. Bronislaw Malinowski, who is regarded as the father of modern anthropology, offers a characterization of magic, which he attempts to distinguish from religion. The piece by Émile Durkheim, the father of modern sociology, presents his definition of religion, and the categories of sacred and profane. Max Weber's piece is taken from his seminal study of the relationship between Protestant values and the capitalist economic agenda. These social scientific approaches stand in contrast with the phenomenologists and psychologists included here. Not all the early psychologists took a sympathetic approach to religious belief. The selection from Freud illustrates this line of psychological analysis of the origin and role of religion. However, William James takes religion and the individual's religious experience more seriously on its own terms. The piece by James is culled from the chapter on mysticism in his classic study, *The Varieties of Religious Experience*. James concedes the possibility of true religion arising from a profound mystical experience, a subjective state which does not yield adequately to objective study and thus does not refute or compel belief for those lacking that experience. The selection from Rudolph Otto's influential *The Idea of the Holy* reiterates this theme of experience, but situates its origin in some sacred reality that exists beyond the individual. Mircea Eliade, one of the giants in the formative decades of the scholarly study of religion, also utilizes the notion of sacrality, its origins and manifestations, as a pivotal feature for classification. His work points to patterns and themes that might provide a structure and framework for the transcultural, comparative study of religious phenomena.

Part 3 of the *Reader* is dedicated to contemporary voices that correlate with the early, classic, or foundational writings presented in Part 2. Thus the pieces by Hick and Nasr are examples purporting the merits and methods of philosophical and confessional stances in the study of religions. In contrast to these, Pratap Kumar is more firmly within the norms of a secular scholarly study of religion in his examination of the stances of believers versus non-believers engaged in the study of religious traditions. John Makransky, however, works to carve out a space in between these positions by arguing that religious studies and theology need not be so mutually exclusive. He acknowledges that the bracketing of normative judgments created room for the study of non-Christian religions, but he asserts that at the same time this has constrained scholars' ability to engage with these traditions' values due to what he suggests are outdated notions of a "value neutral" position. The part (3b) on contemporary social scientific perspectives in the study of religion is notably large. This is because the social sciences continue to contribute much towards our understanding of religion, particularly through their examinations of myths, rituals, and symbols in other societies and cultures. Wendy Doniger O'Flaherty, for example, uses an Indian myth as an interpretive lens through which to explore the differences between religious insiders and scholars of religion. The selections by Victor Turner and Catherine Bell deal with ritual. Turner's piece presents his highly influential theory of liminality, which although derived from his studies of rites of passage in tribal African society, has proved to be applicable in a wide range of contexts, including social movements and religious rites such as pilgrimage. Catherine Bell's chapter addresses the theme of intellectual categorization, demonstrating how "ritual" is a conceptual category that can be extended beyond utilitarian academic and linguistic functions to garner a life of its own. Thus, although the piece is concerned with the concept of ritual, it actually offers a post-modern analysis of the limitations of linguistic categorization in academic discourse.

Talal Asad's article critiques attempts to construct universal definitions of religion, such as the seminal attempt made by Clifford Geertz in his "Religion as a Cultural System." Asad argues that any religious configuration cannot be separated from its particular historical contexts and the structures of power within which it is embedded. Robert Bellah's piece pushes the margins of what circumscribes the boundaries of religion, by arguing that a civil religion exists in America that in compelling ways resembles other religious traditions, and which is therefore worthy of similar attention by scholars of religion. While Asad and Bellah look at symbolic forms, rituals, political structures, and the like in their examination of how societies and cultures construct religion, Mary Douglas and Sam Gill focus on symbols differently in their contributions. Although renowned for her contributions to anthropological theory, Douglas offers a compelling analysis of the dietary laws presented in a Judeo-Christian scripture, the Book of Leviticus. Applying structural analysis and a sort of textual anthropology, she offers a rationale for the rules concerning religious dietary prohibitions and permissions. Gill explores how "art" objects in non-literate societies may have symbolic significance derived more from their cultural and religious contexts than from their aesthetic appeal.

To round out Part 3, we include two representative voices of phenomenological and psychological approaches, Ninian Smart and Justin Barrett, respectively. Smart offers an influential set of categories or dimensions as well as a list of approaches through which religion may and should be studied. His inclusion of the experiential dimension and call for imaginative participation allows him to be classified as sympathetic to the phenomenological approach, which requires taking into consideration believers' accounts of their own worldviews and experiences. Barrett's article is a walkthrough of the study of religious belief from the perspective of cognitive psychology, or the cognitive science of religion. The cognitive science of religion seeks to explain how, for instance, evolutionary mind–brain functional developments in all human beings may naturally lead to the construction of religious ideas and practices. This relatively new psychological approach emphasizes methods and techniques from natural sciences, and has garnered significant attention and funding in recent years.

In **Parts 4 and 5** we move away from efforts to parallel contemporary perspectives with classic or foundational ones, and look directly at current lines of thought on religion and issues that engage scholars and students in the field. In **Part 4** Daniel Dennett, one of the more influential voices in the philosophy of the cognitive sciences and evolutionary biology, offers an argument for religion as a natural outgrowth of human evolutionary development. Jacques Berlinerblau presents a case for a scrupulously secular reading of the Bible (and by extension all other religious texts). Both scholars strive to assert that religion and religious phenomena should be studied with a rigorously secular approach, rather than being regarded as privileged or sacrosanct. Huston Smith, author of one of the most influential early introductory textbooks on world religions, evaluates the distinctions among traditional, modern, and post-modern understandings of reality. Thomas Tweed illustrates the problems faced in trying to situate persons within the rubric of a particular tradition – in his example, Buddhism – and offers some criteria for how one might place persons within a category and rationales for such a choice.

Rodney Stark's essay presents a summary of arguments towards a theory of religion as an intrinsically rational human behavior, where in past studies it has been characterized as irrational and in tension with rational thought and action. William Paden explores how the notion of a "world" can be usefully applied to the study of religious systems. Leila Ahmed's work is included in this collection for various reasons. It is the conclusion of her study of women and gender in Islam, and serves as an example of feminist scholarship in action. Moreover, it offers prescriptions on how the feminist agenda in the study of religion may be furthered. The essay reads well in tandem with the selection by Rita Gross, which offers clear prescriptions on the scholarly study of religion, and in particular how a feminist orientation may be situated within the discipline, without breaching such parameters as the preference for objectivity.

Part 5 presents selections that examine the current state of the discipline, some of its challenges, and its prospects. Donald Wiebe's piece contains an argument that religious studies still tends to fail in its capacity to break free from its theologically based origins, and fully embrace a secular and objectively oriented stance in its approach. J. Z. Smith problematizes the terms "religion" and "religious studies," provocatively arguing that they share certain characteristics, and, among other prescriptions, proposing that the category of religion is a creation of religious studies scholars. Frank Reynolds, using the example of Buddhism, explores the challenges entailed in teaching about religious traditions at university, where post-modernist sensibilities are normative, and proposes that such instruction be serviceably set within the broad framework of liberal education. The collection ends with a chapter by Gregory Alles, who speculates on the issues, challenges, and impact of the discipline from a global perspective. We thought it fitting to include such a selection in a reader designed for students of the discipline, because it may provide fuel for discussions that attempt to appraise religious studies holistically and envision its development into the future with the broadest sensibilities.

PART 1

The Discipline: Its History and Fundamental Perspectives

1 The Study of Religion in Historical Perspective

Eric J. Sharpe

Eric John Sharpe (1933–2000) was born in Manchester, England, and received his doctorate in religious studies and theology from the University of Uppsala, Sweden. He researched on Christian–Hindu interactions during the last two centuries, and made contributions to the study of new religious movements. During his career he taught at the universities of Lancaster, Manchester, and Sydney. He is also well known for his survey of English translations of the Hindu scripture, the *Bhagavad-Gita*, and for his work on methodology and the historical development of the discipline of religious studies. In the selection that follows, Sharpe provides a succinct overview of the historical development of the discipline of religious studies from its earliest practitioners to its current orientations.

Motive, Material, Method

The academic study of anything requires that those involved should consider at least three questions: why, what and how? The first demands that we examine our *motive*; the second makes us consider our *material* – what do we accept as admissible evidence? The third, and most difficult, level of inquiry is concerned with *method*: how do we deal with the material we have at hand? How do we organise it, and with what end in view ("motive" again)? A century ago, it was not uncommon to speak in this connection of "the science of religion" (German: *Religionswissenschaft*) – a form of words no longer current in English. What has been identified as the foundation document carried the title *Introduction to the Science of Religion* (Friedrich Max Müller 1873). According to Müller, such a science of religion was to be "based on an impartial and truly scientific comparison of all, or at all events, of the most important religions of mankind" (1873: 34). It was, then, to be impartial and scientific by the standards of the age and based on the best material available at the time.

The history of the study of religion since the Enlightenment can never be told in full. There is simply too much of it, and it is subdivided in too many ways: by period, by geographical and cultural area and by the "disciplines" cherished by most academics. The one history can be described as being made up of many smaller histories – for instance the history of the study of everything from Animism and Anabaptism to Zoroastrianism and Zen Buddhism. The field may be divided by subject matter; along national lines; depending on where in the world the tradition of study has been pursued; in relation to events in world and local history; and so on, virtually *ad infinitum*. No one can cover the whole of the area.

The words "the study of religion" obviously convey different meanings to different people. For most of human history and in most cultures, they would have conveyed no meaning at all. To "study" in the sense of standing back to take a coolly uncommitted view of anything, was not unknown in the ancient world, but it was uncommon, being cultivated by "philosophers" – lovers of wisdom – but hardly elsewhere. Similarly, where what we call "religion" is concerned: gods, goddesses, spirits, demons, ghosts and the rest, people knew and generally respected them (along with what it was hoped was the right way to please, or at least not to offend them); "religion" they did not.

These supernatural beings – who were they? In the ancient world, they were envisaged in human terms: a hierarchy reaching all the way from a royal family down through nobles and artisans to mischief-makers: imps and demons of the sort who spread disease and curdle milk. There were the ghosts of the departed, still in many ways close at hand and with their remains buried nearby. (The unburied tended to turn into peculiarly nasty ghosts.) Sun, moon and stars watched; storms rampaged; forests and mountains brooded; powerful animals marked out their territories. "Power" was perhaps the key to the world as archaic man saw it – power of heat over cold, light over darkness, life over death – and those who knew how to control that power became themselves powerful.

The process must have begun at some point in time, somewhere in the world, but we have no way of knowing when or where that point might have been (absolute origins of anything are always out of reach). When our records, such as they are, begin – numerical dates are worse than useless in such matters – we are already able to sense the presence of something or someone like a proto-shaman: at one and the same time a ruler and a servant of the spirits, a controller of rituals and an interpreter of laws and customs. From what we know of later shamanism, it would seem that such persons were servants of their respective societies by virtue of their knowledge of the spirit-world and their ability to establish and maintain contact with it. Shamanism "proper" belongs in the context of hunter-gatherer societies, and as the structure of human societies changed, so too did the function of mediation between the tangible, everyday world and the unseen forces that were believed to control it.

The shaman was chosen and prepared for his (or in some cases, her) work, by aptitude, discipline and application, and by initiation – a pattern that survived most tenaciously in the trade guilds and those of the learned professions, which (untypically in the modern West) treasured their own past. In more complex societies – that of the agriculturalists and fisherfolk in their settled environments, that of the city-dwellers within their walls, and so on down to our own day and its bizarre preoccupation with economics – the functions of the shaman (serving the people by mediating between one order of being and another) have multiplied and diversified in an intriguing way.

This is not to say that the Pope or the Archbishop of Canterbury, or for that matter the Chief Rabbi or the Dalai Lama, or the Shankaracharya of Puri, are cryptoshamans: merely that their training on the one hand and their functions on the other, are of a kind one recognises. (How well or how indifferently individuals may fill high offices has no bearing on the question.) Each has a position in an ongoing tradition, and is responsible for its continuation. Here we have the first, and the dominant, sense in which what we call "the study of religion" functions. It is appropriate to call this a *discipline* in the strictest sense, an apprenticeship in which a pupil (*discipulus*) is taught by a master (*magister*) inside the bounds of a system, within the frontiers of which both knew precisely what was to be taught to whom, and why. Since the wellbeing of individuals and societies depended in large measure on the maintenance of what it is perfectly proper to call "law and order" much of what had to be learned was concerned with these concepts and their ramifications.

In many cultures, "law" (in Sanskrit, *dharma*, in Hebrew, *torah* and in Latin, *religio*, even the much misunderstood Australian Aboriginal word "dreaming") and "religion" are almost synonymous. What one supposes began as habit hardened first into custom and eventually into law, on the basis of which boundaries could be set up and wars fought. In the ancient world, no one expected laws, or religions, to be all of one kind. The "when in Rome … " principle was, and often still is, no more than common sense: deities, like humans and animals, were to some extent territorial, and to pay one's respects to a *genius loci* was no more than courtesy. Customs differed in much the same way as languages differed, and normally even the learned would know very little of what went on outside the family. "Study" was for the most part concerned only with the family's (tribe's, nation's) traditions, history, sacred places and the rituals associated with them. In time, as more of this material was committed to writing, the study of those writings assumed a central place in the student's apprenticeship: often through memorisation and constant repetition and chanting, in a setting in which the student's submissive obedience was simply taken for granted. This pattern of education is still operative today, though unevenly; generally speaking, Judaism, Islam, the ancient traditions of the East – varieties of Hinduism and Buddhism – have held fast to the method where instruction in the secular West has not.

What did the student make of other peoples' traditions, their deities, their rituals and their laws? In the ancient world, there were, roughly speaking, three alternatives: to ignore them altogether (the majority view), to observe them as curiosities, without taking them too seriously, and to condemn them as evil. Let us consider the second and third of these.

Greek and Roman "philosophers" and historians were in many cases intrigued by the customs of the various peoples they met around the Mediterranean and as far afield as northern Europe. Perhaps they did not take their own national myths and rituals too seriously. At all events, the Greek and Roman historiographers, beginning with Herodotus (died approx. 420 BCE) showed a certain amount of interest in other people's behaviour where gods and the like were concerned. Berosus and Manetho (both third century BCE) wrote about ancient Egypt and Mesopotamia, Herodotus having previously written about the Persians. In the second century BCE Pausanias compiled an extensive and invaluable account of rituals and places of worship in his native Greece. The Romans for their part made fewer contributions, though special mention may be made of the accounts of the customs of the Celtic and Germanic tribes contained in "war reports" like Caesar's *De bello Gallico* and Tacitus' *Germania*. Such writings as these (and there were many more) were compiled as information and entertainment, and to some extent propaganda: not as systematic accounts of anything. Tacitus "studied" Celtic and Germanic tribes because they were troublesome to the Roman legions, and that was all.

The Hebraic attitude to such things could not have been more different. Israel knew all about "the nations" and their deities, and trusted none of them. To the extent that other people's religion appears in the Hebrew Scriptures/Old Testament, it does so under a black cloud. Egypt and Mesopotamia – oppression. Canaan – apostasy. Persia – a brief glimpse of light. Rome – more oppression, this time apparently terminal, as the Temple was laid waste and the people scattered. Understanding? What was there to understand, except that the gods of the nations were impostors, small-time crooks, perhaps not without local influence, but entirely incapable of any act of creation. Least of all could they create a world, as Yahweh had done. They were mere "idols", man-made and powerless. It is all summed up in two verses, "For all the gods of the peoples are idols; but the Lord made the heavens" (Ps. 96:5); and "The gods who did not make the heavens and the earth shall perish from the earth and from under the heavens" (Jer. 10:11).

There was the additional frightening possibility that "idols" were nests of "evil spirits" – unseen vermin whose existence was never properly explained, but whose malevolence no one in the ancient world seriously [would] have doubted.

We find a partial relaxation of this uncompromising attitude in respect of the worship of natural phenomena – sun, moon and stars. These were at least God's creations, and not man-made objects, and may therefore be admired for the sake of their Creator, to whom ideally they ought to point the way. Human beings, however, are incorrigibly obtuse, and go off in pursuit of "idols" even so. A classical statement of this attitude is to be found in Paul's Letter to the Romans (1:20–23):

> Ever since the creation of the world his invisible nature, namely, his eternal power and deity, has been clearly perceived in the things that have been made … [but to no avail] Claiming to be wise, they became fools, and exchanged the glory of the immortal God for images resembling mortal man or birds or animals or reptiles …

All of this carried over into early Christianity, later Judaism and later still, Islam. There is one God, who has created, and will ultimately judge, the world; he has made his will known to humanity through his servants the Prophets, though his power may be recognised in what he has created. To "study" in this connection was to know and obey the will of God, as set forth in successive writings – historical records, prophecies, hymns, statutes and apocalyptic, visionary writings. We have no need to enter into further details, except to point out that in Judaism the heart of the matter is the Law (Torah) itself, in Christianity the person and work of Jesus Christ, and in Islam again the Law, as revealed afresh to Muhammad; in all three traditions, the dividing line between truth and falsehood was sharply marked (in some modern versions of Judaism and especially Christianity, it has grown less so, modernism and Islam meanwhile remaining largely irreconcilable).

All this stands out in sharp contrast to the spirit of detached inquiry we find in Greek philosophy. Where the Classical cultures had philosophers, the Judaeo-Christian-Muslim tradition had prophets and their disciples, whose business was less to inquire than to obey. The tension between them has been felt repeatedly in Western religious and intellectual history, and it is well that we recognise where it all began. On the one side there are the conservatives, who love and respect tradition and continuity; on the other there are the inquirers, the radicals, the freethinkers (or however else fashion may label them). The terminology is constantly changing, but today's alternatives would seem to be "fundamentalist" (meaning conservative) and "pluralist" (which may mean anything, but is obviously anti-fundamentalist).

What of the Orient in all this? Here we must be brief, but in the Hindu and Buddhist traditions, to "study religion" has always meant to place oneself under spiritual guidance, either by private arrangement with a guru, or as a member of a community of monks or nuns. In either case, the disciple's relationship to a guru has always been paramount: to be accepted as a disciple, or a novice, is to be prepared to show unquestioning obedience to the guru in everything, however trivial or apparently unreasonable. Not until you have made your submission in faith (Sanskrit: *shraddha*) to a teacher, can you begin to be taught. *What* is to be taught, it is entirely up to the guru to decide. The process of teaching and learning is strictly one-way, from the guru to the disciple, whose role is generally limited to the asking of respectful questions and absorbing the teacher's answers, either in writing or (more often) by memorisation – a method still common enough in our own day, despite repeated attempts to discourage it.

We who live in the age of information, with every conceivable fact instantly available to anyone capable of pressing the right computer keys in the right order, find it hard to imagine a time when very little was known about our world and its inhabitants, and what little was known, had to be fitted into existing paradigms. At the end of the first millennium, the West divided religion into four categories, and only four: Christendom, Jewry, Islam and "paganism" – an *omnium gatherum* for everything that did not sort under the first three. As to the study of religion, one studied within the framework of one's own tradition. To be sure, there was a certain curiosity value in other people's customs: travellers' tales have never lacked an audience, and although the genre invited exaggeration and a concentration on the previously unknown and the bizarre, world literature between the fifth and the fifteenth centuries (the "dark ages" of Western culture) was full of fresh information concerning people's beliefs and customs, myths and rituals.

In his fascinating book *The Discoverers* (1983) Daniel Boorstin wrote that:

> The world we now view from the literate West – the vistas of time, the land and the seas, the heavenly bodies and our own bodies, the plants and animals, history and human societies past and present – had to be opened for us by countless Columbuses. ...
>
> (p. xv)

Discoveries are not inventions. One discovers what is already there to be discovered; one invents what is *not* already there. Discovery is in a sense the archaeology of ideas, the finding afresh of what, somewhere and at some time, was once common knowledge but which the world has since forgotten. But having discovered, one has to find some way of incorporating the new information into one's existing frames of reference. In the Christian West, that meant in practice sorting each new wave of information into the categories set forth in the Bible, with occasional footnotes supplied by "the ancients". There were true and false gods and goddesses; there was the sin of idolatry; there were sacrifices offered to "demons" and various related abominations. This was the only viable principle of measurement: by reference to the (so far) unquestioned and unquestionable data of revelation, as stated in Holy Writ and interpreted by the Holy Church. Not until the advent of evolutionary theory toward the end of the nineteenth century did the would-be student of religion have an alternative method to fall back upon.

"Discoveries" came thick and fast, once navigation had become a tolerably exact business, and exploration by sea (as distinct from the overland treks of antiquity) developed. Judaism and Islam were already known, though little understood – in Islam's case, against a background of fear fuelled by the Crusades. The Enlightenment (German, *Aufklärung*) was more interested in China and its (apparently) rational approach to religion than in alternative monotheism or pagan superstitions. Most of the Enlightenment's information about China came directly from the reports of Jesuit missionaries, among whom the first was Matteo Ricci (1552–1610), who idealised Chinese "religion" as a system without "priestcraft" (the bugbear of the Age of Reason), but in possession of high moral virtues. At much the same time other Jesuits were writing about the indigenous peoples of north America in similar terms; the phrase "the noble savage" seems to have been coined by John Dryden (1631–1700) in his *Conquest of Granada* (1670), the point being that virtue can and does flourish beyond the boundaries of Western urban civilisation. The "noble savage" was (or seemed to be) the antithesis of modern urban man – an image which has since proved remarkably resilient.

What manner of religion might "the noble savage" have known and observed? On this point, the unorthodox Western intelligentsia in the seventeenth and especially the

But a blanket condemnation of "miracles" and the supernatural was one thing; proposing a plausible alternative was another matter entirely. Before the middle years of the nineteenth century, though there was no shortage of fresh material, there was no comprehensive method with which to treat it, once one had abandoned the hard-and-fast "truth-versus-falsehood" categories of Christian tradition. Evolution filled that gap from the 1880s on.

Say "evolution" and one thinks at once of Charles Darwin and his epoch-making book *On the Origin of Species* (1859). Darwin had very little to say directly about religion, either for or against (Ellegård 1958). Some of his contemporaries were however less cautious. The most widely read of those writing in English was the popular philosopher Herbert Spencer (1820–1904), who took Darwin's biological theory and made it into a universal explanation of life on earth and its social institutions – government, language, literature, science, art and of course religion. All these things began with simple forms: *homo sapiens* had evolved out of something prior to and simpler than man (exactly what, no one knew, though the hunt for "fossil man" was pursued with diligence); religion had therefore evolved out of something cruder than *Hymns Ancient and Modern*. What that "something" might be, no one could possibly know (Trompf 1990). Conjecture was inevitable. Of the various theories put forward in the late nineteenth century, that labelled "animism" has stood the test of time better than most. The term was launched by the Oxford anthropologist E. B. Tylor, in his important book *Primitive Culture* (1871), who declared that religion began with "a belief in Spiritual Beings", prompted by reflection on the phenomena of dream and death. Suppose that I dream about my father, who died in 1957 (I do, as it happens): is that evidence that he is still alive in some other order of being? If majorities count, most of the world's population has always believed so. There is then at least some reason to inscribe "animism" on religion's birth certificate, as indeed those wanting religion without revelation urged.

But might there perhaps be some even earlier stage, less explicit than animism? Tylor's successor at Oxford, R. R. Marett, thought there was, and called it "preanimism", without dreams and reflections on the mystery of death, but with a sense of the uncanny and of supernatural power (Polynesian/Melanesian *mana*). Marett's book *The Threshold of Religion* (1909) set out the arguments.

A quite different attack on the animistic theory came from the Scottish man of letters Andrew Lang (1844–1912), who had begun as a classicist and specialist on Homer, was for a time a disciple of Tylor, but in the end struck out on his own. From his Tylorian years comes his first anthropological book, *Custom and Myth* (1884). *Myth, Ritual and Religion* (1887) marks a transition, and his mature position was stated in *The Making of Religion* (1898). Lang's final argument was that there was no way in which animism was capable of evolving into ethical monotheism. Again and again the anthropological evidence had recorded belief in "high gods" – conceptions of a Supreme Being, divine rulers and creators – which the evolutionists had simply chosen to ignore or dismiss as proof of "the missionaries" tampering with the evidence. Lang tried to let the evidence speak for itself. He never claimed to have cracked the code, merely that " … alongside of their magic, ghosts, worshipful stones … most of the very most backward races have a very much better God than many races a good deal higher in civilisation … " (Sharpe 1986: 63).

Lang was a public figure only in what he wrote. Having resigned his Oxford fellowship on his marriage, he held no further academic position, living entirely by his pen. His versatility was extraordinary – historian, novelist, minor poet, psychic researcher, biographer, translator of Homer: he was sometimes ironical and often inaccurate, but never dull. His anthropological investigations were undertaken almost in his spare time, though he once confessed that given the opportunity, he might have devoted more time to anthropology. As it was, his hints and suggestions proved extremely fruitful. When he died in 1912, the Austrian ethnologist Wilhelm Schmidt had just published the first volume of his massive work *Der Ursprung der Gottesidee* (in the end twelve volumes in all), in which Lang's "high gods" were taken very seriously indeed.

Another celebrated Scottish anthropologist to leave his mark on the study of religion was James George Frazer (1854–1951), still remembered as the tireless and unworldly author of *The Golden Bough* (1922), a compendium of practically everything sorting under what was then called "primitive" religion, including folklore (domestic anthropology). For many years now, Frazer has been branded the archetypal "armchair anthropologist", all of whose material was second-hand, having been raked together by casual observers whose motives were variable and whose accuracy was open to question. The criticism was justified up to a point, but Frazer did what he could to verify his sources, and was well aware of the risks he was running. In any case, the task of pulling together the growing bodies of evidence concerning archaic and vernacular religions needed to be undertaken by someone.

Frazer might well have become the first professor of comparative religion in the UK. In 1904 he was approached with a view to taking up such a post at the University of Manchester, but in the end declined, on the grounds that he was not a fit and proper person to instruct young men preparing for the Christian ministry. One wonders what might have become of the study of religion at Manchester, had Frazer's scruples been overcome!

The History of Religion School

Between about 1890 and the outbreak of the First World War in 1914, a prominent position in Protestant religious scholarship was occupied by a group of fairly young biblical scholars, most of them Germans, known collectively as *die Religionsgeschichtliche Schule* (the history of religion (not "religions") school). Their leaders were Wilhelm Bousset on the New Testament and Hermann Gunkel on the Old Testament side, and their chief theorist was Ernst Troeltsch (1865–1923), who, almost alone of the group, is still read today, thanks largely to his book *Die Absolutheit des Christentums und die Religionsgeschichte* (1902, belated Eng. tr. *The Absoluteness of Christianity and the History of Religions*, 1971). The principles of the movement were threefold: first, to focus on religion rather than on theology; second, to concentrate on popular expressions of religion rather than on high-level statements about religion; and thirdly, to examine closely the environment of the Old and New Testaments, rather than merely treating them as the free-floating (and divinely inspired) texts of orthodox tradition. The productivity of the young men making up the movement was remarkable, though relatively little of their work found its way into English. The trouble was that, like the deists of the seventeenth and eighteenth centuries, they were generally political radicals, socialists and populists at a time and in a country where socialism was held to be only one step removed from treason.

To the members of the school, the world of scholarship nevertheless owes a great deal, for liberating the study of the Bible from its dogmatic straitjacket, for opening up the worlds of "later Judaism" and the Hellenistic mystery religions, and for demonstrating that conspicuous piety is no substitute for sound scholarship where the study of religion is concerned. Special mention may be made of their work on the religious traditions of ancient Iran, Egypt and Mesopotamia. Iran was important mainly because of the towering figure of the prophet Zoroaster/Zarathustra (perhaps c.1200 BCE), whose teachings seemed to anticipate those of the Judaeo-Christian tradition at a number of points, in particular eschatology (death, judgement and the future life). Also, there were myriad points of contact between Iran and India. There emerged a new label, "Indo-European", as an alternative to "Aryan" as a blanket term for everything from the languages of north India to those of northern Europe. (The sinister overtones of "Aryan" as the equivalent of "non-Jewish" came later.)

Other advances that were registered toward the end of the nineteenth century in the academic study of religion concerned Egypt and Mesopotamia, thanks in both cases to the decipherment of what had previously been unreadable scripts, hieroglyphic and cuneiform respectively. We cannot go into details, but in both cases sober history and wild surmise combined. In Egypt's case, speculation went all the way from the bizarre theories of the Mormons (invented before the hieroglyphs had been deciphered) to the Egyptian origins of monotheism, which Sigmund Freud wrote about and may even have believed in, and the universal diffusionism of the Australian Grafton Elliot Smith, which claimed Egypt as the cradle of the whole of Western civilisation. A controversial expression of what came to be called "pan-Babylonism" was a series of lectures on "Babylon and the Bible" (*Babel und Bibel*), delivered in Berlin by Friedrich Delitzsch in 1902–5, which claimed that everything of value in the Old Testament was copied from Babylonian sources – the creation and flood narratives, the Sabbath, the notion of sin and much more.

The "father" of the history of religion school (as distinct from its propagandists) had been the great historian Adolf (von) Harnack (1851–1930). In 1901 Harnack, also lecturing in Berlin, had argued *against* the widening of the theological curriculum to include non-biblical religions, chiefly on the grounds that the result would be dilettantism and superficiality. If comparative religion were to be taught at the universities, it should be in faculties of arts/ humanities, and not under the aegis of theology. (Eventually, this was more or less what happened.) A somewhat different point of view was that of the Swedish scholar Nathan Söderblom (1866–1931), who argued in his Uppsala inaugural lecture of 1901 that there should be no artificial barrier between biblical religion and the rest, and that comparative religion (*religionshistoria*) should be an essential part of the theological curriculum. Three years later comparative religion in fact became an integral though subordinate part of the theological programme of the University of Manchester.

The trouble, though, was that often, the advocates of *Religionsgeschichte* (comparative religion) were at best indifferent and at worst hostile to theology as the churches understood it and the faculties taught it. And of course vice versa. Hence in most universities the study of "other religions" came to be scattered around departments of history, anthropology, classics, Semitic studies and the like, and kept separate from theology. So it remained until the onset of "the religious studies movement" in the 1960s.

Psychology and the Mystics

The years around the turn of the nineteenth to twentieth century saw the emergence of many new "sciences", among them "the science of religion". Within that science there were soon sub-sciences, of which the psychology of religion and the sociology of religion were the most significant. If two books were to be picked out as foundation documents of these sub-sciences, they might well be William James' *The Varieties of Religious Experience* (1977) on the psychological side, and Émile Durkheim's *The Elementary Forms of the Religious Life* (1915) on the sociological, though neither marks an absolute beginning. The difference between them is easily stated. Whereas the psychology of religion was, to begin with, concerned only with the individual's mental processes as they relate to religion, the sociology of religion saw (and still sees) religion as a collective, social phenomenon.

In both cases the formative years were the 1890s. This has nothing to do with the character of religion itself, which has always involved individuals and societies in equal measure. In psychology's case, the initial question concerned the mechanism by which the individual comes to experience sensations and feelings that he or she identifies as supernatural, and the consequences to which this may lead. The old alternatives had been divine inspiration on the one hand, and demonic deception on the other (speaking here in Judaeo-Christian terms). But suppose there were nothing supernatural involved. What then?

Interestingly enough, a number of the first psychologists of religion were Americans. Religious individualism was endemic in nineteenth-century America, especially among the heirs of the Enlightenment, such as Emerson and the New England Transcendentalists. "Individualism ... was common enough in the Europe of the nineteenth century; in America, it was part of the very air men breathed" (Nisbet 1965: 4). This was due in part to the importance of the individual "conversion experience" as the major criterion by which the genuineness of religion was judged. Sectarian extremism was also common, some parts of America even coming to resemble a menagerie of frequently warring sects. Add to this the impact of phenomena as diverse as exploration, industrialisation, migration, half-understood Darwinism and not least the Civil War, and it is not hard to grasp the fascinated energy with which intellectuals tackled religious questions. Here an important book was Andrew Dickson White's *A History of the Warfare of Science with Theology in Christendom* (1955). White, the first President of Cornell University, was writing too early to incorporate psychology into his account; he was not irreligious, but was passionately opposed to the imposition of "theological" limits on free enquiry.

The first psychologists of religion in America are all but forgotten today – Granville Stanley Hall, James H. Leuba and Edwin D. Starbuck among them. Starbuck is worth a special mention as the first to work with questionnaires as a means of gathering material. How do you find out what people experience as "religion"? Simple: ask them! The results of his enquiries took shape in his book *The Psychology of Religion* (1899). Starbuck also taught a course in the psychology of religion at Harvard in 1894–95. The major emphasis of his questionnaires was on "religious experience" in general, and the experience of conversion in particular. The method as such was deeply flawed, but won approval as a means of breaking away from the crude choice between divine inspiration and demonic deception as explanations of "the conversion experience".

Starbuck's material was used (and duly acknowledged) by his Harvard teacher William James in preparation for the lectures delivered in Scotland and published in 1977 as *The Varieties of Religious Experience* – one of the few religious classics of the twentieth century. William James, (1842–1910), the elder brother of the novelist Henry James, came of Swedenborgian stock, though his personal religion was an undogmatic theism. He trained as a doctor, but never practised medicine. Then he became fascinated by the infant science of psychology, and for years worked on his one and only book, *The Principles of Psychology* (1890) – all his later publications were tidied-up lectures, *Varieties* being his unquestioned masterpiece.

James was writing (or rather, speaking) as what he called a "radical empiricist", a pragmatist who was convinced that where religion was concerned, judgement is possible only on a basis of the results to which it leads – religion is what religion does, not what it claims to be able to do. He drew a famous distinction between two religious temperaments: that of the "healthy-minded" – positive, optimistic, relatively unconcerned with the problem of evil – and that of "the sick soul" – obsessed with the sense of its own unworthiness, inadequacy and (in Christian terms) sin. "Let sanguine healthymindedness do its best with its strange power of living in the moment and ignoring and forgetting, still the evil background is really there to be thought of, and the skull will grin in at the banquet" (James 1977: 140).

James also anticipated in *Varieties* what in the 1960s was to become one of the bugbears of the study of religion, by introducing the subject of artificially induced "religious" experience through drugs, even going so far as to experiment himself with nitrous oxide ("laughing gas") and to suggest that if there should be supernatural revelation, the "neurotic" temperament might be better able to receive it than the well-adjusted.

There were major flaws in James' approach to his subject, and this may be the time to mention them briefly. One was entirely deliberate, namely, his exclusion of religion's social dimension from his inquiry: "religion" he limited to "the feelings, acts, and experiences of individual men in their solitude, so far as they apprehend themselves to stand in relation to whatever they may consider the divine" (James 1977: 31). How far individuals feel, act and experience because of the environment in which they live, with all its precedents, images, taboos, expectations and the rest, he does not discuss. More important was the assumption, shared by all those who have ever used questionnaire material, that the individual actually knows, fully consciously, what he or she believes and why – and this is not always safe, as Freud and Jung were shortly to show.

Lectures XVI and XVII in *Varieties*, James devoted to the subject of "Mysticism", which we might perhaps characterise as religious experience at its most intensive. Wisely, he did not attempt to define this notoriously slippery word, but identified "ineffability", "noetic quality" (the quality of self-authenticating knowledge), "transiency" and "passivity" as a "mystical group" of states of consciousness (James 1977: 380–82). Whether mysticism is therefore to be welcomed or avoided had long been disputed territory. *Mystik* had long been regarded by theologians (especially those of the Catholic tradition) as something entirely positive, a mark of divine favour; *Mysticismus* was the word used by German-speaking rationalists to denote irrationality and delusion in religion, in practically the same sense as "enthusiasm". The English language was in the unfortunate position of having only one word to cover both senses. Either way, "mysticism" came in the years around the turn of the century to serve as a catch-all term for all that sorted under the categories of visions, voices, trances and what today we call "altered states of consciousness"; but also to label religious intensity. At the back of all this was what was the mystic's desire to achieve oneness with the Ultimate Reality – or alternatively, a mental disorder of some kind, depending on one's presuppositions.

One cannot "study" mystics, except to the extent that they are prepared to write or speak about their experiences. There was however no lack of such material, and beginning in the years around the turn of the century there appeared a number of significant works on the subject. The first of these was W. R. Inge's *Christian Mysticism* (1899), followed by, among others, James' *Varieties*, Nathan Söderblom's *Uppenbarelsereligion* (*The Religion of Revelation*, 1903, which drew the important distinction between theistic and non-theistic expressions of religious faith), Friedrich von Hügel's massive *The Mystical Element of Religion* (1908), Rufus Jones' *Studies in Mystical Religion* (1909) and Evelyn Underhill's *Mysticism* (1940). At the end of this line we may perhaps place J. B. Pratt's *The Religious Consciousness* (1920). It is perhaps worth noting that the last four authors mentioned were Roman Catholic, Quaker, uneasy Anglican and Unitarian respectively: clearly religious experience bore no particular relation to Christian denominationalism. Pratt's horizon was however wider: he had a lively interest in India, writing with regard to Buddhism that he had " … tried to enable the reader to understand a little *how it feels to be a Buddhist*" (Sharpe 1986: 115f. emphasis in original).

It was slightly ironical that Pratt's book should have been called *The Religious Consciousness*, since by the time it appeared, Freud, Jung and their respective bands of followers had most effectively called in question the very idea of consciousness as a decisive factor in human conduct. The new psychologists, wrote Sir John Adams in 1929, " ... know exactly what they want and are quite clear about the way they propose to attain it. There is a lion in their path; they want that lion killed and decently buried. This lion is Consciousness ... " (Sharpe 1986: 197). The Freudians, the Jungians and the rest of the psychoanalytical establishment did not pretend to scholarship in the area of religion, and some of their ventures into the field were quite bizarre; their profession was medicine, after all. But whereas Freud and his followers treated religion as part of the problem where mental health was concerned, the Jungians took a more positive view of religious mythology and symbolism. The psychoanalytical cause became fashionable in the years following the insanity of the First World War, not least in America, and cast a long shadow.

As an example, we may quote the case of the American anthropologist Margaret Mead (1902–78), author of the celebrated *Coming of Age in Samoa* (1928), which proved, entirely to its author's satisfaction, that adolescence can be practically pain-free, once the sexual restraints imposed by society have been relaxed. Mead was a protegée of Franz Boas, a determined Freudian. Margaret Mead was no more than 23 when she did the field-work on which her book was based, and many years later one of her chief Samoan informants confessed that the girls who had supplied her with material had been pulling her leg (Freeman 1983). It did not matter. Her teacher Franz Boas wrote that: "The results of her painstaking investigation confirm the suspicion long held by anthropologists, that much of what we ascribe to human nature is no more than a reaction to the restraints put upon us by civilisation" (Mead 1928: viii). "Field-work" was of the essence, no matter how poorly equipped the investigator – an attitude which passed in the course of time to the study of religion.

Psychoanalysis aside, other issues divided students of religion in the early years of the twentieth century. Another relatively new science was the science of sociology – collective, rather than individual human behaviour. A key concept in this connection was "holiness/sacredness" (the adjectives "sacred" and "holy" are generally interchangeable; "the sacred" and "the holy" are on the other hand abstractions).

There were two alternatives: on the psychological (and often the theological) side, what was up for investigation was "what the individual does with his/her own solitariness"; on the sociological side, what communities do under the heading of "religion". At the time when William James was most influential, there was a strong current of thought flowing in precisely the opposite direction: toward the assessment of religion's social functions, past and present. Out of the second of these there emerged *the sociology of religion*, which over the years was to assume a more and more dominant role as an academic sub-discipline.

One can do sociology in two different but connected ways. First, as an evolutionary science. Although Darwin was first and foremost a biologist, it was not long before his admirers applied the evolutionary model to (among much else) the development of human societies. Here the prophetic voice was that of the popular philosopher Herbert Spencer (1820–1904), whose *First Principles* (1862) argued that "the law of organic evolution is the law of all evolution" in every field of human activity, and not just in biology: "this same advance from the simple to the complex, through successive differentiations, holds uniformly" (Spencer 1862: 148). Spencer held that the simplest, and therefore the earliest, form of religion had been the worship (or at least fear) of the dead, especially those who had been powerful during their lifetimes: "The rudimentary form of all religion is the propitiation of dead ancestors … " (Spencer 1901). This "ghost theory" (as it came to be called) has the merit of sometimes being at least partly true. Examples are not hard to come by. But it leaves out too much to serve as a general theory of the origin of religion.

Shortly before Spencer's death, there had been published a centenary edition of an influential book by the German theologian Friedrich Schleiermacher (1768–1834), *Über die Religion: Reden an die Gebildeten unter ihren Verachtern* (1799; Eng. tr. *On Religion: Speeches to its Cultured Despisers*, 1893). It was important on two counts: first, because it argued that the only way to study religion adequately is not in terms of the bloodless intellectual abstractions of "natural religion" (which is in actual fact neither natural nor religion), but in and through the religious beliefs and practices of actual living human beings – a point made many years earlier by Charles de Brosses, but taken insufficiently seriously since. And second, because to Schleiermacher, the heart of religion was to be found, not in rules and regulations, hierarchies, hassocks and hymnbooks, but in the individual's experience of (or sense of) and dependence upon a power infinitely greater than his own. The reissue of Schleiermacher's *Über die Religion* in 1899 could not have come at a more opportune moment. Darwinism was all very well; the rule of law was an efficient sergeant-major in an unruly world, but left little room for creative individuality. It was however Schleiermacher's editor who made the greater long-term impression.

Rudolf Otto (1869–1937) was a philosopher and theologian by training and temperament, with Indology as another area of interest and expertise. Today however he tends to be remembered for only one book, *Das Heilige* (1917; Eng. tr. *The Idea of the Holy*, 1923), which argued that what is essential in religion is the individual's experience of "the holy", even at one point requesting that the reader who has had no such experience to read no further! But experience of what, precisely? Trying to explain, Otto coined the word "numinous" (*das Numinose*), a sense of the presence of a *numen* (deity, supernatural being). This in its turn gives rise to a perception, or apprehension, of a *mysterium* which is both *tremendum* (scary) and *fascinans* (intriguing).

The words "holy" and "sacred" are adjectives, which need to be related to someone or something if they are to make sense, and are not easily turned into nouns ("holy scripture", "holy mountain", "holy day", "sacred cow", "sacred site" make sense as the abstract nouns "the holy" and "the sacred" do not).

A few years before the appearance of Otto's book there appeared in France Émile Durkheim's *Les Formes Élémentaires de la Vie Religieuse* (1912; Eng. tr. *The Elementary Forms of the Religious Life*, 1915). Here we have the opposite argument: that (put crudely) religion is a social phenomenon, resting not on the individual's feeling-states but on the needs of the community. Families, tribes and nations set up symbols of their own collective identity – from totem poles to national flags – which are "sacred" through their associations.

On this view, every human community invents its own sacred symbols. The supernatural does not enter into it, the closest approximation being "power" (the Melanesian/Polynesian *mana* and similar power-words, which Durkheim mistakenly believed to be impersonal, but which always turn out to be associated with spiritual beings who possess them). It is therefore the community which decrees what is, and what is not, "sacred" in its own cultural terms.

The Phenomenology of Religion

Between the outbreak of the First World War in 1914 and the end of the second in 1945, the study of religion in the West became fragmented. The old idealism had been shattered in the trenches of the battlefield, and in 1920, religion itself, let alone the study of religion, seemed to have no future worth speaking of. On the Christian theological front, the tradition of scholarship was maintained by a very few idealists in the face of growing opposition from the disciples of Karl Barth, Emil Brunner and the other "dialectical" theologians, in whose eyes "religion" was as dust and ashes compared to the Gospel, and who declined to study it further. The conservatives were what they had always been: intent on doing battle with "the world" on as many fronts as possible. Meanwhile, the anthropologists, Orientalists, philologists and the rest cultivated their respective gardens.

Comparative religion had been trying to compare religions as totalities, as systems, as competing solutions of the world's problems. This was unsound. Religions are totalities only in the pages of textbooks, and what believers actually believe, and how they believe, may bear little resemblance to what they are supposed to believe and do. The student, intent on examining religions and writing their histories, was faced with an impossible task. One alternative was to divide the field functionally, by themes and characteristics, and to attempt on that basis limited comparisons: prayer with prayer, sacrifice with sacrifice, images of deity with images of deity. In all this it was important to examine, not what the textbooks say, but what is actually there to be observed, the *phenomena* involved in the business of religion. The point had been made by Charles de Brosses in the 1760s and by Friedrich Schleiermacher in 1799: that the student of religion must concentrate, not on what people might do, ought to do or what the textbooks say they are supposed to do, but on what they actually do, and the ways in which they actually behave. But people do, and have done, so many things. How can anyone grasp the field as a whole?

It was with an eye to resolving this difficulty that the term "the phenomenology of religion" was pressed into service. As we have said, limited comparisons were still possible, provided that they were based on either reliable information or careful observation. However, in the early years of the twentieth century, "phenomenology" acquired another set of meanings, having to do less with the material than the mind-set of the observer. The name of the philosopher Edmund Husserl is often mentioned in this connection, though his contribution to the study of religion was at best indirect. "Philosophical" phenomenology aimed at the elimination of subjectivity (and hence dogmatic bias) from the inquirer's process of thought. As such, the ideal was and is unattainable, and it was unfortunate that for a time in the 1970s, a few phenomenological catch-words (*epoché*, the suspension of judgement, and *eidetic vision*, the gift of seeing things as wholes, as well as "phenomenology" itself) found their way into the vocabulary of the study of religion. In the inter-war years, the trend was best represented by the Dutch scholar Gerardus van der Leeuw (1890–1950), author of *Phänomenologie der Religion* (1933; Eng. tr. *Religion in Essence and Manifestation*, 1938).

Practically all the first phenomenologists of religion were Protestant Christian theologians – Chantepie de la Saussaye, Nathan Söderblom, Rudolf Otto, Edvard Lehmann, William Brede Kristensen (" … there exists no other religious reality than the faith of the believers … ") and C. Jouco Bleeker. An exception was the enigmatic German scholar Friedrich Heiler, whose chaotic book *Erscheinungsformen und Wesen der Religion* (1961) rounded off the series. In all these cases, phenomenology was a religious as much as a scholarly exercise. Those making up the between-the-wars generation of scholars we now call phenomenologists were deeply committed to the principle that the causes of sound learning and sound religion were not two causes, but one. The enemies of sound learning were all too often captive to unsound religion – unsound because (among other things) unhistorical and therefore almost inevitably authoritarian. Faced with such a configuration, one may distance oneself altogether from religious praxis; or one may try to bring the religious community (that is, the faculties of theology) round to one's way of thinking. Most opted for the first of these alternatives; the very few who chose the latter, though they won a few battles, ultimately lost the war – not because of the innate superiority of theological thinking, but due to the corrosive influence of secularisation on religious thought in general.

Tools of the Trade

Over the past century or so, the study of religion has gradually acquired an extensive body of reference material for the use of students. The idea that it might be possible to bring together all the world's knowledge and publish it in encyclopaedia form belongs to the Enlightenment. Today we are more modest, but the genre has survived. As far as religion is concerned, an important landmark was James Hastings' *Encyclopaedia of Religion and Ethics* (1908–26); in German, there was *Die Religion in Geschichte und Gegenwart* (1909–13), a fourth edition is currently in preparation. *The Encyclopedia of Religion* (16 vols, edited by Mircea Eliade) appeared in the US in 1987. Given the new situation created by the Internet, it is unlikely that there will be any more.

Compact dictionaries and handbooks are by now legion, as are "world religions" text-books for student use. Special mention may be made of *The New Penguin Dictionary of Religions* (1997) and *A New Handbook of Living Religions* (1998), both edited by John R. Hinnells. On the textbook front, Ninian Smart's *The World's Religions* (1989, an updated version of a book first published in 1969 as *The Religious Experience of Mankind*) has proved an excellent *gradus ad parnassum* for generations of religious studies students.

Concerning scholarly journals, we must be brief. They have never been other than variable in quality, and though these days every effort is made to guard professional standards, the level of readability is often depressingly low. There is the additional factor that the fragmentation of the study of religion in recent years has resulted in more and more specialist journals, which can only be read with profit by fellow specialists. Among the best "general" journals in English are *Religion* (UK/US), *Journal of the American Academy of Religion* (US), *Journal of Religion* (US) and *Numen* (international).

Congresses, Conferences, Consultations

In 1993 there was celebrated the centenary of the Chicago "World's Parliament of Religions", though this time relabelled "Parliament of World Religions" – a shift in meaning no one bothered to examine at all closely. Both were propaganda exercises, but for different causes: 1893 for religious oneness (monism), 1993 for religious diversity (pluralism). There would be little point in listing even a selection of the myriad conferences, congresses and consultations that have punctuated the years between, increasingly frequently since the advent of air travel in the 1960s. Opinions differ as to their importance, though it is probably true to say that the best are the smallest (the most satisfying conference I have ever attended numbered no more than thirty-five or so participants). It would however be churlish to deny their social function or the opportunity they provide for younger voices to make themselves heard among their peers.

Developments since the 1960s

In the immediate post-war years, where religion was studied seriously, the pattern was still largely that of the earlier part of the century. There was still the same broad alternative that there had been all century: most of those committed to the study of religion were equally committed to the community sponsoring it. Theology/ divinity, in one or another form, was still dominant; independent studies were few and far between, and "comparative religion" remained, as far as the West was concerned, something of a playground for liberal eccentrics. The world political scene was dominated by the threats and posturings of the "Cold War", in which context it no longer seemed far-fetched to hope that the great world religions might some day make common cause against the common enemy of "godless communism"; and by rapid decolonisation, beginning with India/Pakistan/Sri Lanka immediately after the war and sweeping through most of Africa (except, for the time being, the far south) soon thereafter. The Chinese Cultural Revolution, the Korean and Vietnam wars – these and many smaller conflicts all left their mark, even on such apparently arcane subjects as the study of religion. The creation of the State of Israel, and waves of Arab-Israeli conflict, left wounds which still today have not healed. The dismal record might be prolonged.

The consequences for the study of religion were profound, and lasting. Still in the 1950s it was simply taken for granted that religion was "all about words", and since these had been written in a vast variety of languages, many of them no longer spoken, the student's first duty was to become as much of a philologist as possible in the time available, with a view to reading ancient texts "in the original". (Pre-literate societies were generally left to the anthropologists to deal with on their own functional terms.) Latin and perhaps Greek had been learned in secondary school; Hebrew, Arabic, Sanskrit, Pali, Mandarin and Japanese had not. The principle, however, still stood. The inevitable outcome was that the study of religion remained a sub-department of the study of (for the most part ancient) history, with a little philosophy added for good measure.

The times, however, were a-changing, and between 1960 and 1970 all these assumptions had been challenged. Certainly old style studies survived, for the time being, but the historical-philological approach was suffering greatly from the attentions, not of scholars, but of politicians and administrators (and their paymasters) whose sights were set at a different level, philology became problematical, as language teaching at the secondary level declined; "history" even more so. The so-called "educational" reforms which began in the 1960s in the West played their part. Most important, however, was the reading of the place of religion in history that emerged in the mid-to-late 1960s.

It is impossible in this connection to overlook the impact of the Second Vatican Council (1962–65), not only on the Roman Catholic Church, but on the whole of world Christianity. Vatican II (Second Vatican Council), in a manner of speaking, launched the idea of inter-religious dialogue on a poorly prepared world. A concept had found its *kairos*. Within a very few years, it became axiomatic that the study of religion could only justify itself on "dialogical" principles – the assumption of course being that religion is far more than an aspect of ancient history. Once, it had been self-evident that the Western-trained historian should have the last word in all matters of importance. This was no longer as obvious as it had once been.

The reassessment began in the 1950s. An early expression was a little book by Huston Smith, *The Religions of Man* (1964), which expressed the hope that history might remember "our years" " … not for the release of nuclear power nor the spread of Communism but as the time in which all the peoples of the world first had to take one another seriously" (Smith 1964). An important part of the "taking seriously" process was the new readiness on the part of Western scholars to listen to the voices of people of other faiths explaining what they believed and why. Earlier this process had been haphazard, though the Chicago

World's Parliament of Religions in 1893 had established the principle, and exotics like Radhakrishnan and Suzuki had continued the mission. The day of the vernacular (primitive, primal, pre-literate) religions, on the other hand, had still not dawned.

As to the object of the exercise, some controversy was caused when in 1958 the German scholar Friedrich Heiler, a passionate internationalist, declared at an international conference in Tokyo that the only worthy objective of the study of religion was "true tolerance and co-operation on behalf of mankind" (Sharpe 1986: 272). For a number of years thereafter, the question of the "pure versus applied" alternatives in the study of religion tended to dominate professional discussion. Although a mere recital of names would serve no purpose, the "pure" camp was for the most part made up of classically trained historians and philologists, whose chief concerns were with history – and fairly remote history at that. In these circles, "objectivity", in the sense of single-minded concentration on one's object of study (usually a text), was still an attainable ideal, and was contrasted with "speculative" philosophy on the one hand, and with dogmatic theology on the other. This was scarcely a new point of view: rather it was the remnant of an old debate, prodded into life once more. "Pure" scholarship could see no value in the study of religion unless it contributed directly to a better understanding among the nations.

Beginning in the mid-1960s, the ideal of scholarly objectivity began to be frozen out of the day-to-day study of religion. New words were coined, among them "postcolonial" and "post-modern", neither of which carried any very precise meaning, but both of which marked out a new territory. "Deconstruction" was another neologism. All indicated extreme impatience with the intellectual and ideological past, with a history most of its advocates took little trouble to understand, and with every last form of idealism.

A forum for discussions of this order was provided by the new departments of (usually) religious studies that were founded between the late 1960s and the late 1970s. (Some tertiary institutions opted for other forms of words, "religion studies", "studies in religion" or whatever; a few retained the time-honoured "comparative religion".) Before the 1960s, despite the West's multifarious colonial involvements, little notice had been taken of what "the natives" believed or did, and why; comparative religion had always been a cinderella subject in faculties of theology/divinity. But in the new post-war climate of opinion, it was decided that religion and its structures and functions world-wide, being far too important a matter to be left to the churches, was to be an object of study. By common consent, the pioneer department of religious studies was that founded at the University of Lancaster in 1967. Many others followed, the University of Sydney not until 1977, the University of Tromsø in Norway not before 1993. An important point was that the study of religion at university level should be entirely free from Church (or other) sponsorship and control. There were to be no more heresy trials; every expression of religion was in principle open to investigation: there was to be no proselytism. As far as was humanly possible, every manifestation of religion was to be treated with "sympathy" and "understanding".

Given these excellent principles, it was unfortunate that the one religious tradition frequently denied a fair hearing was … Christianity. Disillusion reached a new pitch of intensity during the 1960s; the Vietnam war was one obvious cause, postcolonial guilt was another, sexual (or gender) politics yet another. So it was that when the so-called "new religious movements" (NRMs) in the vernacular, "sects" or "cults" – Transcendental Meditation (TM), International Society of Krishna Consciousness (ISKCON), the Unification Church and the rest – began to appear in the mid-to-late 1960s, they enjoyed immediate and in some cases lasting success.

The NRMs were extremely diverse in origin: some had their roots in the Hindu tradition (TM, ISKCON), others in Buddhism, one in Korean Shamanism (the "Moonies"), others again in fringe Christianity (the Children of God). What all had in common was their clientèle and their basis in charismatic leadership. The old faculties of divinity/theology would have taken no notice of them: the new departments of religious studies quickly incorporated them into their curricula, as exercises in sociology, psychology – and in some cases, participant observation free from the discomfort that frequently attends field-work.

Religious Studies and Phenomenology

The post-war situation was one in which old patterns of belief and behaviour were being questioned and reshaped. The demise of colonialism had created a new international, intercultural and inter-religious community, by no means "one nation" but at least a world in which a degree of tolerance of one another's religious idiosyncracies was a high priority. The sectarian squabbles and polemics of the past had, it was hoped, been laid to rest once and for all. There was a large element of left-leaning politics in what emerged in the late 1960s and early 1970s. Its chief ingredient was dogmatic egalitarianism: privilege based on accidents of birth is unacceptable, and no one can claim as a privilege what is not in principle open to everyone as a right. Religion, with all its hierarchies, resources, ranks and exclusivity, was an obvious target, as it had been since the Enlightenment. Christianity was an even more obvious target, given its place in Western, "colonialist" and capitalist culture.

Other factors contributed. The Roman Catholics' Second Vatican Council (1962–65) had embraced the principles of religious freedom (*Dignitatis Humanae*) and improved inter-religious relations (*Ad Gentes*, *Nostra Aetate*), chiefly in the hope of righting the wrongs of anti-Semitism, but with far wider implications. Instead of confrontation, as in the past, "dialogue" was now the order of the day, and inevitably, this gave a great boost to the intercultural study of religion. For some years, the incidence of ex-priests and ex-nuns in religious education (further impelled to move on by the "anti-abortion, anti-contraception" decrees of the late 1960s) became unusually high.

Methods and Methodologies

In recent years it has become more and more common for sessions, sections and sometimes whole conferences to be devoted to "problems of method in the study of religion", the third of the Ms we mentioned at the outset. This in itself is evidence of widespread uncertainty in the field consequent on the erosion of old intellectual assumptions. The most successful of those known to the present writer was that held in Turku/Åbo, Finland, in August 1973. Others have been notably less worthwhile, though there would be little point in identifying them. A frequently recurring topic of late has been the age-old tension between theological and non-theological ways of studying religion, which seems no closer to a resolution now than it was a century ago. In 1996 I was privileged to be asked to present a "position paper" on this subject to the American Academy of Religion. Poor health prevented me from attending, but my paper was duly discussed. In it, I am afraid that I quoted Omar Khayyam:

> Myself when young did eagerly frequent
> Doctor and Saint, and heard great Argument

> About it and about: but evermore
> Came out by the same Door as in I went.

(Song 27)

"Methods," wrote Åke Hultkrantz some years ago, "are the crutches of science". The healthy have no need of them; the busy have little time for them. There is a danger that the "second-order" student may spend so much time studying other people's methods (and quoting them at length, after the manner of social scientists) that there is little time left for the actual study of religion, let alone its practice.

Those who deplore what they see as the "re-theologising" of the study of religion deserve closer examination than we can give them here. One or two points may however be made. First, that (with the possible exception of the old USSR and its satellites) the study of religion had never been wholly "de-theologised"; many and perhaps most of our intellectual forerunners were, as we say, "believers". They were not on the other hand obscurantists – prompting the reflection that the post-1960s generation is so far removed from genuine liberalism in religion as to be unable to acknowledge what it once was, namely, the ability to grasp more than one side of an argument and the reasons behind each.

It needs perhaps to be added that after about 1970, the meaning of "theology" became more and more indistinct. What remained was "theology as history of ideas" on the one hand, and "theology as social ethics, with an occasional mention of God".

Methodological Issues

It is time to attempt an assessment of the study of religion after the years of discovery, progress and reappraisal (and of course conflict) we have passed in rapid review. What have we learned from our academic past? Sometimes the problems we face today seem substantially the problems our forebears wrestled with in the past, and our descendants will no doubt still be debating a century from now. Arguably the most persistent of these concerns the religious allegiance (or lack of it) of the student: does the student function best as an insider or as an outsider? To this one can only answer that the insider knows by experience what to the outsider is mere conjecture; the insider is allowed access to "mysteries" which remain barred to the uninitiated. On the mundane level of such things as history and geography, on the other hand, the outsider may well be the better informed of the two. Whether the outsider can enter imaginatively into the insider's "spiritual experience" is extremely doubtful. In many of today's secular societies, the issue may in any case be a red herring, since what the media unfailingly dub "sectarian" (i.e. religious) conflict generally proves on closer examination to be a matter of territory and resources, history and ethnicity, rather than religion as such.

Another cardinal issue is that of secularisation, the process whereby religious ways of thinking and behaving are replaced by secular (from the Latin, *saeculum*, this world) substitutes. The process passes through three stages: *rejection* of religion and its replacement by secular authority, usually that of "science"; *adaptation* of the old to the new values; and *reaction*, intransigent reaffirmation of the old ways in their entirety. It is at this third, reactive stage that there is created the much-maligned and much-feared phenomenon of fundamentalism and fundamentalists.

Fundamentalism and conservatism are not synonyms. A conservative is one who loves and respects the old ways and the old traditions, and is reluctant to see them change; a fundamentalist is one who tries to battle the corrosive influence of the new and to re-establish the absolute authority of a holy book (the Bible, the Qur'an, the Veda), a law, a community and its traditional values. The fundamentalist is permanently on the defensive, and may be given to paranoia in the face of real or imagined enemies. By its very nature, fundamentalism is a matter for semi-sociological research. Taking the longer view, despite the vast attention that has always been paid to the texts of holy scripture, their *functions* in the community remain imperfectly understood.

An overlapping subject for investigation is that of leadership. Fundamentalists seldom or never interpret scripture for themselves, but rely on the directives of a charismatic leader and the exegetical tradition of which he or she is part. The holy book is read (or listened to) selectively, after having been passed through the filter of a holy tradition – of which the individual fundamentalist generally remains unaware. The nature of religious community leadership then stands out as a matter of great importance, not least in the sectarian context.

Pluralism

Space permits only one last addition to the list of unfinished religious studies business: the issue of pluralism. Once, "pluralism" meant no more than variety or diversity, and as such was an unremarkable fact of religious life. Recently, however, it has taken on a further, ideologically fuelled meaning: the unconditional right of every religious or other community to be itself and maintain its own traditions, practices and attitudes. Like every idealistic programme, that of pluralism (or in political terms, "multiculturalism") is flawed. It tends to assume, for instance, that religious toleration and mutual acceptance is a normal and natural state of human affairs. History indicates otherwise. If, as we suggested at the beginning of this essay, religion and law are virtually inseparable in many societies (for instance Islam), a plurality of laws is as unacceptable as a plurality of gods was in ancient Israel, and for precisely the same reasons: peace and national cohesion.

Where religion is closely allied with nationalism and ethnicity, as it so often is, an extra dimension is added. Conformity is loyalty, dissent is potential or actual treachery – a totalitarian point of view reserved in secular societies for extremist politics. In educational terms, this has led in the West to the insistence that where religious studies are taught, such teaching must be ideologically sound, value-free (the old mirage of "objectivity") and politically innocuous. Secular educators in pluralist societies may go so far as to forbid every expression of overt religiosity – public prayer in schools, the wearing of distinctive items of clothing, even the celebration of religious festivals, outside the circle of the faithful.

Clearly, the study of religion is not what it was to students of my generation. As the theologians have retreated – or at least redefined themselves – the social sciences have come to the fore. What are they hoping to "understand"? Not as a rule the finer points of a Coptic text written two thousand years or so ago, or even an English or German text written less than a hundred years ago. The emphasis in departments of religious studies over the past thirty or so years has been tending more and more in the direction of contemporary issues, as pursued in departments of sociology and anthropology, where you use languages to communicate with the living, and not only to settle accounts with the dead.

It has become somewhat fashionable in recent years to call in question one of the basic assumptions of 1970s-style religious studies: that the student's business is to *understand* religious belief and behaviour, irrespective of time and place. The counterclaim now is that "understanding" is in the blood, and not in the brain; you cannot pretend to understand what you were not *born* to understand, and to claim otherwise is arrogance and cultural neo-imperialism. Thus only women can understand women, only African Americans can understand African Americans, only gay people can understand other gay people, only Jews can understand Jews, and so on *ad infinitum*. So where the troubles of the study of religion initially had to do with gaining access to the material, later the problems shifted to method (what to do with it once you have it), now we are troubled as never before by motive: whose interests the study of religion is serving. The liberal ideal of disinterested scholarship pursued for its own sake is little mentioned in current debate.

In educational terms, it matters very little under what "disciplinary" or administrative label the study of religion is pursued, provided that it is done with diligence and imagination by people who know what they are about, who are motivated by old-fashioned curiosity more than by the desire to score political points, beat a drum or make a career, and who respect the most frequently broken of the Ten Commandments, that which *orders* you not to bear false witness against your neighbour (whether alive or dead makes no difference). The history of the study of religion is the story of people of all ages and cultures and political affiliations, who believe certain things about the world in which they live (or have lived), and because of that belief, behave in certain ways. They have done all the things people have always done: they have celebrated times and seasons with music and dance, food and drink; they have waged war and made peace; they have wondered, as we all still wonder, what it all means and what, if anything, lies on the far side of death. The study of religion is about all of these things, and many more. Let no one pretend that he or she is unaffected by these matters. To those who make such claims, I am tempted to say: "Sir, Madam, James, Jane – with respect, I do not believe you." Because when all the dross has been cleared away, the fact of our mortality will remain to tantalise us until it is too late for it to matter.

Bibliography

Boorstin, D. J., *The Discoverers*. New York, Vintage Books, 1983.

Capps, W. H., *Religious Studies: The Making of a Discipline*. Minneapolis MN, Fortress Press, 1995.

Cook, S. A., *The Study of Religions*. London, A. & C. Black, 1914.

Daniel, G., *The Idea of Prehistory*. Harmondsworth, Penguin, 1964.

De Vries, J., *The Study of Religion: A Historical Approach*. Trans. K. W. Bolle, New York, Harcourt, Brace & World, 1967.

Durkheim, É., *The Elementary Forms of the Religious Life*. Trans. J. W. Swain, London, George Allen & Unwin, 1915.

Eliade, M. (ed.), *Encyclopedia of Religion*. 16 vols, New York, Macmillan, 1987.

Ellegård, A., *Darwin and the General Reader*. Göteborg (Gothenburg, Sweden), Acta Universitatis Gothoburgensis 7, 1958.

Evans-Pritchard, E. E., *Theories of Primitive Religion*. Oxford, Clarendon Press, 1965.

Feldman, B. and Richardson, R. D., *The Rise of Modern Mythology*, 1680–1860. Bloomington, Indiana, Indiana University Press, 1972.

Frazer, J. G., *The Golden Bough*. Abridged edn, London, Macmillan, 1922.

Freeman, D., *Margaret Mead and Samoa: The Making and Unmaking of an Anthropological Myth*. Cambridge, Harvard University Press, 1983.

Hastings, J. (ed.), *Encyclopaedia of Religion and Ethics*. Edinburgh, T. & T. Clark, 1908–26.

Heiler, F., *Erscheinungsformen und Wesen der Religion*. Stuttgart, publisher unknown, 1961.

Hinnells, J. R. (ed.), *The New Penguin Dictionary of Religions*. London, Penguin, 1997.

——(ed.), *A New Handbook of Living Religions*. Harmondsworth, Penguin, 1998.

Hügel, F. von, *The Mystical Element of Religion*. 2 vols, London, Dent, 1908.

Hurd, W., *New Universal History of the Religious Rites, Ceremonies and Customs of the Whole World*. London, publisher unknown, 1788.

Inge, W. R., *Christian Mysticism*. London, Methuen, 1899.

James, W., *The Principles of Psychology*. 2 vols, New York, H. Holt& Co., 1890.

——*The Varieties of Religious Experience*. The Gifford Lectures 1901–2, reprinted Glasgow, Collins, 1977.

Jones, R. M., *Studies in Mystical Religion*. London, Macmillan & Co., 1909.

Lang, A., *Custom and Myth*. London, Longmans & Co., 1884.

——*Myth, Ritual and Religion*. 2 vols, London, Longmans & Co., 1887.

——*The Making of Religion*. London, Longmans & Co., 1898.

Leeuw, G. van der, *Religion in Essence and Manifestation: A Study in Phenomenology*. Trans. J. E. Turner, London, George Allen & Unwin, 1938.

Marett, R. R., *The Threshold of Religion*. London, Methuen, 1909.

Mead, M., *Coming of Age in Samoa*. New York, Morrow, 1928.

Müller, F. M., *Introduction to the Science of Religion*. London, Longmans, Green and Co., 1873.

Nisbet, R. A., *Emile Durkheim*. Englewood Cliffs NJ, Prentice-Hall, 1965.

Otto, R., *The Idea of the Holy*. Trans. J. W. Harvey, London, Humphrey Milford, 1923.

Pratt, J. B., *The Religious Consciousness: A Psychological Study*. New York, Macmillan, 1920.

Schiele, F. M. (ed.), *Die Religion in Geschichte und Gegenwart*. 5 vols, Tübingen, publisher unknown, 1909–13.

Schleiermacher, F., *On Religion: Speeches to its Cultured Despisers*. Trans. John Oman, London, publisher unknown, 1893.

Schmidt, W., *The Origin and Growth of Religion: Facts and Theories*. London, Methuen, 1931.

Sharpe, E. J., *Understanding Religion*. London, Duckworth, 1983.

——*Comparative Religion: A History*. London, Duckworth, 1975. Second edition, London, Duckworth, and La Salle, Open Court, 1986.

Smart, N., *The World's Religions*. Cambridge, Cambridge University Press, 1989.

Smith, H., *The Religions of Man*. New York, Harper & Row, 1964.

Söderblom, Nathan, *Uppenbarelsereligion* (*The Religion of Revelation*). Uppsala, Schultz, 1903.

Spencer, H., *First Principles*. London, Williams & Norgate, 1862.

——*Essays: Scientific, Political and Speculative*. 3 vols, London, Williams & Norgate, 1901.

Starbuck, E. D., *The Psychology of Religion: An Empirical Study of the Growth of Religious Consciousness*. London, Scott, 1899.

Troeltsch, Ernst, *Die Absolutheit des Christentums und die Religionsgeschichte* (1902, belated Eng. tr. David Reid, *The Absoluteness of Christianity and the History of Religions*, 1971). John Knox Press, Louisville, 1971.

Trompf, G. W., *In Search of Origins*. London, Oriental University Press, 1990.

Tylor, E. B., *Primitive Culture*. London, John Murray, 1871.

Underhill, E., *Mysticism: A Study in the Nature and Development of Man's Spiritual Consciousness*. 13th edn, London, Methuen, 1940.

Waardenburg, J., *Classical Approaches to the Study of Religion: Aims, Methods and Theories of Research*. 2 vols, The Hague and Paris, Mouton, 1973–74.

White, A. D., *A History of the Warfare of Science with Theology in Christendom*. 2 vols, London, Arco, 1955.

QUESTIONS FOR REVIEW AND DISCUSSION

1. What are the three questions that Sharpe feels anyone engaged in academic study should consider and of these which is the most difficult? What might the challenges be when considering this question?

2. What were the general attitudes towards the religious beliefs and customs of others among the early Greeks, Romans, Hebrews, and Christians? Do you think these attitudes have changed among contemporary westerners, and if so, in what ways?

3. What were Andrew Lang's main critiques of the theory of animism as the origin of religion? Speculate on what might be other hypothetical contenders for the origin or first forms of religion.

4. What are some of the qualities of mystical experience according to William James, and what are some of the shortcomings of his characterization of religion according to Sharpe?
5. What are the main points of difference between the focus on religion taken by Rudolph Otto versus that by Emile Durkheim?
6. What, according to Sharpe, are some of the best English-language scholarly journals on the study of religion? Can you suggest the names of other journals to add to this list?
7. How does Sharpe contrast religious conservatives and fundamentalists?
8. How does Sharpe characterize the current shape of the "study of the religion"? Are there other characteristics that you discern are among the current expectations of studying religion?

2 Methodology and the Study of Religion: Some Misgivings

Wilfred Cantwell Smith

Wilfred Cantwell Smith (1916–2000) was born in Toronto and received his doctorate in oriental languages from Princeton University. He was the founder of the Institute of Islamic Studies at McGill University, and also taught for over a decade at Harvard. Among his most influential books is *The Meaning and End of Religion*, where he asserts that "religion" is a conceptual label assigned by outsiders to the faith of others. The term "religion" eventually gets picked up by "insiders," in response to the outsiders' perspective. In the following selection, Smith offers a trenchant critique of academic approaches that give primary value to method over the object of study, namely religious phenomena. Moreover, Smith insists on a "humane" attitude towards the object of study, contrasting approaches encouraged by other scholars in this collection. We thought it best to present some of these contrasting prescriptions on approaches to the study of religion at the outset of an anthology dedicated to theories and methods.

***

At a conference called by the School of Religion of the University of Iowa in 1974 on "Methodology and the World Religions" Smith began his talk with a story from the Daoist philosopher, Chuang Tzu:

> Once when Hsi Shih, the most beautiful of women, was frowning and beating her breast, an ugly woman saw her and thought, "Now I have found out how to become more beautiful!" So she went home to her village and did nothing but frown and beat her breast. When the rich men of the village saw her, they bolted themselves into their houses and dared not come out; when the poor people of the village saw her they took wife and child by the hand and ran at top speed. This woman had seen that someone frowning was beautiful and thought that she had only to frown in order to become more beautiful.

Smith used this tale that illustrates the folly of thoughtless mimicry to justify to his colleagues his critique of methodology. He was defending his statement that methodology is "the massive red herring of modern scholarship, the most significant obstacle to intellectual progress, and the chief distraction from rational understanding of the world."[1]

These are very strong words. I state the point starkly so as to make clear that the gulf is wide, and appears also to be deep. Obviously, I have not understood what is meant by 'methodology,' or I should not feel this way about it. Obviously, I have not made myself understood, when I think I see the primary values of humane scholarship threatened by it, else my friends would have salvaged me from my errors ere now (or I them from theirs).

If there be any perspicacity in my position, there has certainly been no perspicuity.

I have come to Iowa in the hopes of learning what is so wrong with my understanding of scholarship in the humanities, or my formulation of it, or my perception of my colleagues' formulations. In this presentation, I am making a serious effort to formulate my reservations. I hope that I can make these sufficiently clear as to be intelligible; and I would plead with you to help me to see where I am wrong, insofar as I am. Let me at the outset make what may seem a concession. When I affirm that the emphasis on method in modern university thinking disturbs or alienates me, I have to admit to myself that I too in some sense prize method, and stress it, and give loyalty to it; and I expect my students to do so. Now that I am teaching undergraduates, I find myself devoting much time and effort to hammering away in an attempt to inculcate method, especially in written work submitted – and rigorously. Yet there is a difference here. For when I think and feel this way, I have in mind the academic method generically. First and foremost, it is rational; and there are many other attributes that one might list: it is critical, analytical, systematic, deliberate, comparative, public, cumulative. It is inductive, and in some sense empirical. One could prolong the list. There are more specific matters also, such as acknowledging indebtedness rather than plagiarizing, and giving exact rather than vague references when citing authorities, and so on. Involved are a scrupulous attention to detail; fastidious precision in the reporting of it; relentless honesty.

Nevertheless, except for the fact that mathematics would seem to be an exception to the inductive-empirical matter, this academic method is, as I have said, generic for *all* university studies; it is not particular, differing from discipline to discipline.

In other words, in my vision of academic procedure and rational inquiry there is no specific method for one subject differentiating it from another. Academic method is what all scholars have in common, not what differentiates them. (We shall be returning to this.)

A second point, also weighty, is that this general academic method is preamble, is subordinate. A good academic learns it, assimilates it, forgets it – in the sense that it is taken so much for granted that he moves on from there to the substance of his work. Ideally, he absorbs it to the point where he is unconscious of it, not self-conscious about it.

My divergence, and my restlessness, then, on this issue, are much deeper than most of my friends can understand. For the divergence, I think of three possible explanations: a geographic, a chronological, and what some might call a "disciplinary." For the first: I come out of a university tradition historically derived from Britain, whereas the recent academic patterns of this country intellectually derive from Germany. This might explain how it is that, after happy years in Canada, Britain, and India, I was never able to feel quite intellectually at home in this country. Another way of seeing the issue would be as a polarity between the old and the new. This could make my understanding of scholarship, which I might be predisposed to call a traditional or even a classical view, rather that of an old fogey: the outlook of a person who has simply not caught up with modern intellectual developments. Still a third interpretation would analyse the difference between my position and the prevalent one as fundamentally a divergence between the humane and the natural sciences. According to this view, concepts and orientations derived from, and presumably appropriate to, the natural sciences would have been taken over into the study of human affairs; by the social sciences deliberately and proudly – they explicitly boast that they are imitating the natural sciences in their methods and outlooks – and even by many humanists, under the great weight of the prestige of the natural, and nowadays perhaps also the social, sciences.

I should guess that all three of these interpretations probably hold some water; that all are relevant. None of them contributes anything however, to determining what is right and what is wrong; what legitimate, and what damaging. The stress on methodology and "discipline" may have become strong because of German, or of contemporary, or of natural science influences; and yet any or all of these might be reasons why it was to be deplored, as well as why it was to be applauded. Whatever the reasons, my vision of authentic humane scholarship and the pursuit of a genuinely rational interpretation of the world seems to lean towards a substantially different conceptualization from the currently dominant one; and I am looking for rational, rather than circumstantial, arguments as to why I should adopt a different one, one that seems to me to bode ill for our enterprise.

Let me look just a little more closely at those three possible grounds for divergence. On the first, I have little to say, since I do not know enough about the history of universities over the past century and am far from confident about interpreting what little I know ...

On the chronological matter, I speak with more confidence. Whatever the cultural or sociological provenance, the temporal sequence is clear. There would seem no question but that there has been, over the last several decades, a powerful shift in academic studies from *subject-matter* to *discipline.* Let no one underestimate the deep significance of that development. I invite you to join me in deploring it; or at the very least, to join me in ferreting out and considering some of its implications.

The faculty members of a university used to divide up their work among themselves according to differing objects of investigation; more recently, by differing methods of investigation. It was assumed in the former case that each scholar would find methods that were appropriate, fruitful, to his field; in the latter case, that each will find things to examine that are presumably appropriate to his methods. Classically, one department was discriminated from another by what it studied; nowadays, by how it studies.

As I understand it, a Ph.D. in, for instance, anthropology, is in a certain sense a certification that the recipient has learned the methods of anthropology, has demonstrated that he knows how to apply them, and is launched on the world with this equipment. What makes him an anthropologist is his grasp of those methods and his reliability in applying them. Once he has them, he may apply them wherever he finds them applicable. In the old days, when anthropology was a subject, it tended to study "primitive" societies on remote islands. Now that it is a discipline, its methods may be applied to an investigating of the local stamp club, a women's political movement, the Trobriand Islanders, or whatever.

Now not all departments of an Arts faculty have become "disciplines" in this sense. English literature, for example, may or might develop certain procedures peculiar to it; nonetheless, it is defined by the content of its subject matter, and cannot be defined by its procedures. The Classics, again, are distinguished from any other part of the Arts faculty by the boundaries of what they study; boundaries in time and space, and to some extent in language. The method by which they study what they study is totally undefined; they may bring to bear upon their data any methods, which they themselves or anybody else may have dreamed up, that prove rewarding. It follows not only that their activity is not characterized by any specific method, but also that the criterion of whether a given method is appropriate or not is the pragmatic one of whether it helps to illuminate within their field that in which at a given moment they are interested. The method used not only cannot define their work, but neither can it justify it. A scholar in the Classics must at every point justify whatever method it be that he brings to bear, not only by its theoretical but also its practical legitimacy, in actually advancing his and his readers' knowledge and under-standing of the subject matter. If upon data from the classical world he brings to bear the methods of Freudian psychoanalysis, Marxian economics, Thomist metaphysics, chemical carbon-dating, McLuhan literary criticism, or anything else, or thinks up new methods *ad hoc*, this is fine insofar as, and only insofar as, it advances the world's knowledge of and insight into that classical world. This means, *inter alia*, that the use of method is always under judgment by something outside itself. Hence the scholar becomes (incidentally) critical of method; but not idolatrous of it.

I once met a young American social scientist in India who was studying the role there of Muslims in political parties. I pointed out to him that in one of his studies, of an election, as reported in an interesting article that he had given me to read, he had omitted consideration of something that, I suggested, though subtle, was of quite central importance for an understanding of Muslim behaviour, including this instance. He responded, in a quite casual and unruffled manner, that his methods were unable to handle matters of that kind, and therefore he had left them out. He said this without embarrassment, without weeping, without resigning his academic appointment.

What has happened to our universities, when presumably reputable members of them will admit without blushing that their work distorts – deliberately, knowingly – what it purports to describe?

Now there are two possible answers to this sort of criticism, I suppose. One is that since sociology explicitly and admittedly is limited in its apprehensions, a full understanding of, let us say, Muslim political behaviour in India would be given by inter-disciplinary study. I shall return to this point in a moment. The other answer (not unrelated) that an apologist might give for the situation that I have just criticized might be that the sociologist in describing the political behaviour of Muslims in India is not, strictly, aspiring to describe, to represent, to understand that particular behaviour, but is aspiring rather to construct eventually theories of political behaviour generally; so that the role of this particular study, concerning this particular group of persons in India at this particular election, was aimed at contributing to an eventual universal theory of political behaviour of all men everywhere. One must in the meantime, he would concede, take note of peculiar people like Muslims, and special countries like India, in order to refine that theory, in order that the universal, abstract truth to which one aspires be not gross, over-simplified, premature. And even that final abstract truth might remain in principle unattainable; yet the business of sociology is supposed to be to approximate ever closer and closer to it, since sociology is a "science." (By the way, maybe the man was a political scientist rather than a sociologist; I do not exactly remember, and it makes no difference.)

It seems to me that the aspiration here is not a knowledge of the real world, but an abstract formula. I suppose that I was offended partly because the chap emerged as not really interested in either the Muslims or in India. His interest was in sociological theory.

The interest in abstract theory rather than in concrete actuality, in universal general-ization rather than particular fact, reminds some people of science. Let me turn, then, to the third matter in the analysis of the methodological enthusiasm: the influence of the natural sciences. Those who champion the new orientation often argue that it is more scientific …

It is also my impression, which I am prepared to discuss quite spiritedly, that the position on the study of man that I champion is in fact more scientific than the one that I reject: both in the sense of being a closer parallel to the natural sciences' studies, and in the sense of being more likely to be acknowledged as such by natural scientists. If students of religion proceed on a rigorously humanist base, oriented primarily to the reality that they study, and secondly to interpreting what is observed in theories always and drastically subordinate to the matters under investigation and to the questions being asked, I should be inclined to predict that in that case our university colleagues in the natural sciences would recognize our work as academically not merely legitimate but indeed as substantially parallel to theirs; that an accusation of being unscientific would come not from them but from our, humanists', work as in fact more closely comparable to theirs than is the work of the methodological enthusiasts among the self-styled social or behavioural sciences.

... Yet in any case I insist that it does not really matter; the test of our validity is not whether we are scientific, nor whether we can establish a claim to be so; but whether we are successful in knowing and in understanding and in making intelligible man's religious life. Our duty, as members of the university, is not to be scientific, but to be rational – in ways appropriate to our subject matter – and effective.

This subject matter, which is human, is so profoundly different from the subject matter of the natural sciences, the physical world, and especially in the religious dimension of our immensely complicated, subtle human life, that it would be a dereliction of our duty if, rather than working out our own principles of study, we were to settle for simply importing notions from a radically other field. However "scientific" the methodological obsession may be, or may appear to be, if it gets in the way of our understanding what we are supposed to be studying, as I fear that it may, then it is out of place in our work.

To subordinate one's understanding of man to one's understanding of science is inhumane, inept, irrational, unscientific.

It is unscientific in a double sense. For apart from the question of the ultimate inherent difference between man and merely physical objects, there is the preliminary fact that there is more to science itself than technology. No wonder, then, that there is much more to the humanities than technique.

Humane knowing – the knowledge of man by man – is an exercise in the meeting between persons, be it across the centuries or across the world. It is, therefore, not technical, not subordinate to methodological rules. In personal relations, whether face-to-face or mediated by man's symbolic forms of expression, the use of technical procedures, unless rigorously subordinated to primarily personalist considerations, is not merely inappropriate but potentially disruptive. Man cannot know man except in mutuality: in respect, trust, and equality, if not ultimately love.

Thus it is not only that the methodology concern seems more interested in ideas than in the real world. It is also that when applied to the real world it is in danger of subordinating it to men's ideas, and even purposes. The prominence in recent Western thought given to the concept of method in epistemology goes back perhaps to Descartes, who in his fundamentally non-scientific, non-humble search for indubitable, absolute knowledge took as his model mathematics, thus focusing not on the objective world and empirical reality and on observation but on logical constructs, on ideas, and pure theory. Yet in its modern version, the outlook is not contemplative but utilitarian. It smacks of Aristotle's practical intellect, rather than theoretical. Bacon, inaugurating the humanistic age, said that knowledge is virtue. The notion of method, the interest in methodology, smack to me of Bacon here, rather than of Socrates. Certainly they smack of Buber's I-It rather than his I-Thou. It is my impression, as I have suggested, that the best scientists are themselves not technicians, but profoundly human; reverent in the fact of an awesomely given universe. They are primarily oriented to reality, not to ideas. And their knowledge is a virtue.

However that may be, we in the human sectors betray our task if we adopt an orientation to knowledge as technique, lending itself to manipulation and control, even to prediction (which infringes human dignity and freedom). The generating of that kind of scientific knowledge that is deliberately conceived as available to be applied, is not our task. The goal of the humanities is to know and to understand; may one not say that knowledge for understanding differs from knowledge for use?

Let me report another incident from my experience in Asia, this time from Lebanon, and with an anthropologist whom I met. This gentleman, a Westerner, admitted to me quite bluntly that he was in fact not at all interested in his Lebanese villagers as persons, nor indeed in the Middle East as an area. He had come out for a year's research from this country, he said, in order to test in that village in Lebanon certain general theories that the discipline of anthropology back home had formulated; he hoped to use his findings to confirm, to rebut, or more probably to refine those theories, and at the end of his year he would return to his academic appointment in this country, publish his results, and hope because of them to get a promotion, or at least a raise in salary. His ambition was by means of his publications to advance his own academic career; simultaneously to advance the so-called "science" of anthropology. (The concept of "academic career," by the way, is a recent development, and a very sad one.) In other words, this intellectual was using persons for his own private purposes, or for the purposes of advancing Western science. This, I feel deeply in either case, is immoral – not to say, sinful.

Now that that man was wicked is perhaps only incidentally interesting; there are many wicked persons on earth, and you might feel that it would distract us if we took time off to lament that fact. Germane to our discussion, however, are two points. One is that the sinfulness was built into his methodology; built in, one might say, to the fact that he made method dominant in his study of persons. We all fall short of ideals; but let us not have ideals that inherently exploit: conceptual frameworks that perceive the relations between persons (in this case knower and known) as technical, mechanical. That there is a method for dealing with persons goes along with the public relations ethos, with the manipulative, with the depersonalization of modern society; but surely it is to be deplored on the academic scene. If you feel that it is going simply too far to assert that the proper relation among persons is love, may we not at least agree that it includes respect, interest, openness, humility? A conception of the academic task, insofar as it involves a study of human beings that stresses method over subject matter is immoral.

Do some of you find that argument irrelevant? Some of my alarm stems from the drift of modern academic study away from moral considerations, as in the increasing use of deliberate deception in psychological and other experiments with human beings: intellectual dishonesty is not scientifically wrong, I suppose that Millman, or Darley and Batson, would say. Even if you do find the moral question irrelevant, however, there is an intellectual facet to the same consideration. The procedure-oriented approach to persons is not merely morally wrong, it is wrong intellectually. For it so happens that human beings are that kind of creature that cannot in fact be understood unless recognized as human, as personal, and treated humanely. To perceive persons as entities, contributing to more rarified theories, is inherently to misunderstand those persons – and therefore, to produce bad theories.

No art historian can be true who does not love his subject. No student of a great scholar of French literature will be as competent as is his teacher, if he has learned all the techniques but none of the appreciation, the sheer affection for the material. Polanyi feels that personal involvement is central even to the natural sciences; certainly in the study of religion, I would distrust any scholar of the Hindus who did not love India, or any interpreter of Islamics who had no Muslim friends.

It so happens that we live in the sort of universe where knowing what concerns man involves more than knowing how to proceed.

Let us turn, then, to that "interdisciplinary" question, proffered as a possible solution to the fact that every methodology inevitably omits something. It is possible that all methodologies put together would still omit something distinctly human. And indeed it is the suspicion that the characteristically religious dimension of human life has in fact proven elusive in even multi-disciplinary projects, that has led some to hope that the study of religion would provide a new methodology out of whose mechanical net this elusive human quality could somehow at last be guaranteed not to escape. The subtle, however, the elusive, the distinctly human, is what formalized method is calculated not to apprehend. The characteristically human is not accessible to technical devices; and most of all, the religious does not lend itself to formalized impersonalism. "We cannot engineer our way into the sacred," as I have heard a colleague put it.

Since I reject the concept "discipline," then, I am hardly mollified by the "interdisciplinary" gambit. The concept 'interdisciplinary' I regard as at best a ladder that may help some to climb out of a hole into which the true humanist has never fallen, and I think it important not to fall. It does at least recognize that something is awry with the notion, and the practice, of "discipline." It fails to recognize, however, what that something awry is.

This fact is somewhat demonstrated in that social scientists, each recognizing that his own methodology needs supplementing in order to arrive at a valid understanding of any concrete thing (as distinct from some abstract theory), nonetheless is inclined to add to his own, in his multi-disciplinary projects, only other social-science disciplines, leaving out humanities studies of the same topic. Or, if they be included, he wishes their results in a form that he can "use"; that is, in order for them to be serviceable he insists that they be conformed to his over-all categories. For his purposes, humane knowledge must be abstracted, depersonalized, rendered, technical and detachable. The contribution must conform to the notion that knowledge is technical.

It is not that I reject multi-lateral approaches; or that the classical humanist was in any sense tempted to do so. On the contrary: in the classical view of studying "subject," the problem was solved before it arose. The traditional British academic concept of an undergraduate "Honours" course, for example, has recently been criticized as overly specialized. (The University of Toronto, for instance, has recently abandoned this pattern, and on these grounds.) In fact, however, it was specialized in an older sense of concentrating on something specific and objective, but not in the modern sense of concentrating on only one aspect or dimension of, as it were, everything. Thus the student in Honours History might "specialize," to use that term, in, let us say, English history generally and specifically in the 17th century or the city of London in the decade of the 1640s; but he was expected, and encouraged, to look at whatever it was that he was thus concentratedly looking at with as much and as diverse assistance as he could muster from the psychological, the numismatic, the art-historical, or whatever.

Let us return to my example of the sociologist in India, for whom knowledge was not a knowledge of India, concretely, not of Muslims, personally, but a knowledge ideally of sociology, of theory. I would contend that no matter how many bits of knowledge of this type one might add together, one would still not arrive at a knowledge of that particular Muslim situation in India – nor indeed, of any other particular situation. I used never to understand how the mediaeval philosophers could consider the possibility that God could know anything, without knowing particulars. I am equally perplexed by a notion of sciences of man that might consist of spectacularly brilliant, and even in some sense true, theories, but that did not take the form of a direct knowledge (*connaissance* rather than *savoir*) of human history, in its actuality, diversity, and solidity.

We are becoming involved here in a philosophic issue with which I have been wrestling some of late: the problem of epistemology and of truth, and the nature of knowledge. Especially at issue is whether the object of man's knowledge is a proposition, or a state of affairs. There is perhaps a modern tendency to favour the former; and if knowledge is of propositions, there is a further question as to whether we approach closer to or recede further from true knowledge as the proposition becomes more generalized, more abstract.

Also at issue is the question of analysis and synthesis. The natural sciences found for a time that their knowledge advanced by their focusing on more and more distinct areas of inquiry. The smallest unit of human affairs, the individual person, the atom of the human sciences, however, is more complicated than anything else in the universe. Moreover, not only are we complicated; we integrate. However fine our analysis, we cannot understand man unless we understand synthesis.

The point here is that in humane study it is the individual student who is expected to do the integrating. A well-educated man, in the classical model, was one who understood the complexity, and multivalence, of every human affair; while the good scholar was he who could illuminate that affair, in its complexity and multi-valence. As he went on in depth, he learned more and more not about a particular method, but about a particular thing.

Thus, let us take an example from our own field, a study of the *Hajj*, the Pilgrimage to Makkah. A good historian of religion will learn all that he can learn from any insights that are or can be made to be pertinent: sociological, philological, historical, psychological, typological (sometimes called "phenomenological"), introspective, and to add something of my own, asking Muslims – and many more. Indeed, he will use these approaches, and not merely profit from others' use of them. Yet what he has specialized upon is something in the real world: namely, the *Hajj*. I have been called a methodological pluralist. Rather, I take methods so lightly that I hardly deserve to have it so dignified. When Bleeker speaks of a "right" methodology for "the science of Religion," I quake.

We have come, then, to the specific matter of the study of religion. So far I have been talking rather about methodology and the humanities at large, where I claim that the methodological emphasis threatens to disrupt knowledge, to distort it, and to obstruct understanding. Certainly my feeling that an academic department is best characterized in terms of what it studies, not how, comes saliently into play in our own particular academic enterprise.

In many universities, the question as to whether there should be a religion department in the Liberal Arts faculty was interpreted as asking, essentially, does the study of religion have its own methodology. Fortunately it does not; and I can think of nothing more calculated to damage the academic study of religion than its acquiring one, whether out of pressure to appear respectable among colleagues, or whether out of a genuine supposition that this is a good way to study human affairs. Given the uniquely subtle, elusive, volatile quality of the religious, it is surely probable that the one thing that we are most desirous of attempting to understand in our study would be precisely what would be omitted by any formalized, pre-conceived procedure or, more subtly, by our relying on any procedure; supposing, as it were, that it could do our work for us.

On this particular point I chuckled to myself over the fact that one of the most major, and most definitely *religious*, attainments of my own scholarly study in Islamics, the understanding of the meaning of the word *islam* and its relation to the concept "religion," I arrived at in part by the somewhat mechanical, although in the end revealing, procedure of going through a list of 25,000 book-titles in Arabic, arranged in alphabetical order, and listing in chronological order the 84 titles that I culled from among them in which the Arabic word *islam* occurs. It amuses me to think how excessively stupid it would be if I were to teach my students, or if anybody else were to imagine, that the way to arrive at insight in religious matters is to count book-titles! *Pace* Chuang Tzu and that ugly woman. ... Any scholar worth his salt would surely be too proud to follow any one else's method, too humble to suppose that others would wish to follow his, to say nothing of too engrossed in his subject matter to be distracted by generic theorizing about abstractions. Method should be developed out of the particular problem that one is considering, not vice versa, and it should be ephemeral, subordinate, and fundamentally dispensable. If the result at which I arrived were not able to be confirmed by totally different procedures, and indeed were it not able to have been arrived at in the first place through some drastically other method equally well, then I should regard its conclusions as unreliable.

In fact, in the religious field, so prone are outsiders to misinterpret that I myself always feel decidedly tentative about any conclusion until I have double and triple-checked. (And may we not accent the point that it is not the method that I check, but the results?)

Indeed, might we not set up as a principle that the validity of the result reached by any particular method, a question much exercising the methodological enthusiasts, is tested best not merely by evaluating that method, rationally and for aptness, but by ascertaining whether those results are convincing judged by other criteria, including whether they are confirmed by a quite other method?

This is doubly so, in that particular results are in fact never reached simply as a result of using a given method. Much more is involved than that. The Dutch scholar van der Leeuw wrote a quite good book called originally *Phenomenology of Religion*. (That phrase became a sub-title in the English-language version, which, since it was published in England, was called primarily *Religion in Essence and Manifestation*.) Because he had accomplished something quite significant in this particular study, a number of people rushed about to seize upon his method, and felt that if they copied it, they too would write good books. So far has this now gone that Phenomenology of Religion itself has become a subject of study; we shall return to this. Meanwhile, one may simply note that those who copied this Dutchman's method seemed not to ask themselves about his person, his sensitivity, his intelligence, his insightfulness, his sympathy, and so on. Indeed, I am left wondering whether the emphasis on method is not designed to relieve us of as much of the personal as possible, in the hopes of by-passing the really difficult challenges. Into the writing of a book of that kind goes a whole series of factors, of which it is surely obvious that method is only one, and of which it is not at all obvious that it is anywhere near the top in order of importance.

It would seem to me relatively easy to argue, and indeed to demonstrate, that the attitude, the philosophy, and the general orientation of an author are of major consequence for any scholarly study: are at least equally important, and usually more important, than the method employed. I speak a little tentatively here, because it seems to me that some of my friends talk about methodology when they mean not something pertaining to method but what I would call rather, conceptual framework, ideology, presuppositions, or the like. The preconceptions with which any scholar approaches any given problem or task undoubtedly colour the conclusions to which he comes. I am inclined, accordingly, to give a great deal of attention, in the critical appraisal of academic work, to this matter of conceptual starting-point. In one's own work, and in the educating of students who come into our field, one may well stress the matter of being self-conscious about one's preconceptions and ideological stance. Often, in fact, a given method is almost predictably derived from the preconceptions of the person using it. (In passing, I may elaborate this to remark that, in illustration, the behavioural sciences' stress on methodology is itself a product of the, to my mind, fundamentally false preconceptual framework of the behaviour sciences.)

I said just now that when a significant book appears in our field, there is a tendency to pounce upon its method and to focus upon that, for imitation by all concerned. The fad even goes to the point of setting it up for separate study itself. Thus "the Phenomenology of Religion" has become something that is studied as such, even though there be nothing in the objective world to which that rubric is the corresponding intellectualization. To study phenomenology of religion is not to study the real world. Or, if that be going too far, let me put it this way: that to study phenomenology of religion is to turn from an interest in the centuries-long history of religion in Asia and to concern oneself with the recent history of thought in Europe indeed. Phenomenology is a minor movement in Western thought, interesting to people who happen to be interested in that sort of thing; but it should be dealt with as a particular subject matter, ancillary to the study of religion itself.

Last September the Department of Religion at Columbia University wrote to me, and I presume to others, saying that they were "looking for a person with a clear grasp of methodological issues in the study of religion, with interest in specific contemporary methods such as phenomenology and structuralism, who also has an area of depth in specific forms of religion phenomena." One may note here the primary interest in method, with substantive knowledge as an additive extra, rather than vice versa. They did not wish someone who knew a particular religious tradition, or any other concrete empirical matters primarily, and "who also has" a competence in questions of method; but the other way round. Some universities, similarly, make a course on phenomenology of religion an introductory freshman offering (though van der Leeuw himself admitted to his course on that subject only doctoral candidates in their final year of study).

. . .

On receiving the letter from Columbia I was bold enough to write back asking why they felt that the modern phenomenologists and structuralists were any more important, interesting, or worthy of a full-scale appointment than other theorists. Van der Leeuw and Lévi-Strauss have come up with some interesting ideas about religion, no doubt; but I asked those at Columbia whether they really regarded them as more illuminating in this realm than, let us say, Hegel and Plotinus – or for that matter, than Samkara. The answer, as might be expected, was that these (at least, the first two) were already covered, under Philosophy of Religion. My point, of course, was that the new writers are theorists of religion in the same sense as were the older ones. Why should the old course not be expanded to cover the new luminaries in the field? I, at least, cannot see how one can do more than (a) study the data; and (b) study interpretations of the data.

What is it that a person knows, who knows structuralism?

QUESTIONS FOR REVIEW AND DISCUSSION

1. Although critical of methodology, Smith upholds and promotes certain canons of scholarly method. What are these?
2. What does Smith mean when he asserts that "to subordinate one's understanding of man to one's understanding of science, ... is unscientific"?

3. What sort of research or attitude to research does Smith characterize as "immoral" or even "sinful" and why? Do you agree with Smith's evaluation and condemnation of valuing the application of method over the persons studied?

4. What other rationales does Smith offer in his critique of method besides the moral objections? Do you find these compelling?

5. What are Smith's objections to the concept of "discipline"? Do you think it is appropriate to call religious studies a discipline?

Note

1 W. C. Smith, "Methodology and the Study of Religion: Some Misgivings," in Robert D. Baird, ed., *Methodological Issues in Religious Studies* (Chico, CA: New Horizons Press, 1975, p. 2).

3 Premises Concerning Religious Studies

Hillary P. Rodrigues

Hillary Peter Rodrigues (1953—) was born in Mumbai, India, and received his doctorate in Religious Studies from McMaster University. A specialist in Eastern religions, he has authored books and articles on the philosophies of contemporary Indian religious teachers and on the Hindu tradition. His contributions include work on the history, iconographic forms, and ritual worship of the great goddess, Durgā. He edits *Studying Religions in Practice*, an instructive series of anthologies for undergraduates designed to meld theory and method in the discipline with the study of religious practices. He has co-authored *Introduction to the Study of Religion* with John S. Harding. A former chair of the Departments of Anthropology and of Religious Studies, Rodrigues currently teaches at the University of Lethbridge, Canada, where he has been honored with the Distinguished Teaching Award and the Board of Governors Chair in Teaching. The following selection draws inspiration from such sources as Bruce Lincoln's "Theses on Method," and attempts to present a succinct articulation of key premises on the doing of religious studies.

1. Despite confusion that may derive from the term, "religious studies" does not refer to efforts to enhance one's personal religious life. Rather it is a scholarly discipline directed at augmenting knowledge of personal, social, and assorted phenomena that are collectively regarded as religion.

Commentary: Like scholars in a variety of other academic disciplines, such as media studies or cultural studies, where media and cultures are the objects of study, the religious studies student strives to understand the full compass of the human religious response. Just as a biologist may study bears without the intent of becoming more bear-like, or an art historian art, but not to become a better artist, so too, religious studies scholars study religion, not to become more effectively religious, but to augment our understanding of the salient constellation of human activities that are broadly designated "religion." Note also that one need not be a bird to be an ornithologist, or an artist to be an art historian.

2. Although it is difficult to generate a definition of religion that will satisfy everyone, the human phenomenon of religion is as evident and apparent as music or art, and is an adequately distinct category of study.

Commentary: There are personal, social, and cultural practices that may be at the margins of what one's personal definition of religion circumscribes. Just as what one considers "music" may simply be "noise" to another, or what one regards as extraordinary art may look like infantile scribbles or painting to another, people vary in what they exclude or are willing to include within the parameters of their definitions. In that vein, one person's religious beliefs may be thought of by others as outright delusion, and some person's religious activities may be abhorrent to others. Nevertheless, despite disagreements about just where to draw the boundaries, few would disagree that there are such entities as music, or art, or religion. Scholars of religion, either consciously, or unconsciously through the features they choose to examine, assert the parameters of what they consider to belong to the category of religion.

3. Among the varied characteristics of religion is its tendency to be circumscribed by a special status, which is designated with privileged labels such as pure, sacred, transcendent, holy, immaculate, eternal, supernatural, divine, and so on. These ennobling characteristics are placed in contrast with the non-religious, which are designated as impure or polluted, profane, worldly, unholy, stained, transient, natural, human, and so on.

Commentary: People often invest portions of their personal and collective lives – portions of their thoughts, feelings, and activities – with the highest significance in their hierarchical grading of facets of reality. Thus health is generally valued over illness, beauty over ugliness, and so on. Religion is a constellation of those ideas, moods, motivations, and deeds that generally occupies the apex of this hierarchy. Put differently, religion circumscribes people's most cherished notions about the nature of reality, their place within that reality, and how they ought to live their lives in relationship to that perspective. For instance, for some persons, reality consists of transcendental realms known as heaven and hell, and the immanent realm known as earth or the manifest universe. Other beings, such as angels and demons, gods, or a supreme God, may be believed to inhabit the transcendental realms. These persons may believe that human beings are created by the supreme God, inhabit the earthly or manifest realm, and are placed here to undergo an ordeal before leaving this realm. Life is a test, with God the supreme judge, and one ought to live in a particular manner, holding particular beliefs, and performing particular ritual actions in daily, weekly, yearly or lifelong cycles as part of the examination process. Passing the ordeal may lead a person to the bliss of heaven for eternity, while failure can lead to a horrific eternity in hellish realms. In contrast to this worldview, some persons believe that one is reborn repeatedly in any of the three realms, and the ultimate purpose of existence is to gain freedom from the cycles of rebirth. Others do not believe in any realm other than the manifest one, and discard notions of rebirth, transcendental beings of any kind, or eternal existence in any transcendental realm. Each such individual or social group holds their beliefs to be the highest truth about reality, so true, in fact, and so special, that the beliefs may be designated as being beyond question. Furthermore, they may even believe that questioning or investigating the reality of their worldview is taboo or sinful, and may carry with it undesirable consequences.

4. Since what is designated as being "religious" within these views of reality varies – even contrasts dramatically – from individual to individual, among social groups, and through the course of history, it suggests that there is nothing intrinsically sacrosanct about the categories so designated. In the discipline of religious studies, these "religious" categories are certainly not treated with sacred reverence. They are only special to the religious studies scholar because they constitute a valid object of one's inquiry (i.e., a so-called religious phenomenon).

Commentary: Religious studies scholars do not accept the sanctified status conferred upon any religious worldview. Sometimes what is regarded as sacred by one group is profane to another. Scholarly study would be inhibited if one preferentially accepted one worldview over another, or the sacred categories of one group over another's. For instance, how would one effectively study the nature and implications of a monotheistic or non-theistic worldview, if one accepted that polytheism was the truth about reality? In religious studies, all worldviews and their components are open to scrutiny, particularly those that are designated as special and off-limits, because these are precisely where one is likely to encounter the objects of one's study: "religious phenomena." Just because a group designates a particular book to have been composed by a divine being and thus treats it with the utmost respect does not mean that it is intrinsically sacred and should not be examined as objectively as any other piece of writing. Just because a group designates a particular practice (e.g., human sacrifice or bodily mutilation) as highly sacred, does not mean that it is beyond inquiry. Etiquette would suggest that one not summarily treat disrespectfully that towards which some individual or group shows respect. However, intellectual honesty and scholarly rigor should not be sacrificed on the altar of social decorum. Religion is not sacred to religious studies scholars when engaged in the activities of the discipline.

5. Religious studies scholars should not restrict their investigations to the parameters delineated or designated by the religious phenomena under study. Whatever is thought pertinent to the study is open to examination.

Commentary: Religious "insiders" (i.e., believers in a particular worldview; members who belong to a particular religious community) may indicate to the scholar what constitutes the valid boundaries for investigation, but these injunctions need not be heeded. For instance, just because a religious community considers a particular set of texts to be the works of their founder, and have designated them with the stamp of approval and authority, does not mean that scholars should only study those texts, and not examine other works that make rival claims. It can be intellectually beneficial to examine materials (e.g., beliefs, works, activities, historical events) that are ignored or even repudiated by insiders, since these may provide insights into the values, interests, historical development, and objectives of a religious group or tradition. The construction of religious worldviews often requires the erection of boundaries that exclude as well as include. Thus, examining materials, listening to voices, etc., at the periphery, where demarcations occur between what is inside and what is outside, may reveal much about a religion's identity formation, its appeal to would-be converts, its methods of persuasion, its promises and powers, as well as the permeability of its borders.

6. In religious studies, method is subordinate to the object of study. The discipline of religious studies is shaped by what is studied, namely, the phenomenon of religion, and not by a particular academic technique. Acceptable methods are diverse, culled from other disciplinary orientations, and applied as suited to the scholar's investigative needs as dictated by the phenomenon being examined.

Commentary: Just as professional carpenters might have an assortment of tools in their toolkits, religious studies scholars may choose from a wide array of methods in their work. When building a chair a carpenter may need various types of saws at certain phases of the work, and drills, hammers, nails, planes, and so on at other stages. So, too, the scholar may need to apply the methods of literary analysis, translation, historical study, participant observation, and so on, in order to decipher a religious phenomenon effectively. For instance, understanding contemporary religious practices among Balinese Hindus may call more for the use of participant observation – a method generally associated with the discipline of anthropology – than, say, the scriptural analysis of Vedic Indian Hindu texts. And yet the study of those texts might shed necessary light on the litany of prayers uttered by Balinese priests during their contemporary ritual activities.

7. The discipline of religious studies does not have as its primary objective the support or denigration of any religious phenomenon. The religious studies scholar's main intent should be to understand the nature of religious phenomena as fully and truthfully as possible, and transmit that understanding to others as effectively as possible.

Commentary: Just as a nuclear physicist is encouraged to be neither favourably nor negatively disposed to a plutonium atom, but to strive to understand how it is put together, and theorize as truthfully and dispassionately about the subatomic processes at work within it, so too, religious studies scholars should take a dispassionate stance to the particular outcomes of their investigations. One may certainly have a passionate interest in the object of study – of obvious benefit in generating motivation and zeal in one's work – but scholars should not be favourably predisposed towards particular outcomes of their investigations. In other words, if the rigorous examination of evidence accumulated offers no substantive proof for the claims made by a religious tradition (e.g., the existence of the founder, the divine source of a scripture, miraculous occurrences, women's roles and participation, tolerant and non-violent attitudes to other belief systems, historical events), the scholar should not obscure the results of their findings in order to support the claims or to not offend adherents of that tradition, or to try to ensure that a religious tradition presents a pleasant countenance. However, despite valuing rigorous critical analysis in one's research, the religious studies approach is not primarily concerned with "debunking" the claims of religions and their various worldviews and values, any more than a student of literature or film would constantly be attempting to ascertain how "truly" a world is depicted in literature or on screen. Instead, the general thrust in religious studies is to understand as best as possible such features as: the structure and dynamics of religious phenomena, when, where, how and by whom they are produced, maintained, and transformed, to whom they appeal and why, and how they interact with other features, designated as "non-religious," in those particular systems.

8. Should a scholar simultaneously be an "insider" to a particular religious tradition, she or he should exercise care – when engaged in the doing of religious studies – not to be partial to that tradition. On the same note, a religious studies scholar should not be partial to "outsider" traditions out of a misplaced sense of respectfulness. The scholar's stance is to strive for impartiality, and an even-handed, rigorous application of objective analysis, critical thinking, and open-minded intellectual curiosity.

Commentary: Students sometime erroneously grant to religious phenomena an exalted status, because adherents dictate that the religious entities are exalted. On a related note, while one may be quite capable of placing one's own tradition under a critical, scholarly lens, there is often a tendency to be inadequately critical or even uncritical of other religious traditions, particularly those that are dominant in other societies and cultures. This is sometimes the result of an erroneous overcompensation based on "othering." Cultural imperialism and religious intolerance by western nations in the past often led to the denigration of other cultures and religions. Thus there is sometimes a tendency to cede to these cultures and traditions a favourable status, by way of overcompensation, and to engage in uncritical examination and appraisal of those traditions, precisely because of their "otherness." Religious studies scholars regard religious phenomena as fundamentally mediated by and to human beings, despite the claims by religious adherents to transcendental sources for their beliefs. And all human activities are open to and require egalitarian intellectual inquiry and examination, regardless of the cultural or purportedly divine milieus from which they emanate. Efforts should be made to avoid favoritism of any kind.

9. Hegemonic religious discourse is not *the* authentic religious tradition. A holistic understanding derives from attending to all discursive strands that constitute a tradition.

Commentary: Since the religious studies stance regards religion as a human activity, it does not accept as axiomatic that the "real" religion is what is purveyed only by authoritative persons, groups, texts, or voices within that tradition. A holistic understanding requires attention to the voices of all persons and phenomena (texts, activities, etc.) within a religious tradition's compass. While certain of these voices may work to constitute a dominant discourse, these should not be privileged. Marginalized voices, contesting voices, dominated voices, and the perspectives and actions of all other groups within a tradition, beyond the margins of a tradition's hegemonic forms, need adequate scholarly attention.

10. The discipline of religious studies itself derives from a particular worldview and its consequent orientations. The scholar's task is to apply the same critical apparatus to the canons and practices of these disciplinary orientations, so that their obscure features are made visible and rendered comprehensible.

Commentary: It is mandatory that the critical analytic lens be regularly turned to the discipline of religious studies, so that it may itself be better understood. Since all worldviews, including religious and rationally constructed ones, are malleable, dynamic entities, they undergo shifts and changes through time, and across cultures. The regular examination and scrutiny of these processes can further our knowledge of how we choose to learn, why we do so, and how better to refine our means of understanding. In other words, critically examining the history, theories and methods of the discipline of religious studies is held to be as crucial an aspect of the discipline as the study of religious phenomena. Just as carpenters must attend to the condition of their tools and not just the wooden objects they fabricate, so too, we must attend to our disciplinary assumptions, orientations, objectives, and productions.

QUESTIONS FOR REVIEW AND DISCUSSION

1. Does Rodrigues indicate the parameters that bound religious phenomena? Can you suggest certain essential characteristics of such phenomena?
2. What does Rodrigues suggest that religious studies scholars should take as the basis of their investigations? Do you think this is reasonable?
3. Rodrigues suggests that method should be subordinate to the object of study. Does he discard the study of theory and method entirely? What place should the study of the discipline have in the discipline of religious studies?

4. Rodrigues suggests that one should strive for holism and impartiality. To what extent are these unattainable ideals?
5. What is meant by hegemonic discourse? Do you agree with Rodrigues that it is partial and inadequate in the study of religious phenomena?
6. List two additional premises to Rodrigues's list of ten.

PART 2

The Older Strata: Early, Classic, or Foundational Writings

A. Philosophy and Theology

Early Examples from the West and East

Classic Examples of Nineteenth-century Philosophizing on Religion

Examples of Foundational Theorists in Feminist Studies of Religion

B. Classic Social Scientific Perspectives (Sociological and Anthropological)

C. Classic Phenomenological and Psychological Perspectives

4 Allegory of the Cave

Plato

Plato (429?–347? BCE), one of the most influential of the early Greek philosophers, was probably born in Athens or Aegina sometime between 429 and 423 BCE. Well educated and travelled, Plato established a school of learning near Athens, known as the Academy, which endured until its closure in the sixth century CE by the Christian emperor Justinian. Plato regarded Socrates as one of his most influential teachers, and Aristotle was his most influential student. Plato generally presented his ideas in the form of dialogues in which Socrates is the main character, with whom other characters engage in philosophical discussion. The following selection, popularly known as the "Allegory of the Cave," is taken from *The Republic*, a Platonic/Socratic dialogue written in about 380 BCE and dealing with what constitutes a just society and its leaders. The conversation in the Allegory is between Socrates [S] and Plato's brother Glaucon [G] and deals with the characteristics of the person ideally suited to govern.

A Dialogue between Socrates and Glaucon

[S] And now, I said, let me show in a figure how far our nature is enlightened or unenlightened: −Behold! human beings living in a underground den, which has a mouth open towards the light and reaching all along the den; here they have been from their childhood, and have their legs and necks chained so that they cannot move, and can only see before them, being prevented by the chains from turning round their heads. Above and behind them a fire is blazing at a distance, and between the fire and the prisoners there is a raised way; and you will see, if you look, a low wall built along the way, like the screen which marionette players have in front of them, over which they show the puppets.

[G] I see.

[S] And do you see, I said, men passing along the wall carrying all sorts of vessels, and statues and figures of animals made of wood and stone and various materials, which appear over the wall? Some of them are talking, others silent.

[G] You have shown me a strange image, and they are strange prisoners.

[S] Like ourselves, I replied; and they see only their own shadows, or the shadows of one another, which the fire throws on the opposite wall of the cave?

[G] True, he said; how could they see anything but the shadows if they were never allowed to move their heads?

[S] And of the objects which are being carried in like manner they would only see the shadows?

[G] Yes, he said.

[S] And if they were able to converse with one another, would they not suppose that they were naming what was actually before them?

[G] Very true.

[S] And suppose further that the prison had an echo which came from the other side, would they not be sure to fancy when one of the passers-by spoke that the voice which they heard came from the passing shadow?

[G] No question, he replied.

[S] To them, I said, the truth would be literally nothing but the shadows of the images.

[G] That is certain.

[S] And now look again, and see what will naturally follow if the prisoners are released and disabused of their error. At first, when any of them is liberated and compelled suddenly to stand up and turn his neck round and walk and look towards the light, he will suffer sharp pains; the glare will distress him, and he will be unable to see the realities of which in his former state he had seen the shadows; and then conceive someone saying to him, that what he saw before was an illusion, but that now, when he is approaching nearer to being and his eye is turned towards more real existence, he has a clearer vision, – what will be his reply? And you may further imagine that his instructor is pointing to the objects as they pass and requiring him to name them, – will he not be perplexed? Will he not fancy that the shadows which he formerly saw are truer than the objects which are now shown to him?

[G] Far truer.

[S] And if he is compelled to look straight at the light, will he not have a pain in his eyes which will make him turn away to take and take in the objects of vision which he can see, and which he will conceive to be in reality clearer than the things which are now being shown to him?

[G] True, he now said.

[S] And suppose once more, that he is reluctantly dragged up a steep and rugged ascent, and held fast until he's forced into the presence of the sun himself, is he not likely to be pained and irritated? When he approaches the light his eyes will be dazzled, and he will not be able to see anything at all of what are now called realities.

[G] Not all in a moment, he said.

[S] He will require to grow accustomed to the sight of the upper world. And first he will see the shadows best, next the reflections of men and other objects in the water, and then the objects themselves; then he will gaze upon the light of the moon and the stars and the spangled heaven; and he will see the sky and the stars by night better than the sun or the light of the sun by day?

[G] Certainly.

[S] Last of he will be able to see the sun, and not mere reflections of him in the water, but he will see him in his own proper place, and not in another; and he will contemplate him as he is.

[G] Certainly.

[S] He will then proceed to argue that this is he who gives the season and the years, and is the guardian of all that is in the visible world, and in a certain way the cause of all things which he and his fellows have been accustomed to behold?

[G] Clearly, he said, he would first see the sun and then reason about him.

[S] And when he remembered his old habitation, and the wisdom of the den and his fellow-prisoners, do you not suppose that he would felicitate himself on the change, and pity them?

[G] Certainly, he would.

[S] And if they were in the habit of conferring honours among themselves on those who were quickest to observe the passing shadows and to remark which of them went before, and which followed after, and which were together; and who were therefore best able to draw conclusions as to the future, do you think that he would care for such honours and glories, or envy the possessors of them? Would he not say with Homer,

> Better to be the poor servant of a poor master, and to endure anything, rather than think as they do and live after their manner?

[G] Yes, he said, I think that he would rather suffer anything than entertain these false notions and live in this miserable manner.

[S] Imagine once more, I said, such a one coming suddenly out of the sun to be replaced in his old situation; would he not be certain to have his eyes full of darkness?

[G] To be sure, he said.

[S] And if there were a contest, and he had to compete in measuring the shadows with the prisoners who had never moved out of the den, while his sight was still weak, and before his eyes had become steady (and the time which would be needed to acquire this new habit of sight might be very considerable) would he not be ridiculous? Men would say of him that up he went and down he came without his eyes; and that it was better not even to think of ascending; and if any one tried to loose another and lead him up to the light, let them only catch the offender, and they would put him to death.

[G] No question, he said.

[S] This entire allegory, I said, you may now append, dear Glaucon, to the previous argument; the prison-house is the world of sight, the light of the fire is the sun, and you will not misapprehend me if you interpret the journey upwards to be the ascent of the soul into the intellectual world according to my poor belief, which, at your desire, I have expressed whether rightly or wrongly God knows. But, whether true or false, my opinion is that in the world of knowledge the idea of good appears last of all, and is seen only with an effort; and, when seen, is also inferred to be the universal author of all things beautiful and right, parent of light and of the lord of light in this visible world, and the immediate source of reason and truth in the intellectual; and that this is the power upon which he who would act rationally, either in public or private life must have his eye fixed.

[G] I agree, he said, as far as I am able to understand you.

[S] Moreover, I said, you must not wonder that those who attain to this beatific vision are unwilling to descend to human affairs; for their souls are ever hastening into the upper world where they desire to dwell; which desire of theirs is very natural, if our allegory may be trusted.

[G] Yes, very natural.

[S] And is there anything surprising in one who passes from divine contemplations to the evil state of man, misbehaving himself in a ridiculous manner; if, while his eyes are blinking and before he has become accustomed to the surrounding darkness, he is compelled to fight in courts of law, or in other places, about the images or the shadows of images of justice, and is endeavouring to meet the conceptions of those who have never yet seen absolute justice?

[G] Anything but surprising, he replied.

[S] Anyone who has common sense will remember that the bewilderments of the eyes are of two kinds, and arise from two causes, either from coming out of the light or from going into the light, which is true of the mind's eye, quite as much as of the bodily eye; and he who remembers this when he sees any one whose vision is perplexed and weak, will not be too ready to laugh; he will first ask whether that soul of man has come out of the brighter light, and is unable to see because unaccustomed to the dark, or having turned from darkness to the day is dazzled by excess of light. And he will count the one happy in his condition and state of being, and he will pity the other; or, if he have a mind to laugh at the soul which comes from below into the light, there will be more reason in this than in the laugh which greets him who returns from above out of the light into the den.

[G] That, he said, is a very just distinction.

[S] But then, if I am right, certain professors of education must be wrong when they say that they can put a knowledge into the soul which was not there before, like sight into blind eyes.

[G] They undoubtedly say this, he replied.

[S] Whereas, our argument shows that the power and capacity of learning exists in the soul already; and that just as the eye was unable to turn from darkness to light without the whole body, so too the instrument of knowledge can only by the movement of the whole soul be turned from the world of becoming into that of being, and learn by degrees to endure the sight of being, and of the brightest and best of being, or in other words, of the good.

[G] Very true.

[S] And must there not be some art which will effect conversion in the easiest and quickest manner; not implanting the faculty of sight, for that exists already, but has been turned in the wrong direction, and is looking away from the truth?

[G] Yes, he said, such an art may be presumed.

[S] And whereas the other so-called virtues of the soul seem to be akin to bodily qualities, for even when they are not originally innate they can be implanted later by habit and exercise, that of wisdom more than anything else contains a divine element which always remains, and by this conversion is rendered useful and profitable; or, on the other hand, hurtful and useless. Did you never observe the narrow intelligence flashing from the keen eye of a clever rogue – how eager he is, how clearly his paltry soul sees the way to his end; he is the reverse of blind, but his keen eyesight is forced into the service of evil, and he is mischievous in proportion to his cleverness.

[G] Very true, he said.

[S] But what if there had been a circumcision of such natures in the days of their youth; and they had been severed from those sensual pleasures, such as eating and drinking, which, like leaden weights, were attached to them at their birth, and which drag them down and turn the vision of their souls upon the things that are below – if, I say, they had been released from these impediments and turned in the opposite direction, the very same faculty in them would have seen the truth as keenly as they see what their eyes are turned to now.

[G] Very likely.

[S] Yes, I said; and there is another thing which is likely, or rather a necessary inference from what has preceded, that neither the uneducated and uninformed of the truth, nor yet those who never make an end of their education, will be able ministers of State; not the former, because they have no single aim of duty which is the rule of all their actions, private as well as public; nor the latter, because they will not act at all except upon compulsion, fancying that they are already dwelling apart in the islands of the blest.

[G] Very true, he replied.

[S] Then, I said, the business of us who are the founders of the State will be to compel the best minds to attain that knowledge which we have already shown to be the greatest of all – they must continue to ascend until they arrive at the good; but when they have ascended and seen enough we must not allow them to do as they do now.

[G] What do you mean?

[S] I mean that they remain in the upper world: but this must not be allowed; they must be made to descend again among the prisoners in the den, and partake of their labours and honours, whether they are worth having or not.

[G] But is not this unjust? he said; ought we to give them a worse life, when they might have a better?

[S] You have again forgotten, my friend, I said, the intention of the legislator, who did not aim at making any one class in the State happy above the rest; the happiness was to be in the whole State, and he held the citizens together by persuasion and necessity, making them benefactors of the State, and therefore benefactors of one another; to this end he created them, not to please themselves, but to be his instruments in binding up the State.

[G] True, he said, I had forgotten.

[S] Observe, Glaucon, that there will be no injustice in compelling our philosophers to have a care and providence of others; we shall explain to them that in other States, men of their class are not obliged to share in the toils of politics: and this is reasonable, for they grow up at their own sweet will, and the government would rather not have them. Being self-taught, they cannot be expected to show any gratitude for a culture which they have never received. But we have brought you into the world to be rulers of the hive, kings of yourselves and of the other citizens, and have educated you far better and more perfectly than they have been educated, and you are better able to share in the double duty. Wherefore each of you, when his turn comes, must go down to the general underground abode, and get the habit of seeing in the dark. When you have acquired the habit, you will see ten thousand times better than the inhabitants of the den, and you will know what the several images are, and what they represent, because you have seen the beautiful and just and good in their truth. And thus our State which is also yours will be a reality, and not a dream only, and will be administered in a spirit unlike that of other States, in which men fight with one another about shadows only and are distracted in the struggle for power, which in their eyes is a great good. Whereas the truth is that the State in which the rulers are most reluctant to govern is always the best and most quietly governed, and the State in which they are most eager, the worst.

[G] Quite true, he replied.

[S] And will our pupils, when they hear this, refuse to take their turn at the toils of State, when they are allowed to spend the greater part of their time with one another in the heavenly light?

[G] Impossible, he answered; for they are just men, and the commands which we impose upon them are just; there can be no doubt that every one of them will take office as a stern necessity, and not after the fashion of our present rulers of State.

[S] Yes, my friend, I said; and there lies the point. You must contrive for your future rulers another and a better life than that of a ruler, and then you may have a well-ordered State; for only in the State which offers this, will they rule who are truly rich, not in silver and gold, but in virtue and wisdom, which are the true blessings of life. Whereas if they go to the administration of public affairs, poor and hungering after their own private advantage, thinking that hence they are to snatch the chief good, order there can never be; for they will be fighting about office, and the civil and domestic broils which thus arise will be the ruin of the rulers themselves and of the whole State.

[G] Most true, he replied.

[S] And the only life which looks down upon the life of political ambition is that of true philosophy. Do you know of any other?

[G] Indeed, I do not, he said.

QUESTIONS FOR REVIEW AND DISCUSSION

1. Make a sketch of the situation in the cave/den as Socrates asks Glaucon to imagine it. What is Socrates' purpose for constructing this scenario? What might the cave represent?

2. What does Socrates imagine as the situation of a person who is initially freed from confinement but still within the cave? What might this condition of freedom represent? Glaucon generally agrees with Socrates throughout this dialogue. Do you concur with him?

3. What do Socrates and Glaucon concur to be the predicament of the person forcibly dragged out into the sunlight? What might this condition of further freedom represent?

4. What would be the likely feelings of the individual who had seen the broader reality outside the cave towards those still within it?

5. What, according to Socrates, would be the likely predicament of the person reentering the cave?

6. Plato's allegory of the cave, when presented apart from its context in *The Republic*, circulates independently and is interpreted in a wide variety of ways. Essentially, the darkness of the cave and the delusions of its inhabitants are interpreted as the human condition prior to some profound transformative experience (e.g., a spiritual awakening, realization, or insight). What sort of interpretations can you envision for the allegory?

7. How does Socrates interpret his allegory to Glaucon? How does he extrapolate it to notions of education? What point is Socrates trying to make when discussing the "narrow intelligence" of the "clever rogue"?

8. What does Socrates propose would facilitate the acquisition of the highest wisdom? Do you agree with his suggestions?

9. Does Socrates imply that people have attained the state of the highest realization? What does he propose that they be obliged to do? Why should they be coerced into public office?

5   The Difference between Exoteric and Esoteric Buddhism

(Benkenmitsu nikyō ran)

Kūkai

Kūkai (774–835) brought the Shingon ("True Word") school of Buddhism to Japan, where he is best known by his posthumous name, Kōbō Daishi, the great teacher who spread the Buddhist law. He is famous as a Buddhist virtuoso who was responsible for many cultural contributions. Kūkai's writings include several works that could be described as comparative religion, including *Ten Stages of Religious Consciousness*, which lists gradations of non-Buddhist perspectives at the bottom, places Mahayana stages of development above other forms of Buddhism, and ranks esoteric teachings from his Shingon school at the peak of religious consciousness. Thirty-three years earlier, at the age of twenty-four, he wrote *Indications of the Goals of the Three Teachings*, which compares the three major East Asian traditions of Confucianism, Daoism, and Buddhism through a story in which Tortoise Hair presents Confucian arguments, Nothingness speaks for Daoism, and Mendicant X triumphs as the representative for Buddhism. At the age of forty-one, halfway between those works, Kūkai wrote the following selection contrasting esoteric and exoteric teachings in an exercise of comparative religion that reflects on general categories while also reinforcing a partisan position in favor of Shingon.

There are three bodies[1] of the Buddha and two forms of Buddhist doctrine. The doctrine revealed by the Nirmanakaya Buddha [Shakyamuni Buddha] is called Exoteric; it is apparent, simplified, and adapted to the needs of the time and to the capacity of the listeners. The doctrine expounded by the Dharmakaya Buddha [Mahāvairocana] is called Esoteric; it is secret and profound and contains the final truth. The sutras used in Exoteric Buddhism number in the millions. The collection is divided by some into ten and by others into fifty-one other parts.[2] They speak of One, Two, Three, Four, and Five Vehicles.[3] In discussing practices, they believe that the Six Paramitas[4] are the most important and explain that in order to attain enlightenment a period of three aeons is needed. The great Sage has explained these matters clearly.

According to the Esoteric *Vajraśekhara Sutra*, the Buddha, manifested in human form, preached the doctrines of the Three Vehicles for the sake of bodhisattvas who were yet to advance to the Ten Stages of Bodhisattvahood, for the followers of Hinayana, and for ordinary people; the Sambhogakaya Buddha taught the doctrine of One Vehicle for the bodhisattvas in the Ten Stages of Bodhisattvahood. Both of these teachings are Exoteric. The Dharmakaya Buddha, for his own enjoyment, with his own retinue,[5] preached the doctrine of the Three Mysteries. This is Esoteric. This doctrine of the Three Mysteries is concerned with the innermost spiritual experience of the Dharmakaya Buddha, and the bodhisattvas in the Ten Stages of Bodhisattvahood or even those who are nearly equal to the Buddha cannot penetrate it, much less the Hinayanists and ordinary people, who cannot cross its threshold. It is thus said in the *Shih-ti-ching lun*[6] and in the *Shih-moho-yen lun*[7] that this experience is beyond their capacity. Also the *Ch'eng-wei-shih lun*[8] and the *Mādhya-mika-kārikās*[9] deplore that it transcends words and thought determinations. Its transcendence is spoken of, however, from the viewpoint of those who have not yet been enlightened and not from the viewpoint of the enlightened ones. I shall give clear evidence for this in the following pages, on the basis of sutras and commentaries. It is hoped that those who aspire to attain enlightenment will understand their meaning clearly.

Being entangled in the net of Exoteric Buddhism, people wear themselves out like male goats dashing themselves against fences; being blocked by the barriers of the Mahayana teachings of provisional nature,[10] they give up advancing further. They are exactly like those who, wishing to rest there, believe in an illusory city,[11] or like children who take a yellow willow leaf to be gold.[12] How can they hope to preserve the glorious treasures which lie within themselves, numberless as the sands of the Ganges? It is as if they were to discard ghee and look for milk, or to throw away precious pearls and pick up fish eyes. They are cut off from their Buddha-seed; they are victims of a mortal disease before which even the King of Medicine would fold his hands in despair, a disease for which even a rain of nectar would be of no avail.

If men and women once grasp the fragrance of this [Esoteric Buddhism], they will have in their minds a clear understanding, as things are reflected in the magic mirror of the Emperor of Ch'in, and the differences between the provisional and the real doctrines will naturally be resolved. Evidence to this effect is abundant in the sutras and commentaries, and I will reveal part of it in the hope of assisting beginners.

QUESTION: The transmitters of the Dharma in ancient times composed extensive discourses advocating the six schools[13] and expounded the Tripitaka so abundantly that the texts could not be stored even in a large library, and people grew tired of opening them. Why then do you bother to write this book? What is its worth?

ANSWER: There is much to be expressed; therefore, it should be written. Everything transmitted by former masters is Exoteric Buddhist teachings. Here I am concerned with the Esoteric Buddhist teaching about which people have not had an adequate understanding. I should like to compile, therefore, a handy guide book for your reflection, quoting pertinent passages from sutras and commentaries.

QUESTION: What are the differences between the Exoteric Buddhist teachings and the Esoteric Buddhist teaching?

ANSWER: The teachings expounded by the Nirmanakaya Buddha in order to help others, responding to the needs of the time, are called Exoteric. What was expounded by the Dharmakaya Buddha for his own enjoyment, on his innermost spiritual experience, is called Esoteric.

QUESTION: The fact that the Nirmanakaya Buddha preached is agreed upon by all schools. As to the Dharmakaya Buddha, however, we understand that he is formless and imageless, that he is totally beyond verbalization and conceptualization, and that therefore there is no way of explaining him or showing him. Sutras and commentaries describe him in this way. Why do you now assert that the Dharmakaya Buddha preaches? What is your evidence for this?

ANSWER: Now and again the sutras and commentaries refer to this preaching. Misled by their biased preconceptions, people overlook these pertinent passages. Indeed, their meanings will be revealed only in accordance with the capacity of the reader: the same water may be seen as emerald by heavenly beings and as burning fire by hungry ghosts; the same darkness may be seen as light by nocturnal birds and as darkness by men.

QUESTION: If what you have said is really true and is given in the teachings of the Buddha, why have the former transmitters of the Dharma not discussed it?

ANSWER: The sermons of the Tathagata were delivered in accordance with the particular diseases in the minds of his audience; manifold remedies were provided, depending on their varied capacities. The sermons thus adapted to the capacity of his listeners were in many cases provisional and seldom final. When the bodhisattvas composed the commentaries, they wrote faithfully on the basis of the sutras which were provisional in nature. It is therefore said in the commentary on the *Daśabhūmika Sutra* written by Vasubandhu that "only the way to enlightenment can be talked about [and not the enlightenment itself],"[14] and also in the commentary on *The Awakening of Faith* written by Nāgārjuna that "the perfect sea of enlightenment cannot be talked about."[15] These works were based on the [provisional] sutras and were not intended to advocate the final truth.

The masters of the Dharma who transmitted the Exoteric Buddhist teachings interpreted the [passages of] profound significance [appearing in the Exoteric Buddhist texts] in the light of their shallow doctrines and failed to find any Esoteric import in them. Faithfully transmitting the Exoteric Buddhist teachings from master to disciple, they discussed Buddhism according to the tenets of their particular schools. They so eagerly supported their beliefs that they found no time to meditate on those [passages] which might have been disadvantageous to their doctrines. In the meantime, Buddhism had spread eastward in China and gradually gained a significant role there. The Buddhist texts translated from the time of Emperor Ming of the Later Han Dynasty to that of Empress Wu of the T'ang Dynasty were all Exoteric. During the reigns of Emperors Hsüan-tsung and Tai-tsung, when Masters Vajrabodhi and Pu-k'ung were active, the Esoteric Buddhist teaching flourished and its profound meaning was discussed enthusiastically. The new medicine had not long been in use, and the old disease was not yet cured. [The Chinese masters of Exoteric Buddhism]—even when they came across passages [of Esoteric significance] such as the statement in the *Laṅkāvatāra Sutra* that "the Dharmakaya Buddha preaches,"[16] or in the *Ta-chih-tu lun* that "the Dharmakaya Buddha is endowed with an exquisite form"[17]—interpreted them according to their imagination or were governed by the professed doctrines of their schools. It was indeed a pity that these wise masters of ancient times failed to appreciate the taste of ghee [the final truth].

QUESTION: If this is the case, in which sutras and commentaries are the differences between the Exoteric and the Esoteric Buddhist teachings given?

ANSWER: [To this question, Kūkai gives the titles of six sutras and three commentaries,[18] and then passages from these and other texts[19] with short remarks of his own at the end of a quotation or a group of quotations. These quotations occupy the major part of the work. In the last section, he remarks:] The foregoing quotations from sutras and commentaries prove that differences exist between Exoteric Buddhism and Esoteric Buddhism and that the latter was preached by the Dharmakaya Buddha himself. It is hoped that learned readers will deliberate on them and remove their misconceptions.

QUESTION: According to your assertion, what the Dharmakaya Buddha preached on his innermost spiritual experience is Esoteric, and all other Buddhist teachings are Exoteric. Then why is the word Esoteric applied to some sutras preached by the Shakyamuni

Buddha [Nirmana-kaya]? We also wonder in which group we should include the dharani teachings imparted by that Buddha?

ANSWER: The meanings of exoteric and esoteric are manifold. If the more profound is compared with the less profound, the former is to be called esoteric and the latter, exoteric. This is the reason why we often find the term esoteric introduced in non-Buddhist scriptures as well. Among the teachings given by the Tathagata, various distinctions between exoteric and esoteric have been made. The Hinayana doctrines explained by the Buddha can be called esoteric when compared to the doctrines given by non-Buddhist teachers. In the same way, when the Mahayana doctrines are compared with the Hinayana doctrines, the former are esoteric and the latter, exoteric. Even in the Mahayana itself, the teaching of the One Vehicle is esoteric in contrast to the teachings of the Three Vehicles. In order to distinguish the dharani section from other lengthy discourses, we call it esoteric. The teaching given by the Dharmakaya Buddha is the most profound, while the teachings of the Nirmanakaya are apparent and simplified; hence, the former is called esoteric.

The term esoteric is also used in the senses of "conceal" or "hidden," that is, "sentient beings conceal," and "hidden by the Tathagata." Since sentient beings conceal their original nature, that is, true enlightenment, they "conceal" themselves through illusions derived from ignorance. The doctrine revealed by the Nirmanakaya Buddha is adapted to the needs of the time and is, as it were, an effective medicine to cure the diseases of the mind. Thus the Buddha who preaches for the benefit of others keeps his innermost spiritual experience hidden and does not reveal it in his instructions. It is hidden even from those bodhisattvas who are nearly equal to the Buddha; it transcends the range of understanding of those who are in the Ten Stages of Bodhisattvahood. This is the so-called experience "hidden by the Tathagata."

In this way, the meanings of the term esoteric are many, but the term in its proper sense should be applied only to the secret teaching revealing the innermost experience of the ultimate Dharmakaya Buddha. The dharani section preached by the Nirmanakaya is also called esoteric, but when it is compared to the teaching of the Dharmakaya Buddha, it is not final. Among the teachings called esoteric, there are the provisional and the final; they should be classified properly according to the context.

QUESTIONS FOR REVIEW AND DISCUSSION

1. What are the essential differences between exoteric and esoteric doctrines according to Kūkai? To whom does Kūkai attribute teaching each type of doctrine and for what purpose?
2. Do you think this selection by Kūkai is appropriate for the Philosophy and Theology section? Why or why not?
3. Most of this short work by Kūkai is in a question and answer format. How does this compare with the dialogue format presented by Plato? What is Kūkai attempting to achieve with this format? Is it effective? Why or why not?
4. In one of these "answers," Kūkai indicates that "meanings will be revealed only in accordance with the capacity of the reader." What does this tell us about esoteric doctrines, interpretations, and perspectives?

5. Which eras or stages of transmission does Kūkai describe as more associated with exoteric vs. esoteric doctrines? Do Buddhist masters always know both exoteric and esoteric interpretations?

6. In Kūkai's final "answer" in this piece, he indicates other meanings and uses for the terms exoteric and esoteric. What are some examples? What does Kūkai offer as a general rule for how this distinction between esoteric and exoteric is made?

7. Is the label, esoteric vs. exoteric, consistently applied to a set of teachings or can the same doctrine be described with either label depending on the context? Do these terms always refer to Buddhist doctrines?

8. Kūkai also offers an ultimate designation for the term esoteric "in its proper sense." What does he describe as this final application of the term? What role might Kūkai's assessment play within the tradition?

Notes

1 *Trikāya.* See Part Two, p. 84, n. 17.

2 This unusual classification is based on a description given in a commentary to *The Awakening of Faith (Shih-mo-ho-yen lun).* Authorship of the commentary is attributed to one Nāgārjuna, about whom nothing is known. Kūkai used this commentary extensively in writing the *Difference* as well as other works. The author of the commentary is not the founder of the Mādhyamika school of Buddhism of second-century India. T32, p. 593a.

3 One Vehicle—the universal teaching which enables all sentient beings to attain enlightenment; Two Vehicles—Mahayana and Hinayana; Three Vehicles—Śrāvakayāna, Pratyekabuddhayāna, and Bodhisattvayāna; Four Vehicles—Three Vehicles and Buddhayāna; and Five Vehicles—Three Vehicles, Vehicle for men, and that for heavenly beings.

4 See *Indications*, n. 115.

5 His retinue consists of those surrounding him in the mandalas, who are manifestations of Mahā-vairocana himself. Thus, dialogues between Mahāvairocana and his own manifestations—Buddhas, Bodhisattvas, Devas, and others—are none other than a monologue in the form of a dialogue carried on by Mahāvairocana himself for his own enjoyment *(jiju hōraku).*

6 The commentary on the *Daśabhūmika Sutra*, written by Vasubandhu and translated by Bodhiruci. T26, p. 132b.

7 The commentary on *The Awakening of Faith* attributed to Nāgārjuna. T32, p. 601c. Cf. n. 2, above.

8 The commentary on the *Trimsikā* translated by Hsüan-tsang. T31, p. 57b.

9 T30, p. 24a.

10 According to the T'ien-t'ai and Hua-yen doctrines, Mahayana is divided into two types: provisional and real. The provisional does not hold that all sentient beings will attain enlightenment. Here reference is made to the doctrine of Yogācāra which recognizes a group of sentient beings, *icchantika*, the cursed ones, who will never attain enlightenment.

11 The story of the illusory city appears in the *Lotus Sutra*. The Buddha showed the illusory city to a traveler who was unwilling to go farther in order to encourage him and to arouse in him the energy to pursue the final goal, Nirvana. T9, p. 25c.

12 In the *Nirvana Sutra* a man who attaches himself to any Mahayana teaching of provisional type is compared to a child who stops crying when given a withered yellow leaf by his parents, which he takes for genuine gold. T12, p. 485c.

13 Kusha, Jōjitsu, Hossō, Sanron, Ritsu, and Kegon.

14 *Shih-ti-ching lun.* T26, p. 132b.

15 *Shih-mo-ho-yen lun.* T32, p. 601c.

16 T16, p. 525b.

17 The commentary on the *Mahāprajñāpāramitā Sutra* attributed to Nāgārjuna and translated by Kumārajīva. T25, p. 13c.

18 They are: T1125, T867, T870, T848, T671, T865, T1665, T1509, T1668.

19 T26l, T310, T997, T1566, T1861, T1866.

6 The Teleological Argument

William Paley

William Paley (1743–1805) was born in Peterborough, England and studied and lectured at Cambridge University. An ordained clergyman, he rose in rank to assume vicarages, and the roles of archdeacon and chancellor. His *Principles of Moral and Political Philosophy* (1786) was a highly influential textbook in university classrooms. He is regarded as a Christian apologist, and is best remembered for his teleological argument for the existence of God. He presented this argument in *Natural Theology* (1802), which is from where the selection that follows is taken. Paley's clear articulation is often used as the classic presentation of the "argument from design," or the "watchmaker analogy."

Chapter I: State of the Argument

In crossing a heath, suppose I pitched my foot against a stone, and were asked how the stone came to be there; I might possibly answer, that, for any thing I knew to the contrary, it had lain there forever: nor would it perhaps be very easy to show the absurdity of this answer. But suppose I had found a watch upon the ground, and it should be inquired how the watch happened to be in that place; I should hardly think of the answer which I had before given, that, for anything I knew, the watch might have always been there. Yet why should not this answer serve for the watch as well as for the stone? Why is it not as admissible in the second case, as in the first? For this reason, and for no other, viz. that, when we come to inspect the watch, we perceive (what we could not discover in the stone) that its several parts are framed and put together for a purpose, e.g. that they are so formed and adjusted as to produce motion, and that motion so regulated as to point out the hour of the day; that, if the different parts had been differently shaped from what they are, of a different size from what they are, or placed after any other manner, or in any other order, than that in which they are placed, either no motion at all would have been carried on in the machine, or none which would have answered the use that is now served by it.

... We take notice that the wheels are made of brass in order to keep them from rust; the springs of steel, no other metal being so elastic; that over the face of the watch there is placed a glass, a material employed in no other part of the work, but in the room of which, if there had been any other than a transparent substance, the hour could not be seen without opening the case. This mechanism being observed (it requires indeed an examination of the instrument, and perhaps some previous knowledge of the subject, to perceive and understand it; but being once, as we have said, observed and understood), the inference, we think, is inevitable, that the watch must have had a maker: that there must have existed, at some time, and at some place or other, an artificer or artificers who formed it for the purpose which we find it actually to answer; who comprehended its construction, and designed its use.

I. Nor would it, I apprehend, weaken the conclusion, that we had never seen a watch made; that we had never known an artist capable of making one; that we were altogether incapable of executing such a piece of workmanship ourselves, or of understanding in what manner it was performed; all this being no more than what is true of some exquisite remains of ancient art, of some lost arts, and, to the generality of mankind, of the more curious productions of modern manufacture. Does one man in a million know how oval frames are turned? Ignorance of this kind exalts our opinion of the unseen and unknown artist's skill, if he be unseen and unknown, but raises no doubt in our minds of the existence and agency of such an artist, at some former time, and in some place or other. Nor can I perceive that it varies at all the inference, whether the question arise concerning a human agent, or concerning an agent of a different species, or an agent possessing, in some respects, a different nature.

II. Neither, secondly, would it invalidate our conclusion, that the watch sometimes went wrong, or that it seldom went exactly right. The purpose of the machinery, the design, and the designer, might be evident, and in the case supposed would be evident, in whatever way we accounted for the irregularity of the movement, or whether we could account for it or not. It is not necessary that a machine be perfect, in order to show with what design it was made: still less necessary, where the only question is, whether it were made with any design at all.

III. Nor, thirdly, would it bring any uncertainty into the argument, if there were a few parts of the watch, concerning which we could not discover, or had not yet discovered, in what manner they conduced to the general effect; or even some parts, concerning which we could not ascertain, whether they conduced to that effect in any manner whatever. For, as to the first branch of the case; if by the loss, or disorder, or decay of the parts in question, the movement of the watch were found in fact to be stopped, or disturbed, or retarded, no doubt would remain in our minds as to the utility or intention of these parts, although we should be unable to investigate the manner according to which, or the connexion by which, the ultimate effect depended upon their action or assistance; and the more complex is the machine, the more likely is this obscurity to arise. Then, as to the second thing supposed, namely, that there were parts which might be spared, without prejudice to the movement of the watch, and that we had proved this by experiment, – these superfluous parts, even if we were completely assured that they were such, would not vacate the reasoning which we had instituted concerning other parts. The indication of contrivance remained, with respect to them, nearly as it was before.

IV. Nor, fourthly, would any man in his senses think the existence of the watch, with its various machinery, accounted for, by being told that it was one out of possible combinations of material forms; that whatever he had found in the place where he found the watch, must have contained some internal configuration or other; and that this configuration might be the structure now exhibited, viz. of the works of a watch, as well as a different structure.

V. Nor, fifthly, would it yield his inquiry more satisfaction to be answered, that there existed in things a principle of order, which had disposed the parts of the watch into their present form and situation. He never knew a watch made by the principle of order; nor can he even form to himself an idea of what is meant by a principle of order, distinct from the intelligence of the watch-maker.

VI. Sixthly, he would be surprised to hear that the mechanism of the watch was no proof of contrivance, only a motive to induce the mind to think so.

VII. And not less surprised to be informed, that the watch in his hand was nothing more than the result of the laws of metallic nature. It is a perversion of language to assign any law, as the efficient, operative cause of any thing. A law presupposes an agent; for it is only the mode, according to which an agent proceeds: it implies a power; for it is the order, according to which that power acts. Without this agent, without this power, which are both distinct from itself, the law does nothing; is nothing. The expression, "the law of metallic nature," may sound strange and harsh to a philosophic ear; but it seems quite as justifiable as some others which are more familiar to him, such as "the law of vegetable nature," "the law of animal nature," or indeed as "the law of nature" in general, when assigned as the cause of phænomena, in exclusion of agency and power; or when it is substituted into the place of these.

VIII. Neither, lastly, would our observer be driven out of his conclusion, or from his confidence in its truth, by being told that he knew nothing at all about the matter. He knows enough for his argument: he knows the utility of the end: he knows the subserviency and adaptation of the means to the end. These points being known, his ignorance of other points, his doubts concerning other points, affect not the certainty of his reasoning. The consciousness of knowing little, need not beget a distrust of that which he does know.

Chapter II: State of the Argument (Continued)

Suppose, in the next place, that the person who found the watch, should, after some time, discover that, in addition to all the properties which he had hitherto observed in it, it possessed the unexpected property of producing, in the course of its movement, another watch like itself (the thing is conceivable); that it contained within it a mechanism, a system of parts, a mould for instance, or a complex adjustment of lathes, files, and other tools, evidently and separately calculated for this purpose; let us inquire, what effect ought such a discovery to have upon his former conclusion.

I. The first effect would be to increase his admiration of the contrivance, and his conviction of the consummate skill of the contriver. Whether he regarded the object of the contrivance, the distinct apparatus, the intricate, yet in many parts intelligible mechanism, by which it was carried on, he would perceive, in this new observation, nothing but an additional reason for doing what he had already done, – for referring the construction of the watch to design, and to supreme art. If that construction without this property, or which is the same thing, before this property had been noticed, proved intention and art to have been employed about it; still more strong would the proof appear, when he came to the knowledge of this further property, the crown and perfection of all the rest.

II. He would reflect, that though the watch before him were, in some sense, the maker of the watch, which was fabricated in the course of its movements, yet it was in a very different sense from that, in which a carpenter, for instance, is the maker of a chair; the author of its contrivance, the cause of the relation of its parts to their use. With respect to these, the first watch was no cause at all to the second: in no such sense as this was it the author of the constitution and order, either of the parts which the new watch contained, or of the parts by the aid and instrumentality of which it was produced. We might possibly say, but with great latitude of expression, that a stream of water ground corn: but no latitude of expression would allow us to say, no stretch of conjecture could lead us to think, that the stream of water built the mill, though it were too ancient for us to know who the builder was. What the stream of water does in the affair, is neither more nor less than this; by the application of an unintelligent impulse to a mechanism previously arranged, arranged independently of it, and arranged by intelligence, an effect is produced, viz. the corn is ground. But the effect results from the arrangement. The force of the stream cannot be said to be the cause or author of the effect, still less of the arrangement. Understanding and plan in the formation of the mill were not the less necessary, for any share which the water has in grinding the corn: yet is this share the same as that which the watch would have contributed to the production of the new watch, upon the supposition assumed in the last section. Therefore,

III. Though it be now no longer probable that the individual watch, which our observer had found, was made immediately by the hand of an artificer, yet doth not this alteration in anywise affect the inference, that an artificer had been originally employed and concerned in the production. The argument from design remains as it was. Marks of design and contrivance are no more accounted for now, than they were before. In the same thing, we may ask for the cause of different properties. ... No answer is given to this question, by telling us that a preceding watch produced it. There cannot be design without a designer; contrivance without a contriver; order without choice; arrangement, without any thing capable of arranging; subserviency and relation to a purpose, without that which could intend a purpose; means suitable to an end, and executing their office, in accomplishing that end, without the end ever having been contemplated, or the means accommodated to it. Arrangement, disposition of parts, subserviency of means to an end, relation of instruments to a use, imply the presence of intelligence and mind. No one, therefore, can rationally believe that the insensible, inanimate watch, from which the watch before us issued, was the proper cause of the mechanism we so much admire in it; – could be truly said to have constructed the instrument, disposed its parts, assigned their office, determined their order, action, and mutual dependency, combined their several motions into one result, and that also a result connected with the utilities of other beings. All these properties, therefore, are as much unaccounted for as they were before.

IV. Nor is any thing gained by running the difficulty farther back, i.e. by supposing the watch before us to have been produced from another watch, that from a former, and so on indefinitely. Our going back ever so far, brings us no nearer to the least degree of satisfaction upon the subject. Contrivance is still unaccounted for. We still want a contriver. A designing mind is neither supplied by this supposition, nor dispensed with. If the difficulty were diminished the further we went back, by going back indefinitely we might exhaust it. ... A chain, composed of an infinite number of links, can no more support itself than a chain composed of a finite number of links. ... This very much resembles the case before us. The machine which we are inspecting, demonstrates, by its construction, contrivance and design. Contrivance must have had a contriver; design, a designer; whether the machine immediately proceeded from another machine or not. That circumstance alters not the case. ... It is the same with any and every succession of these machines; a succession of ten, of a hundred, of a thousand; with one series, as with another; a series which is finite, as with a series which is infinite. In whatever other respects they may differ, in this they do not. In all equally, contrivance and design are unaccounted for.

The question is not simply, "How came the first watch into existence?," which question, it may be pretended, is done away by supposing the series of watches thus produced from one another to have been infinite, and consequently to have had no-such first, for which it was necessary to provide a cause. This, perhaps, would have been nearly the state of the question, if no thing had been before us but an unorganized, unmechanized substance, without mark or indication of contrivance. It might be difficult to show that such substance could not have existed from eternity, either in succession (if it were possible, which I think it is not, for unorganized bodies to spring from one another), or by individual perpetuity. But that is not the question now. To suppose it to be so, is to suppose that it made no difference whether we had found a watch or a stone. As it is, the metaphysics of that question have no place; for, in the watch which we are examining, are seen contrivance, design; an end, a purpose; means for the end, adaptation to the purpose. And the question which irresistibly presses upon our thoughts, is, whence this contrivance and design? The thing required is the intending mind, the adapting hand, the intelligence by which that hand was directed. This question, this demand, is not shaken off, by increasing a number or succession of substances, destitute of these properties; nor the more, by increasing that number to infinity. ... It is in vain, therefore, to assign a series of such causes, or to allege that a series may be carried back to infinity; for I do not admit that we have yet any cause at all of the phænomena, still less any series of causes either finite or infinite. Here is contrivance, but no contriver; proofs of design, but no designer.

V. Our observer would further also reflect, that the maker of the watch before him, was, in truth and reality, the maker of every watch produced from it; there being no difference (except that the latter manifests a more exquisite skill) between the making of another watch with his own hands, by the mediation of files, lathes, chisels, etc. and the disposing, fixing, and inserting of these instruments, or of others equivalent to them, in the body of the watch already made in such a manner as to form a new watch in the course of the movements which he had given to the old one. It is only working by one set of tools, instead of another.

The conclusion of which the first examination of the watch, of its works, construction, and movement, suggested, was, that it must have had, for the cause and author of that construction, an artificer, who understood its mechanism, and designed its use. This conclusion is invincible. A second examination presents us with a new discovery. The watch is found, in the course of its movement, to produce another watch, similar to itself; and not only so, but we perceive in it a system or organization, separately calculated for that purpose. What effect would this discovery have, or ought it to have, upon our former inference? What, as hath already been said, but to increase, beyond measure, our admiration of the skill which had been employed in the formation of such a machine? Or shall it, instead of this, all at once turn us round to an opposite conclusion, viz. that no art or skill whatever has been concerned in the business, although all other evidences of art and skill remain as they were, and this last and supreme piece of art be now added to the rest? Can this be maintained without absurdity? Yet this is atheism. ...

Chapter VI: The Argument Cumulative

Were there no example in the world of contrivance, except that of the eye, it would be alone sufficient to support the conclusion which we draw from it, as to the necessity of an intelligent Creator. It could never be got rid of; because it could not be accounted for by any other supposition, which did not contradict all the principles we possess of knowledge; the principles, according to which, things do, as often as they can be brought to the test of experience, turn out to be true or false. Its coats and humours, constructed, as the lenses of a telescope are constructed, for the refraction of rays of light to a point, which forms the proper action of the organ; the provision in its muscular tendons for turning its pupil to the object, similar to that which is given to the telescope by screws, and upon which power of direction in the eye, the exercise of its office as an optical instrument depends; the further provision for its defence, for its constant lubricity and moisture, which we see in its socket and its lids, in its gland for the secretion of the matter of tears, its outlet or communication with the nose for carrying off the liquid after the eye is washed with it; these provisions compose altogether an apparatus, a system of parts, a preparation of means, so manifest in their design, so exquisite in their contrivance, so successful in their issue, so precious, and so infinitely beneficial in their use, as, in my opinion, to bear down all doubt that can be raised upon the subject. And what I wish, under the title of the present chapter, to observe is, that if other parts of nature were inaccessible to our inquiries, or even if other parts of nature presented nothing to our examination but disorder and confusion, the validity of this example would remain the same. If there were but one watch in the world, it would not be less certain that it had a maker. If we had never in our lives seen any but one single kind of hydraulic machine, yet, if of that one kind we understood the mechanism and use, we should be as perfectly assured that it proceeded from the hand, and thought, and skill of a workman, as if we visited a museum of the arts, and saw collected there twenty different kinds of machines for drawing water, or a thousand different kinds for other purposes. Of this point, each machine is a proof, independently of all the rest. So it is with the evidences of a Divine agency. The proof is not a conclusion which lies at the end of a chain of reasoning, of which chain each instance of contrivance is only a link, and of which, if one link fail, the whole falls; but it is an argument separately supplied by every separate example. An error in stating an example, affects only that example. The argument is cumulative, in the fullest sense of that term. The eye proves it without the ear; the ear without the eye. The proof in each example is complete; for when the design of the part, and the conduciveness of its structure to that design is shown, the mind may set itself at rest; no future consideration can detract any thing from the force of the example.

QUESTIONS FOR REVIEW AND DISCUSSION

1. Why does Paley distinguish between our likely responses to the origin of a stone or a watch encountered in a field?
2. How does Paley refute arguments that the watch might have been created by means other than by purposeful design?
3. If the watch were capable of replicating itself, what effects does Paley suggest this capacity would have on the observer?
4. How does Paley address the concern of infinite regress, in which the watch that was found may have been produced by another watch and so on, ad infinitum?
5. Paley eventually shifts his argument to the human body, and uses the eye as an example of design. What is his argument concerning the creation of the human being, using the eye as an example?
6. Evaluate Paley's argument assessing its strengths and its weaknesses.

7 *The Essence of Christianity*

Ludwig Feuerbach

Ludwig Feuerbach (1804–72) was born in Bavaria and studied in Heidelberg and Berlin. His shift in institutions reflects movement from theology to Hegelian philosophy as well as an increasing rejection of religion, including Christianity. His 1828 dissertation argued for the universality of Reason and despite a series of well-received publications on Philosophy in the following decade, his academic career was curtailed due to reactions against his criticism of Christianity, which were radical for the times and included an anonymous work (correctly linked to him) that satirized popular Christian belief in a personal deity and individual life after death. He came to reject Hegel's thought as well, and through his writing and embrace of atheism and eventually communism, Feuerbach is often described as connecting the contrasting figures of Hegel and Marx. The essay below is from his especially influential 1841 book, *The Essence of Christianity.* Although not his final word on religion, this book was most influential for the theoretical shift to describing religion as imaginative, human projection. In the introduction to this work, Feuerbach locates the origin of religion in an essential difference between humans and animals and identifies the nature and divinity of humans in terms of reason, love, and will. The translator, Marian Evans, is better known by her pen name, George Eliot.

Chapter XXVII: Concluding Application

In the contradiction between Faith and Love which has just been exhibited, we see the practical, palpable ground of necessity that we should raise ourselves above Christianity, above the peculiar stand-point of all religion. We have shown that the substance and object of religion is altogether human; we have shown that divine wisdom is human wisdom; that the secret of theology is anthropology; that the absolute mind is the so-called finite subjective mind. But religion is not conscious that its elements are human; on the contrary, it places itself in opposition to the human, or at least it does not admit that its elements are human. The necessary turning-point of history is therefore the open confession, that the consciousness of God is nothing else than the consciousness of the species; that man can and should raise himself only above the limits of his individuality, and not above the laws, the positive essential conditions of his species; that there is no other essence which man can think, dream of, imagine, feel, believe in, wish for, love and adore as the *absolute*, than the essence of human nature itself.[1]

Our relation to religion is therefore not a merely negative, but a critical one; we only separate the true from the false; – though we grant that the truth thus separated from falsehood is a new truth, essentially different from the old. Religion is the first form of self-consciousness. Religions are sacred because they are the traditions of the primitive self-consciousness. But that which in religion holds the first place – namely, God – is, as we have shown, in itself and according to truth, the second, for it is only the nature of man regarded objectively; and that which to religion is the second – namely, man – must therefore be constituted and declared the first. Love to man must be no derivative love; it must be original. If human nature is the highest nature to man, then practically also the highest and first law must be the love of man to man. *Homo homini Deus est*: – this is the great practical principle: – this is the axis on which revolves the history of the world. The relations of child and parent, of husband and wife, of brother and friend – in general, of man to man – in short, all the moral relations are *per se* religious. Life as a whole is, in its essential, substantial relations, throughout of a divine nature. Its religious consecration is not first conferred by the blessing of the priest. But the pretension of religion is that it can hallow an object by its essentially external co-operation; it thereby assumes to be itself the only holy power; besides itself it knows only earthly, ungodly relations; hence it comes forward in order to consecrate them and make them holy.

But marriage – we mean, of course, marriage as the free bond of love[2] – is sacred in itself, by the very nature of the union which is therein effected. That alone is a religious marriage, which is a true marriage, which corresponds to the essence of marriage – of love. And so it is with all moral relations. Then only are they moral, – then only are they enjoyed in a moral spirit, when they are regarded as sacred in themselves. True friendship exists only when the boundaries of friendship are preserved with religious conscientiousness, with the same conscientiousness with which the believer watches over the dignity of his God. Let friendship be sacred to thee, property sacred, marriage sacred, – sacred the well-being of every man; but let them be sacred *in and by themselves.*

In Christianity the moral laws are regarded as the commandments of God; morality is even made the criterion of piety; but ethics have nevertheless a subordinate rank, they have not in themselves a religious significance. This belongs only to faith. Above morality hovers God, as a being distinct from man, a being to whom the best is due, while the remnants only fall to the share of man. All those dispositions which ought to be devoted to life, to man – all the best powers of humanity, are lavished on the being who wants nothing. The real cause is converted into an impersonal means, a merely conceptional, imaginary cause usurps the place of the true one. Man thanks God for those benefits which have been rendered to him even at the cost of sacrifice by his fellow-man. The Gratitude which he expresses to his benefactor is only ostensible: it is paid, not to him, but to God. He is thankful, grateful to God, but unthankful to man.[3] Thus is the moral sentiment subverted into religion! Thus does man sacrifice man to God! The bloody human sacrifice is in fact only a rude, material expression of the inmost secret of religion. Where bloody human sacrifices are offered to God, such sacrifices are regarded as the highest thing, physical existence as the chief good. For this reason life is sacrificed to God, and it is so on extraordinary occasions; the supposition being that this is the way to show him the greatest honour. If Christianity no longer, at least in our day, offers bloody sacrifices to its God, this arises, to say nothing of other reasons, from the fact that physical existence is no longer regarded as the highest good. Hence the soul, the emotions are now offered to God, because these are held to be something higher. But the common case is, that in religion man sacrifices some duty towards man – such as that of respecting the life of his fellow, of being grateful to him – to a religious obligation, – sacrifices his relation to man to his relation to God. The Christians, by the idea that God is without wants, and that he is only an object of pure adoration, have certainly done away with many pernicious conceptions.

But this freedom from wants is only a metaphysical idea, which is by no means part of the peculiar nature of religion. When the need for worship is supposed to exist only on one side, the subjective side, this has the invariable effect of one-sidedness, and leaves the religious emotions cold; hence, if not in express words, yet in fact, there must be attributed to God a condition corresponding to the subjective need, the need of the worshipper, in order to establish reciprocity.[4] All the positive definitions of religion are based on reciprocity. The religious man thinks of God because God thinks of him; he loves God because God has first loved him. God is jealous of man; religion is jealous of morality;[5] it sucks away the best forces of morality; it renders to man only the things that are man's, but to God the things that are God's; and to him is rendered true living emotion, – the heart.

When in times in which peculiar sanctity was attached to religion, we find marriage, property, and civil law respected, this has not its foundation in religion, but in the original, natural sense of morality and right, to which the true social relations are sacred *as such*. He to whom the Right is not holy for its own sake will never be made to feel it sacred by religion. Property did not become sacred because it was regarded as a divine institution, but it was regarded as a divine institution because it was felt to be in itself sacred. Love is not holy because it is a predicate of God, but it is a predicate of God because it is in itself divine. The heathens do not worship the light or the fountain because it is a gift of God, but because it has of itself a beneficial influence on man, because it refreshes the sufferer; on account of this excellent quality they pay it divine honours.

Wherever morality is based on theology, wherever the right is made dependent on divine authority, the most immoral, unjust, infamous things can be justified and established. I can found morality on theology only when I myself have already defined the Divine Being by means of morality. In the contrary case, I have no criterion of the moral and immoral, but merely an *un*moral, arbitrary basis, from which I may deduce anything I please. Thus, if I would found morality on God, I must first of all place it in God: for Morality, Right, in short, all substantial relations, have their only basis in themselves, can only have a real foundation – such as truth demands – when they are thus based. To place anything in God, or to derive anything from God, is nothing more than to withdraw it from the test of reason, to institute it as indubitable, unassailable, sacred, without rendering an account why. Hence self-delusion, if not wicked, insidious design is at the root of all efforts to establish morality, right, on theology. Where we are in earnest about the right we need no incitement or support from above. We need no Christian rule of political right: we need only one which is rational, just, human. The right, the true, the good, has always its ground of sacredness in itself, in its quality, where man is in earnest about ethics, they have in themselves the validity of a divine power. If morality has no foundation in itself, there is no inherent necessity for morality; morality is then surrendered to the groundless arbitrariness of religion.

Thus the work of the self-conscious reason in relation to religion is simply to destroy an illusion: – an illusion, however, which is by no means indifferent, but which, on the contrary, is profoundly injurious in its effect on mankind; which deprives man as well of the power of real life as of the genuine sense of truth and virtue: for even love, in itself the deepest, truest emotion, becomes by means of religiousness merely ostensible, illusory, since religious love gives itself to man only for God's sake, so that it is given only in appearance to man, but in reality to God.

And we need only, as we have shown, invert the religious relations – regard that as an end which religion supposes to be a means – exalt that into the primary which in religion is subordinate, the accessory, the condition, – at once we have destroyed the illusion, and the unclouded light of truth streams in upon us. The sacraments of Baptism and the Lord's Supper, which are the characteristic symbols of the Christian religion, may serve to confirm and exhibit this truth.

The Water of Baptism is to religion only the means by which the Holy Spirit imparts itself to man. But by this conception it is placed in contradiction with reason, with the truth of things. On the one hand, there is virtue in the objective, natural quality of water; on the other, there is none, but it is a merely arbitrary medium of divine grace and omnipotence. We free ourselves from these and other irreconcilable contradictions, we give a true significance to Baptism, only by regarding it as a symbol of the value of water itself. Baptism should represent to us the wonderful but natural effect of water on man. Water has, in fact, not merely physical effects, but also, and as a result of these, moral and intellectual effects on man. Water not only cleanses man from bodily impurities, but in water the scales fall from his eyes: he sees, he thinks more clearly; he feels himself freer; water extinguishes the fire of appetite. How many saints have had recourse to the natural qualities of water in order to overcome the assaults of the devil! What was denied by Grace has been granted by Nature. Water plays a part not only in dietetics, but also in moral and mental discipline. To purify oneself, to bathe, is the first, though the lowest of virtues.[6]

In the stream of water the fever of selfishness is allayed. Water is the readiest means of making friends with Nature. The bath is a sort of chemical process, in which our individuality is resolved into the objective life of Nature. The man rising from the water is a new, a regenerate man. The doctrine that morality can do nothing without means of grace has a valid meaning if, in place of imaginary, supernatural means of grace, we substitute natural means. Moral feeling can effect nothing without Nature; it must ally itself with the simplest natural means. The profoundest secrets lie in common everyday things, such as supra-naturalistic religion and speculation ignore, thus sacrificing real mysteries to imaginary, illusory ones; as here, for example, the real power of water is sacrificed to an imaginary one. Water is the simplest means of grace or healing for the maladies of the soul as well as of the body. But water is effectual only where its use is constant and regular. Baptism, as a single act, is either an altogether useless and unmeaning institution, or, if real effects are attributed to it, a superstitious one. But it is a rational, a venerable institution, if it is understood to typify and celebrate the moral and physical curative virtues of water.

But the sacrament of water required a supplement. Water, as a universal element of life, reminds us of our origin from Nature, an origin which we have in common with plants and animals. In Baptism we bow to the power of a pure Nature-force; water is the element of natural equality and freedom, the mirror of the golden age. But we men are distinguished from the plants and animals, which together with the inorganic kingdom we comprehend under the common name of Nature; – we are distinguished from Nature. Hence we must celebrate our distinction, our specific difference. The symbols of this our difference are bread and wine. Bread and wine are, as to their materials, products of Nature; as to their form, products of man. If in water we declare: Man can do nothing without Nature; by bread and wine we declare: Nature needs man, as man needs Nature. In water, human mental activity is nullified; in bread and wine it attains self-satisfaction. Bread and wine are supernatural products, – in the only valid and true sense, the sense which is not in contradiction with reason and Nature. If in water we adore the pure force of Nature, in bread and wine we adore the supernatural power of mind, of consciousness, of man. Hence this sacrament is only for man matured into consciousness; while Baptism is imparted to infants. But we at the same time celebrate here the true relation of mind to Nature: Nature gives the material, mind gives the form. The sacrament of Baptism inspires us with thankfulness towards Nature, the sacrament of bread and wine with thankfulness towards man. Bread and wine typify to us the truth that Man is the true God and Saviour of man.

Eating and drinking is the mystery of the Lord's Supper; – eating and drinking is, in fact, in itself a religious act; at least, ought to be so.[7] Think, therefore, with every morsel of bread which relieves thee from the pain of hunger, with every draught of wine which cheers thy heart, of the God who confers these beneficent gifts upon thee, – think of man! But in thy gratitude towards man forget not Gratitude towards holy Nature! Forget not that wine is the blood of plants, and flour the flesh of plants, which are sacrificed for thy well-being! Forget not that the plant typifies to thee the essence of Nature, which lovingly surrenders itself for thy enjoyment. Therefore forget not the gratitude which thou owest to the natural qualities of bread and wine! And if thou art inclined to smile that I call eating and drinking religious acts, because they are common every-day acts, and are therefore performed by multitudes without thought, without emotion; reflect, that the Lord's Supper is to multitudes a thoughtless, emotionless act, because it takes place often; and, for the sake of comprehending the religious significance of bread and wine, place thyself in a position where the daily act is unnaturally, violently interrupted. Hunger and thirst destroy not only the physical but also the mental and moral powers of man; they rob him of his humanity of understanding, of consciousness. Oh! if thou shouldst ever experience such want, how wouldst thou bless and praise the natural qualities of bread and wine, which restore to thee thy humanity, thy intellect! It needs only that the ordinary course of things be interrupted in order to vindicate to common things an uncommon significance, *to life, as such, a religious import*. Therefore let bread be sacred for us, let wine be sacred, and also let water be sacred! Amen.

QUESTIONS FOR REVIEW AND DISCUSSION

1. What is Feuerbach's view of religion? Does it originate from a human or divine source? Is its ultimate object human or divine?
2. What is Feuerbach's view of morality in relationship with religion and divine authority? Does his assessment relate specifically to Christianity or can it be extended to religion more generally? What do you think about his characterization of morality?
3. Feuerbach asserts that "the work of the self-conscious reason in relation to religion is simply to destroy an illusion." How does this view compare with other authors in this volume, such as Plato or Freud?
4. Does Feuerbach argue that "reason and Nature" or "religion and the supernatural" are ultimately most valid and true? What do you think of how he makes his argument with reference to sacraments of water, bread and wine?
5. What is his argument concerning whether eating and drinking should be considered sacred as well as the appropriate role of gratitude?
6. Evaluate Feuerbach's overall argument assessing its strengths and its weaknesses.
7. What is Feuerbach's objective in writing this article? Would you consider this selection to be theology, philosophy, or some other form of religious studies?

Notes

1 Including external Nature; for as man belongs to the essence of Nature, – in opposition to common materialism; so Nature belongs to the essence of man, – in opposition to subjective idealism; which is also the secret of our "absolute" philosophy, at least in relation to Nature. Only by uniting man with Nature can we conquer the supranaturalistic egoism of Christianity.

2 Yes, only as the free bond of love; for a marriage the bond of which is merely an external restriction, not the voluntary, contented self-restriction of love, in short, a marriage which is not spontaneously concluded, spontaneously willed, self-sufficing, is not a true marriage, and therefore not a truly moral marriage.

3 "Because God does good through government, great men and creatures in general, people rush into error, lean on creatures and not on the Creator; – they do not look from the creature to the Creator. Hence it came that the heathens made gods of kings. For they cannot and will not perceive that the work or the benefit comes from God, and not merely from the creature, though the latter is a means, through which God works, helps us and gives to us." – Luther (T. iv. p. 237).

4 "They who honour me, I will honour, and they who despise me shall be lightly esteemed." – i Sam. ii. 30. "*Jam se, o bone pater, vermis vilissimus et odio dignissimus sempiterno, tamen confidit amari, quoniam as sentit amare, imo quia se amari praesentit, non redamare confunditur. ... Nemo itaque se amari diffidat, qui jam amat.*" – Bernardus ad Thomam (Epist. 107). A very fine and pregnant sentence. If I exist not for God, God exists not for me; if I do not love, I am not loved. The *passive* is the active certain of itself, the object is the subject certain of itself. To love is to be man, to be loved is to be God. I am loved, says God; I love, says man. It is not until later that this is reversed, that the passive transforms itself into the active, and conversely.

5 "The Lord spake to Gideon: The people are too many that are with thee, that I should give Midian into their hands; Israel might glorify itself against me and say: My hand has delivered me," – i.e., "*Ne Israel sibi tribuat, quae mihi debentur.*" Judges vii. 2. "Thus saith the Lord: Cursed is the man that trusteth in man. But blessed is the man that trusteth in the Lord and whose hope is in the Lord." – Jer. xvii. 5. "God desires not our gold, body and possessions, but has given these to the emperor (that is, to the representative of the world, of the state), and to us through the emperor. But the heart, which is the greatest and best in man, he has reserved for himself; – this must be our offering to God – that we believe in him." – Luther (xvi. p. 505).

6 Christian baptism also is obviously only a relic of the ancient Nature-worship, in which, as in the Persian, water was a means of religious purification. (S. Rhode: *Die heilige Sage*, &c., pp. 305, 426.) Here, however, water baptism had a much truer, and consequently a deeper meaning, than with the Christians, because it rested on the natural power and value of water. But indeed for these simple views of Nature which characterized the old religions, our speculative as well as theological supra-naturalism has neither sense nor understanding. When therefore the Persians, the Hindus, the Egyptians, the Hebrews, made physical purity a religious duty, they were herein far wiser than the Christian saints, who attested the supra-naturalistic principle of their religion by physical impurity. Supra-naturalism in theory becomes anti-naturalism in practice. Supra-naturalism is only a euphemism for anti-naturalism.

7 "Eating and drinking is the easiest of all work, for men like nothing better: yea, the most joyful work in the whole world is eating and drinking, as it is commonly said: Before eating, no dancing, and, On a full stomach stands a merry head. In short, eating and drinking is a pleasant necessary work; – that is a doctrine soon learned and made popular. The same pleasant necessary work takes our blessed Lord Christ and says: 'I have prepared a joyful, sweat and pleasant meal, I will lay on you no hard heavy work. I institute a supper,' &c." – Luther (xvi. 222).

8   After the Death of God the Father

Mary Daly

Mary Daly (1928–2010) was born in New York State and received doctorates in religion from St. Mary's College and in sacred theology and in philosophy from the University of Fribourg, in Switzerland. She described herself as a "radical lesbian feminist," and the publication of her first book, *The Church and the Second Sex* (1968) was a springboard for a chequered relationship with Boston College, where she taught. The selection that follows traces her arguments presented in greater detail in *Beyond God the Father* (1973), one of her most influential books. In it she explores misogynistic attitudes embedded within religions, and whether there is a way to move religion beyond its patriarchal orientations.

Women's Liberation and the Transformation of Christian Consciousness

The women's liberation movement has produced a deluge of books and articles. Their major task has been exposition and criticism of our male-centered heritage. In order to reveal and drive home to readers the oppressive character of our cultural institutions, it was necessary to do careful research to trot out passages from leading philosophers, psychologists, statesmen, poets, historians, saints and theologians which make the reader's hair stand on end by the blatancy of their misogynism. Part of the task also has been the tracing of the subtle psychological mechanisms by which society has held men up and women down. This method of exposition and analysis reached its crescendo within this past year when Kate Millet's *Sexual Politics* rocketed her into the role of American counterpart to Simone de Beauvoir.

As far as the level of creative research is concerned that phase of the work is finished. The skeletons in our cultural closet have been hauled out for inspection. I do not mean to imply that there are not countless more of the same to be uncovered (just the other day I noticed for the first time that Berdyaev blandly affirms there is "something base and sinister in the female element." Etcetera). Nor do I mean that the task of communicating the message is over. Millions have yet to hear the news, let alone to grasp its import. Certainly it would be a mistake and a betrayal to trivialize the fact that our culture is so diseased. That has always been a major tactic in the fine art of suppressing the rage of women. No, what I am saying is that Phase One of critical research and writing in the movement has opened the way for the logical next step in creative thinking. We now have to ask how the women's revolution can and should change our whole vision of reality. What I intend to do here is to sketch some of the ways in which it can influence Western religious thought.

The Judaic-Christian tradition has served to legitimate sexually imbalanced patriarchal society. Thus, for example, the image of the Father God, spawned in the human imagination and sustained as plausible by patriarchy, has in turn rendered service to this type of society by making its mechanisms for the oppression of women appear right and fitting. If God in "his" heaven is a father ruling "his" people, then it is in the "nature" of things and according to divine plan and the order of the universe that society be male-dominated. Theologian Karl Barth found it appropriate to write that woman is "ontologically" subordinate to man. Within this context a mystification of roles takes place: the husband dominating his wife represents God himself. What is happening, of course, is the familiar mechanism by which the images and values of a given society are projected into a realm of beliefs, which in turn justify the social infrastructure. The belief system becomes hardened and objectified, seeming to have an unchangeable independent existence and validity of its own. It resists social change which would rob it of its plausibility. Nevertheless, despite the vicious circle, change does occur in society, and ideologies die, though they die hard.

As the women's revolution begins to have its effect upon the fabric of society, transforming it from patriarchy into something that never existed before – into a diarchal situation that is radically new – it will, I believe, become the greatest single potential challenge to Christianity to rid itself of its oppressive tendencies or go out of business. Beliefs and values that have held sway for thousands of years will be questioned as never before. It is also very possibly the greatest single hope for survival of religious consciousness in the West.

At this point it is important to consider the objection that the liberation of women will only mean that new characters will assume the same old roles, but that nothing will change essentially in regard to structure, ideology, or values. This objection is often based upon the observation that the very few women in "masculine" occupations seem to behave very much as men do. This is really not to the point for it fails to recognize that the effect of tokenism is not to change stereotypes or social systems but to preserve these. What I am discussing here is an emergence of women such as has never taken place before. It is naive to assume that the coming of women into equal power in society generally and in the church in particular will simply mean uncritical acceptance of values formerly given priority by men. Rather, I suggest that it will be a catalyst for transformation of our culture.

The roles and structures of patriarchy have been developed and sustained in accordance with an artificial polarization of human qualities into the traditional sexual stereotypes. The image of the person in authority and the accepted understanding of "his" role have corresponded to the eternal masculine stereotype, which implies hyperrationality, "objectivity," aggressivity, the possession of dominating and manipulative attitudes toward persons and environment and the tendency to construct boundaries between the self (and those identified with the self) and "the other." The caricature of a human being which is represented by this stereotype depends for its existence upon the opposite caricature – the eternal feminine (hyper-emotional, passive, self-abasing, etc.). By becoming whole persons women can generate a counterforce to the stereotype of the leader as they challenge the artificial polarization of human characteristics. There is no reason to assume that women who have the support of their sisters to criticize the masculine stereotype will simply adopt it as a model for themselves. More likely they will develop a wider range of qualities and skills in themselves and thereby encourage men to engage in a comparably liberating procedure (a phenomenon we are beginning to witness already in men's liberation groups). This becoming of whole human beings will affect the values of our society, for it will involve a change in the fabric of human consciousness.

Accordingly, it is reasonable to anticipate that this change will affect the symbols which reflect the values of our society, including religious symbols. Since some of these have functioned to justify oppression, women and men would do well to welcome this change. Religious symbols die when the cultural situation that supported them ceases to give them plausibility. This should pose no problem to authentic faith, which accepts the relativity of all symbols and recognizes that fixation upon any of them as absolute in itself is idolatrous.

The becoming of new symbols is not a matter that can arbitrarily be decided around a conference table. Rather, they grow out of a changing communal situation and experience. This does not mean that theologically we are consigned to the role of passive spectators. We are called upon to be attentive to what the new experience of the becoming of women is revealing to us, and to foster the evolution of consciousness beyond the oppressiveness and imbalance reflected and justified by symbols and doctrines throughout the millennia of patriarchy.

This imbalance is apparent first of all in the biblical and popular image of the great patriarch in heaven who rewards and punishes according to his mysterious and arbitrary will. The fact that the effects of this image have not always been humanizing is evident to any perceptive reader of history. The often cruel behavior of Christians toward unbelievers and even toward dissenters among themselves is shocking evidence of the function of that image in relation to values and behavior.

Sophisticated thinkers, of course, have never intellectually identified God with an elderly parent in heaven. Nevertheless it is important to recognize that even when very abstract conceptualizations of God are formulated in the mind, images have a way of surviving in the imagination in such a way that a person can function on two different and even apparently contradictory levels at the same time. Thus one can speak of God as spirit and at the same time imagine "him" as belonging to the male sex. Such primitive images can profoundly affect conceptualizations which appear to be very refined and abstract. Even the Yahweh of the future, so cherished by the theology of hope, comes through on an imaginative level as exclusively a He-God, and it is perhaps consistent with this that theologians of hope have attempted to develop a political theology which takes no explicit cognizance of the devastation wrought by sexual politics.

The widespread conception of the "Supreme Being" as an entity distinct from this world but controlling it according to plan and keeping human beings in a state of infantile subjection has been a not too subtle mask of the divine patriarch. The Supreme Being's plausibility, and that of the static worldview which accompanies this projection has, of course, declined. This was a projection grounded in specifically patriarchal infrastructures and sustained as subjectively real by the usual processes of generating plausibility. The sustaining power of the social infrastructures has been eroded by a number of developments in recent history, including the general trend toward democratization of society and the emergence of technology with the accompanying sense of mastery over the world and man's destiny. However, it is the women's movement which appears destined to play the key-role in the overthrow of such oppressive elements in traditional theism, precisely because it strikes at the source of the imbalance reflected in traditional beliefs.

The women's movement will present a growing threat to patriarchal religion less by attacking it than by simply leaving it behind. Few of the leaders in the movement evince an interest in institutional religion having recognized it as an instrument of their betrayal. Those who see their commitment to the movement as consonant with concern for the religious heritage are aware that the Christian tradition is by no means bereft of elements which foster genuine experiences and intimations of transcendence. The problem is that their liberating potential is choked off in the surrounding atmosphere of the images, ideas, values, and structures of patriarchy. What will, I think, become possible through the social change coming from radical feminism is a more acute and widespread perception of qualitative differences between those conceptualizations of God and of the human relationship to God which are oppressive in their implications, and those which encourage self-actualization and social commitment.

The various theologies that hypostatize transcendence invariably use this "God" to legitimate oppression, particularly that of women. These are irredeemably anti-feminine and therefore anti-human. In contrast to this, a more authentic language of transcendence does not hypostatize or objectify God and consequently does not lend itself to such use. So for example, Tillich's way of speaking about God as ground and power of being would be very difficult to use for the legitimation of any sort of oppression. It grows out of awareness of that reality which is both transcendent and immanent, not reducible to or adequately represented by such expressions as person, father, supreme being. Awareness of this reality is not achieved by playing theological games but by existential courage. I am not saying that a liberated consciousness necessarily will use Tillich's language of transcendence. That of Whitehead, James, Jaspers, to mention a few – or an entirely new language – may do as well or better. But it remains true that the driving revelatory force which will make possible an authenticity of religious consciousness is courage in the face of anxiety.

Since the projections of patriarchal religion have been blocking the dynamics of existential courage by offering the false security of alienation – that is, of self-reduction to stereotyped roles – there is reason to see hope for the emergence of genuine religious consciousness in the massive challenge to patriarchy which is now in its initial stages. The becoming of women may be not only the doorway to deliverance from the omnipotent Father in all of his disguises – a deliverance which secular humanism has passionately fought for – but also a doorway to something, that is, the beginning for many of a more authentic search for transcendence, that is, for God.

The imbalance in Christian ideology resulting from sexual hierarchy is manifested not only in the doctrine of God but also in the notion of Jesus as the unique God-man. A great deal of Christian doctrine concerning Jesus has been docetic, that is, it has not really seriously accepted the fact that Jesus was a human being. An effect of the liberation of women will very likely be the loss of plausibility of Christological formulas which come close to reflecting a kind of idolatry in regard to the person of Jesus. As it becomes better understood that God is transcendent and unobjectifiable – or else not at all – it will become less plausible to speak of Jesus as the Second Person of the Trinity who "assumed" a human nature. Indeed, the prevalent emphasis upon the total uniqueness and supereminence of Jesus will, I think, become less meaningful. To say this is not at all to deny his extraordinary character and mission. The point is to attempt a realistic assessment of certain ways of using his image (which in all likelihood he himself would repudiate). It is still not uncommon for priests and ministers, when confronted with the issue of women's liberation, to assert that God become incarnate uniquely as a male, and then to draw arguments for male supremacy from this. Indeed, the tradition itself tends to justify such assertions. The underlying – and often explicit – assumption in the minds of theologians down through the centuries has been that the divinity could not have deigned to become incarnate in the "inferior" sex, and the "fact" that "he" did not do so reinforces the belief in masculine superiority. The transformation of society by the erosion of male dominance will generate serious challenges to such assumptions of the Christological tradition.

It will, I think, become increasingly evident that exclusively masculine symbols for the ideal of "incarnation" will not do. As a uniquely masculine divinity loses credibility, so also the idea of a unique divine incarnation in a human being of the male sex may give way in the religious consciousness to an increased awareness of the divine presence in all human beings, understood as expressing and in a real sense incarnating – although always inadequately – the power of being. The seeds of this awareness are already present, of course, in the traditional doctrine that all human beings are made to the image of God and in a less than adequate way in the doctrine of grace. Now it should become possible to work out with increasing realism the implication in both of these doctrines that human beings are called to self-actualization and to the creation of a community that fosters the becoming of women and men. It means that no completely adequate models can be taken from the past. It may be that we will witness a remythologizing of Western religion. Certainly, if the need for parental symbols for God persists, something like the Father-Mother God proposed by Mary Baker Eddy will be more acceptable to the new woman and the new man than the Father God of the past. A symbolism for incarnation of the divine in human beings may continue to be needed in the future, but it is highly unlikely that women or men will continue to find plausible that symbolism which is epitomized in the image of the Virgin kneeling in adoration before her own son. Perhaps this will be replaced by the emergence of bisexual imagery which is not hierarchical. The experience of the past brought forth a new Adam and a new Eve. Perhaps the future will bring a new Christ and a new Mary. For the present, it would appear that we are being called upon to recognize the poverty of all symbols and the fact of our past idolatry regarding them, and to turn to our own resources for bringing about the radically new in our own lives.

The manifestation of God in Jesus was an eschatological event whose fulfilled reality lies in the future. The Jesus of the Gospels was a free person who challenged ossified beliefs and laws. Since he was remarkably free of prejudice against women and treated them as equals insofar as the limitations of his culture would allow, it is certain that he would be working with them for their liberation today. This awakening of women to their human potentiality by creative action as they assume equal partnership with men in society can bring about a manifestation of God in themselves which will be the Second Coming of God incarnate, fulfilling the latent promise in the original revelation that men and women are made to the image of God.

Behind the Mask

It should be evident, then, that women's liberation is an event that can challenge authoritarian, exclusive and non-existential notions of faith and revelation. Since women have been extra-environmentals, to use a McLuhanish term, that is, since they have not been part of the authority structure which uses "faith" and "revelation" to reinforce the mechanisms of alienation, their emergence can effect a more widespread criticalness of idolatry which is often masked by these ideas. There could result from this a more general understanding, of faith as a state of ultimate concern and commitment and a heightened sense of relativity concerning the symbols it uses to express this commitment. An awareness might also emerge – not merely in the minds of a theological elite, but in the general consciousness – that revelation is an ongoing experience.

The becoming of women implies also a transvaluation of values in Christian morality. As the old order is challenged and as men and women become freed to experience a wholeness of personality which the old polarizations impeded, the potentiality will be awakened for a change in moral consciousness which will go far beyond Nietzsche's merely reactionary rejection of Christian values.

Much of the traditional theory of Christian virtue appears to be the product of reactions on the part of men – perhaps guilt reactions – to the behavioral excesses of the stereotypic male. There has been theoretical emphasis upon charity, meekness, obedience, humility, self-abnegation sacrifice, service. Part of the problem with this moral ideology is that it became generally accepted not by men but by women, who have hardly been helped by an ethic which reinforced their abject situation. This emphasis upon the passive virtues, of course, has not challenged exploitativeness but supported it. Part of the syndrome is the prevailing notion of sin as an offense against those in power, or against "God" (the two are often equated). Within the perspective of such a privatized morality the structures themselves of oppression are not seen as sinful.

Consistent with all of this is the fact that the traditional Christian moral consciousness has been fixated upon the problems of reproductive activity in a manner totally disproportionate to its feeble political concern. This was summed up several years ago in Archbishop Roberts' remark that "if contraceptives had been dropped over Japan instead of bombs which merely killed, maimed and shriveled up thousands alive, there would have been a squeal of outraged protest from the Vatican to the remotest Mass center in Asia." Pertinent also is Simone de Beauvoir's remark that the church has reserved its uncompromising humanitarianism for man in the fetal condition. Although theologians today acknowledge that this privatized morality has failed to cope with the structures of oppression, few seriously face the possibility that the roots of this distortion are deeply buried in the fundamental and all-pervasive sexual alienation which the women's movement is seeking to overcome.

It is well-known that Christians under the spell of the jealous God who represents the collective power of his chosen people can use religion to justify that "us and them" attitude which is disastrous in its consequences for the powerless. It is less widely understood that the projection of "the other" – easily adaptable to national, racial and class differences – has basically and primordially been directed against women. Even the rhetoric of racism finds its model in sexism.

The consciousness-raising which is beginning among women is evoking a qualitatively new understanding of the subtle mechanisms which produce and destroy "the other," and a consequent empathy with all of the oppressed. This gives grounds for the hope that their emergence can generate a counterforce to the exploitative mentality which is destroying persons and the environment. Since the way men and women are seen in society is a prime determinant in the whole social system and ideology, radical women refuse to see their movement as simply one among others. What I am suggesting is that it might be the only chance for the turning of human beings from a course leading to the deterioration and perhaps the end of life on this planet.

Those who see their concern for women's liberation as consonant with an evolving Christianity would be unrealistic to expect much comprehension from the majority of male ecclesiastics. Such writers as Gordon Rattrey Taylor (*The Biological Time Bomb*), Robert Francoeur (*Utopian Motherhood*), and others keep beeping out the message that we are moving into a world in which human sexuality is no longer merely oriented to reproduction of the species – which means that the masculine and feminine mystiques are doomed to evaporate. Within the theological community, however, the predictable and almost universal response has been what one might call the ostrich syndrome. Whereas the old theology justified sexual oppression, the new theology for the most part simply ignores it and goes on in comfortable compatibility with it, failing to recognize its deep connection with such other major problems as war, racism and environmental pollution. The work of fostering religious consciousness which is explicitly incompatible with sexism will require an extraordinary degree of creative rage, love and hope.

QUESTIONS FOR REVIEW AND DISCUSSION

1. What is Daly's objective in writing this article? Would you consider what she has done to be theology or religious studies?

2. What examples does Daly provide of the Judeo-Christian religious tradition legitimating patriarchal societies? What other examples have been pointed out by feminist interpreters in the decades since this early critique? Does Daly's critique hold true for other religious traditions?

3. Does Daly envision the increasing role of women in power-sharing roles in religious traditions as genuinely transformative of society? Is she calling for women to assume the same characteristics as males in dominant roles in society?

4. What religious images in particular does Daly envision as undergoing transformation? How, according to Daly, does the image of Jesus play into patriarchal discourse?

5. Does Daly see hope for the equal place of women within a transformed Judeo-Christian tradition?

6. Daly envisions a sort of "Second Coming" of God through the successes of the feminist challenge to patriarchal Christianity. What does she mean by this? How might it transform the notion of revelation?

7. What social changes does Daly envision resulting from the successes of the feminist movement? How might sexuality be affected?

8. Here, Daly is considerably "restrained" in her force of expression, in comparison with her later works, to which the label "radical" may be much more easily applied. Does a "restrained" or "radical" voice better serve her purposes?

9 The Coming of Lilith: Toward a Feminist Theology

Judith Plaskow

Judith Plaskow (1947–) was born in Brooklyn, New York, and obtained her doctorate from Yale Divinity School. She teaches at Manhattan College in New York, and is a past president of the American Academy of Religion (AAR), the preeminent association for religious studies scholars world-wide. Plaskow is the co-founder of the *Journal of Feminist Studies in Religion,* whose subject matter is her primary area of expertise and scholarly contribution. An earlier version of the following selection "The Coming of Lilith" (1972) is found in a Church Women United collection, entitled, "Women Exploring Theology at Grailville," and it was reprinted in *Womanspirit Rising* (1979). It is one of Plaskow's first publications, and is included in this anthology as a classic of early feminist theology, and not representative of the full sweep of her work. In "The Coming of Lilith," Plaskow uses/constructs/expands a Jewish Midrash (rabbinic legend) in which the first man created by God in the Garden of Eden, Adam, had a first wife, Lilith, prior to the better-known Eve. Lilith was created in the same way as Adam, was thus equal to him, and was unwilling to subordinate herself to him. The article serves as an example of reconfiguring or constructing Jewish theology in alignment with feminist realities and ideals.

The present questioning of theological language, premises, methods, and systems by women in every relation to religious life has critical and constructive sides. Women are both articulating the problems with traditional theology and struggling for ways to express their new relationships with their traditions and themselves. If the feminist theology, which is just beginning to emerge from this struggle has any one distinctive characteristic, it may well be its faithfulness to those experiences that engender it; content and process are inseparable. Since the felt need for such theology arises through the consciousness-raising experience, this theology constantly needs to measure itself against and recapture the richness of feeling and insight gained through consciousness raising, finally becoming a continuation of it. Thus much feminist theology may be communal theology, for, in sharing the theological task, content and process have the chance to come together in a very real way. In this paper, I would like to share the results—fragmentary as they are—of one group's attempt to do theology communally in the hopes that our questions will be taken up by other women and our process made part of an ongoing one.

It is not self-evident that theology must remain close to the experiences that generate it. Experience may provide the occasion for general, abstract reflection or argument. There are reasons why, in the case of feminist theology, the close relation between content and process seems imperative. Not surprisingly, these reasons have to do with the nature of consciousness raising itself. Through consciousness raising, I come to affirm the value of my experience as a woman person, the value of my whole, not only intellectual self. I affirm my experience with and through other women in a process that is communal in essence. I cannot then write a theology that abstracts from my experience and ignores part of myself, or that abstracts from the community of which I am a part.

These considerations form the framework within which to see our group's work. Our group process reflected them, and the content of our discussions further developed them. The question with which we began was whether we could find in the women's movement a process, event, or experience that somehow expresses the essence of the movement and that might function as a central integrating symbol for a theology of liberation. Aware that such a symbol would have value only as it arises out of and remains close to the life of the movement, we proceeded to explore this question by sharing and reflecting on our experiences as women in the women's movement. We then discussed the ways in which these experiences are similar to or are religious experiences, and finally, attempted to reflect theologically on what we had done.

The Women's Movement

Becoming involved in the women's movement means moving from isolation as a woman to community. Through the telling my story, I reach out to other women. Through their hearing, which both affirms my story and makes it possible, they reach out to me. I am able to move, gradually, from defensiveness to openness, from fear of questioning, to a deep and radical questioning of the premises from which I have lived my life. I experience relief; my anger has been heard, and I am not alone. But I am also frightened; I am undermining my own foundations. The walls come tumbling down. *Anger, fear, rage, joy, celebration, rejoicing, high, flying, bursting forth, pregnant with newness, pregnant with possibility, hearing, wholeness*—these were the words we began with in attempting to describe our consciousness-raising experiences. What we wanted to do was to move from these words or experiences to one central word symbol or experience that captured them all. Mary Daly's "sisterhood of man" was in our minds from the start of our discussion, but it was not quite what we were looking for. We felt that sisterhood happens between women because of something else happening to them—an individual process of coming-to-wholeness within community—and we wanted to try to get at that something else.

The "Yeah, Yeah Experience"

We arrived at a term for part of our experience quite spontaneously. One of us said something, and the others responded excitedly, "Yeah, yeah." Somehow, this triggered a double recognition. We saw ourselves in the experience to which we responded, and we also recognized ourselves as women come together, recognizing our common experience with other women. We spent the next hour trying to define the "yeah, yeah experience."

The "yeah, yeah experience" is, first of all, *the process through which we come to be sisters*. It may be the experience that brings me into the movement. I read an article by another woman, defending myself against it, and all of a sudden, undeniably, a piece of my life is there before me on the page. ("Yeah, yeah.") I attend a meeting, a lecture, "just to see what it's all about," and I am "converted," turned around, the pieces of my life fall together in a new way. ("Yeah, yeah.") The "yeah, yeah experience" is all the many individual moments of recognition and illumination through which I come to a new awareness of my situation and myself. I talk to other women, and one describes as her hangup something I thought was peculiar to me—and everyone else is nodding too. I read, I hear, I talk about the oppression of women, and all at once, it's *our* oppression.

Thus the affirmative, early Beatles, sound of "yeah, yeah" is not meant to suggest that the "yeah, yeah experience" is always a joyful one. It can, of course, express deep joy—joy in sharing, joy in self-recognition, joy as I increase my freedom in relation to my past. But I can also say "yeah, yeah" as I put my finger on a hidden source of bitterness, as I hear my own anger spoken, or as I articulate my rage on behalf of my sisters' past and my own. In all cases, however, I express my conviction and my openness. I move forward; I respond toward a future where anything can happen.

My response, although sometimes an affirmation of only a limited area of agreement, is a response of my whole person. When I say "yeah, yeah," I am moved, and I move. I move physically, toward the one who spoke, and I move figuratively, into the consciousness-raising process. I affirm my sister and encourage her to go on while I myself enter the dialogue.

The "yeah, yeah experience" is thus a different way of thinking from our usual "yes, but" reasoning, which is inherently nondialogical and out of touch with its own basis in experience. "Yes, but" thinking focuses on the logic of the speaker or the argument advanced, to the exclusion of the awareness of being addressed by the speaker or argument. When I say "yeah, yeah" on the other hand, I do not forget logic or the fact that genuine disagreement may be, should be part of the dialogue into which I have entered. But I commit my whole person to speak and to really hear. This true speaking and hearing is a possibility for all persons. The "yeah, yeah experience" is potentially universal.

Sisterhood

The value of my being with and for others that develops through the "yeah, yeah experience" finds its expression in sisterhood. But sisterhood is not only what evolves through the "yeah, yeah experience"; it is in some sense its presupposition. Sisterhood grows through my speaking and hearing, but were it not already partly there, I could not begin to speak and hear.

The experience of sisterhood is many-sided. It has, first of all, both a general and a specific dimension. In affirming my own womanhood—or personhood as woman—I affirm it in all women. But I also and particularly affirm those women with whom I share the experience of affirmation. (The other side of this—sisterhood as presupposition—would be that in affirming all women I affirm myself as a woman.) This does not mean that, in community, I acknowledge in myself the characteristics of the "eternal feminine" or make peace with my assigned role. On the contrary, what I proclaim is precisely my freedom as a woman over these limited stereotypes.

Thus this experience is, secondly, both deeply personal and intensely political. I affirm myself as a woman, but only as I enter into a new, and hitherto silent, community. In saying yes to myself, where I and my society had said only no, I open the possibility of seeing other women as persons and friends; I discover a source of energy for personal and social growth and change. I acquire a sense of freedom that is rooted in my new consciousness of personal integrity and wholeness; I express it by uniting with other women in the common task of creating our future. I am freed to repossess or to try to free myself from parts of my past, but I can do this effectively only as I work for interpersonal and institutional change in the present.

But sisterhood, more than an experience of community, *is* a community. It is a place where women can "get themselves together," begin to understand, and thus begin to overcome their common oppression. It is a place where women can begin to act out their new sense of wholeness, making their own decisions for their own lives. Thus the non-hierarchically structured women's movement refuses to replace one set of authorities with another. Instead, women who have rejected the myth of their own powerlessness create, in community, alternatives to a stunted past.

The Women's Movement as a Religious Experience

Throughout our discussion of the women's movement, we found ourselves both repeatedly seeing our experiences in the movement as religious experiences and repeatedly questioning the value of doing so. While the words *grace, illumination, mission,* and *conversion* kept cropping up in our conversation, we recognized that women who do not think in religious categories, who would in fact reject them, share the experiences we expressed in this language. We did not wish imperialistically to insist that their experiences too are "really" religious despite their refusal to recognize the fact. Moreover, if we asked what we added to the "root" experiences by calling them *religious*, there was nothing specific we could identify. On the other hand, we did feel this was a valid way of looking at our experiences in the women's movement, a way that could enrich our understanding of both these experiences and of religious experience itself.

We began our discussion of the women's movement with the "yeah, yeah experience" rather than with sisterhood because we wanted to get more precisely at the experience of coming-to-wholeness that sisterhood presupposes. If our discussion of the "yeah, yeah experience" got at part of this process, our discussion of religious experience dealt with it from another angle. We saw the stages of consciousness raising as analogous to the stages in a religious journey, culminating in the experience of full, related, selfhood.

Again and again we came back to the word *graceful* to describe certain of our experiences with other women. At moments I can never plan or program, I am given to myself in a way I cannot account for by studying the organic progression of my past. Listening to another woman tell her story, I *concentrate* on words spoken and experienced as if our lives depended on them, and indeed they do. And yet I could not say what enables me to be really there, hearing, in a way that makes me feel that I had never really heard before—or been listened to as I am now. Nor could I say why precisely at this moment I become aware of myself as a total person, why I feel myself as whole, integrated, free, fully human. Some of this feeling we hoped to convey through the "yeah, yeah experience." "Yeah, yeah" is my response to an illumination that includes the intellect but is more than intellectual. In this moment in which I transcend it, I feel sharply the limits of the taken-for-granted definition of myself and my capabilities.

This is where the experience of grace can also become the experience of conversion. Seeing myself in a new way, I am called to the transformation of myself. I must become the possibilities I already am in my moment of vision, for I am really not yet those possibilities. The call necessitates a decision, a response.

Here two factors come into play. The feeling of wholeness, which is also a call to self-transformation, is not continuous with my previous development. But this does not mean that I have skipped over a "stage" in my life. I must still decide whether and how to change myself and, having decided, work slowly through the difficulties and pain that my decision entails. My clear perception of the limits of my upbringing, of the lost opportunities and confining decisions of my past does not relieve me of a lifetime of questioning and reques-tioning assumptions that I reject but cannot entirely overcome. On the other hand, there is a sense in which, once I have made a decision, I am already on the other side. At least I have overcome the fear that can only express itself in defensiveness. I have defined my goals and released the source of energy to achieve them.

Once again, the importance of sisterhood as a community comes into play. I make my decision for self-transformation in the context of a community whose support is ongoing. The continuing process of questioning, growth, and change remains collective. Thus, not only is my decision reinforced, but my energies for change are pooled with the group's energies. This expresses itself in a communal sense of mission. After a certain amount of time spent on consciousness raising, a group generally feels the need to move outward, to become involved in projects that translate its goals into reality and that reach and bring in other women. Strengthened in themselves, its members feel ready and anxious to spread the good word to others.

This sense of community also expresses itself—and this is the last way in which we looked at the women's movement as a religious experience—in the formation of embryonic rituals and symbols. Telling our stories has become a ritualized way of getting into the consciousness raising experience. Calling each other "sister," feeling a new freedom to touch and hug one another are concrete expressions of the new bonds between us. We have our heretics and our infidels; we have defined the "others" in a way that conditions behavior toward them: the token woman, the pussycat, and, of course, the male chauvinist pig. We have our political symbols: the woman symbol, the clenched fist. We indulge in ritual language corrections; we call all women "Ms." We are writing our songs, and we are beginning to find and define our peculiar forms of celebration.

Theological Process

With regard to this list of rituals, the first task we envisaged for theology in relation to the women's movement was a critical one. We needed a critical principle to act as a bulwark against the tendency to absolutize either particular issues in the movement or the movement itself. We needed to move beyond defining "others" and, instead, to find those others in ourselves. We saw the need to regard every center, every feminist goal, as only provisional. Beyond each of our "ultimate" perspectives is a still broader one from which ours is judged limited.

With reference to our main, constructive task, we found it easier to discuss the women's movement and religious experience than to reflect theologically on either. What is theology? What does it mean to apply a theological process? Is feminist theology the expression of a new religion? How can we relate ourselves to the old without destroying our new experiences through the attempt to understand them in terms of old forms? These were crucial questions we felt we had to, but could not, answer. There were times we found ourselves getting into some rather traditional discussions—the ambiguity of grace that is both fulfilled and "not yet" fulfilled; the question of which comes first, sisterhood or the "yeah, yeah experience," grace or the experience of grace. Many of the things we talked about set off old associations. There is a clear relation, for example, between the true speaking and hearing of the "yeah, yeah experience" and the I-Thou relation in Martin Buber. We considered what it would mean to write a systematic theology that affirmed the experiences we had been discussing—choosing a philosophical framework, our texts, our rabbis, or our saints. But we were worried about the disappearance of the four of us sitting there, our coming together, behind the framework we would create. We clearly needed a form that would grow out of the content and process of our time together.

Our Story: The Coming of Lilith

It was here that we realized that, although we had failed to come up with a single event or symbol that captured all of feminist experience, there had emerged out of our discussion many of the central elements of a myth. We had a journey to go on, an enemy (or enemies) to vanquish, salvation to be achieved both for ourselves and for humanity. If we found ourselves with a myth, moreover, this was particularly appropriate to our experience, for we had come together to do theology by beginning with our stories. It was no coincidence, then, that we arrived back at the story form.

We recognized the difficulties of "inventing" a myth, however, and so we wanted to tell a story that seemed to grow naturally out of our present history. We also felt the need for using older materials that would carry their own reverberations and significance, even if we departed freely from them. We chose, therefore, to begin with the story of Lilith, demon of the night, who, according to rabbinic legend was Adam's first wife. Created equal to him, for some unexplained reason she found that she could not live with him, and flew away. Through her story, we could express not only our new image of ourselves, but our relation to certain of the elements of our religious traditions. Since stories are the heart of tradition, we could question and create tradition by telling a new story within the framework of an old one. We took Lilith for our heroine, and yet, most important, not Lilith alone. We try to express through our myth the process of our coming to do theology together. Lilith by herself is in exile and can do nothing. The real heroine of our story is sisterhood, and sisterhood is powerful.

In the beginning, the Lord God formed Adam and Lilith from the dust of the ground and breathed into their nostrils the breath of life. Created from the same source, both having been formed from the ground, they were equal in all ways. Adam, being a man, didn't like this situation, and he looked for ways to change it. He said, "I'll have my figs now, Lilith," ordering her to wait on him, and he tried to leave to her the daily tasks of life in the garden. But Lilith wasn't one to take any nonsense; she picked herself up, uttered God's holy name, and flew away. "Well now, Lord," complained Adam, "that uppity woman you sent me has gone and deserted me." The Lord, inclined to be sympathetic, sent his messengers after Lilith, telling her to shape up and return to Adam or face dire punishment. She, however, preferring anything to living with Adam, decided to stay where she was. And so God, after more careful consideration this time, caused a deep sleep to fall on Adam and out of one of his ribs created for him a second companion, Eve.

For a time, Eve and Adam had a good thing going. Adam was happy now, and Eve, though she occasionally sensed capacities within herself that remained undeveloped, was basically satisfied with the role of Adam's wife and helper. The only thing that really disturbed her was the excluding closeness of the relationship between Adam and God. Adam and God just seemed to have more in common, both being men, and Adam came to identify with God more and more. After a while, that made God a bit uncomfortable too, and he started going over in his mind whether he may not have made a mistake letting Adam talk him into banishing Lilith and creating Eve, seeing the power that gave Adam.

Meanwhile Lilith, all alone, attempted from time to time to rejoin the human community in the garden. After her first fruitless attempt to breach its walls, Adam worked hard to build them stronger, even getting Eve to help him. He told her fearsome stories of the demon Lilith who threatens women in childbirth and steals children from their cradles in the middle of the night. The second time Lilith came, she stormed the garden's main gate, and a great battle ensued between her and Adam in which she was finally defeated. This time, however, before Lilith got away, Eve got a glimpse of her and saw she was a woman like herself.

After this encounter, seeds of curiosity and doubt began to grow in Eve's mind. Was Lilith indeed just another woman? Adam had said she was a demon. Another woman! The very idea attracted Eve. She had never seen another creature like herself before. And how beautiful and strong Lilith looked! How bravely she had fought! Slowly, slowly, Eve began to think about the limits of her own life within the garden.

One day, after many months of strange and disturbing thoughts, Eve, wandering around the edge of the garden, noticed a young apple tree she and Adam had planted, and saw that one of its branches stretched over the garden wall. Spontaneously, she tried to climb it, and struggling to the top, swung herself over the wall.

She did not wander long on the other side before she met the one she had come to find, for Lilith was waiting. At first sight of her, Eve remembered the tales of Adam and was frightened, but Lilith understood and greeted her kindly. "Who are you?" they asked each other, "What is your story?" And they sat and spoke together, of the past and then of the future. They talked for many hours, not once, but many times. They taught each other many things, and told each other stories, and laughed together, and cried, over and over, till the bond of sisterhood grew between them.

Meanwhile, back in the garden, Adam was puzzled by Eve's comings and goings, and disturbed by what he sensed to be her new attitude toward him. He talked to God about it, and God, having his own problems with Adam and a somewhat broader perspective, was able to help out a little—but he was confused, too. Something had failed to go according to plan. As in the days of Abraham, he needed counsel from his children. "I am who I am," thought God, "but I must become who I will become."

And God and Adam were expectant and afraid of the day Eve and Lilith returned to the garden, bursting with possibilities, ready to rebuild it together.

QUESTIONS FOR REVIEW AND DISCUSSION

1. What does Plaskow seem to mean by consciousness raising? How does it relate to the link between experience and "doing theology"?
2. What does Plaskow mean by the "yeah, yeah experience"? How does it differ from "yes, but" reasoning? What might be the strengths and limitations of each approach?
3. What are some of the intrinsic qualities of "sisterhood," as Plaskow conceives it? How does it differ from other types of social collectives?
4. In what ways are the "yeah, yeah experience," and notions of "sisterhood" related to a form of religious experience in Plaskow's explanation? Could one consider the women's movement to be a religious experience? Why? Or why not?
5. What does it mean to "apply a theological process"? Is feminist theology a new religion or is it a part of an existing, evolving religious tradition?
6. What purposes might myth serve in encapsulating and articulating theological perspectives?
7. What does the Lilith myth as framed in this article convey to readers?
8. Is the Lilith myth as framed in this article an example of Christian theology? Jewish theology? Feminist theology? What is this myth's relationship to the discipline of religious studies? What is this article's relationship to the discipline of religious studies?

10 The Art of Magic and the Power of Faith

Bronislaw Malinowski

Bronislaw Malinowski (1884–1942) was born in Krakow, Poland and received his doctorate in philosophy from Jagiellonian University in Poland. He obtained another doctorate in anthropology from the University of London. He taught at the London School of Economics, establishing it as a renowned centre for the study of anthropology. Malinowski's *Argonauts of the Western Pacific* (1922) is one of the most influential ethnographies ever written, and was based on his fieldwork in the Trobriand Islands. He is renowned for making fieldwork an indispensable component of anthropological studies. His approach is sometimes classified as psychological functionalism, because he often sought to explain the functions of cultural behaviours in terms of the psychological underpinnings. It had an influence on the development of American cultural anthropology and contrasted with the structural functionalism of his colleague, Radcliffe-Brown, who helped shape the character of British social anthropology. The selection that follows comes from *Magic, Science, and Religion and Other Essays* (1948), in which he explores the relationship among those three seemingly disparate, but often overlapping categories.

Magic – the very word seems to reveal a world of mysterious and unexpected possibilities! Even for those who do not share in that hankering after the occult, … , even for the clear scientific mind the subject of magic has a special attraction. Partly perhaps because we hope to find in it the quintessence of primitive man's longings and of his wisdom and that, whatever it might be, is worth knowing. Partly because "magic" seems to stir up in everyone some hidden mental forces, some lingering hopes in the miraculous, some dormant beliefs in man's mysterious possibilities. Witness to this is the power which the words magic, spell, charm, to bewitch, and to enchant, possess in poetry, where the inner value of words, the emotional forces which they still release, survive longest and are revealed most clearly.

Yet when the sociologist approaches the study of magic, there where it still reigns supreme, where even now it can be found fully developed – that is, among the Stone Age savages of today – he finds to his disappointment an entirely sober, prosaic, even clumsy art, enacted for purely practical reasons, governed by crude and shallow beliefs, carried out in a simple and monotonous technique. This was already indicated in the definition of magic given above when in order to distinguish it from religion we described it as a body of purely practical acts, performed as a means to an end. Such also we have found it when we tried to disentangle it from knowledge and from practical arts, in which it is so strongly enmeshed, superficially so alike that it requires some effort to distinguish the essentially different mental attitude and the specifically ritual nature of its acts. Primitive magic – every field anthropologist knows it to his cost – is extremely monotonous and unexciting, strictly limited in its means of action, circumscribed in its beliefs, stunted in its fundamental assumptions. Follow one rite, study one spell, grasp the principles of magical belief, art and sociology in one case, and you will know not only all the acts of the tribe, but, adding a variant here and there, you will be able to settle as a magical practitioner in any part of the world yet fortunate enough to have faith in that desirable art.

1. The Rite and the Spell

Let us have a look at a typical act of magic, and choose one which is well-known and generally regarded as a standard performance – an act of black magic. Among the several types which we meet in savagery, witchcraft by the act of pointing the magical dart is, perhaps, the most widespread of all. A pointed bone or a stick, an arrow or the spine of some animal, is ritually, in a mimic fashion, thrust, thrown, or pointed in the direction of the man to be killed by sorcery. We have innumerable recipes in the oriental and ancient books of magic, in ethnographic descriptions and tales of travelers, of how such a rite is performed. But the emotional setting, the gestures and expressions of the sorcerer during the performance, have been but seldom described. Yet these are of the greatest importance. If a spectator were suddenly transported to some part of Melanesia and could observe the sorcerer at work, not perhaps knowing exactly what he was looking at, he might think that he had either to do with a lunatic or else he would guess that here was a man acting under the sway of uncontrolled anger. For the sorcerer has, as an essential part of the ritual performance, not merely to point the bone dart at his victim, but with an intense expression of fury and hatred he has to thrust it in the air, turn and twist it as if to bore it in the wound, then pull it back with a sudden jerk. Thus not only is the act of violence, or stabbing, reproduced, but the passion of violence has to be enacted.

We see thus that the dramatic expression of emotion is the essence of this act, for what is it that is reproduced in it? Not its end, for the magician would in that case have to imitate the death of the victim, but the emotional state of the performer, a state which closely corresponds to the situation in which we find it and which has to be gone through mimetically.

I could adduce a number of similar rites from my own experience, and many more, of course, from other records. Thus, when in other types of black magic the sorcerer ritually injures or mutilates or destroys a figure or object symbolizing the victim, this rite is, above all, a clear expression of hatred and anger. Or when in love magic the performer has really or symbolically to grasp, stroke, fondle the beloved person or some object representing her, he reproduces the behavior of a heartsick lover who has lost his common sense and is overwhelmed by passion. ... Or else in an act, recorded by myself, to ward off the evil powers of darkness, a man has ritually to tremble, to utter a spell slowly as if paralyzed by fear. And this fear gets hold also of the approaching sorcerer and wards him off.

All such acts, usually rationalized and explained by some principle of magic, are *prima facie* expressions of emotion. The substances and paraphernalia used in them have often the same significance. Daggers, sharp-pointed lacerating objects, evil-smelling or poisonous substances, used in black magic; scents, flowers, inebriating stimulants, in love magic; valuables, in economic magic – all these are associated primarily through emotions and not through ideas with the end of the respective magic.

Besides such rites, however, in which a dominant element serves to express an emotion, there are others in which the act does forecast its result, or, to use Sir James

Frazer's expression, the rite imitates its end. Thus, in the black magic of the Melanesians recorded by myself, a characteristic ritual way of winding-up the spell is for the sorcerer to weaken the voice, utter a death rattle, and fall down in imitation of the rigor of death. It is, however, not necessary to adduce any other examples, for this aspect of magic and the allied one of contagious magic has been brilliantly described and exhaustively documented by Frazer. Sir James has also shown that there exists a special lore of magical substances based on affinities, relations, on ideas of similarity and contagion, developed with a magical pseudo-science.

But there are also ritual proceedings in which there is neither imitation nor forecasting nor the expression of any special idea or emotion. There are rites so simple that they can be described only as an immediate application of magical virtue, as when the performer stands up and, directly invoking the wind, causes it to rise. Or again, as when a man conveys the spell to some material substance which afterwards will be applied to the thing or person to be charmed. The material objects used in such ritual are also of a strictly appropriate character – substances best fitted to receive, retain, and transmit magical virtue, coverings designed to imprison and preserve it until it is applied to its object.

But what is the magical virtue which figures not only in the last-mentioned type of act but in every magical rite? For whether it be an act expressing certain emotions or a rite of imitation and foreshadowing or an act of simple casting, one feature they have always in common: the force of magic, its virtue, must always be conveyed to the charmed object. What is it? Briefly, it is always the power contained in the spell, for, and this is never sufficiently emphasized, the most important element in magic is the spell. The spell is that part of magic which is occult, handed over in magical filiation, known only to the practitioner. To the natives knowledge of magic means knowledge of spell, and in an analysis of any act of witchcraft it will always be found that the ritual centers round the utterance of the spell. The formula is always the core of the magical performance.

The study of the texts and formulas of primitive magic reveals that there are three typical elements associated with the belief in magical efficiency. There are, first, the phonetic effects, imitations of natural sounds, such as the whistling of the wind, the growling of thunder, the roar of the sea, the voices of various animals. These sounds symbolize certain phenomena and thus are believed to produce them magically. Or else they express certain emotional states associated with the desire which is to be realized by means of the magic.

The second element, very conspicuous in primitive spells, is the use of words which invoke, state, or command the desired aim. Thus the sorcerer will mention all the symptoms of the disease which he is inflicting, or in the lethal formula he will describe the end of his victim. In healing magic the wizard will give word pictures of perfect health and bodily strength. In economic magic the growing of plants, the approach of animals, the arrival of fish in shoals are depicted. Or again the magician uses words and sentences which express the emotion under the stress of which he works his magic, and the action which gives expression to this emotion. The sorcerer in tones of fury will have to repeat such verbs as "I break – I twist – I burn – I destroy," enumerating with each of them the various parts of the body and internal organs of his victim. In all this we see that the spells are built very much on the same pattern as the rites and the words selected for the same reasons as the substances of magic.

Thirdly there is an element in almost every spell to which there is no counterpart in ritual. I mean the mythological allusions, the references to ancestors and culture heroes from whom this magic has been received. And that brings us to perhaps the most important point in the subject, to the traditional setting of magic.

2. The Tradition of Magic

Tradition, which, as we have several times insisted, reigns supreme in primitive civilization, gathers in great abundance round magical ritual and cult. In the case of any important magic we invariably find the story accounting for its existence. Such a story tells when and where it entered the possession of man, how it became the property of a local group or of a family or clan. But such a story is not the story of its origins. Magic never "originated," it never has been made or invented. All magic simply "was" from the beginning an essential adjunct of all such things and processes as vitally interest man and yet elude his normal rational efforts. The spell, the rite, and the thing which they govern are coeval.

Thus, in Central Australia, all magic existed and has been inherited from the *alcheringa* times, when it came about like everything else. In Melanesia all magic comes from a time when humanity lived underground and when magic was a natural knowledge of ancestral man. In higher societies magic is often derived from spirits and demons, but even these, as a rule, originally received and did not invent it. Thus the belief in the primeval natural existence of magic is universal. As its counterpart we find the conviction that only by an absolutely unmodified immaculate transmission does magic retain its efficiency. The slightest alteration from the original pattern would be fatal. There is, then, the idea that between the object and its magic there exists an essential nexus. Magic is the quality of the thing, or rather, of the relation between man and the thing, for though never man-made it is always made for man. In all tradition, in all mythology, magic is always found in the possession of man and through the knowledge of man or man-like being. It implies the performing magician quite as much as the thing to be charmed and the means of charming. It is part of the original endowment of primeval humanity, of the *mura-mura* or *alcheringa* of Australia, of the subterrestrial humanity of Melanesia, of the people of the magical Golden Age all the world over.

Magic is not only human in its embodiment, but also in its subject matter: it refers principally to human activities and states, hunting, gardening, fishing, trading, love-making, disease, and death. It is not directed so much to nature as to man's relation to nature and to the human activities which affect it. Moreover, the effects of magic are usually conceived not as a product of nature influenced by the charm, but as something specially magical, something which nature cannot produce, but only the power of magic. The graver forms of disease, love in its passionate phases, the desire for a ceremonial exchange and other similar manifestations in the human organism and mind, are the direct product of the spell and rite. Magic is thus not derived from an observation of nature or knowledge of its laws, it is a primeval possession of man to be known only through tradition and affirming man's autonomous power of creating desired ends.

Thus, the force of magic is not a universal force residing everywhere, flowing where it will or it is willed to. Magic is the one and only specific power, a force unique of its kind, residing exclusively in man, let loose only by his magical art, gushing out with his voice, conveyed by the casting forth of the rite.

It may be here mentioned that the human body, being the receptacle of magic and the channel of its flow, must be submitted to various conditions. Thus the magician has to keep all sorts of taboos, or else the spell might be injured, especially as in certain parts of the world, in Melanesia for instance, the spell resides in the magician's belly, which is the seat of memory as well as of food. When necessary it is summoned up to the larynx, which is the seat of intelligence, and thence sent forth by the voice, the main organ of the human mind. Thus, not only is magic an essentially human possession, but it is literally and actually enshrined in man and can be handed on only from man to man, according to very strict rules of magical filiation, initiation, and instruction. It is thus never conceived as a force of nature, residing in things, acting independently of man, to be found out and learned by him, by any of those proceedings by which he gains his ordinary knowledge of nature.

4. Magic and Experience

So far we have been dealing mainly with native ideas and with native views of magic. This has led us to a point where the savage simply affirms that magic gives man the power over certain things. Now we must analyze this belief from the point of view of the sociological observer. Let us realize once more the type of situation in which we find magic. Man, engaged in a series of practical activities, comes to a gap; the hunter is disappointed by his quarry, the sailor misses propitious winds, the canoe builder has to deal with some material of which he is never certain that it will stand the strain, or the healthy person suddenly feels his strength failing. What does man do naturally under such conditions, setting aside all magic, belief and ritual? Forsaken by his knowledge, baffled by his past experience and by his technical skill, he realizes his impotence. Yet his desire grips him only the more strongly; his anxiety, his fears and hopes, induce a tension in his organism which drives him to some sort of activity. Whether he be savage or civilized, whether in possession of magic or entirely ignorant of its existence, passive inaction, the only thing dictated by reason, is the last thing in which he can acquiesce. His nervous system and his whole organism drive him to some substitute activity. Obsessed by the idea of the desired end, he sees it and feels it. His organism reproduces the acts suggested by the anticipations of hope, dictated by the emotion of passion so strongly felt.

The man under the sway of impotent fury or dominated by thwarted hate spontaneously clenches his fist and carries out imaginary thrusts at his enemy, muttering imprecations, casting words of hatred and anger against him. The lover aching for his unattainable or irresponsive beauty sees her in his visions, addresses her, and entreats and commands her favors, feeling himself accepted, pressing her to his bosom in his dreams. The anxious fisherman or hunter sees in his imagination the quarry enmeshed in the nets, the animal attained by the spear; he utters their names, describes in words his visions of the magnificent catch, he even breaks out into gestures of mimic representation of what he desires. The man lost at night in the woods or the jungle, beset by superstitious fear, sees around him the haunting demons, addresses them, tries to ward off, to frighten them, or shrinks from them in fear, like an animal which attempts to save itself by feigning death.

These reactions to overwhelming emotion or obsessive desire are natural responses of man to such a situation, based on a universal psycho-physiological mechanism. They engender what could be called extended expressions of emotion in act and in word, the threatening gestures of impotent anger and its maledictions, the spontaneous enactment of the desired end in a practical impasse, the passionate fondling gestures of the lover, and so on. All these spontaneous acts and spontaneous works make man forecast the images of the wished-for results, or express his passion in uncontrollable gestures, or break out into words which give vent to desire and anticipate its end.

And what is the purely intellectual process, the conviction formed during such a free outburst of emotion in words and deeds? First there surges a clear image of the desired end, of the hated person, of the feared danger or ghost. And each image is blended with its specific passion, which drives us to assume an active attitude towards that image. When passion reaches the breaking point at which man loses control over himself, the words which he utters, his blind behavior, allow the pent-up physiological tension to flow over. But over all this outburst presides the image of the end. It supplies the motive-force of the reaction, it apparently organizes and directs words and acts towards a definite purpose. The substitute action in which the passion finds its vent, and which is due to impotence, has subjectively all the value of a real action, to which emotion would, if not impeded, naturally have led.

As the tension spends itself in these words and gestures the obsessing visions fade away, the desired end seems nearer satisfaction, we regain our balance, once more at harmony with life. And we remain with a conviction that the words of malediction and the gestures of fury have traveled towards the hated person and hit their target; that the imploration of love, the visionary embraces, cannot have remained unanswered, that the visionary attainment of success in our pursuit cannot have been without a beneficial influence on the pending issue. In the case of fear, as the emotion which has led us to frenzied behavior gradually subsides, we feel that it is this behavior that has driven away the terrors. In brief, a strong emotional experience, which spends itself in a purely subjective flow of images, words, and acts of behavior, leaves a very deep conviction of its reality, as if of some practical and positive achievement, as if of something done by a power revealed to man.

This power, born of mental and physiological obsession, seems to get hold of us from outside, and to primitive man, or to the credulous and untutored mind of all ages, the spontaneous spell, the spontaneous rite, and the spontaneous belief in their efficiency must appear as a direct revelation from some external and no doubt impersonal sources.

When we compare this spontaneous ritual and verbiage of overflowing passion or desire with traditionally fixed magical ritual and with the principles embodied in magical spells and substances, the striking resemblance of the two products shows that they are not independent of each other. Magical ritual, most of the principles of magic, most of its spells and substances, have been revealed to man in those passionate experiences which assail him in the impasses of his instinctive life and of his practical pursuits, in those gaps and breaches left in the ever-imperfect wall of culture which he erects between himself and the besetting temptations and dangers of his destiny. In this I think we have to recognize not only one of the sources but the very fountainhead of magical belief. ...

5. Magic and Science

With all the strength which magic draws from the spontaneous belief and spontaneous ritual of intense desire or thwarted emotion, with all the force given it by the personal prestige, the social power and success common in the magician and practitioner still there are failures and breakdowns, and we should vastly underrate the savage's intelligence, logic, and grasp of experience if we assumed that he is not aware of it and that he fails to account for it.

First of all, magic is surrounded by strict conditions: exact remembrance of a spell, unimpeachable performance of the rite, unswerving adhesion to the taboos and observances which shackle the magician. If any one of these is neglected, failure of magic follows. And then, even if magic be done in the most perfect manner, its effects can be equally well undone: for against every magic there can be also counter-magic. If magic, as we have shown, is begotten by the union of man's steadfast desire with the wayward whim of chance, then every desire, positive or negative, may – nay, must – have its magic. Now in all his social and worldly ambitions, in all his strivings to catch good fortune and trap propitious luck, man moves in an atmosphere of rivalry, of envy, and of spite. For luck, possessions, even health, are matters of degree and of comparison, and if your neighbor owns more cattle, more wives, more health, and more power than yourself, you feel dwarfed in all you own and all you are. And such is human nature that a man's desire is as much satisfied by the thwarting of others as by the advancement of himself. To this sociological play of desire and counter-desire, of ambition and spite, of success and envy, there corresponds the play of magic and counter-magic, or of magic white and black.

In Melanesia, where I have studied this problem at first hand, there is not one single magical act which is not firmly believed to possess a counter-act which, when stronger, can completely annihilate its effects. In certain types of magic, as for instance, that of health and disease, the formulas actually go in couples. A sorcerer who learns a performance by which to cause a definite disease will at the same time learn the formula and the rite which can annul completely the effects of his evil magic. In love, again, not only does there exist a belief that, when two formulas are performed to win the same heart, the stronger will override the weaker one, but there are spells uttered directly to alienate the affections of the sweetheart or wife of another. Whether this duality of magic is as consistently carried out all the world over as in the Trobriands it is difficult to say, but that the twin forces of white and black, of positive and negative, exist everywhere is beyond doubt. Thus the failures of magic can always be accounted for by the slip of memory, by slovenliness in performance or in observance of a taboo, and, last not least, by the fact that someone else has performed some counter-magic.

We are now in a position to state more fully the relation between magic and science already outlined above. Magic is akin to science in that it always has a definite aim intimately associated with human instincts, needs, and pursuits. The magic art is directed towards the attainment of practical aims. Like the other arts and crafts, it is also governed by a theory, by a system of principles which dictate the manner in which the act has to be performed in order to be effective. In analyzing magical spells, rites, and substances we have found that there are a number of general principles which govern them. Both science and magic develop a special technique. In magic, as in the other arts, man can undo what he has done or mend the damage which he has wrought. In fact, in magic, the quantitative equivalents of black and white seem to be much more exact and the effects of witchcraft much more completely eradicated by counter-witchcraft than is possible in any practical art or craft. Thus both magic and science show certain similarities, and, with Sir James Frazer, we can appropriately call magic a pseudo-science.

And the spurious character of this pseudo-science is not hard to detect. Science, even as represented by the primitive knowledge of savage man, is based on the normal universal experience of everyday life, experience won in man's struggle with nature for his subsistence and safety, founded on observation, fixed by reason. Magic is based on specific experience of emotional states in which man observes not nature but himself, in which the truth is revealed not by reason but by the play of emotions upon the human organism. Science is founded on the conviction that experience, effort, and reason are valid; magic on the belief that hope cannot fail nor desire deceive. The theories of knowledge are dictated by logic, those of magic by the association of ideas under the influence of desire. As a matter of empirical fact the body of rational knowledge and the body of magical lore are incorporated each in a different tradition, in a different social setting and in a different type of activity, and all these differences are clearly recognized by the savages. The one constitutes the domain of the profane; the other, hedged round by observances, mysteries, and taboos, makes up half of the domain of the sacred.

6. Magic and Religion

Both magic and religion arise and function in situations of emotional stress: crises of life, lacunae in important pursuits, death and initiation into tribal mysteries, unhappy love and unsatisfied hate. Both magic and religion open up escapes from such situations and such impasses as offer no empirical way out except by ritual and belief into the domain of the supernatural. This domain embraces, in religion, beliefs in ghosts, spirits, the primitive forebodings of providence, the guardians of tribal mysteries; in magic, the primeval force and virtue of magic. Both magic and religion are based strictly on mythological tradition, and they also both exist in the atmosphere of the miraculous, in a constant revelation of their wonder-working power. They both are surrounded by taboos and observances which mark off their acts from those of the profane world.

Now what distinguishes magic from religion? We have taken for our starting-point a most definite and tangible distinction: we have defined, within the domain of the sacred, magic as a practical art consisting of acts which are only means to a definite end expected to follow later on; religion as a body of self-contained acts being themselves the fulfilment of their purpose. We can now follow up this difference into its deeper layers. The practical art of magic has its limited, circumscribed technique: spell, rite, and the condition of the performer form always its trite trinity. Religion, with its complex aspects and purposes, has no such simple technique, and its unity can be seen neither in the form of its acts nor even in the uniformity of its subject matter, but rather in the function which it fulfils and in the value of its belief and ritual. Again, the belief in magic, corresponding to its plain practical nature, is extremely simple. It is always the affirmation of man's power to cause certain definite effects by a definite spell and rite. In religion, on the other hand, we have a whole supernatural world of faith: the pantheon of spirits and demons, the benevolent powers of totem, guardian spirit, tribal all-father, the vision of the future life, create a second supernatural reality for primitive man. The mythology of religion is also more varied and complex as well as more creative. It usually centers round the various tenets of belief, and it develops them into cosmogonies, tales of culture heroes, accounts of the doings of gods and demigods. In magic, important as it is, mythology is an ever-recurrent boasting about man's primeval achievements.

Magic, the specific art for specific ends, has in every one of its forms come once into the possession of man, and it had to be handed over in direct filiation from generation to generation. Hence it remains from the earliest times in the hands of specialists, and the first profession of mankind is that of a wizard or witch. Religion, on the other hand, in primitive conditions is an affair of all, in which everyone takes an active and equivalent part. Every member of the tribe has to go through initiation, and then himself initiates others. Everyone wails, mourns, digs the grave and commemorates, and in due time everyone has his turn in being mourned and commemorated. Spirits are for all, and everyone becomes a spirit. The only specialization in religion – that is, early spiritualistic mediumism – is not a profession but a personal gift. One more difference between magic and religion is the play of black and white in witchcraft, while religion in its primitive stages has but little of the contrast between good and evil, between the beneficent and malevolent powers. This is due also to the practical character of magic, which aims at direct quantitative results, while early religion, though essentially moral, has to deal with fateful, irremediable happenings and supernatural forces and beings, so that the undoing of things done by man does not enter into it. The maxim that fear first made gods in the universe is certainly not true in the light of anthropology.

In order to grasp the difference between religion and magic and to gain a clear vision of the three-cornered constellation of magic, religion, and science, let us briefly realize the cultural function of each. The function of primitive knowledge and its value have been assessed already and indeed are not difficult to grasp. By acquainting man with his surroundings, by allowing him to use the forces of nature, science, primitive knowledge, bestows on man an immense biological advantage, setting him far above all the rest of creation. The function of religion and its value we have learned to understand in the survey of savage creeds and cults given above. We have shown there that religious faith establishes, fixes, and enhances all valuable mental attitudes, such as reverence for tradition, harmony with environment, courage and confidence in the struggle with difficulties and at the prospect of death. This belief, embodied and maintained by cult and ceremonial, has an immense biological value, and so reveals to primitive man truth in the wider, pragmatic sense of the word.

What is the cultural function of magic? We have seen that all the instincts and emotions, all practical activities, lead man into impasses where gaps in his knowledge and the limitations of his early power of observation and reason betray him at a crucial moment. Human organism reacts to this in spontaneous outbursts, in which rudimentary modes of behavior and rudimentary beliefs in their efficiency are engendered. Magic fixes upon these beliefs and rudimentary rites and standardizes them into permanent traditional forms. Thus magic supplies primitive man with a number of ready-made ritual acts and beliefs, with a definite mental and practical technique which serves to bridge over the dangerous gaps in every important pursuit or critical situation. It enables man to carry out with confidence his important tasks, to maintain his poise and his mental integrity in fits of anger, in the throes of hate, of unrequited love, of despair and anxiety. The function of magic is to ritualize man's optimism, to enhance his faith in the victory of hope over fear. Magic expresses the greater value for man of confidence over doubt, of steadfastness over vacillation, of optimism over pessimism.

Looking from far and above, from our high places of safety in developed civilization, it is easy to see all the crudity and irrelevance of magic. But without its power and guidance early man could not have mastered his practical difficulties as he has done, nor could man have advanced to the higher stages of culture. Hence the universal occurrence of magic in primitive societies and its enormous sway. Hence do we find magic an invariable adjunct of all important activities. I think we must see in it the embodiment of the sublime folly of hope, which has yet been the best school of man's character.

QUESTIONS FOR REVIEW AND DISCUSSION

1. How does Malinowski define magic, and what is his opinion of it? What do you think of his assessment?

2. What example of a magical act does Malinowski provide? What are the key features that he identifies as accompanying the actions? What does he identify as the most important element in magic? What does Malinowski discern as the three features that accompany belief in magical efficiency?

3. What does Malinowski mean when he says that magic is human in its embodiment and its subject matter?

4. What does Malinowski regard as the fountainhead of magical beliefs? Do you agree?

5. For what reasons does Malinowski regard magic as pseudo-science? Do you agree?
6. How does Malinowski differentiate magic from religion? Do you agree?
7. What does Malinowski see as the cultural functions of magic, science, and religion?
8. Malinowski dramatically contrasts the world-views and culture of "primitives" or "savages" with those of "civilized" societies? Are such contrasts justified?

11 Definition of Religious Phenomena and of Religion

Émile Durkheim

Émile Durkheim (1858–1917) was born in Épinal, France and received his doctorate from the University of Paris. A pioneer in social scientific studies of society, he is often regarded as the father of the modern discipline of sociology. He held France's first professorship in sociology at the University of Bordeaux, but went on to teach primarily at the Sorbonne. His works include *The Rules of Sociological Method* (1895), where he set forth the fundamentals of approaching society as an object of study, and *Suicide* (1897), where he demonstrates his method in action. He demonstrated that suicide, mostly regarded as an interior, individualistically driven act, was related to factors such as social marginalization, discord, and alienation. Durkheim's contributions to the study of religion are mostly found in *The Elementary Forms of the Religious Life* (1912), in which he argues that religion is primarily derived from the community of adherents, who individually experience their collective sentiments symbolically projected as a transcendent power. In the selection that follows, derived from *Elementary Forms*, Durkheim establishes his definitions of religion, and the categories of sacred and profane, based on what he regards as the most fundamental form of religion.

If we are going to look for the most primitive and simple religion which we can observe, it is necessary to begin by defining what is meant by a religion; for without this, we would run the risk of giving the name to a system of ideas and practices which has nothing at all religious about it, or else of leaving to one side many religious facts, without perceiving their true nature.

That this is not an imaginary danger, and that nothing is thus sacrificed to a vain formalism of method, is well shown by the fact that owing to his not having taken this precaution, a certain scholar to whom the science of comparative religions owes a great deal, Professor Frazer, has not been able to recognize the profoundly religious character of the beliefs and rites which will be studied below, where, according to our view, the initial germ of the religious life of humanity is to be found. So this is a prejudicial question, which must be treated before all others. It is not that we dream of arriving at once at the profound characteristics which really explain religion: these can be determined only at the end of our study. But that which is necessary and possible, is to indicate a certain number of external and easily recognizable signs, which will enable us to recognize religious phenomena wherever they are met with, and which will deter us from confounding them with others. We shall proceed to this preliminary operation at once …

Leaving aside all conceptions of religion in general, let us consider the various religions in their concrete reality, and attempt to disengage that which they have in common; for religion cannot be defined except by the characteristics which are found wherever religion itself is found. In this comparison, then, we shall make use of all the religious systems which we can know, those of the present and those of the past, the most primitive and simple as well as the most recent and refined; for we have neither the right nor the logical means of excluding some and retaining others. For those who regard religion as only a natural manifestation of human activity, all religions, without any exception whatsoever, are instructive; for all, after their manner, express man, and thus can aid us in better understanding this aspect of our nature. Also, we have seen how far it is from being the best way of studying religion to consider by preference the forms which it presents among the most civilized peoples.

But to aid the mind in freeing itself from these usual conceptions which, owing to their prestige, might prevent it from seeing things as they really are, it is fitting to examine some of the most current of the definitions in which these prejudices are commonly expressed, before taking up the question on our own account.

One idea which generally passes as characteristic of all that is religious, is that of the supernatural. By this is understood all sorts of things which surpass the limits of our knowledge; the supernatural is the world of the mysterious, of the unknowable, of the un-understandable. Thus religion would be a sort of speculation upon all that which evades science or distinct thought in general. ... In all events, it is certain that this idea does not appear until late in the history of religions; it is completely foreign, not only to those peoples who are called primitive, but also to all others who have not attained a considerable degree of intellectual culture. ... These definitions set aside, let us set ourselves before the problem.

First of all, let us remark that in all these formulæ it is the nature of religion as a whole that they seek to express. They proceed as if it were a sort of indivisible entity, while, as a matter of fact, it is made up of parts; it is a more or less complex system of myths, dogmas, rites and ceremonies. Now a whole cannot be defined except in relation to its parts. It will be more methodical, then, to try to characterize the various elementary phenomena of which all religions are made up, before we attack the system produced by their union. This method is imposed still more forcibly by the fact that there are religious phenomena which belong to no determined religion. Such are those phenomena which constitute the matter of folklore. In general, they are the debris of passed religions, unorganized survivals; but there are some which have been formed spontaneously under the influence of local causes. In our European countries Christianity has forced itself to absorb and assimilate them; it has given them a Christian colouring, Nevertheless, there are many which have persisted up until a recent date, or which still exist with a relative autonomy; celebrations of May Day, the summer solstice or the carnival, beliefs relative to genii, local demons, etc., are cases in point. If the religious character of these facts is now diminishing, their religious importance is nevertheless so great that they have enabled Mannhardt and his school to revive the science of religions. A definition which did not take account of them would not cover all that is religious.

Religious phenomena are naturally arranged in two fundamental categories: beliefs and rites. The first are states of opinion, and consist in representations; the second are determined modes of action. Between these two classes of facts there is all the difference which separates thought from action.

The rites can be defined and distinguished from other human practices, moral practices, for example, only by the special nature of their object. A moral rule prescribes certain manners of acting to us, just as a rite does, but which are addressed to a different class of objects. So it is the object of the rite which must be characterized, if we are to characterize the rite itself. Now it is in the beliefs that the special nature of this object is expressed. It is possible to define the rite only after we have defined the belief.

All known religious beliefs, whether simple or complex, present one common characteristic: they presuppose a classification of all the things, real and ideal, of which men think, into two classes or opposed groups, generally designated by two distinct terms which are translated well enough by the words *profane* and *sacred* (*profane, sacré*). This division of the world into two domains, the one containing all that is sacred, the other all that is profane, is the distinctive trait of religious thought; the beliefs, myths, dogmas and legends are either representations or systems of representations which express the nature of sacred things, the virtues and powers which are attributed to them, or their relations with each other and with profane things. But by sacred things one must not understand simply those personal beings which are called gods or spirits; a rock, a tree, a spring, a pebble, a piece of wood, a house, in a word, anything can be sacred. A rite can have this character; in fact, the rite does not exist which does not have it to a certain degree. There are words, expressions and formulae which can be pronounced only by the mouths of consecrated persons; there are gestures and movements which everybody cannot perform. If the Vedic sacrifice has had such an efficacy that, according to mythology, it was the creator of the gods, and not merely a means of winning their favour, it is because it possessed a virtue comparable to that of the most sacred beings. The circle of sacred objects cannot be determined, then, once for all. Its extent varies infinitely, according to the different religions. That is how Buddhism is a religion: in default of gods, it admits the existence of sacred things, namely, the four noble truths and the practices derived from them.

Up to the present we have confined ourselves to enumerating a certain number of sacred things as examples: we must now show by what general characteristics they are to be distinguished from profane things.

One might be tempted, first of all, to define them by the place they are generally assigned in the hierarchy of things. They are naturally considered superior in dignity and power to profane things, and particularly to man, when he is only a man and has nothing sacred about him. One thinks of himself as occupying an inferior and dependent position in relation to them; and surely this conception is not without some truth. Only there is nothing in it which is really characteristic of the sacred. It is not enough that one thing be subordinated to another for the second to be sacred in regard to the first. Slaves are inferior to their masters, subjects to their king, soldiers to their leaders, the miser to his gold, the man ambitious for power to the hands which keep it from him; but if it is sometimes said of a man that he makes a religion of those beings or things whose eminent value and superiority to himself he thus recognizes, it is clear that in any case the word is taken in a metaphorical sense, and that there is nothing in these relations which is really religious.

On the other hand, it must not be lost to view that there are sacred things of every degree, and that there are some in relation to which a man feels himself relatively at his ease. An amulet has a sacred character, yet the respect which it inspires is nothing exceptional. Even before his gods, a man is not always in such a marked state of inferiority; for it very frequently happens that he exercises a veritable physical constraint upon them to obtain what he desires. He beats the fetish with which he is not contented, but only to reconcile himself with it again, if in the end it shows itself more docile to the wishes of its adorer. To have rain, he throws stones into the spring or sacred lake where the god of rain is thought to reside; he believes that by this means he forces him to come out and show himself. Moreover, if it is true that man depends upon his gods, this dependence is reciprocal. The gods also have need of man; without offerings and sacrifices they would die. We shall even have occasion to show that this dependence of the gods upon their worshippers is maintained even in the most idealistic religions.

But if a purely hierarchic distinction is a criterium at once too general and too imprecise, there is nothing left with which to characterize the sacred in its relation to the profane except their heterogeneity. However, this heterogeneity is sufficient to characterize this classification of things and to distinguish it from all others, because it is very particular: it is absolute. In all the history of human thought there exists no other example of two categories of things so profoundly differentiated or so radically opposed to one another. The traditional opposition of good and bad is nothing beside this; for the good and the bad are only two opposed species of the same class, namely morals, just as sickness and health are two different aspects of the same order of facts, life, while the sacred and the profane have always and everywhere been conceived by the human mind as two distinct classes, as two worlds between which there is nothing in common. The forces which play in one are not simply those which are met with in the other, but a little stronger; they are of a different sort. In different religions, this opposition has been conceived in different ways. Here, to separate these two sorts of things, it has seemed sufficient to localize them in different parts of the physical universe; there, the first have been put into an ideal and transcendental world, while the material world is left in full possession of the others. But howsoever much the forms of the contrast may vary, the fact of the contrast is universal.

This is not equivalent to saying that a being can never pass from one of these worlds into the other: but the manner in which this passage is effected when it does take place, puts into relief the essential duality of the two kingdoms. In fact, it implies a veritable metamorphosis. This is notably demonstrated by the initiation rites, such as they are practiced by a multitude of peoples. This initiation is a long series of ceremonies with the object of introducing the young man into the religious life: for the first time, he leaves the purely profane world where he passed his first infancy, and enters into the world of sacred things. Now this change of state is thought of, not as a simple and regular development of pre-existent germs, but as a transformation *totius substantiae*—of the whole being. It is said that at this moment the young man dies, that the person that he was ceases to exist, and that another is instantly substituted for it. He is re-born under a new form. Appropriate ceremonies are felt to bring about this death and re-birth, which are not understood in a merely symbolic sense, but are taken literally. Does this not prove that between the profane being which he was and the religious being which he becomes, there is a break of continuity?

This heterogeneity is even so complete that it frequently degenerates into a veritable antagonism. The two worlds are not only conceived of as separate, but as even hostile and jealous rivals of each other. Since men cannot fully belong to one except on condition of leaving the other completely, they are exhorted to withdraw themselves completely from the profane world, in order to lead an exclusively religious life. Hence comes the monasticism which is artificially organized outside of and apart from the natural environment in which the ordinary man leads the life of this world, in a different one, closed to the first, and nearly its contrary. Hence comes the mystic asceticism whose object is to root out from man all the attachment for the profane world that remains in him, From that come all the forms of religious suicide, the logical working-out of this asceticism; for the only manner of fully escaping the profane life is, after all, to forsake all life.

The opposition of these two classes manifests itself outwardly with a visible sign by which we can easily recognize this very special classification, wherever it exists. Since the idea of the sacred is always and everywhere separated from the idea of the profane in the thought of men, and since we picture a sort of logical chasm between the two, the mind irresistibly refuses to allow the two corresponding things to be confounded, or even to be merely put in contact with each other; for such a promiscuity, or even too direct a contiguity, would contradict too violently the dissociation of these ideas in the mind. The sacred thing is par excellence that which the profane should not touch, and cannot touch with impunity. To be sure, this interdiction cannot go so far as to make all communication between the two worlds impossible; for if the profane could in no way enter into relations with the sacred, this latter could be good for nothing. …

Thus we arrive at the first criterium of religious beliefs. Undoubtedly there are secondary species within these two fundamental classes which, in their turn, are more or less incomparable with each other. But the real characteristic of religious phenomena is that they always suppose a bipartite division of the whole universe, known and knowable, into two classes which embrace all that exists, but which radically exclude each other. Sacred things are those which the interdictions protect and isolate; profane things, those to which these interdictions are applied and which must remain at a distance from the first. Religious beliefs are the representations which express the nature of sacred things and the relations which they sustain, either with each other or with profane things. Finally, rites are the rules of conduct which prescribe how a man should comport himself in the presence of these sacred objects.

When a certain number of sacred things sustain relations of coordination or subordination with each other in such a way as to form a system having a certain unity, but which is not comprised within any other system of the same sort, the totality of these beliefs and their corresponding rites constitutes a religion. From this definition it is seen that a religion is not necessarily contained within one sole and single idea, and does not proceed from one unique principle which, though varying according to the circumstances under which it is applied, is nevertheless at bottom always the same: it is rather a whole made up of distinct and relatively individualized parts. Each homogeneous group of sacred things, or even each sacred thing of some importance, constitutes a centre of organization about which gravitate a group of beliefs and rites, or a particular cult; there is no religion, howsoever unified it may be, which does not recognize a plurality of sacred things. Even Christianity, at least in its Catholic form, admits, in addition to the divine personality which, incidentally, is triple as well as one, the Virgin, angels, saints, souls of the dead, etc. Thus a religion cannot be reduced to one single cult generally, but rather consists in a system of cults, each endowed with a certain autonomy. Also, this autonomy is variable. Sometimes they are arranged in a hierarchy, and subordinated to some predominating cult, into which they are finally absorbed; but sometimes, also, they are merely rearranged and united. The religion which we are going to study will furnish us with an example of just this latter sort of organization.

At the same time we find the explanation of how there can be groups of religious phenomena which do not belong to any special religion; it is because they have not been, or are no longer, a part of any religious system. If, for some special reason, one of the cults of which we just spoke happens to be maintained while the group of which it was a part disappears, it survives only in a disintegrated condition. That is what has happened to many agrarian cults which have survived themselves as folklore. In certain cases, it is not even a cult, but a simple ceremony or particular rite which persists in this way.

Although this definition is only preliminary, it permits us to see in what terms the problem which necessarily dominates the science of religions should be stated. When we believed that sacred beings could be distinguished from others merely by the greater intensity of the powers attributed to them, the question of how men came to imagine them was sufficiently simple: it was enough to demand which forces had, because of their exceptional energy, been able to strike the human imagination forcefully enough to inspire religious sentiments. But if, as we have sought to establish, sacred things differ in nature from profane things, if they have a wholly different essence, then the problem is more complex. For we must first of all ask what has been able to lead men to see in the world two heterogeneous and incompatible worlds, though nothing in sensible experience seems able to suggest the idea of so radical a duality to them.

However, this definition is not yet complete, for it is equally applicable to two sorts of facts which, while being related to each other, must be distinguished nevertheless: these are magic and religion. Magic, too, is made up of beliefs and rites. Like religion, it has its myths and its dogmas; only they are more elementary, undoubtedly because, seeking technical and utilitarian ends, it does not waste its time in pure speculation. It has its ceremonies, sacrifices, lustrations, prayers, chants and dances as well. The beings which the magician invokes and the forces which he throws in play are not merely of the same nature as the forces and beings to which religion addresses itself; very frequently, they are identically the same. ... Whatever relations there may be between these two sorts of institutions, it is difficult to imagine their not being opposed somewhere; and it is still more necessary for us to find where they are differentiated, as we plan to limit our researches to religion, and to stop at the point where magic commences.

Here is how a line of demarcation can be traced between these two domains.

The really religious beliefs are always common to a determined group, which makes profession of adhering to them and of practising the rites connected with them. They are not merely received individually by all the members of this group; they are something belonging to the group, and they make its unity. The individuals which compose it feel themselves united to each other by the simple fact that they have a common faith. A society whose members are united by the fact that they think in the same way in regard to the sacred world and its relations with the profane world, and by the fact that they translate these common ideas into common practices, is what is called a Church. In all history, we do not find a single religion without a Church. Sometimes the Church is strictly national, sometimes it passes the frontiers; sometimes it embraces an entire people (Rome, Athens, the Hebrews), sometimes it embraces only a part of them (the Christian societies since the advent of Protestantism); sometimes it is directed by a corps of priests, sometimes it is almost completely devoid of any official directing body. But wherever we observe the religious life, we find that it has a definite group as its foundation. Even the so-called private cults, such as the domestic cult or the cult of a corporation, satisfy this condition; for they are always celebrated by a group, the family or the corporation. Moreover, even these particular religions are ordinarily only special forms of a more general religion which embraces all; these restricted Churches are in reality only chapels of a vaster Church which, by reason of this very extent, merits this name still more.

It is quite another matter with magic. To be sure, the belief in magic is always more or less general; it is very frequently diffused in large masses of the population, and there are even peoples where it has as many adherents as the real religion. But it does not result in binding together those who adhere to it, nor in uniting them into a group leading a common life. There is no Church of magic. Between the magician and the individuals who consult him, as between these individuals themselves, there are no lasting bonds which make them members of the same moral community, comparable to that formed by the believers in the same god or the observers of the same cult. The magician has a clientele and not a Church, and it is very possible that his clients have no other relations between each other, or even do not know each other; even the relations which they have with him are generally accidental and transient; they are just like those of a sick man with his physician. The official and public character with which he is sometimes invested changes nothing in this situation; the fact that he works openly does not unite him more regularly or more durably to those who have recourse to his services …

Religion, on the other hand, is inseparable from the idea of a Church. From this point of view, there is an essential difference between magic and religion. But what is especially important is that when these societies of magic are formed, they do not include all the adherents to magic, but only the magicians; the laymen, if they may be so called, that is to say, those for whose profit the rites are celebrated, in fine those who represent the worshippers in the regular cults, are excluded. Now the magician is for magic what the priest is for religion, but a college of priests is not a Church, any more than a religious congregation which should devote itself to some particular saint in the shadow of a cloister, would be a particular cult. A Church is not a fraternity of priests; it is a moral community formed by all the believers in a single faith, laymen as well as priests. But magic lacks any such community …

There still remain those contemporary aspirations towards a religion which would consist entirely in internal and subjective states, and which would be constructed freely by each of us. But howsoever real these aspirations may be, they cannot affect our definition, for this is to be applied only to facts already realized, and not to uncertain possibilities. One can define religions such as they are, or such as they have been, but not such as they more or less vaguely tend to become. It is possible that this religious individualism is destined to be realized in facts; but before we can say just how far this may be the case, we must first know what religion is, of what elements it is made up, from what causes it results, and what function it fulfils—all questions whose solution cannot be foreseen before the threshold of our study has been passed. It is only at the close of this study that we can attempt to anticipate the future.

Thus we arrive at the following definition: *A religion is a unified system of beliefs and practices relative to sacred things, that is to say, things set apart and forbidden—beliefs and practices which unite into one single moral community called a Church, all those who adhere to them.* The second element which thus finds a place in our definition is no less essential than the first; for by showing that the idea of religion is inseparable from that of the Church, it makes it clear that religion should be an eminently collective thing.

QUESTIONS FOR REVIEW AND DISCUSSION

1. What two fundamental categories does Durkheim discern in all religious phenomena?
2. According to Durkheim, what are the two major opposing categories constructed by religious beliefs?
3. What does Durkheim mean when he speaks of the heterogeneity of the categories of sacred and profane?
4. What does Durkheim observe as characteristics that distinguish magic from religion?
5. What does Durkheim mean by a "Church"?
6. What is a key feature in Durkheim's definition of religion that makes it a fundamentally social phenomenon?

12 Asceticism and the Spirit of Capitalism

Max Weber

Max Weber (1864–1920) was born in Erfurt, Thuringia, Germany, and received his doctorate in law from the University of Berlin, where he later taught. His initial interest in legal history and its relationship to society and economics blossomed into his most famous work, *The Protestant Ethic and the Spirit of Capitalism* (1905), from which the selection that follows (chapter 5) is taken. This led to other studies in the sociology of religion, which included examinations of ancient Judaism and the religions of China and India. Such works, together with his studies of political sociology, including his examinations of bureaucracy and social strata, make him one of the most influential social theorists of the twentieth century. In the selection below, Weber looks at the relationship between the ascetic values of Protestantism and their relationship to the capitalistic spirit in societies where Protestantism flourishes.

In order to understand the connection between the fundamental religious ideas of ascetic Protestantism and its maxims for everyday economic conduct, it is necessary to examine with especial care such writings as have evidently been derived from ministerial practice. For in a time in which the beyond meant everything, when the social position of the Christian depended upon his admission to the communion, the clergyman, through his ministry, Church discipline, and preaching, exercised an influence (as a glance at collections of *consilia, casus conscientia,* etc., shows) which we modern men are entirely unable to picture. In such a time the religious forces which express themselves through such channels are the decisive influences in the formation of national character.

For the purposes of this chapter, though by no means for all purposes, we can treat ascetic Protestantism as a single whole. But since that side of English Puritanism which was derived from Calvinism gives the most consistent religious basis for the idea of the calling, we shall, following our previous method, place one of its representatives at the centre of the discussion. Richard Baxter stands out above many other writers on Puritan ethics, both because of his eminently practical and realistic attitude, and, at the same time, because of the universal recognition accorded to his works, which have gone through many new editions and translations. He was a Presbyterian and an apologist of the Westminster Synod, but at the same time, like so many of the best spirits of his time, gradually grew away from the dogmas of pure Calvinism. At heart he opposed Cromwell's usurpation as he would any revolution. He was unfavourable to the sects and the fanatical enthusiasm of the saints, but was very broad-minded about external peculiarities and objective towards his opponents. He sought his field of labour most especially in the practical promotion of the moral life through the Church. In the pursuit of this end, as one of the most successful ministers known to history, he placed his services at the disposal of the Parliamentary Government, of Cromwell, and of the Restoration until he retired from office under the last, before St. Bartholomew's day. His *Christian Directory* is the most complete compendium of Puritan ethics, and is adjusted to the practical experiences of his own ministerial activity. In comparison we shall see Spener's *Theologische Bedenken*, as representative of German Pietism, Barclay's *Apology for the Quakers* and some other representatives of ascetic ethics, which, however, in the interest of space, will be limited as far as possible.

Now, in glancing at Baxter's *Saints' Everlasting Rest*, or his *Christian Directory*, or similar works of others, one is struck at first glance by the emphasis placed, in the discussion of wealth and its acquisition, on the ebionitic elements of the New Testament. Wealth as such is a great danger; its temptations never end and its pursuit is not only senseless as compared with the dominating importance of the Kingdom of God, but it is morally suspect. Here asceticism seems to have turned much more sharply against the acquisition of earthly goods than it did in Calvin, who saw no hindrance to the effectiveness of the clergy in their wealth, but rather a thoroughly desirable enhancement of their prestige. Hence he permitted them to employ their means profitably. Examples of the condemnation of the pursuit of money and goods may be gathered without end from Puritan writings, and may be contrasted with the late mediaeval ethical literature, which was much more open-minded on this point. Moreover, these doubts were meant with perfect seriousness; only it is necessary to examine them somewhat more closely in order to understand their true ethical significance and implications. The real, moral objection is to relaxation in the security of possession, the enjoyment of wealth with the consequence of idleness and the temptations of the flesh, above all of distraction from the pursuit of a righteous life. In fact, it is only because possession involves this danger of relaxation that it is objectionable at all. For the saints' everlasting rest is in the next world; on earth man must, to be certain of his state of grace, "do the works of Him who sent him, as long as it is yet day." Not leisure and enjoyment, but only activity serves to increase the glory of God, according to the definite manifestations of His will.

Waste of time is thus the first and in principle the deadliest of sins. The span of human life is infinitely short and precious to make sure of one's own election. Loss of time through sociability, idle talk, luxury, even more sleep than is necessary for health, six to at most eight hours, is worthy of absolute moral condemnation. It does not yet hold, with Franklin, that time is money, but the proposition is true in a certain spiritual sense. It is infinitely valuable because every hour lost is lost to labour for the glory of God. Thus inactive contemplation is also valueless, or even directly reprehensible if it is at the expense of one's daily work. For it is less pleasing to God than the active performance of His will in a calling. Besides, Sunday is provided for that, and, according to Baxter, it is always those who are not diligent in their callings who have no time for God when the occasion demands it.

Accordingly, Baxter's principal work is dominated by the continually repeated, often almost passionate preaching of hard, continuous bodily or mental labour. It is due to a combination of two different motives. Labour is, on the one hand, an approved ascetic technique, as it always has been in the Western Church, in sharp contrast not only to the Orient but to almost all monastic rules the world over. It is in particular the specific defence against all those temptations which Puritanism united under the name of the unclean life, whose role for it was by no means small. The sexual asceticism of Puritanism differs only in degree, not in fundamental principle, from that of monasticism; and on account of the Puritan conception of marriage, its practical influence is more far-reaching than that of the latter. For sexual intercourse is permitted, even within marriage, only as the means willed by God for the increase of His glory according to the commandment, "Be fruitful and multiply." Along with a moderate vegetable diet and cold baths, the same prescription is given for all sexual temptations as is used against religious doubts and a sense of moral unworthiness: "Work hard in your calling." But the most important thing was that even beyond that labour came to be considered in itself the end of life, ordained as such by God. St. Paul's "He who will not work shall not eat" holds unconditionally for everyone. Unwillingness to work is symptomatic of the lack of grace.

Here the difference from the mediaeval viewpoint becomes quite evident. Thomas Aquinas also gave an interpretation of that statement of St. Paul. But for him labour is only necessary *naturali ratione* for the maintenance of individual and community. Where this end is achieved, the precept ceases to have any meaning. Moreover, it holds only for the race, not for every individual. It does not apply to anyone who can live without labour on his possessions, and of course contemplation, as a spiritual form of action in the Kingdom of God, takes precedence over the commandment in its literal sense. Moreover, for the popular theology of the time, the highest form of monastic productivity lay in the increase of the *Thesaurus ecclesie* through prayer and chant.

Not only do these exceptions to the duty to labour naturally no longer hold for Baxter, but he holds most emphatically that wealth does not exempt anyone from the unconditional command. Even the wealthy shall not eat without working, for even though they do not need to labour to support their own needs, there is God's commandment which they, like the poor, must obey. For everyone without exception God's Providence has prepared a calling, which he should profess and in which he should labour. And this calling is not, as it was for the Lutheran, a fate to which he must submit and which he must make the best of, but God's commandment to the individual to work for the divine glory. This seemingly subtle difference had far-reaching psychological consequences, and became connected with a further development of the providential interpretation of the economic order which had begun in Scholasticism.

The phenomenon of the division of labour and occupations in society had, among others, been interpreted by Thomas Aquinas, to whom we may most conveniently refer, as a direct consequence of the divine scheme of things. But the places assigned to each man in this cosmos follow *ex causis naturalibus* and are fortuitous (contingent in the Scholastic terminology). The differentiation of men into the classes and occupations established through historical development became for Luther, as we have seen, a direct result of the divine will. The perseverance of the individual in the place and within the limits which God had assigned to him was a religious duty. This was the more certainly the consequence since the relations of Lutheranism to the world were in general uncertain from the beginning and remained so. Ethical principles for the reform of the world could not be found in Luther's realm of ideas; in fact it never quite freed itself from Pauline indifference. Hence the world had to be accepted as it was, and this alone could be made a religious duty. But in the Puritan view, the providential character of the play of private economic interests takes on a somewhat different emphasis. True to the Puritan tendency to pragmatic interpretations, the providential purpose of the division of labour is to be known by its fruits. On this point Baxter expresses himself in terms which more than once directly recall Adam Smith's well-known apotheosis of the division of labour. The specialization of occupations leads, since it makes the development of skill possible, to a quantitative and qualitative improvement in production, and thus serves the common good, which is identical with the good of the greatest possible number. So far, the motivation is purely utilitarian, and is closely related to the customary viewpoint of much of the secular literature of the time.

But the characteristic Puritan element appears when Baxter sets at the head of his discussion the statement that "outside of a well-marked calling the accomplishments of a man are only casual and irregular, and he spends more time in idleness than at work", and when he concludes it as follows: "and he [the specialized worker] will carry out his work in order while another remains in constant confusion, and his business knows neither time nor place ... therefore is a certain calling the best for everyone." Irregular work, which the ordinary labourer is often forced to accept, is often unavoidable, but always an unwelcome state of transition. A man without a calling thus lacks the systematic, methodical character which is, as we have seen, demanded by worldly asceticism.

The Quaker ethic also holds that a man's life in his calling is an exercise in ascetic virtue, a proof of his state of grace through his conscientiousness, which is expressed in the care and method with which he pursues his calling. What God demands is not labour in itself, but rational labour in a calling. In the Puritan concept of the calling the emphasis is always placed on this methodical character of worldly asceticism, not, as with Luther, on the acceptance of the lot which God has irretrievably assigned to man.

Hence the question whether anyone may combine several callings is answered in the affirmative, if it is useful for the common good or one's own, and not injurious to anyone, and if it does not lead to unfaithfulness in one of the callings. Even a change of calling is by no means regarded as objectionable, if it is not thoughtless and is made for the purpose of pursuing a calling more pleasing to God, which means, on general principles, one more useful. It is true that the usefulness of a calling, and thus its favour in the sight of God, is measured primarily in moral terms, and thus in terms of the importance of the goods produced in it for the community. But a further, and, above all, in practice the most important, criterion is found in private profitableness. For if that God, whose hand the Puritan sees in all the occurrences of life, shows one of His elect a chance of profit, he must do it with a purpose. Hence the faithful Christian must follow the call by taking advantage of the opportunity. "If God show you a way in which you may lawfully get more than in another way (without wrong to your soul or to any other), if you refuse this, and choose the less gainful way, you cross one of the ends of your calling, and you refuse to be God's steward, and to accept His gifts and use them for Him, when He requireth it: you may labour to be rich for God, though not for the flesh and sin."

Wealth is thus bad ethically only in so far as it is a temptation to idleness and sinful enjoyment of life, and its acquisition is bad only when it is with the purpose of later living merrily and without care. But as a performance of duty in a calling it is not only morally permissible, but actually enjoined. The parable of the servant who was rejected because he did not increase the talent which was entrusted to him seemed to say so directly. To wish to be poor was, it was often argued, the same as wishing to be unhealthy; it is objectionable as a glorification of works and derogatory to the glory of God. Especially begging, on the part of one able to work, is not only the sin of slothfulness, but a violation of the duty of brotherly love according to the Apostle's own word. The emphasis on the ascetic importance of a fixed calling provided an ethical justification of the modern specialized division of labour. In a similar way the providential interpretation of profit-making justified the activities of the business man. The superior indulgence of the seigneur and the parvenu ostentation of the *nouveau riche* are equally detestable to asceticism.

But, on the other hand, it has the highest ethical appreciation of the sober, middle-class, self-made man. "God blesseth His trade" is a stock remark about those good men who had successfully followed the divine hints. The whole power of the God of the Old Testament, who rewards His people for their obedience in this life, necessarily exercised a similar influence on the Puritan who, following Baxter's advice, compared his own state of grace with that of the heroes of the Bible, and in the process interpreted the statements of the Scriptures as the articles of a book of statutes.

Of course, the words of the Old Testament were not entirely without ambiguity. We have seen that Luther first used the concept of the calling in the secular sense in translating a passage from Jesus Sirach. But the book of Jesus Sirach belongs, with the whole atmosphere expressed in it, to those parts of the broadened Old Testament with distinctly traditionalistic tendency, in spite of Hellenistic influences. It is characteristic that down to the present day this book seems to enjoy a special favour among Lutheran German peasants just as the Lutheran influence in large sections of German Pietism has been expressed by a preference for Jesus Sirach.

The Puritans repudiated the Apocrypha as not inspired, consistently with their sharp distinction between things divine and things of the flesh. But among the canonical books that of Job had all the more influence. On the one hand it contained a grand conception of the absolute sovereign majesty of God, beyond all human comprehension, which was closely related to that of Calvinism. With that, on the other hand, it combined the certainty which, though incidental for Calvin, came to be of great importance for Puritanism, that God would bless His own in this life – in the book of Job only – and also in the material sense. The Oriental quietism, which appears in several of the finest verses of the Psalms and in the Proverbs, was interpreted away, just as Baxter did with the traditionalistic tinge of the passage in the 1st Epistle to the Corinthians, so important for the idea of the calling.

But all the more emphasis was placed on those parts of the Old Testament which praise formal legality as a sign of conduct pleasing to God. They held the theory that the Mosaic Law had only lost its validity through Christ in so far as it contained ceremonial or purely historical precepts applying only to the Jewish people, but that otherwise it had always been valid as an expression of the natural law, and must hence be retained. This made it possible, on the one hand, to eliminate elements which could not be reconciled with modern life. But still, through its numerous related features, Old Testament morality was able to give a powerful impetus to that spirit of self-righteous and sober legality which was so characteristic of the worldly asceticism of this form of Protestantism.

Thus when authors, as was the case with several contemporaries as well as later writers, characterize the basic ethical tendency of Puritanism, especially in England, as English Hebrews they are, correctly understood, not wrong. It is necessary, however, not to think of Palestinian Judaism at the time of the writing of the Scriptures, but of Judaism as it became under the influence of many centuries of formalistic, legalistic, and Talmudic education. Even then one must be very careful in drawing parallels. The general tendency of the older Judaism toward a naive acceptance of life as such was far removed from the special characteristics of Puritanism. It was, however, just as far – and this ought not to be overlooked – from the economic ethics of mediaeval and modern Judaism, in the traits which determined the positions of both in the development of the capitalistic ethos. The Jews stood on the side of the politically and speculatively oriented adventurous capitalism; their ethos was, in a word, that of pariah-capitalism. But Puritanism carried the ethos of the rational organization of capital and labour. It took over from the Jewish ethic only what was adapted to this purpose.

To analyse the effects on the character of peoples of the penetration of life with Old Testament norms – a tempting task which, however, has not yet satisfactorily been done even for Judaism – would be impossible within the limits of this sketch. In addition to the relationships already pointed out, it is important for the general inner attitude of the Puritans, above all, that the belief that they were God's chosen people saw in them a great renaissance. Even the kindly Baxter thanked God that he was born in England, and thus in the true Church, and nowhere else. This thankfulness for one's own perfection by the grace of God penetrated the attitude toward life of the Puritan middle class, and played its part in developing that formalistic, hard, correct character which was peculiar to the men of that heroic age of capitalism.

Let us now try to clarify the points in which the Puritan idea of the calling and the pre-mium it placed upon ascetic conduct was bound directly to influence the development of a capitalistic way of life. As we have seen, this asceticism turned with all its force against one thing: the spontaneous enjoyment of life and all it had to offer. This is perhaps most char-acteristically brought out in the struggle over the Book of Sports which James I and Charles I made into law expressly as a means of counteracting Puritanism, and which the latter ordered to be read from all the pulpits. The fanatical opposition of the Puritans to the ordinances of the King, permitting certain popular amusements on Sunday outside of Church hours by law, was not only explained by the disturbance of the Sabbath rest, but also by resentment against the intentional diversion from the ordered life of the saint, which it caused. And, on his side, the King's threats of severe punishment for every attack on the legality of those sports were motivated by his purpose of breaking the anti-authoritarian ascetic tendency of Puritanism, which was so dangerous to the State. The feudal and monarchical forces protected the pleasure seekers against the rising middle-class morality and the anti-authoritarian ascetic conventicles, just as today capitalistic society tends to protect those willing to work against the class morality of the proletariat and the anti-authoritarian trade union.

As against this the Puritans upheld their decisive characteristic, the principle of ascetic conduct. For otherwise the Puritan aversion to sport, even for the Quakers, was by no means simply one of principle. Sport was accepted if it served a rational purpose, that of recreation necessary for physical efficiency. But as a means for the spontaneous expression of undisciplined impulses, it was under suspicion; and in so far as it became purely a means of enjoyment, or awakened pride, raw instincts or the irrational gambling instinct, it was of course strictly condemned. Impulsive enjoyment of life, which leads away both from work in a calling and from religion, was as such the enemy of rational asceticism, whether in the form of seigneurial sports, or the enjoyment of the dance-hall or the public-house of the common man.

Its attitude was thus suspicious and often hostile to the aspects of culture without any immediate religious value. It is not, however, true that the ideals of Puritanism implied a solemn, narrow-minded contempt of culture. Quite the contrary is the case at least for sci-ence, with the exception of the hatred of Scholasticism. Moreover, the great men of the Puritan movement were thoroughly steeped in the culture of the Renaissance. The sermons of the Presbyterian divines abound with classical allusions and even the Radicals, although they objected to it, were not ashamed to display that kind of learning in theological polemics. Perhaps no country was ever so full of graduates as New England in the first generation of its existence. The satire of their opponents, such as, for instance, Butler's *Hudibras*, also attacks primarily the pedantry and highly trained dialectics of the Puritans. This is partially due to the religious valuation of knowledge which followed from their attitude to the Catholic *fides implicita*.

But the situation is quite different when one looks at non-scientific literature and especially the fine arts. Here asceticism descended like a frost on the life of "Merrie old England." And not only worldly merriment felt its effect. The Puritan's ferocious hatred of everything which smacked of superstition, of all survivals of magical or sacramental salvation, applied to the Christmas festivities and the May Pole and all spontaneous religious art. That there was room in Holland for a great, often uncouthly realistic art proves only how far from completely the authoritarian moral discipline of that country was able to counteract the influence of the court and the regents (a class of rentiers), and also the joy in life of the parvenu bourgeoisie, after the short supremacy of the Calvinistic theocracy had been transformed into a moderate national Church, and with it Calvinism had perceptibly lost in its power of ascetic influence.

The theatre was obnoxious to the Puritans, and with the strict exclusion of the erotic and of nudity from the realm of toleration, a radical view of either literature or art could not exist. The conceptions of idle talk, of superfluities, and of vain ostentation, all designations of an irrational attitude without objective purpose, thus not ascetic, and especially not serving the glory of God, but of man, were always at hand to serve in deciding in favour of sober utility as against any artistic tendencies. This was especially true in the case of decoration of the person, for instance clothing. That powerful tendency toward uniformity of life, which today so immensely aids the capitalistic interest in the standardization of production, had its ideal foundations in the repudiation of all idolatry of the flesh.

Of course we must not forget that Puritanism included a world of contradictions, and that the instinctive sense of eternal greatness in art was certainly stronger among its leaders than in the atmosphere of the Cavaliers. Moreover, a unique genius like Rembrandt, however little his conduct may have been acceptable to God in the eyes of the Puritans, was very strongly influenced in the character of his work by his religious environment. But that does not alter the picture as a whole. In so far as the development of the Puritan tradition could, and in part did, lead to a powerful spiritualization of personality, it was a decided benefit to literature. But for the most part that benefit only accrued to later generations.

Although we cannot here enter upon a discussion of the influence of Puritanism in all these directions, we should call attention to the fact that the toleration of pleasure in cultural goods, which contributed to purely aesthetic or athletic enjoyment, certainly always ran up against one characteristic limitation: they must not cost anything. Man is only a trustee of the goods which have come to him through God's grace. He must, like the servant in the parable, give an account of every penny entrusted to him, and it is at least hazardous to spend any of it for a purpose which does not serve the glory of God but only one's own enjoyment. What person, who keeps his eyes open, has not met representatives of this viewpoint even in the present? The idea of a man's duty to his possessions, to which he subordinates himself as an obedient steward, or even as an acquisitive machine, bears with chilling weight on his life. The greater the possessions the heavier, if the ascetic attitude toward life stands the test, the feeling of responsibility for them, for holding them undiminished for the glory of God and increasing them by restless effort. The origin of this type of life also extends in certain roots, like so many aspects of the spirit of capitalism, back into the Middle Ages. But it was in the ethic of ascetic Protestantism that it first found a consistent ethical foundation. Its significance for the development of capitalism is obvious. This worldly Protestant Asceticism, as we may recapitulate up to this point, acted powerfully against the spontaneous enjoyment of possessions; it restricted consumption, especially of luxuries. On the other hand, it had the psychological effect of freeing the acquisition of goods from the inhibitions of traditionalistic ethics. It broke the bonds of the impulse of acquisition in that it not only legalized it, but (in the sense discussed) looked upon it as directly willed by God. The campaign against the temptations of the flesh, and the dependence on external things, was, as besides the Puritans the great Quaker apologist Barclay expressly says, not a struggle against the rational acquisition, but against the irrational use of wealth.

But this irrational use was exemplified in the outward forms of luxury which their code condemned as idolatry of the flesh, however natural they had appeared to the feudal mind. On the other hand, they approved the rational and utilitarian uses of wealth which were willed by God for the needs of the individual and the community. They did not wish to impose mortification on the man of wealth, but the use of his means for necessary and practical things. The idea of comfort characteristically limits the extent of ethically permissible expenditures. It is naturally no accident that the development of a manner of living consistent with that idea may be observed earliest and most clearly among the most consistent representatives of this whole attitude toward life. Over against the glitter and ostentation of feudal magnificence which, resting on an unsound economic basis, prefers a sordid elegance to a sober simplicity, they set the clean and solid comfort of the middle-class home as an ideal.

On the side of the production of private wealth, asceticism condemned both dishonesty and impulsive avarice. What was condemned as covetousness, Mammonism, etc., was the pursuit of riches for their own sake. For wealth in itself was a temptation. But here asceticism was the power "which ever seeks the good but ever creates evil"; what was evil in its sense was possession and its temptations. For, in conformity with the Old Testament and in analogy to the ethical valuation of good works, asceticism looked upon the pursuit of wealth as an end in itself as highly reprehensible; but the attainment of it as a fruit of labour in a calling was a sign of God's blessing. And even more important: the religious valuation of restless, continuous, systematic work in a worldly calling, as the highest means to asceticism, and at the same time the surest and most evident proof of rebirth and genuine faith, must have been the most powerful conceivable lever for the expansion of that attitude toward life which we have here called the spirit of capitalism.

When the limitation of consumption is combined with this release of acquisitive activity, the inevitable practical result is obvious: accumulation of capital through ascetic compulsion to save. The restraints which were imposed upon the consumption of wealth naturally served to increase it by making possible the productive investment of capital. How strong this influence was is not, unfortunately, susceptible to exact statistical demonstration. In New England the connection is so evident that it did not escape the eye of so discerning a historian as Doyle. But also in Holland, which was really only dominated by strict Calvinism for seven years, the greater simplicity of life in the more seriously religious circles, in combination with great wealth, led to an excessive propensity to accumulation.

That, furthermore, the tendency which has existed everywhere and at all times, being quite strong in Germany today, for middle-class fortunes to be absorbed into the nobility, was necessarily checked by the Puritan antipathy to the feudal way of life, is evident. English Mercantilist writers of the seventeenth century attributed the superiority of Dutch capital to English to the circumstance that newly acquired wealth there did not regularly seek investment in land. Also, since it is not simply a question of the purchase of land, it did not there seek to transfer itself to feudal habits of life, and thereby to remove itself from the possibility of capitalistic investment. The high esteem for agriculture as a peculiarly important branch of activity, also especially consistent with piety, which the Puritans shared, applied (for instance in Baxter) not to the landlord, but to the yeoman and farmer, in the eighteenth century not to the squire, but the rational cultivator. Through the whole of English society in the time since the seventeenth century goes the conflict between the squirearchy, the representatives of "merrie old England," and the Puritan circles of widely varying social influence. Both elements, that of an unspoiled naive joy of life, and of a strictly regulated, reserved self-control, and conventional ethical conduct are even today combined to form the English national character. Similarly, the early history of the North American colonies is dominated by the sharp contrast of the adventurers, who wanted to set up plantations with the labour of indentured servants and live as feudal lords, and the specifically middle-class outlook of the Puritans.

As far as the influence of the Puritan outlook extended, under all circumstances – and this is, of course, much more important than the mere encouragement of capital accumulation – it favoured the development of a rational bourgeois economic life; it was the most important, and above all the only consistent influence in the development of that life. It stood at the cradle of the modern economic man.

To be sure, these Puritanical ideals tended to give way under excessive pressure from the temptations of wealth, as the Puritans themselves knew very well. With great regularity we find the most genuine adherents of Puritanism among the classes which were rising from a lowly status, the small bourgeois and farmers, while the *beati possidentes,* even among Quakers, are often found tending to repudiate the old ideals. It was the same fate which again and again befell the predecessor of this worldly asceticism, the monastic asceticism of the Middle Ages. In the latter case, when rational economic activity had worked out its full effects by strict regulation of conduct and limitation of consumption, the wealth accumulated either succumbed directly to the nobility, as in the time before the Reformation, or monastic discipline threatened to break down, and one of the numerous reformations became necessary.

In fact the whole history of monasticism is in a certain sense the history of a continual struggle with the problem of the secularizing influence of wealth. The same is true on a grand scale of the worldly asceticism of Puritanism. The great revival of Methodism, which preceded the expansion of English industry toward the end of the eighteenth century, may well be compared with such a monastic reform. We may hence quote here a passage from John Wesley himself which might well serve as a motto for everything which has been said above. For it shows that the leaders of these ascetic movements understood the seemingly paradoxical relationships which we have here analysed perfectly well, and in the same sense that we have given them. He wrote:

> I fear, wherever riches have increased, the essence of religion has decreased in the same proportion. Therefore I do not see how it is possible, in the nature of things, for any revival of true religion to continue long. For religion must necessarily produce both industry and frugality, and these cannot but produce riches. But as riches increase, so will pride, anger, and love of the world in all its branches. How then is it possible that Methodism, that is, a religion of the heart, though it flourishes now as a green bay tree, should continue in this state? For the Methodists in every place grow diligent and frugal; consequently they increase in goods. Hence they proportionately increase in pride, in anger, in the desire of the flesh, the desire of the eyes, and the pride of life. So, although the form of religion remains, the spirit is swiftly vanishing away. Is there no way to prevent this – this continual decay of pure religion? We ought not to prevent people from being diligent and frugal; we must exhort all Christians to gain all they can, and to save all they can; that is, in effect, to grow rich.

There follows the advice that those who gain all they can and save all they can should also give all they can, so that they will grow in grace and lay up a treasure in heaven. It is clear that Wesley here expresses, even in detail, just what we have been trying to point out. As Wesley here says, the full economic effect of those great religious movements, whose significance for economic development lay above all in their ascetic educative influence, generally came only after the peak of the purely religious enthusiasm was past. Then the intensity of the search for the Kingdom of God commenced gradually to pass over into sober economic virtue; the religious roots died out slowly, giving way to utilitarian worldliness. Then, as Dowden puts it, as in Robinson Crusoe, the isolated economic man who carries on missionary activities on the side takes the place of the lonely spiritual search for the Kingdom of Heaven of Bunyan's pilgrim, hurrying through the marketplace of Vanity. When later the principle "to make the most of both worlds" became dominant in the end, as Dowden has remarked, a good conscience simply became one of the means of enjoying a comfortable bourgeois life, as is well expressed in the German proverb about the soft pillow. What the great religious epoch of the seventeenth century bequeathed to its utilitarian successor was, however, above all an amazingly good, we may even say a pharisaically good, conscience in the acquisition of money, so long as it took place legally. Every trace of the *deplacere vix potest* has disappeared.

A specifically bourgeois economic ethic had grown up. With the consciousness of standing in the fullness of God's grace and being visibly blessed by Him, the bourgeois business man, as long as he remained within the bounds of formal correctness, as long as his moral conduct was spotless and the use to which he put his wealth was not objectionable, could follow his pecuniary interests as he would and feel that he was fulfilling a duty in doing so. The power of religious asceticism provided him in addition with sober, conscientious, and unusually industrious workmen, who clung to their work as to a life purpose willed by God.

Finally, it gave him the comforting assurance that the unequal distribution of the goods of this world was a special dispensation of Divine Providence, which in these differences, as in particular grace, pursued secret ends unknown to men. Calvin himself had made the much-quoted statement that only when the people, i.e. the mass of labourers and craftsmen, were poor did they remain obedient to God. In the Netherlands (Pieter de la Court and others), that had been secularized to the effect that the mass of men only labour when necessity forces them to do so. This formulation of a leading idea of capitalistic economy later entered into the current theories of the productivity of low wages. Here also, with the dying out of the religious root, the utilitarian interpretation crept in unnoticed, in the line of development which we have again and again observed. Mediaeval ethics not only tolerated begging but actually glorified it in the mendicant orders. Even secular beggars, since they gave the person of means opportunity for good works through giving alms, were sometimes considered an estate and treated as such. Even the Anglican social ethic of the Stuarts was very close to this attitude. It remained for Puritan Asceticism to take part in the severe English Poor Relief Legislation which fundamentally changed the situation. And it could do that because the Protestant sects and the strict Puritan communities actually did not know any begging in their own midst.

On the other hand, seen from the side of the workers, the Zinzendorf branch of Pietism, for instance, glorified the loyal worker who did not seek acquisition, but lived according to the apostolic model, and was thus endowed with the charisma of the disciples. Similar ideas had originally been prevalent among the Baptists.

Now naturally the whole ascetic literature of almost all denominations is saturated with the idea that faithful labour, even at low wages, on the part of those to whom life offers no other opportunities, is highly pleasing to God. In this respect Protestant Asceticism added in itself nothing new. But it not only deepened this idea most powerfully, it also created the force which was alone decisive for its effectiveness: the psychological sanction of it through the conception of this labour as a calling, as the best, often in the last analysis the only means of attaining certainty of grace. And on the other hand it legalized the exploitation of this specific willingness to work, in that it also interpreted the employer's business activity as a calling. It is obvious how powerfully the exclusive search for the Kingdom of God only through the fulfilment of duty in the calling, and the strict asceticism which Church discipline naturally imposed, especially on the propertyless classes, was bound to affect the productivity of labour in the capitalistic sense of the word. The treatment of labour as a calling became as characteristic of the modern worker as the corresponding attitude toward acquisition of the business man. It was a perception of this situation, new at his time, which caused so able an observer as Sir William Petty to attribute the economic power of Holland in the seventeenth century to the fact that the very numerous dissenters in that country (Calvinists and Baptists) "are for the most part thinking, sober men, and such as believe that Labour and Industry is their duty towards God."

Calvinism opposed organic social organization in the fiscal-monopolistic form which it assumed in Anglicanism under the Stuarts, especially in the conceptions of Laud, this alliance of Church and State with the monopolists on the basis of a Christian, social ethical foundation. Its leaders were universally among the most passionate opponents of this type of politically privileged commercial, putting-out, and colonial capitalism. Over against it they placed the individualistic motives of rational legal acquisition by virtue of one's own ability and initiative. And, while the politically privileged monopoly industries in England all disappeared in short order, this attitude played a large and decisive part in the development of the industries which grew up in spite of and against the authority of the State. The Puritans (Prynne, Parker) repudiated all connection with the large-scale capitalistic courtiers and projectors as an ethically suspicious class. On the other hand, they took pride in their own superior middle-class business morality, which formed the true reason for the persecutions to which they were subjected on the part of those circles. Defoe proposed to win the battle against dissent by boycotting bank credit and withdrawing deposits. The difference of the two types of capitalistic attitude went to a very large extent hand in hand with religious differences. The opponents of the Nonconformists, even in the eighteenth century, again and again ridiculed them for personifying the spirit of shopkeepers, and for having ruined the ideals of old England. Here also lay the difference of the Puritan economic ethic from the Jewish; and contemporaries (Prynne) knew well that the former and not the latter was the bourgeois capitalistic ethic.

One of the fundamental elements of the spirit of modern capitalism, and not only of that but of all modern culture: rational conduct on the basis of the idea of the calling, was born – that is what this discussion has sought to demonstrate – from the spirit of Christian asceticism. One has only to re-read the passage from Franklin, quoted at the beginning of this essay, in order to see that the essential elements of the attitude which was there called the spirit of capitalism are the same as what we have just shown to be the content of the Puritan worldly asceticism, only without the religious basis, which by Franklin's time had died away. The idea that modern labour has an ascetic character is of course not new. Limitation to specialized work, with a renunciation of the Faustian universality of man which it involves, is a condition of any valuable work in the modern world; hence deeds and renunciation inevitably condition each other today. This fundamentally ascetic trait of middle-class life, if it attempts to be a way of life at all, and not simply the absence of any, was what Goethe wanted to teach, at the height of his wisdom, in the *Wanderjahren*, and in the end which he gave to the life of his Faust. For him the realization meant a renunciation, a departure from an age of full and beautiful humanity, which can no more be repeated in the course of our cultural development than can the flower of the Athenian culture of antiquity.

The Puritan wanted to work in a calling; we are forced to do so. For when asceticism was carried out of monastic cells into everyday life, and began to dominate worldly morality, it did its part in building the tremendous cosmos of the modern economic order. This order is now bound to the technical and economic conditions of machine production which today determine the lives of all the individuals who are born into this mechanism, not only those directly concerned with economic acquisition, with irresistible force. Perhaps it will so determine them until the last ton of fossilized coal is burnt. In Baxter's view the care for external goods should only lie on the shoulders of the "saint like a light cloak, which can be thrown aside at any moment." But fate decreed that the cloak should become an iron cage.

Since asceticism undertook to remodel the world and to work out its ideals in the world, material goods have gained an increasing and finally an inexorable power over the lives of men as at no previous period in history. Today the spirit of religious asceticism – whether finally, who knows? – has escaped from the cage. But victorious capitalism, since it rests on mechanical foundations, needs its support no longer. The rosy blush of its laughing heir, the Enlightenment, seems also to be irretrievably fading, and the idea of duty in one's calling prowls about in our lives like the ghost of dead religious beliefs. Where the fulfilment of the calling cannot directly be related to the highest spiritual and cultural values, or when, on the other hand, it need not be felt simply as economic compulsion, the individual generally abandons the attempt to justify it at all. In the field of its highest development, in the United States, the pursuit of wealth, stripped of its religious and ethical meaning, tends to become associated with purely mundane passions, which often actually give it the character of sport.

No one knows who will live in this cage in the future, or whether at the end of this tremendous development, entirely new prophets will arise, or there will be a great rebirth of old ideas and ideals, or, if neither, mechanized petrification, embellished with a sort of convulsive self-importance. For of the fast stage of this cultural development, it might well be truly said: "Specialists without spirit, sensualists without heart; this nullity imagines that it has attained a level of civilization never before achieved."

But this brings us to the world of judgements of value and of faith, with which this purely historical discussion need not be burdened. The next task would be rather to show the significance of ascetic rationalism which has only been touched in the foregoing sketch for the content of practical social ethics, thus for the types of organization and the functions of social groups from the conventicle to the State. Then its relations to humanistic rationalism, its ideals of life and cultural influence; further to the development of philosophical and scientific empiricism, to technical development and to spiritual ideals would have to be analysed. Then its historical development from the mediaeval beginnings of worldly asceticism to its dissolution into pure utilitarianism would have to be traced out through all the areas of ascetic religion. Only then could the quantitative cultural significance of ascetic Protestantism in its relation to the other plastic elements of modern culture be estimated.

Here we have only attempted to trace the fact and the direction of its influence to their motives in one, though a very important point. But it would also further be necessary to investigate how Protestant Asceticism was in turn influenced in its development and its character by the totality of social conditions, especially economic. The modern man is in general, even with the best will, unable to give religious ideas a significance for culture and national character which they deserve. But it is, of course, not my aim to substitute for a one-sided materialistic an equally one-sided spiritualistic causal interpretation of culture and of history. Each is equally possible, but each, if it does not serve as the preparation, but as the conclusion of an investigation, accomplish equally little in the interest of historical truth.

QUESTIONS FOR REVIEW AND DISCUSSION

1. What are some of the attitudes to wealth that Weber discovers in the manuals of Puritan ethics, and how do these contrast with earlier Calvinist attitudes? How do these attitudes translate into attitudes to time?

2. How do Puritan ways of thinking about labour, as expressed in Baxter's writings, vary from the earlier notions by Thomas Aquinas and St. Paul? In what ways do they resemble the ideas of Adam Smith?

3. In Weber's analysis, how do the Puritan and Quaker ethics of work as a "calling" differ from Luther's attitude to work? Is wealth problematic in itself, or only under certain criteria?

4. What were Puritan attitudes to sports, the arts, and other forms of consumption of luxuries, according to Weber? What was the attitude to payment for such diversions?

5. In Weber's view, how do the ascetic values of Puritanism towards labor and wealth lead to the rise of a bourgeois economic ethic, in which the unequal distribution of goods is the result of Divine Providence? How do these attitudes work in the justification of low wages for workers, and the workers' acceptance of these?

6. How does the notion of a calling and the accompanying ascetic sentiments it engenders, combined with the accumulation of capital, influence the development of capitalism, according to Weber?

7. According to Weber, how have these attitudes changed, despite leaving their mark on modern Western society? Can you think of other instances where the traces of these Protestant attitudes are visible in modern society? What are their implications? Can you think of alternate attitudes to work, wealth, entertainment, etc., in other cultures or religious traditions?

8. Weber has highlighted a link between religion and economics. In what other ways might religious values and practices appear to affect social, economic, or political realities?

13 Mysticism

William James

William James (1842–1910) was born in New York City as a member of a wealthy, famous, and well-connected family. He attended various schools in Europe and the United States, including Harvard School of Medicine. He finished his MD and shifted from Physiology to Psychology, where he made pioneering contributions, including the first American psychology laboratory and the massive two-volume 1890 publication, *The Principles of Psychology.* James applied his pragmatic philosophical and psychological outlook to the study of religion with particular focus on religious experience, conversion, and mysticism. His approach invokes the scientific method and differs from Freud to the extent that James takes seriously the reality and potentially positive contribution of religious experiences. James delivered the prestigious Gifford Lectures in 1901–2, which he published as *The Varieties of Religious Experience.* Our selections on mysticism are excerpted from chapters 16 and 17 of this influential book.

Over and over again in these lectures I have raised points and left them open and unfinished until we should have come to the subject of Mysticism. Some of you, I fear, may have smiled as you noted my reiterated postponements. But now the hour has come when mysticism must be faced in good earnest, and those broken threads wound up together. One may say truly, I think, that personal religious experience has its root and centre in mystical states of consciousness; so for us, who in these lectures are treating personal experience as the exclusive subject of our study, such states of consciousness ought to form the vital chapter from which the other chapters get their light. Whether my treatment of mystical states will shed more light or darkness, I do not know, for my own constitution shuts me out from their enjoyment almost entirely, and I can speak of them only at second hand. But though forced to look upon the subject so externally, I will be as objective and receptive as I can; and I think I shall at least succeed in convincing you of the reality of the states in question, and of the paramount importance of their function.

First of all, then, I ask, What does the expression 'mystical states of consciousness' mean? How do we part off mystical states from other states?

The words 'mysticism' and 'mystical' are often used as terms of mere reproach, to throw at any opinion which we regard as vague and vast and sentimental, and without a base in either facts or logic. For some writers a 'mystic' is any person who believes in thought-transference, or spirit-return. Employed in this way the word has little value: there are too many less ambiguous synonyms. So, to keep it useful by restricting it, I will do what I did in the case of the word 'religion,' and simply propose to you four marks which, when an experience has them, may justify us in calling it mystical for the purpose of the present lectures. In this way we shall save verbal disputation, and the recriminations that generally go therewith.

1. Ineffability.—The handiest of the marks by which I classify a state of mind as mystical is negative. The subject of it immediately says that it defies expression, that no adequate report of its contents can be given in words. It follows from this that its quality must be directly experienced; it cannot be imparted or transferred to others. In this peculiarity mystical states are more like states of feeling than like states of intellect. No one can make clear to another who has never had a certain feeling, in what the quality or worth of it consists. One must have musical ears to know the value of a symphony; one must have been in love one's self to understand a lover's state of mind. Lacking the heart or ear, we cannot interpret the musician or the lover justly, and are even likely to consider him weak-minded or absurd. The mystic finds that most of us accord to his experiences an equally incompetent treatment.

2. Noetic quality.—Although so similar to states of feeling, mystical states seem to those who experience them to be also states of knowledge. They are states of insight into depths of truth unplumbed by the discursive intellect. They are illuminations, revelations, full of significance and importance, all inarticulate though they remain; and as a rule they carry with them a curious sense of authority for after-time.

These two characters will entitle any state to be called mystical, in the sense in which I use the word. Two other qualities are less sharply marked, but are usually found. These are:

3. Transiency.—Mystical states cannot be sustained for long. Except in rare instances, half an hour, or at most an hour or two, seems to be the limit beyond which they fade into the light of common day. Often, when faded, their quality can but imperfectly be reproduced in memory; but when they recur it is recognized; and from one recurrence to another it is susceptible of continuous development in what is felt as inner richness and importance.

4. Passivity.—Although the oncoming of mystical states may be facilitated by preliminary voluntary operations, as by fixing the attention, or going through certain bodily performances, or in other ways which manuals of mysticism prescribe; yet when the characteristic sort of consciousness once has set in, the mystic feels as if his own will were in abeyance, and indeed sometimes as if he were grasped and held by a superior power. This latter peculiarity connects mystical states with certain definite phenomena of secondary or alternative personality, such as prophetic speech, automatic writing, or the mediumistic trance. When these latter conditions are well pronounced, however, there may be no recollection whatever of the phenomenon and it may have no significance for the subject's usual inner life, to which, as it were, it makes a mere interruption. Mystical states, strictly so called, are never merely interruptive. Some memory of their content always remains, and a profound sense of their importance. They modify the inner life of the subject between the times of their recurrence. Sharp divisions in this region are, however, difficult to make, and we find all sorts of gradations and mixtures.

These four characteristics are sufficient to mark out a group of states of consciousness peculiar enough to deserve a special name and to call for careful study. Let it then be called the mystical group.

Our next step should be to gain acquaintance with some typical examples. Professional mystics at the height of their development have often elaborately organized experiences and a philosophy based thereupon. But you remember what I said in my first lecture: phenomena are best understood when placed within their series, studied in their germ and in their over-ripe decay, and compared with their exaggerated and degenerated kindred. The range of mystical experience is very wide, much too wide for us to cover in the time at our disposal. Yet the method of serial study is so essential for interpretation that if we really wish to reach conclusions we must use it. I will begin, therefore, with phenomena which claim no special religious significance, and end with those of which the religious pretensions are extreme.

The simplest rudiment of mystical experience would seem to be that deepened sense of the significance of a maxim or formula which occasionally sweeps over one. "I've heard that said all my life," we exclaim, "but I never realized its full meaning until now." "When a fellow-monk," said Luther, "one day repeated the words of the Creed: 'I believe in the forgiveness of sins,' I saw the Scripture in an entirely new light; and straightway I felt as if I were born anew. It was as if I had found the door of paradise thrown wide open."[1] This sense of deeper significance is not confined to rational propositions. Single words,[2] and conjunctions of words, effects of light on land and sea, odors and musical sounds, all bring it when the mind is tuned aright. Most of us can remember the strangely moving power of passages in certain poems read when we were young, irrational doorways as they were through which the mystery of fact, the wildness and the pang of life, stole into our hearts and thrilled them. The words have now perhaps become mere polished surfaces for us; but lyric poetry and music are alive and significant only in proportion as they fetch these vague vistas of a life continuous with our own, beckoning and inviting, yet ever eluding our pursuit. We are alive or dead to the eternal inner message of the arts according as we have kept or lost this mystical susceptibility.

A more pronounced step forward on the mystical ladder is found in an extremely frequent phenomenon, that sudden feeling, namely, which sometimes sweeps over us, of having 'been here before,' as if at some indefinite past time, in just this place, with just these people, we were already saying just these things. As Tennyson writes:

> Moreover, something is or seems,
> That touches me with mystic gleams,
> Like glimpses of forgotten dreams—
> Of something felt, like something here;
> Of something done, I know not where;
> Such as no language may declare.[3]

Sir James Crichton-Browne has given the technical name of 'dreamy states' to these sudden invasions of vaguely reminiscent consciousness.[4] They bring a sense of mystery and of the metaphysical duality of things, and the feeling of an enlargement of perception which seems imminent but which never completes itself. In Dr. Crichton-Browne's opinion they connect themselves with the perplexed and scared disturbances of self-consciousness which occasionally precede epileptic attacks. I think that this learned alienist takes a rather absurdly alarmist view of an intrinsically insignificant phenomenon. He follows it along the downward ladder, to insanity; our path pursues the upward ladder chiefly. The divergence shows how important it is to neglect no part of a phenomenon's connections, for we make it appear admirable or dreadful according to the context by which we set it off ...

... The next step into mystical states carries us into a realm that public opinion and ethical philosophy have long since branded as pathological, though private practice and certain lyric strains of poetry seem still to bear witness to its ideality. I refer to the consciousness produced by intoxicants and anaesthetics, especially by alcohol. The sway of alcohol over mankind is unquestionably due to its power to stimulate the mystical faculties of human nature, usually crushed to earth by the cold facts and dry criticisms of the sober hour. Sobriety diminishes, discriminates and says no; drunkenness expands, unites, and says yes. It is in fact the great exciter of the Yes function in man. It brings its votary from the chill periphery of things to the radiant core. It makes him for the moment one with truth. Not through mere perversity do men run after it. To the poor and the unlettered it stands in the place of symphony concerts and of literature; and it is part of the deeper mystery and tragedy of life that whiffs and gleams of something that we immediately recognize as excellent should be vouchsafed to so many of us only in the fleeting earlier phases of what in its totality is so degrading a poisoning. The drunken consciousness is one bit of the mystic consciousness, and our total opinion of it must find its place in our opinion of that larger whole.

Nitrous oxide and ether, especially nitrous oxide, when sufficiently diluted with air, stimulate the mystical consciousness in an extraordinary degree. Depth beyond depth of truth seems revealed to the inhaler. This truth fades out, however, or escapes, at the moment of coming to; and if any words remain over in which it seemed to clothe itself, they prove to be the veriest nonsense. Nevertheless, the sense of a profound meaning having been there persists; and I know more than one person who is persuaded that in the nitrous oxide trance we have a genuine metaphysical revelation.

Some years ago I myself made some observations on this aspect of nitrous oxide intoxication, and reported them in print. One conclusion was forced upon my mind at that time, and my impression of its truth has ever since remained unshaken. It is that our normal waking consciousness, rational consciousness as we call it, is but one special type of consciousness, whilst all about it, parted from it by the filmiest of screens, there lie potential forms of consciousness entirely different. We may go through life without suspecting their existence; but apply the requisite stimulus, and at a touch they are there in all their completeness, definite types of mentality which probably somewhere have their field of application and adaptation. No account of the universe in its totality can be final which leaves these other forms of consciousness quite disregarded. How to regard them is the question— for they are so discontinuous with ordinary consciousness. Yet they may determine attitudes though they cannot furnish formulas, and open a region though they fail to give a map. At any rate, they forbid a premature closing of our accounts with reality. Looking back on my own experiences, they all converge towards a kind of insight to which I cannot help ascribing some metaphysical significance. The keynote of it is invariably a reconciliation. It is as if the opposites of the world, whose contradictoriness and conflict make all our difficulties and troubles, were melted into unity ...

... Certain aspects of nature seem to have a peculiar power of awakening such mystical moods. Most of the striking cases which I have collected have occurred out of doors.

... The well-known passage from Walt Whitman is a classical expression of this sporadic type of mystical experience.

> I believe in you, my Soul ...
> Loaf with me on the grass, loose the stop from your throat; ...
> Only the lull I like, the hum of your valved voice.

I mind how once we lay, such a transparent summer morning.
Swiftly arose and spread around me the peace and knowledge that pass all the argument
     of the earth,
And I know that the hand of God is the promise of my own,
And I know that the spirit of God is the brother of my own,
And that all the men ever born are also my brothers and the women my sisters and
     lovers,
And that a kelson of the creation is love.[5]

I could easily give more instances, but one will suffice. I take it from the Autobiography of
J. Trevor.[6]

> One brilliant Sunday morning, my wife and boys went to the Unitarian Chapel in
> Macclesfield. I felt it impossible to accompany them—as though to leave the sunshine
> on the hills, and go down there to the chapel, would be for the time an act of spiritual
> suicide. And I felt such need for new inspiration and expansion in my life. So, very
> reluctantly and sadly, I left my wife and boys to go down into the town, while I went
> further up into the hills with my stick and my dog. In the loveliness of the morning,
> and the beauty of the hills and valleys, I soon lost my sense of sadness and regret. For
> nearly an hour I walked along the road to the 'Cat and Fiddle,' and then returned. On
> the way back, suddenly, without warning, I felt that I was in Heaven—an inward state
> of peace and joy and assurance indescribably intense, accompanied with a sense of
> being bathed in a warm glow of light, as though the external condition had brought
> about the internal effect—a feeling of having passed beyond the body, though the
> scene around me stood out more clearly and as if nearer to me than before, by reason
> of the illumination in the midst of which I seemed to be placed. This deep emotion
> lasted, though with decreasing strength, until I reached home, and for some time after,
> only gradually passing away.

The writer adds that having had further experiences of a similar sort, he now knows
them well.

> "The spiritual life," he writes, "justifies itself to those who live it; but what can we say
> to those who do not understand? This, at least, we can say, that it is a life whose
> experiences are proved real to their possessor, because they remain with him when
> brought closest into contact with the objective realities of life. Dreams cannot stand this
> test. We wake from them to find that they are but dreams. Wanderings of an over-
> wrought brain do not stand this test. These highest experiences that I have had of
> God's presence have been rare and brief—flashes of consciousness which have com-
> pelled me to exclaim with surprise—God is *here*!—or conditions of exaltation and
> insight less intense, and only gradually passing away. I have severely questioned the
> worth of these moments. To no soul have I named them, lest I should be building my
> life and work on mere phantasies of the brain. But I find that, after every questioning
> and test, they stand out to-day as the most real experiences of my life, and experiences
> which have explained and justified and unified all past experiences and all past growth.
> Indeed, their reality and their far-reaching significance are ever becoming more clear
> and evident. When they came, I was living the fullest, strongest, sanest, deepest life. I
> was not seeking them. What I was seeking, with resolute determination, was to live

more intensely my own life, as against what I knew would be the adverse judgment of the world. It was in the most real seasons that the Real Presence came, and I was aware that I was immersed in the infinite ocean of God."[7]

Even the least mystical of you must by this time be convinced of the existence of mystical moments as states of consciousness of an entirely specific quality, and of the deep impression which they make on those who have them. A Canadian psychiatrist, Dr. R.M. Bucke, gives to the more distinctly characterized of these phenomena the name of cosmic consciousness. "Cosmic consciousness in its more striking instances is not," Dr. Bucke says, "simply an expansion or extension of the self-conscious mind with which we are all familiar, but the superaddition of a function as distinct from any possessed by the average man as self-consciousness is distinct from any function possessed by one of the higher animals."

> The prime characteristic of cosmic consciousness is a consciousness of the cosmos, that is, of the life and order of the universe. Along with the consciousness of the cosmos there occurs an intellectual enlightenment which alone would place the individual on a new plane of existence—would make him almost a member of a new species. To this is added a state of moral exaltation, an indescribable feeling of elevation, elation, and joyousness, and a quickening of the moral sense, which is fully as striking, and more important than is the enhanced intellectual power. With these come what may be called a sense of immortality, a consciousness of eternal life, not a conviction that he shall have this, but the consciousness that he has it already.[8]

… We have now seen enough of this cosmic or mystic consciousness, as it comes sporadically. We must next pass to its methodical cultivation as an element of the religious life. Hindus, Buddhists, Mohammedans, and Christians all have cultivated it methodically.

In India, training in mystical insight has been known from time immemorial under the name of yoga. Yoga means the experimental union of the individual with the divine. It is based on persevering exercise; and the diet, posture, breathing, intellectual concentration, and moral discipline vary slightly in the different systems which teach it. The yogi, or disciple, who has by these means overcome the obscurations of his lower nature sufficiently, enters into the condition termed samadhi, "and comes face to face with facts which no instinct or reason can ever know." He learns—

> That the mind itself has a higher state of existence, beyond reason, a superconscious state, and that when the mind gets to that higher state, then this knowledge beyond reasoning comes. … All the different steps in yoga are intended to bring us scientifically to the superconscious state or samadhi. … Just as unconscious work is beneath consciousness, so there is another work which is above consciousness, and which, also, is not accompanied with the feeling of egoism. … There is no feeling of I, and yet the mind works, desireless, free from restlessness, objectless, bodiless. Then the Truth shines in its full effulgence, and we know ourselves—for Samadhi lies potential in us all—for what we truly are, free, immortal, omnipotent, loosed from the finite, and its contrasts of good and evil altogether, and identical with the Atman or Universal Soul.[9]

The Vedantists say that one may stumble into super-consciousness sporadically, without the previous discipline, but it is then impure. Their test of its purity, like our test of religion's value, is empirical: its fruits must be good for life. When a man comes out of Samadhi, they assure us that he remains "enlightened, a sage, a prophet, a saint, his whole character changed, his life changed, illumined."[10]

The Buddhists use the word 'samadhi' as well as the Hindus; but 'dhyana' is their special word for higher states of contemplation. There seem to be four stages recognized in dhyana. The first stage comes through concentration of the mind upon one point. It excludes desire, but not discernment or judgment: it is still intellectual. In the second stage the intellectual functions drop off, and the satisfied sense of unity remains. In the third stage the satisfaction departs, and indifference begins, along with memory and self-consciousness. In the fourth stage the indifference, memory, and self-consciousness are perfected. [Just what 'memory' and 'self-consciousness' mean in this connection is doubtful. They cannot be the faculties familiar to us in the lower life.] Higher stages still of contemplation are mentioned—a region where there exists nothing, and where the meditator says: "There exists absolutely nothing," and stops. Then he reaches another region where he says: "There are neither ideas nor absence of ideas," and stops again. Then another region where, "having reached the end of both idea and perception, he stops finally." This would seem to be, not yet Nirvana, but as close an approach to it as this life affords.[11]

In the Mohammedan world the Sufi sect and various dervish bodies are the possessors of the mystical tradition. The Sufis have existed in Persia from the earliest times, and as their pantheism is so at variance with the hot and rigid monotheism of the Arab mind, it has been suggested that Sufism must have been inoculated into Islam by Hindu influences. We Christians know little of Sufism, for its secrets are disclosed only to those initiated. To give its existence a certain liveliness in your minds, I will quote a Moslem document, and pass away from the subject.

Al-Ghazzali, a Persian philosopher and theologian, who flourished in the eleventh century, and ranks as one of the greatest doctors of the Moslem church, has left us one of the few autobiographies to be found outside of Christian literature. Strange that a species of book so abundant among ourselves should be so little represented elsewhere—the absence of strictly personal confessions is the chief difficulty to the purely literary student who would like to become acquainted with the inwardness of religions other than the Christian.

M. Schmolders has translated a part of Al-Ghazzali's autobiography into French:[12]

"The Science of the Sufis," says the Moslem author, "aims at detaching the heart from all that is not God, and at giving to it for sole occupation the meditation of the divine being. Theory being more easy for me than practice, I read [certain books] until I understood all that can be learned by study and hearsay. Then I recognized that what pertains most exclusively to their method is just what no study can grasp, but only transport, ecstasy, and the transformation of the soul. How great, for example, is the difference between knowing the definitions of health, of satiety, with their causes and conditions, and being really healthy or filled. How different to know in what drunkenness consists—as being a state occasioned by a vapor that rises from the stomach— and *being* drunk effectively. Without doubt, the drunken man knows neither the definition of drunkenness nor what makes it interesting for science. Being drunk, he knows nothing; whilst the physician, although not drunk, knows well in what drunkenness consists, and what are its predisposing conditions. Similarly there is a difference between knowing the nature of abstinence, and *being* abstinent or having one's soul detached from the world.—Thus I had learned what words could teach of Sufism, but what was left could be learned neither by study nor through the ears, but solely by giving one's self up to ecstasy and leading a pious life. ... "[13]

... This incommunicableness of the transport is the keynote of all mysticism. Mystical truth exists for the individual who has the transport, but for no one else. In this, as I have said, it resembles the knowledge given to us in sensations more than that given by conceptual thought. Thought, with its remoteness and abstractness, has often enough in the history of philosophy been contrasted unfavorably with sensation. It is a commonplace of metaphysics that God's knowledge cannot be discursive but must be intuitive, that is, must be constructed more after the pattern of what in ourselves is called immediate feeling, than after that of proposition and judgment. But our immediate feelings have no content but what the five senses supply; and we have seen and shall see again that mystics may emphatically deny that the senses play any part in the very highest type of knowledge which their transports yield.

In the Christian church there have always been mystics. Although many of them have been viewed with suspicion, some have gained favor in the eyes of the authorities. The experiences of these have been treated as precedents, and a codified system of mystical theology has been based upon them ...

... Mystical conditions may, therefore, render the soul more energetic in the lines which their inspiration favors. But this could be reckoned an advantage only in case the inspiration were a true one. If the inspiration were erroneous, the energy would be all the more mistaken and misbegotten. So we stand once more before that problem of truth which confronted us at the end of the lectures on saintliness. You will remember that we turned to mysticism precisely to get some light on truth. Do mystical states establish the truth of those theological affections in which the saintly life has its root?

In spite of their repudiation of articulate self-description, mystical states in general assert a pretty distinct theoretic drift. It is possible to give the outcome of the majority of them in terms that point in definite philosophical directions. One of these directions is optimism, and the other is monism. We pass into mystical states from out of ordinary consciousness as from a less into a more, as from a smallness into a vastness, and at the same time as from an unrest to a rest. We feel them as reconciling, unifying states. They appeal to the yes-function more than to the no-function in us. In them the unlimited absorbs the limits and peacefully closes the account. Their very denial of every adjective you may propose as applicable to the ultimate truth,—He, the Self, the Atman, is to be described by 'No! no!' only, say the Upanishads[14]—though it seems on the surface to be a no-function, is a denial made on behalf of a deeper yes. Whoso calls the Absolute anything in particular, or says that it is this, seems implicitly to shut it off from being that—it is as if he lessened it. So we deny the 'this,' negating the negation which it seems to us to imply, in the interests of the higher affirmative attitude by which we are possessed. The fountain-head of Christian mysticism is Dionysius the Areopagite. He describes the absolute truth by negatives exclusively.

> The cause of all things is neither soul nor intellect; nor has it imagination, opinion, or reason, or intelligence; nor is it reason or intelligence; nor is it spoken or thought. It is neither number, nor order, nor magnitude, nor littleness, nor equality, nor inequality, nor similarity, nor dissimilarity. It neither stands, nor moves, nor rests. ... It is neither essence, nor eternity, nor time. Even intellectual contact does not belong to it. It is neither science nor truth. It is not even royalty or wisdom; not one; not unity; not divinity or goodness; nor even spirit as we know it.[15]

But these qualifications are denied by Dionysius, not because the truth falls short of them, but because it so infinitely excels them. It is above them. It is *super*-lucent, *super*-splendent, *super*-essential, *super*-sublime, *super everything* that can be named. Like Hegel in his logic, mystics journey towards the positive pole of truth only by the 'Methode der Absoluten Negativität.'[16]

... I have now sketched with extreme brevity and insufficiency, but as fairly as I am able in the time allowed, the general traits of the mystic range of consciousness. It is on the whole pantheistic and optimistic, or at least the opposite of pessimistic. It is anti-naturalistic, and harmonizes best with twice-bornness and so-called other-worldly states of mind.

My next task is to inquire whether we can invoke it as authoritative. Does it furnish any *warrant for the truth* of the twice-bornness and supernaturality and pantheism which it favors? I must give my answer to this question as concisely as I can.

In brief my answer is this—and I will divide it into three parts:—

(1) Mystical states, when well developed, usually are, and have the right to be, absolutely authoritative over the individuals to whom they come.
(2) No authority emanates from them which should make it a duty for those who stand outside of them to accept their revelations uncritically.
(3) They break down the authority of the non-mystical or rationalistic consciousness, based upon the understanding and the senses alone. They show it to be only one kind of consciousness. They open out the possibility of other orders of truth, in which, so far as anything in us vitally responds to them, we may freely continue to have faith.

I will take up these points one by one.

1. As a matter of psychological fact, mystical states of a well-pronounced and emphatic sort *are* usually authoritative over those who have them.[17] They have been 'there,' and know. It is vain for rationalism to grumble about this. If the mystical truth that comes to a man proves to be a force that he can live by, what mandate have we of the majority to order him to live in another way? We can throw him into a prison or a madhouse, but we cannot change his mind—we commonly attach it only the more stubbornly to its beliefs.[18] It mocks our utmost efforts, as a matter of fact, and in point of logic it absolutely escapes our jurisdiction. Our own more 'rational' beliefs are based on evidence exactly similar in nature to that which mystics quote for theirs. Our senses, namely, have assured us of certain states of fact; but mystical experiences are as direct perceptions of fact for those who have them as any sensations ever were for us. The records show that even though the five senses be in abeyance in them, they are absolutely sensational in their epistemological quality, if I may be pardoned the barbarous expression—that is, they are face to face presentations of what seems immediately to exist.

The mystic is, in short, *invulnerable*, and must be left, whether we relish it or not, in undisturbed enjoyment of his creed. Faith, says Tolstoy, is that by which men live. And faith-state and mystic state are practically convertible terms.

2. But I now proceed to add that mystics have no right to claim that we ought to accept the deliverance of their peculiar experiences, if we are ourselves outsiders and feel no private call thereto. The utmost they can ever ask of us in this life is to admit that they establish a presumption. They form a consensus and have an unequivocal outcome; and it would be odd, mystics might say, if such a unanimous type of experience should prove to be altogether wrong. At bottom, however, this would only be an appeal to numbers, like the appeal of rationalism the other way; and the appeal to numbers has no logical force. If we acknowledge it, it is for 'suggestive,' not for logical reasons: we follow the majority because to do so suits our life.

But even this presumption from the unanimity of mystics is far from being strong. In characterizing mystic states as pantheistic, optimistic, etc., I am afraid I over-simplified the truth. I did so for expository reasons, and to keep the closer to the classic mystical tradition. The classic religious mysticism, it now must be confessed, is only a 'privileged case.' It is an *extract*, kept true to type by the selection of the fittest specimens and their preservation in 'schools.' It is carved out from a much larger mass; and if we take the larger mass as seriously as religious mysticism has historically taken itself, we find that the supposed unanimity largely disappears. To begin with, even religious mysticism itself, the kind that accumulates traditions and makes schools, is much less unanimous than I have allowed. It has been both ascetic and antinomianly self-indulgent within the Christian church.[19] It is dualistic in Sankhya, and monistic in Vedanta philosophy, I called it pantheistic; but the great Spanish mystics are anything but pantheists. They are with few exceptions non-metaphysical minds, for whom 'the category of personality' is absolute. The 'union' of man with God is for them much more like an occasional miracle than like an original identity.[20] How different again, apart from the happiness common to all, is the mysticism of Walt Whitman, Edward Carpenter, Richard Jefferies, and other naturalistic pantheists, from the more distinctively Christian sort.[21] The fact is that the mystical feeling of enlargement, union, and emancipation has no specific intellectual content whatever of its own. It is capable of forming matrimonial alliances with material furnished by the most diverse philosophies and theologies, provided only they can find a place in their framework for its peculiar emotional mood. We have no right, therefore, to invoke its prestige as distinctively in favor of any special belief, such as that in absolute idealism, or in the absolute monistic identity, or in the absolute goodness, of the world. It is only relatively in favor of all these things—it passes out of common human consciousness in the direction in which they lie.

So much for religious mysticism proper. But more remains to be told, for religious mysticism is only one half of mysticism. The other half has no accumulated traditions except those which the text-books on insanity supply. Open any one of these, and you will find abundant cases in which 'mystical ideas' are cited as characteristic symptoms of enfeebled or deluded states of mind. In delusional insanity, paranoia, as they sometimes call it, we may have a diabolical mysticism, a sort of religious mysticism turned upside down. The same sense of ineffable importance in the smallest events, the same texts and words coming with new meanings, the same voices and visions and leadings and missions, the same controlling by extraneous powers; only this time the emotion is pessimistic: instead of consolations we have desolations; the meanings are dreadful; and the powers are enemies to life. It is evident that from the point of view of their psychological mechanism, the classic mysticism and these lower mysticisms spring from the same mental level, from that great subliminal or trans-marginal region of which science is beginning to admit the existence, but of which so little is really known. That region contains every kind of matter: 'seraph and snake' abide there side by side. To come from thence is no infallible credential. What comes must be sifted and tested, and run the gauntlet of confrontation with the total context of experience, just like what comes from the outer world of sense. Its value must be ascertained by empirical methods, so long as we are not mystics ourselves.

Once more, then, I repeat that non-mystics are under no obligation to acknowledge in mystical states a superior authority conferred on them by their intrinsic nature.[22]

3. Yet, I repeat once more, the existence of mystical states absolutely overthrows the pretension of non-mystical states to be the sole and ultimate dictators of what we may believe. As a rule, mystical states merely add a supersensuous meaning to the ordinary outward data

of consciousness. They are excitements like the emotions of love or ambition, gifts to our spirit by means of which facts already objectively before us fall into a new expressiveness and make a new connection with our active life. They do not contradict these facts as such or deny anything that our senses have immediately seized.[23] It is the rationalistic critic rather who plays the part of denier in the controversy, and his denials have no strength, for there never can be a state of facts to which new meaning may not truthfully be added, provided the mind ascend to a more enveloping point of view. It must always remain an open question whether mystical states may not possibly be such superior points of view, windows through which the mind looks out upon a more extensive and inclusive world. The difference of the views seen from the different mystical windows need not prevent us from entertaining this supposition. The wider world would in that case prove to have a mixed constitution like that of this world, that is all. It would have its celestial and its infernal regions, its tempting and its saving moments, its valid experiences and its counterfeit ones, just as our world has them; but it would be a wider world all the same. We should have to use its experiences by selecting and subordinating and substituting just as is our custom in this ordinary naturalistic world; we should be liable to error just as we are now; yet the counting in of that wider world of meanings, and the serious dealing with it, might, in spite of all the perplexity, be indispensable stages in our approach to the final fullness of the truth.

In this shape, I think, we have to leave the subject. Mystical states indeed wield no authority due simply to their being mystical states. But the higher ones among them point in directions to which the religious sentiments even of non-mystical men incline. They tell of the supremacy of the ideal, of vastness, of union, of safety, and of rest. They offer us *hypotheses*, hypotheses which we may voluntarily ignore, but which as thinkers we cannot possibly upset. The supernaturalism and optimism to which they would persuade us may, interpreted in one way or another, be after all the truest of insights into the meaning of this life.

"Oh, the little more, and how much it is; and the little less, and what worlds away!" It may be that possibility and permission of this sort are all that the religious consciousness requires to live on. In my last lecture I shall have to try to persuade you that this is the case. Meanwhile, however, I am sure that for many of my readers this diet is too slender. If supernaturalism and inner union with the divine are true, you think, then not so much permission, as compulsion to believe, ought to be found. Philosophy has always professed to prove religious truth by coercive argument; and the construction of philosophies of this kind has always been one favorite function of the religious life, if we use this term in the large historic sense. But religious philosophy is an enormous subject, and in my next lecture I can only give that brief glance at it which my limits will allow.

QUESTIONS FOR REVIEW AND DISCUSSION

1. Why does James indicate that this is an especially vital chapter in his book?
2. How does James' position ("my own constitution shuts me out from their [mystical states'] enjoyment almost entirely") vary from Freud's dismissal of "oceanic" states that Freud had not experienced?
3. What are the four marks that justify calling a religious experience mystical? Which do you find most compelling to qualify for this label?
4. How does James address the inherent difficulty of assessing the ineffable?
5. How does James claim that phenomena are best understood? Do you agree?

6. Although in our abridged selection you do not have the full range of examples presented by James, do you agree that "Even the least mystical of you must by this time be convinced of the existence of mystical moments as states of consciousness of an entirely specific quality, and of the deep impression which they make on those who have them"?

7. How does James bring Yoga from India into his study? Comment on his use of examples from Buddhism, Hinduism, and Sufism. Does he emphasize similarity or difference among mystical strands in these traditions?

8. Summarize James' main points with regard to whether we can invoke mystic consciousness as authoritative. Do you find effective the way he differentiates between ways that these states should, or need not, be taken as authoritative?

9. How does James call into question the unanimity of religious mysticism?

10. By what rationale does James argue the weakness of rationalistic critics of mystical states?

11. What do you think of James' writing style as well as the types of examples and arguments he employs?

12. What do you think are the sorts of relationships between mystical experience and religious traditions?

13. How might scholars of religion study mysticism and mystical experience?

Notes

1 Newman's *Securus judicat orbis terrarum* is another instance.

2 'Mesopotamia' is the stock comic instance.—An excellent old German lady, who had done some traveling in her day, used to describe to me her *Sehnsucht* that she might yet visit 'Philadelphia,' whose wondrous name had always haunted her imagination. Of John Foster it is said that "single words (as chalcedony), or the names of ancient heroes, had a mighty fascination over him. 'At any time the word *hermit* was enough to transport him.' The words *woods* and *forests* would produce the most powerful emotion." *Foster's Life*, by RYLAND, New York, 1846, p. 3.

3 The Two Voices. In a letter to Mr. B.P. Blood, Tennyson reports of himself as follows: "I have never had any revelations through anaesthetics, but a kind of waking trance—this for lack of a better word—I have frequently had, quite up from boyhood, when I have been all alone. This has come upon me through repeating my own name to myself silently, till all at once, as it were out of the intensity of the consciousness of individuality, individuality itself seemed to dissolve and fade away into boundless being, and this not a confused state but the clearest, the surest of the surest, utterly beyond words—where death was an almost laughable impossibility—the loss of personality (if so it were) seeming no extinction, but the only true life. I am ashamed of my feeble description. Have I not said the state is utterly beyond words?"
Professor Tyndall, in a letter, recalls Tennyson saying of this condition: "By God Almighty! there is no delusion in the matter! It is no nebulous ecstasy, but a state of transcendent wonder, associated with absolute clearness of mind." *Memoirs of Alfred Tennyson*, ii. 473.

4 *The Lancet*, July 6 and 13, 1895, reprinted as the *Cavendish Lecture, on Dreamy Mental States*, London, Bailliere, 1895. They have been a good deal discussed of late by psychologists. See, for example, BERNARD-LEROY: *L'Illusion de Fausse Reconnaissance*, Paris, 1898.

5 Whitman in another place expresses in a quieter way what was probably with him a chronic mystical perception: "There is," he writes, "apart from mere intellect, in the make-up of every superior human identity, a wondrous something that realizes without argument, frequently without what is called education (though I think it the goal and apex of all education deserving the name), an intuition of the absolute balance, in time and space, of the whole of this multifariousness, this revel of fools, and incredible make-believe and general unsettledness, we call *the*

world; a soul-sight of that divine clue and unseen thread which holds the whole congeries of things, all history and time, and all events, however trivial, however momentous, like a leashed dog in the hand of the hunter. [Of] such soul-sight and root-centre for the mind mere optimism explains only the surface."

Whitman charges it against Carlyle that he lacked this perception. *Specimen Days and Collect*, Philadelphia, 1882, p. 174.

6 *My Quest for God*, London, 1897, pp. 268, 269, abridged.

7 Op. cit., pp. 256, 257, abridged.

8 *Cosmic Consciousness: a study in the evolution of the human Mind*, Philadelphia, 1901, p. 2.

9 My quotations are from VIVEKANANDA, *Raja Yoga*, London, 1896. The completest source of information on Yoga is the work translated by VIHARI LALA MITRA: *Yoga Vasishta Maha Ramayana*, 4 vols., Calcutta. 1891–99.

10 A European witness, after carefully comparing the results of Yoga with those of the hypnotic or dreamy states artificially producible by us, says: "It makes of its true disciples good, healthy, and happy men. … Through the mastery which the yogi attains over his thoughts and his body, he grows into a 'character.' By the subjection of his impulses and propensities to his will, and the fixing of the latter upon the ideal of goodness, be becomes a 'personality' hard to influence by others, and thus almost the opposite of what we usually imagine a 'medium' so-called, or 'psychic subject' to be." KARL KELLNER: *Yoga: Eine Skizze*, Munchen, 1896, p. 21.

11 I follow the account in C.F. KOEPPEN: *Die Religion des Buddha*, Berlin, 1857, i. 585 ff.

12 For a full account of him, see D.B. MACDONALD: *The Life of Al-Ghazzali*, in the *Journal of the American Oriental Society*, 1899, vol. xx. p. 71.

13 A. SCHMOLDERS: *Essai sur les ecoles philosophiques chez les Arabes*, Paris, 1842, pp. 54–68, abridged.

14 MULLER'S translation, part ii. p. 180.

15 T. DAVIDSON'S translation, in *Journal of Speculative Philosophy*, 1893, vol. xxii. p. 399.

16 "Deus propter excellentiam non immerito Nihil vocatur." Scotus Erigena, quoted by ANDREW SETH: *Two Lectures on Theism*, New York, 1897, p. 55.

17 I abstract from weaker states, and from those cases of which the books are full, where the director (but usually not the subject) remains in doubt whether the experience may not have proceeded from the demon.

18 Example: Mr. John Nelson writes of his imprisonment for preaching Methodism: "My soul was as a watered garden, and I could sing praises to God all day long; for he turned my captivity into joy, and gave me to rest as well on the boards, as if I had been on a bed of down. Now could I say, 'God's service is perfect freedom,' and I was carried out much in prayer that my enemies might drink of the same river of peace which my God gave so largely to me." *Journal*, London, no date, p. 172.

19 RUYSBROECK, in the work which Maeterlinck has translated, has a chapter against the antinomianism of disciples. H. DELACROIX'S book (*Essai sur le mysticisme speculatif en Allemagne au XIVme Siecle*, Paris, 1900) is full of antinomian material. Compare also A. JUNDT: *Les Amis de Dieu au XIVme Siecle*, These de Strasbourg, 1879.

20 Compare PAUL ROUSSELOT: *Les Mystiques Espagnols*, Paris, 1869, ch. xii.

21 See CARPENTER'S *Towards Democracy*, especially the latter parts, and JEFFERIES'S wonderful and splendid mystic rhapsody, *The Story of my Heart*.

22 In chapter i of book ii of his work *Degeneration*, 'MAX NORDAU' seeks to undermine all mysticism by exposing the weakness of the lower kinds. Mysticism for him means any sudden perception of hidden significance in things. He explains such perception by the abundant uncompleted associations which experiences may arouse in a degenerate brain. These give to him who has the experience a vague and vast sense of its leading further, yet they awaken no definite or useful consequent in his thought. The explanation is a plausible one for certain sorts of feeling of significance; and other alienists (WERNICKE, for example, in his *Grundriss der Psychiatrie*, Theil ii., Leipzig, 1896) have explained 'paranoiac' conditions by a laming of the association-organ. But the higher mystical flights, with their positiveness and abruptness, are surely products of no such merely negative condition. It seems far more reasonable to ascribe them to inroads from the subconscious life, of the cerebral activity correlative to which we as yet know nothing.

23 They sometimes add subjective *audita et visa* to the facts, but as these are usually interpreted as transmundane, they oblige no alteration in the facts of sense.

14 *The Future of an Illusion*

Sigmund Freud

Sigmund Freud (1856–1939) was born in Freiberg, Moravia, in what was then part of the Austrian Empire and is now in the Czech Republic. He is most closely associated with Vienna, fifty miles to the south, where he became a leading intellectual and the founding father of psychoanalysis after having first studied medicine and later taught neuropathology at the University of Vienna. Although more famous for his theories and therapies of psychoanalysis, his perspective on religion was influential and interrelated with his study of neuroses. *Totem and Taboo* (1912–13) employs psychoanalytic insights related to the Oedipus complex to explain the origins of totemism, cultural taboos, and to an extent, religion itself. *Moses and Monotheism* (1939) proposes developments in Judaism and Christianity that reject the assumptions of scholars and theologians in favor of psychoanalytic postulations. However, it was Freud's *The Future of an Illusion* (1927) that most influenced the field. We have included selections from this work including ideas that still resonate today about religion as illusory wish fulfillment that has provided some benefit but ultimately fails to meet scientific standards of authentication. For Freud, clinging to religion's illusions in modern times is diagnosed as a sort of collective neurosis that stunts the development of civilization.

Chapter III

Wherein lies the special value of religious ideas?

We have discussed the hostility toward culture engendered by the pressure culture exerts and the renunciations of drives it demands. If one imagines its prohibitions lifted – thus one may now take any woman one wishes as sexual objects; may without hesitation kill one's rival in love, or anyone else standing in the way; may take anything belonging to another person without asking permission – how marvelous, what a sequence of satisfactions life would be! But one soon discovers the first problem: all others have just the same wishes I do, and will treat me no more gently than I treat them. Essentially, then, if cultural restrictions are abolished, only one person can become unlimitedly happy: a tyrant, a dictator who has seized for himself all the means of power. And even he has every reason to hope others will at least observe the one cultural commandment: "Thou shalt not kill."

But how ungrateful, indeed how short-sighted, to aim to abolish culture! Only a state of nature would remain – harder by far to bear. True, nature would demand of us no restrictions of drives: she would let us do as we pleased. But she has her own highly effective means of constraining us. She kills us – coldly, cruelly, recklessly, it seems to us – and perhaps through the very sources of our satisfaction. Precisely because of these dangers with which we are threatened by nature, we joined together and created culture, which, among other things, is intended to make possible our communal life. Indeed, the chief task of culture, its actual *raison d'être*, is to defend us against nature.

Clearly, culture already does this well enough in many aspects, and will certainly do so much better in the future. But no one is fooled into thinking that nature is already conquered; few dare hope she will ever be completely subject to humankind. There are the elements, which seem to mock all human force; the earth, which quakes and is torn asunder, burying all humanity and its works; water, which floods and drowns everything in a great cataclysm, and storms, which blow away the refuse; there are diseases, only recently recognized as the attacks of other organisms; and finally there is the painful riddle of death, against which no healing herb has yet been discovered nor probably ever will be. With these forces nature rises up against us, magnificent, cruel, inexorable, again showing us our weakness and helplessness, from which we planned to extricate ourselves through the work of culture. One of the few pleasant and uplifting impressions of humanity one can have is presented when, faced with a natural disaster, humanity forgets its cultural disunity – all the internal difficulties and hostilities – and remembers the great communal task: preserving itself against the overwhelming power of nature.

Just as is true for humanity in general, life is hard to bear for the individual. The culture of which one is a member imposes on one a certain degree of privation, and other people, too, create a measure of suffering – despite the precepts of the culture or as a consequence of its imperfection. There are also the injuries inflicted by untamed nature – the individual calls it fate. We would expect the consequence of this situation to be a continuing state of anxious expectation and a heavy blow to innate narcissism. We already know how the individual reacts to the injuries culture and others inflict: by developing a corresponding, measure of resistance to the institutions of the culture – hostility toward it. But how does one defend oneself against the overwhelming forces of nature, of fate, which threaten the individual and all others?

Culture frees one from this task; it performs this task for everyone equally. It is also noteworthy that nearly all cultures do the same in this respect. Culture never ceases to carry out its task of defending humankind against nature, but perpetrates it by other means. The task here is multifaceted. Humankind's seriously threatened self-regard requires solace; the terrors of the world and of life must be eliminated. And human curiosity – albeit driven by the strongest practical interest – wants an answer too.

With the very first step – humanization of nature – much is already attained. Impersonal forces and fates are unapproachable, eternally unfamiliar. But if passions rage in the elements as they do in the human soul; if death itself is nothing arbitrary, but the violent act of an evil will; if nature is filled with beings like those in one's own society, then one can breathe a sigh of relief, then one feels at home in the uncanny and can mentally work through one's senseless anxiety. One may still be defenseless, but is no longer helplessly paralyzed. At least one can react. And perhaps one is not defenseless after all. Against these violent supermen outside, one can apply the same methods used within society. One can try to conjure them up, placate them, bribe them – and through such influence rob them of some of their power. Such a substitution of natural science by psychology not only produces immediate relief, but also shows the way to further mastery of the situation.

Indeed, this situation is nothing new. It has an infantile prototype – is, in fact, only the continuation of that prototype, for one has been in a similar state of helplessness once before: as a small child in relation to one's parent. There was reason to fear them, especially the father, yet one could be sure of his protection against the dangers one knew at the time. Thus it was natural to regard the two situations as similar. Here, too, as in dream life, wishing came into its own. A premonition of death may come over the sleeper, may seek to place him in the grave. But the dreamwork knows how to choose the condition under which even that feared event becomes a wish fulfillment: the dreamer sees himself in an old Etruscan tomb he had climbed down into, happy to satisfy his archaeological interests. Similarly, one does not simply turn the forces of nature into human beings to be associated with as with equals: that would do no justice to the overpowering impression they create. Rather, one gives them the character of a father – turns them into gods. Here one follows not only an infantile prototype, but, as I have sought to demonstrate, a phylogenetic one as well.

As time progresses, humankind first observes the regularity and conformity to law of natural phenomena; thus, the forces of nature lose their human traits. Yet human helplessness remains, and with it the human longing for a father. The gods, too, remain, retaining their threefold task: warding off the terrors of nature, providing reconciliation with the cruelty of fate (particularly as it appears in death), and providing compensation for the sufferings and privations imposed on humankind by cultural, communal life.

Gradually, though, there is a shift of accent in these functions. It is observed that natural forces develop on their own, based on internal necessities. Indeed, the gods are the lords of nature; they have established nature as it is, and can now leave it to its own devices. Only rarely, in so-called miracles, do they intervene, as if to provide assurance that they have given up nothing of their original sphere of power. As for the vicissitudes of fate, an uncomfortable foreboding remains that the perplexity and helplessness of the human race cannot be ameliorated. Here, above all, the gods fail; if they themselves create fate, then one must declare their determinations inscrutable. The most gifted nation of Antiquity begins to grasp that Moira [Fate] stands above the gods and that the gods themselves have their own fates. The more autonomous nature becomes, and the more the gods recede from it, the more earnestly all expectations concentrate on the third function assigned to them and the more morality becomes their actual domain. The task of the gods is now to provide compensation for the inadequacies and hurts of culture, to fix their attention on the sufferings people inflict on one another in their communal life, and to watch over the execution of the precepts of culture, so inadequately observed by humankind. The precepts of culture themselves are ascribed divine origin; they are raised above human society and extended to nature and the universe.

Thus a store of ideas is created, born of the need to make human helplessness bearable, and constructed with the material of recollections of the helplessness of one's own childhood and that of the childhood of the human race. It is clear that these ideas protect humankind in two directions – against the dangers of nature and fate, and against the injuries originating from within human society itself. In summary: life in this world serves a higher purpose – one difficult to guess, but certainly signifying a perfecting of human nature. The spiritual part of humankind, the soul, which through time has so slowly and reluctantly separated itself from the body, is probably seen as the object of this elevation and exaltation. Thus, whatever happens in this world results from the intentions of an intelligence superior to us, which, albeit through ways and detours difficult to follow, ultimately steers everything toward the good – that is, toward a state of affairs pleasant for us. Over each one of us watches a kindly Providence, stern only in strong and ruthless forces of nature. Death itself is no destruction, no return to an inorganic lifeless state, but the start of a new type of existence on the path of higher development. On the other hand, the same moral laws our cultures have established also govern all that occurs in the universe, but they are safeguarded by a supreme judicial authority with incomparably more might and consistency. All good is ultimately rewarded, and all evil punished – if not in this form of life, then in the later existences commencing after death. Thus all the terrors, sufferings, and hardships of life are destined for annihilation. Life after death, which adjoins our earthly life just as the invisible portion of the spectrum adjoins the visible portion, brings all the perfection we may have missed here. And the superior wisdom that governs this progression, the perfect goodness that expresses itself therein, the justice that asserts itself therein – these are the attributes of the divine beings who also created us and the whole universe, or rather, these are the attributes of the one divine being into whom, in our culture, all the ancient gods have been subsumed. The people that first succeeded in this concentration of the divine attributes were not a little proud of this advance. It had exposed the paternal core that had always been hidden behind every divine figure. Essentially, this was a return to the historical beginnings of the idea of God. Now that God was a single individual, relations toward him could regain the intimacy and intensity of the child's relationship to the father. But having done so much for the father, one also wanted to be rewarded, or at least to be the only beloved child, the chosen people. Very much later, pious America claims to be "God's own country," and for one form in which humanity worships the deity, this is certainly correct. The religious ideas reviewed above have of course undergone a long development and have been adopted by various cultures at various phases. From these phases, I have selected just one, which more or less corresponds to the final form in our contemporary white Christian culture. One can easily see that not all the parts of this whole accord equally well with the others, that not all the urgent questions receive an answer, and that the contradiction supplied by daily experience can be dismissed only with difficulty. But such as they are, these ideas – broadly speaking, religious ones – are deemed the most precious possession of culture, as the most valuable thing it has to offer its members, far more valued than any skill in winning treasure from the earth, in providing humankind with sustenance, or in preventing disease, etc. People believe they could not bear life if they did not attribute to these ideas the value claimed for them. And now we must ask: what are these ideas in the light of psychology? What is the source of their high regard? And, to continue timidly, what is their true worth?

Chapter IV

An investigation that proceeds uninterrupted, like a monologue, is not completely free of danger. One may too easily yield to the temptation to push aside thoughts that seek to interrupt, and end up instead with a feeling of uncertainty, which in the end one tries to overpower through excessive assertiveness. I will therefore imagine an opponent who attends to my arguments with mistrust; here and there I will let him express himself.

I hear him saying: *"You have repeatedly used the formulation 'culture creates these religious ideas,' 'culture places them at the disposal of its members.' Something about this strikes me as strange. I cannot even say why, but that does not sound as obvious as saying that culture has created regulations for the distribution of the products of labor, or concerning rights over wife and child."*

Nevertheless, I think I am justified in expressing myself that way. I have attempted to show that religious ideas have proceeded from the same need as all other cultural achievements: from the need to defend oneself against the crushing, overwhelming force of nature. There was also a second motive – the urge to correct the painfully felt imperfections of culture. Furthermore, it is especially accurate to say that culture gives the individual these ideas, for one finds them already available; they are presented complete, and one would not be in a position to find them independently. It is the heritage of many generations that one is entering, and which one absorbs just like the multiplication table, geometry, etc. There is admittedly a difference here, but it lies elsewhere and cannot yet be clarified. The feeling of strangeness you mention may arise in part from the fact that we are usually presented with this store of religious ideas as a divine revelation. But that in itself is already part of the religious system, and entirely disregards the known historical development of these ideas and their differences at different times and in different cultures.

"*Another point, which strikes me as more important. You would have it that the humanization of nature proceeds from the need to put an end to human perplexity and helplessness in the face of nature's dreaded forces, to enter into a relation which them, and ultimately to influence them. But such a motive seems superfluous. Clearly primitive man has no choice, no other way of thinking. It is natural for him, as if innate, to project his existence into the universe and to regard all the processes he observes as the expressions of beings basically like himself. That is the only method of understanding at his disposal. And it is by no means an obvious outcome, but rather a remarkable coincidence, if he succeeds in satisfying one of his great needs by thus giving free rein to his natural inclinations.*"

I do not find that so remarkable. Do you think human thought has no practical motives – is merely the expression of a disinterested curiosity? That is highly unlikely, I believe, rather, that humankind, even when personifying the forces of nature, follows an infantile prototype. Humans learned from the persons in their earliest surroundings that the way to influence them is to establish a relationship with them; and therefore, with the same intent, they later treat everything else they encounter just as they treated those persons. Thus I am not contradicting your descriptive observation; it is really natural for humans to personify everything they want to understand so as to control it later – mental mastery as preparation for physical mastery – but I also provide a motive and a genesis for this peculiar trait of human thought.

"*And now a third point. You have previously discussed the origin of religion, in your book* Totem and Taboo *[1913].*[1] *But there things look different. Everything is the son–father relationship; God is the exalted father; longing for the father is the root of the need for religion. Since then, you seem to have discovered the factor of human weakness and helplessness, to which, it is true, the greatest role in the formation of religion is generally ascribed, and now you transfer everything that was previously the father complex to helplessness. May I ask you to clarify this change?*"

I shall be glad to reply; I was only waiting for the invitation. If it really is a change. In *Totem and Taboo* it was not the intention to explain the origin of religions, but only that of totemism. Can you, from any standpoint you know of, explain the fact that the first form in which the protecting deity revealed itself to humankind was that of an animal, that there was a prohibition on killing and eating that animal, and that even so it was the ceremonial custom to kill and eat it communally once a year? This is exactly what occurs in totemism. And it is certainly not helpful to argue whether totemism should be designated as a religion. It is intimately connected with later god-religions. The totem animals become the sacred animals of the gods; the earliest, but most profound moral restrictions – those on murder and incest – arise from totemism. Whether or not you agree with the conclusions of *Totem and Taboo*, I hope you will admit that in that volume several highly remarkable and disparate facts are brought together as a consistent whole.

Why the animal god did not suffice in the long run, and was replaced by a human one – that was hardly touched on in *Totem and Taboo*; other problems in the formation of religion are not even mentioned there. Do you feel that such a limitation is identical to a denial? My work is a good example of the strict isolation of the contribution psychoanalytic observation can make in solving the problem of religion. If I now seek to add the other, less deeply hidden part, you should not accuse me of contradiction, as you previously accused me of one-sidedness. It is of course, my task to point out the connections between what I said earlier and what I am asserting now, between the deeper and the manifest motivation, between the father complex and human helplessness and the need for protection.

These connections are not hard to find. These are the relations of the child's helplessness to the helplessness of the adult, which continues that of the child such that, as we might expect, the psychoanalytic motivation for the formation of religion is clearly the infantile contribution to its manifest motivation. Let us transport ourselves into the mental life of the young child. You probably remember the choice of object in the *dependent* type that psychoanalysis speaks of. The libido follows the paths of the narcissistic needs and clings to the objects that ensure their satisfaction. Thus the mother, who satisfies the child's hunger, becomes the first love-object and certainly the first protection against all the vague, threatening dangers of the external world as well – the first protection against anxiety, we can say.

In this function, the mother is soon replaced by the stronger father; this function remains his for the duration of childhood. But the child's relation to the father is marked by a peculiar ambivalence. The father himself is a danger, perhaps due to the child's earlier relation to the mother. Thus one fears him no less than one longs for him and admires him. The signs of this ambivalence in the relation to the father are deeply imprinted in all religions, as demonstrated in *Totem and Taboo*. As one grows up, one finds that it is one's lot to remain always a child, and that one can never manage without protection from strange, superior powers; one then lends these the features of the father figure; one creates for oneself the gods – whom one fears, whose favor one seeks to gain, and yet whom one assigns the task of protection. Thus the motive of longing for a father is identical to the need for protection from the consequences of human powerlessness. The defense against helplessness in childhood lends its characteristic features to the reaction to the helplessness the adult must acknowledge; this reaction is the formation of religion. But I do not intend to investigate further the development of the god-idea; here, we are concerned with the complete store of religious ideas as transmitted by culture to the individual.

Chapter V

And now we take up again the thread of our investigation: what, then, is the psychological significance of religious ideas and in what category shall we classify them? Initially, the question is not at all easy to answer. After eliminating various formulations, we will stand by just one: religious ideas are teachings and pronouncements about facts and states of external (or internal) reality that convey something one has not discovered for oneself and which assert the right to be believed. Since they provide information on what is most important and interesting for us in life, they are especially highly valued. Those who know nothing of them are very ignorant; those who have taken them up in their store of knowledge can consider themselves much enriched.

There are, of course, many such teachings about a diverse range of things in this world. Every class at school is full of them. Let us take the geography class. There, we hear that Konstanz lies on the Bodensee. A student song adds: "If you don't believe it, go and see." I have been there, by chance, and can confirm that this beautiful city does lie on the shore of a wide body of water known by all who live around it as the Bodensee. Indeed, I am now fully convinced of the correctness of this geographical claim. In this connection I recall another, quite peculiar experience. I was already a grown man when I first stood on the hill of the Athenian Acropolis, among the temple ruins, with my gaze on the blue sea. Into my contentment there entered a feeling of amazement that brought forth the thought: "So it's really just as we learned at school!" What a shallow and feeble belief I must have acquired in the real truth of what I heard there, if I could be so amazed that day! But I do not want to overemphasize the significance of that experience. There is another possible explanation for my amazement; it did not occur to me at the time and is thoroughly subjective, relating to the special character of the place.

Thus, all such teachings demand belief in their content, but not without justifying their claim of authority. They present themselves as the summarized result of a lengthy thought process based on observation and clearly also on inference. To anyone with the intention of going through this process independently, rather than accepting its result, they show the way. Further, the source of the knowledge proclaimed by the teaching is always added when that source is not as obvious as it is with geographical claims. For instance, the earth is spherical; as proofs of this claim one adduces Foucault's pendulum experiment, the behavior of the horizon, and the possibility of circumnavigating the earth. Since, as all involved realize, it is impracticable to send all schoolchildren on voyages around the world, one is content to let school learning be accepted on "faith and belief", but for those who wish to convince themselves personally, we know that the path remains open.

Let us measure religious doctrines with the same ruler. If we ask the basis for their claim that they must be believed, we receive three answers, and these show a remarkably poor mutual accord. First, these doctrines deserve belief because our forefathers already believed in them; second, we have proofs that have been passed down to us from those early times; and third, it is forbidden to question their authority in the first place. Any such attempt was formerly met with the harshest punishments, and even today society regards it with disapproval, should anyone raise the question again.

This third point must provoke our strongest reservations. Indeed, such a prohibition can only have one motivation: society understands perfectly well the insecurity of the claim it makes for its religious doctrines. Otherwise it would certainly be very willing to provide the necessary data to those desiring to find conviction on their own. Thus, with a feeling of mistrust not easily assuaged, we shall proceed to an examination of the two other arguments. We ought to believe because our forefathers believed. But those ancestors of ours were far more ignorant than we, and believed in things we could not possibly accept today. The possibility arises that religious doctrines, too, could fall in that category. The proofs our ancestors have left us are set down in writings that themselves bear every characteristic of unreliability. They are full of contradictions; they are reworked and falsified, and, where they report actual confirmations, are themselves unconfirmed. It does not help much when divine revelation is claimed as the source of their wording, or indeed merely of their content, for this claim is itself among the doctrines whose reliability is being investigated. Obviously, no pronouncement can prove itself.

Thus we reach the remarkable finding that precisely those communications from our store of cultural assets that could be the most significant for us, those assigned the task of solving the riddles of the universe and of reconciling us with the sufferings of life – precisely these have the very weakest confirmation. If it could not be better proven, we would never accept such an indifferent matter as the fact that whales bear young rather than laying eggs.

This state of affairs is in itself a very remarkable psychological problem. And no one should think the preceding comments on the impossibility of verifying religious doctrines hold anything new. This impossibility has been sensed at all times – and certainly also by those ancestors who left us this legacy. Many of them probably harbored the same doubts we do, but the pressure exerted on them was so great that they dared not express them. And since then countless people have tormented themselves with just the same doubts, which they wanted to suppress because they felt obliged to believe; many shining intellects have broken down over this conflict, and many people's characters have suffered damage through the compromises in which they sought a solution.

If all the evidence presented for the credibility of religious teachings stems from the past, the next step is to look around and see whether the present, which we can better evaluate, can also provide such evidence. If in this way we could free just one element of the religious system from doubt, the whole system would gain enormously in credibility. Here the activities of the spiritists are of interest; they are convinced of the continued existence of the individual soul, and seek to prove this one point of religious doctrine beyond all doubt. Unfortunately they cannot prove that the appearances and utterances of the spirits they invoke are not merely the products of their own mental activity. They have summoned up the spirits of the greatest individuals, of the most eminent thinkers, but all the utterances and messages received from them have been so inane, so hopelessly devoid of sense, that the only credible thing one notes is the spirits' ability to adapt themselves to the circle of people conjuring them up.

One must now recall two attempts that seem like desperate efforts to evade the problem. One of these, violent in nature, is ancient; the other is subtle and modern. The first is the *credo quia absurdum* [I believe because it is absurd] of the early Church Fathers. It seeks to assert that religious doctrines are outside the realm of reason – above reason. One must sense their truth within oneself; one need not understand them. But this *credo* is of interest only as a personal confession; as a claim to authority it is not binding. Shall I be obliged to believe every absurdity? And if not, why this particular one? There is no higher court than the court of reason. If the truth of religious doctrines depends on an inner experience attesting to that truth, what shall one do with the many people who have not had that rare experience? One can require of all people that they apply the gift of reason they possess, but one cannot, on the basis of a motive existing only for a very few, set up an obligation for all. If one person, based on a state of ecstasy experienced as deeply moving, has gained an unshakable conviction in the real truth of religious doctrines, how is that significant for others?

The second attempt is that of the philosophy of "as if." This argument claims that in our mental activity there are a great number of assumptions whose baselessness and even absurdity we fully realize. These are called fictions, but given various practical reasons, it is claimed that we must act "as if" we believed in them. This is said to be the case with religious doctrines because of their incomparable importance for maintaining human society. This argument is not far removed from the *credo quia absurdum*. But I think the demand made by this "as if" could only be made by a philosopher. A person whose thinking is uninfluenced by the artifice of philosophy will never be able to accept it: for such a person, the admission of absurdity, of being contrary to reason, puts the matter to rest. Precisely in handling one's most important interests, one cannot be expected to renounce the certainties one demands for all one's normal activities. This reminds me of one of my children, who was characterized at a young age by his high regard for accordance with reality. When the children were being told a story and were listening with fixed attention, he would come up and ask: "Is that a true story?" On hearing that it was not, he would leave with an expression of disdain. It is only to be expected that people will soon treat the tales of religion in a similar way, despite any support expressed for "as if."[2]

But now they still behave in a different manner entirely; in the past, too, religious ideas, despite their obvious lack of confirmation, have had the very strongest influence on humankind. That is a new psychological problem. The question arises: Wherein lies the inner force of these doctrines and to what do they owe their effectiveness, which has no need for approval by reason?

Chapter VI

I think we have made sufficient preparation for an answer to both questions. The answer will be found if we regard the mental origin of religious ideas. These, promulgated as doctrines, are not residues of experience or final results of thought. They are illusions – fulfillments of the oldest, strongest and most fervent wishes of humanity. The secret of their strength is in the strength of those wishes. We already know that the frightening impression of helplessness in childhood awakened the need for protection – protection through love – once provided by the father; and the realization that this helplessness will continue throughout. One's entire life necessitated clinging to the existence of a father albeit now a more powerful one. Through the kind rule of divine Providence, anxiety over the dangers of life is assuaged; the introduction of a moral world order ensures the fulfillment of the demand for justice, so often unmet in human society. The extension of earthly existence through a future life provides the framework in space and time within which these wish fulfillments are to occur. Answers to the riddles posed by human curiosity, such as those asking about the origin of the universe or the relation between body and mind, are developed corresponding to the underlying assumptions of this system. It is a great relief for the individual psyche if the childhood conflicts arising from the father complex – conflicts never fully surmounted – are taken from the psyche and given a solution acceptable to all.

In saying that all those things are illusions, I must narrow down the meaning of the word. An illusion is not identical to an error, and is not necessarily an error. Aristotle's belief that vermin spontaneously generate from filth (a belief uneducated people still retain today) was an error, as was the belief among a former generation of physicians that *tabes dorsalis* results from sexual excess. It would be wrong to call these errors illusions. On the other hand Columbus's belief that he had discovered a new sea route to India was an illusion. In this error, the part played by his wish is very clear. One may designate as an illusion the claim of certain nationalists that the Indo-European peoples constitute the only race capable of culture, or the belief, demolished only by psychoanalysis, that the child is a being without sexuality. For illusions, the characteristic aspect remains their derivation from human wishes. In this respect they resemble psychiatric delusions, but they differ from them too – even disregarding the more complex framework of delusions. In delusions, we emphasize as the essential thing their contradiction to reality. Illusions, though, need not necessarily be false, i.e., unrealizable or in contradiction to reality. For instance, a bourgeois girl may have the illusion that a prince will come to carry her off to his home as his bride. This is possible, and cases of this sort have occurred. That the Messiah will come and establish a golden age is much less likely; based on one's personal orientation, one will classify this belief as an illusion or as analogous to a delusion. In any case, examples of illusions that have turned out to be true are not easy to find, but the illusion of alchemists that metals could be transformed into gold might be such a case. The wish to have a large amount of gold, as much as possible, has been significantly dampened by our contemporary insights into the conditioning factors of wealth, but chemistry no longer regards the transformation of metals into gold as impossible. Thus we call a belief an illusion when wish fulfillment is prominent in its motivation; in doing so we disregard its relation to reality, just as the illusion itself abjures confirmations.

Having now completed this orientation, we can turn once again to religious doctrines. We can now reiterate: all of them are illusions – indemonstrable – and no one can be forced to hold them true, to believe in them. Some of them are so unlikely, so very much in contradiction with everything we have laboriously learned about the reality of the world, that one may – with appropriate consideration of the psychological differences – compare them to delusions. As to the reality value of most of them, one can make no judgment. Just as they are indemonstrable, they are likewise irrefutable. We still know too little to approach them critically. Only slowly do the riddles of the universe unveil themselves to our investigations; for many questions, science still cannot provide answers today. But scientific work is the only path that can lead us to knowledge of reality outside ourselves. Again, it is merely illusion to expect anything from intuition and introspection; these can only give us information about our own mental life – information difficult to interpret – never information about the questions that religious doctrine answers so effortlessly. It would be criminal to let one's own arbitrary opinion enter the void and, according to one's own personal estimation, to declare one aspect or another of the religious system more acceptable or less so. For such an approach, these questions are too significant – one might even say too sacred.

Here, one must be prepared for an objection, *"So, if even dogged skeptics admit that the claims of religion cannot be refuted by reason, why shouldn't I believe in them, since so much speaks for them: tradition, agreement among people, and the comforting nature of their content?"* Indeed, why not? Just as no one can be forced to believe, no one can be forced to disbelieve. But we should not deceive ourselves into thinking that with such justifications we are treading on the paths of correct thought. If the term "weak excuse," was ever appropriate, it certainly is here. Ignorance is ignorance; no right to believe derives from it. In other matters, sensible persons will never behave so carelessly or be satisfied with such feeble justifications for their opinions or the side they choose. Only in the highest and most sacred matters does one permit oneself such behavior. These are really just efforts to pretend to oneself or others that one still holds firmly to religion when one has long since become free of it. When questions of religion are involved people commit every possible sort of insincerity and intellectual sloppiness. Philosophers overextend the meaning of words until they contain hardly anything of their original sense. They designate as "God" some hazy abstraction they have created for themselves; then, before all the world, they are deists, believers in God, and they can even boast that they have perceived a higher, purer notion of God, though their God is now only an insubstantial shadow, no longer the powerful personality of religious doctrine. Critics continue to describe as "deeply religious" anyone who has admitted to a feeling of man's smallness and powerlessness within the scope of the universe. Yet it is not this feeling that constitutes the essence of religiosity. Rather, it is the next step – the reaction to this feeling, which seeks a remedy for it. The person who goes no further, who humbly accepts the minimal part humans play in the universe, is actually irreligious in the truest sense of the word.

Stating a position on the truth value of religious doctrines is not within the plan of this investigation. For us, it suffices that we have recognized them, in their psychological nature, as illusions. But we need not conceal the fact that this finding also has a powerful influence on our attitude to the question many people surely see as the most important. We know approximately at what times religious doctrines were created, and by what sorts of people. If we also discover the motives underlying this creation, our stance toward the problem of religion will undergo a marked shift. We tell ourselves that it would be very nice if there were a God – creator of the world and kindly Providence – if there were a moral world order and a life in the hereafter, but it is quite obvious that all of this is just as we would wish. And it would be even more remarkable if our poor, ignorant, unfree ancestors had succeeded in finding the solution to all these difficult riddles of the universe.

... Chapter X

"That really sounds marvelous! A human race that has renounced all illusions and has thereby become capable of making life on earth bearable for itself! However, I cannot share your expectations. Not because I am the stubborn reactionary you may take me for. No, because of my prudence. It seems to me that we have now switched roles: you prove to be the enthusiast, who allows himself to be carried away by illusions, and I argue for the claims of reason, the right of skepticism. What you have been explicating here seems to me to be constructed on the basis of errors which, given your example, I may be permitted to call illusions, for they reveal clearly enough the influence of your wishes. You place your hopes on a scenario in which generations uninfluenced by religious doctrines in early childhood will easily achieve the longed-for primacy of intelligence over the life of drives. Surely that is an illusion: in this decisive point, human nature is not likely to change. Unless I am mistaken – one knows so little about other cultures – there are people even today that do not grow up under the pressure of a religious system, but these come no closer to your ideal than do other groups. If you want to eliminate religion in our European culture, that can only be done through another system of doctrines, and from the very start, in its own defense, that system would take on all the psychological characteristics of religion, the same sanctity, inflexibility, intolerance, and the same prohibition of thought. You must have something like this to satisfy the requirements of education. In any case you cannot do without education. The path from the infant to the civilized person is long; too many children would lose their way, failing to fulfill their life's tasks in a timely manner if left, unguided, to their own development. The doctrines applied in their education will always limit their thinking at an older age – just as you accuse religion of doing today. Do you not see that; it is the indelible inborn defect of our culture and every culture that it compels the child, dominated by drives and weak in intellect, to make decisions which only the mature intelligence of the adult can justify? But our culture cannot do otherwise, given the compression into a few childhood years of humanity's development through the ages, and only through affective forces can children be made to deal with the task assigned them. Such, then, are the prospects for your 'primacy of the intellect.'

"Now you should not be surprised if I argue for the retention of the religious system of instruction as the basis of education and of human communal life. This is a practical problem, not a question of reality value. Since, in the interest of preserving our culture, we cannot wait to influence individuals until they have become culturally mature (and many would never achieve that anyway), and since we must impose on growing children some system of doctrines intended to function in them as basic tenets beyond criticism, the religious system seems to me the most suitable for that purpose by far. Precisely, of course, due to its wishfulfilling and consoling power, in which you claim to have recognized the 'illusion.' In view of the difficulties involved in learning anything about reality – indeed, given doubts as to whether we can even do so – we must not overlook the fact that human needs are also part of reality, an important part indeed, and one that especially concerns us.

"I see another advantage of religious doctrine in one of its characteristics which you seem to find particularly offensive. It permits a conceptual purification and sublimation through which most aspects evincing the traces of primitive and infantile thinking can be wiped away. What then remains a store of ideas science no longer contradicts and cannot disprove. Such restructurings of religious doctrine, which you have condemned as half-measures and compromises, make it possible to avoid the rift between the uneducated mass and the philosophical thinker; they preserve the commonality between them that is so important for the defense of culture. Accordingly, there would be no fear that the man of the people will find out that the upper strata of society 'no longer believe in God.' Now I think I have shown that your efforts are merely an attempt to replace a well-tested and affectively valuable illusion by another one, untested and indifferent."

I hope you will not think I am unreceptive to your criticism. I know how hard it is to avoid illusions; maybe the hopes I have confessed are also illusory. But I insist on one difference. My illusions – beyond the fact that there is no punishment for not sharing them – are not uncorrectable, as are those of religion; they do not possess a delusional character. If experience shows – not to me, but to others after me who think as I do – that we have erred, we will renounce our expectations. Just take my attempt for what it is. A psychologist who does not deceive himself about how hard it is to find one's way in this world is striving to assess the development of humankind in accordance with the small insights he has gained through a study of mental processes in the individual during development from child to adult. While he is thus engaged, the idea imposes itself upon him that religion is like a childhood neurosis, and he is optimistic enough to assume that humankind will overcome this neurotic phase, just as so many children outgrow their similar neurosis. These insights from individual psychology may be inadequate, their extension to the human race unjustified, the noted optimism unfounded; I admit all these uncertainties. But often it is impossible to refrain from speaking one's mind – with the excuse that one is not presenting one's thoughts as anything more than they are worth.

And there are two points I must still dwell on. First: the weakness of my position does not signify any strengthening of yours. I think you are defending a lost cause. We may repeatedly emphasize that the human intellect is powerless compared to human drives, and we may be correct in doing so. But there is something special about this weakness; the voice of the intellect is soft, but it does not rest until it is heard. In the end, after countless rejections, it does find a hearing. This is one of the few points where one may be optimistic about the future of humankind, but in itself the point is not insignificant. To it still more hopes can be connected. The primacy of the intellect certainly lies far, far ahead, but probably not infinitely far. The intellect will presumably choose the same goals whose realization you expect from your god – a realization reduced to a human scale, of course, to the extent that external reality, *Ananke* [Necessity], permits; these goals are human love and the limitation of suffering. We may therefore tell ourselves that our mutual opposition is only temporary, not irreconcilable. We hope for the same things, but you are more impatient, more ambitious, and – why should I not say it? – more self-serving than I and those who think as I do. You want a state of bliss to begin immediately after death; you demand the impossible of that blissful state, and will not give up the claims of the individual. Of those wishes, our God *Lógos* [Reason][3] will fulfill what nature outside us permits but very gradually, only in the unforeseeable future, and for new human generations. He does not promise any compensation for us, who suffer greatly from life. On the way to this distant goal your religious doctrines will have to be dropped, even if the first attempts fail, even if the first substitute constructs prove unfounded. You know why: in the long run nothing can withstand reason and experience, and religion's contradiction to both is all too tangible. Even reformed religious ideas cannot escape this fate so long as they seek to salvage a portion of the consolatory content of religion. Indeed, if they restrict themselves to proclaiming a higher spiritual being whose qualities are indeterminable, whose intentions are indiscernible, they will be safe from the objections of science, but then they will also be abandoned by human interest.

And second: notice the difference between your attitude to illusion and mine. You must define the religious illusion with all your might. If it becomes discredited – and it is certainly under significant threat – then your world collapses; your only alternative is to despair of everything of culture and the future of humankind. From such serfdom I am, we are, free. Since we are prepared to renounce a good part of our infantile wishes, we can endure it if some of our expectations prove to be illusions.

Perhaps education freed from the pressure of religious doctrines will not change human psychology to any great extent. Our god *Lógos* is perhaps not particularly almighty, and can only fulfill a small part of what his predecessors promised. If we must face up to this, we will accept it with resignation. We will not, for all that, lose our interest in the world and in life: in one area we have solid ground which you lack. We believe it is possible for scientific work to learn something about the reality of the world; through such knowledge we will be able to increase our power and in accord with it we will be able to arrange our life. If this belief is an illusion, then we are in the same position as you are, but through its numerous and significant successes science has given us proof that it is no illusion. Science has many open enemies and even more hidden ones among those who cannot forgive her for having weakened religious faith and for her threat to overthrow it. People reproach her for how little she has taught us and for the incomparably greater amount she has left in darkness. But in doing so, they forget how young she is, how difficult were her beginnings, and how infinitesimally short has been the period of time since the human intellect has had the strength for scientific tasks. Are we not all wrong to base our judgments on excessively brief periods of time? We should take geologists as our example. People complain about the uncertainty of science – how she announces as a law today what the next generation recognizes as erroneous and replaces with a new law considered valid just as briefly. But this is unfair and in part untrue. The transformations of scientific opinion are developments, progress – not overthrow of the old order. A law initially taken as valid without limitation proves to be a special case of a more general regularity or is limited by another law, undiscovered until later; a rough approximation of the truth is replaced by a more meticulously adapted one, which in turn awaits further steps toward perfection. In various fields, science has not yet advanced beyond a phase of research in which hypotheses are tested that soon must be rejected as inadequate; in other fields, there is already an assured and nearly unchangeable core of knowledge. Finally an attempt has been made to radically devalue scientific endeavor based on the judgment that such an endeavor, bound to the conditions of our own organization, can produce only subjective results, while the real nature of things outside us remains inaccessible to it. Here, several factors crucial for understanding scientific work are being ignored. 1) Our organization – i.e., our mental apparatus – evolved precisely in the attempt to gain knowledge of the external world, and must accordingly have realized in its structure a certain amount of expediency. 2) It is itself a component of the very world we seek to investigate, and readily allows such investigation. 3) The task of science is fully described if we limit it to showing how the world must appear to us, given the particulars of our organization. 4) The final results of science, precisely because of how they are acquired, are determined not only by our organization but by what has affected that organization. 5) The problem of the nature of the world, approached without considering our mental apparatus engaged in perception, is an empty abstraction, without practical interest.

No, our science is no illusion. But an illusion it would be to think we can get elsewhere what science cannot give us.

QUESTIONS FOR REVIEW AND DISCUSSION

1. How does Freud connect the origins of religion with human needs to "defend oneself against the overwhelming forces of nature"? What is the role of the "humanization of nature"?

2. Freud indicates that attempts to placate and bribe natural forces continue an "infantile prototype" of relationship within a family. What is this prototype and how does it work according to Freud?

3. What kinds of evidence does Freud appeal to in his argument? What do you think of the style of his approach or the substance of his conclusions?

4. In chapter IV, Freud poses as a critic to raise and then respond to three points. How does Freud defend his assertion that "religious ideas have proceeded from the same need as all other cultural achievements"? Do you agree?

5. In your own words, what are the other two points that Freud presents as critiques? What is his response to each? Is this rhetorical device effective?

6. What answer does Freud supply to his own question at the beginning of section VI? That is, "What, then, is the psychological significance of religious ideas and in what category shall we classify them?"

7. Freud expresses reservations about the basis for belief in religious claims. Paraphrase the three answers that Freud indicates are given to justify belief and his objections to each.

8. Freud objects most strongly to the claim about religious doctrines that "it is forbidden to question their authority in the first place." Do you see similar concerns expressed by other authors in this volume?

9. How does Freud differentiate "illusion" from "error" and from "delusion"? Religious doctrines best fit which of these categories according to Freud? Do you agree?

10. How does Freud answer the "dogged skeptics [who] admit that the claims of religion cannot be refuted by reason" but ask why not believe in them anyway "since so much speaks for them: tradition, agreement among people, and the comforting nature of their content?"

11. Freud acknowledges that some of his ideas may be illusions that are later shown to be errors, but he indicates that his claims can be corrected and therefore are not delusional. How does this contrast with his assessment of religious claims? Does he seem confident that reason, intellect, and experience will prevail over religious claims that cannot be substantiated? Why? Do you agree?

Notes

1 Sigmund Freud, 1913, *Totem and Taboo*; Trans. by A. A. Brill, New York: Moffat, Yard & Co., 1918; Bartleby.com, 2010.

2 I hope I am committing no injustice in letting the philosopher of "as if" represent a view which is not unfamiliar to other thinkers: "We include in the group of fictions not only indifferent theoretical operations but also conceptions created by the noblest minds, to which the heart of the nobler part of mankind clings and which mankind will not allow to be taken away. And this we certainly do not wish to do. We will allow all that to remain as *practical fiction*, but it perishes as *theoretical truth*" (Hans Vaihinger, 1922: 68). [Freud's note, it appears in Freud's original at the end of the fourth sentence of this paragraph.]

3 The paired gods Lógos [Reason] and Anánke [Necessity] of the Dutch writer Multatuli (1862). [Freud's note. Multatuli was the *nom de plume* of Eduard Douwes Dekker (1820–87), a Dutch author, satirist, and philosopher best known for his anti-colonial novel *Max Havelaar* (1860).]

15 The Analysis of 'Mysterium'

Rudolph Otto

Rudolph Otto (1869–1937) was born near Hanover, Germany, in the village of Peine in what was Prussia at that time. He was trained and taught in theology at several universities, including the University of Marburg's Divinity school, where he served as professor. The following selection is chapter 5 in Otto's famous 1915 work, *Das Heilige* (we excerpt here from its 1923 translation, *The Idea of the Holy*). Unlike social scientific attempts to explain (or even explain away) religion, Otto declared it uniquely irreducible and characterized by a feeling of mystery, awe, terror, and fascination. In *The Idea of the Holy* Otto warns that those who have not had a "deeply-felt religious experience" should "read no farther." In other words, there is an essence of religion accessible to some but beyond the grasp of others. This division hinges on experience and is not a matter that can be settled by scholarship and rational argument alone. Otto's claims reflect his theological training but also exert influence on phenomenological approaches. The line between approaches is blurred in a figure such as Otto. In fact, he wrote doctoral theses on both Martin Luther and Immanuel Kant. Although his Christian theological training remains clearly evident, Otto travelled extensively, studied multiple languages and traditions, and engaged in comparative religion with wide-ranging examples focused on religious experience in an effort to understand religion as a whole.

> *Ein begriffener Gott ist kein Gott.*
> "A God comprehended is no God."
>
> (Tersteegen)

We gave to the object to which the numinous consciousness is directed the name *mysterium tremendum*, and we then set ourselves first to determine the meaning of the adjective *tremendum*—which we found to be itself only justified by analogy—because it is more easily analysed than the substantive idea *mysterium*. We have now to turn to this, and try, as best we may, by hint and suggestion, to get to a clearer apprehension of what it implies.

The "Wholly Other"

It might be thought that the adjective itself gives an explanation of the substantive; but this is not so. It is not merely analytical; it is a synthetic attribute to it; i.e. *tremendum* adds something not necessarily inherent in *mysterium*. It is true that the reactions in consciousness that correspond to the one readily and spontaneously overflow into those that correspond to the other; in fact, anyone sensitive to the use of words would commonly feel that the idea of "mystery" (*mysterium*) is so closely bound up with its synthetic qualifying attribute "aweful" (*tremendum*) that one can hardly say the former without catching an echo of the latter, "mystery" almost of itself becoming "aweful mystery" to us. But the passage from the one idea to the other need not by any means be always so easy. The elements of meaning implied in "awefulness" and "mysteriousness" are in themselves definitely differ-ent. The latter may so far preponderate in the religious consciousness, may stand out so vividly, that in comparison with it the former almost sinks out of sight; a case which again could be clearly exemplified from some forms of mysticism. Occasionally, on the other hand, the reverse happens, and the *tremendum* may in turn occupy the mind without the *mysterium*.

This latter, then, needs special consideration on its own account. We need an expression for the mental reaction peculiar to it; and here, too, only one word seems appropriate, though, as it is strictly applicable only to a "natural" state of mind, it has here meaning only by analogy: it is the word "stupor". *Stupor* is plainly a different thing from *tremor;* it signifies blank wonder, an astonishment that strikes us dumb, amazement absolute. Taken, indeed, in its purely natural sense, *mysterium* would first mean merely a secret or a mystery in the sense of that which is alien to us, uncomprehended and unexplained; and so far *mysterium* is itself merely an ideogram, an analogical notion taken from the natural sphere, illustrating, but incapable of exhaustively rendering, our real meaning. Taken in the religious sense, that which is "mysterious" is—to give it perhaps the most striking expression—the "wholly other" (Θάτερον, *anyad, alienum*) that which is quite beyond the sphere of the usual, the intelligible, and the familiar, which therefore falls quite outside the limits of the "canny", and is contrasted with it, filling the mind with blank wonder and astonishment.

This is already to be observed on the lowest and earliest level of the religion of primitive man, where the numinous consciousness is but an inchoate stirring of the feelings. What is really characteristic of this stage is *not*—as the theory of Animism would have us believe—that men are here concerned with curious entities, called "souls" or "spirits", which happen to be invisible. Representations of spirits and similar conceptions are rather one and all early modes of "rationalizing" a precedent experience, to which they are subsidiary. They are attempts in some way or other, it little matters how, to guess the riddle it propounds, and their effect is at the same time always to weaken and deaden the experience itself. They are the source from which springs, not religion, but the rationalization of religion, which often ends by constructing such a massive structure of theory and such a plausible fabric of interpretation, that the "mystery" is frankly excluded.[1] Both imaginative "myth", when developed into a system, and intellectualist Scholasticism, when worked out to its completion, are methods by which the fundamental fact of religious experience is, as it were, simply rolled out so thin and flat as to be finally eliminated altogether.

Even on the lowest level of religious development the essential characteristic is therefore to be sought elsewhere than in the appearance of "spirit" representations. It lies rather, we repeat, in a peculiar "moment" of consciousness, to wit, the *stupor* before something "wholly other", whether such an other be named "spirit" or "daemon" or "deva", or be left without any name. Nor does it make any difference in this respect whether, to interpret and pre-serve their apprehension of this "other", men coin original imagery of their own or adapt imaginations drawn from the world of legend, the fabrications of fancy apart from and prior to any stirrings of daemonic dread.

In accordance with laws of which we shall have to speak again later, this feeling or con-sciousness of the "wholly other" will attach itself to, or sometimes be indirectly aroused by means of, objects which are already puzzling upon the "natural" plane, or are of a surprising or astounding character; such as extraordinary phenomena or astonishing occurrences or things in inanimate nature, in the animal world, or among men. But here once more we are dealing with a case of association between things specifically different— the "numinous" and the "natural" moments of consciousness—and not merely with the gradual enhancement of one of them—the "natural"—till it becomes the other. As in the case of "natural fear" and "daemonic dread" already considered, so here the transition from natural to daemonic amazement is not a mere matter of degree. But it is only with the latter that the complementary expression *mysterium* perfectly harmonizes, as will be felt perhaps more clearly in the case of the adjectival form "mysterious". No one says, strictly and in earnest, of a piece of clockwork that is beyond his grasp, or of a science that he cannot understand: "That is 'mysterious' to me."

It might be objected that the mysterious is something which is and remains absolutely and invariably beyond our understanding, whereas that which merely eludes our under-standing for a time but is perfectly intelligible in principle should be called, not a "mystery", but merely a "problem". But this is by no means an adequate account of the matter. The truly "mysterious" object is beyond our apprehension and comprehension, not only because our knowledge has certain irremovable limits, but because in it we come upon something inherently "wholly other", whose kind and character are incommensurable with our own, and before which we therefore recoil in a wonder that strikes us chill and numb.[2]

This may be made still clearer by a consideration of that degraded offshoot and travesty of the genuine "numinous" dread or awe, the fear of ghosts. Let us try to analyse this experience. We have already specified the peculiar feeling-element of "dread" aroused by the ghost as that of "grue", grisly horror.[3] Now this "grue" obviously contributes something to the attraction which ghost-stories exercise, in so far, namely, as the relaxation of tension ensuing upon our release from it relieves the mind in a pleasant and agreeable way. So far, however, it is not really the ghost itself that gives us pleasure, but the fact that we are rid of it. But obviously this is quite insufficient to explain the ensnaring attraction of the ghost-story. The ghost's real attraction rather consists in this, that of itself and in an uncommon degree it entices the imagination, awakening strong interest and curiosity; it is the weird thing itself that allures the fancy. But it does this, not because it is "something long and white" (as someone once defined a ghost), nor yet through any of the positive and con-ceptual attributes which fancies about ghosts have invented, but because it is a thing that "doesn't really exist at all", the "wholly other", something which has no place in our scheme of reality but belongs to an absolutely different one, and which at the same time arouses an irrepressible interest in the mind.

But that which is perceptibly true in the fear of ghosts, which is, after all, only a car-icature of the genuine thing, is in a far stronger sense true of the "daemonic" experience itself, of which the fear of ghosts is a mere off-shoot. And while, following this main line of development, this element in the numinous consciousness, the feeling of the "wholly other", is heightened and clarified, its higher modes of manifestation come into being, which set the numinous object in contrast not only to everything wonted and familiar (i.e. in the end, to nature in general), thereby turning it into the "supernatural", but finally to the world itself, and thereby exalt it to the "supramundane", that which is above the whole world-order.

In mysticism we have in the "beyond" again the strongest stressing and over-stressing of those non-rational elements which are already inherent in all religion. Mysticism continues to its extreme point this contrasting of the numinous object (the numen), as the "wholly other", with ordinary experience. Not content with contrasting it with all that is of nature or this world, mysticism concludes by contrasting it with Being itself and all that "is", and finally actually calls it "that which is nothing". By this "nothing" is meant not only that of which nothing can be predicated, but that which is absolutely and intrinsically other than and opposite of everything that is and can be thought. But while exaggerating to the point of paradox this *negation* and contrast—the only means open to conceptual thought to apprehend the *mysterium*—mysticism at the same time retains the *positive quality* of the "wholly other" as a very living factor in its over-brimming religious emotion.

But what is true of the strange "nothingness" of our mystics holds good equally of the *sūnyam* and the *sūnyatā*, the "void" and "emptiness" of the Buddhist mystics. This aspiration for the "void" and for becoming void, no less than the aspiration of our western mystics for "nothing" and for becoming nothing, must seem a kind of lunacy to anyone who has no inner sympathy for the esoteric language and ideograms of mysticism, and lacks the matrix from which these come necessarily to birth. To such a one Buddhism itself will be simply a morbid sort of pessimism. But in fact the "void" of the eastern, like the "nothing" of the western, mystic is a numinous ideogram of the "wholly other".

These terms "supernatural" and "transcendent"[4] give the appearance of positive attributes, and, as applied to the mysterious, they appear to divest the *mysterium* of its originally negative meaning and to turn it into an affirmation. On the side of conceptual thought this is nothing more than appearance, for it is obvious that the two terms in question are merely negative and exclusive attributes with reference to "nature" and the world or cosmos respectively. But on the side of the feeling-content it is otherwise; that *is* in very truth positive in the highest degree, though here too, as before, it cannot be rendered explicit in conceptual terms. It is through this positive feeling-content that the concepts of the "transcendent" and "supernatural" become forthwith designations for a unique "wholly other" reality and quality, something of whose special character we can *feel*, without being able to give it clear conceptual expression.

QUESTIONS FOR REVIEW AND DISCUSSION

1. Otto and James both focus on religious experience. How do they differ with regard to their methods, emphases, and conclusions?
2. Although not universally accessible to any student of religion through the faculty of reason alone, Otto claims that a mysterious experience of the holy is fundamentally important to understand religion and the divine. This position is in contrast to Freud, who seems to dismiss "Oceanic" states of consciousness that he himself has not experienced. James appears to occupy a place in between, in that he asserts that mystical states are both real and important even though he acknowledges his lack of mystical experience. What do you think about these contrasting positions with regard to the academic study of religion?
3. The subtitle of *The Idea of the Holy* is "*An Inquiry into the non-rational factor in the idea of the divine and its relation to the rational*". What is Otto's position on "*the non-rational factor in the idea of the divine*"?
4. Why do you think Otto invokes Latin terms, such as *mysterium* and *tremendum*? Do you find his use of these terms effective? Although you are reading a translation from the original German, what is your assessment of Otto's use of terminology and language more generally?

5. What does Otto see as the relationship between representation of spirits, systems of myth, and intellectualist Scholasticism on the one hand and religious experience on the other?

6. Why does Otto assert that there is such an essential difference between the natural and the numinous moments of consciousness (as well as with consciousness of the "wholly other" and experience of *mysterium*)? How would his overall position and arguments change if he instead indicated that the differences were just a matter of degree?

7. How does Otto connect mysticism to the "wholly other" both in terms of negation and as a "living factor in its over-brimming religious emotion"? Otto illustrates his point with reference to Buddhist and western mystics. What is his assessment of characterizations of Buddhism as a "morbid sort of pessimism"?

8. What is your sense of the roles of feeling, emotion, and experience relative to conceptualization for Otto? Do you agree? Why or why not?

Notes

1 A spirit or soul that has been conceived and comprehended no longer prompts to "shuddering", as is proved by Spiritualism. But it thereby ceases to be of interest for the psychology of religion.

2 In *Confessions*, ii. 9. I, Augustine very strikingly suggests this stiffening, benumbing element of the "wholly other" and its contrast to the rational aspect of the numen; the *dissimile* and the *simile*:

> "Quid est illud, quod interlucet mihi et percutit cor meum sine laesione? Et inhorresco et inardesco. *Inhorresco*, in quantum *dissimilis* ei sum. Inardesco, in quantum similis ei sum."
>
> ("What is that which gleams through me and smites my heart without wounding it? I am both a-shudder and a-glow. A-shudder, in so far as I am unlike it, a-glow in so far as I am like it.")

3 *gruseln, gräsen.*

4 Literally, supramundane: *überweltlich.*

16 Approximations: The Structure and Morphology of the Sacred

Mircea Eliade

Mircea Eliade (1907–86) was born in Bucharest, Romania. His comparative studies and prodigious publishing in various genres from scholarship to fiction began in Romania and moved on to further studies and travel in Italy and India, as well as an academic post in Paris, before he joined the University of Chicago's Divinity School. Eliade became a towering figure of the Chicago School and sought to establish a "New Humanism" led by a "History of Religions" that not only took religion as valuable and irreducible, but also studied it comparatively with close attention to Asian and ancient forms, myths, symbols, and rituals. Eliade's views on religion have exerted tremendous influence since the middle of the twentieth century and have also been targeted for critical reappraisal in recent decades. Along with his studies of yoga and shamanism he wrote seminal books such as *Patterns in Comparative Religion* (1949), *The Myth of the Eternal Return: Or, Cosmos and History* (1949), and *The Sacred and the Profane* (1959). Eliade also served as the editor-in-chief of the foremost reference resource for this field, *The Encyclopedia of Religion* (1987).

AUTHOR'S FOREWORD TO *PATTERNS IN COMPARATIVE RELIGION*

Modern science has restored a principle which was seriously endangered by some of the confusions of the nineteenth century: *"It is the scale that makes the phenomenon."* Henri Poincaré queried with some irony whether "a naturalist who had studied elephants only under the microscope would think he knew enough about those animals?" The microscope shows the structure and mechanism of the cells, a structure and mechanism which are the same in all multicellular organisms. But is that all there is to know? At the microscopic level one cannot be certain. At the level of human eyesight, which does at least recognize the elephant as a phenomenon of zoology, all uncertainty departs. In the same way, a religious phenomenon will only be recognized as such if it is grasped at its own level, that is to say, if it is studied *as* something religious. To try to grasp the essence of such a phenomenon by means of physiology, psychology, sociology, economics, linguistics, art or any other study is false; it misses the one unique and irreducible element in it—the element of the sacred. Obviously there are no *purely* religious phenomena; no phenomenon can be solely and exclusively religious. Because religion is human it must for that very reason be something social, something linguistic, something economic—you cannot think of man apart from language and society.

But it would be hopeless to try and explain religion in terms of any one of those basic functions which are really no more than another way of saying what man is. It would be as futile as thinking you could explain *Madame Bovary* by a list of social, economic and political facts; however true, they do not affect it as a work of literature.

I do not mean to deny the usefulness of approaching the religious phenomenon from various different angles; but it must be looked at first of all in itself, in that which belongs to it alone and can be explained in no other terms. It is no easy task. It is a matter, if not of giving an exact definition of the religious phenomenon, at least of seeing its limits and setting it in its true relation to the other things of the mind. And, as Roger Caillois remarks at the beginning of his brilliant short book, *L'Homme et le sacré*: "At bottom, the only helpful thing one can say of the sacred in general is contained in the very definition of the term: that it is the opposite of profane. As soon as one attempts to give a clear statement of the nature, the *modality* of that opposition, one strikes difficulty. No formula, however elementary, will cover the labyrinthine complexity of the facts." Now, in my researches, what have primarily interested me are these facts, this labyrinthine complexity of elements which will yield to no formula or definition whatever. Taboo, ritual, symbol, myth, demon, god—these are some of them; but it would be an outrageous simplification to make such a list tell the whole story. What we have really got to deal with is a diverse and indeed chaotic mass of actions, beliefs and systems which go together to make up what one may call the religious phenomenon.

This book deals with a twofold problem: first, what *is* religion and, secondly, how far can one talk of the history of religion? As I doubt the value of beginning with a definition of the religious phenomenon, I am simply going to examine various "hierophanies"—taking that term in its widest sense as anything which manifests the sacred. We shall, therefore, only be able to consider the problem of the *history* of religious forms after having examined a certain number of them. A treatise on religious phenomena starting with the simplest and working up to the most complex does not seem to me to be called for, given the aims I have set myself in this book—I mean the sort of treatise that starts with the most elementary hierophanies (*mana*, the unusual, etc.), going on to totemism, fetishism, the worship of nature and spirits, thence to gods and demons, and coming finally to the monotheistic idea of God. Such an arrangement would be quite arbitrary; it presupposes an evolution in the religious phenomenon, from the simple to the complex, which is a mere hypothesis and cannot be proved; we have yet to meet anywhere a simple religion, consisting only of the most elementary hierophanies; and it would, besides, run counter to the aim I intend—that of seeing just what things *are* religious in nature and what those things reveal.

The path I have followed is, if not easier, at least surer. I have begun this study with an account of certain cosmic hierophanies, the sacred revealed at different cosmic levels—sky, waters, earth, stones. I have chosen these classes of hierophany not because I consider them the earliest (the historical problem does not yet arise), but because describing them explains on the one hand the dialectic of the sacred, and on the other what sort of forms the sacred will take. For instance, a study of the hierophanies of sky and water will provide us with data enabling us to understand both exactly what the manifestation of the sacred means at those particular cosmic levels, and how far those hierophanies constitute autonomous forms. I then go on to the biological hierophanies (the rhythm of the moon, the sun, vegetation and agriculture, sexuality, etc.), then local hierophanies (consecrated places, temples, etc.) and lastly myths and symbols. Having looked at a sufficient quantity of such material, we shall be ready to turn in a future book to the other problems of the history of religions: "divine forms", man's relations with the sacred, and handling of it (rites, etc.), magic and religion, ideas on the soul and death, consecrated persons (priest, magician, king, initiate, etc.), the relationships of myth, symbol and ideogram, the possibility of laying the foundations for a history of religions, and so on.

This does not mean that I shall discuss each subject separately as in articles in an encyclopaedia, carefully avoiding any mention of myth or symbol, for instance, in the chapter on aquatic or lunar hierophanies; nor do I promise that all discussion of divine figures will be restricted to a chapter on "gods". In fact, the reader may be surprised to find quite a lot about gods of sky and air in the chapter on hierophanies of the sky, and to observe in that same chapter references to, and even discussions upon, symbols, rites, myths and ideograms. The nature of the subject necessitates constant overlaps between the subject matter of one chapter and another. It is not possible to talk of the sacredness attributed to the sky without mentioning the divine figures that reflect or share that sacredness, some of the sky myths, the rites connected with its worship, the symbols and ideograms in which it is personified. Each one in its own way shows some modality of the sky religion or its history. But since each myth, rite and "divine figure" is discussed in its proper place, I do not hesitate to use these terms in their precise meaning in the chapter about the sky. In the same way, when dealing with the hierophanies of earth, vegetation and farming, my concern is with the manifestations of the sacred at these bio-cosmic levels; all analysis of the forms of the gods of vegetation and agriculture will be left to the chapter on these forms. But that does not mean that I do not allude to the gods, rites, myths or symbols of vegetation and agriculture in the preliminary study. The object of these preliminary chapters is to examine as closely as possible the pattern to be found in the cosmic hierophanies, to see what we can discover from the sacred as expressed in the sky, in water, in vegetation, and so on.

If one is to weigh the advantages and disadvantages of this method of proceeding, I think the former are considerably greater, and that for more than one reason:

(1) We are dispensed from any *a priori* definition of the religious phenomenon; the reader can make his own reflections on the nature of the sacred as he goes.
(2) The analysis of each group of hierophanies, by making a natural division among the various modalities of the sacred, and showing how they fit together in a coherent system, will at the same time clear the ground for the final discussion on the essence of religion.
(3) By examining the "lower" and "higher" religious forms simultaneously, and seeing at once what elements they have in common, we shall not make the mistakes that result from an *evolutionist* or *occidentalist* perspective.
(4) Religious wholes are not seen in bits and pieces, for each class of hierophanies (aquatic, celestial, vegetal, etc.) forms in its own way, a whole, both morphologically (for we have to deal with gods and myths and symbols and every sort of thing) and historically (for often enough the study must spread over a great many cultures widely divergent in time and space).
(5) Each chapter will present one particular modality of the sacred, a series of relationships between man and the sacred, and, in these relationships, a series of "historical moments".

This, and this only, is what I mean by calling this book "Patterns in Comparative Religion"; what I intend is to introduce my readers to the labyrinthine complexity of religious data, their basic patterns, and the variety of cultures they reflect. I have endeavoured to give each chapter a different plan and even a different style, to escape from the monotony which threatens every didactic work, and I have so arranged the paragraphing as to make reference as easy as possible. But the point of this book cannot be grasped except by reading it right through; it is in no sense a handbook for reference. The bibliographies are intended as a spur to elementary research; they are in no case exhaustive. I have, however, tried to include in them representatives of as many schools and methods as possible.

A great part of the morphological analyses and the methodological conclusions of this book was given as lectures in my courses on the history of religions at the University of Bucharest, and in two series of lectures at the École des Hautes Études of the Sorbonne (*Recherches sur la morphologie du sacré*, 1946; *Recherches sur la structure des mythes*, 1948). For this English edition, corrections have been made in the text, and the bibliographies have been brought up to date.

APPROXIMATIONS: THE STRUCTURE AND MORPHOLOGY OF THE SACRED

1. "Sacred" and "Profane"

All the definitions given up till now of the religious phenomenon have one thing in common: each has its own way of showing that the sacred and the religious life are the opposite of the profane and the secular life. But as soon as you start to fix limits to the notion of the sacred you come upon difficulties—difficulties both theoretical and practical. For, before you attempt any definition of the phenomenon of religion, you must know where to look for the evidence, and, first and foremost, for those expressions of religion that can be seen in the "pure state"—that is, those which are "simple" and as close as possible to their origins. Unfortunately, evidence of this sort is nowhere to be found; neither in any society whose history we know, nor among the "primitives", the uncivilized peoples of today. Almost everywhere the religious phenomena we see are complex, suggesting a long historical evolution.

Then, too, assembling one's material presents certain important practical difficulties. Even if one were satisfied with studying only one religion, a lifetime would scarcely be long enough to complete the research, while, if one proposed to compare religions, several lifetimes would not suffice to attain the end in view. Yet it is just such a comparative study that we want, for only thus can we discover both the changing morphology of the sacred, and its historical development. In embarking, therefore, on this study, we must choose a few among the many religions which have been discovered by history, or ethnology, and then only some of their aspects or phases.

This choice, even if confined to the major manifestations, is a delicate matter. If we want to limit and define the sacred, we shall have to have at our disposal a manageable number of expressions of religion. If it starts by being difficult, the diversity of those expressions becomes gradually paralysing. We are faced with rites, myths, divine forms, sacred and venerated objects, symbols, cosmologies, theologoumena, consecrated men, animals and plants, sacred places, and more. And each category has its own morphology—of a branching and luxuriant richness. We have to deal with a vast and ill-assorted mass of material, with a Melanesian cosmogony myth or Brahman sacrifice having as much right to our consideration as the mystical writings of a St. Teresa or a Nichiren, an Australian totem, a primitive initiation rite, the symbolism of the Borobudur temple, the ceremonial costumes and dances of a Siberian shaman, the sacred stones to be found in so many places, agricultural ceremonies, the myths and rites of the Great Goddesses, the enthroning of an ancient king or the superstitions attaching to precious stones. Each must be considered as a hierophany in as much as it expresses in some way some modality of the sacred and some moment in its history; that is to say, some one of the many kinds of experience of the sacred man has had. Each is valuable for two things it tells us: because it is a hierophany, it reveals some modality of the sacred; because it is a historical incident, it reveals some attitude man has had towards the sacred. For instance, the following Vedic text addressing a dead man: "Crawl to your Mother, Earth! May she save you from the void!" This text shows the nature of earth worship; the earth is looked upon as the Mother, *Tellus Mater*; but it also shows one given stage in the history of Indian religions, the moment when Mother Earth was valued—at least by one group—as a protectress against the void, a valuation which was to be done away with by the reform of the Upanisads and the preaching of Buddha.

To return to where we began, each category of evidence (myths, rites, gods, superstitions, and so on) is really equally important to us if we are to understand the religious phenomenon. And this understanding will always come about in relation to history. Every hierophany we look at is also an historical fact. Every manifestation of the sacred takes place in some historical situation. Even the most personal and transcendent mystical experiences are affected by the age in which they occur. The Jewish prophets owed a debt to the events of history, which justified them and confirmed their message; and also to the religious history of Israel, which made it possible for them to explain what they had experienced. As a historical phenomenon—though not as personal experience—the nihilism and ontologism of some of the Mahāyāna mystics would not have been possible without the Upanisad speculations, the evolution of Sanskrit and other things. I do not mean that every hierophany and every religious experience whatsoever is a unique and never-to-be-repeated incident in the working of the spirit. The greatest experiences are not only alike in content, but often also alike in their expression. Rudolf Otto discovered some astonishing similarities between the vocabulary and formulae of Meister Eckhardt and those of Śankara.

The fact that a hierophany is always a historical event (that is to say, always occurs in some definite situation) does not lessen its universal quality. Some hierophanies have a purely local purpose; others have, or attain, world-wide significance. The Indians, for instance, venerate a certain tree called *aśvattha*; the manifestation of the sacred in that particular plant species has meaning only for them, for only to them is the *aśvattha* anything more than just a tree. Consequently, that hierophany is not only of a certain time (as every hierophany must be), but also of a certain place. However, the Indians also have the symbol of a cosmic tree *(Axis Mundi)*, and this mythico-symbolic hierophany is universal, for we find Cosmic Trees everywhere among ancient civilizations. But note that the *aśvattha* is venerated because it embodies the sacred significance of the universe in constant renewal of life; it is venerated, in fact, because it embodies, is part of, or symbolizes the universe as represented by all the Cosmic Trees in all mythologies. (Cf. § 99.) But although the *aśvattha is* explained by the same symbolism that we find in the Cosmic Tree, the hierophany which turns a particular plant-form into a sacred tree has a meaning only in the eyes of that particular Indian society.

To give a further example—in this case a hierophany which was left behind by the actual history of the people concerned: the Semites at one time in their history adored the divine couple made up of Ba'al, the god of hurricane and fecundity, and Belit, the goddess of fertility (particularly the fertility of the earth). The Jewish prophets held these cults to be sacrilegious. From their standpoint—from the standpoint, that is, of those Semites who had, as a result of the Mosaic reforms, reached a higher, purer and more complete conception of the Deity—such a criticism was perfectly justified. And yet the old Semitic cult of Ba'al and Belit *was* a hierophany: it showed (though in unhealthy and monstrous forms) the religious value of organic life, the elementary forces of blood, sexuality and fecundity. This revelation maintained its importance, if not for thousands, at least for hundreds of years. As a hierophany it held sway till the time when it was replaced by another, which—completed in the religious experience of an elite—proved itself more satisfying and of greater perfection. The "divine form" of Yahweh prevailed over the "divine form" of Ba'al; it manifested a more perfect holiness, it sanctified life without in any way allowing to run wild the elementary forces concentrated in the cult of Ba'al, it revealed a spiritual economy in which man's life and destiny gained a totally new value; at the same time it made possible a richer religious experience, a communion with God at once purer and more complete. This hierophany of Yahweh had the final victory; because it represented a universal modality of the sacred, it was by its very nature open to other cultures; it became, by means of Christianity, of world-wide religious value. It can be seen, then, that some hierophanies are, or can in this way become, of universal value and significance, whereas others may remain local or of one period—they are not open to other cultures, and fall eventually into oblivion even in the society which produced them.

2. Difficulties of Method

But, to return to the great practical difficulty I mentioned earlier: the extreme diversity of the material we are faced with. To make matters worse, there seems no limit to the number of spheres whence we have drawn these hundreds of thousands of scraps of evidence. For one thing (as with all historical material), what we have to hand has survived more or less by chance (not merely in the case of written texts but also of monuments, inscriptions, oral traditions and customs). For another, what has chanced to survive comes to us from many different sources. If, for instance, we want to piece together the early history of the Greek religion, we must make do with the very few texts that have come down to us, a few inscriptions, a few mutilated monuments and some votive objects; in the case of the Germanic or Slavonic religions, we are obliged to make use of simple folklore, with the inevitable risks attaching to its handling and interpretation. A runic inscription, a myth recorded several centuries after it had ceased to be understood, a few symbolic pictures, a few protohistoric monuments, a mass of rites, and the popular legends of a century ago—nothing could be more ill-assorted than the material available to the historian of Germanic and Slavonic religion. Such a mixture of things would not be too bad if one were studying only one religion, but it is really serious when one attempts a comparative study of religions, or tries to grasp a great many different modalities of the sacred.

It is exactly as if a critic had to write a history of French literature with no other evidence than some fragments of Racine, a Spanish translation of La Bruyère, a few texts quoted by a foreign critic, the literary recollections of a few travellers and diplomats, the catalogue of a provincial library, the notes and exercise books of a schoolboy, and a few more hints of the same sort. That is really all the material available to a historian of religions: a few fragments from a vast oral priestly learning (the exclusive product of one social class), allusions found in travellers' notes, material gathered by foreign missionaries, reflections drawn from secular literature, a few monuments, a few inscriptions, and what memories remain in local traditions. All the historical sciences are, of course, tied to this sort of scrappy and accidental evidence. But the religious historian faces a bolder task than the historian, whose job is merely to piece together an event or a series of events with the aid of the few bits of evidence that are preserved to him; the religious historian must trace not only the *history* of a given hierophany, but must first of all understand and explain the modality of the sacred that that hierophany discloses. It would be difficult enough to interpret the meaning of a hierophany in any case, but the heterogeneous and chancy nature of the available evidence makes it far, far worse. Imagine a Buddhist trying to understand Christianity with only a few fragments of the Gospels, a Catholic breviary, various ornaments (Byzantine icons, Baroque statues of the saints, the vestments, perhaps, of an Orthodox priest), but able, on the other hand, to study the religious life of some European village. No doubt the first thing our Buddhist observer would note would be a distinct difference between the religious life of the peasants and the theological, moral and mystical ideas of the village priest. But, while he would be quite right to note the distinction, he would be wrong if he refused to judge Christianity according to the traditions preserved by the priest on the grounds that he was merely a single individual—if he only held to be genuine the experience represented by the village as a community. The modalities of the sacred revealed by Christianity are in fact more truly preserved in the tradition represented by the priest (however strongly coloured by history and theology) than in the beliefs of the villagers. What the observer is interested in is not the one moment in the history of Christianity, or one part of Christendom, but the Christian religion as such. The fact that only one man, in a whole village, may have a proper knowledge of Christian ritual, dogma and mysticism, while the rest of the community are ill-informed about them and practise an elemental cult tinctured with superstition (with, that is, the remains of outworn hierophanies) does not, for his purpose at least, matter at all. What does matter is to realize that this single man has kept more completely, if not the original experience of Christianity, at least its basic elements and its mystical, theological and ritual values.

We find this mistake in method often enough in ethnology. Paul Radin felt he had the right to reject the conclusions reached by the missionary Gusinde in his researches because his enquiries were limited to one man. Such an attitude would be justified only if the object of the enquiry were a strictly sociological one: if it were the religious life of a Fuegian community at a given time; but when it is a question of discovering what capacity the Fuegians have of experiencing religion, then the position is quite different. And the capacity of primitives to know different modalities of the sacred is one of the most important problems of religious history. Indeed, if one can show (as has been done in recent decades) that the religious lives of the most primitive peoples are in fact complex, that they cannot be reduced to "animism", "totemism", or even ancestor-worship, that they include visions of Supreme Beings with all the powers of an omnipotent Creator-God, then these evolutionist hypotheses which deny the primitive any approach to "superior hierophanies" are nullified.

3. The Variety among Hierophanies

The comparisons I have used to illustrate the tenuousness of the evidence the religious historian has at his disposal are, of course, imaginary examples and must be taken as such. My first object is to justify the method I have used in this book. How far—considering the diversity and tenuousness of our evidence—are we right to speak of different "modalities of the sacred"? That those modalities exist is proved by the fact that a given hierophany may be lived and interpreted quite differently by the religious elite and by the rest of the community. For the throng who come to the temple of Kalighat in Calcutta every autumn Durgā is simply a goddess of terror to whom goats are sacrificed; but for a few initiated *sāktas* Durgā is the manifestation of cosmic life in constant and violent regeneration. It is very likely that among those who adore the *lingam* of Siva, a great many see it only as an archetype of the generative organ; but there are others who look to it as a sign, an "image" of the rhythmic creation and destruction of the universe which expresses itself in forms, and periodically returns to its primal, pre-formal unity, before being reborn. Which is the true meaning of Durgā and Siva—what is deciphered by the initiates, or what is taken up by the mass of the faithful? In this book I am trying to show that both are equally valuable; that the meaning given by the masses stands for as authentic a modality of the sacred manifested in Durgā or Siva as the interpretation of the initiates. And I can show that the two hierophanies fit together—that the modalities of the sacred which they reveal are in no sense contradictory, but are complementary, are parts of a whole. That is my warrant for giving equal weight to what records an experience of the masses, and what reflects only the experience of an elite. Both categories are necessary—to enable us not only to trace the history of a hierophany, but, even more important, to establish the modalities of the sacred which that hierophany manifests.

These observations—which are amply illustrated later on in this book—may be applied to the great variety of hierophanies I spoke of earlier. For—as I have said—this evidence is not only heterogeneous in origin (some coming from priests and initiates, some from the masses, some presenting the merest allusions, fragments and sayings, some whole texts), but also in form. For instance, plant hierophanies (or the sacred as expressed in vegetation) are to be found equally in symbols (like the Cosmic Tree) or "popular" rites (like "bringing home the May", the burning of logs, or agricultural ceremonies), in beliefs bound up with the idea that mankind originated from plants, in the mystical relationships which have existed between certain trees and certain individuals or societies, in the superstitions relative to the fertilizing power of fruits or flowers, in the stories of dead heroes being changed into plants, in the myths and rites of the gods of vegetation and agriculture, and so on. These things differ, not only in their history (compare, for instance, the symbol of the Cosmic Tree among the Indians and the Altai peoples with the belief of some primitive peoples that the human race is descended from a vegetable species)—but even in structure. Which should we take as our models in trying to understand plant hierophanies? The symbols, the myths, the rites, or the "divine forms"?

The safest method, clearly, is to make use of all these kinds of evidence, omitting no important type, and always asking ourselves what *meaning* is revealed by each of these hierophanies. In this way we shall get a coherent collection of common traits which, as we shall see later, will make it possible to formulate a *coherent* system of the various modalities of vegetation cult. We shall see in this way that every hierophany in fact supposes such a system; a popular custom bearing a certain relation to "bringing home the May" implies the same sacred meaning of plants expressed in the ideogram of the Cosmic Tree; some hierophanies are not at all clear, are indeed almost cryptic, in that they only reveal the sacred meaning embodied or symbolized in plant life in part, or, as it were, in code, while others (more truly *manifestations*) display the sacred in all its modalities as a whole. For instance, what I should describe as a cryptic, or insufficiently clear, *local* hierophany is the custom of carrying a green branch in solemn procession at the beginning of the spring; whereas what I should call a "clear" hierophany is the symbol of the Cosmic Tree. Yet both reveal the same modality of the sacred embodied in plant life: the rhythm of rebirth, the never-ending life that vegetation contains, reality manifested in recurring creation, and so on. What must be emphasized at once is that *all* these hierophanies point to a system of coherent statements, to a theory of the sacred significance of vegetation, the more cryptic hierophanies as much as the others.

The theoretical consequences attendant on these remarks will be dealt with at the end of this book after we have examined enough of our material. For the moment it is enough to show that neither the variety of sources for the evidence (coming partly from the religious elite, partly from the uneducated masses, some being the product of cultured civilizations, some of primitive societies, etc.), nor the variety of forms it takes (myths, rites, divine forms, superstitions and so on), forms any obstacle to the understanding of any hierophany. Whatever the practical difficulties it causes, this very variety is what makes it possible for us to discover all the different modalities of the sacred—for symbol and myth will give a clear view of the modalities that a rite can never do more than suggest. A symbol and a rite (say) are on such different levels that the rite can never reveal what the symbol reveals. But let me say again, the hierophany present in one agricultural rite presupposes the entire system—the different modalities of the sacredness of vegetation revealed to us by all the other agricultural hierophanies all over the world.

Perhaps I can make these preliminary remarks clearer if I state the problem differently. When a sorceress burns a wax doll containing a lock of her victim's hair she does not have in mind the entire theory underlying that bit of magic—but this fact does not affect our understanding of sympathetic magic. What does matter to our understanding is to know that such an action could only have happened after people had satisfied themselves by experiment, or established theoretically, that nails, hair, or anything a person has worn preserve an intimate relation with their owner even when separated from him. This belief is based on the notion of a "space-connection" between the most distant things whereby they are linked by means of a kind of sympathy governed by its own specific laws—organic coexistence, formal or symbolic analogy, and functional symmetry. The sorceress can only believe what she does to have any effect in so far as this "space-connection" exists. Whether she knows what it is or not, whether or not she understands the "sympathy" that connects the lock of hair with the person concerned does not matter at all. It is extremely unlikely that most of those sorceresses to be found today have a view of the world that corresponds with the magical practices they perform. Yet, even if those who perform them do not subscribe to the theories which underlie them, the practices themselves can tell us much of the world from which they come. We do not arrive at the mental universe of archaic man by logical investigation, by means of men's explicit beliefs; it is preserved to us in myths, symbols and customs which still, in spite of every sort of corruption, show clearly what they meant when they began. In a way they are a kind of "living fossils"—and sometimes a single fossil is enough for us to reassemble a whole organism.

4. The Multiplicity of Hierophanies

I shall return to the examples I have quoted here and support them more fully later on in this book. For the moment let them give a first approximation—not towards defining the idea of the sacred, but towards familiarizing us with the evidence we have to deal with. I have given each piece of evidence the title *hierophany*, because each expresses some one modality of the sacred. The modalities of that expression and the ontological value to be accorded to it are two questions which must be left to the end of this study. For the moment we shall consider each separate thing—rite, myth, cosmogony or god—as a hierophany; in other words, we shall see each as a manifestation of the sacred in the mental world of those who believed in it.

What I propose is by no means always easy. To the Western mind, which almost automatically relates all ideas of the sacred, of religion, and even of magic to certain historical forms of Judaeo-Christian religious life, alien hierophanies must appear largely as aberrations. Even for those disposed to consider certain aspects of exotic—and particularly of Oriental—religions quite sympathetically, it is hard to understand the sacred value attached to stones, say, or the mystique of eroticism. And even if he can see some justification for these queer hierophanies (labelling them "fetishism" or something of the sort), it is quite certain that there are others the modern man will never come to accept, which he cannot see as having the value of a hierophany at all, in which he can discern no modality of the sacred. Walter Otto noted in his *Die Götter Griechenlands* how difficult it is for a modern to find any religious meaning in "perfect forms", one of the categories of the divine current among the ancient Greeks. The difficulty is even greater when it comes to considering a symbol as a manifestation of the sacred, to thinking of the seasons, the rhythm or the fullness of forms (any and every form) as so many modes of the sacred. In the pages that follow I shall try to show that they were held to be such by primitive cultures. If only we can get away from the prejudices of the lecture-room, can consider such beliefs not simply as pantheism, fetishism, infantilism and so on, but as what they actually meant to those who held them, we shall be better able to understand the past and present meaning of the sacred in primitive cultures; and at the same time our chances of understanding the modes and the history of religion will increase too.

We must get used to the idea of recognizing hierophanies absolutely everywhere, in every area of psychological, economic, spiritual and social life. Indeed, we cannot be sure that there is *anything*—object, movement, psychological function, being or even game—that has not at some time in human history been somewhere transformed into a hierophany. It is a very different matter to find out *why* that particular thing should have become a hierophany, or should have stopped being one at any given moment. But it is quite certain that anything man has ever handled, felt, come in contact with or loved *can* become a hierophany. We know, for instance, that all the gestures, dances and games children have, and many of their toys, have a religious origin—they were once the gestures and objects of worship. In the same way musical and architectural instruments, means of transport (animals, chariots, boats and so on) started by being sacred objects, sacred activities. It is unlikely that there is any animal or any important species of plant in the world that has *never* had a place in religion. In the same way too, every trade, art, industry and technical skill either began as something holy, or has, over the years, been invested with religious value. This list could be carried on to include man's everyday movements (getting up, walking, running), his various employments (hunting, fishing, agriculture), all his physiological activities (nutrition, sexual life, etc.); perhaps too the essential words of the language, and so on. Obviously it would be wrong to imagine the whole of mankind's having gone through all these stages; to see every society in turn reaching the sacred in all these ways. Such an evolutionist hypothesis might have been conceivable a few generations ago, but it is now completely impossible. But somewhere, at a given time, each human society chose for itself a certain number of things, animals, plants, gestures and so on, and turned them into hierophanies; and as this has been going on for tens of thousands of years of religious life, it seems improbable that there remains anything that has not at some time been so transfigured.

5. The Dialectic of Hierophanies

I mentioned at the beginning of this chapter that all the definitions that have ever been given of the religious phenomenon make the sacred the opposite of the profane. What I have just said—that anything whatever can become at any given moment a hierophany—may seem to contradict all these definitions. If anything whatever may embody separate values, can the sacred–profane dichotomy have any meaning? The contradiction is, in fact, only a surface one, for while it is true that anything at all can become a hierophany, and that in all probability there is nothing that has not, somewhere, some time, been invested with a sacred value, it still remains that no one religion or race has ever been found to contain all these hierophanies in its history. In other words, in every religious framework there have always been profane beings and things beside the sacred. (The same cannot be said of physiological actions, trades, skills, gestures and so on, but I shall come to this distinction later.) Further: while a certain class of things may be found fitting vehicles of the sacred, there always remain some things in the class which are not given this honour.

For instance, in the so-called "worship of stones" not all stones are held to be sacred. We shall always find that *some* stones are venerated because they are a certain shape, or because they are very large, or because they are bound up with some ritual. Note, too, that it is not a question of actually worshipping the stones; the stones are venerated precisely because they are not simply stones but hierophanies, something outside their normal status as things. The dialectic of a hierophany implies a more or less clear choice, a singling-out. A thing becomes sacred in so far as it embodies (that is, reveals) something other than itself. Here we need not be concerned with whether that something other comes from its unusual shape, its efficacy or simply its "power"—or whether it springs from the thing's fitting in with some symbolism or other, or has been given it by some rite of consecration, or acquired by its being placed in some position that is instinct with sacredness (a sacred zone, a sacred time, some "accident"—a thunderbolt, crime, sacrilege or such). What matters is that a hierophany implies a *choice*, a clear-cut separation of this thing which manifests the sacred from everything else around it. There is always something *else*, even when it is some whole sphere that becomes sacred—the sky, for instance, or a certain familiar landscape, or the "fatherland". The thing that becomes sacred is still separated in regard to itself, for it only becomes a hierophany at the moment of stopping to be a mere profane something, at the moment of acquiring a new "dimension" of sacredness.

This dialectic shows itself very clearly at the elementary level of those vivid hierophanies so often mentioned in ethnological writings. Everything unusual, unique, new, perfect or monstrous at once becomes imbued with magico-religious powers and an object of veneration or fear according to the circumstances (for the sacred usually produces this double reaction). "When a dog," writes A. C. Kruyt, "is always lucky in hunting, it is *measa* (ill-starred, a bringer of evil), for too much good luck in hunting makes the Toradja uneasy. The mystic virtue by means of which the animal is enabled to seize his prey must necessarily be fatal to his master; he will soon die, or his rice-crop will fail, or, more often still, there will be an epidemic among his cattle or his pigs. This belief is general throughout Central Celebes."[1] Perfection in any sphere is frightening, and this sacred or magic quality of perfection may provide an explanation for the fear that even the most civilized societies seem to feel when faced with a genius or a saint. Perfection is not of this world. It is something different, it comes from somewhere else.

This same fear, this same scrupulous reserve, applies to everything alien, strange, new— that such astonishing things should be present is the sign of a force that, however much it is to be venerated, may be dangerous. In the Celebes, "if the fruit of the banana appears, not at the end of the stalk but in the middle, it is *measa*. ... People usually say that it entails the death of its owner. ... When a certain variety of pumpkin bears two fruits upon a single stem (a similar case to a twin birth) it is *measa*. It will cause a death in the family of the man who owns the field in which it is growing. The pumpkin-plant must be pulled up, for nobody must eat it."[2] As Edwin W. Smith says, "it is especially strange, unusual things, uncommon sights, new-fangled habits, strange foods and ways of doing things that are regarded as manifestations of the hidden powers."[3] At Tana, in the New Hebrides, all disasters were attributed to the white missionaries who had just come.[4] This list could easily be made longer.[5]

6. The Taboo and the Ambivalence of the Sacred

I will come later to the question, how far such things can be considered hierophanies. They are in any case kratophanies, that is manifestations of power, and are therefore feared and venerated. This ambivalence of the sacred is not only in the psychological order (in that it attracts or repels), but also in the order of values; the sacred is at once "sacred" and "denied". Commenting on Virgil's phrase *auri sacra fames*, Servius[6] remarks quite rightly that *sacer* can mean at the same time accursed and holy. Eustathius[7] notes the same double meaning with *hagios*, which can express at once the notion "pure" and the notion "polluted".[8] And we find this same ambivalence of the sacred appearing in the early Semitic world[9] and among the Egyptians.[10]

All the negative valuations of "defilement" (contact with corpses, criminals and so on) result from this ambivalence of hierophanies and kratophanies. It is dangerous to come near any defiled or consecrated object in a profane state—without, that is, the proper ritual preparation. What is called taboo—from a Polynesian word that the ethnologists have taken over—means just that: it is the fact of things', or places', or persons', being cut off, or "forbidden", because contact with them is dangerous. Generally speaking, any object, action or person which either has naturally, or acquires by some shift of ontological level, force of a nature more or less uncertain, is, or becomes, taboo. The study of the nature of taboos and of things, persons or actions that are taboo, is quite a rich one. You can get some idea of this by glancing through Part II of Frazer's *The Golden Bough, Taboo and the Perils of the Soul*, or Webster's huge catalogue in his book *Taboo*. Here I will simply quote a few examples from Van Gennep's monograph, *Tabou et totémisme à Madagascar*.[11] The Malagasy word that corresponds to *taboo* is *fady, faly*, which means what is "sacred, forbidden, out of bounds, incestuous, ill-omened"[12]—really, in other words, what is dangerous.[13] ...

[Eliade continues this section 6 and adds: 7. Mana, 8. The Structure of Hierophanies, 9. The Revaluation of Hierophanies, and 10. The Complexity of "Primitive" Religion to complete the chapter.]

QUESTIONS FOR REVIEW AND DISCUSSION

1. In his foreword to *Patterns in Comparative Religion*, what is Eliade's point about the importance of scale? What is his assessment of functionalist approaches to religion or approaches that account for religion from within a related discipline, such as psychology or sociology?

2. In the foreword, Eliade identifies "what *is* religion?" as one of the two key problems addressed by his book; however, he also discounts "the value of beginning with a definition of the religious phenomenon." Why do you think this is? What does he propose in place of starting with a definition of religion?

3. In the foreword to *Patterns in Comparative Religion* Eliade lists five advantages to the design of his study in contrast to other approaches, such as a "treatise on religious phenomena starting with the simplest and working up to the most complex." In your own words, paraphrase Eliade's purpose for this book and the rationale he presents for his methods.

4. In "Approximations," what are some of the theoretical and practical difficulties that Eliade outlines for this study of the sacred?

5. Eliade acknowledges the dizzying, even paralyzing, diversity of religious expressions, which he in turn draws upon to illustrate and reinforce his arguments. How does he characterize the relationship between local manifestations of the sacred and universal value?

6. What problems of method does Eliade point out with regard to the materials available to the historian of religion? What makes the job of the "religious historian" so much more difficult and bold than that of the historian? Do you agree?

7. What is Eliade's position with regard to studying religious practices or understandings of the masses vs. the elites? Do you agree with his position?

8. Eliade indicates that rather than choosing to focus only on symbols, or myths, or rites, or divine forms, "The safest method, clearly, is to make use of all these kinds of evidence, omitting no important type, and always asking ourselves what *meaning* is revealed by each of these hierophanies." How is this assertion supported by the structure of his book, *Patterns in Comparative Religion*, or by his life's work more generally?

9. What is Eliade's point with regard to the relationship of cryptic vs. clear hierophanies?

10. Eliade declares that "We must get used to the idea of recognizing hierophanies absolutely everywhere." What are the challenges he indicates for the Western student in this regard and what are the rewards for overcoming this challenge?

11. How does Eliade reconcile the quotation in question 10 with his distinction between sacred and profane?

Notes

1 Translated and quoted by Lévy-Bruhl in *Primitives and the Supernatural*, London, 1936, pp. 45–46.
2 Kruyt, quoted by Lévy-Bruhl, p. 191.
3 Quoted by Lévy-Bruhl, p. 192.
4 Lévy-Bruhl, p. 164.
5 Cf, for instance, Lévy-Bruhl, *Primitive Mentality*, London, 1923, pp. 36, 261–64, 352 sq; H. Webster, *Taboo, A Sociological Study*, Standford, 1942, pp. 230 ff.
6 *Ad. Aen.*, iii. 75.
7 *Ad Iliadem*, xxiii, 429.
8 Cf. Harrison, *Prolegomena to the Study of Greek Religion*, 3rd ed., Cambridge, 1922, p. 59.
9 Cf. Robertson Smith, *The Religion of the Semites*, 3rd ed., London, 1927, pp. 446–54.
10 Cf. W. F. Albright, *From the Stone Age to Christianity*, 2nd ed., Baltimore, 1946, p. 321, n. 45.
11 Paris, 1904.
12 Van Gennep, p. 12.
13 Van Gennep, p. 23.

PART 3

The Newer Strata: Contemporary Voices in the Scholarly Study of Religion

17 On Doing Philosophy of Religion

John Hick

John Hick (1922–2012) was born in Yorkshire, England, and received his doctorate in philosophy from Oxford. He taught at Claremont Graduate University and the University of Birmingham. Although raised with fundamentalist Christian beliefs, he converted to evangelical Christianity, and ultimately was granted membership as a Quaker (Religious Society of Friends). He is known for his contributions to the philosophy of religion, but conducted from a confessional or "religious insider" perspective. He regarded himself as a philosopher and a theologian. His Christian theology is said to be pluralistic and inclusivist, in that it allows for engagement with other faiths, which hold truths of equal validity and from which Christians may themselves learn. The following article is a talk given at the University of Birmingham, in which he offered an informal view of what philosophy of religion meant to him and how it ought to be conducted.

We have to start from where we are and what we are. As I see it, one of the most important things about us is that we are fragments of a much larger whole, and any possible completeness cannot lie in an isolated individual completeness but in a right relationship to the rest of the whole. Physically we are sub-microscopic dots in the vastness of the universe. As human beings we are one among some six billion others. As personalities we are incomplete, imperfect, idiosyncratic, always needing the complementarity of others. As thinkers we can only operate from a partial point of view, with limited abilities, with biases and prejudices, and with a very limited range of experience. Trying to look at myself in this light, in relation to work in the philosophy of religion, the only kind of which I am capable is the kind in which I have been trained, which is the post-logical positivist kind broadly called analytical. This began as linguistic analysis but has long since broadened out considerably to include metaphysics. You identify a problem, learn what has been said about it by major thinkers past and present, examine critically what they have said, and occasionally come up with a new suggestion of your own. You are naturally attached to this and will defend it against criticism – the process whereby it is tested in debate. You have to remember that it is an hypothesis, not a revealed truth, and you have to be ready to modify and develop it, and if necessary in the last resort to abandon it. But as in the sciences failed hypotheses can also contribute to the larger process of truth seeking.

But if a philosophical hypothesis is to contribute, either by being tenable or by being seen not to be tenable, it has to be formulated as clearly and precisely as possible. So analytical philosophers try not to go in for vague but impressive sounding language which cannot be cashed as usable intellectual currency. Further, so far as I am concerned, life is too short to spend it on authors who cannot think clearly enough to write clearly. Reading them is okay for the young, who quite rightly will try anything because they think they have all the time in the world; and in this way, hopefully, they develop discrimination. But as time becomes more precious, you tend to discriminate more severely. Nevertheless as I read stuff whose approach or method is alien to me, I have to recognise that there is plenty of good work going on in ways which are not to my own taste. But personally I benefit more, whether I agree with them or not, from lucid thinkers such as Anselm, Aquinas, Descartes, Leibniz, Spinoza, Locke, Berkeley, Hume, Kant (who was difficult but never vague), Russell, Moore, Popper, Hartshorne, Quine, Wittgenstein (who was clear though never systematic), more than such as Hegel, Heidegger, Gadamer, Derrida, etc.

The other side of our fragmentariness is that we only have a limited responsibility. We are not responsible for finding the whole Truth, but only for contributing the little that we can to the search. Again, we are not responsible for the state of the whole world, let alone the whole universe. We can take the Dalai Lama's advice: when you have the power to change things for the better, you must do so, but when you can't, don't worry about the fact that you can't.

Another limitation, or example, of fragmentariness, is that I am a westerner and, like all of us, an heir to the western Enlightenment. I have often had it pointed out to me by colleagues of the eastern cultures, particularly in India, how western are the presuppositions of so many of us whom they meet. They see in us, for example, individualism as opposed to their more communal outlook, binary either/or logic as opposed to their tendency to both/and thinking, and suspicion of the mystical as opposed to their tendency to embrace it. But more than a year spent at different times in India and Sri Lanka, and shorter times in Africa, has taught me that there are different ways of being human, which are the great cultures of the earth, and that the culture in which I happen to have been born, and which has formed me, is not normative for all humanity. Therefore we have to accept our own fragmentariness and our need for the balancing influence of others. This is one reason, incidentally, why Christian theology ought to be, although it still usually isn't, done as though in the presence of people of the other world faiths.

More individually, I like order and clarity and dislike chaos, vagueness, and cloudiness. I prefer to leave my desk empty rather than littered with unfinished business. And so in my metaphysical speculations I am probably trying to tidy up the universe in my own mind by finding a systematic picture of it! Question: are systematic thinkers generally also tidy in other aspects of their lives? And unsystematic thinkers generally untidy? Certainly the very systematic Kant was famously tidy, and the very unsystematic Donald Mackinnon, who was a colleague in Cambridge, was incredibly untidy. Note that if there are these correlations, this in no way invalidates either kind of work. It just means that it requires different kinds of minds to do different kinds of intellectual job.

Moving on, what is the philosophy of religion? It is analogous to the philosophy of science, of law, of mind, of morality (i.e. ethics), of knowledge (i.e. epistemology), etc. It is thus not itself a religious exercise but a meta exercise, and it can be carried out by non-religious as much as by religious people. So my own main project in the epistemology of religion, which has been to try to see what in the light of contemporary epistemology a viable religious interpretation of religion would look like, could in principle be done by an atheist. The difference between myself and the atheist would consist in the philosophically extraneous fact that I do and the atheist does not see life in a religious light which can make use of such an interpretation. In actual fact most of those who spend their time on the philosophy of religion do so because they are philosophers for whom religion is very important and thus worth thinking about. But religion can also be important to people, not because it has value to them, but because they feel threatened by it and need continually to assure themselves of its falsity. They are as obsessed with religion as any Christian fundamentalist. They are indeed the mirror image of Christian fundamentalists, and disapprove of the likes of me for not upholding the antiquated theology which they love to attack.

Now my own philosophy of religion manifesto. I hold that from our point of view within it the universe is ambiguous as between religious and naturalistic interpretations. Complete and consistent accounts of both kinds are possible, at least in principle, each including within it an account of the other. To accept either is, and is equally – I want to stress that word 'equally' – an act of faith in the sense that it commits one to a view which cannot be proved, or in any precise sense of the word probabilified, and which therefore *may* be mistaken. This is something that naturalistic thinkers find it as hard as religious thinkers to accept. They don't like to think of naturalism as a faith, though in fact it is.

Concerning this ambiguity, on the religious side the traditional theistic arguments are not conclusive, although they are intellectually fascinating and should certainly form part of a philosophical education. Nor is the modern revival of the ontological argument by Hartshorne and Malcolm, based on Anselm's so called second form of the argument; nor is Plantinga's version, using possible worlds logic, and nor again is Swinburne's cumulative argument using Bayes' probability theorem. I won't bore you here with these, or with the 'fine tuning' argument in astro-physics propounded by Barrow and Tipler and many others, which is also suggestive but also inconclusive.

Let us now use the word 'God' as our familiar western term for the putative Ultimate Reality to which the religions point, without at this stage defining that reality as an infinite person, or three infinite persons, or in any other specific way. The right approach for a religious interpretation of religion is, I believe, not an argument directly for the existence of such a reality, but an argument for the rationality of trusting religious experience as a mediated awareness of that reality – about which more presently.

On the other side, although the naturalistic assumption is pervasive in all our minds, and is indeed completely dominant as an unquestioned assumption of our western culture, its very dominance hides foundations which are as shaky and inadequate as the theistic arguments. For the only religion-proof form of naturalism requires strict materialism, or as a more friendly name for it, physicalism – the view that nothing exists but the physical universe, including of course human brains and their activity. For if there is further reality beyond the physical, this constitutes a gaping hole in a thoroughgoing naturalism. If naturalistic thinkers are not willing to commit themselves to strict physicalism they ought to be aware that their position has thereby ceased to be religion-proof. In a universe in which there is reality beyond the physical it is impossible to exclude the divine *a priori*.

But there are serious logical and empirical flaws in strict physicalism. The logical flaw is that the physical universe is law-governed and proceeds by cause and effect, so that everything that happens is determined. It is true that the physicists speak of indeterminacy in the movements of the ultimate quanta of energy. But (a) there is a question whether this simply means that we cannot predict the movements of the ultimate particles, not that a theoretical omniscient mind could not predict them, and (b) even if there is genuine quantum indeterminacy, this is swamped in the large scale statistical regularities which constitute the 'laws' of nature – somewhat as the fact that we cannot predict when a given individual will die does not affect the statistical death rates of large populations. And physical objects at our level of awareness are multi-billion populations of the ultimate particles. And so according to physicalism all events, at least on the scale of which we are conscious, including crucially the continuous electro-chemical activity which constitutes the functioning of our own brains, are determined. But in that case we meet the contradiction, which has been pointed out by 20th century philosophers such as Karl Popper, and which Epicurus pointed out long ago when he said that 'He who says that all things happen of necessity cannot criticise another who says that not all things happen of necessity. For he has to admit that the assertion itself happens of necessity'. So there is a practical contradiction at the heart of any strictly physicalist position – practical as in the case of the man who saws off the branch on which he is sitting.

So when Susan Greenfield for example, Professor of Pharmacology at Oxford, says in her recent fascinating popular TV programme about the brain that freewill is an illusion, and holds that more research is needed to find out just where in the brain the illusion is created, she is revealing a complete lack of philosophical sophistication. This on two counts. First, she presumably thinks that, in coming to the conclusion that free will is an illusion she was making a rational judgment based on evidence, and does not realise that, according to her own conclusion, her brain came by physical necessity to that conclusion, and differs in this respect from many other brains, such as for example (amongst many others), that of Wolf Singer, Director of the Max Planck Institute for Brain Research in Frankfurt who is, if Susan Greenfield is right, programmed by physical necessity to conclude that mental 'attributes transcend the reach of purely neurobiological reductionism' (*From Brains to Consciousness*, ed. Rose, Penguin Books, 1998, p. 241). And second, like so many neuro-scientists, she fails to appreciate the elementary point that the fact that mental events are always correlated with brain events does not mean that they are identical with brain events.

But there are also empirical, in the sense of observational, difficulties involved in physicalism. I am not myself very impressed by the ESP experiments done by Rhine at Duke University and by many others elsewhere, probably because I have an irrational distrust of statistical data; but I am impressed by some of the anecdotal evidence – 'anecdotal' being a scientist's disparaging word for real life human testimony as distinguished from laboratory experiments. Law courts work largely on the basis of real life human testimony, as indeed does much of ordinary life, and it seems to me a perfectly valid basis on which to form beliefs about events of a kind that can only very unreliably be produced at will in a lab. Let me give an example which came to my attention only a few weeks ago of anecdotally evidenced ESP. I was having lunch with a former neighbour who has recently retired from being a judge. He is a standard agnostic, but he told me of an experience that has left him extremely puzzled. A barrister a generation older than himself had been his pupil master and mentor and had been almost like a father to him. When the older man was dying of cancer the judge visited him every day and spent as much time as he could with him. One day the old man seemed to be approaching a critical state, and when the judge left for the night he asked the nurse in charge to ring him if the patient became worse, saying that he would want to come at any time. Then he went home. At three in the morning he suddenly woke with a very strong sense or feeling that the old man was present there with him in his bedroom, not physically present, not seen or heard, but nevertheless very definitely there. In the morning the nurse told him that she had not rung him during the night because the end came too suddenly, but the patient had died at 3 a.m. He saw the medical record which confirmed the time. He could not believe that his experience at 3 a.m. could have been pure coincidence, and he asked me what I made of it. I said that a minimal interpretation would be unconscious telepathic contact between himself and the patient. The literature of parapsychology contains innumerable examples, sometimes in the form of what are known as crisis apparitions. Some of the most impressive of these come from the time before telephone and radio, when messages from, say, India to Britain took many weeks. They are cases, typically from the 19th century, of a husband in India being quite unexpectedly killed in an accident and of his wife in England seeing an apparition of him at that same time and being aware that he had died, the wife having told others about this both orally and in writing very soon afterwards and long before the official news came. This telepathic explanation was a relief to the judge, since it did not commit him to a belief in any kind of life after death. But for our present purpose it is important to see that if such telepathic interactions, i.e. non-physical effects of one mind on another, occur, this is *as* fatal to strict physicalism as would be a proven life after death.

I should add here that Soviet researchers at the Institute for Brain Research in Leningrad, before and up to the second world war, who were of course dogmatic materialists, were nevertheless interested in telepathy, which they found to be a genuine phenomenon, and worked on it because their authorities thought it might possibly have some military use. They devised experiments to find out what kind of physical radiation from brain to brain was involved. They put the telepathic sender and receiver, one in a screening chamber of sheet iron and the other in a screening chamber lined with lead. This was to confirm that when you cut out known forms of radiation, telepathy does not occur. But to their surprise the screening made no difference to the positive results. They also found that distance between the two subjects, varying from 25 metres to 1,700 kilometres, made no difference and that there was no time–distance correlation, as there is with all known forms of radiation. And so they left the presumed physical nature of telepathy as something yet to be discovered, their materialist faith being too strong to admit a non-physical mind to mind causation.

Now I suppose that nothing in this area can be said to be 100% certain. But it does seem to me more rational to conclude that ESP occurs, and is not a physical effect, and therefore that there is more to reality than matter, than to maintain a dogmatic physicalism regardless of the evidence. It is also necessary, as I pointed out earlier, to affirm intellectual and volitional freedom because to profess to deny it on rational grounds is be in a self-contradictory position. But in that case the physicalist, or naturalistic, assumption is simply a local cultural consensus taken, as a cultural consensus always is, as established fact. For if there is reality beyond the physical, or in addition to the physical, the door is open to religious possibilities.

So the situation thus far is that, on the one hand, there are no religious phenomena – and ESP as such is not a religious phenomenon – that cannot in principle be described in purely naturalistic terms. But on the other hand, the assumption that the naturalistic account is correct does not have a privileged status over against a religious account. It only seems so from the point of view of an already existing naturalistic faith. The exceptions to this statement are those in which a religious picture contradicts known, or highly probable, conclusions of any of the special sciences – as, for example, in the case of 'creationists' who believe that the world was created some four thousand years ago. And of course the churches, from the time of Galileo to Darwin, have been habitually behind the times and have needlessly involved themselves in contradictions of this kind. But that is a problem for the churches, not for philosophers. Setting the churches' self-created problem aside, the naturalistic picture is threatened by the fact that it can only be totally consistent and religion-proof if it accepts a strict physicalism, to embrace which as a freely reasoned belief is self-refuting, and which also has at least a potential problem, I would say an actual problem, with ESP.

But on the other side, a religious picture is threatened by the appalling problem of human and animal suffering and human wickedness, the ancient problem of evil. For the great world faiths are all, though in different ways and with different qualifications, forms of cosmic optimism. And so the fact of evil constitutes the biggest obstacle there is to all major forms of religious belief. Any religious interpretation of the universe has to recognise the extreme toughness and non-human-centredness of any creative process that is taking place, and has to set this within a very large view, involving many lives in many worlds. I have attempted this in *Evil and the God of Love* and *Death and Eternal Life*, and cannot attempt to summarise all that here. For our present purpose I simply have to leave it as a vast acknowledged problem.

But how to justify accepting religious experience as cognitive? This is a difficult area because 'religious experience' covers such a vast field ranging from manifestly human imaginings expressing hopes and fears and prejudices, to profoundly impressive and valuably transformative experiences. We have to take the matter in three stages. First, we live all the time by the principle that what seems to be so is so, unless we have adequate reason to doubt it. In other words, it is in general rational to trust our experience. Otherwise we would walk into walls, get run over by traffic, etc., etc. This principle is of course always subject to the proviso that we have no good reason to suspect our experience in a particular case to be erroneous or hallucinatory. But apparently cognitive experience is, so to speak, innocent until proved guilty. This basic principle, I suggest, applies to religious as much as to sense experience, for both are apparently cognitive. And so instead of assuming that it is guilty until proved innocent, we should assume that it is innocent until proved guilty. And so the question becomes, on what grounds have we – our modern western society – judged it to be guilty, delusory?

Well, the paradigm of experience that we all accept as cognitive is sense experience, because (1) it forces itself upon us, so that (2) everyone participates in it, and (3) it is uniform – or very largely so – throughout the world. If we did not experience the physical world correctly for the kind of physical organism that we are, the world would eliminate us. In contrast, religious experience (1) is not compulsory, so that (2) not everyone at any given time seems to participate in it, and (3) it is not uniform throughout the world, but on the contrary takes many different forms. At first glance these differences discredit religious experience. But on second thoughts, not. The second and third factors both depend on the first, the compulsoriness of sense experience versus the non-compulsoriness of religious experience. But I suggest that this is appropriately correlated with the different putative objects of these two types of experience. Our natural or physical environment has to force itself upon us as sheer brute fact if we are to survive within it. But if we are living at the same time within an interpenetrating supra-natural environment, may this not be of such a kind that it does *not* force itself upon us? Is it not of the very nature of value-laden reality that it can only be freely recognised? Suppose the Transcendent to which the religions point is such that the only appropriate human recognition of it is a self-committing cognitive choice, reorientating us, or beginning to reorient us, towards a reality of limitless value – in traditional religious terms, a faith response involving the whole person? Will not this be, in its very nature, a response that cannot be forced? And if the religious response is in its essential nature free, it is not surprising that we do not find everyone making that response. It may be that ultimately everyone will, but at present not.

But what about the third factor, the immense variety of forms of religious experience around the world, in contrast to the global uniformity of sense experience? Does not this discredit it? Not, I suggest, if we apply another epistemological principle which is well established elsewhere. This is the principle that was succinctly expressed by Thomas Aquinas when he wrote that 'Things known are in the knower according to the mode of the knower' (*S.T.*, II/II, Q. 1, art. 2). But this has a much wider application than he realised – which provokes the thought that almost everything has been said before, but often by people who did not know that they were saying it! Its most massive and influential development is of course in Kant's first *Critique*. But Kant applied it only to sense experience and did not extend it to religious experience. Consequently his own epistemology of religion was quite different from that which I am going very briefly to outline. He held that in the case of sense experience there is a reality beyond us, which is somehow affecting us all the time, but that the form that our awareness of it takes is always and necessarily determined by the structure of human consciousness. And so he sought to identify the categories (substance, causation, etc.) that are necessary for experience to occur within a unitary finite consciousness. What I want to take from him, however, is not his complex categorical system but only his basic insight that we cannot be aware of things as they are in themselves, unobserved, but always and only as they appear to us with our distinctive, and distinctively limited, cognitive apparatus. Our world, as we consciously perceive it, is partly our own construction, a fact that requires the distinction between the world as it is in itself and as to appears to us. This is a commonplace today in cognitive psychology as well as in epistemology. To develop a concept of Wittgenstein's, though in a way that he himself did not authorise, all experiencing is experiencing-as.

So my neo- or quasi- or, if you like, pseudo-Kantian suggestion is that whereas Kant held that God is a necessary postulate of the moral life, I suggest that a transcendent Ultimate Reality, or the Real, is a necessary postulate of the religious life in its global variety. This Reality is experienced by human beings in a manner analogous to that in which, according to Kant, we experience the world, namely by informational input from external reality being interpreted by the mind in terms of its own categorial scheme and thus coming to consciousness as meaningful phenomenal experience. But whereas Kant held that the categories of thought structuring sense experience are universal throughout the human species, the categories of thought which structure religious experience are historically formed and vary from culture to culture. The two key concepts are those of deity, which presides over the monotheisms and polytheisms, and of the non-personal absolute, which presides over the non-theistic religions. These basic categories are, to use Kant's language, then schematised or made concrete, not as in Kant's system in terms of the abstract form of time, but in terms of the filled time of history and culture, as a range of specific god figures (Jahweh, the Heavenly Father, Allah, Vishnu, Shiva, etc.), and specifically conceived absolutes (Brahman, Nirvana, the Tao, etc.), which thus constitute the personae and impersonae of the Real in relation to humanity. And although there is not time to expand this here, this hypothesis requires that the Real in itself is, in relation to the human mind, ineffable, or as I would rather say transcategorial, i.e. beyond the range of our human conceptual systems. And if we ask, as well we may, why we should postulate a transcategorial Ultimate Reality, the answer is that this constitutes the difference between a religious and a naturalistic understanding of the universe. A religious interpretation of the universe will be founded on the basic faith that religious experience is not purely projection, but is responsive projection. If we then take account not only of one tradition but of religious experience globally, then I suggest that we shall require the two tier model of the transcategorial noumenal reality and its varied phenomenal manifestations to human consciousness.

It follows that religious experience is not to be taken at face value as an experience of the Ultimate Reality as it is in itself but rather as an experience formed jointly by the universal presence of the Real and our own varying religious conceptualities and spiritual practices. And if we now ask how it is that the ineffable Real can affect us, the answer has to be that given by the mystics, namely that there is an aspect or dimension of our own nature that is inherently responsive to, or akin to, or on one view even continuous with, the Real. This is the image of God within us, or what the Quakers call that of God in everyone, or the atman which we all are in the depths of our being and which is ultimately identical with Brahman, or the universal Buddha nature which is obscured within us by self-concern, but the recovery of which is a salvific transformation, or again the Tao within which answers to the Tao without.

Religious experience, then, I am suggesting, is to a greater or lesser degree a fragmentary response to the Real. But we have to note that religious concepts can also inform modes of experience that are in no degree responses to the Real, but entirely projections of human hatred, greed, and prejudice. The criterion, which is taught in all the great traditions, lies in the fruits of such experience in human life, namely in a gradual transformation from natural self-centredness towards a universal compassion, feeling with and for others, and acting accordingly.

All this is not an argument that those who do not currently participate in the wide range of human religious experience should accept it as authentically cognitive. They are not under any obligation to do so. For they are operating with a more restricted range of data than those for whom religious experience is an important part of their data. As a large intermediate group, many ordinary religious believers who do participate in this mode of experience, though only very rarely and slightly, can properly be influenced by the existence of the saints or mahatmas in whom we see very clearly the fruits of the religious response. However if there is nothing at all in your experience that resonates, however feebly, to the reports of the saints, then you have no reason to think that they are more in touch with reality than the rest of us. On the contrary, they must be more deeply deluded. So my argument is the comparatively modest one that, as rational beings, those who *do* participate in the wide field of religious experience are fully entitled to trust it as genuinely cognitive, as an enhanced awareness of reality, though one that involves all the time our own human conceptual systems and human imagination.

So the two basic contrary responses to the ambiguity of the universe consist in two different ways of experiencing our existence within it. In one way our life is, at least sometimes, experienced as taking place in relation to, or in the presence of, an Ultimate Reality, variously conceived and experienced as one or other of its humanly formed personae or impersonae. One aspect of this is the sense of an overarching meaning in life, going beyond the individual meanings which we find or construct for ourselves, in our relationships to others, in the use of our skills, in the creation of beauty or the discovery of truth, and so on. The more ultimate meaning of our lives depends on what kind of universe we believe ourselves to be part of, and more particularly whether we believe that we exist within a cosmic process leading to a limitlessly desirable future. For the meaning of the present moment depends, in important measure, on the future to which it is leading – a point that Sartre made very well. The outcome determines retrospectively the meaning of the events leading to that outcome. If the process of existence is not leading anywhere, then we are just contingently fortunate or unfortunate in the circumstances of our lives, but with more misfortune than good fortune being presently evident in human life as a whole. And that's all there is to it. If on the other hand the cosmic optimism of the great religious traditions is well founded, this gives to our present situation, both in its fortunate and its unfortunate aspects, the positive character that Julian of Norwich expressed in her famous saying, which she repeats a number of times, that in the end 'all shall be well, and all shall be well, and all manner of thing shall be well'. This was not for her a guarantee against accidents and illnesses, hardships, pains, sorrows, failures, death. It did not mean that we may not face all manner of sorrows and disasters, as well as all the wealth of good things that also happen to us. It means that beyond all this, and within all this, we can have an ultimate trust. In practice, let it be admitted, this can often be so difficult as to be beyond the capacity of almost anyone. Even Jesus, as he died, is said to have felt deserted by God. But nevertheless, according to the religions, the structure of the universe – meaning not just the physical universe but the totality of reality – is such that the cosmic optimism which they teach is objectively well founded.

So, to conclude, my basic epistemological argument is that it is *as* rational for those who participate sufficiently in the religious response to the universe to adopt and try to live in terms of a religious conception of it, as it is for those who do not currently participate in that response to adopt a naturalistic interpretation of it. I would add however that we seem to have an inborn tendency to experience the natural in terms of the supra-natural. This tendency can be repressed or perverted, as in Soviet Russia, Maoist China, and Nazi Germany, and also in a quite different way in our own contemporary western secular culture. But we are ourselves part of the totality of reality, and it may well be that the religious aspect of our nature answers to the character of the totality. At any rate, I maintain that it is just as reasonable, just as rational, just as intellectually responsible, to take the risk of trusting the religious aspect of our nature as it is to take the opposite risk of suppressing it – which is not, needless to say, a risk of perdition, but of being blind, at least for now, to an enormously important and transforming range of reality.

I would also add, however, that from a religious point of view it is entirely possible for many people to be responding in their lives to the universal presence of the transcendent Real in a felt imperative to value and serve their fellow humans both near and far, without using religious concepts to structure that awareness. In other words, there can be, and are, 'secular' servants of humanity who may also attain the level of saintliness. If the religions are right, there is a great deal more for them still to discover, but the discovery – in this life or beyond – will be wholly positive, not a 'judgment' but a welcome!

QUESTIONS FOR REVIEW AND DISCUSSION

1. What is the purpose of philosophy as implied by Hick, and what sort of philosopher does he regard himself to be?
2. What does Hick mean by "fragmentariness" and what implications does it have for philosophy or theology from his perspective? Do you agree?
3. How does Hick distinguish between the implications of philosophy of religion for an atheist versus a believer?
4. What does Hick see as the ambiguities inherent in the religious world-view? What are his criticisms of pure physicalism?
5. Does Hick's concession to anecdotal evidence about extra-sensory perceptions and phenomena strengthen his argument?
6. What does Hick regard as the largest obstacle to forms of religious belief? Do you agree, or can you think of other obstacles?
7. How does Hick modify Kant's argument that we are limited by our cognitive apparatus to make a case for transcategorical Absolute Reality, and the diversity of religions? Evaluate his argument.
8. What, according to Hick, is religious experience? Is it necessary for an atheist to believe in it as an authentic cognition?
9. Does Hick regard the religious world-view as more or less "rational" than the naturalistic one? What do you think?

18 Islam and the Encounter of Religions

Seyyed Hossein Nasr

Seyyed Hossein Nasr (1933–) was born in Tehran and his distinguished career includes teaching, training scholars, and publishing widely in both Iran and North America. He earned science degrees from MIT and Harvard followed by a doctorate from Harvard in the history of science alongside his extensive Islamic studies. Even at MIT he had decided that Islamic and perennial philosophy would better address his intellectual and existential questions than would his studies in the natural sciences. This led him back to Iran for more traditional forms of Islamic philosophical study and an influential academic career there until the 1979 revolution. He left Iran and delivered the prestigious Gifford Lectures in Scotland in 1980, which became the book *Knowledge and the Sacred*. He has written dozens of books and many times that number of articles and remains engaged in religious practice as well as wide-ranging activities from interfaith dialogue to lectures and scholarship about Sufism, traditional philosophy, and various topics within and beyond Islam. Since 1984 Nasr has served as Professor of Islamic Studies at George Washington University.

> Lo! We did reveal the Torah, wherein is guidance and a light, by which the Prophets who surrendered (unto Allah) judged the Jews, and the rabbis and the priests (judged) by such of Allah's Scriptures as they were bidden to observe, and thereunto were they witnesses. So fear not mankind, but fear Me. And barter not My revelations for a little gain. Whoso judgeth not by that which Allah hath revealed: such are disbelievers.
>
> (Quran, V, 44)

> *The difference among creatures comes from the outward* FORM (nām);
> *When one* PENETRATES *into the inner meaning* (ma'nā) *there is peace.*
> *Oh marrow of existence! It is because of the point of view in question*
> *That there has* COME *into being differences among the Muslim, Zoroastrian and Jew.*
>
> (*Rûmî*)

Section I

Because it is concerned with the inner meaning *(ma'nā)* through the penetration of the outward form *(nām)*, Sufism is by nature qualified to delve into the mysterious unity that underlies the diversity of religious forms. It is, moreover, the only aspect of Islam that can do full justice to the more profound questions of comparative religion, questions which cannot be ignored without violating the nature of religion itself. Moreover, the spread of modern influences into the Islamic world has made a serious study of comparative religion into an imperative need; the way to meet this need is to make use of all the keys stored in the treasury of Sufi wisdom wherewith to open doors which would otherwise remain locked and thus help to solve many intellectual problems by drawing on the metaphysical insight provided by the esoteric teachings of Islam as contained in Sufism.

In considering the problem of comparative religion from the Islamic point of view, it must be remembered at the outset that the metaphysical and theological significance of the presence of other religions differs depending on whether one is considering homogeneous traditional civilizations or the modern world, in which a homogeneous world-view is no longer to be found. For traditional man, Muslim or otherwise, that is, a man whose life and thought are moulded by a set of principles of transcendent origin and who lives in a society in which these principles are manifested in every sphere, other religious traditions appear as alien worlds which do not concern him as an immediate spiritual reality save in exceptional cases which only go to prove the rule. Before modern times the founder of each religion appeared as the sun in the solar system in which his followers were born, lived and died. The founders of other religions were either not known—just as when the sun shines one can no longer observe the stars, which are nevertheless suns in their own right—or in certain cases such as that of Islam itself they were relegated to the rank of stars in the firmament, which do not have the same significance as the sun although they too are suns at the centre of their own solar systems.

Just as man is mentally and psychologically constituted in such a way as to live in a physical world with only one sun, even if modern astronomy assures him of the presence of others, so he is constituted religiously and spiritually to live under the light of the particular sun who is the founder of the religion to which he belongs. In normal times a man's religion is *the* religion, and in fact each religion addresses itself to a humanity which, for it, is humanity as such. The exclusiveness of a religion is a symbol of its divine origin, of the fact that it comes from the Absolute, of its being in itself a total way of life. Under normal circumstances there would be no need to take cognizance of the metaphysical significance of other traditions, just as normally man needs only to know of the sun of his own solar system in order to live a normal life on earth. Even if modern astronomy teaches him that there are myriads of other suns in the Universe, he relegates this knowledge to the background of his mind and continues to live as if his sun were the only one. The immediate experience of the physical world in which he lives presents to him a picture that has something absolute in its nature because of its symbolic content. Man was created to live in precisely such a world where there is only one sun in the sky so that the normal appearance of a single sun in the firmament corresponds to the natural structure of man's mind and psyche, and alone constitutes a natural and meaningful environment for him.

Likewise, in the religious sphere, man has been created to live in a homogeneous religious tradition, one in which the values of his religion are for him *the* values, absolute and binding. As long as the traditional divisions of humanity continued to subsist it was unnecessary, or, one might even say redundant, to seek to penetrate into the meaning of other traditions except in the particular circumstances when two religious traditions came in direct contact with one other. But even here the significance of this encounter was not the same as it is today when the homogeneity of the traditional climate itself is broken in the West and to a greater or lesser extent in other parts of the world where the modernist outlook has taken root. For centuries Christian and Jewish minorities have lived within the Islamic world and there has been even occasional religious contact between the respective communities; but each community has lived in its own traditional world. The necessity for the study of one tradition by another in such a case has not been at all the same as that faced by a modern educated person who, having been touched by the effect of modern thought, is forced to consider the problems of other religions on a different basis, a basis which concerns the nature of religion itself.

It might then be said that the necessity for studying other religious traditions is brought about by the particular conditions of the modern world, where the bounds of both the astronomical and religious universe have been broken. The dilemma of wishing to be able to remain faithful to one's own religion and yet come to accept the validity of other traditions is one of the results of the abnormal conditions that modern man faces and is a consequence of the anomalous conditions in which he lives. Yet it is a problem that he must face on pain of losing faith in religion itself. For a traditional Muslim living in Fez or Mashhad it is not necessary to be concerned with the verities of Buddhism or Christianity. Nor is it urgent for a peasant in the hills of Italy or Spain to learn about Hinduism. But for a person for whom the homogeneity of a religious culture has been ruptured by modern secularist philosophies or, alternatively, affected by contact with the authentic spirituality of foreign traditions, it is no longer possible to ignore the metaphysical and theological implications of the presence of other religions. If he does so, he falls into the danger of either losing his own religion or having a conception of the Divinity which, to say the least, places a limit upon the Divine Mercy.

The very plurality of religious forms has been used by some as an argument against the validity of all religions. The insistence upon this view, stated in so many different forms today, itself proves the urgency of the study of other religions today for the sake of preserving religion itself. Moreover, this task is placed upon the shoulders of either those who have come into contact with the modern mentality and yet remain spiritually inclined, or else of those who thanks to exceptional circumstances are enabled to carry out this task. Traditional authorities are completely within their rights to address a traditional audience without the need of referring to other religious forms. But there are also those whose vocation it is to provide the keys with which the treasury of wisdom of other traditions can be unlocked, revealing to those who are destined to receive this wisdom the essential unity and universality and at the same time the formal diversity of tradition and revelation. [1] The most powerful defence for religion in the face of modern scepticism is precisely the universality of religion, the realization of the basic truth that God has addressed man many times, in each case saying 'I' and speaking in a language that is suitable for the particular humanity to which the revelation is addressed.[2]

The difficulty of studying the relation between religions seriously arises, of course, only when one is concerned with the truth of religion itself. For the sceptic or the 'scientific' observer or the syncretist the problem never transcends that of historical events and phenomena or of sentimental attitudes; it is not with such an approach that we are concerned here. The essential problem that the study of religion poses is how to preserve religious truth, traditional orthodoxy, the dogmatic theological structures of one's own religion and yet gain knowledge of other traditions and accept them as spiritually valid ways and roads to God. For one who is colour-blind it matters little what colours make up the rainbow. And it is precisely here that the very forces that have made the study of other religions religiously and metaphysically necessary have also made such a study difficult.

Modernism has either destroyed religious faith or else has narrowed it. Men of old were not only less sceptical than modern man but also less narrow in their faith. Today everyone congratulates himself on having an open mind; one can agree that it is good to have the windows of the mind open provided the mind also has walls. If a room has no walls it does not matter very much whether the windows are open or closed. Once man rejects revelation and tradition there is little virtue in religious open-mindedness because there is no longer a criterion for distinguishing the true from the false. Faith has narrowed in the case of many Christians as well as Muslims, Hindus, and others; here one is speaking, not about those who have fallen outside of the tradition, and therefore have no faith either narrow or broad, but about those who remain within it, but whose religious faith has become narrowly constricted as a result of the onslaught of modernism. Just to cite the case of Islam, modernism has not only caused some men to have their faith weakened but it has also produced certain movements against the most universal aspect of Islam, namely Sufism. Often a simple peasant has a more universal conception of Islam than a university-educated rationalist.

Another difficulty that modernism places in the way of a serious study of other religions is its own negation of the very metaphysical principles that underlie all religions. The 'science' of comparative religion or *Religionswissenschaft* began during the age of rationalism and came into its own as a separate discipline during the nineteenth century. The history of this discipline carries with it the limitations and prejudices of the period of its formation.[3] The 'age of enlightenment' saw itself as the final perfection of civilization and studied other religions as a prelude to Christianity with which it somehow identified itself despite its own rebellion against the Christian tradition. This attitude has continued to subsist to a certain degree. That is why to this day Islam receives the least satisfactory treatment at the hands of those interested in comparative religion. Coming after Christianity, it simply does not fit into the pre-conceived pattern that other religions were simple and childish imitations of something that reached its perfection with Christianity through the process of evolution, which everything is supposed somehow to undergo.[4]

Likewise, the nineteenth century left its own mark upon this discipline by impregnating it with theories of linear historical progress and the like, as well as the theory mentioned above, these being the best guarantee of not understanding a religious tradition and its spiritual significance. Phenomenology, which has criticized the shortcomings of the historical method and emphasized the morphological study of all religious manifestations, has been in a sense an improvement, but even that has not been sufficient. What has been lacking is true metaphysics, which alone can reveal the transparency of forms and bring to light their inner meaning. The study of religions began in the West when, on the one hand, the true metaphysical aspect of the Christian tradition had become eclipsed and nearly forgotten and, on the other hand, secular philosophies had become dominant which were from the beginning opposed to the very idea of the Transcendent and the *scientia sacra* which lies hidden within every religion. The study of religions, therefore, has been coloured by the mentality of modern Western man and seen under categories which have been either borrowed from later developments of Christianity or from reactions against Christianity.[5] But in any case that metaphysical background which is indispensable for a study in depth of religion has generally been lacking.

It is not, therefore, without interest for the discipline of comparative religion itself to see how the problem of the encounter of religions is seen from the point of view of other traditions. Such a knowledge provides one more vision of a reality which surrounds us, but it is a vision from another perspective than the familiar one, and therefore reveals another aspect of this encompassing reality. Whatever any orthodox religion has to say about the relation between religions is itself a precious insight into the real nature of religion as such and helps to explain the juxtaposition of religions in the spiritual space in which they are situated. It is with this end in view that the study of the problem of the encounter of religions from the Islamic point of view can be fruitful, since in this way it will also be possible to bring into focus the metaphysical and theological implications of the presence of other religious traditions for Islam itself.

The metaphysical background which was absent when the study of comparative religion began in the West has always been alive within the Islamic tradition as within other living Oriental traditions. According to it reality is comprised not of just the single psychophysical level in which ordinary men live but of multiple states of being standing hierarchically one above the other. Each state of being possesses its own objective reality, the degree of its reality depending on how intense is the light of Being which illuminates it.

At the origin stands the source of all existence, the Absolute which is at once Being and above-Being (the *dhât* of Sufism). The basis of all metaphysical doctrine is the distinction between the Absolute and the relative. The task of all traditional cosmology is to elucidate the science of forms belonging to each state of being. In Islam all metaphysics is contained in the first *Shahâdah*, *Lâ ilâha ill'Allâh* (there is no divinity but the Divine), which means ultimately that only the Absolute is absolute, all else is relative; and all cosmology is contained in principle in the second *Shahâdah*, *Muhammadun rasûl Allâh* (Muhammad is the messenger of God), which means that all that is positive in the Universe, of which Muhammad is the supreme symbol, comes from God.

If then the source of all things, all beings, all forms, is the Transcendent Reality, every being must have an external and an internal aspect, one which manifests it outwardly and another which connects it inwardly to the spiritual world. It is said in the Quran that God is both the Outward *(al-zâhir)* and the Inward *(al-bâtin)*. One might also say, using the language of Sufism, that each thing in the Universe has an outward form *(sûrah)* and an inner essence *(ma'nâ)*. The form belongs to the world of multiplicity and the essence leads to Unity which is the Origin of all things. This is especially true of religion, that direct manifestation of the Divine in the human order. It too must have a form and an essence. And so religions can be studied either in their forms, which should then be described and compared, or in their essence, which leads to their inner unity because the source of all reality and therefore all religion is God who is One. But inasmuch as the essence comes before the form and links it with the higher orders of being it is precisely through the essence that the significance of the form can be understood. Only by gaining a vision of Unity can man come to realize the unity of all that exists. Only in understanding the essence of a religion can its forms become understood as intelligible symbols rather than opaque facts.

Islam's relation to other religions has been dictated by this metaphysical doctrine which underlies its whole intellectual edifice. It has studied both the forms of other religions and, in certain instances, their essence. And today it stands equipped with the necessary intellectual and spiritual means of carrying out this study in the new circumstances which the modern world has placed before it.

A characteristic of Islam which is particularly pertinent in regard to this question is the synthesizing and integrating power of the Islamic revelation, which allows the grace of the prophets and saints of previous religions—especially of the Abrahamic line—to reach the Muslim within the context provided by the grace of the Prophet of Islam. For a Christian all the grace of God is centred in the personality of Christ, without whom there would be no other channel of grace open to man. For the Muslim, within the firmament of Islam, in which the Prophet is like the full moon, other great prophets and saints are like stars which shine in the same firmament, but they do so by virtue of the grace of Muhammad—upon whom be peace. A Muslim can pray to Abraham or Christ, not as Jewish or Christian prophets, but as Muslim ones, and in fact often does so, as seen in the popular 'prayer of Abraham' in the Sunni world and the *Du'ā-yi wārith* in Shi'ite Islam. The synthesizing power of Islam has made possible the integration of previous spiritual poles within the world of Islam and the effective operation of their particular grace within that world. This feature of Islam, so important in the ritual life of Muslims, has also the greatest significance in the intellectual and spiritual aspects of the problem of comparative religion from the Islamic point of view.

Section II

At first sight it may seem strange that, despite the features described above, Islam is, of all the major religions of the world today, the one that has displayed the least amount of interest in the study of the history and doctrines of other religions although its own point of view about religion is the most universal possible. Very few works have been written in this field in Persian and even fewer in Arabic except for translations from European sources.[6] And in recently established programmes in the field of religion in America and England there are fewer Muslim students than those of any other major tradition.

The reason for this relative neglect of the discipline of comparative religion by Muslims is that Islam is not at all disturbed theologically by the presence of other religions. The existence of other traditions is taken for granted, and in fact Islam is based on the conception of the universality of revelation. The Quran among all sacred scriptures is the one that speaks the most universal language,[7] and Muslims believe in the existence of a large number of prophets (traditionally given as 124,000) sent to every people.[8] The spiritual anthropology depicted in the Quran makes of prophecy a necessary element of the human condition. Man is truly man only by virtue of his participation in a tradition. Adam, the first man, was also the first prophet. Man did not evolve from polytheism to monotheism. He began as a monotheist and has to be gradually reminded of the original message of unity *(al-tawhîd)* which he is ever in danger of forgetting. Human history consists of cycles of prophecy, with each new prophecy beginning a new cycle of humanity.

Islam also considers itself to be the reassertion of the original religion, of the doctrine of Unity, which always was and always will be. That is why it is called the primordial religion *(al-dîn al-hanîf)*; it comes at the end of this human cycle to reassert the essential truth of the primordial tradition.[9] It is thus like the *sanâtana dharma* of Hinduism, and on the metaphysical plane has a profound affinity with this tradition, which some Sufis have in fact called the '*Sharî'ah* or religion of Adam'. Not only have some of the most authoritative Muslim scholars of the sub-continent during the Moghul period called the Hindus '*ahl al-kitâb*, belonging to the chain of prophets preceding Islam and beginning with Adam, but also some of the Muslim Indian commentators have considered the prophet Dhu'l-Kifl mentioned in the Quran to be the Buddha of Kifl (Kapilavasta) and the 'Fig Tree' of Surah 95 to be the Bodi Tree under which the Buddha received his illumination. Muslims have always had an innate feeling of possessing in their purest form the doctrines that all religions have come to proclaim before. In Islamic gnosis, or Sufism, this truth is *al-tawhîd* in its metaphysical sense, the eternal wisdom, the *religio perennis*, which Islam has come to reveal in its fullness. For the Sharî'ite Muslim it is the doctrine of monotheism which he believes to have been revealed by every prophet. That is why at the end of the cycle the appearance of the Mahdi brings to light the common inner meaning of all religions.

These and other more contingent factors have made Muslims less interested in the study of other religions than is the case with Christians, Hindus and others. But nevertheless it is necessary today to remind the modern educated Muslims of the universality of their own tradition and of the historical contacts Islam has made with other religions, a fact that has been gradually forgotten in recent times in many circles. Moreover it is necessary to apply the universal principles contained within Islam to study other traditions in the light of the anomalous conditions that the modern world has brought about.[10]

To understand the encounter of Islam with other religions it must be remembered that Islam itself comprises an exoteric and an esoteric dimension, namely a Divine Law or *Shari'ah* and a spiritual way or *Tariqah*. Moreover Islam has cultivated different arts and sciences and intellectual perspectives. It has its own schools of theology, philosophy and theosophy *(hikmah)*—understood in its original sense before modern usage had debased the word. It has had its own historians and scholars, geographers and travellers. Through all of these channels Islam has encountered other religions, and the profundity of the encounter has depended each time on the perspective in question.

If we exclude the modern period with its rapid means of communication, it can be said with safety that Islam has had more contact with other traditions than any other of the world religions. It encountered Christianity and Judaism in its cradle and during its first expansion northward. It met the Iranian religions, both Zoroastrianism and Manichaeism, in the Sassanid Empire. It gradually absorbed small communities in which remnants of late Hellenistic cults continued, especially the Sabaean community of Harran, which considered itself the heir to the most esoteric aspect of the Greek tradition. It met Buddhism in north-west Persia, Afghanistan, and Central Asia, and Hinduism in Sind and later in many parts of the Indian sub-continent. There was even contact with Mongolian and Siberian Shamanism on the popular level, mostly through the Turkish tribes who had followed Shamanism before their conversion to Islam. Moreover the Muslims of Sinkiang were in direct contact with the Chinese tradition.

In fact, of all the important religious traditions of Asia—putting aside Shintoism which was limited to Japan—there is none with which Muslims have had no early intellectual contact, save for the Chinese tradition with which contact on a religious and intellectual level by the main part of the Muslim world happened only after the Mongol invasion. As for the Chinese Muslim Community, it remained more or less separated from its co-religionists further West so that its knowledge of the Chinese tradition was not generally shared. Only an occasional traveller like Ibn Battûtah provided the Muslim intelligentsia with a knowledge of things Chinese. Yet, even with regard to the Chinese tradition the Muslims preserved a sense of respect. The prophetic *hadîth* 'Seek knowledge, even in China' was known by all, and some Persian Sufis have made specific reference to the Divine origin of the Chinese tradition. Farîd al-Din 'Attâr in his *Mantiq al-tayr (Conference of the Birds)*, speaking of the Sîmurgh who symbolizes the Divine Essence and his feather which symbolizes divine revelation, writes:

> An astonishing thing! The first manifestation of the Simurgh took place in China in the middle of the night. One of his feathers fell on China and his reputation filled the world. Everyone made a picture of this feather, and from it formed his own system of ideas, and so fell into a turmoil. This feather is still in the picture-gallery of that country; hence the saying, 'Seek knowledge, even in China!'
>
> But for his manifestation there would not have been so much noise in the world concerning this mysterious Being. This sign of his existence is a token of his glory. All souls carry an impression of the image of his feather. Since the description of it has neither head nor tail, beginning nor end, it is not necessary to say more about it.[11]

As for the encounter of Islam with the Judaeo-Christian tradition, this has persisted throughout nearly fourteen centuries of the history of Islam. Judaism and Christianity themselves are in a sense 'contained' in Islam inasmuch as the latter is the final affirmation of the Abrahamic tradition of which Judaism and Christianity are the two earlier manifestations. However there is no question of historical borrowing here as some orientalists have sought to show; the *Sharî'ah* is a Divine Law similar in many ways to Talmudic law, but not borrowed from it or based upon it; Christ plays a very important role in Islam, but this is not a distortion of the Christian conception of Christ. The latter is, independently of Christianity, a part of the Islamic religious view. Christ and Moses, as well as the other ancient Hebrew prophets, play a part in Islam independently of any possible historical borrowing from Judaism and Christianity. The similarities that exist come only from the common transcendent archetype of Judaism, Christianity and Islam.

Encounters with Judaism and Christianity during the early Islamic centuries were mostly polemical and concerned with theological questions; it can, in fact, be said that the problems faced by Philo and the early Church Fathers, versus the rational demonstration of articles of faith such as the immortality of the soul, resurrection of the body and creation *ex-nihilo*, influenced early Muslim theologians in adopting similar arguments for the defence of Islam against rationalistic criticism.[12] Usually most of the early Muslim works on the history of religion (*al-Milal wa'l-nihal*) contain chapters devoted to Judaism and Christianity, some of which like *al-Mughni* of Qâdî 'Abd al-Jabbâr are precious documents for present-day knowledge of certain aspects of the Eastern Church and of the eastern Christian communities. The figures of Moses and Christ appear in nearly every Muslim religious work, especially those of the Sufis, such as the *Futûhât al-makkiyyah* of Ibn 'Arabî, the *Mathnawî* of Rûmî, or the *Gulshan-i râz* of Shabistarî. Nearly every experience undergone by these prophets, such as the vision of the burning bush by Moses, or Christ's miracle of raising the dead to life, plays an important part in the exposition of Sufi doctrine.[13] Needless to say, all these sources rejected the ideas of divine filiation and incarnation in Christianity, neither of which ideas is in conformity with the Islamic perspective, and occasionally works were written with the express purpose of refuting these doctrines.[14]

It must not be thought that contact between the Muslim and the Christian and Jewish communities has been constant over the ages. During the first centuries of Islam, especially the early Abbasid period, debates between the different communities were common. After the Crusades the bitterness brought about by political events caused the Muslim and Christian communities in the Near East, where their physical contact is closest, to be completely isolated from one another. The same situation is now developing in regard to Judaism as a result of the situation in Palestine. Yet in other parts of the Muslim world where socio-political events did not bring about lasting friction, study of both Christianity and Judaism continued, often with much sympathy, and there have been occasional contacts of a theological and spiritual order between these various communities. Only a century ago the Persian Sufi poet Hâtif Isfahânî praised Christianity as being an affirmation of Divine Unity provided its doctrine of trinity is understood in its metaphysical significance. In his memorable poem *(Tarjf band)* he writes:

> In the church I said to a Christian charmer of hearts,
> 'O thou in whose net the heart is captive!
> O thou to the warp of whose girdle each hair-tip
> of mine is separately attached!
> How long wilt thou continue not to find the way

to the Divine Unity? How long wilt thou impose
on the One the shame of the Trinity?
How can it be right to name the One True God "Father",
"Son", and "Holy Ghost"?'
She parted her sweet lips and said to me, while
with sweet laughter she poured sugar from her lips:
'If thou art aware of the Secret of the Divine Unity
do not cast on us the stigma of infidelity!
In three mirrors the Eternal Beauty cast a ray
from His effulgent countenance.
Silk does not become three things
if thou callest it *Parniyân, Harir,* and *Parand.*'[15]
While we were thus speaking, this chant
rose up beside us from the church bell:
'He is One and there is naught save He:
There is no God save Him alone!'[16]

During this century the great Algerian Sufi, Shaykh Ahmad al-'AIawî, echoed this same view when he called for the joining of hands of all religions to combat modern unbelief and showed particular interest in Christianity, whose doctrines he knew well.[17] Altogether the contact between Islam and the Judaeo-Christian tradition over the centuries has been immense both on the formal and informal planes. This heritage provides all that is needed for a meaningful encounter between these religions today.

As for the Iranian religions, Islam encountered them also early in its career as it subdued the Sassanid Empire and penetrated into the Iranian plateau. During the three or four centuries when Islam gradually became completely dominant in Persia it had numerous contacts with these religions and especially with Zoroastrianism and Manichaeism. It even influenced some of the later Zoroastrian writings produced in the early Islamic period in the same way that elements of Zoroastrianism were integrated into certain perspectives of Islamic intellectual life.[18] Debates carried on with followers of Iranian religions in Basra and Baghdad itself are recorded in early theological and historical sources. From the beginning the Zoroastrians were accepted as a 'People of the Book' while the Manichaeans were opposed on fundamental theological grounds. Nevertheless the influence of the latter, especially in regard to cosmogonical and cosmological ideas, is to be seen in certain Ismâ'îlî cosmologies and most likely also in some of the writings of Muhammad ibn Zakariyyâ' al-Râzâ. Manichaean beliefs have also been described by many scholars such as Ibn al-Nadîm and Bîrûnî, and in fact Muslim works serve as a valuable source for present-day knowledge of certain aspects of Manichaeism.[19]

Zoroastrianism had more intimate contact with Islam than did Manichaeism. But here again the situation has not been the same in all Muslim lands. Zoroastrianism, although known on the popular level everywhere, was not as much studied in the Arab part of the Muslim world as in Persia which had been its ancient home.[20] In Persia Zoroastrianism provided first of all a vocabulary for Sufi poets like Hâfiz who often speak of the 'fire-temple', the Zoroastrian priest, etc., as symbols of the Sufi centre *(khâniqâh* or *zâwiyah)*, the spiritual master, and so on;[21] this manner of speaking, however, does not at all imply an historical influence of Zoroastrianism upon Sufism. Rather is it a means whereby the Sufi asserted the independence of esotericism from the exoteric forms of the revelation, in the sense that esotericism does not derive from exotericism but directly from God who is the source of the revelation containing both dimensions. Zoroastrian angelology and cosmology were also resuscitated by Shihâbal-Din Suhrawardî, the founder of the school of Illumination or *Ishrâq*, who made these symbols transparent in the light of Islamic gnosis.[22] In this domain there was also an influence of the *Ishrâqî* school itself upon certain schools of later Zoroastrianism such as the movement connected with the name of Adhar Kaywan.

It is when we turn to the Indian religions—essentially Hinduism and Buddhism—that from the Islamic point of view the question of understanding and penetrating into religious forms becomes more difficult. This difficulty is brought about not only because of the mythological language of the Indian traditions which is different from the 'abstract' language of Islam, but also because in going from the one tradition to the others one moves from the background of the Abrahamic traditions to a different spiritual climate. Nevertheless Islam has had profound contact with the religions of India on both the formal and metaphysical planes. Already through the Indian sciences which had reached the Muslims both through Pahlavi and directly from Sanskrit, some knowledge had been gained of Indian culture during the early Islamic period. But it is thanks to the incomparable *Tahqîq mâ li'l-hind* or *India* of Bîrûnî, a work unique in the exactitude of its compilation, that medieval Muslims gained a knowledge of Hinduism, especially the Vishnavite school with which Bîrûnî seems to have been best acquainted.[23] He was also responsible for the translation of the *Patañjali Yoga* into Arabic, and in fact inaugurated a tradition of contact with Hinduism which, although interrupted by several gaps in time, continued through Amir Khusraw Dihlawî, to Abu'l-Fadl, Dârâ Shukûh, and the vast movement of translation of Hindu works into Persian in the Moghul period.[24]

On the religious plane, although the Zoroastrians were definitely included among *the ahl al-kitâb* or 'people of the Book', there was a debate among the general Muslim public as to where Hinduism stood, although as already mentioned many of the *ulamâ of* India definitely considered Hindus as 'people of the Book'. It goes without saying that in India itself the Muslims certainly did not treat the Hindus as simple pagans or idol-worshippers like those of Arabia but came to respect them as possessing a religion of their own. As already mentioned, many Sufis in India called Hinduism the religion of Adam, and such an orthodox Naqshbandî saint as Mirzâ Mazhar Jân Jânân considered the Vedas as divinely inspired. There was, in fact, in Islam a presentiment of the primordial character of Hinduism which moved many Muslim authors to identify Brahman with Abraham. This connection may seem strange linguistically but it contains a deep metaphysical significance. Abraham is, for Islam, the original patriarch identified with the primordial religion *(al-din al-hanîf)* which Islam came to reassert and reaffirm. The connection of the name of the *barâhimah* (namely Hindus) with Abraham was precisely an assertion of the primordial nature of the Hindu tradition in the Muslim mind.

The Sufi master 'Abd al-Karim al-Jîlî writes in his *al-Insân al-kâmil:*

> The people of the book are divided into many groups. As for the *barâhimah* [Hindus] they claim that they belong to the religion of Abraham and that they are of his progeny and possess special acts of worship. ... The *barâhimah* worship God absolutely without [recourse to] prophet or messenger. In fact, they say there is nothing in the world of existence except that it be the created of God. They testify to His Oneness in Being, but deny the prophets and messengers completely. Their worship of the Truth is like that of the prophets before their prophetic mission. They claim to be the children of Abraham—upon whom be peace—and say that they possess a book written for them by Abraham—upon whom be peace—himself, except that they say that it came from

His Lord. In it the truth of things is mentioned and it has five parts. As for the four parts they permit their reading to everyone. But as for the fifth part they do not allow its reading except to a few among them, because of its depth and unfathomableness. It is well known among them that whoever reads the fifth part of their book will of necessity come into the fold of Islam and enter into the religion of Muhammad—upon whom be peace.[25]

Al-Jîlî distinguishes between Hindu metaphysics and the daily practice of the Hindus and identifies especially their metaphysical doctrines with the doctrine of Divine Unity in Islam. His reference to the 'Fifth Veda' signifies precisely the inner identity of the esoteric and metaphysical doctrines of the two traditions. He, like the other Sufis, sought to approach Hinduism through a metaphysical penetration into its mythological structure to reveal the presence of the One behind the veil of the many. In this domain his approach was not basically different from the attitude of those Sufis who tried to interpret the Christian Trinity as an assertion rather than a negation of Divine Unity.

The translation of Hindu works into Persian during the Moghul period is an event of great spiritual significance whose full import has not as yet been explored, especially by non-Persian and non-Indian Muslims. The central figure in this movement was the prince Dârâ Shukûh who was responsible for the translation of the *Bhagavad-Gîtâ*, the *Yoga Vasishtha*, and, most important of all, the *Upanishads*. It was from his Persian version that the Latin translation of Anquetil-Duperron was made, a translation which influenced many of the nineteenth-century European philosophers like Schelling and a copy of which was owned by the mystic poet William Blake.[26]

Whatever the significance of this translation has been for the spread of Hindu studies in the West, it is even more significant for the question of the religious encounter between Hinduism and Islam today. In the same way that the Crusades nearly destroyed amicable contacts between Islam and Christianity in the Near East, the events of the past century have embittered the contact between Hinduism and Islam in the Indian sub-continent itself, and perhaps a land like Persia, where there has been both the historical contact with Hinduism and lack of bitter political encounters during recent times, could be a more suitable place for making a basic study of the relations between Hinduism and Islam on the highest level.

Be that as it may, the translations of Dârâ Shukûh do not at all indicate a syncretism or eclecticism as one finds in certain other mixed movements in India. Dârâ was a Sufi of the Qâdiriyyah order and a devout Muslim. He believed the *Upanishads* to be the 'Hidden Books' to which the Quran refers (lvi. 77–80) and wrote that: 'They contain the essence of unity and they are secrets which have to be kept hidden!'[27] His *Majma' al-bahrayn* is an attempt to show the identity of the Muslim and Hindu doctrines of unity. It is enough to read Dârâ Shukûh's translation of any of the *Upanishads* to realize that he was not only translating words into Persian but also ideas into the framework of Sufism. His translations contain a Sufi view of the *Upanishads* and, far from being an attempt to syncretize, represent a serious effort to create a bridge between Hindu and Islamic metaphysics. His translations and numerous others of such Hindu classics as the *Râmâyana*, the *Mahâbhârata* and the *Yoga Vasishtha*, upon which the Persian sage Mîr Abu'l-Qâsim Findiriskî wrote a commentary, are a veritable treasure which should become known to the Muslim world at large and not remain confined to the Persians and the Muslims of the Indo-Pakistani sub-continent.[28] These writings, as well as those of other Sufi masters in Muslim India such as Ghawth 'Alî Shâh, the Sufi expositor of Tantrism, and many others, who have often given the most penetrating explanations of Hindu metaphysics and mythology, can serve as a basis for a serious study of the Hindu tradition in the light of modern conditions.

It is surprising that although Islam had so much contact with Buddhism there is much less about this tradition in Muslim sources than about Hinduism. Of course, through the translation of the *Pancha Tântra* into Arabic from Pahlavi as well as through other literary sources and oral traditions, something was known of the personality of the Buddha as a wise man, and he was often identified with the figure of Hermes as the origin of wisdom.[29] Many of the common sources of religious schools and sects considered Buddhism as a branch of Hinduism,[30] and even Bîrûnî in his *India* devoted little attention to it.

The most serious and noteworthy study of Buddhism in Islamic annals outside the works written more recently by Indian Muslims comes rather late, in the eighth/fourteenth century, in the universal history of Rashîid al-Din Faa'lallâh.[31] The chapter devoted to Buddhism, a religion which must have attracted new attention with the coming of the Mongols, is based mostly upon collections of traditions and the direct assistance of a Kashmiri lama named Kâmalashrî-Bakhshî. The chapter includes an account of Indian mythology drawn mostly from the *Purânas* and the best Muslim description of the Yuga cycles, but all seen from the Buddhist rather than the Hindu point of view. The most outstanding aspect of the work, however, is the account of the life of the Buddha,[32] which is unique in Islamic writings. He is considered a prophet with a book called *Abi dharma* containing the quintessence of truth. As is to be expected, the Muslims see all 'divine descents' or *Avatâras* as prophets in the Islamic sense, so that such a treatment of the Buddha should not be in any way surprising. This valuable account of the life of Shakyamuni became well known and was incorporated in several later Persian works on universal history. But there was no further work of any great significance in this field as there was in the case of Hinduism, mostly because the same opportunity of direct contact with Buddhism did not present itself later save in western China, where the Muslim community continued to live relatively isolated from the main stream of Islamic intellectual life.

Section III

This analysis of some of the features of the historical contact between Islam and other religions has revealed the fact that during its history Islam has felt the presence of other traditions on different levels, and in different modes, which may be enumerated as essentially: the *Sharî'ah*; theology; history; science, philosophy, and learning; and finally Sufism or esotericism. On each level the encounter with other religions has had a meaning and continues to do so and each encounter can contribute to the total understanding of other traditions.

On the level of *the Sharî'ah* Islam has always seen other religions as a Divine Law like itself. Many medieval jurists referred to the *shar'* of other prophets and peoples, and Islamic Law itself gives freedom within the Islamic world *(dâr al-islâm)* for other people having their own Divine Law to follow their own ways within their community, wherein they enjoy complete religious independence. Many studies have been made of what one might call 'comparative religious law' in which the religious injunctions of different communities have been described and compared. The Muslim jurists were also the first to develop the science of international law, of trying to provide means whereby relations between peoples following differing codes of law could be established. This description and morphological study of the sacred laws of other religions is one that can in fact be pursued today on the basis established by the classical jurists.

Theological debates occurred early between Muslims and followers of other faiths, incited especially by the Mu'tazilites who were interested in this subject. Also discussions about different religions were held with some of the Shi'ite Imams and often by adherents of these religions themselves, as is recorded in Shi'ite sources such as Ibn Bâbûyan. Likewise, Ismâ'îlî authors continued to interest themselves in other religions particularly because of their emphasis upon the cycles of prophecy and the universality of esotericism.[33] There grew from these theological debates the numerous works on 'sects' or *al-Milal wa'l-nihal*, to the extent that one can say that the Muslims were the founders of the science of comparative religion. Many outstanding theologians—Shi'ites and Sunnis alike—wrote works of this kind like *Kitâb al-maqâlât wa'l-firaq* of Sa'd ibn 'Abdallâh al-Ash'ari al-Qumi, the *Kitâb firaq al-shi'ah* of al-Nawbakhtî, the *Farq bayn al-firaq* of al-Baghdâdî, the *Maqâlât al-islâmiyyîn* of Abu'l-I Hasan al-Ash'arî, the founder of Ash'arite theology,[34] *al-Fasl* of Ibn Hazm, *I'tiqâdât firaq al-muslimîn* of Fakhr al-Dîn al-Râzî, and the best-known work of this kind, *al-Milal wa'l-nihal* of al-Shahristânîi. All of these authors were outstanding theologians and their approach is primarily theological and usually polemical. But inasmuch as again in modern times theological debates have come to take place, especially between Christianity, Judaism and Islam, these works can serve as a basis and provide a background for the task that lies ahead in this domain.

Then there is the tradition of historians who tried to describe simply in as objective a manner as possible what they saw or read of other religions and religious cultures. We see such an approach in the writings of universal historians like al-Mas'ûdî and al-Ya'qûbî. Al-Mas'ûdî also wrote a special treatise on religions, entitled *al-Maqâ-lât ft usûl al-diyânât*. There are the *Fihrist* of Ibn al-Nadîm and the *Bayân al-adyân* of Abu'l-Ma'âlî Muhammad ibn 'Ubaydallâh, where a very fair account of religions is given, and there are references by both Bîrûnî and Nâsir-i Khusraw to Abu'l-'Abbas Irân-shahrî, who is said to have studied the doctrines of other religions with genuine interest. There is the incomparable Bîrûnî himself who, not only in his *India* but also in the *Chronology of Ancient Nations* and many other works, has provided a wealth of information about so many different religions. This tradition continued in later universal histories up to very recent times in such works as the *Nâsikh al-tawârîkh* which was compiled in Persia only about a century ago. But these later works were mostly repetitions of earlier ones when it came to religious matters. This tradition of objective accounts of other religions could again serve as a basis for contemporary works in Muslim languages on Hinduism, Buddhism, Shintoism, and even the religions of the American Indians, as well as on Christianity and Judaism; however many such works in Islamic languages have been compiled by non-Muslim authors for reasons other than that of creating understanding between religions. Such descriptive accounts should be based upon genuine sources; and especially as far as the Oriental traditions are concerned, they should not be an echo of the mistakes and prejudices of Western works translated into Arabic, Persian, Turkish, etc., as is in fact often the case.[35]

In the sphere of science and philosophy and learning in general the integration of elements from these fields into the Islamic world-view meant also contact with the religion of the civilizations from which the material in question came. It must be remembered that in a traditional civilization every science is connected in one way or another with the religious principles of that civilization. The Indian medicine and astronomy that the Muslims soon absorbed also brought them into contact with certain Hindu cosmological ideas. Indian and Persian works on natural history acquainted Muslims with the religious conception of nature present in these works. As for the Graeco-Hellenistic sciences, although the Muslims were not interested in the Olympic pantheon, through Greek philosophical and scientific works they came to learn of the Orphic-Pythagorean element of the Greek tradition, which interested them immensely, precisely because it was an assertion of the doctrine of Divine Unity. If they called Plato the *imâm* of the philosophers and Plotinus 'the Shaykh of the Greeks' (namely, their Sufi master) it was again because in their writings they saw the expression of that metaphysical doctrine that Islam was to expound later. In the *Ishrâqî* theosophy of Suhrawardî, moreover, there is continuous reference to the universality of a wisdom which was shared by all nations of old and which found its universal expression in Islamic gnosis.[36] It is that wisdom which Steuben, Leibniz and the Neoscholastics were later to call the *philosophia perennis*, an expression to which A. K. Coomaraswamy quite rightly added the epithet *et universalis*.

It is, however, on the level of esotericism, in the perspective of Sufism, that the most profound encounter with other traditions has been made and where one can find the indispensable ground for the understanding in depth of other religions today. The Sufi is one who seeks to transcend the world of forms, to journey from multiplicity to Unity, from the particular to the Universal. He leaves the many for the One and through this very process is granted the vision of the One in the many. For him all forms become transparent, including religious forms, thus revealing to him their unique origin. Sufism or Islamic gnosis is the most universal affirmation of that perennial wisdom which stands at the heart of Islam and in fact of all religion as such.[37] It is this supreme doctrine of Unity—which is itself unique *(al-tawhîd wâhid)*—that the Sufis call the 'religion of love' and to which Ibn 'Arabî refers in his well-known verses in the *Tarjumân al-ashwâq*.[38] This love is not merely sentiment or emotions, it is the realized aspect of gnosis. It is a transcendent knowledge that reveals the inner unity of religions. Shabistarî in his *Gulshan-i râz* refers to this very truth when he says:

> Necessary Being is as Heaven and Hell as contingent,
> 'I' and 'You' are the Hades veil between them.
> When this veil is lifted up from before you,
> There remains not the bond of sects and creeds.
> All the authority of the law is over this 'I' of yours,
> Since that is bound to your soul and body,
> When 'I' and 'You' remain not in the midst,
> What is mosque, what is synagogue, what is fire temple?[39]

Although not all Sufis have dealt specifically with the question of other traditions, some have gone into detailed discussion of this matter. Ibn 'Arabî, one of the Sufis whose vocation it was to expound the doctrines of Sufism in their fullness, asserts openly the doctrine of the universality of revelation. He writes:

> Know that when God, the Exalted, created the creatures He created them in kinds and in each kind He placed the best and chose from the best the élite. These are the faithful *(mu'minûn)*. And He chose from the faithful the élite, who are the saints, and from these élite the quintessence. These are the prophets *(anbiyâ')*. And from this quintessence He chose the finest parts and they are the prophets who bring a Divine Law. ... [40]

Ibn 'Arabî and al-Jîlî after him also elaborated the doctrine of the Logos according to which the founder of each religion is an aspect of the universal logos, which they identify with the 'Reality of Muhammad' *(al-haqîqat al-muhammadiyyah)*.[41] The masterpiece of Ibn 'Arabî, the *Fusûs al-hikam* or *Bezels of Wisdom*, is in fact an exposition of the particular spiritual genius of each prophet as 'a Word of God'. Moreover, the Sufis believe that in the same way that each being in the Universe is the theophany *(tajalli)* of a Divine Name, so does each religion reveal an aspect of the Divine Names and Qualities. The multiplicity of religions is a direct result of the infinite richness of the Divine Being. Al-Jîlî writes:

> There is nothing in existence except that it worships God the Most High in its state and speech and acts, nay in its essence and qualities. And everything in existence obeys God Most High. But acts of worship differ because of the difference of the exigencies of the Divine Names and Qualities.[42]

The Sufis not only assert the unity of revelation but also consider themselves as the guardians of Islam and, moreover, of all traditions. To quote al-Jîlî once again,

> The [gnostics] are the investigators of the truth upon whom God has constructed the foundations of existence. The spheres of the worlds rotate about them. They are the centre of God's attention in the world, nay, the centre of God's [theophany] in existence. ... God has erected the foundation of religion, nay, the foundation of all religions upon the ground of their gnosis.[43]

The Sufis have lived throughout Islamic history with a consciousness of the universality of the wisdom whose means of attainment they bear within their doctrines and methods. But some have had the special vocation to speak explicitly on this matter while others have remained silent. Jalâl al-Dîn Rûmî, who even had some Christian and Jewish disciples and whose *Mathnawî* is replete with verses asserting the universality of tradition, writes in his *Fihi mâ fihi*, or *Discourses*, with direct allusion to different traditions:

> I was speaking one day amongst a group of people, and a party of non-Muslims were present. In the middle of my address they began to weep and to register emotion and ecstasy.
>
> Someone asked: What do they understand and what do they know? Only one Muslim in a thousand understands this kind of talk. What did they understand, that they should weep?
>
> The Master answered: It is not necessary that they should understand the inner spirit of these words. The root of the matter is the words themselves, and that they do understand. After all, every one acknowledges the Oneness of God, that He is the Creator and Provider, that He controls everything, that to Him all things shall return, and that it is He who punishes and forgives. When anyone hears these words, which are a description and commemoration of God, a universal commotion and ecstatic passion supervenes, since out of these words comes the scent of their Beloved and their Quest.
>
> Though the ways are various, the goal is one. Do you not see that there are many roads to the Kaaba? For some the road is from Rum, for some from Syria, for some from Persia, for some from China, for some by sea from India and Yemen. So if you consider the roads, the variety is great and the divergence infinite; but when you consider the goal, they are all of one accord and one. The hearts of all are at one upon the Kaaba. The hearts have one attachment, an ardour and a great love for the Kaaba, and in that there is no room for contrariety. That attachment is neither infidelity nor

faith; that is to say, that attachment is not confounded with the various roads which we have mentioned. Once they have arrived there, that disputation and war and diversity touching the roads—this man saying to that man, 'You are false, you are an infidel', and the other replying in kind—once they have arrived at the Kaaba, it is realized that the warfare was concerning the roads only, that their goal was one …

To resume: now all men in their inmost hearts love God and seek Him, pray to Him and in all things put their hope in Him, recognizing none but Him as omnipotent and ordering their affairs. Such an apperception is neither infidelity nor faith. Inwardly it has no name. …

Now the literalists take the Holy Mosque to be that Kaaba to which people repair. Lovers, however, and the elect of God, take the Holy Mosque to mean union with God. …

Continuing to expound the meaning of this union above the world of forms, he adds:

If I were to occupy myself with expounding that subtlety, even the saints who have attained God would lose the thread of discourse. How then is it possible to speak of such mysteries and mystic states to mortal men? … One man does not see a camel on the top of a minaret; how then shall he see the thread of a hair in the mouth of the camel?[44]

Not everyone may be able to see the camel on the top of the minaret, much less to distinguish the hair in its mouth. But those who are possessed of such a vision are bound by duty to explain to others to the greatest extent possible what they have seen. Scholarship today can do much in bringing to life unedited texts and making known many chapters in the history of contact between Islam and other religions that have been forgotten. But it remains for the Sufis to expound the metaphysical background in the light of which particular forms can be studied and understood. That is not to say that only the perfect saint, the *wâsil* (one who has reached the goal), can speak of the inner unity of religions. Only such a person can speak from realized and lived experience. But others who are endowed with intellectual intuition can anticipate intellectually the Centre where all the radii meet, the summit which all roads reach. Only such a vision of the Centre can provide a meaningful dialogue between religions, showing both their inner unity and formal diversity which itself contributes to the richness of modern man's spiritual life and which is given as a compensation for the spiritually starved environment in which he lives.

As far as Islam is concerned the key necessary for opening the door towards a true encounter with other religions has already been provided by Sufism. It is for contemporary Muslims to use this key and to apply the established principles to the particular condition presented to the Islamic world today. It is only through the possession of a metaphysical doctrine of distinguishing between the true and the false, grounded in traditional orthodoxy, that so many pitfalls which exist in the way of a serious study of religions can be averted. And it is only through such a doctrine that a firm basis can be established for a more formal encounter with other religions on the theological and social planes.

He who has gained a vision of that mountain top that touches the Infinite rests assured that climbers who are following other paths are nevertheless his companions on this journey which is the only meaningful journey of life itself. His certainty comes not only from the vision of the peak but also from his knowledge that those paths that have been chosen for man by God Himself do ultimately lead to the top, whatever turns they may make on the way. As far as Islam is concerned this knowledge is already contained within the treasure-house of Islamic wisdom. It is for contemporary Muslims to seek this wisdom, to make it their own and then to make use of it in conformity with their real needs.

QUESTIONS FOR REVIEW AND DISCUSSION

1. What is the role of Sufism, according to Nasr, with regard to comparative religion? Why does he indicate that this is important?
2. How does Nasr use solar metaphors for founders of religions in traditional religions to explain obstacles to comparative religion? Is this effective?
3. What does Nasr mean by "the necessity for studying other religious traditions is brought about by the particular conditions of the modern world"? What implications does this have for philosophy or theology from his perspective? Is this true for all people in modern times or only for some? Do you agree?
4. How does Nasr distinguish between the implications of philosophy of religion for an atheist versus a believer?
5. To whom does the task of studying other religions fall? What are the stakes? Who is free to address a traditional audience without reference to other religious traditions?
6. What does Nasr see as the essential problem posed by the study of religion for those who are concerned with the truth of religion? Why is this not a problem for "the 'scientific' observer or the syncretist"? Do you agree with Nasr that the study of other religions is both more difficult and more religiously necessary for such an adherent who is interested in religious truth?
7. What does Nasr regard as the negative effects of modernism for religious faith, for Islam, and for serious study of other religions? What are some of the related limitations and prejudices from the formative period of the "science" of comparative religion? Do you agree?
8. How does Nasr assess phenomenology among the approaches in religious studies? What does it lack? What does he see as the relationship between Christianity and the categories used in the study of religion? How does Nasr think that Islam and other religious traditions' perspectives on the encounter of religions can remedy these problems and contribute to greater understanding?
9. What, according to Nasr, is religious experience? Is it necessary for an atheist to believe in it as an authentic cognition?
10. Why does Nasr shift to the metaphysical background of Islam? What are some of the key points he makes about this understanding of reality from within the tradition? Why is Islamic revelation described by Nasr as particularly pertinent? What do you think about his approach and style of argument and presentation?
11. How does Nasr explain the relative neglect of comparative religion by Muslims? What are some examples of encounters between Islam and other religions in pre-modern times? How do encounters with Hinduism and Buddhism differ from each other and from the encounters between Islam and various traditions outlined by Nasr?
12. What are the various levels and modes of contact between Islam and other religions? Which meanings and contributions are associated with each level? Why

does Nasr present the level of esotericism and perspective of Sufism as the most profound encounter and best ground for understanding?

13. What do you think of Nasr's assertion at the end of his essay about the potential benefits of religious studies scholarship? What is it that "those who are possessed of such a vision are bound by duty to explain"? What does he indicate is the responsibility of contemporary Muslims?

Notes

1 Several authors in the West have, in fact, during the past half-century presented to the world this cardinal teaching, men like René Guénon, Amanda Coomaraswamy, Titus Burckhardt, Marco Pallis, Martin Lings, and expecially Frithjof Schuon, whose many works, particularly *The Transcendent Unity of Religions*, have revealed with unparalleled lucidity the essential unity and, at the same time, the formal diversity of the great traditions of the world. It is a tragedy for the academic discipline of comparative religion that except for a very few cases no serious attention has been paid to these writings.

   On another level one may mention the works of such scholars as Mircea Eliade, Heinrich Zimmer, Jean Herbert, Eugen Herrigel, Rudolf Otto, Henry Corbin and Louis Massignon, whose findings contribute much to a genuine understanding of other religions. Also among Catholic authors or those sympathetic to the point of view of Catholicism such figures as Simone Weil, Bernard Kelly, Elémire Zolla and Dom A. Graham speak in a language which has contributed profitably to an effective discourse between religions. See W. Stoddart, 'Catholicism and Zen', *Tomorrow*, vol. XII, no. 4, Autumn, 1964, pp. 289–96.

2 The Holy Quran says 'And We never sent a messenger save with the language of his folk, that he might make (the message) clear for them' (XIV, 4).

3 For an account of the phases that the discipline of comparative religion has undergone and the influences that have shaped it see M. Eliade, 'The Quest for the "Origins" of Religion', *History of Religions*, vol. IV, no. 1, Summer, 1964, pp. 156 ff.

4 'So little is the Western historian of religions nowadays equipped in Islamics that this discipline, to which he has hardly contributed anything, does not seem to need him. Even today, no historian of religions proper has had anything to say that would catch the attention of the men of knowledge in the Islamics field.' Isma'il R. A. al-Faruqi, 'History of Religions: Its nature and significance for Christian education and the Muslim-Christian Dialogue', *Numen*, vol. XII, fasc. 1, Jan., 1965, p. 40. Some may object to this statement by pointing to men like W. C. Smith or R. C. Zachner who have made well-known contributions to Islamic and Iranian studies. But such men were in fact first Islamicists and Iranologists and only later went into the field of the history of religions.

5 There has been some study of other religions by Hindus as well, but for the most part by modernized Hindus who have usually expounded a shallow 'universalism' which can only end in a mere humanitarianism or in the pseudo-spiritual cults which have sprung up everywhere in the West today. Even some genuine Hindu *bhaktas* have contributed to this situation because once out of their traditional environment, which 'thinks' for them, they do not have the power of discernment to be able to distinguish between the multitude of forms in civilizations which are alien to them.

6 Although the author's own knowledge of the situation of other Muslim languages is limited, the same seems to be true of Turkish, Urdu, etc., except that naturally in Urdu, Bengali and other languages of the Muslims of the Indo-Pakistani sub-continent many works can be found concerning Hindu religion and culture. But even here, since the partition of the sub-continent, very few works of substance free from transient factors and sentimental considerations have seen the light of day. The Urdu language is rich in works dealing with Hinduism, including not only translations of Hindu sacred texts (mostly from translations that had been made previously into Persian), but also new works on different aspects of Hinduism written often by Hindus themselves but in Urdu. Some Muslims also have written outstanding expositions of Hindu doctrines, such as the work of Habib al-Rabmân Shastri composed in 1930 on the theory of *rasa*, which received very favourable comments from Hindu circles. But nearly all of these works belong also to the last decades of the

last century and the early period of this century. See M. H. Askari, 'Tradition et modernisme dans le monde indo-pakistanais', *Etudes Traditionnelles*, May–June and July–August 1970, pp. 98–125.

7 The Holy Quran states: 'And for every nation there is a messenger' (X, 48).

8 This large number of prophets indicates implicitly that all nations must have been given a religion sent to them by God. Although generally only the Abrahamic tradition has been considered, the principle of the universality of revelation applies to all nations, and Muslims applied it outside the Abrahamic family when faced with Zoroastrianism in Persia and Hinduism in India.

9 See F. Schuon, *Understanding Islam*, chapter I.

10 One cannot overlook the fact that there are some – although still few in number – among Westernized Muslims who, in their extreme degree of Westernization, have also begun to take an interest in Hinduism, Zen, and other oriental disciplines, but usually of the spurious kind. For them also a direct and authentic contact between Islam and these traditions can be of the greatest aid in becoming oriented spiritually. There are a few who have had direct contact with authorities belonging to these traditions, but their number is extremely limited.

11 Farid ud-Din Attâr, *The Conference of the Birds*, trans. S. C. Nott, London, 1954, p. 13. See also H. Ritter, *Das Meer der Seele*, Leiden, 1955, pp. 607–68.

12 The many writings of H. A. Wolfson, especially his *Philo* and his *Philosophy of the Kalâm*, have amply demonstrated the result of this interaction between Jewish, Christian, and Muslim theologians and the influence of Judaeo-Christian theological arguments upon the *Kalâm* itself.

13 Christ is given the supreme position of the universal 'Seal of Sanctity' (*Khâtam al-wilâyah*) and is believed to be the one who will bring the cycle to a close after the advent of the Mahdf. Ibn 'Arabi writes of Christ in his *Futûhât* (VI, 215):

> Oui, le Sceau des Saints est un Apôtre
> Qui n'aura point d'égal dans le monde!
> Il est l'Esprit et il est le fils de l'Esprit et de la mère Marie
> C'est là un rang qu'aucun autre ne pourra atteindre.
> Il descendra parmi nous en arbiter juste
> Mais non point selon les principes de sa proper loi qui aura cessé
> Il tuera le porc et confondra l'iniquité;
> Allah sera seul son guide ...

M. Hayak, *Le Christ de l'Islam*, Paris, 1959, p. 260.

14 An outstanding example of a work of this kind is al-Ghazzâli's refutation of the divinity of Christ, in which, using the text of the Gospels, he argued that Christ was given special permission by God – a permission that is unique among prophets – to use the type of language that he employed concerning his union and filial relationship with God, but that in reality he never attributed divinity to himself as is commonly understood by Christians. See al-Ghazzâli, *Réfutation excéllente de la Divinité de Jésus-Christ d'après les Evangiles*, ed. and trans. R. Chidiac, Paris, 1939.

15 These are three different words for silk.

16 Trans. By E. G. Browne in his *A Literary History of Persia*, vol. IV, Cambridge, 1930, pp. 293–94.

17 See M. Lings, *A Moslem Saint of the Twentieth Century*, where the Shaykh's interest in other religions is amply treated in the opening chapters.

18 See W. H. Baily, *Zoroastrian Problems in the Ninth Century Books*, Oxford, 1943.

19 All the Muslim sources pertaining to Manichaeism are assembled in S. H. Taqizadeh, *Mâni wa dîn-I û*, Tehran, 1335.

20 Even today many people in the Arab Near East refer to the Hindus as *majâs* or Zoroastrians, not making a distinction on the popular level between the Indian and Iranian traditions.

21 The symbolism of Hâfiz's delicate and exquisite language has never been fully expounded in any Western language. One of the best translations and commentaries upon him is *The Divân*, written in the fourteenth century by *Khwâja Shamsu-d-Din Muhammad-i-Hâfiz-I Shirâzi*, otherwise known as *Lisânu-l-Ghaib* and *Tarjunânu-l-Asrâr* by Lieut. Col. H. Wilberforce Clarke, Calcutta, 2 vols, 1891.

22 See S. H. Nasr, *Three Muslim Sages*, chapter II; also S. H. Nasr, 'Suhrawardi' in *A History of Muslim Philosophy*. See also the many studies of H. Corbin on prolegomena and *Les Motifs zoroastriens dans la philosophie de Sohrawardf*, Tehran, 1946–1325.

23 For a summary of Bîrûnî's views on Hinduism see A. Jeffery, 'Al-Biruni's Contribution to Comparative Religion', in *Al-Biruni Commemoration Volume*, Calcutta, 1951, pp. 125–60; also S. H. Nasr, *An Introduction to Islamic Cosmological Doctrines*, Chapter V.

24 For two different views of the interaction between Islam and Hinduism in India see Tara Chand, *The Influence of Islam on Indian Culture*, Allahabad, 1954, and A. Ahmad, *Studies in Islamic Culture in its Indian Environment*, Oxford, 1964, which also contains a rich bibliography on the subject.

25 *Al-Insân al-kâmil*, Cairo, 1304, II, pp. 78 and 87. Of course many authors of works on religious sects denied this connection, like al-Shahristâni, who writes: 'There are those among the people who believe they [the Hindus] are called *Bardhimah* because of their affiliation to Abraham – upon whom be peace. But this is wrong, for they are a people especially known to have denied prophecy completely and totally.' *Al-Milai wa'l-nibal*, Cairo, 1347, IV, p. 135. Needless to say this theological criticism does not in any way detract from the metaphysical significance of the assertion of al-Jîlî.

   Regarding the relation between Hinduism and Islam as the first and last tradition of this human cycle see R. Guénon, 'The Mysteries of the Letter Nûn', in *Art and Thought*, ed. K. B. Iver, London, 1947, pp. 166–68; see also the series of articles by M. Valsân entitled, 'Le Triangle de l'Androgyne et le monosyllable "Om"', in *Etudes traditionnelles* of 1964 and 1965.

26 The Persian text of the *Upanishads* has been edited in a modern edition by Tara Chand and J. Na'ini as *Sirr-I akbar*. Tehran, 1957–60. See the English introduction of Tara Chand concerning Dârâ Shukûh's writings and their significance. The Persian translations of Dârâ Shukûh were also important for the preservation of Hindu doctrines for the Hindus themselves in the eighteenth and nineteenth century so that a nineteenth-century Hindu translator of the *Upanishads* refers to Dârâ Shukûh as one of the revivers of Hinduism along with Shankarâ-charyâ and Vyasa. See M. H. Askari, 'Tradition et modernism ... ', p. 120.

27 *Ibid.*, p. 45 of Tara Chand's introduction.

28 The profound comparative study of the *Yoga Vasishtha* by Mir Findiriski is a highlight of Hindu–Muslim metaphysical studies perhaps even surpassing in depth the works of Dârâ Shukûh. A study is currently being made of this work by the Persian scholar, Fatbaliâh Mujtabâ'I.

29 See S. H. Nasr, *Islamic Studies*, chapter IV.

30 Al-Shahristânî divides the Hindus into three groups, one of whom he calls *ashâb al-budadah* or Buddhists. He says that the first *budd* was called *shâkin* (Shakyamuni) and below him stands the rank of *al-bardt sa'tyah* (?) most likely meaning the Boddhisattiva. He also gives some account of Buddhist asceticism and moral teachings. Op. cit., pp. 139 ff.

31 See K. Jahn, 'On the mythology and religion of the Indians in the medieval Moslem tradition', in *Mélanges Henri Massé*, pp. 185–97.

32 See K. Jahn, 'Kâmalashri-Rashid al-Din's "Life and teaching of the Buddha"', *Central Asiatic Journal*, vol. II, 1956, pp. 81–128.

33 See, for example, the *Kashf al-mahjûb* of Abû Yaqûb Sijistânî, ed. H. Corbin, Jamil'al Tehran, 1949, pp. 77–79, on the necessity of the plurality of prophets and religions because of changing conditions of the people to whom revelation is addressed. The author adds that each prophet reveals an aspect of the truth and the Divine Law so that it is necessary to have many prophets to reveal the different aspects of truth and also reaffirm what came before in the way of revelation. Likewise Nâsir-I Khuraw in his *Jâmil' al-bikmatayn*, ed. H. Corbin and M. Mo'in, Tehran, 1953, speaks of Christ as the 'Word of God' and of the universality of the prophetic chain before the Prophet of Islam. The universality of revelation is a permanent theme of both Twelve-Imâm Sh'ite and Ismâ'ili theology as it is with Sufism in general, although the standpoint remains within the bounds of the Abrahamic tradition.

34 This important work edited by H. Ritter as *Die dogmarischen Lehren der Ashanger des Islam*, Wiesbaden, 1963, as well as al-Ash'arf's *Maqâlat al-mulhidin*, which is its complementary volume dealing more directly with non-Islamic groups and sects, reveals how much interest the study of religions held for even those Muslim theologians who tried to oppose rationalistic discourse on religion and were the defenders of the letter of the revelation.
   Some theologians dealt even in their theological works with the history of religions, which they treated in a separate section; al-iji in his *al-Mawâqif* provides an example.

35 The very commendable work of Kenneth Morgan and a few others in America and England should here be mentioned, their aim being to provide means of learning about religions based on the writings of those who believe in them and live within their world-view; this method of

approaching the subject could also be adopted by Muslims with advantage. If Muslims want to know about Christianity it is best to seek this knowledge from a Christian who believes in it, not one who has 'outgrown' it in his own mind. And for even stronger reasons they should want to hear from a Buddhist about Buddhism or a Hindu about Hinduism or to learn of these religions from the very few Western authors who have either themselves had direct contact with these traditions or are particularly endowed both through inner sympathy and innate intelligence to understand the forms and symbols of other religions than their own. The large number of second-hand works on comparative religion now being translated from European languages into Arabic, Persian, etc., calls for a definite Muslim answer before, in yet another field of study, the minds of modern educated Muslims become fatally contaminated. Until now only a few works based on genuine sources have appeared, but they are far too few to answer the need for such literature today.

36 The figure of Hermes invoked by Suhrawardi and many other Muslim sages as the bringer of a revelation which was the origin of all philosophy or rather theosophy, signifies belief in the universality of wisdom, the *religio perennis*.
For the importance of the figure of Hermes as the symbol of a primodial religion see M. Eliade, 'The Quest for the "Origins of Religion"', pp. 154–56. However, it is of great significance that the hermetic movement in the Renaissance was essentially against the all-embracing medieval Christian tradition, whereas in Islam the figure of Hermes fitted perfectly well into Islamic prophetology.

37 It is this gnosis which stands as the best proof of the truth of religion as such because the Gnostic sees religion as an inseparable aspect of human existence. There is no better proof of the existence of God than man, who confirms his creator through his theomorphic nature and particularly through his intelligence which stands as the proof of the Absolute that is its real object.
'Human nature is general and human intelligence in particular cannot be understood apart from the phenomenon of religion, which characterizes them in the most direct and most complete way possible. If we can grasp the transcendent nature (not the "psychological" nature) of the human being, we thereby grasp the nature of revelation, of religion, of tradition; we understand their possibility, their necessity, their truth. And in understanding religion, not only in a particular form or according to some verbal specification, but also in its formless essence, we understand the religions, that is to say, the meaning of their plurality and their diversity; this is the plane of gnosis, of the *religio perennis*, whereon the extrinsic antimonies of dogma are explained and resolved.' F. Schuon, 'Religio Perennis' in *Light on the Ancient Worlds*, p. 142.

38
> My heart has become capable of every form; it is
> a pasture for gazelles and a convent for Christians
> And a temple for idols and the pilgrim's Ka'ba and
> the tables of the Torah, and the book of the Koran.
> I follow the religion of Love: whatever way Love's camels
> Take, that is my religion and my faith.

> *Tarjumân al-ashwâq*, trans. by R. A. Nicholson, London, 1911, p. 67;
> see also S. H. Nasr, *Three Muslim Sages*, pp. 116–18.

It need hardly be pointed out that this vision of the transcendent unity of religions stands at the very antipodes of the modern syncretisms and pseudo-spiritualities which have been growing during the past few decades as a result of the weakening of tradition in the West. Not only do they not succeed in transcending forms but they fall beneath them, opening the door to all kinds of evil forces affecting those who are unfortunate enough to be duped by their so-called universalism.

39 *Gulshan-I râz*, p. 31.
40 *Al-Futûhât al-makkiyyah*, Cairo, 1293, vol. II, pp. 73–75.
41 This fundamental doctrine expounded mostly in the *Fusûs* of Ibn 'Arabî and the *Al-Insân al-kâmil* of al-Jîlî has been explained with remarkable clarity in the introduction and notes of the masterly translations of these works by T. Burckhardt, *La Sagesse des prophètes* and *De l'homme universel*.
The doctrine of the Logos according to Ibn 'Arabî is also summarized in his *Shajarat al-kawn*. See the translation of it by A. Jeffery in *Studia Islamica*, vol. X, pp. 43–77, and vol. XI, pp. 113–60. His notes and explanations, however, do not at all accord with the Islamic view.
42 *Al-Insân al-kâmil*, II, pp. 76–77.
43 *Ibid.*, p. 83.

In fact has not this assertion of this great medieval Sufi been realized during this century by those who have sought to defend all traditions against forces that threaten not only a particular religion but religion itself?

44 *Discourses of Rûmî*, trans. by A. J. Arberry, London, 1961, pp. 108–12. One must be grateful to Professor Arberry for making available to the outside world this rather remarkable work of Rûmî which reveals an aspect of Sufism not often found in more formal Sufi texts.

19 Insiders and Outsiders: Studying Hinduism Non-Religiously?

P. Pratap Kumar

P. Pratap Kumar (1952—) received his doctorate from the University of California at Santa Barbara. A specialist in the Hindu religious tradition he is currently professor at the University of KwaZulu Natal, South Africa. Among his publications are books on the Hindu goddess Lakshmi within the Vishnu worshipping traditions of South India, and on South Asian religions in diaspora. His *Methods and Theories in the Study of Religion* (2004) explores the discipline of religious studies through perspectives drawn from Indian religious traditions. The selection that follows illustrates this approach. The article focuses on the insider/outsider concept frequently used in religious studies, highlights its complexity when applied to a tradition such as Hinduism, and demonstrates how these complexities can offer general guidance for theoretical and methodological approaches in the discipline.

Recent General Trends in the Study of Religion

In the last few years there has been a great deal of concern in the academy about ignoring the insiders' views and opinions in the study of religions. Never before has the rift between the social-scientific study of religion and the theological or faith-based study of religion been more pronounced than it is currently. This is quite poignantly reflected in the recent issue of the *Journal of the American Academy of Religion*. In its March 2006 issue, *JAAR* carried a number of essays on what it called "On the Future of the Study of Religion in the Academy." What is interesting is that the essays are generally cast in the context of the relationship between theology and religious studies, thereby signaling that the study of religion as it evolved—as shown in the review essay "Religious Studies: A Bibliographic Essay" by Slavica Jakelic and Jessica Starling (2006)—still has to settle its score with theology.

It might be worthwhile to identify some of the issues raised by various authors included in this special issue. Ellen T. Armour sees theology speaking normatively from within the tradition, while religious studies speaks descriptively from the outside (2006, 9). She agrees with her respondent, Peter Ochs, that the AAR (American Academy of Religion) is a mediating place for "religious houses" and "academic theories" (2006, 20). Playing on the discourse of alterity, Jose Cabezón implicitly argues in favor of "theory parity." He notes that within the academy "an increasing number of scholars are choosing to 'come out' as believers and practitioners" (2006, 33). This "coming out," he suggests, has problematized the distinction between scholars (us) who claim to be critical and have theory and those (practitioners) who do not. He is keen for scholars to discover indigenous theories in an effort to move towards what he calls "theory pluralism" (2006, 34). This paradigm shift therefore includes: (I) theory pluralism; (2) challenges posed by non-Western, non-academic, religious believers; (3) the self-disclosure of scholars' religious identities; and (4) the movement toward institutionalizing non-Western theologies (2006, 36). It is interesting to note that, while he calls for theory pluralism and is clearly critical of Western academic domination of theory in the study of religion, he does not seem to mind universalizing the category "theology" and applying it to the non-Western religions (see his fourth component of the paradigm shift). Cabezón's respondent, theologian William Schweiker, rightly cautions that when "we need to theorize with religious sources, one does not want to repeat problems of the past by assuming that the 'dialectic alterity' is answered by merely replacing Christian with non-Christian sources" (2006, 43). And Cabezón readily agrees! Gavin Flood's essay is a natural extension of Cabezón's call for including in theory the non-Western sources. For example, Flood calls for the inclusion of "theological expression of traditions" in the social-scientific study of religion (2006, 54). He then makes the problematic suggestion that "[r]eligious studies can function as an arena that allows the self-articulation of traditions to reflect upon themselves." He goes on to elaborate:

> Philology and historical research might show that the *daśanāmi* order was not in fact founded by Sankara, a claim that conflicts with the traditional view. But while not being benign, Religious Studies needs to be hospitable in allowing a plurality of discourses to function within it and providing an arena for encounter between traditions that would not otherwise happen. Islamic Theology, for example, should not be excluded from the academy on *a priori* grounds, but the incorporation of that theology entails its encountering other theologies and secular contestation. But Religious Studies can provide this forum for argument.
>
> (2006, 56)

The problem in this proposal is that, while Flood wants, on the one hand, to give credence to the traditional view on the *daśanāmi* order notwithstanding what historians have to say, he wants, on the other hand, Islam to listen to the secular viewpoint, which is what was given in the case of the *daśanāmi* order in the first place. If the traditional view is going to ignore it and maintain its ahistorical view of their beliefs, then the question is how religious studies should accommodate both and not make a common-sense comment. He further compounds the problems of his proposal by saying "[i]t is the degree to which traditional theologies accept forms of secular reasoning that determines their degree of participation in the academy" (2006, 56). If that is the case, then the traditional view should be modified in the light of what the philologists and historians have found about the *daśanāmi* order. It seems as if Flood wants to have his cake and yet eat it! If that is not enough, he compounds it further by saying: "Religious Studies can offer space in which different forms of reasoning and reflection upon texts and practices can develop within a horizon of expectation that no areas of tradition can be placed outside of method as developed within the secular academy" (2005, 56). If no areas of tradition can be placed outside of the method developed in the secular academy (at least he recognizes it is a secular academy and not a religious order), then how is it possible for traditional theologies not to accept the findings of secular methodologies? What then is the point of religious studies being asked to "offer space" and give "hospitality to traditions"? In any case, what is even more problematic is that this reduces religious studies to a halfway home, what his respondent, Nancy Levene, called "theology laundering" (2006, 61).

While Flood wants to see religious studies as some sort of service station for religious traditions, Paul Griffiths pronounces a gloomy future for the academic study of religion, primarily because of the narrow view he holds about religion: "construed to denote human action that springs from desire for closer union … with God of Abraham, Isaac, Jacob, and Jesus, as distinct from any particular being in the cosmos" (2006, 68). In this sense, he considers religion to be a natural kind. The problem with his view is that he takes God as the direct object of theology, as if God is an entity in the cosmos. Indeed, that is how he begins his essay: "The formal object of theology, for example, is God" (2006, 66). He does not wait to ask the simple question as to how we may know God cognitively. He seems to assume theology (Christian theology) will disclose it. What about someone who does not share in that or any theology? On the one hand, he speaks as an insider to the tradition (Catholic) and seems to expect the outsiders to know in the same way. As such, the difficulty that he has with J. Z. Smith and Bruce Lincoln stems from his inability to concede that religion could be constructed in other ways and hence could belong to an "artificial kind," to use his own words. Griffiths's view that the academic study of religion could flourish within the embrace of theology simply reinforces the fallacy: that theology somehow has a direct knowledge of God or some such entity and that the outsiders to the theological discourse cannot have access to such knowledge without the help of theology.

Such a fallacious starting point simply widens the gap between theology and the academic study of religion. Instead, what might be of help is to actually look at what theologians themselves do in doing theology. So, what do they do? They study texts, rituals, doctrines, and so on within the confines of a tradition. But in studying and interpreting these data they are just as cognitively engaged as any social scientist. In other words, they do not have any more evidence at their disposal than a social scientist or historian might. If the theologian can read the texts, study the rituals and their interpretations, so can the historian of religions. To the extent that these texts, doctrines, and rituals are available through language that we share, they are accessible as data to anyone who has access to them. Even the commentaries and internal debates on the various doctrines are no longer closed to the academic scholars. We are not living in a time when the Vatican has exclusive knowledge of the Bible or the Hindu Brahmin priests have exclusive ownership of the brahmanical texts. There was a time when a non-Brahmin was prevented from even listening to the Vedic chants by mistake, and if anyone was found in that act, it is said that hot liquid metal was poured into his ears. Thankfully we do not live in those times. Now, once something is committed to language, it is available to all those who share in that language. So, the brahmanical texts that were once closed to the outside world are now open to any scholar through the painstaking work of the early Indologists—most of whom were outsiders to the tradition. Ironically, today most of the practitioners in fact learn Hinduism through these non-practicing scholarly writings. And here Robert Segal (2006) is right in saying that the scholar knows more about a tradition than the insiders—and, I might add, this includes the insider theologians.

But what about personal religious experience? Well, it is just as inaccessible to the scholar of religion as it is to the theologian. For it is individual, and unless such individuals share it through language, it is closed to anyone. But once it is expressed in language, the possibility exists for the academic scholar to access it either through texts or through engaging in a participant observation. What is available to the theologian is therefore available to the academic scholar and what is not available to the academic scholar *vis-à-vis* individual religious experience or exclusive commentarial traditions is not available to theologians in general, for they are peculiar to those individuals and secret societies.

So the question really is not who knows how much, but, rather, whether knowledge of religions is exclusive to theologians or insiders once it is linguistically made available. As already suggested, one of the stark realities of today is that knowledge is no longer private or privileged. This is evidenced from our daily life. Matters of sexuality, for instance, were once considered either private or adult-only information. But thanks to the information revolution that privilege is no longer possible. For example, HIV/AIDS has directly made it possible for us to discuss the use of condoms in public debates and media advertising. Thus the claim, whether implicit or explicit, that religious knowledge is better known to the insiders/theologians is seriously problematic.

While this gives us a sample of where the academy is situated in terms of debates on the future of the study of religion as a general field, an analogous debate is raging within the academy in specific areas of study. And this has to do with the recent debates in RISA (Religion in South Asia, an electronic discussion network) on the issue of Hinduism textbooks used by the California Department of Education. It might therefore be worthwhile to consider some of the issues that this debate has raised for scholars of religion in general.

Textbooks on Hinduism and the California Department of Education

The issue of the insider vs. the outsider in the study of religion may be exemplified in the recent debate on the California textbook controversy. The Hindu Education Foundation in the USA launched the debate with several US-based scholars, with others from elsewhere vigorously participating in it. The Hindu Education Foundation wanted the textbook for teaching Hinduism for sixth graders to be revised, for they felt "the textbook[s] adopt[s] an anthropological/outsider viewpoint that does injustice to the dignity of Hindu dharma, etc."[1] Brian Hatcher brought this to the attention of scholars who are on the RISA list and expressed concern "about the ways we can successfully present the goals of our scholarly study while being sensitive to insider sentiments." Other scholars were concerned about "blurring ... the lines between issues of serious scholarly debate, those of clearer [*sic*] sectarian interest (and sometimes of clearly anti-Islamic sentiment), and questions regarding minor factual details."[2] Another commentator who saw himself "as a scholar, a practitioner, a parent and a teacher of Hinduism in the community" thought somewhat differently. He wrote:

> it was clear to me that there were significant problems in the treatment and representation of the Hindu and I am not here referring to the issue of the Aryan invasion. In many instances, there were cheap humorous shots at the tradition and misleading simplifications of Hindu teachings and insights. It is important that, as scholars, we recognize the legitimacy of these concerns and not see only the hand of "extremism" in all community initiated efforts. Although it is true that the organizations lobbying for textbook changes are not academic in nature, it is wrong for us in the scholarly community to dismiss them impulsively when there are genuine issues about the representation of Hinduism.[3]

Generally, scholars are sensitive about religious communities' sentiment and feelings and this is evidenced from another comment on the same RISA list. One scholar poignantly said:

> I'm aware of the debates that the discussions over California textbooks' representation of India have occasioned, and I have gotten emails from several directions about it. There is certainly no disagreement about removing stereotypes, demeaning representations, and subtle biases. I would always support such efforts. You speak of factual

mistakes and misinformation, but that's precisely where there is a lot of disagreement. It's not self-evident that one version of the "facts" is correct and the others are wrong. This is what scholars of history (political or cultural or whatever) spend their work lives doing—trying to gather and evaluate evidence for various possible ways in which we can understand what happened in the past. Scholars argue, present competing theories, search for new evidence, discuss and share information, develop new approaches and methods, etc.[4]

From this one example it is evident how difficult it has become for the insiders and outsiders of a religious tradition to engage meaningfully in academic discussions. On the one side academic scholars of religion cautioned about Hindu fundamentalist agendas:

> I believe that the role of scholars of South Asian religion is of critical importance. California Educators are seeking the advice of "experts" and those who have been most vocal and present in the debates have favored a "Hindu Dharma" centered approach. While the desire to honor the "insider" perspective is noble, we need to be vigilant about the alliances we form. The HEF (Hindu Education Foundation) was founded by the HSS (Hindu Swayamsevak Sangh—RSS's International wing). The politics and agendas are quite clear.
>
> (RISA mailing list, December 1, 2006)

On the other hand, religiously inclined scholars are concerned about misrepresentations. But underlying all of this is the question of who represents Hinduism or, as a special issue of the *Journal of the American Academy of Religion* put it: "Who speaks for Hinduism?" (68/4 [2000]). To further explore this issue, let me summarize some of the essential points of the essays presented in this volume.

Who Speaks for Hinduism?

The *JAAR* essays, introduced by Sara Caldwell and Brian K. Smith, are broadly linked to the general problem of "who speaks for religion," that is, any religion. The question that reverberates in these essays is whether "non-South Asians can speak" for Hinduism (McDermott 2000, 721). Or, as John Stratton Hawley puts it, "Can the subaltern speak?" (2000, 718). In answering this question, various responses were made by the scholars who contributed to the volume—some are Western and some thought they were indigenous scholars or practitioners and academics at the same time. Hawley, a Western scholar of Hinduism, felt disqualified to speak for Hinduism in the face of Dhareshvar, a native scholar's categorical rejection of Hinduism as a Western theory (2000, 712). However, McDermott, also a Western scholar, sees the possibility of several voices contributing to the academic discussion of Hinduism. She says, "the scholarly conversation will change, improve, and deepen as more voices—whether from India or from New York—enrich the discussion" (2000, 730). William Harman, another Western scholar, plays it even safer: "Scholars of religion have a special responsibility when *we* speak of religious traditions to which we do not belong. We must represent what we find there, but because we have chosen—for one reason or another—not to be participants in that tradition, we cannot credibly dictate how that tradition should function" (2000, 739). Brian K. Smith is more optimistic about religious studies scholars being in a position to speak for Hinduism:

Unless we are all ready to take up another occupation, it is, it seems to me, precisely our *svadharma*, our legitimate duty, to speak about and for Hinduism—to our students, to the general public, and to our colleagues in other fields within religious studies and other related disciplines. And while it is certainly not incumbent on us to simply reproduce the discourse of selected indigenous religious authorities, it does seem troubling when scholars go so far as to silence or ignore not only these authorities but also those who view them as such.

(2000, 748)[5]

Responses from scholars of Indian origin also varied. For instance, Arvind Sharma, using Advaita logic, renders the problem of "insider-outside" irrelevant. He says,

The great advantage of the outsider is that the outsider can be objective. However, to the extent that an insider from a tradition can objectify his or her own tradition, the insider can also perpetually distance him- or herself from his or her tradition and, *to that extent*, the outsider's claim to perceptual objectivity no longer remains unique … [W]hat is really happening is that the *contents* of the insider's and outsider's knowledge have been shown to be capable of being similar, or even identical, to a much greater extent than might be obvious at first sight. But that does not mean that the knowledges themselves—as the *insider's* knowledge and the *outsider's* knowledge—cease to remain distinct.

(2000, 258)

Vasudha Narayanan argued for a multiplicity of voices in speaking for Hinduism. These include local goddesses, musicians and dancers, women poets, women patrons, and "lower" caste Hindus (2000, 776). In her analysis of Indian textual studies, Laurie Patton (2000) agrees with the idea that people who speak for Hinduism need not do so based on race or religion. She calls for an exchange of scholarship between Indian scholars and their Western counterparts. Deepak Sarma (2000), a practitioner of Madhva tradition (a South Indian Vaishnava branch), struggles between being an insider and an outsider (as an academic). John Thatamanil (2000), an Indian Christian theologian currently teaching in the USA, proposes a joint venture between theologians and religionists in the academic study of religion. Douglas Brooks, a scholar of Tantra, suggests that scholars of Hinduism are just as qualified to speak for Hinduism—the important thing, however, is the integrity of the scholar. He says, "Who speaks for Hinduism is less a matter of authority than one of integrity" (2000, 824). This applies to both scholars' statements as well as those that are made by religious authorities. He argues:

Scholars should indeed judge the integrity and validity of religious claims in their contexts. Just because our subject is religion or Hinduism and we may be neither religious nor Hindu by birth, this creates no exemption. Likewise, being of any religious persuasion, including Hindu by birth or by choice, neither qualifies nor disqualifies a work as scholarship. There is no privileged authority conferred by birth, culture, or religious persuasion in contexts of academic study.

(2000, 825)

He seems to indicate that in order for academic scholars to engage in theological writing,[6] one should receive the authority from the "inside authority," as illustrated in his case through Swami Chidvilasananda (2000, 827).

After these many different strands on the issue comes the wisdom statement in the form of a response by Donald S. Lopez (2000). He restates the dilemma, as expressed by many of the voices before him, and provides a diagnosis and a possible cure. The dilemma is that the religious studies departments in North America are trying to teach the Hinduism of "lentils"[7] when the students, who are predominantly of South Asian descent, are eager to hear of the Hinduism of "liberation." By this Lopez refers to the historical development of Hinduism. His cure is as follows:

> The solution may lie more simply in an appeal to history. It would seem that any class on any religion might begin with some discussion of why it is that that class is being taught at that college or university: why, institutionally speaking, the students and teacher are sitting together in that classroom at the beginning of the semester.

(2000, 834)

These views are helpful to both theologically oriented scholars and those who have their sympathy for the "insider" sensibilities. But my restlessness remains, for I view the study of Hinduism as someone who has no religious interest in religion. Among the above responses, only Brooks refers to someone who could be non-religious. For me, the issues involved in studying Hinduism are but a case-in-point for those involved in comparatively studying religion in general. That is, if J. Z. Smith's oft-quoted statement that "It [i.e. religion] is created by the scholar's imaginative acts of comparison and generalization" (1982, 217) is something to go by, then not only religion but also the very notion of Hinduism is a product of scholarly comparisons and generalizations. Moreover, it is important to emphasize that Hinduism is a product of both scholarly engagement with the data and also a product of the engagement of native pundits and nationalist intellectuals from South Asia. For this reason, it does not really matter whether one accepts Hinduism as a homogeneous religion or several religions with several schemes of salvations and their attendant philosophies. What matters is the data, and how that data are interrogated by a theory. If there is sufficient evidence in the data and the data are analyzed clearly to show a theoretical point (for instance that Hinduism as a single monolithic and homogeneous religion does not exist on the ground), then it is for the theory to interrogate such a claim. And it does not need to be discredited as a "deconstructionist" theory as though there is something inherently wrong in the theory. The same could apply to psychoanalysis as a theory. The scholarly enterprise does not preclude a theory simply because it comes from a murky past or simply because some of us do not like it. Instead, scholars should credit or discredit a theory based on the credibility of the data, method, and their analysis. Whether the method of collecting the data, method of analyzing them, and the method of interpreting them is available to someone else is, therefore, equally important. It is of no great help if an insider knows something and no one else can have access to it even by deploying the dubious phenomenological methods of empathy and eidetic vision.[8] On the other hand, if the insider wants to influence knowledge about a religion, in this case Hinduism, then he or she should place it in the public domain. Once it is in the public domain, scholars from outside can use it as well.

My point here is that our knowledge of any religion depends on the extent to which we possibly can know. What is outside our knowledge can become part of our theory. This limitation does not exclude the insiders. Even insiders too have such limitations. For instance, women in orthodox Hindu families are not permitted to know some of the traditions. The extent to which they (i.e. Hindu women) describe Hinduism is therefore contingent upon their knowledge of the tradition. One might call it Hinduism of "lentils" but that is Hinduism too.

Is Hinduism an Exception?

Notwithstanding the fact that Hindu texts have been studied in conventional formats in the orthodox brahmanical centers, the study of Hinduism in its modern form certainly began with European interest in South Asia with all its cultural diversity and complexity. For this reason alone, the construction (or misconstruction) of Hinduism has been attributed to the Orientalist scholars who received help from the native pundits in translations and interpretations of texts. Nevertheless, to the extent that those data were then analyzed and interpreted (or reinterpreted) in the metropolitan centers of Europe, a legacy was created that has European hallmarks to it, for getting the data from native sources was only a part of the story of Hinduism. How that data was later shaped by scholars, missionaries, and colonial administrators is what has raised questions about the "authenticity" of those interpretations. One of the lasting legacies of this is the fact that, unlike the study of Judaism, Christianity, Islam and these days even Buddhism (all of which have been populated by believers[9]), the study of Hinduism for the most part remained in the Western academy.

This has raised the question whether the study of Hinduism is an exception. To a certain extent, it seems so. First, as Hawley points out, religion in general is seen as a way of life in India and "almost never taught as an academic discipline in public universities"; "Even in the Hindu university at Banaras and the Muslim one at Aligarh there was no Department of Hindu Studies, Islamic Studies or Religion in general" (2000, 715). Second, there is the quibble from within Hinduism whether Brahmins are the only authority to speak for Hinduism, or whether those who practice Hinduism (i.e. lentil Hinduism), or even the Dalits and non-Sanskritic practitioners, could also speak for Hinduism. This, of course, has affected the academic study of Hinduism. Brian K. Smith thinks that as secular scholars we have no right to ask whether Brahmins could speak for Hinduism (2000, 747). Vasudha Narayanan asks us to listen to the local goddesses (2000, 768), whereas Sarma asks us to listen to the *Apta Gurus* (trustworthy teachers) (2000, 781). Third, as Brooks informs us: "Our colonial history notwithstanding, Hinduism is not merely the same religion in different places and contexts. Hinduism is, if you will, a plural religion or even a 'religions' to be studied comparatively" (2000, 825). For the three above reasons, one might accord Hinduism a special place in the study of religion, in that it has been predominantly studied by non-native scholars and only recently have native scholars, as well as scholars of WASH (White Anglo-Saxon Hindus)[10] background begun to engage in the study of Hinduism.

However, granting Hinduism such special status does not help much in placing the study of Hinduism within the context of the study of religion. What matters to me is the place of Hinduism in the broader scope of the study of religion. How does studying Hinduism shape or influence the study of religion in general? Two comments are instructive in this regard:

> While many different theologians may say, with authority, many different things about the unified essence of "Hinduism," it is the outside scholar's task to compare and analyze these different strands and construct his or her own conceptualization of "Hinduism" on the basis of such work and reflection upon it.
>
> (B. K. Smith 2000, 746)

Scholars should indeed judge the integrity and validity of religious claims in their contexts. Just because our subject is religion or Hinduism and we may be neither religious nor Hindus by birth, this creates no exemption. Likewise, being of any religious persuasion, including Hindu by birth or by choice, neither qualifies nor disqualifies a work as scholarship. (Brooks 2000, 825)

Taken together, these two comments may help us move forward, for the problems that confronted the study of Hinduism can be of great assistance in understanding the broader scope of the study of religion. We learn lessons from the past. We now know that much of our understanding of Hinduism both as a religion as well as an academic engagement by professionally trained scholars, has been influenced by Orientalist scholarship that was assisted by native Brahmin pundits. We are also poignantly aware of the fact that many subaltern voices, be they non-Sanskrit goddesses or emerging native scholars who are religiously inclined, are not part of that understanding. From the comments quoted above two important insights might be gleaned. First, the comment by Smith reminds us about our task of comparativism and, second, the comment by Brooks reminds us of our integrity as scholars. Given the vast diversity that exists within the religion called Hinduism, the "insider scholar–outsider scholar" distinction collapses at some point. That is, the insider to the Madhava tradition becomes an outsider to the Shaiva Siddhanta tradition and perhaps to everything else within what we have included as Hinduism. In this sense, he or she stands more or less in the same predicament as the outside scholar does—of being ignorant of the other tradition and being reliant on another insider. As such, Hinduism as a broader phenomenon has no insiders *per se*. Its so-called participants are all insiders and outsiders at the same time.

This means that, whether one is an insider or an outsider, if one wants to construct Hinduism in the broader sense, there is no escape from comparativism—which to me is the basis for constructing a discussion on religion. That is, just as scholars of Hinduism, both insiders and outsiders, need to compare the data before them to understand Hinduism in its broader scope, so too the study of religion engages in comparing the vast amount of data gleaned from different religions. It is here that the experience of our comparisons within the study of Hinduism might be useful in understanding how comparisons of differences as well as similarities could happen in the study of religion. In this sense, Hinduism is no exception and does not stand alone but joins as a collaborator in the broader study of religion. From a scholarly comparativist perspective, data selection and their analysis is something that belongs to a scholar's choice and hence the theory based on the analysis is one that belongs to the scholar too. This means that it is the scholar who constructs what Hinduism is and what it means within the theoretical analysis of the data. If the data are chosen only from Vedanta materials, then there is every possibility that what that scholar constructs about Hinduism reflects those data—hence the divergence of views on what constitutes Hinduism. But to the extent that it is constructed by scholars it belongs to the scholar's imagination, as J. Z. Smith tells us. This is why definitions and theories are constantly contested and reviewed. That is, after all, the purpose of scholarship and no one needs to get upset if some scholar uses psychoanalysis as a theoretical tool to analyze the data that he or she have selected for the purpose of proposing a thesis. All such scholarship means to examine is whether there is sufficient evidence for the thesis and if the integrity of the scholar and his or her scholarship can be maintained.

Conclusion

I have suggested that studying Hinduism provides a case-in-point for the study of religion in the broader and more generic sense—not that religion as a social phenomenon exists, but it does so as a conceptual tool for our scholarly comparative analysis. Similarly, I suggest that

Hinduism as a social phenomenon does not exist, but it does exist as a conceptual tool for our purposes of comparison and generalization. I think, therefore, that it does not make much of a difference whether or not religious Hindus think it exists, but that we as scholars think it does, whether it is in the form of a single, homogeneous unit or in all its diversity. It matters to us that it exists because we as scholars have created it, and did so for our scholarly analysis. And this we did for our purposes of generalizations. And these generalizations allow us to understand and conceptualize the vast amount of data comparatively, however incomplete they may be. As Jonathan Smith clarifies: "The 'general' differs from the universal in that it admits to exceptions; it differs from the 'particular' in that it is highly selective. Both characteristics guarantee that generalizations are always corrigible" (2004, 31).

A couple of hundred years ago, the people whom we today call Hindu perhaps did not think of their religious traditions as Hinduism, but contemporary practitioners might do so; what began as our scholarly conceptual tool has become so vastly used by lay people that there today seems to be no clear distinction between how scholars have used it, and how lay people have become used to relating to it. Some religiously oriented scholars as well as lay people may still buy the questionable historical narrative of a continuous story of Hinduism, beginning with the Vedic gods and traversing through the Upanishads and ending eventually at the temple-based gods such as Rama, Krishna, Shiva, and the goddess of all varieties.[11] Scholarly analyses of Hinduism may see it as different religions with different soteriologies as suggested by the work of scholars such as von Stietencron (1995), or with some continuities and discontinuities, as in the work of Axel Michaels (2004). Whether one subscribes on scholarly grounds to the radical diversity theory in what we call Hinduism or to the homogeneity theory, what remain important are the data and the theoretical framework that is brought to bear on the thesis. But in either case, the category "Hinduism" has not been given up in favor of something else, just as in the case of the category "religion." That is, how data are related to the principal category of analysis, namely, Hinduism, matters. In relating the data to our categories of analysis, it is eminently important to take into account the "meaning within the cultures that produced them, and their meaning within the history of scholarship on them" (J. Z. Smith 2004, 10).

That is to say, in our understanding of Hinduism it is not only what religious insiders say about it, but equally important is what scholarly analyses have constructed over many years of scholarship. After all, when there was no such notion prevalent among lay practitioners and believers whom we have identified as Hindus, it is the outsiders (i.e. missionaries and colonial administrators) who have been credited with having produced the concept of Hinduism. No doubt, in the many years of its use, native pundits, nationalist intellectuals, and politicians have made use of it in abundance. For this reason it is less important to ask who speaks for Hinduism as far as the academy is concerned; rather, we ought to ask about who studies or who can study Hinduism. Obviously as many voices have already indicated it has to be those who are professionally trained and in possession of conceptual and analytical tools that should study it. It therefore matters very little whether one is an insider or an outsider. Even if one is a Madhva follower and has insider access to data, the only reason scholars would read his or her analysis is because such a person has gone through the rigor of academic training. Access to data is only one part of our engagement as scholars. What we do with them is far more important. Criticality is central to our scholarship. It is what gives us a sense of where to get off the train. Otherwise the tragedy of Eliade's method will befall scholars!

So, I want to conclude this piece by turning to Eliade and returning to J. Z. Smith, but with a point. As much as Mircea Eliade dabbled in alchemy, he could never become a professor of chemistry! In the last few decades a good deal of scholarship went along the path of phenomenologists such as Eliade, hoping to enter into the world of religious people, be they Hindus or others. Such engagements became so close to the data that they missed analytical criticality. The best example is Eliade himself. Being phenomenologically enthusiastic he entered the world of religious cultures and ideas to the extent that he nearly reconstructed what he thought was human consciousness. In his *The Myth of the Eternal Return* (1974), for instance, he simply reaffirmed what he saw in many ritual societies, such that by performing the sacred ritual one is continually re-enacting the cosmic act of the divine and thereby celebrating the divine act. But when "the chips are down" (to use J. Z. Smith's own phrase, which, he reports, often mystified Eliade), this is what J. Z. Smith had to say when he reconsidered Eliade's approach after many years of his own scholarship:

> One finds in many archaic cultures a profound faith in the cosmos as ordered in the beginning and a joyous celebration of the primordial act of ordering as well as a deep sense of responsibility for the maintenance of that order through repetition of the myth, through ritual, through norms of conduct, or through taxonomy. *But it is equally apparent that in some cultures the structure of order, the gods that won or ordained it, creation itself, are discovered to be evil and oppressive. In such circumstances, one will rebel against the paradigms and seek to reverse their power.*
>
> (2004, 15, emphasis added)[12]

Smith then added, "I concluded that what was required was a 'phenomenology of rebellion'" (2004, 15).

In other words, the most important aspect of our academic engagement is to go beyond religious limitations and push the analysis to explain what needs to be explained. In doing so, theories are deployed. If a theory does not work, either the scholar can revisit his or her theory after further examination of missing data or another promising young scholar might take it up as a doctoral dissertation. For me, this is the eminent example I see in Jonathan Smith's work. He relentlessly continued to revise his theories, so much so that he could only describe his work as a series of "persistent preoccupations." In a similar way, we may persistently argue about who speaks for Hinduism and who studies it and what it means. But the category "Hinduism" will continue to dominate our notions of religion in South Asia. It is purely a non-religious, conceptual tool that helps us to analyze data that we find in the plethora of traditions in South Asia. Deploying it religiously simply discredits it; it fails when it is deployed religiously. But it challengingly becomes meaningful when used as an analytical tool—it can bring coherence to a vast amount of disparate data not because it has any essence in it, but because it is our attempt at generalization. It is, therefore, far more fruitful to engage with it non-religiously.

Such a view frees one from the limitations of both theology and the insider traditions. Such a view of religion can also help to free the academic study of religion from the uncomfortable embrace of theology.

QUESTIONS FOR REVIEW AND DISCUSSION

1. What are some of the conflicting positions on the relationship between religious studies and theology identified by Kumar at the beginning of his paper?

2. What does Kumar note about a theologian or a religious studies scholar's access to materials for study?
3. What was the California Textbook Controversy? Outline some of the positions taken by various scholars – insiders and outsiders – on the degree to which they may speak accurately about a religious tradition such as Hinduism.
4. What is Kumar's position on who may speak effectively about a religious tradition?
5. What does Kumar have to say about whether or not Hinduism is a special case? What do you think about the status of Hinduism among the world's major religious traditions?
6. What features about the study of Hinduism does Kumar use to extrapolate to the scholarly study of religions in general?
7. Does Kumar conclude that insiders or outsiders are better suited to study religion? What criteria are most important for him in the study of religion? Do you agree?
8. What is the gist of J. Z. Smith's critique of Eliade's phenomenology according to Kumar? From your readings of Eliade, do you agree with Smith's critique?

Notes

1 This was posted by Brian Hatcher on the RISA mailing list, December 1, 2005.
2 Posted by Stuart Sarbacker, RISA mailing list, December 1, 2005.
3 Posted by Anantanand Rambachan, Saint Olaf College, RISA mailing list, December 1, 2005.
4 Posted by Linda Hess, RISA mailing list, December 1, 2005.
5 Smith is referring to what he calls the deconstructionist scholars who objected to Orientalist scholars' generalizations of Hinduism. He has in mind scholars such as von Stietencron.
6 Brooks wants to allow scholars of Hinduism (by implication I would think scholars of religion) to do any genre of scholarship – "Scholars of Hinduism need not limit themselves to any one genre of scholarship, be it strictly descriptive and 'critical' or theological" (2000, 829).
7 Lopez derives the metaphor from Vasudha Narayanan's (2000) idea of Hinduism of practice.
8 It might be interesting and curious to note the detour of J. Z. Smith into phenomenology and then out of it. Smith says: "In several papers written in 1959–60, I sharply criticized what was taken to be 'phenomenology of religion,' coupled with a long paper in which I argued that Sartre's *Being and Nothingness* was a useful model for a properly anthropological phenomenology, even though I ended by confessing that I could not see how to apply it to problems of mythic thought. My work on Hesiod still retained too much phenomenological vocabulary; it was my excited reading of Lévi-Strauss's 'Four Winnebago Myths' that purged that. I rewrote the Hesiod piece several times during 1960–61, striving to make it into a purely structuralist essay as I understood structuralism at that time" (2004, 7).
9 This point has been made by Brooks (2000, 827).
10 Brooks identified himself as one (2000, 823).
11 Lopez rightly suggests concerning this narrative, "As compelling as this story might seem, it is not true" (2000, 833).
12 No wonder, the gods in the Vedic myths were reversed in the Zoroastrian myths as demons!

References

Armour, Ellen T. 2006. "Theology in Modernity's Wake." *Journal of the American Academy of Religion* 74:7–15.

Brooks, Douglas R. 2000. "Taking Sides and Opening Doors: Authority and Integrity in the Academy's Hinduism." *Journal of the American Academy of Religion* 68:817–30.

Cabezón, Jose Ignacio. 2006. "The Discipline and Its Other: The Dialectic of Alterity in the Study of Religion." *Journal of the American Academy of Religion* 74:21–38.

Eliade, Mircea. 1971.*The Quest: History and Meaning in Religion*. Chicago: University of Chicago Press.

———. 1974. *The Myth of the Eternal Return, or Cosmos and History*. Trans. W. R. Trask. Princeton: Princeton University Press.

Flood, Gavin. 2006. "Reflections on Tradition and Inquiry in the Study of Religions.*" Journal of the American Academy of Religion* 74:47–58.

Griffiths, Paul J. 2006."On the Future of the Study of Religion in the Academy." *Journal of the American Academy of Religion* 74:66–74.

Harman, William. 2000. "Speaking about Hinduism and Speaking against It." *Journal of the American Academy of Religion* 68:733–40.

Hawley, John Stratton. 2000. "Who Speaks for Hinduism—and Who Against?" *Journal of the American Academy of Religion* 68:711–20.

Jakelic, Slavica, and Jessica Starling. 2006. "Religious Studies: A Bibliographic Essay." *Journal of the American Academy of Religion* 74:194–211.

Levene, Nancy. 2006. "Response to Flood." *Journal of the American Academy of Religion* 74:59–63.

Lopez, Donald S. 2000. "Response: Pandit's Revenge." *Journal of the American Academy of Religion* 68:831–35.

McDermott, Rachel Fell. 2000. "New Age Hindus, New Age Orientalism, and the Second-Generation South Asian." *Journal of the American Academy of Religion* 68:721–32.

Michaels, Axel. 2004. *Hinduism: Past and Present*. Princeton: Princeton University Press.

Narayanan, Vasudha. 2000. "Diglossic Hinduism: Liberation and Lentils." *Journal of the American Academy of Religion* 68:761–80.

Ochs, Peter. 2006. "Response to Armour." *Journal of the American Academy of Religion* 68:16–18.

Patton, Laurie L. 2000. "Fire, the Kali Yuga, and Textual Reading." *Journal of the American Academy of Religion* 68:805–16.

Sarma, Deepak. 2000. "Let the Apta (Trustworthy) Hindu Speak!" *Journal of the American Academy of Religion* 68:781–90.

Schweiker, William. 2006. "Response to Cabezon." *Journal of the American Academy of Religion* 74:39–44.

Segal, Robert A. 2006. "All Generalizations Are Bad: Postmodernism on *Theories.*" *Journal of the American Academy of Religion* 74:157–71.

Sharma, Arvind. 2000. "Who Speaks for Hinduism? A Perspective from Advaita Vedanta." *Journal of the American Academy of Religion* 68:751–60.

Smith, Brian K. 2000. "Who Does, Can, and Should Speak for Hinduism?" *Journal of the American Academy of Religion* 68:741–50.

Smith, Jonathan Z. 1982. *Imagining Religion: From Babylon to Jonestown*. Studies in the History of Judaism. Chicago: University of Chicago Press.

———. 2004. *Relating Religion: Essays in the Study of Religion*. Chicago: University of Chicago Press.

Stietencron, Heinrich von. 1995. "Religious Configurations in Pre-Muslim India and the Modern Concept of Hinduism." Pages 51–81 in V. Dalmia and H. von Stietencron (eds), *Representing Hinduism: The Construction of Religious and National Identity*. New Delhi: Sage.

Thatamanil, John J. 2000. "Managing Multiple Religious and Scholarly Identities: An Argument for a Theological Study of Hinduism." *Journal of the American Academy of Religion* 68:791–804.

20 Contemporary Academic Buddhist Theology: Its Emergence and Rationale

John Makransky

John Makransky (1953−) received his doctorate in Buddhist Studies from the University of Wisconsin-Madison. He specializes in doctrines of enlightenment and forms of meditation, ritual, and devotion in Indian and Tibetan Buddhism. He is both a professor of Buddhism and Comparative Theology at Boston College and a meditation teacher who studied twenty-five years in four lineages of Tibetan Buddhism. Makransky became a lama in the Nyingma order of Nyoshul Khenpo in 2000. His article in this volume is informed by this nexus of training and teaching both within the tradition and within the academic world. He is also a co-chair of the Buddhist Critical-Constructive Reflection Group at the American Academy of Religion. This signals the ongoing discussion about the relationship between Buddhist insights and scholarship about Buddhism as does the book he co-edited with Roger Jackson, *Buddhist Theology: Critical Reflections by Contemporary Buddhist Scholars.*

The "scientific study of religions" is a twentieth century phenomenon. It emerged in the Western academy as a child of the Western enlightenment through a methodology designed to distinguish it from Christian theological study. Central to it has been the method of "epoché": bracketing judgments of normative truth and value so as to open a new space in the academy for the in-depth study of non-Christian religions, free from the presumption of their normative inferiority to Christianity. With its emergence, the study of religion in the academy became segregated into two separate institutional niches. In North America and Europe, religious studies (or "history of religions") departments were created in hundreds of colleges and universities, while university divinity schools and departments of theology remained the loci of Christian theological studies. The meteoric rise of religious studies in colleges and universities made many new things possible. It has given millions of students a much more intimate knowledge and appreciation of world religions than previously possible, and continues to educate the wider public through many new kinds of publication and media. Of special importance to the present discussion, religious studies departments have also created new opportunities for non-Christian graduate students to engage in the critical study of their own religious traditions within the Western academy.

The latter development, though broadly welcomed, has had unintended and largely unacknowledged consequences: it has released new forces of interest in the academy. Religious studies method, by withholding normative judgments, opened space in the academy for new kinds of study of non-Christian religions, but did not provide the space to apply such findings to the theological concerns of those religions. The training of non-Christian scholars in the contemporary study of religions (including their own) has triggered, in some, a natural impulse to apply such knowledge to the theological needs of their traditions. This is an interest not merely to describe their tradition at a distance (from the bracketed, "value neutral" position of religious studies) but precisely to clarify the truth and value of their tradition from a critical perspective located within it. Thus, the training of non-Christian scholars in the religious studies academy has generated a strong new interest in critical, constructive theology that fits neither within the established method of religious studies nor under the rubric of Christian theology, the previous main locus of such work in Western culture.

This has had further unintended consequences. The religious studies framework that permits non-Christian religions to be taken newly seriously in the West excludes their being taken seriously on their own terms. Under the rubric of religious studies, the functionally secular Western academy mines world religions for its use: to generate research findings, publications, conferences to explore whatever may be of current interest and benefit to the academy. The "value neutral" method of religious studies was of course never value neutral. Rather, it implicitly established a value in religions divorced from the normative interests of their own religious communities: a value found exclusively in their capacity to fulfill the intellectual, social, and economic interests of the Western academy.

This contributes to the current re-evaluation of the assumptions upon which the separation between theological studies and religious studies was originally constructed. As Francis Schussler Fiorenza has pointed out, the "science of religion" was constructed upon late nineteenth century presuppositions about the nature of disciplinary knowledge which late twentieth century criticism largely rejects, while the ahistorical presuppositions that previously conditioned theological study have been replaced by the methods of historical and cultural criticism. The domains of religious studies and theological studies are appearing less mutually exclusive than before.[1] The recent turn toward theology on behalf of their religious traditions by non-Christians in the academy who presently possess no clear niche for such work will further contribute to this re-evaluation. Despite the diverse origins of theological interest within the academic study of religions, it is, among other things, good news for Christian theology, which will be enriched by the wider conversation that continues to unfold around it and in dialogue with it.

This renascent interest in theology manifests vividly in the Buddhist studies wing of the religious studies academy, because the increasing prominence of Buddhist studies in the academy has been driven by the contemporary culture's growing interest in Buddhism, and that cultural interest is driven in significant part by an implicit theological concern to tap Buddhism as a source of truth and value for persons' lives. People who seek truth and transformative power in Buddhism include not only those who identify themselves as Contemporary Buddhists, but prominently also Christians, Jews and others for whom Buddhist teaching or practice sheds light upon truths of their own traditions or upon possibilities for integration of those truths into their lives.

The current ground-swell of normative Western interest in Buddhism is by no means a passing fad, any more than previous such ground swells in China, Japan or Tibet. Like other cultures in their stages of Buddhist encounter, the West has just begun to discern its own face in the Buddha's teaching. Some postmodern analysts have argued that this is merely an imaginative projection, and of course it is partly that (as it was in China, Japan, Tibet). But it is not merely that. The remarkable cultural absorption of Buddhist thought and practice we are now witnessing is rooted in an intuitive recognition of its potential power to beneficially transform many aspects of the culture it now touches. As for previous cultures, this is the start of a profound cultural recognition that energizes masses of people across diverse social strata to explore more and more dimensions of Buddhist image, thought and practice over the long term.

Can Buddhist teaching and practice reveal the nature of reality beyond the webs of dichotomous thought? Can it shed light upon holism in embodied experience, beyond dichotomies of mind and body? Can it open new ways to heal body and mind? Can it profoundly affect ways we currently think, write, make music, paint, form relationships, recreate, educate our children? Can it reveal previously unnoticed limitations of post-modern responses to modernism, of feminist responses to patriarchy, of intellectual responses to the environmental crisis? Can it shed new light upon the West's resurgent interest in previously marginalized sources of its own spirituality? Can it shed light on so much because it ultimately derives from a transcendent knowledge (Sanskrit: *Jokottara-jñāna*) whose creative potential is limitlessly adaptable? These are questions that concern truth, value and transformative power. Religious studies, as previously practiced, brackets such questions. But to bracket them is to render the academy irrelevant to the ground-swell of interest in Western culture that generates the increasing presence of Buddhist studies in its midst.

If the contemporary situation generates pressing cultural questions that the religious studies academy has been ill-equipped to address, it generates equally pressing questions for Buddhist tradition that traditional Buddhist teachers have been ill-equipped to address. Is there a systematic coherence to be found within or among the competing Buddhist cultural traditions now planting their roots in Western culture (cultural traditions that have often ignored or disparaged each other)? What contemporary meaning and relevance is to be found in these ancient cultural expressions? What are the possibilities of authentic adaptation?

Such pressing cultural concerns now contribute to an especially strong theological push in Buddhist studies, because a number of its current representatives were set on their course by the same kinds of concerns, which took expression in them both through years of traditional study and practice under Asian Buddhist teachers and through training in the critical methods of the contemporary Western academy. A number of such scholars now find themselves equipped with both sets of tools, and an emerging scholarly purpose defined both by the cultural forces operative in and around them and by the contemporary theological needs of the Buddhist traditions in which they have trained.

The contemporary need of Buddhist tradition for critical reflection is as great as that of Western culture. The two needs are, of course, connected. Buddhist traditions want to communicate themselves in ways accessible to new worlds of interest. But to do this requires not only a knowledge of new languages in which to translate the old ways, but a critical perspective upon the old ways that understands how much of them has been the product of socio-cultural and historical forces that are inapplicable to new socio-cultural settings. Lacking such critical understanding, religious traditions such as Buddhism do unintended harm to persons and to their own reputations in new settings, then repeatedly misdiagnose the sources of harm.[2]

Historical critical consciousness developed in the Western academy which has been the locus of Christian theological study. Christian theologians now routinely inquire into the effects of historical, cultural, political, economic, and social conditions upon previous theological understandings, seeking to contextualize and critique previous perspectives so as to recover or newly emphasize other resources of tradition in light of contemporary knowledge and experience, and thereby to constructively re-engage the truth and value of Christian tradition for fresh re-appropriation. Such theologians view at least some of the critical methods of the contemporary academy as powerful (even providential) tools on behalf of their tradition, to help Christians authentically re-engage and clarify the truth of Christianity for a new time.

Unlike the Christian situation, the new historical and cultural awareness of Buddhism that religious studies has made available in the Western academy has not yet been profoundly integrated with Buddhist religious culture in most of Asia or the West. Historico-cultural critical consciousness, by and large, has remained the province of the Western academy at a great distance from the Asian Buddhist cultures that it studies. Asian Buddhist teachers are not trained in Western critical methods, and frequently have little interest in exploring the implications of critical findings for their own traditions.[3] Such methods are irrelevant to what has previously mattered in Buddhist cultures, where Buddhist teachers and meditation masters have become accomplished through traditional, not contemporary critical, methods. Now Buddhist thought and practice is increasingly introduced into the West by such Asian teachers, and by a number of their outstanding Western students recognized as teachers of Buddhism in their own right. But for the most part, the training of such Western Buddhist teachers in the study of Buddhism has been traditional. Very few have been trained in the critical methods of the academy.

Thus, in contrast to the integration of Christian theology with contemporary critical thought, the rise of Buddhist studies in the religious studies academy has opened a gap between those who transmit the living experience and traditional understanding of Buddhism and those who critically analyze Buddhism to understand the historical and cultural conditions of its development. As Christian theologians know well, the latter findings are crucial for a religious tradition to appropriate if it is to find the voice to speak its truth anew.

This situation contributes to a great irony, which has not gone unnoticed in the West: Buddhist traditions that take pride in their knowledge of all kinds of human conditioning that cause suffering (Second Noble Truth) still lack the critical tools to diagnose the effects of cultural conditioning upon their own previous understanding and current communication, and how that conditioning now contributes to confusion and suffering. Because of this, Asian Buddhist traditions continue to require contemporary persons to conform inappropriately to aspects of ancient cultures that do more harm than good for the very life of their own traditions. One common example of this is the Asian Buddhist transmission of ethnic prejudice to Westerners unawares. Upon introducing Westerners to the Dharma, Asian traditions often continue to claim for themselves the only "pure" transmission of the Buddha's teachings, subtly conforming naive Westerners to the implicit understanding that all other Asian Buddhist cultures or traditions are corrupt. Other such examples appear in some of the essays of this volume.

In recognition of these issues, scholars who were formed both by Buddhist tradition and by the contemporary academy increasingly seek ways to respond both to their own culture's normative interest in Buddhism and to the inner necessity of Buddhist tradition to reflect critically upon itself and find new ways to express itself. Their hope is that, as in the past, such new reflection rooted in long community experience may contribute to authentic new understanding: by critiquing past elements of tradition inappropriate to a new time, recovering or re-emphasizing other elements, critiquing Western models inadequate for a fuller understanding of Buddhism, and exploring the potential of Buddhist experience to shine new light upon a host of contemporary cultural and religious concerns. This is the broad project of contemporary "Buddhist theology."

The term "theology," then, in "Buddhist theology," is used in a broad sense. It includes critical reflection upon Buddhist experience in light of contemporary understanding and critical reflection upon contemporary understanding in light of Buddhist experience. Like that of Christian theologians, it is the work of scholars who stand normatively within their tradition, who look to traditional sources of authority (in sacred text and previous forms of social practice and experience), who re-evaluate prior Buddhist understandings in light of contemporary findings and who seek thereby to contribute to the continuing development of their tradition in its relevance to new times and places.

Although, for reasons noted, the institutional loci for Buddhist theology are still largely undeveloped, we would argue that the forces behind its emergence and continuing evolution are ineluctable. At present Buddhist theology finds expression mostly in the margins of academia: in religious studies conferences where "theology" is still too often viewed with suspicion, in theology conferences where the central focus is Christianity, in settings for inter-religious dialogue, in recent writings on Buddhist ethics and contemporary thought, and now in this volume.

One purpose of this volume, then, is to inspire further exploration of ways that the pressing needs of Western culture and Buddhist tradition for Buddhist critical reflection may be met through new forms of interchange, new cooperative projects, and new institutional settings East and West.

QUESTIONS FOR REVIEW AND DISCUSSION

1. How does Makransky characterize the relationship between the scientific study of religions, theology, the development of religious studies departments, and the study of religions other than Christianity?
2. What does Makransky assert are the unintended consequences of the separation between theology and religious studies with regard to non-Christian religions and methods, such as bracketing judgments of normative truth and value? Do you agree with his assessment?
3. What is Makransky's position on the "value neutral" method of religious studies? What are some examples of the types of questions that are often ignored in the academy due to such methods to bracket out truth claims?
4. What does Makransky have to say about rising Western interest in Buddhism, rising prominence of Buddhist studies within academic religious studies, and increased attention to theological concerns related to Buddhism in both contexts?
5. Do you agree with the parallels Makransky presents between Western interest in Buddhism and earlier phases in the spread of Buddhism to China, Japan, and Tibet?
6. How does Makransky indicate that a lack of engagement with questions of truth, value, and transformative power might be damaging to the growth of Buddhist studies in the academy?
7. Does Makransky conclude that traditional Buddhist teachers are properly equipped to address pressing cultural questions generated by our contemporary situation? Who is best trained and positioned for these questions? Why? What criteria and qualifications does he indicate are most important? Do you agree?
8. To what extent is the contemporary situation for Christian theological study similar or different to that of Buddhist theological study? What is the gap and related irony faced by Buddhist traditions in the West in contrast with Makransky's characterization of greater integration on the Christian side of this comparison?

9. How does Makransky use the term "Buddhist theology"? Do you think the term is appropriate for the larger project he describes? What are some of the barriers faced by this project of Buddhist theology?

Notes

1 See Fiorenza for a seminal analysis of forces in late twentieth century Western thought that push for the fundamental re-evaluation of the distinction between religious and theological studies that was erected on the basis of late nineteenth century thought. The recent resurgence of theological interest instigated by non-Christian entry into the academic study of religion complements and makes more vivid the very issues that Fiorenza has raised.

2 A stunning recent example of this: some Tibetan monks who now introduce Westerners to practices centered on a native Tibetan deity, without informing them that one of its primary functions has been to assert hegemony over rival sects! The current Dalai Lama, seeking to combat the ancient, virulent sectarianisms operative in such quarters, has strongly discouraged the worship of the "protector" deity known as Dorje Shugden, because one of its functions has been to force conformity to the dGe lugs pa sect (with which the Dalai Lama himself is most closely associated) and to assert power over competing sects. Western followers of a few dGe lugs pa monks who worship that deity, lacking any critical awareness of its sectarian functions in Tibet, have recently followed the Dalai Lama to his speaking engagements to protest his strong stance (for non-sectarianism) in the name of their "religious freedom" to promulgate, now in the West, an embodiment of Tibetan sectarianism. If it were not so harmful to persons and traditions, this would surely be one of the funniest examples of the cross-cultural confusion that lack of critical reflection continues to create.

3 Japan is certainly a partial exception to this, but there, too, there remains a tendency to segregate within academic institutions what is viewed as the confessional study of Buddha-dharma from the contemporary critical study of Buddhism.

Bibliography

Batchelor, Stephen (1994). *The Awakening of the West: The Encounter of Buddhism and Western Culture.* London: Aquarian.

Bechert, Heinz and R. Gombrich, eds (1984). *The World of Buddhism.* New York: Facts on File.

Ch'en, Kenneth (1964). *Buddhism in China: A Historical Survey.* Princeton: Princeton University Press.

Cougar, Yves (1987). "Christian Theology." In Mircea Eliade, ed., *The Encyclopedia of Religion.* New York: Macmillan, vol. 14: 455–64.

Dumoulin, Heinrich (1976). *The Cultural, Political, and Religious Significance of Buddhism in the Modern World.* New York: Macmillan.

Fields, Rick (1992). *How the Swans Came to the Lake: A Narrative History of Buddhism in America.* 3rd ed. Boston & London: Shambhala.

Fiorenza, Francis S. (1993). "Theology in the University." *CSSR Bulletin* (22: 2).

Glassé, Cyril (1989). *The Concise Encyclopedia of Islam.* San Francisco: Harper & Row.

de Jong, J. W. (1987). *A Brief History of Buddhist Studies in Europe and North America.* 2nd ed. Delhi: Sri Satguru.

Kitagawa, Joseph (1966). *Religion in Japanese History.* New York: Columbia University Press.

Pereira, Jose (1976). *Hindu Theology: A Reader.* Garden City, NY: Anchor/Doubleday.

Robinson, Richard and Willard Johnson (1997). *The Buddhist Religion: A Historical Introduction.* 4th ed. Belmont, CA: Wadsworth.

Samuel, Geoffrey (1994). *Civilized Shamans: Buddhism in Tibetan Societies.* Washington, DC: Smithsonian.

Schopen, Gregory (1997). *Bones, Stones, and Buddhist Monks: Collected Papers on the Archaeology, Epigraphy, and Texts of Monastic Buddhism in India.* Honolulu: University of Hawaii Press.

Swearer, Donald (1995). *The Buddhist World of Southeast Asia.* Albany: State University of New York Press.

Toben, Arthur A. (1987). "Theology." In Arthur A. Cohen and Paul Mendes-Flohr, eds, *Contemporary Jewish Religious Thought: Original Essays* on *Critical Concepts, Movements, and Beliefs.* New York: Charles Scribner's Sons.

Tracy, David (1987). "Comparative Theology." In Mircea Eliade, ed., *The Encyclopedia of Religion.* New York: Macmillan, vol. 14: 446–55.

Tweed, Thomas (1992). *The American Encounter with Buddhism, 1844–1912: Victorian Culture and the Limits of Dissent.* Bloomington: Indiana University Press.

Warder, A. K. (1980). *Indian Buddhism.* 2nd ed. Delhi: Motilal Banarsidass.

21 Other Scholars' Myths: The Hunter and the Sage

Wendy Doniger O'Flaherty

Wendy Doniger (O'Flaherty) (1940—) was born in New York City and has completed two doctorates, a PhD from Harvard and a DPhil from Oxford. She has also been presented with six honorary doctorates. A specialist in the study of Sanskrit Hindu texts, Doniger has translated several, including the *Kamasutra*, *The Laws of Manu*, and some portions of the *Rig Veda*. She has also written extensively on comparative mythology, and holds the Mircea Eliade Distinguished Service Professor Chair at the University of Chicago. Her writings have sometimes placed her in tension with certain segments of Hindus who feel that her analyses do not portray Hinduism in manners they would prefer. The selection that follows is the first chapter from *Other People's Myths: The Cave of Echoes* (1988). It is a challenging piece to read, because it uses a Hindu myth of a dream within a dream as a metaphor, but it is creative and rewarding in its attempt to illustrate certain differences between scholars of religion and insiders to a religion. Moreover, Doniger offers an embedded critique of various modes of traditional scholarship in religious studies, and offers suggestions for how the history of religions might further humanize its methods.

A myth may be, among many other things, the incarnation of a metaphor.[1] One metaphor that we often use to describe complete sympathy with or understanding of someone else is "getting inside someone else's head." This does not, to my knowledge, occur as a figure of speech in Sanskrit, but the image that it conjures up is often literally depicted in Indian mythology, where a person may "get inside" another person's head (that is, his mind, his mental software) by actually going inside the physical space of his skull (that is, his brain, his mental hardware) and indeed pervading his entire body.[2] The theme of entering someone else's body is a popular one in Indian literature; any respectable yogi can do this trick, which may lead to embarrassing or amusing situations (as when the mind of a yogi enters the body of a whore, and her mind enters his body in return).[3] I propose to use an Indian myth to dramatize our own English metaphor, in order both to demonstrate one of the cross-cultural uses of mythology (that is, to show how we may legitimately see in a myth a meaning different from what its own culture sees in it) and to create an image with which to think about such cross-cultural uses (an image about scholarship).

The Hunter and the Sage

The most striking dramatization I know of the metaphor of "getting inside someone else's head" is a myth that occurs in the *Yogavasishtha*, a Sanskrit philosophical treatise composed in Kashmir sometime between the tenth and twelfth centuries A.D. The myth is the story of a hunter who meets a sage who has entered another man's body and lodged in his head:

> One day a hunter wandered in the woods until he came to the home of a sage, who became his teacher. The sage told him this story:
>
> In the old days, I became an ascetic sage and lived alone in a hermitage. I studied magic. I entered someone else's body and saw all his organs; I entered his head and then I saw a universe, with a sun and an ocean and mountains, and gods and demons and human beings. This universe was his dream, and I saw his dream. Inside his head, I saw his city and his wife and his servants and his son.
>
> When darkness fell, he went to bed and slept, and I slept too. Then his world was overwhelmed by a flood [and fire] at doomsday; I, too, was swept away in the flood, and though I managed to obtain a foothold on a rock, a great wave knocked me into the water again. When I saw that world destroyed at doomsday, I wept. I still saw, in my own dream, a whole universe, for I had picked up his karmic memories along with his dream. I had become involved in that world and I forgot my former life; I thought, "This is my father, my mother, my village, my house, my family."
>
> Once again I saw doomsday. This time, however, even while I was being burnt up by the flames, I did not suffer, for I realized, "This is a just a dream." Then I forgot my own experiences. Time passed. A sage came to my house, and slept and ate, and as we were talking after dinner he said, "Don't you know that all of this is a dream? I am a man in your dream, and you are a man in someone else's dream."
>
> Then I awakened, and remembered my own nature; I remembered that I was an ascetic. And I said to him, "I will go to that body of mine (that was an ascetic)," for I wanted to see my own body as well as the body which I had set out to explore. But he smiled and said, "Where do you think those two bodies of yours are?" I could find no body, nor could I get out of the head of the person I had entered, and so I asked him, "Well, where are the two bodies?"
>
> The sage replied, "While you were in the other person's body, a great fire arose, that destroyed your body as well as the body of the other person. Now you are a house-holder, not an ascetic." When the sage said this, I was amazed. He lay back on his bed in silence in the night, and I did not let him go away; he stayed with me until he died.
>
> The hunter said, "If this is so, then you and I and all of us are people in one another's dreams." The sage continued to teach the hunter and told him what would happen to him in the future. But the hunter left him and went on to new rebirths. Finally, the hunter became an ascetic and found release.[4]

This remarkable story has many meanings that we may use for our own purposes, but first let us try to understand it in its own terms. In its own context, this is a myth about doomsday and ontology. An ascetic sage tells the tale of entering the body of a dreamer who is a married man—entering his breath, his head, and his consciousness. The sage inside the dreamer dreams of the same village that the dreamer was dreaming of, and becomes a householder like him. His "outer," or original, body does not simply decay in the absence of the conscious soul (as it does in many tales of this type);[5] it is destroyed by a fire that burns the hermitage in which the outer body was lodged. This is a strange fire: it came from the doomsday flames that the sage dreamed about when he was lying asleep in that hermitage (and inside the body of the sleeping man that he had entered). Moreover, whereas the first doomsday fire seemed real to him, so that he wept to see it destroy the inner world, this second doomsday fire seemed to him to be nothing but a dream, and a déjà vu dream at that, so that he did not feel any pain when it burnt him. Yet the first fire did not burn his outer body, because he merely saw it in another man's dream, while the second fire did burn his outer body, because he saw it in what had become his own dream, too. Since he had dreamed his outer body into nonexistence, he was physically trapped inside his dream world.

Indeed, the dreams within dreams in this text are even more complex than may appear from the narrative as I have just presented it.[6] For the story of the hunter and the sage is embedded in the *Yogavasishtha* in a complex web of interlocking narratives. As we read the story of the hunter and the sage, we become confused and are tempted to draw charts to figure it all out. It is not clear, for instance, whether the sage has entered the waking world or the sleeping world of the man whose consciousness he penetrates, and whether that person is sleeping, waking, or, indeed, dead at the moment when we meet the sage. But as the tale progresses, we realize that our confusion is neither our own mistake nor the mistake of the author of the text; it is a device of the narrative, constructed to make us realize how impossible and, finally, how irrelevant it is to attempt to determine the precise level of consciousness at which we are existing.[7] We cannot do it, and it does not matter. We can never know whether or not we have become trapped inside the minds of people whose consciousness we have come to share.

Inside the dream village, the new householder (*né* sage) meets another sage, who enlightens him and wakes him up. Yet, although he is explicitly said to awaken, he stays where he is inside the dream; the only difference is that now he knows he is inside the dream. Now he becomes a sage again, but a different sort of sage, a householder sage, inside the dreamer's dream. While he is in this state, he meets the hunter and attempts to instruct him. But the hunter misses the point of the sage's saga: "If this is so ... ," he mutters, and he goes off to get a whole series of bodies before he finally figures it out. The hunter has to experience everything for himself, dying and being reborn;[8] he cannot learn merely by dreaming, as the sage does.

But let us now set aside the metaphysical complexities of this story, its primary locus of meaning for the Hindu reader or hearer, and extract instead a point that we can apply to a very different concern, the nature of the experience of the scholar who studies other people's religions.

Scholars and People

Let us attempt now to get outside the head of the author of that myth and to translate into our own terms the metaphor of the hunter and the sage as ideal types, extreme types never actually encountered in their pure form. If we return to the metaphor that is enacted in this parable, the hunter is the person who cannot get inside other people's heads and so is driven by his emotions to go on being reborn himself over and over again, in order to have the series of experiences that are the necessary prerequisites for enlightenment. But the sage, who can go inside other people mentally, mentally experiences countless lives without ever having to be reborn.[9] There are two different ways in which one can get inside another person's life: one can be reborn inside various bodies, and live many lives, as the hunter does; or one can use mental powers to get inside other people's heads and learn about their lives, as the sage does. Hunters and sages can be taken as two types of people, the sort who have to experience everything physically in order to understand it, and the sort who think that they can understand things merely by learning about them. Hunters are ordinary householders; sages are artists and intellectuals.[10] In Indian terms, sages are Brahmins, hunters are Kshatriyas.

To be a hunter one need not necessarily believe literally in the doctrine of transmigration; one might be able to live several lives within a single rebirth, living a life in one career and then in another, in one country and then in another, with one person and then with another. So too, to be a sage in a myth one might literally enter another person's head, as a yogi does, but to be a sage in real life one might simply enter other people's consciousness through some other, milder means, perhaps by entering their myths. I will use the image of the sage to denote the person who mentally enters the nonphysical essence of other people, in contrast with the hunter who physically, through his body, experiences many lives.

We are all hunters, whether we know it or not, but the ones who know what it means to be a hunter are sages. Since sages believe that they are experiencing many lives, they can do it on purpose; hunters live their multiple lives unknowingly, helplessly. The sage is always part hunter because he is a human being and therefore an emotional, experiential creature; but because he is a sage, he is always trying to be what he cannot be: entirely free from the hunter within him. That is, the sage has a hunter in him in addition to a sage, just as Dr. Jekyll had in him both the evil Mr. Hyde and the good Dr. Jekyll; but the hunter may not have a sage in him, just as Mr. Hyde did not have Dr. Jekyll in him.[11]

The sage in our story enters what in Sanskrit is called *manas* (translated as both "heart" and "mind," in contrast with *hridaya*, usually translated simply as "heart," with which it is cognate). *Manas* is the organ that is responsible for both reason and emotion, the place where one does algebra but also the place where one falls in love. This term provides a good example of the way in which Indian thought fails to distinguish between some of the categories that we tend to think of as inherently polarized,[12] for, as we shall see, we tend to demarcate rather sharply people who are ruled by the heart and people who are ruled by the head. Indians do not do this; the Indian sage experiences life through both the head and the heart, although he tries not to experience it with his body.

E. M. Forster describes a shrine in India that was created when, according to legend, a beheaded warrior contrived somehow to continue to run, in the form of a headless torso, from the top of a hill, where he left his head, to the bottom of the hill, where his body finally collapsed; at the top of the hill is now the Shrine of the Head, and at the bottom, the Shrine of the Body.[13] This seems to me to be a useful parable for much of Western civilization, certainly for that fraction of it that studies religion. A similar metaphor is provided by the mythical beast once described by Woody Allen: the Great Roe, who had the head of a lion and the body of a lion, but not the same lion.[14]

If we apply our root metaphor to scholars of religion (who would be superficially classified, as a group, as sages, in contrast with people who just are religious, the hunters), we might further distinguish within the group of sages a subgroup of hunters, who assume that their own personal experience of religion, their own religiosity, is a sufficient basis on which to understand other people's religions, and another subgroup of sages, who assume that they must go inside other cultures (through their texts, perhaps, or through personal observation of their rituals) in order to understand them.[15] We might then further divide this latter subgroup of sages into a sub-subgroup of hunters who prefer to do their learning by going there, experiencing, doing fieldwork (the more anthropological branch of the family) and another sub-subgroup of classical sages who prefer to do their learning in their armchairs, reading texts (the more classical branch of the family). And, finally, we might go on to divide either of the sub-subgroups of anthropological or classical sages into one sub-sub-subgroup of hunters, who allow themselves to react emotionally to their learning experiences, and another of sages, who attempt to remain as objective as possible toward the people that they are studying.

Scholars of religion tend to regard themselves as Great Roes, not realizing that they have the head and the heart (the *manas*, in Sanskrit) of the same lion.[16] But this is an unfortunate schizophrenia. Good hunters *do* have sages in them, sages that bring some degree of self-awareness to the hunting; bad hunters do not. But good sages, on the other hand, always have good hunters in them. To deny the experiential component is not merely elitist; it is to deny the essential humanitarian component in the study of religion.

Indian aesthetic theory calls the sympathetic reader or member of the audience the one "whose heart is with [the poet or actor]," the *sa-hridaya* (or sym-pathetic), whose heart melts in response to poetry or art.[17] But the narrow-minded scholar's heart is hardened and encrusted by his reading of dry metaphysical texts. The accomplished sage becomes *sa-hridaya* when he shares the heart of the person with whom he sympathizes. The narrow-minded scholar is the sage who wants to live entirely in the head and never in the heart; he is the sage who attempts utterly to deny his inevitable hunter component. The sympathetic scholar is the sage who acknowledges his need to live both in the head and in the heart; who accepts his hunter component, though he attempts to deal with that aspect of his nature with greater self-awareness than that of the hunter who lives only in the heart and never in the head. Just as there are sage hunters, there are hunting sages. The hunting sage is my idea of the right sort of historian of religions.

The Sage's Myth

Let us turn for a moment to the problem faced by sages, people who enter other people's heads. In India, sages are enlightened wise men, gurus or priests. In the West, sages belong to another category of professionals or specialists: scholars, humanists such as classicists and anthropologists. Classicists (by which I mean not just people who read Greek and Latin but, more broadly, all those historians, philologists, and other humanists and social scientists who deal with the past) attempt to enter a world that is perhaps as foreign and unattainable as any world can be—the lost world of people who are now dead, but who may once have lived where we live now, or have spoken ancient forms of languages related to our own. Anthropologists, who do not usually travel in time, make all the greater effort to travel far in space, to the farthest reaches of Otherness. And anthropologists are storytellers: the word for "anthropologist" in Tok Pisin in New Guinea used to be (and unfortunately no longer is) "story-master." But although anthropologists pride themselves on entering other people's heads (that is, their thoughts), they also pride themselves on not entering other people's hearts (that is, their emotions and their lives).[18] Malinowski once remarked, "I see the life of natives as … as remote from me as the life of a dog."[19] Nevertheless, sometimes anthropologists do enter the hearts of the people that they study, just as nonprofessionals (hunters) do.

People who study myths constitute a subcaste of historians of religion, more precisely a half-caste formed through an illicit liaison between anthropologists and classicists. Mythologists, too, are Western sages, and like other sages they are also hunters. To the extent that they are sages, mythologists may enter into other people's heads (that is, understand other people's myths). But to the extent that they are hunters, mythologists, like other sages, may also enter into other people's hearts and bodies (that is, live other people's myths). Like other sages, they do absorb, if only, sometimes, unconsciously, myths that become their myths, that become personally meaningful to them.

It may be recalled that after a while Mr. Hyde took over Dr. Jekyll's life: Dr. Jekyll could not help being Mr. Hyde, and could not get back into his existence as Dr. Jekyll. In our Indian text, the life of the man whose mind the sage entered became the sage's life. In that story, the sage who began his scientific experiment in cold blood became drawn helplessly into the life of the man whose head he had entered (a householder, whom we may call a hunter in the broad sense in which we are using that metaphor). Once he made the dreamer's dream his own dream, he forgot that he was a sage; he became a hunter. Yet, eventually, still within that dream, he awakened to become another sort of sage, a sage inside a hunter.

What meaning does this story have for us? On some deep level, I think all truly creative scholarship in the humanities is autobiographical, but it is particularly evident that people who traffic in myths are caught up in them *volens nolens*. This has certainly been true for me. In 1971, when I was struggling to come to terms with the death of my father (my first major experience of inexplicable and unjust evil), I failed to draw any comfort from Jewish or Christian approaches to the problem, not through any inherent inadequacy in them but simply because they were not my myth; I had never had them. I had grown up with a certain number of Jewish rituals, and with a great number of Jewish social attitudes, but with no myths (unless, of course, one were to count as myths Jewish jokes, which I had in abundance).

Perhaps I was unable to live the Jewish myths when I needed them because I had already unconsciously replaced them with the Hindu myths in which I had been steeped from the age of twelve, when my mother gave me a copy of E. M. Forster's *A Passage to India;* perhaps I simply had an innate affinity for the Hindu myths, an immediate individual response. In any case, I found that I could in fact make some sense of my father's death in terms of the Hindu mythology of death and evil—the subject of the book that I was working on at the time, and had begun some years before the onset of my father's illness.[20] In a certain sense, I had been experiencing, like a hunter, the same events that were narrated in the myth that I had been reading and writing about as a sage, though at first I did not realize that this was the myth that I was in, perhaps because I did not expect someone else's myth to be my myth.

But there was another good reason why I could not use Jewish myths to sustain me then, why, indeed, it would perhaps have been inappropriate to use them to understand my father's death: they had ceased to be his myths, too. The tendency to make use of other people's myths has long been a habit of the Jews, wandering or dispersed as they are.[21] Jews have always lived among Others—have always been the Others wherever they lived. Both of my parents were relentlessly assimilated, secularized, and Enlightened Jewish refugees, he from Poland (a small town not far from Cracow) and she from Vienna (she lived on the street where Sigmund Freud had lived). My father, whose father had been a Talmudic scholar, knew much of Frazer's *The Golden Bough* by heart and taught it to me. He had learned it at New York University, where he had worked his way through school as a stringer for the *New York Times*, going around to all the major churches in Manhattan every Sunday and summarizing the sermons; he was paid by the inch. Eventually it dawned on him that it might be profitable to serve as a kind of matchmaker between those ministers who yearned to see their sermons in print and those ministers who were eager to have at their disposal every week the sermons of the first sort of ministers. Thus he founded in the late 1930s, and published throughout his life, two magazines for the Protestant clergy, *Pulpit Digest* and *Pastoral Psychology*. And from time to time, when he was short of copy, he wrote, under various pseudonyms, sermons that were preached all over America by Protestant clergymen who little dreamed that their homilies had been composed by an East European

Jew. Thus my father was a (Jewish) sage who entered the heads of others (Christians) but always managed to get out again.

In a similar way, I gradually came first to think with and then to feel with the karma theory. The karma theory *tells* us that we have lived other lives, that our souls have had other bodies. But how can we *feel*, as well as accept intellectually, the reality of those other lives if we cannot remember them? Plato constructed his own version of this theory in the myth of Er in the *Republic*,[22] but Plato was not a Neoplatonist and neither Platonism nor Neoplatonism became an integral part of Western thinking about death. It is easier for Hindus to *feel* the theory of rebirth, as they feel themselves to be a part of a larger human group in a way that we do not; they believe that they are joined in nature as well as in culture both with the other people with whom they have present contact and with the people in the past and future to whom they are related. But what about us who are not Hindus? For us, the previous incarnation unrecalled has no existence. For some things in life can be remembered in one's soul; but other things can only be remembered with one's body.

The body remembers some things, and the mind remembers others. But memory is not all there is; there is also a reality of unrecalled experience that gives a kind of validity to our connection with lives that we do not recall. The karma theory recognizes the parallelism between events forgotten within a single life—the events of early childhood, or the things that we repress or that (in Indian mythology) we forget as the result of a curse[23]—and the events forgotten from a previous life. It also recognizes a similarity in the ways in which we sometimes half-recall these various sorts of events, often with a sense of *déjà vu*. We remember something that we cannot remember, from a lost past, through the power of the invisible tracks or traces left behind on our souls by those events; these traces the Hindus call perfumes (*vasanas*).[24]

The karma theory tells us that we have lived lives that we cannot remember and hence cannot feel. Sages can imagine the lives of others, and so live them; and sages are rare. But for those of us who lack the imagination to perceive the infinity of our lives in time, it might be possible to perceive the infinity of our lives in human space. Again, the Indian texts tell us that we are karmically linked to all the other people in the world; they *are us*. I have known and respected this theory for a long time, though I have not always believed it.[25] But for one important moment, I did believe it. It was at a time when I was feeling rather sorry for myself for having only one child; I wished that I had had lots of children, and now it was too late. I felt that having six children would have meant having an entirely different life, not merely six times the life of a woman with one child, and I wanted that life as well as the life that I had. This thought was in my mind as I wandered on a beach in Ireland, and saw a woman with lots and lots of children, very nice children, too, and at their best, as young children often are on a beach. Normally, I would have envied her; but this time, I enjoyed her children. I was happy to watch them. And suddenly I felt that they were mine, that the woman on the beach had had them for me, so that they would be there for me to watch them as they played in the water. Her life was my life too; I felt it then, and I remember it now. What had been an idea to me until then, the idea of my karmic identity with other people, became an experience. I was able to live her life in my imagination.

One way of interpreting my epiphany of the woman on the beach was this realization that my connection to her—and, through her, to every other woman who had ever had or ever would have children—meant that my brief lifespan was expanded into the lifespans of all the other people in the world. This is a very Hindu way of looking at one's relationship with all other people. Woven through the series of individual lives, each consisting of a cluster of experiences, was the thread of the experience itself—in this case, motherhood. That experience would survive when her children and mine were long dead.

I felt then that all the things that one wanted to do and to be existed in eternity; they stood there forever, as long as there was human life on the planet Earth. They were like beautiful rooms that anyone could walk into; and when I could no longer walk into them, they would still be there. They were part of time, and though they could not go on being part of me for much longer, part of me would always be there in them. Something of me would still linger in those things that I had loved, like the perfume or pipe smoke that tells you that someone else has been in a room before you. This is the same "perfume," the same karmic trace of memory, that adheres to the transmigrating soul. And through my connection with the woman on the beach, I would be the people in the future who sensed in that room the perfume that I had left behind, though (unless I was a gifted sage) I would not recognize it as my perfume. Perhaps, since I am not a Hindu, that is as close as I can come to believing that I can remember my other lives: remembering other people's lives as my life. And perhaps it is close enough.

Fire and Ice

Scholars can learn to think with the myths of other cultures. More than that: they sometimes learn to *feel* with them. Thinking (with the head) and feeling (with the heart) when we confront other people's myths has serious implications. There are several things that it does not mean. It does not mean that a scholar of religion should become an apologist for another tradition, let alone convert to it; though conversions of this type do in fact occur from time to time, they are not the usual course of events, and they are hedged with problems. Nor does it mean that mythologists should proselytize for the texts that they study, using them in an attempt to cure the ills of a demythologized age. As we shall see, people other than mythologists certainly do take up foreign myths (just as they convert to foreign religions), but they do not take them up in the same way that the historian of religions takes them up, and in any case it is not the task of the historian of religions to facilitate such conversions. Nor does it imply that the way to study other people's myths is to take them into our own lives; the way to study them is to *study* them, learning the languages in which they were composed, finding all the other myths in the constellation of which they are a part, setting them in the context of the culture in which they were spawned—in short, trying to find out what they mean to the people who have created and sustained them, not what they mean to us. And this is hard enough to do.

But sometimes something happens to us when we study other people's myths; sometimes they enter our hearts as well as our heads. Some scholars have come to think and feel with other people's myths, an enterprise that always affects the construction of a scholar's personal worldview (one's life as a hunter) and may also affect one's professional scholarship (the life as a sage). What happens to the scholarship of sages who take seriously the myths that they study?

There is an entire continuum of ways of interpreting a myth. At one end of the spectrum is the scholarly attempt to find out what the myth meant to the people who created it: this is the method of learning the language and so forth that I have just described. It is also a method that takes serious account of the interpretations offered by believers within the tradition (though the hermeneutics of suspicion would also take into account other scholarly data that might contradict a statement from within the tradition). Such interpretations, based upon the unique characteristics of the particular culture that created this particular version of the myth, can be judged and criticized by the same criteria that would be applied to any academic enterprise. At the other end of the spectrum is the nonscholarly experience of the myth, which deals solely with the meaning that the myth has for the person who encounters it. Such an experience can only take place if the person who interprets the myth believes in certain universals of human experience and sees in the myth not merely a particular cultural version but also a universal theme that has some meaning beyond culture, across cultures. Such interpretations cannot be judged or criticized by any academic criteria; they are purely subjective, valuable only to the person who draws personal meaning from the myth.

But what of the middle ground between these extremes? What of scholars who see, as well as any good scholar can, what the myth means to its parent culture, and find that that interpretation also has meaning for them? Do we understand other peoples better if we *do* take their myths into our lives or if we *do not* take their myths into our lives? Do we understand other people's myths better if we like them, or if we hate them, or if we remain neutral?

Many scholars who have written great studies of religion have been motivated not by love of religion but by hatred of religion, or at least by anger directed against religion, or fear or loathing of religion. Freud and Marx are the most outstanding examples of brilliant haters of religion, but there are others.[26] Hate is, like love, fueled by the heart rather than the head, and emotional fuel has great staying power. Hunters *must* love and hate; ideally, sages do neither, if they remain in the cool realm of the head. But, as we have seen, they do *not* always remain in the realm of the head; they, too, hunt in the heart, and so they, too, may love and hate what they study with the head.

Robert Frost wrote of the power of hate compared with the power of desire (which is, of course, not precisely the same as love, but close enough for poetic license):

> Some say the world will end in fire,
> Some say in ice.
> From what I've tasted of desire
> I hold with those who favor fire.
> But if it had to perish twice,
> I think I know enough of hate
> To say that for destruction ice
> Is also great
> And would suffice.[27]

So hate, like desire, can destroy; and I think that, like desire, hate can create. The Hindus know that hate can even be a way of loving, particularly a way of loving a god: they speak of "hate-love" (*dvesha-bhakti*), a form of devotion in which by trying to destroy or resist a god one is drawn into an ultimately salvational intimate relationship with him. …

But hate may have been a more appropriate academic motivation in the salad days of the academic study of religion, when, like Shakespeare's *Cleopatra*, we were green in judgment, and trying to be cold in blood. Nowadays, when we can, and must, be more subtle in our criticisms of religion, hate has its limits. The attempt to sympathize is always interesting, perhaps because it is ultimately impossible; but the enterprise of killing is ultimately boring. It doesn't take very long to kill something academically—that is, to demonstrate how wrong or bad a religion, or a colleague in the study of religion, may be—but then you're finished; there is nothing left to do.[28] Killing may be amusing while it lasts, but it never lasts very long, and then you're back where you started from; there is nowhere to go *on* to. Hunters have to kill; sages do not. Sages have their opinions, of course, but they have learned to move with a careful tolerance in strange waters. Hate is creative but not generative; scholars who study what they hate go round and round, obsessively, ad infinitum, like an ouroboros biting its own tail forever—or until it burns out.

The issue of the legitimacy of affect (the heart) in the academic study of religion (a discipline of the head) has thus led us to the question of the relative validity of the two different sorts of affect, love and hate. Hate seems to provide an answer to the embarrassing problem of caring about what one teaches when what one teaches is religion. For though in the academy at large (if not in most divinity schools) it is regarded as wrong to care for religion, it is not wrong to care *against* religion. Criticism is more *wissenschaftlich* than praise in all academic disciplines, but particularly in religious studies. Since the Enlightenment, hatred of religion has been a more respectable scholarly emotion than love, particularly hatred for one's own religion.

The problem of affect is thornier when one is studying not the myths of others but one's own myths, a delicate enterprise that has been much discussed. If we teach what we believe in, our subconscious commitment to our own worldview may skew our supposedly innocent approach to the data; the heart may pollute the head. Teachers with such secret agendas (sometimes secret even to themselves) force their theories and their pupils onto a Procrustean Hide-a-Bed. Hunters lead dangerous lives; there are many traps that lie in wait for scholars who bring their lives into their work, who allow too many liberties to the hunters within themselves, who fall into the traps laid for them in the jungles of their unconscious assumptions.

The simultaneous use of heart and head seems to violate many of the unspoken canons of scholarship, particularly the rather nervous scholarship of those of us who study religion.[29] Scholars of religion tend to be particularly gun-shy when it comes to admitting to any sort of personal investment in the subject that they teach, and with good reason: the battle between those who believe that religion has a place in the academic curriculum and those who believe that it does not has had a long and ugly history, beginning from the time when the American Constitution banished the church from the state. Americans have generally assumed that one could not be both pious and educated; this formulation was challenged long ago by William Rainey Harper, the founder of the University of Chicago, but his challenge was never truly accepted, least of all at Chicago. The battle still rages today; diehard creationists still rouse passions with their objection to Darwin, as do fundamentalists with their demands for prayers in schools and their claim that secular humanism is a religion. Religion remains the academic Scarlet Woman, pilloried primarily by those who react against the Reaction of the Moral Majority, but also by those who have always been, rightly, frightened by the power that religion has (like alcohol, sex, and nuclear energy—or drugs, sex, and rock 'n' roll) to do evil as well as good.

Though, still in the academy at large, the love of religion is never considered as academically legitimate as the hatred of religion, the love of *other* people's religions is regarded as at least less illegitimate than the love of one's own. In an attempt to undo the damage done by centuries of scholarship motivated by colonial and missionary hatred (or loathing) of non-Western religions, the scholarship of recent decades has leaned over backward and fallen into awkward postures of cultural relativism.[30] Many historians of religions hope that none of the othernesses of other religions will prove so overwhelming as to prevent us entirely from understanding them. In this, historians of religions endorse Terence's affirmation that "nothing human is alien to me" and Merleau-Ponty's assertion that ethnography is a way of knowing that allows us to see the alien as our own, and our own as the alien. But though many historians of religions acknowledge the ultimate inadequacy of cultural relativism and are willing to confront the ugly shadow side of religious phenomena, I think they still maintain a covert hope of learning to sympathize with, if not necessarily to approve of, that ugliness.[31] It is surely significant that the discipline of the history of religions was born and raised in the context of the World Parliament of Religions, which spawned the still operative optimism that the more you know about other people (even when you do not like what you know), the less likely you will be to kill them. One of the results of this position is that some historians of religions have let down their guard to such a point that they have made their own academic writings about other people's texts into sermons for the truth values of those texts. Such scholars are sometimes accused of committing the deadly academic sin of cryptotheologizing; this is sometimes said even of Mircea Eliade.

I do not think this accusation can be justly applied to all scholars who regard other people's myths as potential vehicles of meaning; I think that there are ways, scholarly ways, of saying that other people's myths may have meaning for us without preaching them. But this must be done with great self-awareness. For if they say that other people's myths are good, scholars are in danger of legitimating these myths just as priests do; and it is not the job of a scholar to replicate the claims of religious believers.

The other side of the coin of cultural relativism is equally slippery. For it is also dangerous for scholars to say that other people's myths are not good, to admit to hating aspects of other people's myths. Bigots, who hate other people's religions, are not a problem peculiar to the academy; bigots may be hunters or sages. But the problem of bigotry takes on an interesting twist when it comes to the study of religions. Relativists often assume that we may say that our own myths are evil, but they tell us that we must not say that other people's myths are evil. It is no longer legitimate to say in print (at least in a scholarly text) that one hates some aspect of other people's religions, that one thinks the Aztecs were nasty to massacre all those children, or the Hindus were/are wrong to burn their widows alive. If we were to make such Eurocentric judgments, it is feared, we would be no better than the Spanish under Cortes or (perish the thought) the British in India. Yet, as Edward Said has demonstrated, at bottom we *are*, and can be, no better (that is, no fairer) than the British;[32] and, as Allan Bloom has demonstrated, relativism when slavishly pursued has profoundly disturbing effects upon our own culture.[33]

Yet I think that if we are going to take other people's myths seriously, we must not feel constrained to love them, or, even if we do love them, to overlook their flaws. Indeed, as with the people that we love, to love deeply is to know deeply, and to know deeply is to be aware of the shadows too. And surely if scholars are to have the right to love other people's myths, they should have the right to hate them as well. There should be a place for honest affect—which must necessarily include the judgment that some myths are good and others are not—within the legitimate study of other people's religions, even for—or, rather, especially for—people who have made the initial judgment that mythology as a whole has meaning for us.

Thus, for instance, I find personally repugnant the Hindu tradition of *suttee* that theoretically exalts widows who burn themselves alive on their husbands' funeral pyres. But I hesitate to call the myth that establishes this tradition a bad myth, for it is a genuine expression of one aspect of a complex worldview that has complex meanings. Before making our judgments, we must first admit our personal revulsion and then attempt to transcend it. First we must find out what may be the Hindu widow's concept of what will happen to her after her death and what will happen to her if she continues to live, and her broader concept of the relationships between wives and husbands, between mothers and children, and between the living and those who have died and those who are yet to be born. Only then may we come to realize that for some women the act of *suttee* may have had a value not unlike the value that we would attribute to the self-sacrifices of heroes of the Resistance at the hands of the Nazis in World War II, or the self-sacrifices of the Christian martyrs: the willing death of the individual for a greater cause. At the same time, we must recognize that other women, who did not necessarily share this worldview, may have been forced, by moral or even physical pressure, to commit *suttee* unwillingly, and thus may have perceived it as we initially perceive it, as a murder. But so long as what the Hindu widow sees in *suttee* remains invisible to us, we have no choice but to view it as a murder; only when the broader context becomes visible are we able to choose to view it as a murder or not.

I myself find the Hindu worldview as a whole both beautiful and meaningful, and I have been able to make many Hindu myths my own myths, to use them to construct my own meanings. But my personal resistance to the institution of *suttee* means that I cannot use the myth of *suttee* as my myth. This poses a further limitation for the goal of "getting inside the head" of a Hindu: there are parts of that head that I don't want to be inside. Moreover, it is evident that the myth of *suttee* has several different meanings for the lives of the people who tell that story—some for those Hindus who approve of *suttee*, others for those who disapprove, and still others, perhaps, for the willing or unwilling widows. And if there are (and there are) Hindus, too, who have not taken *suttee* into their heads, I reserve the right to avoid that particular part of the Hindu head, myself.

The ambivalence that I and other Western historians of religions have experienced in confronting such phenomena as *suttee* is in part a reflection of the fact that it is harder to accept other people's rituals (*suttee*)—or, even more, other people's realities (the woman who is burned alive)—than to accept other people's myths (the story that tells how Sati, the wife of Shiva, established this custom). In the first case, moral relativism would ultimately prevent us from making essential decisions about the one way in which we can act in a given situation (or, in its more extreme form, the way in which anyone should act in that situation). In the second case, *ontological* relativism, relativism about ideas, does not necessarily involve a yes/no decision about any particular action; it merely allows us to consider all the options. Moral relativism does expose us to serious dangers, but these dangers are not necessarily attached to ontological relativism. Ontological relativism is neither cowardly nor inconsistent with the pragmatist position: when forced to make a decision, one does so, but when not forced to do so (and one should not be forced to do so), one does not.

Within all the options that we may consider, we have the right to love some myths and to hate others. By and large, I regard the myths that I have told in this book as laden with perceptions that have meaning for me; this is why I have allowed them to speak for me, to express my opinions about the meaning and use of the telling of myths.

Academic Hardware and Religious Software

Thus historians of religions must fight a war on two fronts. The first battle is against the covert truth claims of theological approaches to religion that masquerade as nontheological approaches, whether these be self-justifying at the expense of other people's religions (bigotry) or self-denegrating at the expense of one's own religion (mindless moral relativism or promiscuous conversion). But the historian of religions must also be on guard against the overt objections of superrationalists, who oppose the study of religion in any form or would allow it to be studied only within the sterile confines of an objectivity that is in any case impossible and probably not even desirable. It is a razor's edge not at all easy to tread, but it is the Middle Way for the humanistic study of religion.

Scholars of religion are not unique in caring about the personal implications of what they teach, but their commitment is usually more vulnerable than that of many of their colleagues in other fields. For though the personal commitment of scholars engaged in the teaching of Marxism, women's studies, black studies, and even regional studies (Chinese, Middle Eastern) is often just as intense and just as potentially disruptive of academic objectivity, scholars of religion have made the most self-conscious effort to be more objective than the chemists, *plus royaliste que le roi*—or, in Martin E. Marty's formulation, "more secular than thou." This is all well and good; if one is going to teach a highly charged subject like religion, one must be more aware, not less aware, of the impossible goal of pure objectivity. It behooves us, even more, perhaps, than it behooves anthropologists or classicists, to play by the rules of the game of scholarship—to learn languages, read commentaries, examine firsthand reports, and take into consideration the various biases of the many people in the chain of transmission that ends with us. Clifford Geertz has stated the problem well: "I have never been impressed by the argument that, as complete objectivity is impossible in these matters (as, of course, it is), one might as well let one's sentiments run loose. As Robert Solow has remarked, that is like saying that as a perfectly aseptic environment is impossible, one might as well conduct surgery in a sewer."[34]

We tell ourselves (and others, particularly our colleagues in the "harder" disciplines) that we study our texts from the outside, in the approved manner of the head, like sages, cool and objective, while we deal with the religious affairs of the heart, if we deal with them at all, from the inside, like hunters, with passion and commitment. We maintain an objective interest in one sort of religion and a subjective faith in another. For historians of religions, the "objective" religion may be obviously other—Hinduism or Islam—but even if we are dealing with our "own" tradition we are prey to a kind of schizophrenia in artificially defining it as "other" for the duration of the period in which we have it under the academic microscope. That our stock-in-trade is ideas about gods rather than ideas about electrons or phonemes is not supposed to bother anyone. The same basic rules should apply; the mental computer follows the same synapses, and we merely change the software to *very* soft software.

But in making such assertions, in attempting to play the game of objectivity with the Big Boys on the playing fields of the harder sciences, we often tend to play down the more subtle but equally genuine sort of objectivity that good scholars of religion can and do bring to their discipline, a critical judgment that allows them to be critical even of their own faith claims. And leaning over backward is not always the best posture in which to conduct a class; it is a posture in which one can easily be knocked over by any well-aimed blow from the opposition (indeed, from either of the two oppositions). Moreover, this pressure often makes scholars of religions deny that they care about religion, which is untrue; we do care, which is why we have chosen this profession, instead of becoming lawyers and making lots of money.

Some scholars—I think of Paul Ricoeur and David Tracy—do manage to accomplish the rapprochement from the heart to the head, using their own religious commitment in their academic study. But others take the safer path, using their academic study of other people's religions in their private religious understanding (the approach from the head to the heart). This latter approach, the way of the sympathetic sage, is, as we have seen, more easily achieved, though it is less often discussed. To write about a religion that one cares about may be academically unfashionable; but to let what one reads and writes affect one's personal religion is academically irrelevant. The assertion that critical objectivity makes it possible for a scholar to deal even with his or her own faith claims, in an academic forum demands a far more delicate defense than the assertion that a scholar may derive new faith claims from the subject matter that is first taken up with critical objectivity.

A cynic might view this second process as merely a disguised form of the first, achieving the same end through a means less susceptible to criticism. I am reminded of the Jesuit who was informed that he was not permitted to smoke while he meditated. Quite right, the Jesuit replied; but surely no one would object if he were to meditate while he was smoking. In fact, I think the two procedures that I have outlined are truly distinct, though my justification for both admittedly rests upon my conviction that it is not necessary for the head and the heart of the scholar of religion to answer to two different masters, that the head and the heart can nourish rather than sabotage one another.

It sometimes seems to me that we arrange our talents and weaknesses like the foolish blind man and lame man in the old story: they agreed to team up, but the lame man carried the blind man on his shoulders. If the blind but physically whole man is the hunter, the experiencer, surely we should let him be led about by the lame sage, the *see-er*, the scholar. As we have seen, though a hunter is basically limited to one side of experience (the physical and emotional), a sage is not necessarily limited to only the other side of experience (the intellectual). In any case, since it is ultimately impossible for the sage to deny the hunter within him, it is best for him to come to terms with his hunter. But more than that; the sage who acknowledges his hunter aspect is a better sage, the sage whose heart melts (in the Indian example) rather than the one who is dried up by his books.

If we return now to the metaphor of "getting inside someone else's head," we realize its more complex implications. For me, it implies the (ultimately unreachable) goal of cross-cultural studies. In attempting to understand Hinduism, I would want to get inside the head of a Hindu, to become in a way a kind of ersatz Hindu. But then, one might say, why not just talk to a Hindu and find out what is inside his head? (This is the "Take-a-Buddhist-to-dinner" approach to the comparative study of world religions.) There are a number of reasons why this is not a satisfactory equivalent for getting inside the head of a Hindu oneself. (1) There are many Hindus, and the one that I talk to might be as ignorant of or mistaken about her own tradition as a Jew or Christian chosen at random might be wrong about her own tradition. (2) There are so many Hinduisms that no single Hindu could speak for the entire tradition. (3) In many ways, a Hindu is the very worst person to ask about Hinduism; he is so bound up in it that he is blind to many of its aspects that an outsider might see.[35] (4) A Hindu would not ask of Hinduism the sorts of questions that I might want to ask of it, might leave out of his necessarily selective summary precisely the sorts of things that I would want to know.

This last objection, in particular, reveals the fact that when I say that I want to get inside the head of a Hindu I really mean that I want to get inside it *but to remain, at the same time, inside my own head*. The sage, at a certain point, realized that he was a sage inside a hunter, that he was running both systems of perception at once. Thus, the ideal scholar at this point is two-headed: he has his own head and the head of the Other. But if we look closer, we see that such a scholar must, in fact, have more heads than the most capitally extravagant Hindu deity. For there are many heads of the Other (many different sorts of Hindus, all of whom one hopes to understand) and, of course, many heads of Us. For each scholar is not only simultaneously hunter and sage but often also simultaneously superstitious and a secular humanist, and many other things. Freud once remarked that when two people made love, there were four people in the bed (the two there, and the two being fantasized); in the study of comparative religion, when we attempt to penetrate not the body but the head of the other, there are always hundreds of people in the head.

Eclecticism in personal cosmologies may be too elusive and idiosyncratic to be subjected to the structures of a public, communal, academic discourse. But eclecticism does have a legitimate place in the evolution of private universes. Eclectics make better hunters, people who use their academic discoveries to enrich their personal worldviews; they embody the positive side of Socrates' famous dictum that the life that is unexamined is not worth living. And I think that they are better sages, too, scholars whose sympathy gives them greater understanding of the subject that they teach; for it is also true that the life that is not lived is not worth examining.[36]

Yet "eclecticism" may be too arrogant a word, implying, perhaps, that we decide what myths are true or make up gods that suit our moods. Perhaps we should find some more modest, passive word to describe what we do in receiving and accepting the myths from other people's religions. Perhaps our myths, like greatness in Shakespeare's formulation,[37] are not something that we are born with, or achieve, but something that we have thrust upon us, to confront not only with our heads but with our hearts.

QUESTIONS FOR REVIEW AND DISCUSSION

1. What are the two purposes that Doniger hopes to accomplish by using the Indian myth of the hunter and the ascetic sage?

2. In the myth that Doniger recounts, what does the ascetic sage experience when he enters the head of a householder with his magical powers? What did the householder, whose head was inhabited by the ascetic sage, dream about when he fell asleep?

3. The ascetic sage also fell asleep and dreamt. How did he, who had fully identified with the householder, survive the two doomsdays, the first in which he was in the householder's dream, and the second, in his own dream?

4. The ascetic sage, in his dream, encountered a dream sage who told him that he was dreaming, and that he was actually an ascetic sage identifying with a householder whose head he was inhabiting. When the ascetic said he would like to return to his own body and see the body of the householder whose head he had entered, the dream sage told him he was unable to return to either body. Why? What did the ascetic sage and dream sage then do?

5. What did the hunter, who was listening to this tale, conclude from this story, and what was his fate? Where do you think the hunter is during his encounter with the sage in the frame story?

6. How does Doniger apply the symbolism in this myth to intellectuals versus ordinary householders, or religious studies scholars versus people who are simply religious? In what way can a sage be a hunter, but a hunter not necessarily be a sage? What is her idea of the hunting sage, and why does she regard this symbol as pointing to the "right sort of historian of religions"?

7. What does Doniger mean by learning to feel with myths? She suggests the possibility of this in addition to certain general ways in which a historian of religions should study myths. What are these general ways? Do you agree with her on "feeling" with myths?

8. What are some of the ways in which myths may be interpreted, by scholars and non-scholars, according to Doniger? What does Doniger see as pitfalls for the scholar of religion within the realities of cultural relativism?

9. What are the points that Doniger is trying to make with her example of the Hindu tradition of suttee and the myths surrounding it? Can you think of other examples from other religious traditions where you find similar issues? Do you agree with her views?

10. What, according to Doniger, are the two fronts on which the scholar of religion must battle?

11. What does she see as a potential limitation of scholars of religion who deny their physical and emotional involvement with experience? What does Doniger mean by being a two-headed scholar? And how does the analogy of the ascetic sage in the householder's head relate to this? What do these "heads" represent?

Notes

1 I shall discuss other definitions of myth in chapter 2, but for now let me cite two that are relevant to this particular usage: David Shulman has said that "a myth is an intuition dramatized by a story" (in "Terror of Symbols and Symbols of Terror: Notes on the myth of Śiva as Sthānu," *History of Religions* 26, 2 [November 1986]: 105), and A. K. Ramanujan has noted that "a myth is a metaphor that has been made concrete and literal" (private communication, 4 August 1985).

2 O'Flaherty, *Dreams*, chap. 4.

3 Maurice Bloomfield, "On the Art of Entering Another's Body: A Hindu Fiction Motif," *Proceedings of the American Philosophical Society* 41 (1917): 1–43. Cf. also the *Bhagavadajjuka-Prahasanam of Bodhayana* (Prayaga: Devabhasaprakasanam, 1979). I know of one remarkable occurrence of this theme in contemporary America, and that is the film *All of Me* (based on Ed Davis's novel *Me Two*), starring Steve Martin and Lily Tomlin and directed by Carl Reiner. In this film, the soul of Tomlin's character leaves her body as she dies and enters the body of Martin's character, who still has his own soul as well and thus becomes, internally, an androgyne (the woman occupies and controls the right half of his body), while externally he remains a man. The comic possibilities of this situation (as, for instance, when he attempts to make love to another woman) are brilliantly developed throughout the film; but it is interesting to note that the figure who makes the entire transformation possible in the first place, and continues to make adjustments throughout the whole film, is an Indian guru.

4 *Yogavasishtha-Maha-Ramayana of Valmiki*, ed. W. L. S. Pansikar, 2 vols. (Bombay, 1918) 6.2.136–57.

5 See O'Flaherty, *Dreams*, pp. 231–34, for a discussion of similar myths about doomsday and ontology.

6 I have greatly abbreviated this story, which occupies 21 chapters (not 21 verses) of the Sanskrit text. In some ways, this condensation makes the story more confusing than it is when one reads it at length; in some ways, it oversimplifies it. In particular, I have omitted the fascinating but here irrelevant fact that the sage falls asleep first in order to become the householder and then falls asleep as the householder; thus he is actually a creature in a dream within a dream. For the implications of this nesting of dreams, see chapter 5 of O'Flaherty, *Dreams*.

7 Ranjini and Gananath Obeyesekere demonstrated the way in which a similar confusion is built into a Buddhist text about revenge and reincarnation, in a paper presented at the Association of Asian Studies, 24 March 1986.

8 See the story of the hundred Rudras and the wild goose in O'Flaherty, *Dreams*, chapter 5.

9 There is another beautiful ancient Indian metaphor for this pair: "Two birds, friends joined together, clutch the same tree. One of them eats the sweet fruit; the other looks on without eating." Rig Veda 1.164.20, translated by Wendy Doniger O'Flaherty in *The Rig Veda* (Harmondsworth, 1981), p. 78.

10 A. K. Ramanujan has argued, in an unpublished paper ("Samskara and Death in Venice"), that the figures of sages in India are "religious" and in the West "artists"; both are capable of seeing and being other beings.

11 Robert Louis Stevenson, *The Strange Case of Dr. Jekyll and Mr. Hyde* (London, 1886). It is interesting to note the names that Stevenson gives to these two characters: Jekyll is a Dr., a sage; Hyde hides, like a hunter, lying in wait for his prey.

12 See O'Flaherty, *Dreams*, introduction and chapter 1. It is significant that although for a long time we defined the moment of death as the moment when the heart stopped working, we now define it as the moment when the brain stops working. I use "head" and "heart" as metaphors as they have often been used in the West, indicating rational, objective, scientific, methodological mental processes on the one hand—the thoughts of sages—and irrational, subjective, artistic, and inspirational mental processes on the other—the emotions of hunters. This is, of course, not merely anatomically incorrect; it is a logically inconsistent way of dividing up reason and emotion.

13 E. M. Forster, *A Passage to India, the Abinger edition*, edited by Oliver Stallybrass (New York, 1978), p. 287.

14 Woody Allen, "Fabulous Tales and Mythical Beasts," in *Without Feathers* (New York, 1976), p. 193.

15 This division is only roughly equivalent to the distinction that is often made, in methodological debates within the history of religions, between phenomenologists and historians. Be that as it may, I do not wish to reactivate that old controversy here.

16 Or, as the late Hans van Buitenen used to say (apparently citing a Dutch proverb), "If I were two dogs, I could play with myself." Another mythical beast that can serve well as a metaphor for the same resolution of opposing tensions in the self-image of the scholar of religion is the armadillo in Rudyard Kipling's *Just So Stories* ("Beginning of the Armadillos"), who was formed when the Stickly-Prickly Hedgehog and the Slow-Solid Tortoise combined forces in order to avoid being eaten by the baby Painted Jaguar. The Jaguar, thrown into confusion by this cross-breed, came back and complained to his mother, who said, "Son, son! ... A Hedgehog is a Hedgehog, and can't be anything but a Hedgehog; and a Tortoise is a Tortoise, and can never be anything else." "But it isn't a Hedgehog, and it isn't a Tortoise," said the baby Jaguar. "It's a little bit of both, and I don't know its proper name." "Nonsense!" said Mother Jaguar. "Everything has its proper name. I should call it 'Armadillo' till I found out the real one. And I should leave it alone."
Yet another mythical beast of ambivalence is the Pushmi-Pullyu in Dr. Doolittle, a creature with a head at each end, which Winston Davis has borrowed (in *Dojo: Magic and Exorcism in Modern Japan*, Stanford, Calif., 1980) to express the tension between two sets of factors that operate when a worshiper is drawn to a particular religion.

17 *Dhvanyaloka of Anandavardhana, with the Dhvanyalokalocana of Abhinavagupta*, ed. D. and K. Pandurang Parab (Bombay, 1891), 2.9; cited by J. L. Masson and M. V. Patwardhan, *Aesthetic Rapture: The Rasadhyaya of the Natyashastra* (Poona, 1970), p. 21.

18 An epidemic of self-conscious discussions of this problem was touched off by Claude Lévi-Strauss in *Tristes Tropiques*, trans. John and Doreen Weightman (New York, 1974).

19 Bronislaw Malinowski, *A Diary in the Strict Sense of the Term*, trans. Norbert Guterman (London, 1967), p. 167. Clifford Geertz's essay, "'From the Native's Point of View': On the Nature of Anthropological Understanding," in *Local Knowledge* (New York, 1983) pp. 55–70, begins with a response to Malinowski's diary.

20 Wendy Doniger O'Flaherty, *The Origins of Evil in Hindu Mythology* (Berkeley, 1976), especially chap. 6, "The Birth of Death." It was Dennis O'Flaherty who pointed out to me the relevance of my work on death to my experience of death.

21 This talent (or weakness, if you will) of a particular sort of Jew must be understood in the context of Judaism as a whole. The overwhelming majority of Jews are of a very different sort. They live and die in the religion of their birth and find it entirely sufficient unto their religious needs. They are the undemythologized (whom we shall encounter in chapter 6). I am not talking about religious conversion, let alone the anti-Semitic proselytizing of such groups as the Jews for Jesus (though it is indeed interesting to note the fascination that Indian gurus seem to have for American Jews, but this is another story—one that has in fact been well discussed by Daniel Gold in *Comprehending the Guru: Toward a Grammar of Religious Perception*, Atlanta, Ga., 1988). I have in mind, rather, the ways in which Jews have been forced, for their very survival, to learn other people's religions, and in some cases to learn from them as well.

22 Plato, *Republic*, book 10.

23 Robert P. Goldman, "Karma, Guilt, and Buried Memories: Public Fantasy and Private Reality in Traditional India," *Journal of the American Oriental Society* 105, 3 (1985): 413–25.

24 A similar concept of physical traces on the transmigrating soul may be seen in Plato's *Gorgias* 524, in which a man who has been whipped bears the marks of the whip upon him when he is judged after his death.

25 My belief in the karma theory was, wrongly, challenged by Robert P. Goldman in his "Karma, Guilt, and Buried Memories."

26 One striking example of a scholar who hated what he wrote about was Julius Eggeling, who devoted his life to the massive Sanskrit text of the Shatapatha Brahmana, his translation of which was published in five volumes in Oxford, from 1882 to 1900. In his introduction (ix) Eggeling complained that "For wearisome prolixity of exposition, characterised by a dogmatic assertion and a flimsy symbolism rather than by serious reasoning, these works are perhaps not equalled any-where" (cited by Wendy Doniger O'Flaherty, *Tales of Sex and Violence: Folklore, Sacrifice, and Danger in the Jaiminiya Brahmana*, Chicago, 1985, p. 4).

27 "Fire and Ice," in *The Complete Poems of Robert Frost* (New York, 1949), p. 268.

28 This is only one point of view, of course; some people find real killing endlessly fascinating. And there are those who would argue that the only way to understand what a butterfly is is to pin it to the wall, dead. But against that view I would set the parable (another version of which was told by Hans Christian Andersen) of the emperor who was given a marvelous nightingale (in some versions of the story it is a live nightingale, in some it is mechanical) that sang sublimely; in order to "understand" it, he took it apart—and of course it never sang again.

29 See James T. Laney, "The Education of the Heart." *Harvard Magazine* 88, 1 (1985): pp. 23–24.

30 Relativism is often called "cheap relativism," but in its more subtle academic forms it has proved quite expensive. For a sophisticated and complex debate on the issue of moral relativity, see Bryan Wilson, *Rationality* (Oxford, 1970), and Martin Hollis and Steven Lukes, eds, *Rationality and Relativism* (Oxford, 1982).

31 Eliade has written much about the need to see beauty in all sorts of religious phenomena; see, in particular, *The Quest: History and Meaning in Religion* (Chicago, 1969). See also my criticism of this aspect of Joseph Campbell's work, in "Origins of Myth-making Man," review of Joseph Campbell's *Historical Atlas of World Mythology*, *New York Times Book Review*, IS December 1983, pp. 3, 24–25.

32 Edward Said, *Orientalism* (New York, 1978).

33 Allan Bloom, *The Closing of the American Mind* (New York, 1987). My favorite epigram on relativism is the old garbled Latin malapropism: *De gustibus nihil nisi bonum*.

34 Clifford Geertz, "Thick Description: Toward an Interpretive Theory of Culture," in *The Interpretation of Cultures* (New York, 1973), p. 30.

35 In this I disagree with Wilfred Cantwell Smith, who has argued, on many occasions, that any statement that one makes about Hinduism, from outside, must be at least theoretically acceptable to at least one Hindu.

36 I think this is a quote from Nietzsche, writing about Socrates. David Tracy used it in a speech at the University of Chicago on 6 November 1985. And Janet Malcolm, in discussing the resistance against the Freudian approach to the unconscious, remarked that "The unexamined life may not be worth living, but the examined life is impossible to live for more than a few moments at a time." (Janet Malcolm, *In the Freud Archives*, New York, 1984), p. 26.

37 *Twelfth Night*, 2.5.159.

22 Liminality and Communitas

Victor Turner

Victor Turner (1920–83) was born in Glasgow and obtained his doctorate in anthropology from the University of Manchester. He conducted fieldwork among the Ndembu tribal people of Zambia, producing studies of their social configurations and rituals. Turner taught at several American universities including Stanford, Cornell, Chicago, and Virginia. He is best known for his theories that developed from his examination of rites of passage (especially the work of Arnold Van Gennep), but which he found applicable to broader social and historical phenomena. Turner's most influential book is *The Ritual Process* (1969) from which the selection that follows is taken. He refers to his own studies of the Ndembu, as well as other examples to develop his theory.

Van Gennep himself defined *rites de passage* as "rites which accompany every change of place, state, social position and age." To point up the contrast between "state" and "transition," I employ "state" to include all his other terms. It is a more inclusive concept than "status" or "office," and refers to any type of stable or recurrent condition that is culturally recognized. Van Gennep has shown that all rites of passage or "transition" are marked by three phases: separation, margin (or *limen*, signifying "threshold" in Latin), and aggregation. The first phase (of separation) comprises symbolic behavior signifying the detachment of the individual or group either from an earlier fixed point in the social structure, from a set of cultural conditions (a "state"), or from both. During the intervening "liminal" period, the characteristics of the ritual subject (the "passenger") are ambiguous; he passes through a cultural realm that has few or none of the attributes of the past or coming state. In the third phase (reaggregation or reincorporation), the passage is consummated. The ritual subject, individual or corporate, is in a relatively stable state once more and, by virtue of this, has rights and obligations vis-à-vis others of a clearly defined and "structural" type; he is expected to behave in accordance with certain customary norms and ethical standards binding on incumbents of social position in a system of such positions.

Liminality

The attributes of liminality or of liminal *personae* ("threshold people") are necessarily ambiguous, since this condition and these persons elude or slip through the network of classifications that normally locate states and positions in cultural space. Liminal entities are neither here nor there; they are betwixt and between the positions assigned and arrayed by law, custom, convention, and ceremonial. As such, their ambiguous and indeterminate attributes are expressed by a rich variety of symbols in the many societies that ritualize social and cultural transitions. Thus, liminality is frequently likened to death, to being in the womb, to invisibility, to darkness, to bisexuality, to the wilderness, and to an eclipse of the sun or moon.

Liminal entities, such as neophytes in initiation or puberty rites, may be represented as possessing nothing. They may be disguised as monsters, wear only a strip of clothing, or even go naked, to demonstrate that as liminal beings they have no status, property, insignia, secular clothing indicating rank or role, position in a kinship system—in short, nothing that may distinguish them from their fellow neophytes or initiands. Their behavior is normally passive or humble; they must obey their instructors implicitly, and accept arbitrary punishment without complaint. It is as though they are being reduced or ground down to a uniform condition to be fashioned anew and endowed with additional powers to enable them to cope with their new station in life. Among themselves, neophytes tend to develop an intense comradeship and egalitarianism. Secular distinctions of rank and status disappear or are homogenized. The condition of the patient and her husband in Isoma had some of these attributes—passivity, humility, near-nakedness—in a symbolic milieu that represented both a grave and a womb. In initiations with a long period of seclusion, such as the circumcision rites of many tribal societies or induction into secret societies, there is often a rich proliferation of liminal symbols.

Communitas

What is interesting about liminal phenomena for our present purposes is the blend they offer of lowliness and sacredness, of homogeneity and comradeship. We are presented, in such rites, with a "moment in and out of time," and in and out of secular social structure, which reveals, however fleetingly, some recognition (in symbol if not always in language) of a generalized social bond that has ceased to be and has simultaneously yet to be fragmented into a multiplicity of structural ties. These are the ties organized in terms either of caste, class, or rank hierarchies or of segmentary oppositions in the stateless societies beloved of political anthropologists. It is as though there are here two major "models" for human interrelatedness, juxtaposed and alternating. The first is of society as a structured, differentiated, and often hierarchical system of politico-legal economic positions with many types of evaluation, separating men in terms of "more" or "less." The second, which emerges recognizably in the liminal period, is of society as an unstructured or rudimentarily structured and relatively undifferentiated *comitatus*, community, or even communion of equal individuals who submit together to the general authority of the ritual elders.

I prefer the Latin term "communitas" to "community," to distinguish this modality of social relationship from an "area of common living." The distinction between structure and communitas is not simply the familiar between "secular" and "sacred," or that, for example, between politics and religion. Certain fixed offices in tribal societies have *many* sacred attributes; indeed, every social position has *some* sacred characteristics. But this "sacred" component is acquired by the incumbents of positions during the *rites of passage*, through which they changed positions. Something of the sacredness of that transient humility and modelessness goes over, and tempers the pride of the incumbent of a higher position or office. ... Liminality implies that the high could not be high unless the low existed, and he who is high must experience what it is like to be low. ...

Dialectic of the Development Cycle

From all this I infer that, for individuals and groups, social life is a type of dialectical process that involves successive experience of high and low, communitas and structure, homogeneity and differentiation, equality and inequality. The passage from lower to higher status is through a limbo of statuslessness. In such a process, the opposites, as it were, constitute one another and are mutually indispensable. Furthermore, since any concrete tribal society is made up of multiple personae, groups, and categories, each of which has its own developmental cycle, at a given moment many incumbencies of fixed positions coexist with many passages between positions. In other words, each individual's life experience contains alternating exposure to structure and communitas, and to states and transitions.

Attributes of Liminal Entities

… Our present focus is upon liminality and the ritual powers of the weak. … In liminality, the underling comes uppermost. Second, the supreme political authority is portrayed "as a slave," recalling that aspect of the coronation of a pope in Western Christendom when he is called upon to be the *"servus servorum Dei."* Part of the rite has, of course, what Monica Wilson has called a "prophylactic function."[1] The chief has to exert self-control in the rites that he may be able to have self-mastery thereafter in face of the temptations of power. But the role of the humbled chief is only an extreme example of a recurrent theme of liminal situations. This theme is the stripping off of preliminal and postliminal attributes.

Let us look at the main ingredients of the Kumukindyila rites. The chief and his wife are dressed identically in a ragged waist-cloth and share the same name—*mwadyi*. This term is also applied to boys undergoing initiation and to a man's first wife in chronological order of marriage. It is an index of the anonymous state of "initiand." These attributes of sexlessness and anonymity are highly characteristic of liminality. In many kinds of initiation where the neophytes are of both sexes, males and females are dressed alike and referred to by the same term. This is true, for example, of many baptismal ceremonies in Christian or syncretist sects in Africa: for example, those of the *Bwiti* cult in the Gabon (James Fernandez; personal communication). It is also true of initiation into the Ndembu funerary association of Chiwila. Symbolically, all attributes that distinguish categories and groups in the structured social order are here in abeyance; the neophytes are merely entities in transition, as yet without place or position.

Other characteristics are submissiveness and silence. Not only the chief in the rites under discussion, but also neophytes in many *rites de passage* have to submit to an authority that is nothing less than that of the total community. This community is the repository of the whole gamut of the culture's values, norms, attitudes, sentiments, and relationships. Its representatives in the specific rites represent the generic authority of tradition. In tribal societies, too, speech is not merely communication but also power and wisdom. The wisdom (*mana*) that is imparted in sacred liminality is not just an aggregation of words and sentences; it has ontological value. That is why, in the *Chisungu* rites of the Bemba, so well described by Audrey Richards, the secluded girl is said to be "grown into a woman" by the female elders—and she is so grown by the verbal and nonverbal instruction she receives in precept and symbol, especially by the revelation to her of tribal sacra in the form of pottery images.[2]

The neophyte in liminality must be a *tabula rasa*, a blank slate, on which is inscribed the knowledge and wisdom of the group, in those respects that pertain to the new status. The ordeals and humiliations, often of a grossly physiological character, to which neophytes are submitted represent partly a destruction of the previous status and partly a tempering of their essence in order to prepare them to cope with their new responsibilities and restrain them in advance from abusing their new privileges. They have to be shown that in themselves they are clay or dust, mere matter, whose form is impressed upon them by society.

Another liminal theme exemplified in the Ndembu installation rites is sexual continence. This is a pervasive theme of Ndembu ritual. Indeed, the resumption of sexual relations is usually a ceremonial mark of the return to society as a structure of statuses. While this is a feature of certain types of religious behavior in almost all societies, in preindustrial society, with its strong stress on kinship as the basis of many types of group affiliation, sexual continence has additional religious force. For kinship, or relations shaped by the idiom of kinship, is one of the main factors in structural differentiation. The undifferentiated character of liminality is reflected by the discontinuance of sexual relations and the absence of marked sexual polarity. ...

The pedagogics of liminality, therefore, represent a condemnation of two kinds of separation from the generic bond of communitas. The first kind is to act only in terms of the rights conferred on one by the incumbency of office in the social structure. The second is to follow one's psychobiological urges at the expense of one's fellows. A mystical character is assigned to the sentiment of humankindness in most types of liminality, and in most cultures this stage of transition is brought closely in touch with beliefs in the protective and punitive powers of divine or preterhuman beings or powers. ...

Millenarian Movements

Among the more striking manifestations of communitas are to be found the so-called millenarian religious movements. ... The attributes of such movements will be well known to most of my readers. Here I would merely recall some of the properties of liminality in tribal rituals that I mentioned earlier. Many of these correspond pretty closely with those of millenarian movements: homogeneity, equality, anonymity, absence of property (many movements actually enjoin on their members the destruction of what property they possess to bring nearer the coming of the perfect state of unison and communion they desire, for property rights are linked with structural distinctions both vertical and horizontal), reduction of all to the same status level, the wearing of uniform apparel (sometimes for both sexes), sexual continence (or its antithesis, sexual community, both continence and sexual community liquidate marriage and the family, which legitimate structural status), minimization of sex distinctions (all are "equal in the sight of God" or the ancestors), abolition of rank, humility, disregard for personal appearance, unselfishness, total obedience to the prophet or leader, sacred instruction, the maximization of religious, as opposed to secular, attitudes and behavior, suspension of kinship rights and obligations (all are siblings or comrades of one another regardless of previous secular ties), simplicity of speech and manners, sacred folly, acceptance of pain and suffering (even to the point of undergoing martyrdom), and so forth.

It is noteworthy that many of these movements cut right across tribal and national divisions during their initial momentum. Communitas, or the "open society," differs in this from structure, or the "closed society," in that it is potentially or ideally extensible to the limits of humanity. In practice, of course, the impetus soon becomes exhausted, and the "movement" becomes itself an institution among other institutions—often one more fanatical and militant than the rest, for the reason that it feels itself to be the unique bearer of universal-human truths. Mostly, such movements occur during phases of history that are in many respects "homologous" to the liminal periods of important rituals in stable and repetitive societies, when major groups or social categories in those societies are passing from one cultural state to another. They are essentially phenomena of transition. This is perhaps why in so many of these movements much of their mythology and symbolism is borrowed from those of traditional *rites de passage*, either in the cultures in which they originate or in the cultures with which they are in dramatic contact.

Hippies, Communitas, and the Powers of the Weak

In modern Western society, the values of communitas are strikingly present in the literature and behavior of what came to be known as the "beat generation," who were succeeded by the "hippies," who, in turn, have a junior division known as the "teeny-boppers." These are the "cool" members of the adolescent and young-adult categories—which do not have the advantages of national *rites de passage*—who "opt out" of the status-bound social order and acquire the stigmata of the lowly, dressing like "bums," itinerant in their habits, "folk" in their musical tastes, and menial in the casual employment they undertake. They stress personal relationships rather than social obligations, and regard sexuality as a polymorphic instrument of immediate communitas rather than as the basis for an enduring structured social tie. The poet Allen Ginsberg is particularly eloquent about the function of sexual freedom. The "sacred" properties often assigned to communitas are not lacking here, either: this can be seen in their frequent use of religious terms, such as "saint" and "angel," to describe their congeners and in their interest in Zen Buddhism. The Zen formulation "all is one, one is none, none is all" well expresses the global, unstructured character earlier applied to communitas. The hippie emphasis on spontaneity, immediacy, and "existence" throws into relief one of the senses in which communitas contrasts with structure. Communitas is of the now; structure is rooted in the past and extends into the future through language, law, and custom. While our focus here is on traditional preindustrial societies it becomes clear that the collective dimensions, communitas and structure, are to be found at all stages and levels of culture and society.

Liminality, Low Status, and Communitas

The time has now come to make a careful review of a hypothesis that seeks to account for the attributes of such seemingly diverse phenomena as neophytes in the liminal phase of ritual, subjugated autochthones, small nations, court jesters, holy mendicants, good Samaritans, millenarian movements, "dharma bums," matrilaterality in patrilineal systems, patrilaterality in matrilineal systems, and monastic orders. Surely an ill-assorted bunch of social phenomena! Yet all have this common characteristic: they are persons or principles that (1) fall in the interstices of social structure, (2) are on its margins, or (3) occupy its lowest rungs. ...

For me, communitas emerges where social structure is not. Perhaps the best way of putting this difficult concept into words is Martin Buber's—though I feel that perhaps he should be regarded as a gifted native informant rather than as a social scientist! Buber uses the term "community" for "communitas": "Community is the being no longer side by side (and, one might add, above and below) but with one another of a multitude of persons. And this multitude, though it moves towards one goal, yet experiences everywhere a turning to, a dynamic facing of, the others, a flowing from I to *Thou*. Community is where community happens."

Buber lays his finger on the spontaneous, immediate, concrete nature of communitas, as opposed to the norm-governed, institutionalized, abstract nature of social structure. Yet, communitas is made evident or accessible, so to speak, only through its juxtaposition to, or hybridization with, aspects of social structure. Just as in Gestalt psychology, figure and ground are mutually determinative, or, as some rare elements are never found in nature in their purity but only as components of chemical compounds, so communitas can be grasped only in some relation to structure. Just because the communitas component is elusive, hard to pin down, it is not unimportant. ... Communitas, with its unstructured character, representing the "quick" of human interrelatedness, what Buber has called *das Zwischen-menschliche*, might well be represented by the "emptiness at the center," which is nevertheless indispensable to the functioning of the structure of the wheel. ...

Communitas breaks in through the interstices of structure, in liminality; at the edges of structure, in marginality; and from beneath structure, in inferiority. It is almost everywhere held to be sacred or "holy," possibly because it transgresses or dissolves the norms that govern structured and institutionalized relationships and is accompanied by experiences of unprecedented potency. The processes of "leveling" and "stripping" to which Goffman has drawn our attention, often appear to flood their subjects with affect. Instinctual energies are surely liberated by these processes, but I am now inclined to think that communitas is not solely the product of biologically inherited drives released from cultural constraints. Rather is it the product of peculiarly human faculties, which include rationality, volition, and memory, and which develop with experience of life in society—just as among the Tallensi it is only mature men who undergo the experiences that induce them to receive *bakologi* shrines.

The notion that there is a generic bond between men, and its related sentiment of "humankindness," are not epiphenomena of some kind of herd instinct but are products of "men in their wholeness wholly attending." Liminality, marginality, and structural inferiority are conditions in which are frequently generated myths, symbols, rituals, philosophical systems, and works of art. These cultural forms provide men with a set of templates or models which are, at one level, periodical reclassifications of reality and man's relationship to society, nature, and culture. But they are more than classifications, since they incite men to action as well as to thought. Each of these productions has a multivocal character, having many meanings, and each is capable of moving people at many psycho-biological levels simultaneously.

There is a dialectic here, for the immediacy of communitas gives way to the mediacy of structure, while, in *rites de passage*, men are released from structure into communitas only to return to structure revitalized by their experience of communitas. What is certain is that no society can function adequately without this dialectic. Exaggeration of structure may well lead to pathological manifestations of communitas outside or against "the law." Exaggeration of communitas, in certain religious or political movements of the leveling type, may be speedily followed by despotism, overbureaucratization, or other modes of structural rigidification. For, like the neophytes in the African circumcision lodge, or the Benedictine monks, or the members of a millenarian movement, those living in community seem to require, sooner or later, an absolute authority, whether this be a religious commandment, a divinely inspired leader, or a dictator. Communitas cannot stand alone if the material and organizational needs of human beings are to be adequately met. Maximization of communitas provokes maximization of structure, which in its turn produces revolutionary strivings for renewed communitas. The history of any great society provides evidence at the political level for this oscillation. ...

Modalities of Communitas

... Essentially, communitas is a relationship between concrete, historical, idiosyncratic individuals. These individuals are not segmentalized into roles and statuses but confront one another rather in the manner of Martin Buber's "I and Thou." Along with this direct, immediate, and total confrontation of human identities, there tends to go a model of society as a homogenous, unstructured communitas, whose boundaries are ideally coterminous with those of the human species. Communitas is in this respect strikingly different from Durkheiman "solidarity," the force of which depends upon an in-group/out-group contrast. ... But the spontaneity and immediacy of communitas—as opposed to the jural-political character of structure—can seldom be maintained for very long. Communitas itself soon develops a structure in which free relationships between individuals become converted into norm-governed relationships between social personae. Thus, it is necessary to distinguish between: (1) *existential* or *spontaneous* communitas, approximately what the hippies today would call "a happening," ... (2) *normative* communitas, where, under the influence of time, the need to mobilize and organize resources, and the necessity for social control among the members of the group in pursuance of these goals, the existential communitas is organized into a perduring social system; and (3) *ideological* communitas, which is a label one can apply to a variety of utopian models of societies based on existential communitas.

Ideological communitas is at once an attempt to describe the external and visible effects—the outward form, it might be said—of an inward experience of existential communitas, and to spell out the optimal social conditions under which such experiences might be expected to flourish and multiply. Both normative and ideological communitas are already within the domain of structure, and it is the fate of all spontaneous communitas in history to undergo what most people see as a "decline and fall" into structure and law. In religious movements of the communitas type, it is not only the charisma of the leaders that is "routinized" but also the communitas of their first disciples and followers. ...

Furthermore, structure tends to be pragmatic and this-worldly; while communitas is often speculative and generates imagery and philosophical ideas. One example of this contrast, to which our seminar gave a great deal of attention, is that kind of normative communitas that characterizes the liminal phase of tribal initiation rites. ...

In our seminar, also, we frequently came across instances, in religion and literature, in which normative and ideological communitas are symbolized by structurally inferior categories, groups, types, or individuals, ranging from the mother's brother in patrilineal societies, to conquered autochthonous peoples, Tolstoy's peasants, Gandhi's *harijans*, and the "holy poor" or "God's poor" of medieval Europe. For example, today's hippies, like yesterday's Franciscans, assume the attributes of the structurally inferior in order to achieve communitas.

Ideological and Spontaneous Communitas

The scattered clues and indications we have encountered in preliterate and preindustrial societies of the existence in their cultures, notably in liminality and structural inferiority, of the egalitarian model we have called normative communitas, become in complex and literate societies, both ancient and modern, a positive torrent of explicitly formulated views on how men may best live together in comradely harmony. Such views may be called, as we have just noted, ideological communitas. In order to convey the wide generality of these formulations of the ideal structureless domain, I would like to adduce, almost at random, evidence from sources far removed from one another in space and time. In these sources, both religious and secular, a fairly regular connection is maintained between liminality, structural inferiority, lowermost status, and structural outsiderhood on the one hand, and, on the other, such universal-human values as peace and harmony between all men, fertility, health of mind and body, universal justice, comradeship and brotherhood between all men, the equality before God, the law or the life force of men and women, young and old, and persons of all races and ethnic groups. And of especial importance in all these utopian formulations is the persisting adhesion between equality and absence of property. ...

To my mind, the "essential We" has a liminal character, since perdurance implies institutionalization and repetition, while community (which roughly equals spontaneous communitas) is always completely unique, and hence socially transient. At times Buber appears to be misled about the feasibility of converting this experience of mutuality into structural forms. Spontaneous communitas can never be adequately expressed in a structural form, but it may arise unpredictably at any time between human beings who are institutionally reckoned or defined as members of any or all kinds of social groupings, or of none. Just as in preliterate society the social and individual developmental cycles are punctuated by more or less prolonged instants of ritually guarded and stimulated liminality, each with its core of potential communitas, so the phase structure of social life in complex societies is also punctuated, but without institutionalized provocations and safe-guards, by innumerable instants of spontaneous communitas.

In preindustrial and early industrial societies with multiplex social relations, spontaneous communitas appears to be very frequently associated with mystical power and to be regarded as a charism or grace sent by the deities or ancestors. Nevertheless, by impetrative ritual means, attempts are made, mostly in the phases of liminal seclusion, to cause the deities or ancestors to bring this charism of communitas among men. But there is no specific social form that is held to express spontaneous communitas. Rather is it expected best to arise in the intervals between incumbencies of social positions and statuses, in what used to be known as "the interstices of the social structure." In complex industrialized societies, we still find traces in the liturgies of churches and other religious organizations of institutionalized attempts to prepare for the coming of spontaneous communitas. This modality of relationship, however, appears to flourish best in spontaneously liminal situations—phases betwixt and between states where social-structural role-playing is dominant, and especially between status equals. ...

Once more we come back to the necessity of seeing man's social life as a process, or rather as a multiplicity of processes, in which the character of one type of phase—where communitas is paramount—differs deeply, even abysmally, from that of all others. The great human temptation, found most prominently among utopians, is to resist giving up the good and pleasurable qualities of that one phase to make way for what may be the necessary hardships and dangers of the next. Spontaneous communitas has something "magical" about it. Subjectively there is in it the feeling of endless power. But this power untransformed cannot readily be applied to the organizational details of social existence. It is no substitute for lucid thought and sustained will. On the other hand, structural action swiftly becomes arid and mechanical if those involved in it are not periodically immersed in the regenerative abyss of communitas. Wisdom is always to find the appropriate relationship between structure and communitas under the given circumstances of time and place, to accept each modality when it is paramount without rejecting the other, and not to cling to one when its present impetus is spent.

QUESTIONS FOR REVIEW AND DISCUSSION

1. What does Turner mean by liminality? What are the characteristics of liminal persons?
2. What does Turner mean by communitas? Why is it a characteristic of groups in liminal situations?

3. In what ways do millenarian movements illustrate the principles of liminality and communitas, according to Turner?
4. In what ways did the counter-culture period of the beat generation and hippie movement embody principles of communitas and liminality, according to Turner? Do you agree with his analysis?
5. What three types of communitas does Turner distinguish? What does he mean by its routinization?
6. What, according to Turner, are some of the characteristics of spontaneous communitas? Can you think of other examples?
7. What is the relationship between communitas and social structure? social hierarchy? social transformation?
8. How, according to Turner, is the liminal state and communitas related to religious notions such as sacredness? Do you agree?
9. Identify and elaborate upon some instances of religious rituals (e.g., sacraments, rites of passage) to which Turner's theory of liminality may be applied.
10. Identify and elaborate upon some religious communities or social configurations to which Turner's theory of communitas may be applied.

Notes

1 Monica Wilson, *Rituals of Kinship among the Nyakyusa* (London: Oxford University Press, 1957), pp. 46–54.
2 Audrey Richards, *Chisungu* (London: Faber and Faber, 1956).

23 Ritual Reification

Catherine Bell

Catherine Bell (1951–2008), a native of New York, received her doctorate in History of Religions from the University of Chicago. Trained in the study of Asian religions, particularly Chinese religions, her most influential contributions were in the area of ritual studies. She worked at the Center for Chinese Studies at the University of California, Berkeley, and taught at Santa Clara University in the department of Religious Studies. She received the American Academy of Religions (AAR) best first book in the History of Religions award in 1994, for *Ritual Theory, Ritual Practice* (1992). The selection that follows is taken from her follow up volume, *Ritual: Perspectives and Dimensions* (1997), and deals with the notion of intellectual reification. This is the tendency to take a category (e.g., ritual), which serves certain pragmatic purposes, and give it greater solidity or "reality" than it actually holds, namely that it is just a conceptual notion or idea.

Discussions of ritual density and change inevitably imply that there is something essential and stable that undergoes variations according to time and place. These discussions and each of the theories of ritual outlined in part I reify ritual, that is assume there is a substantive phenomenon at stake, not simply an abstract analytical category. The spectrum of ritual and ritual-like activities explored in part II appears to give little cause for inferring the substantive existence of some universal form of action best known as ritual. Nonetheless, the reification of ritual has become an important factor in our understanding of the rites around us today and even in the way we are apt to go about doing them. For this reason, the *study* of ritual as a universal mode of action has become an influential part of the context of ritual practice in contemporary Europe and America.

As part I demonstrated, the study of ritual has gone through several historical perspectives that, in hindsight, seem to have had less to do with how people ritualize and more with how Western culture has sorted out relationships between science and religion, on the one hand, and relationships between more technologically developed cultures and more localized tribal cultures, on the other. A number of the formal theories invoked in that section were also vitally concerned with relationship between tradition and modernity, between cultural continuity and social change, between authentic and inauthentic modes of orchestrating cultural communication and, of course, between engaging in a series of religious activities and analyzing this engagement as ritual. Such scholarship purports to identify "ritual" underlying all the permutations of form, variations of place, and changes of time that it documents and organizes. This chapter explores the ways in which scholarly study of certain types of religious and cultural practices has generated the notion of "ritual" and how in turn, this notion has affected these religious and cultural practices.

Repudiating, Returning, Romancing

The emergence of the concept of "ritual" as a universal phenomenon that is substantively manifest in human nature, biology, or culture appears to be the result of a successive layering of scholarly and popular attitudes. These attitudes range from an early modern "repudiation" of ritual at home while finding it prevalent in so-called primitive societies, a subsequent "return" to ritual that recognized it as an important social and cross-cultural phenomenon, followed by a tendency to "romanticize" ritual by both practitioners and theorists as a key mechanism for personal and cultural transformation. The following analysis suggests that these attitudes toward ritual are intrinsic to concerted intellectual efforts to deal with the "other" in the various religious and cultural guises in which this "other" has been perceived.

People talk about the decline and repudiation of ritual in two ways: either in terms of a general stage in an embracing process of social evolution or in terms of particular historical-political situations, such as the 16th-century Protestant Reformation. While the latter situation is usually characterized by specific social circumstances, the first is depicted in terms of more abstract forces of rationalism, secularism, or modernization by which traditional religious communities are dramatically remade by science, pluralism, and individualism. The popular contention that ritual and religion decline in proportion to modernization has been something of a sociological truism since the mid-19th century. The British philosopher Herbert Spencer (1820–1903) was probably among the first to formulate an evolutionary opposition between industrialization of modern culture and the rituals of tribal or feudal cultures, but Max Weber followed up a generation later by contrasting ritual and magic with the rationalism and "disenchantment" of modern life. For the historian Peter Burke, the 19th-century tendency to oppose ritual and reason was itself the product of an earlier opposition, rooted in the ethos of the Reformation, in which ritual came to be seen as artifice and mystification in contrast to the virtues of sincerity, simplicity, and directness. In this ethos, Burke argues, ritual was associated "with the shadow rather than the substance, the letter rather than the spirit, the outer husk rather than the inner kernel."[1] Emerging fields of study focused on ritual as an ideal representation of what was different from reason, what reason needed to explain and, ultimately, enlighten and transform.[2] According to Mary Douglas, among others, these attitudes led comparative studies of religion to elevate ethical Protestant-like religions in contrast to the magical ritualism of primitive, Catholic-like religions.[3]

In the second half of the 20th century, the trend in scholarship began to swing the other way. Burke notes that people began to assume that "that all societies are equally ritualised; they merely practice different rituals. If most people in industrial societies no longer go to church regularly or practice elaborate rituals of initiation, this does not mean that ritual has declined. Instead, new types of ritual—political, sporting, musical, medical, academic, and so on—have taken the place of the traditional ones."[4] From this perspective, ritual is deemed good and healthy, humanly important, universal, and constantly concerned with what Weber, and Geertz after him, called "the Problem of Meaning."[5] Yet this more recent attitude, embodied in the work of both Victor Turner and Clifford Geertz, continues to rely on the opposition between ritual and modernization assumed by Spencer and Weber. This time, however, the opposition casts ritual as a natural mitigator of the harsh and unwanted aspects of modern life. It is possible that 16th- and 19th-century formulations of a modern, secular repudiation of ritual may have contributed to cultural attitudes associated with a decline in ritual participation. There is certainly evidence that the more recent and positive view of ritual promoted by Turner and Geertz has been influential in people's return to ritual. In any case, it is pertinent to ask if the widespread repudiations and returns identified by the theorists have really existed.

There are many sociohistorical situations in which people reject ritual, either their own ritual traditions or those imposed on them by others. In addition to the rejection by 16th-century Protestant reformers of what they saw as papist idolatry and vain superstition, there are many other historical examples, including the rejection of ritual (*li*) by the ancient Taoists, the criticisms of outer ritual form in favor of inner intention by Greek and Roman philosophers, as well as Saint Paul; and a series of movements in Hinduism from the ancient Upanishadic teachers to the early-19th-century Hindu reformer, Ram Mohun Roy. In most cases such criticisms were not attacks on all forms of ritual, just on certain features of pomp, mystery, rigidity, or claims for material efficacy. In the complex milieu of the Reformation, Burke points out, many different understandings of ritual were formulated and challenged. The result was not so much a general repudiation of ritual as a widespread and pluralist debate over different styles and understandings of ritual. As a consequence, he concludes, western Europeans may have become "unusually self-conscious and articulate on the subject."[6]

Typological systems as different as those of Bellah and Douglas, presented earlier, suggest that different types of social order and cultural worldview can be correlated with different styles of ritual. Yet rarely does a society have only one style or one worldview. Usually there are several different cosmological orders more or less integrated with each other but capable of tense differentiation and mutual opposition. Different parts of a society—social classes, economic strata, or ethnic groups—may hold different perspectives on ritual, or the same subgroup may have different attitudes on different occasions. Hence, any repudiation of ritual, like all ritual practice, must be seen as a very contextual thing. For example, when the most radical of the Protestant reformers, the 17th-century Quakers, went so far as to reject even conventional greetings as artificial "bundles of fopperies, fond ceremonies, foolish windings, turnings and crouchings with their bodies," it was in the context of a particular group distinguishing itself from others by taking ideas of inner versus outer spirituality to a new logical extreme.[7]

From this perspective, the evidence for a general, long-term historical process of repudiating ritual begun in 16th-century Europe becomes rather slim. It seems more likely that the century saw the emergence of alternative understandings of ritual that had close links to issues concerning the constitution of personhood, national community, and religious authority. While these clashes would not forbid the future emergence of a general consensus about ritual, the cultural pluralism amplifying the debate can make it difficult to imagine. Certainly there has been no single smooth process of ritual atrophy in European and American culture since then. However, there has been a process in which the emerging disciplines studying religion and culture associated ritual with the primitive, tribal, and nonrational. And despite the variety of other modes of ritual surrounding them in their own societies, such theorists could convince many of a loss of ritual in modern life.

If a general repudiation of ritual in modern industrial society has been somewhat exaggerated, therefore, it is possible that the evidence for a return to ritual has also been overstated. For example, a great deal of attention has been given to the "return" of secular Jews to more demanding forms of orthodoxy. In this context, of course, the word "return" should be examined. In most cases, the people involved had never left orthodoxy; they were born and raised in secular Jewish families and communities. The fact that they are called "those who return" (*baalei teshuvah* in Hebrew) reflects the perspective of the orthodox segment of the Jewish tradition (as well as Zionist interpretations), the view from within the fold, as it were, for whom a secular Jew is a sinner and all Jews who "return" must repent for transgressing correct observance of Jewish law.[8]

The notion of return is also problematic because it rarely means simply picking up the tradition as it has been practiced in the past. Indeed, it is argued that some forms of Jewish orthodoxy to which people are said to return constitute a modern phenomenon, not a traditional one.[9] What is seized upon as tradition is usually a rather new synthesis of custom and accommodation. Many of the secular Jews who have adopted orthodoxy, for example, have no automatic place in the traditional social fabric. Institutional innovations have been necessary, including special yeshivas, synagogue programs, and the quite untraditional Manhattan outreach program for returning singles that has enrolled some 1,200 men and women. In addition, those who convert tend to embrace some aspects of tradition more than others and bring with them new needs to which the tradition must respond. This type of "return" to tradition, therefore, is clearly a force that opens the tradition to many changes. Nonetheless, Jews are embracing orthodoxy in significant numbers; although some research suggests that they do not appear to offset Jews who drift away from orthodox communities.[10]

A variety of reasons have been proposed to explain this type of return to ritual. In most general terms, it is usually analyzed as a form of resistance to secularization, modernization, and, in the case of Judaism in particular, to assimilation.[11] Yet the decision to embrace orthodoxy is itself possible only in a secular society where there are various options for religious affiliation and where the whole issue is considered a matter of individual choice. Hence, if the choice of a return to orthodoxy is a form of resistance to secularism, it also reinforces some of the more central values of secularism, namely, individual choice and a plurality of options. In addition, the most statistically dominant reason for returning to orthodoxy, marriage to an orthodox spouse (by either a secular Jew or a non-Jew), suggests some ambivalence since it indicates that significant numbers of orthodox Jews are marrying outside their communities.[12] The effect of a visit to Israel is another reason commonly given for orthodox conversion, and it is testimony to the emotional impact of experiencing Judaism as a living ethnic culture. Comparably, in America and Europe today, the decision to join a highly ritualized community is often based on an interest in ethnicity as a framework for community, identity, and a sense of tradition and belonging. The sociologist Herbert Danzger finds that the formal belief system is usually less important to the newly orthodox than what Peter Berger called the "plausibility system," that is, the network of people who share the beliefs and make them appear to be a credible understanding of the true nature of things. The family is the most important component of this plausibility system, but the local community or peer group plays a decisive role as well. Identifying with this community by means of dress, residence, and lifestyle—particularly the style of interaction between men and women—can secure one a place in a high-profile, clearly demarcated community.[13]

The decision of women to embrace orthodox Judaism merits particular attention since it is a choice that would seem to fly in the face of the larger movements for women's social and personal emancipation in this century. In exploring the appeal of orthodoxy to young, middle-class, educated women, Lynn Davidman finds the "characteristic dilemmas of modern life, such as feelings of isolation, rootlessness and confusion about gender." As a possible solution to these dilemmas, different women looked to different types of orthodox community—some that took complete control over their lives, others that encouraged them to continue living independently. Yet all of these communities honored women's roles as wives and mothers and held out to their female converts the promise of a religion that gives pride of place to fulfilling domestic life. The primacy accorded women's domestic roles is understood in terms of the importance of a series of rituals governing food preparation and consumption, marital relations, and the observance of the Sabbath and other holidays: Orthodox women say they find in these rituals a deep recognition of their womanhood and their role in the well-being of the family.[14]

Often what is called a return to ritual may be as simple as a heightened interest in symbolism. For example, two Protestant denominations, the United Methodist Church and the Presbyterian Church (U.S.A.), recently "reclaimed," in their words; the Catholic and pre-Reformation practice of receiving a smudge of ashes in the shape of a cross on their foreheads on Ash Wednesday, the beginning of Lent, the forty-day period of preparation for Easter. The use of ashes was originally a Jewish practice reinterpreted by Christians but rejected by Protestant reformers who looked to biblical teachings over external marks of piety. Most of the reasons given for the return to ashes appeal to an emotional resonance with this symbolic reminder of mortality and sin—and a new appreciation of the evocative power of ritual. In the words of Reverend Deborah A. McKinley, spokesperson for the Presbyterian Church (U.S.A.), people "are discovering the importance of ritual action and its ability to draw us beyond the cerebral."[15]

Reverend McKinley's comment reflects the attitude, popular since the early 1970s, that ritual is basically good for you. This is certainly the conviction of much recent scholarship, which has helped to promote and legitimate this perspective among the wider public. The post-Reformation opposition of external form and internal feeling appears displaced by a somewhat different understanding. The same is true for the early modern opposition of rational-industrial to the mystical-tribal. Ritual is now more likely to be seen as a medium of emotional, intuitive expression that is able to express the spiritual states, alternative realities, and the incipient connectedness in which individuals and communities are embedded. While ritual once stood for the status quo and the authority of the dominant social institutions, for many it has become antistructural, revolutionary, and capable of deconstructing inhuman institutions and generating alternative structures. A long-standing concern with the falsity of ritual, conveyed in the negativity of such words as "ritualistic" and "ritualism," has been replaced in many quarters with a desire for ritual as a healing experience. The older conviction that increasing modernization, rational utilitarianism, and individualism would inevitably do away with most forms of traditional ritual life has given way to a heroic championing of ritual as the way to remain human in an increasingly dehumanized world.

In 1982, Douglas argued that most scholars of religion in the postwar period were apt to overemphasize the positive and integrative aspects of religion, implicitly opposing it to modernity in the same way that theology has opposed salvation to worldliness or, in a different debate, scientific rationalism opposed the delusions of traditional religion to the progress of reason.[16] Indeed, the positive and integrative aspects of ritual action are so taken for granted that no effort is made to substantiate them. Vincent Crapanzano's conclusion that Moroccan male initiation rites cruelly traumatize a child in ways that benefit the conservatism of the social group is a rare example of a critical analysis.[17] It is dramatically outweighed by the number of studies attempting to show how initiations are good and healthy social experiences, the lack of which in modern society has resulted in profound sociocultural impoverishment. The assumptions behind this type of statement are never laid out and tested against any empirical evidence.

Since Douglas's criticism of these tendencies toward an indiscriminate affirmation of religion, the opposition of ritual and modernity has actually gone a step further and overly romanticized ritual. It is characterized by testimonies to its creative solutions to the anomie of modern society, which promise among other things, that initiation rites can solve adolescent delinquency and that communing with the earth can rectify our ecological relationships with the environment. A variety of analyses have pushed ritual as a curative for the ills of modernity to the point where ritual appears to act independently of any sociocultural determinism. Indeed, it is set up to act almost salvifically. Aside from all the nonscholarly appeals to the roots of ritual in the "eternal wisdom of ancient peoples," there are theorists who locate ritual in pre-linguistic grammars, in the biogenetic foundation of the "reptilian brain," and in basic, cross-cultural gestures of the human body.[18] All of these views cast ritual as independent of any sociocultural context. They never implicate ritual in the emergence of modernity. Instead, ritual remains a pure, inadequately tapped human resource for ameliorating the evils of modernity—specifically, the personal and communal wholeness fractured by ethnicity, religious ideology, and areligious passivity. Tom Driver writes that "the human longing for ritual is deep," although often frustrated; he extols ritual as essentially liberating and the means of salvation for the modern world. Unable to ignore completely some of the latent contradictions in the position, however, Driver notes that Mohandas Gandhi, the spiritual leader of the Indian independence movement, and Joseph Goebbels, the director of the Nazis' "final solution" for the Jews, were both "consummate ritualist[s]."[19] Yet Driver never analyzes why ritual in the hands of Gandhi was good and in the hands of Goebbels was horrific, or how ritual in general can be so liberating if it can support both men's visions of human aspirations.

The roots of this most recent romanticization of ritual are many and complex, as are its effects. One clear result, however, is a blindness to how contemporary ritual practices are part and parcel of the modern world, often effectively promoting the very forces of modernity that such perspectives implicitly condemn.

The Emergence of "Ritual"

The twists and turns of repudiating, returning, and romancing ritual have been closely intertwined with the emergence of the very concept of ritual as a universal phenomenon accessible to formal identification and analysis. The anthropologist Talal Asad argues that modern use of the term has very specific dates attached to it. The earliest editions of the *Encyclopedia Britannica*, put out between 1771 and 1852, defined ritual as a "book directing the order and manner to be observed in performing divine service in a particular church, diocese, or the like." Even with the addition of references to the rituals of "heathens" like the ancient Romans, it is clear that ritual meant a type of prescriptive liturgical book. Similarly, the entries for "rite" indicated "the particular manner of celebrating divine service, in this or that country," for example, the Roman rite or the Eastern rite. After 1852, there were no entries for either term until 1910, by which time the meaning had clearly shifted. The brief paragraphs of the earlier editions were replaced by a long article with sections on magical elements, interpretation, change, and classification, as well as a bibliography noting the works of the early theorists discussed in part I. For Asad, this shift is "something quite new." Ritual is "no longer a script for regulating practice, but a type of practice" found in all religions and even outside religion, involving expressive symbols intrinsic to the sense of self and workings of society.[20]

To conceive of ritual as a panhuman phenomenon rather than simply to point and gawk at the strange activities of another culture must constitute some form of progress. Yet it is also the result of a drawn-out, complex, and intrinsically political process of negotiating cultural differences and similarities. The observation of ritual commonalities between "our worship" and "their customs" was facilitated by a term, a noun, which asserted a common denominator. At the same time, however, this new commonality effectively relocated "difference." No longer the difference between "our worship" and "their customs," it became the difference between those who sufficiently transcend culture and history to perceive the universal (and scientific) in contrast to those who remain trapped in cultural and historical particularity and are therein so naturally amenable to being the object of study.

Some of the intricacies of this process of negotiating new forms of commonality and difference are preserved in the real-life vignettes of those scholars who literally mapped a frontier, marking out the borders between the newly similar and dissimilar "other." While they emerged as scholars of ritual practices, the people they studied emerged as practitioners of ritual. At one end of the spectrum of experiences and scholars that created this border, there is the story of the Third Cavalry Captain John G. Bourke's reaction to the rites of a secret Zuñi society, the Ne'wekwe (or Nehue-Cue).[21] His initial encounter with them in 1881 provoked intense nausea, which in turn, inspired him to undertake a ten-year study of Zuñi ritual. According to the literary historian Stephen Greenblatt, who has dramatically chronicled some of the themes implicit in Bourke's work, this experience of disgust served to define what was of ethnographic interest, what was "other" (in this case, not Hebrew or Christian) and thus in need of explanation.[22]

At the other end of the "us-them" spectrum, there is the story of Frank Cushing's romantic identification with the Zuñi. An ethnologist sent by the Smithsonian in 1879 to study the Southwest Indians, he acted as Bourke's host. But in contrast to Bourke, Cushing became uncomfortable as an outside observer-scientist putting these people under a type of microscope; he wanted to learn about being Zuñi from the inside. Living with them for many years, he became fluent in their language and so comfortable with their customs that they eventually adopted him into the tribe and initiated him as a priest and war chief. Cushing claimed to think like a Zuñi. It is said that in "going native" he stopped writing about secret Zuñi myths and rituals, unwilling to publish sacred information that had been transmitted to him in confidence. There is some question, however, whether this was the real reason Cushing did not complete several of his ethnographic projects; some suggest that his reticence had less to do with idealism and more to do with sloppy work habits.[23] It is also possible that he was not as well integrated into the tribe as he thought, and his claims to think like a Zuñi may not have been perfectly echoed by the Zuñi themselves. Indeed, they appear to have been very aware of significant peculiarities about Cushing, as shown in the song they composed about him, related by Sam Gill:

> Once they made a White man into a Priest of the Bow
> he was out there with the other Bow priests
> he had black stripes on his body
> the others said their prayers from their hearts
> but he read his from a piece of paper.[24]

Aside from the contrast between prayers said from the heart and those read from the paper, the song also refers to Cushing's striped body paint. According to Gill, the Zuñi refer to paper with writing as something "striped." So it seems that Cushing's reliance on texts and writing—the instruments for the objectification of ritual and of Zuñi culture—was so distinctive that they made it his emblematic sign. In other words, as Gill tells it, they painted him up as a walking piece of writing.[25]

In the annals of ethnographic history and interpretation, many instinctive reactions of disgust or romantic attraction have been used as markers of the differences that make another culture "other," suspect, barbaric, and exotic. Such reactions, moreover, never go in just one direction. Many peoples greeted Europeans and European customs with equal reactions of disgust. Greenblatt notes the reaction of a Native American to the European practice of "collecting and carrying around mucus in handkerchiefs."[26] Early Chinese accounts of Westerners also record many formulations of the "us-them" differences. One early Chinese visitor to the United States graphically described "the red-haired, green-eyed foreign devils with hairy faces" for his audience back home. They were, he continued, "wild and wicked, and paid no regard to the moral precepts of Confucius and the Sages; neither did they worship their ancestors, but pretended to be wiser than their fathers and grand-fathers." Worse yet, men and women "were shameless enough to walk the streets arm in arm in daylight." A later Chinese visitor, more accustomed to these differences, carefully instructed his readers back home in the intricacies and repellent immodesties of that most foreign of rituals, the dinner party, where a man must be prepared to shake a strange woman's hand, offer her his arm, and even engage her in polite conversation.[27] Chinese routinely concluded that Americans had no *li*, that is, no sense of proper behavior.

Somewhere in between the extremes of Bourke's and Cushing's defining encounters with the "other" lies the well-known story of the early sociologist and ordained minister, William Robertson Smith, whose theories were discussed in chapter 1. His career represents a more complex stage in the emergence of the notion and study of ritual. Smith's work on "totemic sacrifice" among the ancient Semitic tribes of the Sinai Desert established the role of ritual in unifying the social group. Using what he presumed was a firsthand account of "the oldest known form of Arabian sacrifice" written by a hermit named Nilus, Smith described how a tribe would tie up a camel and place it on an altar of piled stones. The head of the group would lead them in chanting around the altar three times before inflicting the first wound. Everyone rushed to drink the blood that gushed forth, after which they would all "fall on the victim with their swords, hacking off pieces of the quivering flesh and devouring them raw with such wild haste, that in the short interval between the rise of the day star … and the disappearance of its rays before the rising sun, the entire camel, body and bones, skin, blood and entrails is wholly devoured."[28] Not unlike Bourke's experience of nausea, the brutality of this communal sacrificial meal proved its distance from modern religion; in other words, it testified to the primitiveness of the rite and hence its potential for indicating the origin and essential meaning of all communal rites. Yet even this degree of distance was threatening since it presumed some historical relationship between primitive carnage and modern worship. When Smith brought some of his critical methods of ethnographic ana-lysis to bear on the Bible, even quite indirectly, it provoked a major conflict within the Free Church, a branch of the Church of Scotland, in which he was an ordained minister. In 1881 he was dismissed from his professorship at the Free Church Divinity College of the University of Aberdeen and put on trial in a protracted libel case known in its day as the "Robertson Smith affair."[29] The trial was essentially an accusation of heresy by con-servatives reacting to the implications of his work, particularly the implication that common social forces underlie primitive *and* revealed religions.[30]

It is interesting to note that Robertson Smith himself never aired any doubts about the revealed nature of Christianity. On the contrary, he appears to have been convinced that careful and critical scholarship would only help to unfold the central revelations of the Christian scripture. His interpretation of the typical distinction of his day saw all the "lower" religions mired in the social forces that he was among the first to describe, while Christianity as the revealed truth was able to transcend such determinisms.[31] Smith's attempts to negotiate the relationship between the Bible of belief and the demands of objective scholarship were integral to the emergence of another aspect of the "us-them" boundary, the boundary distinguishing the *practice* of religion from the *study* of it. In Smith's work, this particular boundary followed from how he nearly transgressed the first one: while affirming the distinction between Christianity as revealed religion and all other religions, he also appeared to transgress it with hints of some sort of commonality—the suggestion that perhaps all acts of ritual communion shared a common origin. While such hints were too much for Smith's church, many of his colleagues and students continued to look for the origins and commonalties underlying grossly different forms of religious practice. The splits between church and academy would widen, of course, as scholars distinguished between their practices as a Christian believers and their objective studies, and as the term "ritual" began to be used to talk about common forms of religious practice underlying our liturgies and their barbaric sacrifices.

Although Robertson Smith's tendency to see the ancient rite of totemic sacrifice in as primitive a light as possible did not prevent him from suggesting some modern connections, it seriously misled him in another, rather ironic way. The ancient text on which he relied for a description of this totemic sacrifice was not an authentic account of an ancient tribal ritual at all. It was, in fact, a highly dubious source, a fifth-century Christian text, *The Story of Nilus*, and a type of fictional travelogue in which a witty and sophisticated urban traveler details his hair-raising—and completely fabricated and exaggerated—adventures among stereotypically ferocious desert tribes.[32] Smith mistook this farcical tale for an objective, detached, and reliable account akin to what he himself wished to produce. Since his book laid out the first sociological theory of ritual and was the basis for much subsequent scholarship on ritual, we can wonder what it means that the study of ritual was founded on a pulp tale of primitive barbarism!

The adventures of scholars like Bourke, Cushing, and Robertson Smith along the emerging border between us and them, scholar and practitioner, and theory and data established the basis on which the term "ritual" came to denote group-oriented religious activities that are common, in fundamental ways, to all cultures and peoples.[33] At the same time, as part I demonstrated, the concept of ritual became important to scholarly debates over how to distinguish the magical, the religious, and the rational. The effects of this simultaneous universalization and differentiation are complex. On the one hand, as the foregoing makes very clear, a focus on ritual has enabled scholars to determine the basic similarities among very different ritual practices and traditions. At the same time, however, on a more subtle level, the deployment of "ritual" as a universal has also established new distinctions and borderlands, especially between those who wield such universal categories and thereby transcend their culture and those who, locked in their cultural perspectives, are the recipients of categorizations that may seem meaningless or threatening.[34]

In the end, the history of the concept of ritual suggests that the term has been primarily used to define and mediate plurality and relationships between "us and them,", with the practices of "them" ranging from primitive magic to papist idolatry to the affirmation of traditional wisdom in the face of brutal modernity. Yet there is another important dimension to the emergence of these perspectives on ritual. Approaching ritual as a universal medium of symbolic expression has had significant consequences for the very practice of ritual in Europe and America. In other words, the concept of ritual has influenced how many people in these cultures go about ritualizing today. As parts of the public have come to share an awareness of the cross-cultural similarities among rituals within very different doctrinal systems, social organizations, and cosmological worldviews, "ritual" has emerged for them as a more important focus of attention than the doctrines that appear so tied to particular cultures and histories. Indeed, scholarly studies of "ritual" that demonstrate the evolution and variation of ritual practices over time have been used by components of the larger public as authoritative justifications for making fresh changes in their traditional practices. As a result, the scholarly perspectives on ritual described previously have come to undermine some forms of traditional ritual authority—the authority of having been divinely mandated by God or the ancestors, the authority of seeming to be the way things have been done since time immemorial, and the authority of being the sole possession of this particular community and thus intrinsic to its particular worldview. Hence, the study of ritual practices and the emergence of "ritual as an abstract universal" have the effect of subordinating, relativizing, and ultimately undermining many aspects of ritual practice, even as they point to ritual as a powerful medium of transcultural experience.

While some observers of the current scene see social expressions of a new freedom to ritualize, others see chaotic and idiosyncratic performances that lack all authority. In actual fact, recent forms of ritualization locate their authority in rather nontraditional ways. Most common, perhaps, is an implicit appeal to the authority lodged in the abstract notion of ritual itself. Scholars, ritual inventors, and ritual participants do not usually see how scholarship has constructed this notion of ritual or the type of authority it has acquired. They think of "ritual in general" as something that has been there all along and only now discovered—no matter whether it is thought to be a social constant, a psychological necessity, or a biological determinism. As an abstraction that determines all particular rites and ceremonies, ritual itself becomes a reified construct with the authority to sanction new forms of ritualization that appeal to it as a quintessential human and social dynamic.

There are few ritual leaders and inventors these days who have not read something of the theories of Frazer, van Gennep, Eliade, Turner, or Geertz, either in an original or popularized form. Turner, in particular, by identifying a "ritual process" weaving its way through micro and macro social relations and symbol systems, has been the authority behind much American ritual invention. His books, even when only half-read, legitimize the appeal to ritual as a universal process that authenticates changes in traditional rites or empowers people to invent new ones. The ever increasing corpus of studies on ritual also functions as further testimony to the solidity of ritual as a universal phenomenon and to the legitimacy of activities done in its name. In a typical introduction to a general-audience book on the need for ritual in the modern era, the editor states:

> We take Turner's view that the "betwixt and between" times, the threshold transition times, deserve special attention as constructive "building blocks" for change, or possibly transformation and initiation to another level of consciousness. These liminal or threshold times have a power of their own for both the individual and the culture at large. … Our book is essentially practical, applying basic ideas and patterns of initiation for several age groups.[35]

Here, the abstract patterns "identified" by Turner as common to all initiations—something that has never been proven, and strongly contested by some—are taken as intrinsically human.[36] This view of ritual gives legitimacy to the rites invented by the authors; it also interprets many different personal and cultural experiences as reflecting, and thereby further authenticating, these patterns.

Another book offering advice for creating one's own rituals uses the same logic. It states that "all cultures recognize the need to ritualize major life transitions. In 1929, anthropologist Arnold Van Gennep coined the term 'rite of passage' to describe the universal practice of ceremonializing life's major events."[37] Here the universality of the phenomenon pointed out by van Gennep is the authority behind the rites presented in the book. In a more scholarly study, the author suggests that Turner's model of pilgrimage as a transforming ritual transition should be adopted by the Roman Catholic Church as a central strategy for the pre-Cana activities meant to prepare non-Catholics for marriage in the church.[38] The authority for using this particular ritual structure is not rooted in Catholic doctrine or revelation, although the author does refer to a minor historical precedent for pilgrimage metaphors. Rather, the effective authority for using this ritual pattern is the universality accorded the ritual process described by Turner. The explicit authority vouchsafed to scholars of rituals is certainly significant and perhaps unprecedented. At various times in church deliberations over liturgical matters, the recent tendency has been to consult outside secular scholars. For modern ritualists devising ecological liturgies, crafting new age harmonies, or drumming up a fire in the belly, the taken-for-granted authority to do these things and the accompanying conviction about their efficacy lie in the abstraction "ritual" that scholars have done so much to construct.[39]

We are seeing a new "paradigm" for ritualization. Belief in ritual as a central dynamic in human affairs—as opposed to belief in a particular Christian liturgical tradition or the historical practice of Jewish law—gives ritualists the authority to ritualize creatively and even idiosyncratically. Ritual is approached as a means to create and renew community, transform human identity, and remake our most existential sense of being in the cosmos.[40] Popularized versions of the Turner-Geertz model of "the ritual process" make people expect that these rites can work as a type of social alchemy to transform good intentions into new instincts or weave the threads of raw and broken experiences into a textured fabric of connectedness to other people and things. Ritual practitioners of all kinds in Europe and America now share the sense that their rites participate in something universal. They consider what they do as fundamentally symbolic and having much in common with the equally symbolic practices of Chinese ancestral offerings, Trobriand garden magic, or Turner's accounts of Ndembu healing. And these modern practitioners can reconcile this commonality with personal commitment to the practices of a particular, if newly flexible tradition. This is a fascinating development in the West and one that needs to be examined more closely. There is nothing inherently wrong with it, except that it is clearly not the last word on either ritualization or the concept of ritual. It is a set of attitudes that are as historically determined as the definitions laid out in the earliest editions of the *Encyclopedia Britannica*.[41] Yet in a pragmatic sense, these recent developments may also imply that only now do we have "ritual" as such in European and American cultural life. Only now do people do various rites with a consciousness of participating in a universal phenomenon.

Just as modern theories of ritual have had a powerful effect on how people ritualize, how people ritualize profoundly affects what theorists set about to describe and explain. There is no "scientific" detachment here: ritual theorists, experts, and participants are pulled into a complex circle of interdependence. Recognition of the interdependence makes it easier to consider how our use of the notion of ritual can influence our understanding of people who do not abstract the same experiences in the same way. In other words, our theories of ritual may do a lot to translate Confucian ancestor practices or Trobriand gardening practices into more abstract terms and models that make sense to us. But these analyses do not necessarily help us understand how these activities figure in the worldview of the Chinese or

Trobrianders; they may even distort Chinese and Trobriand cultural experiences. If only now we have "ritual" as such in European and American cultural life, then it may not be inappropriate to contend that what many Chinese and Trobrianders are doing is not "ritual."

With this historical perspective, we can be sympathetic to the critique of anthropologist Talal Asad, who suggests that the category of ritual may not be appropriate to other, non-Christian cultural milieus, such as Islam, which involves very different "technologies of power" and "moral economies of the self." If our historically determined notion of ritual should appear to explain Islamic ritual to our satisfaction, Asad proposes, then perhaps we need to reexamine whether we have constructed categories that inadvertently tell us only what we want to know. Asad fears that Western scholarship is so powerful that it is impossible for Trobriand garden magic to survive in any form but as data for the great mills of scholarly theory. More specifically, he fears that the categories of ritual and religion will influence and even be adopted by those who would not traditionally have defined their lives in these ways.[42] While such developments may foster easier communication and shared values, they may do so by means of political subordination and substantive diminutive of the diversity of human experience.

Western scholarship *is* very powerful. Its explanative power rests not only on tools of abstraction that make some things into concepts and other things in data but also on many other social activities, simultaneously economic and political, that construct a plausibility system of global proportions. Hence, it is quite possible that categories of ritual and non-ritual will influence people who would define their activities differently. If scholarship on ritual as a universal construct has succeeded in creating the beginnings of a shared sense of ritual in many religious and civic practices of Euro-American culture, then we cannot dismiss the concern that such a construct can reach out to restructure practice elsewhere. We may well be in the very process of actually creating ritual as the universal phenomenon we have long taken it to be. Yet creating it has not been our intention, and does not appear to further our more self-conscious goals of understanding.

Richard Schechner concludes his study, *The Future of Ritual*, with a vision in which ritual's pairing of restraint and creativity is the best means by which human beings can avoid complete self-extinction.[43] While his romantic evocation of ritual as a force for global good is not likely to garner the support of empiricists, this sort of vision is tied to practices that could construct as concrete a phenomenon as any empiricist might wish, by encouraging people everywhere to begin to understand their practices as cultural variations on an underlying, universal phenomenon. Certainly the construction of interpretive categories and the propensity to reify them are among the ways by which people have always shaped their world. Abstractions like freedom, human dignity, evil, or true love have had powerful and concrete effects on human affairs. A global discourse on ritual, understood as a transcultural language of the human spirit, is more likely to promote a sense of common humanity and cross-cultural respect than the view that one set of religious rites is the revealed truth itself and the idols worshiped by all other peoples must be destroyed. Yet it is clear that this discourse is being constructed not without violence, loss, and deeply rooted assumptions of cultural hegemony.

In a purely methodological vein, such concerns suggest the need for revised methodologies. The practice theories examined at the close of chapter 3 attempt to focus on activities in such a way as to minimize the amount of preliminary selecting and framing of the data in terms of such powerful categories as ritual, religion, technology, ideology, and so on. There are also attempts to formulate elements basic to "reflexive" and "self-critical" forms of scholarly analysis.[44] There may be other alternatives as well, perhaps even a reconstructed phenomenology—a phenomenology for the post-postmodern era, so to speak—in which the scholar and the conditions of the scholarly project itself are systematically included as part of the total phenomenon under scrutiny. In any case, the links between the emergence of ritual as a category of analysis and the shifts in how people in European and American society ritualize make very clear that ritual cannot be approached as some transparent phenomenon out there in the world waiting to be analyzed and explained. It exists only in sets of complex interactions that we are just beginning to try to map.

Conclusion

The contexts in which ritual practices unfold are not like the props of painted scenery on a theatrical stage. Ritual action involves an inextricable interaction with its immediate world, often drawing it into the very activity of the rite in multiple ways. Exactly how this is done, how often, and with what stylistic features will depend on the specific cultural and social situation with its traditions, conventions, and innovations. Why some societies have more ritual than others, why ritual traditions change or do not change, and why some groups abstract and study "ritual" as some kind of universal phenomenon when others do not— these are questions of context that are at the heart of the dynamics understood as religion and culture.

The way that European and American scholars generate questions about ritual reflects and promotes basic elements of their cultural worldview. The notion of ritual has become one of the ways in which these cultures experience and understand the world. So what does this interest in ritual tell us about ourselves? Most readily, it tells us that we do not live with a seamless worldview; what we do and what we think or believe are routinely distinguished, separated out, and differently weighted. It suggests a certain drive toward transcending the particularities of place, time, and culture by means of the "higher learning" embodied in scientific, artistic, historical and hermeneutical forms of analysis. This interest in transcending the particular suggests a fundamental drive toward world transformation and self-determination. It suggests an eagerness to find or forge spiritual-cultural commonalities among the heterogeneity of beliefs and styles in the world, but primarily in terms that extend our historical experiences as nearly universal. The hubris is not unconstructive, but it now comes face to face with a fresh set of challenges. Whether it can address and solve them is not clear, but these are the issues that ritual and the study of ritual will struggle with in the near future.

The central concern of this study has been to introduce systematically all of the issues, debates, and areas of inquiry that comprise the modern study of ritual. In most cases, this has meant raising open-ended issues, rather than presenting an authoritative consensus. Of course, the topic of ritual is not unique in this regard. Without sacrificing any of the complexity and convolutions involved in the issues, this study has also tried to impose some minimal order on them for the purpose, at least, of suggesting other orderings and contexts. If it was not clear at the beginning, it should be clear by now that "theories," "activities" and "contexts" can be only provisional frameworks. Theories and contexts affect what is seen as ritual and by whom, while those activities deemed to be ritual in turn have theoretic and contextual consequences.

In the end, "ritual" is a relatively new term that we have pressed into service to negotiate a variety of social and cultural differences, including the differentiation of scholarly objectivity and generalization as distinct from cultural particularism and parochialism. The work and hopes of many theorists and practitioners today are pinned to it, and there is no doubt that ritual has become one of the ways in which we structure and interpret our world. As an interpretive tool, it inevitably corrects a bit here and distorts a bit there, or, in terms of practice theory, it addresses problems by shifting the very terrain on which they appeared. In the future, we may have better tools with which to understand what people are doing when they bow their heads, to offer incense to a deity, dance in masks in the plaza, or give a lecture on the meaning of ritual. Yet all these acts are ways of dealing with the world and its perceived forces and sources of power. The form and scope of interpretation differ, and that should not be lightly dismissed, but it cannot be amiss to see in all of these instances practices that illuminate our shared humanity.

QUESTIONS FOR REVIEW AND DISCUSSION

1. What does Bell mean by "repudiation" of ritual, and how does she problematize that term? What evidence does she cite for the tendency to "return" to ritual within Western societies? How do these categories of "repudiation" and "return" play out within scholarly work on rituals?
2. In what ways does Bell suggest ritual has been romanticized? Can you think of other examples of this romanticization? What does Bell point out that such a view of ritual overlooks?
3. Discuss Robertson Smith's analysis of ritual, as presented by Bell, and how it characterizes the dichotomy between "us" and "them," as well as between the practice of religion and its study.
4. What, according to Bell, are some of the effects produced by viewing ritual as a "universal" category?
5. Discuss Bell's observation about the rise of ritualization in response to scholarly constructions of ritual and ritual processes as categories. Can you think of other examples of such responses and ritual creations?
6. Do you concur with the notion that if ritual is consciously constructed in tandem with its reification, then traditional practices may not actually be classified as ritual at all?
7. What does Bell offer by way of conclusion as to what "ritual" is? Do you agree with her assessment?

Notes

1 Burke, "The Repudiation of Ritual," pp. 223–24.
2 For an analysis of stages in the development of a "rational" project to study "religion," see Preus, *Explaining Religion*, pp. 3–103.
3 Douglas, *Purity and Danger*, pp. 18–19.
4 Burke, "The Repudiation of Ritual," p. 223.
5 Geertz, *Interpretation of Culture*, p. 108.
6 Burke, "The Repudiation of Ritual," pp. 224–28, 236.
7 Burke, "The Repudiation of Ritual," p. 233.
8 Janet Aviad, *Return to Judaism: Religious Renewal in Israel* (Chicago: University of Chicago Press, 1983), p. ix.
9 Heilman and Friedman, "Religious Fundamentalism and Religious Jews," pp. 197–264; Heilman, *Defenders of the Faith*, pp. 14–39, 156–58.

10 M. Herbert Danzger, *Returning to Tradition: The Contemporary Revival of Orthodox Judaism* (New Haven: Yale University Press, 1989), pp. 1–2, 328.

11 Aviad, *Return to Judaism*, p. ix.

12 Danzger, *Returning to Tradition*, p. 328.

13 Danzger, *Returning to Tradition*, pp. 330–31; Peter L. Berger, *The Sacred Canopy: Elements of a Sociological Theory of Religion* (New York: Doubleday, 1967), pp. 45–51.

14 Lynn Davidman, *Tradition in a Rootless World: Women Turn to Orthodox Judaism* (Berkeley: University of California Press, 1991), pp. 26, 45, 192, 194. For a personal account, see Shira Dicker, "Mikva," *Tikkun* 7, no. 6 (1992): 62–64.

15 Peter Steinfels, "More Protestants Accept Ashes as Ritual for Lent," *New York Times* (February 24, 1993), p. B12.

16 Mary Douglas, "The Effects of Modernization," 2, 5.

17 Crapanzano, "Rite of Return: Circumcision in Morocco," 15–36.

18 For a discussion of these approaches, see Richard Schechner, *The Future of Ritual Writings on Culture and Performance* (London: Routledge, 1993), pp. 250–51, 253.

19 Tom F. Driver, *The Magic of Ritual*, pp. 8, 33, 79, 99–101.

20 Asad, *Genealogies*, pp. 56–57. The *Oxford English Dictionary* gives a more complicated picture of the evidence that Asad deduces from the *Britannica*, probably because it includes adjectival forms as well.

21 See the excerpt from Bourke's account in Sam D. Gill, *Native American Tradition*, pp. 39–41. Also see Bell, *Ritual Theory, Ritual Practice*, p. 29.

22 Stephen Greenblatt, "Filthy Rites," *Daedalus* 111, no. 3 (Summer 1982): 1–3.

23 Christopher Winters, ed., *International Dictionary of Anthropologists* (New York, Garland, 1991), p. 132.

24 Sam D. Gill, "Nonliterate Traditions and Holy Books: Toward a New Model," *The Holy Book in Comparative Perspective*, ed. Frederick M. Denny and Rodney L. Taylor (Columbia: University of South Carolina Press, 1985), p. 235.

25 Gill, "Nonliterate Traditions and Holy Books," p. 225.

26 Greenblatt, "Filthy Rites," p. 3.

27 R. David Arkush and Leo O. Lee, eds, *Land without Ghosts: Chinese Impressions of America from the Mid-Nineteenth Century to the Present* (Berkeley: University of California Press, 1989), pp. 16, 55–56.

28 Robertson Smith, *Lectures on the Religion of the Semites*, p. 338.

29 T. O. Beidelman, *W. Robertson Smith*, pp. 13–22. As Beidelman notes, the trial was technically for libel but was widely understood to concern heresy (pp. 13, 17).

30 T. O. Beidelman, *W. Robertson Smith*, pp. 13–22. For another application of myth-ritual pattern to Christianity, see E. O. James, "The Sources of Christian Ritual," in Samuel H. Hooke, ed., *The Labyrinth: Further Studies in the Relation between Myth Ritual in the Ancient World* (New York: Macmillan, 1935, pp. 235–60).

31 Beidelman, *W. Robertson Smith*, pp. 26, 30–31.

32 See Joseph Henninger, "Ist der sogenannte Nilus-Bericht eine brauchbare religionsgeschichtliche Quelle?" *Anthropus* 50 (1955): 81–148; see Mircea Eliade, *Occultism, Witchcraft and Cultural Fashions: Essays in Comparative Religion* (Chicago: University of Chicago Press, 1976), pp. 6–7.

33 Just as some anthropologists have argued that the production of texts is integral to this process of creating "ritual" as a transcultural object of study (James Clifford and George E. Marcus, eds, *Writing Cultures: The Poetics and Politics of Ethnography* [Berkeley: University of California, 1986], pp. 1–26), so is a network of scholars defined as professionals distinguished from practitioners. See Bruno Latour, *Science in Action* (Cambridge: Harvard University Press, 1987) and *We Have Never Been Modern*, trans. Catherine Porter (Cambridge: Harvard University Press, 1993).

34 Jack Goody, "Against 'Ritual': Loosely Structured Thoughts on a Loosely Defined Topic," in *Secular Ritual*, ed. Sally F. Moore and Barbara G. Myerhoff (Amsterdam: Van Gorcum, 1977), pp. 25–35.

35 Madhi et al., eds, *Betwixt and Between*, p. ix.

36 Contested primarily on gender grounds, by Bruce Lincoln and Caroline Walker Bynum; see the discussion of the Mukanda ritual in chapter 2 [of Catharine Bell, *Ritual Perspectives and Dimensions*, Oxford: Oxford University Press, 1997].

37 Beck and Metrick, *The Art of Ritual*, p. i.

38 Paul A. Holmes, "A Catechumenate for Marriage: Presacramental Preparation as Pilgrimage," *Journal of Ritual Studies* 6, no. 2 (Summer 1992): 93–113.

39 Victor Turner, Mary Douglas, Ronald Grimes—and I to a lesser extent—have been involved in various forms of consultation as ritual experts. Grimes coined the term "ritology" to designate this form of expertise, describing the ritologist as someone concerned with assessing the effectiveness of rituals. He argues that the ritologist is just an elaboration of an internal process of assessing a rite after its completion, a process that is a common and perhaps necessary part of the ongoing dynamics by which ritual forms are interpreted, reunderstood, and renuanced. See Grimes, *Ritual Criticism*, pp. 3–4, 9.

40 See Tom F. Driver, *The Magic of Ritual.*

41 For a critique of the ability of this perspective on ritual to understand practice in Islam, see Asad, *Genealogies*, pp. 55, 57, 79.

42 Asad, *Genealogies*, pp. 55, 57, 79.

43 Richard Schechner, *The Future of Ritual*, p. 263.

44 Bell, *Ritual, Theory, Ritual Practice*, p. 5.

Works cited

Arkush, R. David, and Leo O. Lee, eds. *Land without Ghosts: Chinese Impressions of America from the Mid-Nineteenth Century to the Present.* Berkeley: University of California Press, 1989.

Asad, Talal. *Genealogies of Religion: Discipline and Reasons of Power in Christianity and Islam.* Baltimore: Johns Hopkins Press, 1993.

Aviad, Janet. *Return to Judaism: Religious Renewal in Israel.* Chicago: University of Chicago Press, 1983.

Beck, Renee, and Sydney B. Metrick. *The Art of Ritual: A Guide to Creating and Performing Your Own Rituals for Growth and Change.* Berkeley, California: Celestial Arts, 1990.

Beidelman, T. O. W. *Robertson Smith and the Sociological Study of Religion.* Chicago: University of Chicago Press, 1974.

Bell, Catherine. *Ritual Theory, Ritual Practice.* New York: Oxford University Press, 1992.

Berger, Peter L. *The Sacred Canopy: Elements of a Sociological Theory of Religion.* New York: Doubleday, 1967.

Burke, Peter. "The Repudiation of Ritual in Early Modern Europe." In *The Historical Anthropology of Early Modern Italy: Essays on Perception and Communication.* Cambridge: Cambridge University Press, 1987.

Bynum, Caroline Walker. "Women's Stories, Women's Symbols: A Critique of Victor Turner's Theory of Liminality." In Robert L. Moore and Frank E. Reynolds, eds. *Anthropology and the Study of Religion.* Chicago: Center for the Scientific Study of Religion, 1984, pp. 105–25.

Clifford, James, and George E. Marcus, eds. *Writing Culture: The Poetics and Politics of Ethnography.* Berkeley: University of California Press, 1986.

Crapanzano, Vincent. "Rite of Return: Circumcision in Morocco." In Werner Muenster-Berger and L. Bryce Boyer, eds. *The Psychoanalytic Study of Society* 9 (1981): 15–36.

Danzger, M. Herbert. *Returning to Tradition: The Contemporary Revival of Orthodox Judaism.* New Haven: Yale University Press, 1989.

Davidman, Lynn. *Tradition in a Rootless World: Women Turn to Orthodox Judaism.* Berkeley: University of California Press, 1991.

Dicker, Shira. "Mikva," *Tikkun* 7, no. 6 (1992): 62–64.

Douglas, Mary. "The Effects of Modernization on Religious Change." *Daedalus in*, no. 1 (Winter 1982): 1–19.

——. *Purity and Danger: An Analysis of Concepts of Pollution and Taboo.* New York: Praeger, 1966.

Driver, Tom F. *The Magic of Ritual: Our Need for Liberating Rites That Transform Our Lives and Our Communities.* San Francisco: Harper Collins, 1991.

Eliade, Mircea. *Occultism, Witchcraft and Cultural Fashions: Essays in Comparative Religion.* Chicago: University of Chicago Press, 1976.

Geertz, Clifford. *The Interpretation of Culture.* New York: Basic Books, 1973.

Gill, Sam D. *Native American Religions: An Introduction.* Belmont, California: Wadsworth, 1982.

——. "Nonliterate Traditions and Holy Books: Toward a New Model." In Frederick M. Denny and Rodney L. Taylor, eds. *The Holy Book in Comparative Perspective*. Columbia: University of South Carolina Press, 1985.

Goody, Jack R. "Against 'Ritual': Loosely Structured Thoughts on a Loosely Defined Topic." In Sally F. Moore and Barbara G. Myerhoff, eds. *Secular Ritual*. Amsterdam: Van Gorcum, 1977, pp. 25–35.

Greenblatt, Stephen. "Filthy Rites." *Daedalus 111* , no. 3 (Summer 1982): 1–16.

Grimes, Ronald L. *Ritual Criticism: Case Studies in Its Practice, Essays on Its Theory*. Columbia: University of South Carolina Press, 1990.

Heilman, Samuel C. *Defenders of the Faith*. New York: Schocken, 1992.

Heilman, Samuel C., and Menachem Friedman. "Religious Fundamentalism and Religious Jews: The Case of the Haredim." In Martin E. Marty and R. Scott Appleby, eds. *Fundamentalisms Observed*. Chicago: University of Chicago Press, 1991, pp. 197–264.

Henninger, Joseph. "Ist der sogenannte Nilus-Bericht eine brauchbare religionsgeschichtliche Quelle?" *Anthropus* 50 (1955): 81–148.

Holmes, Paul A. "A Catechumenate for Marriage: Presacramental Preparation as Pilgrimage." *Journal of Ritual Studies* 6, no. 2 (Summer 1992): 93–113.

James, E. O. "The Sources of Christian Ritual." In Samuel H. Hooke, ed. *The Labyrinth: Further Studies in the Relation between Myth and Ritual in the Ancient World*. New York: Macmillan, 1935, pp. 235–60.

Latour, Bruno. *Science in Action*. Cambridge: Harvard University Press, 1987.

——. *We Have Never Been Modern*. Trans. Catherine Porter. Cambridge: Harvard University Press, 1993.

Lincoln, Bruce. *Emerging from the Chrysalis: Rituals of Women's Initiations, rev. ed*. New York: Oxford University Press, 1991.

Mahdi, Louise Carus, Steven Foster, and Meredith Little, eds. *Betwixt and Between: Patterns of Masculine and Feminine Initiation*. LaSalle, Ill.: Open Court, 1987.

Preuss, J. Samuel. *Explaining Religion: Criticism and Theory from Bodin to Freud*. New Haven: Yale University Press, 1987.

Robertson Smith, William. *Lectures on the Religion of the Semites: The Fundamental Institutions* [1889], New York: KTAV Publishing House, 1969.

Schechner, Richard. *The Future of Ritual: Writings on Culture and Performance*. London: Routledge, 1993.

Steinfels, Peter. "More Protestants Accept Ashes as Ritual for Lent." New York Times. February 24, 1993, p. 612.

Winters, Christopher, ed. *International Dictionary of Anthropologists*. New York: Garland, 1991.

24 The Construction of Religion as an Anthropological Category

Talal Asad

Talal Asad (1932—) was born in Saudi Arabia, grew up in Pakistan, and received his doctorate in anthropology from Oxford University. His work includes studies of colonialism and post-colonialism, in particular how the West has perceived and portrayed the Islamic East. Other studies examine the nature of religion, secularism and its relationship to modernity as it has developed in the formation of the Western state. He currently teaches at the graduate center of the City University of New York. The selection that follows is derived from *Genealogies of Religion: Discipline and Reasons of Power in Christianity and Islam* (1993). It is one of Asad's most notable essays, in part because of its attempt to recommend a shift from understanding religion through the universalist definitions of symbolic anthropology – evident in Clifford Geertz's influential "Religion as a Cultural System" – to a post-structuralist understanding that examines how religious insiders are constructed through the exercise of power and discipline.

In much nineteenth-century evolutionary thought, religion was considered to be an early human condition from which modern law, science, and politics emerged and became detached.[1] In this [twentieth] century most anthropologists have abandoned Victorian evolutionary ideas, and many have challenged the rationalist notion that religion is simply a primitive and therefore outmoded form of the institutions we now encounter in truer form (law, politics, science) in modern life. For these twentieth-century anthropologists, religion is not an archaic mode of scientific thinking, nor of any other secular endeavor we value today; it is, on the contrary, a distinctive space of human practice and belief which cannot be reduced to any other. From this it seems to follow that the essence of religion is not to be confused with, say, the essence of politics, although in many societies the two may overlap and be intertwined.

In a characteristically subtle passage, Louis Dumont has told us that medieval Christendom was one such composite society:

> I shall take it for granted that a change in relations entails a change in whatever is related. If throughout our history religion has developed (to a large extent, with some other influences at play) a revolution in social values and has given birth by scissiparity, as it were, to an autonomous world of political institutions and speculations, then surely religion itself will have changed in the process. Of some important and visible changes we are all aware, but, I submit, we are not aware of the change in the very nature of religion as lived by any given individual, say a Catholic. Everyone knows that religion was formerly a matter of the group and has become a matter of the individual (in principle, and in practice at least in many environments and situations). But if we go

on to assert that this change is correlated with the birth of the modern State, the proposition is not such a commonplace as the previous one. Let us go a little further: medieval-religion was a great cloak – I am thinking of the Mantle of Our Lady of Mercy. Once it became an individual affair, it lost its all-embracing capacity and became one among other apparently equal considerations, of which the political was the first born. Each individual may, of course, and perhaps even will, recognise religion (or philosophy), as the same all-embracing consideration as it used to be *socially*. Yet on the level of social consensus or ideology, the same person will switch to a different configuration of values in which autonomous values (religious, political, etc.) are seemingly juxtaposed, much as individuals are juxtaposed in society.

(1971, 32; emphasis in original)

According to this view, medieval religion, pervading or encompassing other categories, is nevertheless *analytically* identifiable. It is this fact that makes it possible to say that religion has the same essence today as it had in the Middle Ages, although its social extension and function were different in the two epochs. Yet the insistence that religion has an autonomous essence – not to be confused with the essence of science, or of politics, or of common sense – invites us to define religion (like any essence) as a transhistorical and transcultural phenomenon. It may be a happy accident that this effort of defining religion converges with the liberal demand in our time that it be kept quite separate from politics, law, and science – spaces in which varieties of power and reason articulate our distinctively modern life. This definition is at once part of a strategy (for secular liberals) of the confinement, and (for liberal Christians) of the defense of religion.

Yet this separation of religion from power is a modern Western norm, the product of a unique post-Reformation history. The attempt to understand Muslim traditions by insisting that in them religion and politics (two essences modern society tries to keep conceptually and practically apart) are coupled must, in my view, lead to failure. At its most dubious, such attempts encourage us to take up an a priori position in which religious discourse in the political arena is seen as a disguise for political power.

In what follows I want to examine the ways in which the theoretical search for an essence of religion invites us to separate it conceptually from the domain of power. I shall do this by exploring a universalist definition of religion offered by an eminent anthropologist: Clifford Geertz's "Religion as a Cultural System" [reprinted in his widely acclaimed *The Interpretation of Cultures* (1973)]. I stress that this is not primarily a critical review of Geertz's ideas on religion – if that had been my aim I would have addressed myself to the entire corpus of his writings on religion in Indonesia and Morocco. My intention in this chapter is to try to identify some of the historical shifts that have produced our concept of religion as the concept of a transhistorical essence – and Geertz's article is merely my starting point.

It is part of my basic argument that socially identifiable forms, preconditions, and effects of what was regarded as religion in the medieval Christian epoch were quite different from those so considered in modern society. I want to get at this well-known fact while trying to avoid a simple nominalism. What we call religious power was differently distributed and had a different thrust. There were different ways in which it created and worked through legal institutions, different selves that it shaped and responded to, and different categories of knowledge which it authorized and made available. Nevertheless, what the anthropologist is confronted with, as a consequence, is not merely an arbitrary collection of elements and processes that we happen to call "religion." For the entire phenomenon is to be seen in large measure in the context of Christian attempts to achieve a coherence in doctrines and practices, rules and regulations, even if that was a state never fully attained. My argument is that there cannot be a universal definition of religion, not only because its constituent elements and relationships are historically specific, but because that definition is itself the historical product of discursive processes.

A universal (i.e., anthropological) definition is, however, precisely what Geertz aims at: A *religion*, he proposes, is "(1) a system of symbols which act to (2) establish powerful, pervasive, and long-lasting moods and motivations in men by (3) formulating conceptions of a general order of existence and (4) clothing these conceptions with such an aura of factuality that (5) the moods and motivations seem uniquely realistic" (1973, 90). In what follows I shall examine this definition, not only in order to test its interlinked assertions, but also to flesh out the counterclaim that a transhistorical definition of religion is not viable.

The Concept of Symbol as a Clue to the Essence of Religion

Geertz sees his first task as the definition of symbol: "any object, act, event, quality, or relation which serves as a vehicle for a conception – the conception is the symbol's 'meaning'" (91). But this simple, clear statement – in which *symbol* (any object, etc.) is differentiated from but linked to *conception* (its meaning) – is later supplemented by others not entirely consistent with it, for it turns out that the symbol is not an object that serves as a vehicle for a conception, *it is itself the conception.* Thus, in the statement "The number 6, written, imagined, laid out as a row of stones, or even punched into the program tapes of a computer, is a symbol" (91), what constitutes all these diverse representations as versions of the same symbol ("the number 6") is of course *a conception.* Furthermore, Geertz sometimes seems to suggest that even as a conception a symbol has an intrinsic connection with empirical events from which it is merely "theoretically" separable: "the symbolic dimension of social events is, like the psychological, itself theoretically abstractable from these events as empirical totalities" (91). At other times, however, he stresses the importance of keeping symbols and empirical objects quite separate: "there is something to be said for not confusing our traffic with symbols with our traffic with objects or human beings, for these latter are not in themselves symbols, however often they may function as such" (92). Thus, "symbol" is sometimes an aspect of reality, sometimes of its representation.[2]

These divergencies are symptoms of the fact that cognitive questions are mixed up in this account with communicative ones, and this makes it difficult to inquire into the ways in which discourse and understanding are connected in social practice. To begin with we might say, as a number of writers have done, that a symbol is not an object or event that serves to carry a meaning but a set of relationships between objects or events uniquely brought together as complexes or as concepts,[3] having at once an intellectual, instrumental, and emotional significance. If we define symbol along these lines,[4] a number of questions can be raised about the conditions that explain how such complexes and concepts come to be formed, and in particular how their formation is related to varieties of practice. Half a century ago, Vygotsky was able to show how the development of children's intellect is dependent on the internalization of social speech. This means that the formation of what we have here called "symbols" (complexes, concepts) is conditioned by the social relations in which the growing child is involved – by the social activities that he or she is permitted or encouraged or obliged to undertake – in which other symbols (speech and significant movements) are crucial. The conditions (discursive and nondiscursive) that explain how symbols come to be constructed, and how some of them are established as natural or authoritative as opposed to others, then become an important object of anthropological inquiry. It must be stressed that this is not a matter of urging the study of the origin and function of symbols in addition to their meaning – such a distinction is not relevant here. What is being argued is that the authoritative status of representations/discourses is dependent on the appropriate production of other representations/discourses; the two are intrinsically and not just temporally connected.

Systems of symbols, says Geertz, are also *culture patterns*, and they constitute "extrinsic sources of information" (92). Extrinsic, because "they lie outside the boundaries of the individual organism as such, in that inter-subjective world of common understandings into which all human individuals are born" (92). And sources of information in the sense that "they provide a blueprint or template in terms of which processes external to themselves can be given a definite form" (92). Thus, culture patterns, we are told, may be thought of as "models *for* reality" as well as "models *of* reality."[5]

This part of the discussion does open up possibilities by speaking of modeling: that is, it allows for the possibility of conceptualizing discourses in the process of elaboration, modification, testing, and so forth. Unfortunately, Geertz quickly regresses to his earlier position: "culture patterns have an intrinsic double aspect," he writes; "they give meaning, that is objective conceptual form, to social and psychological reality both by shaping themselves to it and by shaping it to themselves" (1973, 93). This alleged dialectical tendency toward isomorphism, incidentally, makes it difficult to understand how social change can ever occur. The basic problem, however, is not with the idea of mirror images as such but with the assumption that there are two separate levels – the cultural, on the one side (consisting of symbols) and the social and psychological, on the other – which interact. This resort to Parsonian theory creates a logical space for defining the essence of religion. By adopting it, Geertz moves away from a notion of symbols that are intrinsic to signifying and organizing practices, and back to a notion of symbols as meaning-carrying objects external to social conditions and states of the self ("social and psychological reality").

This is not to say that Geertz doesn't think of symbols as "doing" something. In a way that recalls older anthropological approaches to ritual,[6] he states that religious symbols act "by inducing in the worshipper a certain distinctive set of dispositions (tendencies, capacities, propensities, skills, habits, liabilities, proneness) which lend a chronic character to the flow of his activity and the quality of his experience" (95). And here again, symbols are set apart from mental states. But how plausible are these propositions? Can we, for example, predict the "distinctive" set of dispositions for a Christian worshiper in modern, industrial society? Alternatively, can we say of someone with a "distinctive" set of dispositions that he is or is not a Christian? The answer to both questions must surely be no. The reason, of course, is that it is not simply worship but social, political, and economic institutions in general, within which individual biographies are lived out, that lend a stable character to the flow of a Christian's activity and to the quality of her experience.

Religious symbols, Geertz elaborates, produce two kinds of dispositions, *moods* and *motivations:* "motivations are 'made meaningful' with reference to the ends towards which they are conceived to conduce, whereas moods are 'made meaningful' with reference to the conditions from which they are conceived to spring" (97). Now, a Christian might say that this is not their essence, because religious symbols, even when failing to produce moods and motivations, are still religious (i.e., true) symbols – that religious symbols possess a truth independent of their effectiveness. Yet surely even a committed Christian cannot be unconcerned at the existence of truthful symbols that appear to be largely powerless in modern society. He will rightly want to ask: What are the conditions in which religious symbols can actually produce religious dispositions? Or, as a nonbeliever would put it: How does (religious) power create (religious) truth?

The relation between power and truth is an ancient theme, and no one has dealt with it more impressively in Christian thought than St. Augustine. Augustine developed his views on the creative religious function of power after his experience with the Donatist heresy, insisting that coercion was a condition for the realization of truth, and discipline essential to its maintenance.

For a Donatist, Augustine's attitude to coercion was a blatant denial of Christian teaching: God had made men free to choose good or evil; a policy which forced this choice was plainly irreligious. The Donatist writers quoted the same passages from the Bible in favour of free will, as Pelagius would later quote. In his reply, Augustine already gave them the same answer as he would give to the Pelagians: the final, individual act of choice must be spontaneous; but this act of choice could be prepared by a long process, which men did not necessarily choose for themselves, but which was often imposed on them, against their will, by God. This was a corrective process of "teaching," *eruditio*, and warning, *admonitio*, which might even include fear, constraint, and external inconveniences: "Let constraint be found outside; it is inside that the will is born."

Augustine had become convinced that men needed such firm handling. He summed up his attitude in one word: *disciplina*. He thought of this *disciplina*, not as many of his more traditional Roman contemporaries did, as the static preservation of a "Roman way of life." For him it was an essentially active process of corrective punishment, "a softening-up process," a "teaching by inconveniences" – *a per motestias eruditio*. In the Old Testament, God had taught his wayward Chosen People through just such a process of *disciplina*, checking and punishing their evil tendencies by a whole series of divinely-ordained disasters. The persecution of the Donatists was another "controlled catastrophe" imposed by God, mediated, on this occasion, by the laws of the Christian Emperors.

Augustine's view of the Fall of mankind determined his attitude to society. Fallen men had come to need restraint. Even man's greatest achievements had been made possible only by a "straight-jacket" of unremitting harshness. Augustine was a great intellect, with a healthy respect for the achievements of human reason. Yet he was obsessed by the difficulties of thought, and by the long, coercive processes, reaching back into the horrors of his own schooldays, that had made this intellectual activity possible; so "ready to lie down" was the fallen human mind. He said he would rather die than become a child again. Nonetheless, the terrors of that time had been strictly necessary; for they were part of the awesome discipline of God, "from the schoolmasters' canes to the agonies of the martyrs," by which human beings were recalled, by suffering, from their own disastrous inclinations. (Brown 1967, 236–38)

Isn't Geertz's formula too simple to accommodate the force of this religious symbolism? Note that here it is not mere symbols that implant true Christian dispositions, but power – ranging all the way from laws (imperial and ecclesiastical) and other sanctions (hellfire, death, salvation, good repute, peace) to the disciplinary activities of social institutions (family, school, city, church) and of human bodies (fasting, prayer, obedience, penance). Augustine was quite clear that power, the effect of an entire network of motivated practices, assumes a religious form because of the end to which it is directed, for human events are the instruments of God. It was not the mind that moved spontaneously to religious truth, but power that created the conditions for experiencing that truth. Particular discourses and practices were to be systematically excluded, forbidden, denounced – made as much as possible unthinkable; others were to be included, allowed, praised, and drawn into the narrative of sacred truth. The configurations of power in this sense have, of course, varied profoundly in Christendom from one epoch to another – from Augustine's time, through the Middle Ages, to the industrial capitalist West of today. The patterns of religious moods and motivations, the possibilities for religious knowledge and truth, have all varied with them and been conditioned by them. Even Augustine held that although religious truth was eternal, the means for securing human access to it were not.

From Reading Symbols to Analyzing Practices

One consequence of assuming a symbolic system separate from practices is that important distinctions are sometimes obscured, or even explicitly denied. "That the symbols or symbol systems which induce and define dispositions we set off as religious and those which place these dispositions in a cosmic framework are the same symbols ought to occasion no surprise" (Geertz 1973, 98). But it does surprise! Let us grant that religious dispositions are crucially dependent on certain religious symbols, that such symbols operate in a way integral to religious motivation and religious mood. Even so, the symbolic process by which the concepts of religious motivation and mood are placed within "a cosmic framework" is surely quite a different operation, and therefore the signs involved are quite different. Put another way, theological discourse is not identical with either moral attitudes or liturgical discourses – of which, among other things, theology speaks. Thoughtful Christians will concede that, although theology has an essential function, theological discourse does not necessarily induce religious dispositions and that, conversely, having religious dispositions does not necessarily depend on a clear-cut conception of the cosmic framework on the part of a religious actor. Discourse involved in practice is not the same as that involved in speaking about practice. It is a modern idea that a practitioner cannot know how to live religiously without being able to articulate that knowledge.

Geertz's reason for merging the two kinds of discursive process seems to spring from a wish to distinguish in general between religious and secular dispositions. The statement quoted above is elaborated as follows:

> For what else do we mean by saying that a particular mood of awe is religious and not secular, except that it springs from entertaining a conception of all-pervading vitality like mana and not from a visit to the Grand Canyon? Or that a particular case of asceticism is an example of a religious motivation except that it is directed toward the achievement of an unconditioned end like nirvana and not a conditioned one like weight-reduction? If sacred symbols did not at one and the same time induce dispositions in human beings and formulate … general ideas of order, then the empirical differentia of religious activity or religious experience would not exist.
>
> (98)

The argument that a particular disposition is religious partly because it occupies a conceptual place within a cosmic framework appears plausible, but only because it presupposes a question that must be made explicit: how do authorizing processes represent practices, utterances, or dispositions so that they can be discursively related to general (cosmic) ideas of order? In short, the question pertains to the authorizing process by which "religion" is created.

The ways in which authorizing discourses, presupposing and expounding a cosmology, systematically redefined religious spaces have been of profound importance in the history of

Western society. In the Middle Ages, such discourses ranged over an enormous domain, defining and creating religion: rejecting "pagan" practices or accepting them;[7] authenticating particular miracles and relics (the two confirmed each other); authorizing shrines; compiling saints' lives, both as a model of and as a model for the Truth; requiring the regular telling of sinful thoughts, words, and deeds to a priestly confessor and giving absolution to a penitent; regularizing popular social movements into Rule-following Orders (for example, the Franciscans), or denouncing them for heresy or for verging on the heretical (for example, the Beguines). The medieval Church did not attempt to establish absolute uniformity of practice; on the contrary, its authoritative discourse was always concerned to specify differences, gradations, exceptions. What it sought was the subjection of all practice to a unified authority, to a single authentic source that could tell truth from falsehood. It was the early Christian Fathers who established the principle that only a single Church could become the source of authenticating discourse. They knew that the "symbols" embodied in the practice of self-confessed Christians are not always identical with the theory of the "one true Church," that religion requires authorized practice and authorizing doctrine, and that there is always a tension between them – sometimes breaking into heresy, the subversion of Truth – which underlines the creative role of institutional power.[8]

The medieval Church was always clear about why there was a continuous need to distinguish knowledge from falsehood (religion from what sought to subvert it), as well as the sacred from the profane (religion from what was outside it), distinctions for which the authoritative discourses, the teachings and practices of the Church, not the convictions of the practitioner, were the final test.[9] Several times before the Reformation, the boundary between the religious and the secular was redrawn, but always the formal authority of the Church remained preeminent. In later centuries, with the triumphant rise of modern science, modern production, and the modern state, the churches would also be clear about the need to distinguish the religious from the secular, shifting, as they did so, the weight of religion more and more onto the moods and motivations of the individual believer. Discipline (intellectual and social) would, in this period, gradually abandon religious space, letting "belief," "conscience," and "sensibility" take its place. *But theory would still be needed to define religion.*

The Construction of Religion in Early Modern Europe

It was in the seventeenth century, following the fragmentation of the unity and authority of the Roman church and the consequent wars of religion, which tore European principalities apart, that the earliest systematic attempts at producing a universal definition of religion were made. Herbert produced a substantive definition of what later came to be formulated as Natural Religion – in terms of beliefs (about a supreme power), practices (its ordered worship), and ethics (a code of conduct based on rewards and punishments after this life) – said to exist in all societies.[10] This emphasis on belief meant that henceforth religion could be conceived as a set of propositions to which believers gave assent, and which could therefore be judged and compared as between different religions and as against natural science (Harrison 1990). The idea of scripture (a divinely produced/interpreted text) was not essential to this "common denominator" of religions partly because Christians had become more familiar, through trade and colonization, with societies that lacked writing. But a more important reason lies in the shift in attention that occurred in the *seventeenth* century from God's words to God's works. "Nature" became the real space of divine writing, and eventually the indisputable authority for the truth of all sacred texts written in merely human language (the Old Testament and the New). ... In this way, Natural Religion not only became a universal phenomenon but began to be demarcated from, and was also supportive of, a newly emerging domain of natural science. I want to emphasize that the idea of Natural Religion was a crucial step in the formation of the modern concept of religious belief, experience, and practice, and that it was an idea developed in response to problems specific to Christian theology at a particular historical juncture.

By 1795, Kant was able to produce a fully essentialized idea of religion which could be counterposed to its phenomenal forms: "There may certainly be different historical *confessions*" he wrote,

> although these have nothing to do with religion itself but only with changes in the means used to further religion, and are thus the province of historical research. And there may be just as many religious *books* (the Zend-Avesta, the Vedas, the Koran, etc.). But there can only be *one religion* which is valid for all men and at all times. Thus the different confessions can scarcely be more than the vehicles of religion; these are fortuitous, and may vary with differences in time or place.
>
> (Kant 1991, 114)

From here, the classification of historical confessions into lower and higher religions became an increasingly popular option for philosophers, theologians, missionaries, and anthropologists in the nineteenth and twentieth centuries. As to whether any particular tribe has existed without any form of religion whatever was often raised as a question,[11] but this was recognized as an empirical matter not affecting the essence of religion itself.

Thus, what appears to anthropologists today to be self-evident, namely that religion is essentially a matter of symbolic meanings linked to ideas of general order (expressed through either or both rite and doctrine), that it has generic functions/features, and that it must not be confused with any of its particular historical or cultural forms, is in fact a view that has a specific Christian history. From being a concrete set of practical rules attached to specific processes of power and knowledge, religion has come to be abstracted and universalized. In this movement we have not merely an increase in religious toleration, certainly not merely a new scientific discovery, but the mutation of a concept and a range of social practices which is itself part of a wider change in the modern landscape of power and knowledge. That change included a new kind of state, a new kind of science, a new kind of legal and moral subject. To understand this mutation it is essential to keep clearly distinct that which theology tends to obscure: the occurrence of events (utterances, practices, dispositions) and the authorizing processes that give those events meaning and embody that meaning in concrete institutions.

Religion as Meaning and Religious Meanings

The equation between two levels of discourse (symbols that induce dispositions and those that place the idea of those dispositions discursively in a cosmic framework) is not the only problematic thing in this part of Geertz's discussion. He also appears, inadvertently, to be taking up the standpoint of theology. This happens when he insists on the primacy of meaning without regard to the processes by which meanings are constructed. "What any particular religion affirms about the fundamental nature of reality may be obscure, shallow, or, all too often, perverse," he writes, "but it must, if it is not to consist of the mere collection of received practices and conventional sentiments we usually refer to as moralism, affirm something" (98–99).

The requirement of affirmation is apparently innocent and logical, but through it the entire field of evangelism was historically opened up, in particular the work of European missionaries in Asia, Africa, and Latin America. The demand that the received practices must *affirm something about the fundamental nature of reality*, that it should therefore always be possible to state meanings for them which are not plain nonsense, is the first condition for determining whether they belong to "religion." The unevangelized come to be seen typically either as those who have practices but affirm nothing, in which case meaning can be attributed to their practices (thus making them vulnerable), or as those who do affirm something (probably "obscure, shallow, or perverse"), an affirmation that can therefore be dismissed. In the one case, religious theory becomes necessary for a correct reading of the mute ritual hieroglyphics of others, for reducing their practices to texts; in the other, it is essential for judging the validity of their cosmological utterances. But always, there must be something that exists beyond the observed practices, the heard utterances, the written words, and it is the function of religious theory to reach into, and to bring out, that background by giving them meaning.

Geertz is thus right to make a connection between religious theory and practice, but wrong to see it as essentially cognitive, as a means by which a disembodied mind can identify religion from an Archimedean point. The connection between religious theory and practice is fundamentally a matter of intervention – of constructing religion in the world (not in the mind) through definitional discourses, interpreting true meanings, excluding some utterances and practices and including others. Hence my repeated question: how does theoretical discourse actually define religion? What are the historical conditions in which it can act effectively as a demand for the imitation, or the prohibition, or the authentication of truthful utterances and practices? How does power create religion?

What kinds of affirmation, of meaning, must be identified with practice in order for it to qualify as religion? According to Geertz, it is because all human beings have a profound need for a general order of existence that religious symbols function to fulfill that need. It follows that human beings have a deep dread of disorder. "There are at least three points where chaos – a tumult of events which lack not just interpretations but *interpretability* – threatens to break in upon man: at the limits of his analytic capabilities, at the limits of his powers of endurance, and at the limits of his moral insight" (100). It is the function of religious symbols to meet perceived threats to order at each of these points (intellectual, physical, and moral):

> The Problem of Meaning in each of its intergrading aspects … is a matter of affirming, or at least recognizing, the inescapability of ignorance, pain, and injustice on the human plane while simultaneously denying that these irrationalities are characteristic of the world as a whole. And it is in terms of religious symbolism, a symbolism relating man's sphere of existence to a wider sphere within which it is conceived to rest, that both the affirmation and the denial are made.
>
> (108)

Notice how the reasoning seems now to have shifted its ground from the claim that religion must affirm something specific about the nature of reality (however obscure, shallow, or perverse) to the bland suggestion that religion is ultimately a matter of having a positive attitude toward the problem of disorder, of affirming simply that in some sense or other the world as a whole is explicable, justifiable, bearable. This modest view of religion (which would have horrified the early Christian Fathers or medieval churchmen)[12] is a product of the only legitimate space allowed to Christianity by post-Enlightenment society, the right to individual *belief*: the human condition is full of ignorance, pain, and injustice, and religious symbols are a means of coming positively to terms with that condition. One consequence is that this view would in principle render any philosophy that performs such a function into religion (to the annoyance of the nineteenth-century rationalist), or alternatively, make it possible to think of religion as a more primitive, a less adult mode of coming to terms with the human condition (to the annoyance of the modern Christian). In either case, the suggestion that religion has a universal function in belief is one indication of how marginal religion has become in modern industrial society as the site for producing disciplined knowledge and personal discipline. As such it comes to resemble the conception Marx had of religion as ideology – that is, as a mode of consciousness which is other than consciousness of reality, external to the relations of production, producing no knowledge, but expressing at once the anguish of the oppressed and a spurious consolation.

Geertz has much more to say, however, on the elusive question of religious meaning: not only do religious symbols formulate conceptions of a general order of existence, they also clothe those conceptions with an aura of factuality. This, we are told, is "the problem of belief." *Religious belief* always involves "the prior acceptance of authority," which transforms experience:

> The existence of bafflement, pain, and moral paradox – of the Problem of Meaning – is one of the things that drives men toward belief in gods, devils, spirits, totemic principles, or the spiritual efficacy of cannibalism, … but it is not the basis upon which those beliefs rest, but rather their most important field of application.
>
> (109)

This seems to imply that religious belief stands independently of the worldly conditions that produce bafflement, pain, and moral paradox, although that belief is primarily a way of coming to terms with them. But surely this is mistaken, on logical grounds as well as historical, for changes in the object of belief change that belief; and as the world changes, so do the objects of belief and the specific forms of bafflement and moral paradox that are a part of that world. What the Christian believes today about God, life after death, the universe, is not what he believed a millennium ago – nor is the way he responds to ignorance, pain, and injustice the same now as it was then. The medieval valorization of pain as the mode of participating in Christ's suffering contrasts sharply with the modern Catholic perception of pain as an evil to be fought against and overcome as Christ the Healer did. That difference is clearly related to the post-Enlightenment secularization of Western society and to the moral language which that society now authorizes.

Geertz's treatment of religious belief, which lies at the core of his conception of religion, is a modern, privatized Christian one because and to the extent that it emphasizes the priority of belief as a state of mind rather than as constituting activity in the world: "The basic axiom underlying what we may perhaps call 'the religious perspective' is everywhere the same: he who would know must first believe" (110). In modern society, where knowledge is rooted either in an a-Christian everyday life or in an a-religious science, the Christian apologist tends not to regard belief as the conclusion to a knowledge process but as its precondition. However, the knowledge that he promises will not pass (nor, in fairness, does he claim that it will pass) for knowledge of social life, still less for the systematic knowledge of objects that natural science provides. Her claim is to a particular state of mind, a sense of conviction, not to a corpus of practical knowledge. But the reversal of belief and knowledge she demands was not a basic axiom to, say, pious learned Christians of the twelfth century, for whom knowledge and belief were not so clearly at odds. On the contrary, Christian belief would then have been built on knowledge – knowledge of theological doctrine, of canon law and Church courts, of the details of clerical liberties, of the powers of ecclesiastical office (over souls, bodies, properties), of the preconditions and effects of confession, of the rules of religious orders, of the locations and virtues of shrines, of the lives of the saints, and so forth. Familiarity with all such (religious) knowledge was a precondition for normal social life, and belief (embodied in practice and discourse) an orientation for effective activity in it – whether on the part of the religious clergy, the secular clergy, or the laity. Because of this, the form and texture and function of their beliefs would have been different from the form and texture and function of contemporary belief – and so too of their doubts and their disbelief.

The assumption that belief is a distinctive mental state characteristic of all religions has been the subject of discussion by contemporary scholars. Thus, Needham (1972) has interestingly argued that belief is nowhere a distinct mode of consciousness, nor a necessary institution for the conduct of social life. Southwold (1979) takes an almost diametrically opposed view, asserting that questions of belief do relate to distinctive mental states and that they are relevant in any and every society, since "to believe" always designates a relation between a believer and a proposition and through it to reality. Harré (1981, 82), in a criticism of Needham, makes the more persuasive case that "belief is a mental state, a grounded disposition, but it is confined to people who have certain social institutions and practices."

At any rate, I think it is not too unreasonable to maintain that "the basic axiom" underlying what Geertz calls "the religious perspective" is *not* everywhere the same. It is preeminently the Christian church that has occupied itself with identifying, cultivating, and testing belief as a verbalizable inner condition of true religion (Asad 1986).

Religion as a Perspective

The phenomenological vocabulary that Geertz employs raises two interesting questions, one regarding its coherence and the other concerning its adequacy to a modern cognitivist notion of religion. I want to suggest that although this vocabulary is theoretically incoherent, it is socially quite compatible with the privatized idea of religion in modern society.

Thus, "the religious perspective," we are told, is one among several – common-sense, scientific, aesthetic – and it differs from these as follows. It differs from the *common-sense* perspective, because it "moves beyond the realities of everyday life to wider ones which correct and complete them, and [because] its defining concern is not action upon those wider realities but acceptance of them, faith in them." It is unlike the *scientific* perspective, because "it questions the realities of everyday life not out of an institutionalized scepticism which dissolves the world's givenness into a swirl of probabilistic hypotheses, but in terms of what it takes to be wider, non-hypothetical truths." And it is distinguished from the *aesthetic* perspective, because "instead of effecting a disengagement from the whole question of factuality, deliberately manufacturing an air of semblance and illusion, it deepens the concern with fact and seeks to create an aura of utter actuality" (112). In other words, although the religious perspective is not exactly rational, it is not irrational either.

It would not be difficult to state one's disagreement with this summary of what common sense, science, and aesthetics are about. But my point is that the optional flavor conveyed by the term *perspective* is surely misleading when it is applied equally to science and to religion in modern society: religion is indeed now optional in a way that science is not. Scientific practices, techniques, knowledges, permeate and create the very fibers of social life in ways that religion no longer does. In that sense, religion today *is* a perspective (or an "attitude," as Geertz sometimes calls it), but science is not. In that sense, too, science is not to be found in every society, past and present. We shall see in a moment the difficulties that Geertz's perspectivism gets him into, but before that I need to examine his analysis of the mechanics of reality maintenance at work in religion.

Consistent with previous arguments about the functions of religious symbols is Geertz's remark that "it is in ritual – that is, consecrated behavior – that this conviction that religious conceptions are veridical and that religious directives are sound is somehow generated" (112). The long passage from which this is taken swings back and forth between arbitrary speculations about what goes on in the consciousness of officiants and unfounded assertions about ritual as imprinting. At first sight, this seems a curious combination of introspectionist psychology with a behaviorist one – but as Vygotsky (1978, 58–59) argued long ago, the two are by no means inconsistent, insofar as both assume that psychological phenomena consist essentially in the consequence of various stimulating environments.

Geertz postulates the function of rituals in generating religious conviction ("In these plastic dramas men attain their faith as they portray it" [114]), but how or why this happens is nowhere explained. Indeed, he concedes that such a religious state is not always achieved in religious ritual: "Of course, all cultural performances are not religious performances, and the line between those that are, and artistic, or even political, ones is often not so easy to draw in practice, for, like social forms, symbolic forms can serve multiple purposes" (113). But the question remains: What is it that ensures the participant's taking the symbolic forms in the way that leads to faith if the line between religious and nonreligious perspectives is not so easy to draw? Mustn't the ability and the will to adopt a religious standpoint be present prior to the ritual performance? That is precisely why a simple stimulus-response model of how ritual works will not do. And if that is the case, then ritual in the sense of a sacred performance cannot be the place where religious faith is attained, but the manner in which it is (literally) played out. If we are to understand how this happens, we must examine not only the sacred performance itself but also the entire range of available disciplinary activities, of institutional forms of knowledge and practice, within which dispositions are formed and sustained and through which the possibilities of attaining the truth are marked out – as Augustine clearly saw.

I have noted more than once Geertz's concern to define religious symbols according to universal, cognitive criteria, to distinguish the religious perspective clearly from nonreligious ones. The separation of religion from science, common sense, aesthetics, politics, and so on, allows him to defend it against charges of irrationality. If religion has a distinctive perspective (its own truth, as Durkheim would have said) and performs an indispensable function, it does not in essence compete with others and cannot, therefore, be accused of generating false consciousness. Yet in a way this defense is equivocal. Religious symbols create dispositions, Geertz observes, which seem uniquely realistic. Is this the point of view of a reasonably confident agent (who must always operate within the denseness of historically given probabilities) or that of a skeptical observer (who can see through the representations of reality to the reality itself)? It is never clear. And it is never clear because this kind of phenomenological approach doesn't make it easy to examine whether, and if so to what extent and in what ways, religious experience relates to something in the real world that believers inhabit. This is partly because religious symbols are treated, in circular fashion, as the precondition for religious experience (which, like any experience, must, by definition, be genuine), rather than as one condition for engaging with life.

Toward the end of his essay, Geertz attempts to connect, instead of separating, the religious perspective and the common-sense one – and the result reveals an ambiguity basic to his entire approach. First, invoking Schutz, Geertz states that the everyday world of common-sense objects and practical acts is common to all human beings because their survival depends on it: "A man, even large groups of men, may be aesthetically insensitive, religiously uncon-cerned, and unequipped to pursue formal scientific analysis, but he cannot be completely lacking in common sense and survive" (119). Next, he informs us that individuals move "back and forth between the religious perspective and the common-sense perspective" (119). These perspectives are so utterly different, he declares, that only "Kierkegaardian leaps" (120) can cover the cultural gaps that separate them. Then, the phenomenological conclusion:

> Having ritually "leapt" … into the framework of meaning which religious conceptions define, and the ritual ended, returned again to the common-sense world, a man is – unless, as sometimes happens, the experience fails to register – changed. *And as he is changed, so also is the common-sense world*, for it is now seen as but the partial form of a wider reality which corrects and completes it.
>
> (122; emphasis added)

This curious account of shifting perspectives and changing worlds is puzzling – as indeed it is in Schutz himself. It is not clear, for example, whether the religious framework and the common-sense world, between which the individual moves, are independent of him or not. Most of what Geertz has said at the beginning of his essay would imply that they are independent (cf. 92), and his remark about common sense being vital to every man's sur-vival also enforces this reading. Yet it is also suggested that as the believer changes his perspective, so he himself changes; and that as he changes, so too is his common-sense world changed and corrected. So the latter, at any rate, is not independent of his moves. But it would appear from the account that the religious world is independent, since it is the source of distinctive experience for the believer, and through that experience, a source of change in the common-sense world: there is no suggestion anywhere that the religious world (or perspective) is ever affected by experience in the common-sense world.

This last point is consistent with the phenomenological approach in which religious symbols are sui generis, marking out an independent religious domain. But in the present context it presents the reader with a paradox: the world of common sense is always common to all human beings, and quite distinct from the religious world, which in turn differs from one group to another, as one culture differs from another; but experience of the religious world affects the common sense world, and so the distinctiveness of the two kinds of world is modified, and the common-sense world comes to differ, from one group to another, as one culture differs from another. The paradox results from an ambiguous phenomenology in which reality is at once the distance of an agent's social perspective from the truth, measurable only by the privileged observer, and also the substantive knowledge of a socially constructed world available to both agent and observer, but to the latter only through the former.[13]

Conclusion

Perhaps we can learn something from this paradox which will help us evaluate Geertz's confident conclusion: "The anthropological study of religion is therefore a two-stage operation: first, an analysis of the system of meanings embodied in the symbols which make up *the religion proper*, and, second, the relating of these systems to social-structural and psychological processes" (125; emphasis added). How sensible this sounds, yet how mistaken, surely, it is. If religious symbols are understood, on the analogy with words, as vehicles for meaning, can such meanings be established independently of the form of life in which they are used? If religious symbols are to be taken as the signatures of a sacred text, can we know what they mean without regard to the social disciplines by which their correct reading is secured? If religious symbols are to be thought of as the concepts by which experiences are organized, can we say much about them without considering how they come to be authorized? Even if it be claimed that what is experienced through religious symbols is not, in essence, the social world but the spiritual,[14] is it possible to assert that conditions in the social world have nothing to do with making that kind of experience accessible? Is the concept of religious training entirely vacuous?

The two stages that Geertz proposes are, I would suggest, one. Religious symbols – whether one thinks of them in terms of communication or of cognition, of guiding action or of expressing emotion – cannot be understood independently of their historical relations with nonreligious symbols or of their articulations in and of social life, in which work and power are always crucial. My argument, I must stress, is not just that religious symbols are intimately linked to social life (and so change with it), or that they usually support dominant political power (and occasionally oppose it). It is that different kinds of practice and discourse are intrinsic to the field in which religious representations (like any representation) acquire their identity and their truthfulness. From this it does not follow that the meanings of religious practices and utterances are to be sought in social phenomena, but only that their possibility and their authoritative status are to be explained as products of historically distinctive disciplines and forces. The anthropological student of *particular* religions should therefore begin from this point, in a sense unpacking the comprehensive concept which he or she translates as "religion" into heterogeneous elements according to its historical character.

A final word of caution. Hasty readers might conclude that my discussion of the Christian religion is skewed towards an authoritarian, centralized, elite perspective, and that consequently it fails to take into account the religions of heterodox believers, of resistant peasantries, of all those who cannot be completely controlled by the orthodox church. Or, worse still, that my discussion has no bearing on nondisciplinarian, voluntaristic, localized cults of noncentralized religions such as Hinduism. But that conclusion would be a misunderstanding of this chapter, seeing in it an attempt to advocate a better anthropological definition of religion than Geertz has done. Nothing could be farther from my intention. If my effort reads in large part like a brief sketch of transmutations in Christianity from the Middle Ages until today, then that is not because I have arbitrarily confined my ethnographic examples to one religion. My aim has been to problematize the idea of an anthropological definition of religion by assigning that endeavor to a particular history of knowledge and power (including a particular understanding of our legitimate past and future) out of which the modern world has been constructed.

QUESTIONS FOR REVIEW AND DISCUSSION

1. Why does Asad choose to start with Geertz's "Religion as a Cultural System" to present his argument? What is the argument that Asad wishes to make?

2. What is Asad's point regarding attending to the conditions under which symbols are constructed? What is his critique of Geertz's notion of symbols as "models *of*" and "models *for*"? Is this critique justified?

3. Asad argues that Geertz sets symbols apart from mental states. Do you agree? What does Asad insist are important components to developing the character and experience of a religious person?

4. Explain Asad's example of St. Augustine's arguments about the role of coercion when dealing with the Donatist heresy. For what purpose does Asad use this example?

5. What, according to Asad, are the processes through which religion becomes an "abstracted and universalized" category, instead of a "concrete set of practical rules attached to specific processes of power and knowledge"?

6. What is Asad's argument that Geertz's definition inadvertently takes up "the standpoint of theology"? Do you agree?

7. What does Asad mean by Geertz's perspectivism, and why does Asad maintain that science in today's world is not a perspective, the way that religion now is? Do you agree?

8. What is Asad's point about the phenomenological approach as it plays out in the relationship between the common-sense and religious perspectives as argued by Geertz? Do you agree with Asad's appraisal?

9. What does Asad propose as a starting point for the anthropological study of religion, and how does it differ from Geertz's proposal? Do you agree with his prescription?

Notes

1 Thus, Fustel de Coulanges (1873). Originally published in French in 1864, this was an influential work in the history of several overlapping disciplines – anthropology, biblical studies, and classics.

2 Compare Peirce's more rigorous account of *representations*. A representation is an object which stands for another so that an experience of the former affords us a knowledge of the latter. There must be three essential conditions to which every representation must conform. It must in the first place like any other object have qualities independent of its meaning. ... In the 2nd place a representation must have a real causal connection with its object. ... In the third place, every representation addresses itself to a mind. It is only in so far as it does this that it is a representation (Peirce 1986, 62).

3 Vygotsky (1962) makes crucial analytical distinctions in the development of conceptual thought: heaps, complexes, pseudoconcepts, and true concepts. Although, according to Vygotsky, these represent stages in the development of children's use of language, the earlier stages persist into adult life.

4 The argument that symbols *organize practice*, and consequently the structure of cognition, is central to Vygotsky's genetic psychology – see especially "Tool and Symbol in Child Development," in Vygotsky 1978. A cognitive conception of symbols has recently been revived by Sperber (1975). A similar view was taken much earlier by Lienhardt (1961).

5 Or, as Kroeber and Kluckhohn (1952, 181) put it much earlier, "Culture consists of patterns, explicit and implicit, of and for behaviour acquired and transmitted by symbols."

6 If we set aside Radcliffe-Brown's well-known preoccupation with social cohesion, we may recall that he too was concerned to specify certain kinds of psychological states said to be induced by religious symbols: "Rites can be seen to be the regulated symbolic expressions of certain sentiments (which control the behaviour of the individual in his relation to others). Rites can therefore be shown to have a specific social function when, and to the extent that, they have for their effect

to regulate, maintain and transmit from one generation to another sentiments on which the constitution of society depends" (1952, 157).

7 The series of booklets known as penitential manuals, with the aid of which Christian discipline was imposed on Western Europe from roughly the fifth to the tenth centuries, contains much material on pagan practices penalized as un-Christian. So, for example, "The taking of vows or releasing from them by springs or trees or lattices, anywhere except in a church, and partaking of food or drink in these places sacred to the folk-*I* deities, are offenses condemned" (quoted in McNeill 1933, 456).

8 The Church always exercised the authority to read Christian *practice* for its religious truth. In this context, it is interesting that the word *heresy* at first designated all kinds of errors, including errors "unconsciously" involved in some activity *(simoniaca haersis)*, and it acquired its specific modern meaning (the verbal formulation of denial or doubt of any defined doctrine of the Catholic church) only in the course of the methodological controversies of the sixteenth century (Chenu 1968, 276).

9 In the early Middle Ages, monastic discipline was the principal basis of religiosity. Knowles (1963, 3) observes that: from roughly the sixth to the twelfth centuries, "monastic life based on the Rule of St. Benedict was everywhere the norm and exercised from time to time a paramount influence on the spiritual, intellectual, liturgical and apostolic life of the Western Church ... the only type of religious life available in the countries concerned was monastic, and the only monastic code was the Rule of St. Benedict." During the period the very term *religious* was therefore reserved for those living in monastic communities; with the later emergence of nonmonastic orders, the term came to be used for all who had taken lifelong vows by which they were set apart from the ordinary members of the Church (Southern 1970, 214). The extension and simultaneous transformation of the religious disciplines to lay sections of society from the twelfth century onward (Chenu 1968) contributed to the Church's authority becoming more pervasive, more complex, and more contradictory than before – and so too the articulation of the concept and practice of lay religion.

10 When Christian missionaries found themselves in culturally unfamiliar territory, the problem of identifying "religion" became a matter of considerable theoretical difficulty and practical importance. For example, the Jesuits in China contended that the reverence for ancestors was a social, not a religious, act, or that if religious, it was hardly different from Catholic prayers for the dead. They wished the Chinese to regard Christianity, not as a replacement, not as a new religion, but as the highest fulfillment of their finest aspirations. But to their opponents the Jesuits appeared to be merely lax. In 1631 a Franciscan and a Dominican from the Spanish zone of Manila travelled (illegally, from the Portuguese viewpoint) to Peking and found that to translate the word *mass*, the Jesuit catechism used the character *tsi*, which was the Chinese description of the ceremonies of ancestor-worship. One night they went in disguise to such a ceremony, observed Chinese Christians participating and were scandalized at what they saw. So began the quarrel of "the rites," which plagued the eastern missions for a century and more (Chadwick 1964, 338).

11 For example, by Tylor in the chapter "Animism" in part 2 of *Primitive Culture* [see chapter 1].

12 When the fifth-century bishop of Javols spread Christianity into the Auvergne, he found the peasants "celebrating a three-day festival with offerings on the edge of a marsh 'Nulla est religio in stagno,' he said: There can be no religion in a swamp" (Brown 1981, 125). For medieval Christians, religion was not a universal phenomenon: religion was a site on which universal truth was produced, and it was clear to them that truth was not produced universally.

13 In the introduction to his 1983 collection of essays, Geertz seems to want to abandon this perspectival approach.

14 Cf. the final chapter in Evans-Pritchard 1956, and also the conclusion to Evans-Pritchard 1965.

Bibliography

Asad, T. 1986. "Medieval Heresy: An Anthropological View." *Social History* II, no. 3.

Brown, P. 1967. *Augustine of Hippo*. London: Faber and Faber.

——. 1981. *The Cult of the Saints: Its Rise and Function in Latin Christianity*. London: SCM.

Burckhardt, J. 1950 [1860]. *The Civilization of the Renaissance in Italy*. London: Phaidon.

Burling, R. 1977. Review of *Political Language and Oratory in Traditional Society*, by Maurice Bloch. *American Anthropologist* 79, no.3.

Burns, E. 1990. *Character: Acting and Being on the Pre-Modern Stage.* New York: St. Martin's.

Butler, C. 1924. *Benedictine Monasticism.* Cambridge: Cambridge Univ. Press.

Butterfield, H. 1931. *The Whig Interpretation of History.* London: Bell.

Bynum, C. W. 1980. "Did the Twelfth Century Discover the Individual?" *Journal of Ecclesiastical History* 31, no. 1.

Caenegem, R. C. van. 1965. "La preuve dans le droit du moyen age occidental." *La Preuve,* Recueils de la societe Jean Bodin pour l'histoire comparative des institutions, vol. 17. Brussels.

Chadwick, O. 1964. *The Reformation.* Harmondsworth, Middlesex: Penguin.

Chenu, M. I. 1968. *Nature, Man, and Society in the Twelfth Century: Essays on Theological Perspectives in the Latin West.* Chicago: Univ. of Chicago Press.

Coulanges, Fustel de. 1873. *The Ancient City: A Study on the Religion, Laws, and Institutions of Greece and Rome.* Boston: Lothrop, Lee and Shepherd.

Dumont, L. 1971. "Religion, Politics, and Society in the Individualistic Universe." *Proceedings of the Royal Anthropological Institute for 1970.*

Evans-Pritchard, E. E. 1956. *Nuer Religion.* Oxford: Clarendon.

——. 1965. *Theories of Primitive Religion.* Oxford: Clarendon.

Geertz, C. 1973. *The Interpretation of Cultures.* New York: Basic Books.

——. 1983. *Local Knowledge: Further Essays in Interpretive Anthropology.* New York: Basic Books.

Harré, R. 1981. "Psychological Variety." In *Indigenous Psychologies,* edited by P. lleelas and A. Lock. London: Academic Press.

Harrison, P. 1990. *"Religion" and the Religions in the English Enlightenment.* Cambridge: Cambridge Univ. Press.

Kant, I. 1991. *Kant: Political Writings.* Edited by H. Reiss. Cambridge: Cambridge Univ. Press.

Knowles, M. IX, ed. 1963. *The Monastic Order in England: 940–1216.* 2d ed. Cambridge: Cambridge Univ. Press.

Kroeber, A. L., and C. Kluckhohn. 1952. *Culture: A Critical Review of Concepts and Definitions.* Papers of the Peabody Museum, vol. 47, no. 1. Cambridge, Mass.: Peabody Museum.

Lea, H. C. 1896. *A History of Auricular Confession and Indulgences in the Latin Church.* 3 vols. Philadelphia: Lea Bros.

Leach, E. R. 1954. *Political Systems of Highland Burma.* London: Bell.

——. 1973. "Ourselves and Others." *Times Literary Supplement,* 6 July.

Leavitt, J. 1986. "Strategies for the Interpretation of Affect." Manuscript.

Leclercq, J. 1957. "Disciplina." In *Dictionnaire de Spiritualite,* 3. Paris: Beauchesne.

——. 1966. "The Intentions of the Founders of the Cistercian Order." *Cistercian Studies* 4.

——. 1971. "Le cloitre est-il une prison?" *Revue d'ascétique et de mystique* 47.

——. 1977. *The Love of Learning and the Desire for God: A Study of Monastic Culture.* 2nd ed. New York: Fordham Univ. Press.

——. 1979. *Monks and Love in Twelfth-Century France.* Oxford: Oxford Univ. Press.

Leclercq, J., and G. Gartner. 1965. "S. Bernard dans l'histoire de l'obeissance monastique." *Annuario De Estudios Medievales 2.*

Le Goff, J. 1980. *Time, Work, and Culture in the Middle Ages.* Chicago: Univ. of Chicago Press.

Lekai, L. J. 1977. *The Cistercians: Ideals and Reality.* Kent, Ohio: Kent State Univ. Press.

Lerner, D. 1958. *The Passing of Traditional Society: Modernizing the Middle East.* New York: Free Press.

Levi, A. 1964. *French Moralists: The Theory of the Passions, 1585 to 1649.* Oxford: Clarendon.

Lienhardt, G. 1961. *Divinity and Experience.* Oxford: Clarendon.

McNeill, J. T. 1933. "Folk-Paganism in the Penitentials." *Journal of Religion* 13.

Needham, R. 1972. *Belief, Language, and Experience.* Oxford: Basil Blackwell.

Peirce, C. S. 1986. *Writings of C. S. Peirce.* Vol. 3. Bloomington: Indiana Univ. Press.

Radcliffe-Brown, A. R. 1952 [1939]. "Taboo." In *Structure and Function in Primitive Society.* London: Cohen and West.

Southern, R. W. 1970. *Western Society and the Church in the Middle Ages.* Harmondsworth, Middlesex: Penguin.

Southwold, M. 1979. "Religious Belief." *Man*, n.s. 14.

Sperber, D. 1975. *Rethinking Symbolism*. Cambridge: Cambridge Univ. Press.

Tylor, E. B. 1871. *Primitive Culture*. London: J. Murray.

Vygotsky, L. S. 1962 [1934]. *Thought and Language*. Cambridge, Mass.: MIT Press.

——. 1978. *Mind in Society*. Cambridge, Mass.: Harvard Univ. Press.

25 Civil Religion in America[1]

Robert N. Bellah

Robert N. Bellah (1927–) is an American sociologist who received his doctorate from Harvard, where he also taught for a decade. The article in this volume, "Civil Religion in America," was published in 1967, at the beginning of his thirty-year career as the Ford Professor of Sociology at the University of California, Berkeley. In this well-known essay, Bellah articulates an overlooked religious dimension. His career has encompassed many regions, eras, and topics that delve into the complexity of society and culture from early work on Japanese religion, such as *Tokugawa Religion: The Values of Pre-Industrial Japan* (1957) to *Habits of the Heart: Individualism and Commitment in American Life* (1985) and *The Good Society* (1991). The breadth and depth of his ongoing contributions to the study of religion is illustrated by the 2011 publication of his most ambitious work, *Religion in Human Evolution: From the Paleolithic to the Axial Age.* His attention to evolutionary psychology, cognitive science, and biology as well as to diverse early civilizations of China, India, Greece, and ancient Israel in this 784-page tome demonstrates Bellah's commitment to the intellectual scope of his own teacher, Talcott Parsons, who "never recognized any disciplinary boundary and tended to define sociology as concerned with the world and its contents."[2]

While some have argued that Christianity is the national faith, and others that church and synagogue celebrate only the generalized religion of "the American Way of Life," few have realized that there actually exists alongside of and rather clearly differentiated from the churches an elaborate and well-institutionalized civil religion in America. This article argues not only that there is such a thing, but also that this religion—or perhaps better, this religious dimension—has its own seriousness and integrity and requires the same care in understanding that any other religion does.[3]

The Kennedy Inaugural

John F. Kennedy's inaugural address of January 20, 1961, serves as an example and a clue with which to introduce this complex subject. That address began:

> We observe today not a victory of party but a celebration of freedom—symbolizing an end as well as a beginning—signifying renewal as well as change. For I have sworn before you and Almighty God the same solemn oath our forebears prescribed nearly a century and three quarters ago.

The world is very different now. For man holds in his mortal hands the power to abolish all forms of human poverty and to abolish all forms of human life. And yet the same revolutionary beliefs for which our forbears fought are still at issue around the globe—the belief that the rights of man come not from the generosity of the state but from the hand of God.

And it concluded:

Finally, whether you are citizens of America or of the world, ask of us the same high standards of strength and sacrifice that we shall ask of you. With a good conscience our only sure reward, with history the final judge of our deeds, let us go forth to lead the land we love, asking His blessing and His help, but knowing that here on earth God's work must truly be our own.

These are the three places in this brief address in which Kennedy mentioned the name of God. If we could understand why he mentioned God, the way in which he did, and what he meant to say in those three references, we would understand much about American civil religion. But this is not a simple or obvious task, and American students of religion would probably differ widely in their interpretation of these passages.

Let us consider first the placing of the three references. They occur in the two opening paragraphs and in the closing paragraph, thus providing a sort of frame for more concrete remarks that form the middle part of the speech. Looking beyond this particular speech, we would find that similar references to God are almost invariably to be found in the pronouncements of American presidents on solemn occasions, though usually not in the working messages that the President sends to Congress on various concrete issues. How, then, are we to interpret this placing of references to God?

It might be argued that the passages quoted reveal the essentially irrelevant role of religion in the very secular society that is America. The placing of the references in this speech as well as in public life generally indicates that religion "has only a ceremonial significance"; it gets only a sentimental nod that serves largely to placate the more unenlightened members of the community before a discussion of the really serious business with which religion has nothing whatever to do. A cynical observer might even say that an American President has to mention God or risk losing votes. A semblance of piety is merely one of the unwritten qualifications for the office, a bit more traditional than but not essentially different from the present-day requirement of a pleasing television personality.

But we know enough about the function of ceremonial and ritual in various societies to make us suspicious of dismissing something as unimportant because it is "only a ritual." What people say on solemn occasions need not be taken at face value, but it is often indicative of deep-seated values and commitments that are not made explicit in the course of everyday life. Following this line of argument, it is worth considering whether the very special placing of the references to God in Kennedy's address may not reveal something rather important and serious about religion in American life.

It might be countered that the very way in which Kennedy made his references reveals the essentially vestigial place of religion today. He did not refer to any religion in particular. He did not refer to Jesus Christ, or to Moses, or to the Christian church; certainly he did not refer to the Catholic church. In fact, his only reference was to the concept of God, a word that almost all Americans can accept but that means so many different things to so many different people that it is almost an empty sign. Is this not just another indication that in America religion is considered vaguely to be a good thing, but that people care so little about it that it has lost any content whatever? Isn't Dwight Eisenhower reported to have said "Our government makes no sense unless it is founded in a deeply felt religious faith—and I don't care what it is,"[4] and isn't that a complete negation of any real religion?

These questions are worth pursuing because they raise the issue of how civil religion relates to the political society on the one hand and to private religious organization on the other. President Kennedy was a Christian, more specifically a Catholic Christian. Thus his general references to God do not mean that he lacked a specific religious commitment. But why, then, did he not include some remark to the effect that Christ is the Lord of the world or some indication of respect for the Catholic church? He did not because these are matters of his own private religious belief and of his own particular church; they are not matters relevant in any direct way to the conduct of his public office. Others with different religious views and commitments to different churches or denominations are equally qualified participants in the political process. The principle of separation of church and state guarantees the freedom of religious belief and association, but at the same time clearly segregates the religious sphere, which is considered to be essentially private, from the political one.

Considering the separation of church and state, how is a president justified in using the word "God" at all? The answer is that the separation of church and state has not denied the political realm a religious dimension. Although matters of personal religious belief, worship, and association are considered to be strictly private affairs, there are, at the same time, certain common elements of religious orientation that the great majority of Americans share. These have played a crucial role in the development of American institutions and still provide a religious dimension for the whole fabric of American life, including the political sphere. This public religious dimension is expressed in a set of beliefs, symbols, and rituals that I am calling American civil religion. The inauguration of a president is an important ceremonial event in this religion. It reaffirms, among other things, the religious legitimation of the highest political authority.

Let us look more closely at what Kennedy actually said. First, he said, "I have sworn before you and Almighty God the same solemn oath our forbears prescribed nearly a century and three quarters ago." The oath is the oath of office, including the acceptance of the obligation to uphold the Constitution. He swears it before the people (you) and God. Beyond the Constitution, then, the president's obligation extends not only to the people but to God. In American political theory, sovereignty rests, of course, with the people, but implicitly, and often explicitly, the ultimate sovereignty has been attributed to God. This is the meaning of the motto, "In God we trust," as well as the inclusion of the phrase "under God" in the pledge to the flag. What difference does it make that sovereignty belongs to God? Though the will of the people as expressed in the majority vote is carefully institutionalized as the operative source of political authority, it is deprived of an ultimate significance. The will of the people is not itself the criterion of right and wrong. There is a higher criterion in terms of which this will can be judged; it is possible that the people may be wrong. The president's obligation extends to the higher criterion.

When Kennedy says that "the rights of man come not from the generosity of the state but from the hand of God," he is stressing this point again. It does not matter whether the state is the expression of the will of an autocratic monarch or of the "people"; the rights of man are more basic than any political structure and provide a point of revolutionary leverage from which any state structure may be radically altered. That is the basis for his reassertion of the revolutionary significance of America.

But the religious dimension of political life as recognized by Kennedy not only provides a grounding for the rights of man that makes any form of political absolutism illegitimate, it also provides a transcendent goal for the political process. This is implied in his final words that "here on earth God's work must truly be our own." What he means here is, I think, more clearly spelled out in a previous paragraph, the wording of which, incidentally, has a distinctly biblical ring:

> Now the trumpet summons us again—not as a call to bear arms, though arms we need—not as a call to battle, though embattled we are—but a call to bear the burden of a long twilight struggle, year in and year out, "rejoicing in hope, patient in tribulation"—a struggle against the common enemies of man: tyranny, poverty, disease and war itself.

The whole address can be understood as only the most recent statement of a theme that lies very deep in the American tradition, namely the obligation, both collective and individual, to carry out God's will on earth. This was the motivating spirit of those who founded America, and it has been present in every generation since. Just below the surface throughout Kennedy's inaugural address, it becomes explicit in the closing statement that God's work must be our own. That this very activist and noncontemplative conception of the fundamental religious obligation, which has been historically associated with the Protestant position, should be enunciated so clearly in the first major statement of the first Catholic president seems to underline how deeply established it is in the American outlook. Let us now consider the form and history of the civil religious tradition in which Kennedy was speaking.

The Idea of a Civil Religion

The phrase "civil religion" is, of course, Rousseau's. In chapter 8, book 4 of *The Social Contract*, he outlines the simple dogmas of the civil religion: the existence of God, the life to come, the reward of virtue and the punishment of vice, and the exclusion of religious intolerance. All other religious opinions are outside the cognizance of the state and may be freely held by citizens. While the phrase "civil religion" was not used, to the best of my knowledge, by the founding fathers, and I am certainly not arguing for the particular influence of Rousseau, it is clear that similar ideas, as part of the cultural climate of the late eighteenth century, were to be found among the Americans. For example, Benjamin Franklin writes in his autobiography,

> I never was without some religious principles. I never doubted, for instance, the existence of the Deity; that he made the world and govern'd it by his Providence; that the most acceptable service of God was the doing of good to men; that our souls are immortal; and that all crime will be punished, and virtue rewarded either here or hereafter. These I esteemed the essentials of every religion; and, being to be found in all the religions we had in our country, I respected them all, tho' with different degrees of respect, as I found them more or less mix'd with other articles, which, without any tendency to inspire, promote or confirm morality, serv'd principally to divide us, and make us unfriendly to one another.

It is easy to dispose of this sort of position as essentially utilitarian in relation to religion. In Washington's Farewell Address (though the words may be Hamilton's) the utilitarian aspect is quite explicit:

Of all the dispositions and habits which lead to political prosperity, Religion and Morality are indispensable supports. In vain would that man claim the tribute of Patriotism, who should labour to subvert these great Pillars of human happiness, these firmest props of the duties of men and citizens. The mere politician, equally with the pious man ought to cherish and respect them. A volume could not trace all their connections with private and public felicity. Let it simply be asked where is the security for property, for reputation, for life, if the sense of religious obligation *desert* the oaths, which are the instruments of investigation in Courts of Justice? And let us with caution indulge the supposition, that morality can be maintained without religion. Whatever may be conceded to the influence of refined education on minds of peculiar structure, reason and experience both forbid us to expect that National morality can prevail in exclusion of religious principle.

But there is every reason to believe that religion, particularly the idea of God, played a constitutive role in the thought of the early American statesmen.

Kennedy's inaugural pointed to the religious aspect of the Declaration of Independence, and it might be well to look at that document a bit more closely. There are four references to God. The first speaks of the "Laws of Nature and of Nature's God" that entitle any people to be independent. The second is the famous statement that all men "are endowed by their Creator with certain inalienable Rights." Here Jefferson is locating the fundamental legitimacy of the new nation in a conception of "higher law" that is itself based on both classical natural law and biblical religion. The third is an appeal to "the Supreme Judge of the world for the rectitude of our intentions," and the last indicates "a firm reliance on the protection of divine Providence." In these last two references, a biblical God of history who stands in judgment over the world is indicated.

The intimate relation of these religious notions with the self-conception of the new republic is indicated by the frequency of their appearance in early official documents. For example, we find in Washington's first inaugural address of April 30, 1789:

It would be peculiarly improper to omit in this first official act my fervent supplications to that Almighty Being who rules over the universe, who presides in the councils of nations, and whose providential aids can supply every defect, that His benediction may consecrate to the liberties and happiness of the people of the United States a Government instituted by themselves for these essential purposes, and may enable every instrument employed in its administration to execute with success the functions allotted to his charge.

No people can be bound to acknowledge and adore the Invisible Hand which conducts the affairs of man more than those of the United States. Every step by which we have advanced to the character of an independent nation seems to have been distinguished by some token providential agency. ...

The propitious smiles of Heaven can never be expected on a nation that disregards the eternal rules of order and right which Heaven itself has ordained. ... The preservation of the sacred fire of liberty and the destiny of the republican model of government are justly considered, perhaps, as deeply, as finally, staked on the experiment intrusted to the hands of the American people.

Nor did these religious sentiments remain merely the personal expression of the President. At the request of both Houses of Congress, Washington proclaimed on October 3 of that same first year as President that November 26 should be "a day of public thanksgiving and prayer," the first Thanksgiving Day under the Constitution.

The words and acts of the founding fathers, especially the first few presidents, shaped the form and tone of the civil religion as it has been maintained ever since. Though much is selectively derived from Christianity, this religion is clearly not itself Christianity. For one thing, neither Washington nor Adams nor Jefferson mentions Christ in his inaugural address; nor do any of the subsequent presidents, although not one of them fails to mention God.[5] The God of the civil religion is not only rather "unitarian," he is also on the austere side, much more related to order, law, and right than to salvation and love. Even though he is somewhat deist in cast, he is by no means simply a watchmaker God. He is actively interested and involved in history, with a special concern for America. Here the analogy has much less to do with natural law than with ancient Israel; the equation of America with Israel in the idea of the "American Israel" is not infrequent.[6] What was implicit in the words of Washington already quoted becomes explicit in Jefferson's second inaugural when he said: "I shall need, too, the favor of that Being in whose hands we are, who led our fathers, as Israel of old, from their native land and planted them in a country flowing with all the necessaries and comforts of life." Europe is Egypt; America, the promised land. God has led his people to establish a new sort of social order that shall be a light unto all the nations.[7] This theme, too, has been a continuous one in the civil religion. We have already alluded to it in the case of the Kennedy inaugural. We find it again in President Johnson's inaugural address:

> They came already here—the exile and the stranger, brave but frightened—to find a place where a man could be his own man. They made a covenant with this land. Conceived in justice, written in liberty, bound in union, it was meant one day to inspire the hopes of all mankind; and it binds us still. If we keep its terms, we shall flourish.

What we have, then, from the earliest years of the republic is a collection of beliefs, symbols, and rituals with respect to sacred things and institutionalized in a collectivity. This religion—there seems no other word for it—while not antithetical to and indeed sharing much in common with Christianity, was neither sectarian nor in any specific sense Christian. At a time when the society was overwhelmingly Christian, it seems unlikely that this lack of Christian reference was meant to spare the feelings of the tiny non-Christian minority. Rather, the civil religion expressed what those who set the precedents felt was appropriate under the circumstances. It reflected their private as well as public views. Nor was the civil religion simply "religion in general." While generality was undoubtedly seen as a virtue by some, as in the quotation from Franklin above, the civil religion was specific enough when it came to the topic of America. Precisely because of this specificity, the civil religion was saved from empty formalism and served as a genuine vehicle of national religious self-understanding.

But the civil religion was not, in the minds of Franklin, Washington, Jefferson, or other leaders, with the exception of a few radicals like Tom Paine, ever felt to be a substitute for Christianity. There was an implicit but quite clear division of function between the civil religion and Christianity. Under the doctrine of religious liberty, an exceptionally wide sphere of personal piety and voluntary social action was left to the churches. But the churches were neither to control the state nor to be controlled by it. The national magistrate, whatever his private religious views, operates under the rubrics of the civil religion as long as he is in his official capacity, as we have already seen in the case of Kennedy. This accommodation was undoubtedly the product of a particular historical moment and of a cultural background dominated by Protestantism of several varieties and by the Enlightenment, but it has survived despite subsequent changes in the cultural and religious climate.

Civil War and Civil Religion

Until the Civil War, the American civil religion focused above all on the event of the Revolution, which was seen as the final act of the Exodus from the old lands across the waters. The Declaration of Independence and the Constitution were the sacred scriptures and Washington the divinely appointed Moses who led his people out of the hands of tyranny. The Civil War, which Sidney Mead calls "the center of American history,"[8] was the second great event that involved the national self-understanding so deeply as to require expression in civil religion. In 1835, Alexis de Tocqueville wrote that the American republic has never really been tried and that victory in the Revolutionary War was more the result of British preoccupation elsewhere and the presence of a powerful ally than of any great military success of the Americans. But in 1861 the time of testing had indeed come. Not only did the Civil War have the tragic intensity of fratricidal strife, but it was one of the bloodiest wars of the nineteenth century; the loss of life was far greater than any previously suffered by Americans.

The Civil War raised the deepest questions of national meaning. The man who not only formulated but in his own person embodied its meaning for Americans was Abraham Lincoln. For him the issue was not in the first instance slavery but "whether that nation, or any nation so conceived, and so dedicated, can long endure." He had said in Independence Hall in Philadelphia on February 22, 1861:

> All the political sentiments I entertain have been drawn, so far as I have been able to draw them, from the sentiments which originated in and were given to the world from this Hall. I have never had a feeling, politically, that did not spring from the sentiments embodied in the Declaration of Independence.[9]

The phrases of Jefferson constantly echo in Lincoln's speeches. His task was, first of all, to save the Union—not for America alone but for the meaning of America to the whole world so unforgettably etched in the last phrase of the Gettysburg Address.

But inevitably the issue of slavery as the deeper cause of the conflict had to be faced. In his second inaugural, Lincoln related slavery and the war in an ultimate perspective:

> If we shall suppose that American slavery is one of those offenses which, in the providence of God, must needs come, but which, having continued through His appointed time, He now wills to remove, and that He gives to both North and South this terrible war as the woe due to those by whom the offense came, shall we discern therein any departure from those divine attributes which the believers in a living God always ascribe to Him? Fondly do we hope, fervently do we pray, that this mighty scourge of war may speedily pass away. Yet, if God wills that it continue until all the wealth piled by the bondsman's two hundred and fifty years of unrequited toil shall be sunk, and until every drop of blood drawn with the lash shall be paid by another drawn with the sword, as was said three thousand years ago, so still it must be said "the judgements of the Lord are true and righteous altogether."

But he closes on a note if not of redemption then of reconciliation—"With malice toward none, with charity for all."

With the Civil War, a new theme of death, sacrifice, and rebirth enters the new civil religion. It is symbolized in the life and death of Lincoln. Nowhere is it stated more vividly than in the Gettysburg Address, itself part of the Lincolnian "New Testament" among the civil scriptures. Robert Lowell has recently pointed out the "insistent use of birth images" in this speech explicitly devoted to "these honored dead": "brought forth," "conceived," "created," "a new birth of freedom." He goes on to say:

> The Gettysburg Address is a symbolic and sacramental act. Its verbal quality is resonance combined with a logical, matter of fact, prosaic brevity. ... In his words, Lincoln symbolically died, just as the Union soldiers really died—and as he himself was soon really to die. By his words, he gave the field of battle a symbolic significance that it has lacked. For us and our country, he left Jefferson's ideals of freedom and equality joined to the Christian sacrificial act of death and rebirth. I believe this is the meaning that goes beyond sect or religion and beyond peace and war, and is now part of our lives as a challenge, obstacle and hope.[10]

Lowell is certainly right in pointing out the Christian quality of the symbolism here, but he is also right in quickly disavowing any sectarian implication. The earlier symbolism of the civil religion had been Hebraic without any specific sense of being Jewish. The Gettysburg symbolism (" ... those who here gave their lives, that that nation might live") is Christian without having anything to do with the Christian church.

The symbolic equation of Lincoln with Jesus was made relatively early. W. H. Herndon, who had been Lincoln's law partner, wrote:

> For fifty years God rolled Abraham Lincoln through his fiery furnace. He did it to try Abraham and to purify him for his purposes. This made Mr. Lincoln humble, tender, forbearing, sympathetic to suffering, kind, sensitive, tolerant; broadening, deepening and widening his whole nature; making him the noblest and loveliest character since Jesus Christ. ... I believe that Lincoln was God's chosen one.[11]

With the Christian archetype in the background, Lincoln, "our martyred president," was linked to the war dead, those who "gave the last full measure of devotion." The theme of sacrifice was indelibly written into the civil religion.

The new symbolism soon found both physical and ritualistic expression. The great number of the war dead required the establishment of a number of national cemeteries. Of these, Gettysburg National Cemetery, which Lincoln's famous address served to dedicate, has been overshadowed only by the Arlington National Cemetery. Begun somewhat vindictively on the Lee estate across the river from Washington, partly with the end that the Lee family could never reclaim it,[12] it has subsequently become the most hallowed monument of the civil religion. Not only was a section set aside for the confederate dead, but it has received the dead of each succeeding American war. It is the site of the one important new symbol to come out of World War I, the Tomb of the Unknown Soldier; more recently it has become the site of the tomb of another martyred President and its symbolic eternal flame.

Memorial Day, which grew out of the Civil War, gave ritual expression to the themes we have been discussing. As Lloyd Warner has so brilliantly analyzed it, the Memorial Day observance, especially in the towns and smaller cities of America, is a major event for the whole community involving a rededication to the martyred dead, to the spirit of sacrifice, and to the American vision.[13] Just as Thanksgiving Day, which incidentally was securely institutionalized as an annual national holiday only under the presidency of Lincoln, serves to integrate the family into the civil religion, so Memorial Day has acted to integrate the local community into the national cult. Together with the less overtly religious Fourth of July and the more minor celebrations of Veterans Day and the birthdays of Washington and Lincoln, these two holidays provide an annual ritual calendar for the civil religion. The public school system serves as a particularly important context for the cultic celebration of the civil rituals.

The Civil Religion Today

In reifying and giving a name to something that, though pervasive enough when you look at it, has gone on only semiconsciously, there is risk of severely distorting the data. But the reification and the naming have already begun. The religious critics of "religion in general," or of the "religion of the 'American Way of Life,'" or of "American Shinto" have really been talking about the civil religion. As usual in religious polemic, they take as criteria the best in their own religious tradition and as typical the worst in the tradition of the civil religion. Against these critics, I would argue that the civil religion at its best is a genuine apprehension of universal and transcendent religious reality as seen in or, one could almost say, as revealed through the experience of the American people. Like all religions, it has suffered various deformations and demonic distortions. At its best, it has neither been so general that it has lacked incisive relevance to the American scene nor so particular that it has placed American society above universal human values. I am not at all convinced that the leaders of the churches have consistently represented a higher level of religious insight than the spokesmen of the civil religion. Reinhold Niebuhr has this to say of Lincoln, who never joined a church and who certainly represents civil religion at its best:

> An analysis of the religion of Abraham Lincoln in the context of the traditional religion of his time and place and of its polemical use on the slavery issue, which corrupted religious life in the days before and during the Civil War, must lead to the conclusion that Lincoln's religious convictions were superior in depth and purity to those, not only of the political leaders of his day, but of the religious leaders of the era.[14]

Perhaps the real animus of the religious critics has been not so much against the civil religion in itself but against its pervasive and dominating influence within the sphere of church religion. As S. M. Lipset has recently shown, American religion at least since the early nineteenth century has been predominantly activist, moralistic, and social rather than contemplative, theological, or innerly spiritual.[15] De Tocqueville spoke of American church religion as "a political institution which powerfully contributes to the maintenance of a democratic republic among the Americans"[16] by supplying a strong moral consensus amidst continuous political change. Henry Bargy in 1902 spoke of American church religion as "*la poésie du civisme*."[17]

It is certainly true that the relation between religion and politics in America has been singularly smooth. This is in large part due to the dominant tradition. As de Tocqueville wrote:

The greatest part of British America was peopled by men who, after having shaken off the authority of the Pope, acknowledged no other religious supremacy: they brought with them into the New World a form of Christianity which I cannot better describe than by styling it a democratic and republican religion.[18]

The churches opposed neither the Revolution nor the establishment of democratic institutions. Even when some of them opposed the full institutionalization of religious liberty, they accepted the final outcome with good grace and without nostalgia for the *ancien régime.*

The American civil religion was never anticlerical or militantly secular. On the contrary, it borrowed selectively from the religious tradition in such a way that the average American saw no conflict between the two. In this way, the civil religion was able to build up without any bitter struggle with the church powerful symbols of national solidarity and to mobilize deep levels of personal motivation for the attainment of national goals.

Such an achievement is by no means to be taken for granted. It would seem that the problem of a civil religion is quite general in modern societies and that the way it is solved or not solved will have repercussions in many spheres. One need only to think of France to see how differently things can go. The French Revolution was anticlerical to the core and attempted to set up an anti-Christian civil religion. Throughout modern French history, the chasm between traditional Catholic symbols and the symbolism of 1789 has been immense.

American civil religion is still very much alive. Just three years ago we participated in a vivid reenactment of the sacrifice theme in connection with the funeral of our assassinated President. The American Israel theme is clearly behind both Kennedy's New Frontier and Johnson's Great Society. Let me give just one recent illustration of how the civil religion serves to mobilize support for the attainment of national goals. On March 15, 1965, President Johnson went before Congress to ask for a strong voting-rights bill. Early in the speech he said:

> Rarely are we met with the challenge, not to our growth or abundance, or our welfare or our society—but rather to the values and the purposes and the meaning of our beloved nation.
>
> The issue of equal rights for American Negroes is such an issue. And should we double our wealth and conquer the stars and still be unequal to this issue, then we will have failed as a people and as a nation.
>
> For with a country as with a person, "What is a man profited, if he shall gain the whole world, and lose his own soul."

And in conclusion he said:

> Above the pyramid on the great seal of the United States it says in Latin, "God has favored our undertaking."
>
> God will not favor everything that we do. It is rather our duty to divine his will. I cannot help but believe that He truly understands and that He really favors the undertaking that we begin here tonight.[19]

The civil religion has not always been invoked in favor of worthy causes. On the domestic scene, an American-Legion type of ideology that fuses God, country, and flag has been used to attack nonconformist and liberal ideas and groups of all kinds. Still, it has been difficult to use the words of Jefferson and Lincoln to support special interests and undermine personal freedom. The defenders of slavery before the Civil War came to reject the thinking of the Declaration of Independence. Some of the most consistent of them turned against not only Jeffersonian democracy but Reformation religion; they dreamed of a South dominated by medieval chivalry and divine-right monarchy.[20] For all the overt religiosity of the radical right today, their relation to the civil religious consensus is tenuous, as when the John Birch Society attacks the central American symbol of Democracy itself.

With respect to America's role in the world, the dangers of distortion are greater and the built-in safeguards of the tradition weaker. The theme of the American Israel was used, almost from the beginning, as a justification for the shameful treatment of the Indians so characteristic of our history. It can be overtly or implicitly linked to the ideal of manifest destiny that has been used to legitimate several adventures in imperialism since the early nineteenth century. Never has the danger been greater than today. The issue is not so much one of imperial expansion, of which we are accused, as of the tendency to assimilate all governments or parties in the world that support our immediate policies or call upon our help by invoking the notion of free institutions and democratic values. Those nations that are for the moment "on our side" become "the free world." A repressive and unstable military dictatorship in South Vietnam becomes "the free people of South Vietnam and their government." It is then part of the role of America as the New Jerusalem and "the last best hope of earth" to defend such governments with treasure and eventually with blood. When our soldiers are actually dying, it becomes possible to consecrate the struggle further by invoking the great theme of sacrifice. For the majority of the American people who are unable to judge whether the people in South Vietnam (or wherever) are "free like us," such arguments are convincing. Fortunately President Johnson has been less ready to assert that "God has favored our undertaking" in the case of Vietnam than with respect to civil rights. But others are not so hesitant. The civil religion has exercised long-term pressure for the humane solution of our greatest domestic problem, the treatment of the Negro American. It remains to be seen how relevant it can become for our role in the world at large, and whether we can effectually stand for "the revolutionary beliefs for which our forbears fought," in John F. Kennedy's words.

The civil religion is obviously involved in the most pressing moral and political issues of the day. But it is also caught in another kind of crisis, theoretical and theological, of which it is at the moment largely unaware. "God" has clearly been a central symbol in the civil religion from the beginning and remains so today. This symbol is just as central to the civil religion as it is to Judaism or Christianity. In the late eighteenth century this posed no problem; even Tom Paine, contrary to his detractors, was not an atheist. From left to right and regardless of church or sect, all could accept the idea of God. But today, as even *Time* has recognized, the meaning of "God" is by no means so clear or so obvious. There is no formal creed in the civil religion. We have had a Catholic President; it is conceivable that we could have a Jewish one. But could we have an agnostic president? Could a man with conscientious scruples about using the word "God" the way Kennedy and Johnson have used it be elected chief magistrate of our country? If the whole God symbolism requires reformulation, there will be obvious consequences for the civil religion, consequences perhaps of liberal alienation and of fundamentalist ossification that have not so far been prominent in this realm. The civil religion has been a point of articulation between the profoundest commitments of Western religious and philosophical tradition and the common beliefs of ordinary Americans. It is not too soon to consider how the deepening theological crisis may affect the future of this articulation.

The Third Time of Trial

In conclusion it may be worthwhile to relate the civil religion to the most serious situation that we as Americans now face, what I call the third time of trial. The first time of trial had to do with the question of independence, whether we should or could run our own affairs in our own way. The second time of trial was over the issue of slavery, which in turn was only the most salient aspect of the more general problem of the full institutionalization of democracy within our country. This second problem we are still far from solving though we have some notable successes to our credit. But we have been overtaken by a third great problem that has led to a third great crisis, in the midst of which we stand. This is the problem of responsible action in a revolutionary world, a world seeking to attain many of the things, material and spiritual, that we have already attained. Americans have, from the beginning, been aware of the responsibility and the significance our republican experiment has for the whole world. The first internal political polarization in the new nation had to do with our attitude toward the French Revolution. But we were small and weak then, and "foreign entanglements" seemed to threaten our very survival. During the last century, our relevance for the world was not forgotten, but our role was seen as purely exemplary. Our democratic republic rebuked tyranny by merely existing. Just after World War I we were on the brink of taking a different role in the world, but once again we turned our backs.

Since World War II the old pattern has become impossible. Every president since Franklin Roosevelt has been groping toward a new pattern of action in the world, one that would be consonant with our power and our responsibilities. For Truman and for the period dominated by John Foster Dulles that pattern was seen to be the great Manichean confrontation of East and West, the confrontation of democracy and "the false philosophy of Communism" that provided the structure of Truman's inaugural address. But with the last years of Eisenhower and with the successive two presidents, the pattern began to shift. The great problems came to be seen as caused not solely by the evil intent of any one group of men. For Kennedy it was not so much a struggle against particular men as against "the common enemies of man: tyranny, poverty, disease and war itself."

But in the midst of this trend toward a less primitive conception of ourselves and our world, we have somehow, without anyone really intending it, stumbled into a military confrontation where we have come to feel that our honor is at stake. We have in a moment of uncertainty been tempted to rely on our overwhelming physical power rather than on our intelligence, and we have, in part, succumbed to this temptation. Bewildered and unnerved when our terrible power fails to bring immediate success, we are at the edge of a chasm the depth of which no man knows.

I cannot help but think of Robinson Jeffers, whose poetry seems more apt now than when it was written, when he said:

> Unhappy country, what wings you have! ...
> Weep (it is frequent in human affairs), weep for
> the terrible magnificence of the means,
> The ridiculous incompetence of the reasons, the
> bloody and shabby
> Pathos of the result.

But as so often before in similar times, we have a man of prophetic stature, without the bitterness or misanthropy of Jeffers, who, as Lincoln before him, calls this nation to its judgment:

When a nation is very powerful but lacking in self-confidence, it is likely to behave in a manner that is dangerous both to itself and to others.

Gradually but unmistakably, America is succumbing to that arrogance of power which has afflicted, weakened and in some cases destroyed great nations in the past.

If the war goes on and expands, if that fatal process continues to accelerate until America becomes what it is not now and never has been, a seeker after unlimited power and empire, then Vietnam will have had a mighty and tragic fallout indeed.

I do not believe that will happen. I am very apprehensive but I still remain hopeful, and even confident, that America, with its humane and democratic traditions, will find the wisdom to match its power.[21]

Without an awareness that our nation stands under higher judgment, the tradition of the civil religion would be dangerous indeed. Fortunately, the prophetic voices have never been lacking. Our present situation brings to mind the Mexican–American war that Lincoln, among so many others, opposed. The spirit of civil disobedience that is alive today in the civil rights movement and the opposition to the Vietnam War was already clearly outlined by Henry David Thoreau when he wrote, "If the law is of such a nature that it requires you to be an agent of injustice to another, then I say, break the law." Thoreau's words, "I would remind my countrymen that they are men first, and Americans at a late and convenient hour,"[22] provide an essential standard for any adequate thought and action in our third time of trial. As Americans, we have been well favored in the world, but it is as men that we will be judged.

Out of the first and second times of trial have come, as we have seen, the major symbols of the American civil religion. There seems little doubt that a successful negotiation of this third time of trial—the attainment of some kind of viable and coherent world order—would precipitate a major new set of symbolic forms. So far the flickering flame of the United Nations burns too low to be the focus of a cult, but the emergence of a genuine transnational sovereignty would certainly change this. It would necessitate the incorporation of vital international symbolism into our civil religion, or, perhaps a better way of putting it, it would result in American civil religion becoming simply one part of a new civil religion of the world. It is useless to speculate on the form such a civil religion might take, though it obviously would draw on religious traditions beyond the sphere of biblical religion alone. Fortunately, since the American civil religion is not the worship of the American nation but an understanding of the American experience in the light of ultimate and universal reality, the reorganization entailed by such a new situation need not disrupt the American civil religion's continuity. A world civil religion could be accepted as a fulfillment and not as a denial of American civil religion. Indeed, such an outcome has been the eschatological hope of American civil religion from the beginning. To deny such an outcome would be to deny the meaning of America itself.

Behind the civil religion at every point lie biblical archetypes: Exodus, Chosen People, Promised Land, New Jerusalem, and Sacrificial Death and Rebirth. But it is also genuinely American and genuinely new. It has its own prophets and its own martyrs, its own sacred events and sacred places, its own solemn rituals and symbols. It is concerned that America be a society as perfectly in accord with the will of God as men can make it, and a light to all nations.

It has often been used and is being used today as a cloak for petty interests and ugly passions. It is in need—as any living faith—of continual reformation, of being measured by universal standards. But it is not evident that it is incapable of growth and new insight.

It does not make any decisions for us. It does not remove us from moral ambiguity, from being, in Lincoln's fine phrase, an "almost chosen people." But it is a heritage of moral and religious experience from which we still have much to learn as we formulate the decisions that lie ahead.

QUESTIONS FOR REVIEW AND DISCUSSION

1. Why does Bellah choose to start with John F. Kennedy's inaugural address of January 20, 1961?
2. What are some of the possible interpretations that Bellah offers for the placing of references to God in this speech by President Kennedy?
3. How does Bellah address the seeming contradiction of the American President using the word "God," considering the separation of church and state? What do you think of his explanation?
4. How does Bellah support his assertion that the civil religion shaped by the first few presidents and other founding fathers "is clearly not itself Christianity"? Did the early leaders quoted by Bellah understand this civil religion as a substitute for Christianity?
5. What analogy is forged between America and Israel in this religious rhetoric? What countries and leaders play key roles in the American civil religion version?
6. What is the importance of the Civil War, Lincoln, and his speeches for civil religion in America?
7. What does Bellah indicate as the holidays most important to the "annual ritual calendar for the civil religion"? What purpose does each serve?
8. Bellah argues that there is a well-institutionalized civil religion in America and that it deserves the same "care in understanding that any other religion does." Do you agree? Why do you think civil religion has not received as much attention?
9. Does Bellah characterize this civil religion as harmful, beneficial, fraudulent, or genuine? Why? What are some examples of harm? What do you think?
10. How does Bellah characterize the relationships between American civil religion, politics, and religion? How does this contrast with France?

Notes

1 At the beginning of the reprint of this essay in Bellah's 1991, *Beyond Belief*, the author acknowledges its original 1967 publication in *Dædalus* and wrote the following for context and clarification:

> This chapter was written for a Dædalus conference on American Religion in May 1966. It was reprinted with comments and a rejoinder in The Religious Situation: 1968, where I defend myself against the accusation of supporting an idolatrous worship of the American nation. I think it should be clear from the text that I conceive of the central tradition of the American civil religion not as a form of national self-worship but as the subordination of the nation to ethical principles that transcend it in terms of which it should be judged. I am convinced that every nation and every people come to some form of religious self-understanding whether the critics like it or not. Rather than simply denounce what seems in any case inevitable, it seems more responsible to seek within the civil religious tradition for those critical principles which undercut the everpresent danger of national self-idolization.

2 Robert N. Bellah, "A response to three readers" at *The Immanent Frame: Secularism, religion, and the public sphere*, a digital forum of the Social Science Research Council (SSRC), posted Feb. 27, 2012 (http://blogs.ssrc.org/tif/author/bellah/ accessed Sept. 19, 2012).

3 Why something so obvious should have escaped serious analytical attention is itself an interesting problem. Part of the reason is probably the controversial nature of the subject. From the earliest years of the nineteenth century, conservative religious and political groups have argued that Christianity is, in fact, the national religion. Some of them from time to time and as recently as the 1950s proposed constitutional amendments that would explicitly recognize the sovereignty of Christ. In defending the doctrine of separation of church and state, opponents of such groups have denied that the national polity has, intrinsically, anything to do with religion at all. The moderates on this issue have insisted that the American state has taken a permissive and indeed supportive attitude toward religious groups (tax exemptions, et cetera), thus favoring religion but still missing the positive institutionalization with which I am concerned. But part of the reason this issue has been left in obscurity is certainly due to the peculiarly Western concept of "religion" as denoting a single type of collectivity of which an individual can be a member of one and only one at a time. The Durkheimian notion that every group has a religious dimension, which would be seen as obvious in southern or eastern Asia, is foreign to us. This obscures the recognition of such dimensions in our society.

4 Dwight D. Eisenhower, in Will Herberg, *Protestant-Catholic-Jew* (Garden City, N.Y.: Doubleday & Co., 1955), p. 97.

5 God is mentioned or referred to in all inaugural addresses but Washington's second, which is a very brief (two paragraphs) and perfunctory acknowledgement. It is not without interest that the actual word "God" does not appear until Monroe's second inaugural, March 5, 1821. In his first inaugural, Washington refers to God as "that Almighty Being who rules the universe," "Great Author of every public and private good," "Invisible Hand," and "benign Parent of the Human Race." John Adams refers to God as "Providence," "Being who is supreme over all," "Patron of Order," "Fountain of Justice," and "Protector in all ages of the world of virtuous liberty." Jefferson speaks of "that Infinite Power which rules the destinies of the universe," and "that Being in whose hands we are." Madison speaks of "that Almighty Being whose power regulates the destiny of nations," and "Heaven." Monroe uses "Providence" and "the Almighty" in his first inaugural and finally "Almighty God" in his second. See *Inaugural Addresses of the Presidents of the United States from George Washington 1789 to Harry S. Truman 1949*, 82d Congress, 2d Session, House Document No. 540, 1952.

6 For example, Abiel Abbot, pastor of the First Church in Haverhill, Massachusetts, delivered a Thanksgiving sermon in 1799, *Traits of Resemblance in the People of the United States of America to Ancient Israel*, in which he said, "It has been often remarked that the people of the United States come nearer to a parallel with Ancient Israel, than any other nation upon the globe. Hence 'Our American Israel' is a term frequently used; and common consent allows it apt and proper." In Hans Kohn, *The Idea of Nationalism* (New York: Macmillan Co., 1961), p. 665.

7 That the Mosaic analogy was present in the minds of leaders at the very moment of the birth of the republic is indicated in the designs proposed by Franklin and Jefferson for the seal of the United States of America. Together with Adams, they formed a committee of three delegated by the Continental Congress on July 4, 1776, to draw up the new device. "Franklin proposed as the device Moses lifting up his wand and dividing the Red Sea while Pharaoh was overwhelmed by its waters, with the motto 'Rebellion to tyrants is obedience to God.' Jefferson proposed the children of Israel in the wilderness 'led by a cloud by day and a pillar of fire at night.'" Anson Phelps Stokes, *Church and State in the United States*, vol. 1 (New York: Harper & Co., 1950), pp. 467–68.

8 Sidney E. Mead, *The Lively Experiment* (New York: Harper & Row, 1963), p. 12.

9 Abraham Lincoln, in Allan Nevins, ed., *Lincoln and the Gettysburg Address* (Urbana, Ill.: Univ. of Ill. Press, 1964), p. 39.

10 Robert Lowell, in *ibid.*, "On the Gettysburg Address," pp. 88–89.

11 William Henry Herndon, in Sherwood Eddy, *The Kingdom of God and the American Dream* (New York: Harper & Row, 1941), p. 162.

12 Karl Decker and Angus McSween, *Historic Arlington* (Washington, D.C., 1892), pp. 60–67.

13 How extensive the activity associated with Memorial Day can be is indicated by Warner: "The sacred symbolic behavior of Memorial Day, in which scores of the town's organizations are involved, is ordinarily divided into four periods. During the year separate rituals are held by many

of the associations for their dead, and many of these activities are connected with later Memorial Day events. In the second phase, preparations are made during the last three or four weeks for the ceremony itself, and some of the associations perform public rituals. The third phase consists of scores of rituals held in all the cemeteries, churches, and halls of the associations. These rituals consist of speeches and highly ritualized behavior. They last for two days and are climaxed by the fourth and last phase, in which all the separate celebrants gather in the center of the business district on the afternoon of Memorial Day. The separate organizations, with their members in uniform or with fitting insignia, march through the town, visit the shrines and monuments of the hero dead, and, finally, enter the cemetery. Here dozens of ceremonies are held, most of them highly symbolic and formalized." During these various ceremonies Lincoln is continually referred to and the Gettysburg Address recited many times. W. Lloyd Warner, *American Life* (Chicago: Univ. of Chicago Press, 1962), pp. 8–9.

14 Reinhold Niebuhr, "The Religion of Abraham Lincoln," in Nevins, ed., *op. cit.*, p. 72. William J. Wolfe of the Episcopal Theological School in Cambridge, Massachusetts, has written: "Lincoln is one of the greatest theologians of America—not in the technical meaning of producing a system of doctrine, certainly not as a defender of some one denomination, but in the sense of seeing the hand of God intimately in the affairs of nations. Just so the prophets of Israel criticized the events of their day from the perspective of the God who is concerned for history, and who reveals His will within it. Lincoln now stands among God's latter day prophets." *The Religion of Abraham Lincoln* (New York, 1963), p. 24.

15 Seymour Martin Lipset, "Religion and American Values in *The First New Nation* (New York: Basic Books, 1964), chap. 4.

16 Alexis de Tocqueville, *Democracy in America*, vol. 1 (Garden City, N.Y.: Doubleday & Co., Anchor Books, 1954), p. 310.

17 Henry Bargy, *La Religion dans la Société aux États-Unis* (Paris, 1902), p. 31.

18 De Tocqueville, *op. cit.*, p. 311. Later he says, "In the United States even the religion of most of the citizens is republican, since it submits the truths of the other world to private judgment, as in politics the care of their temporal interests is abandoned to the good sense of the people. Thus every man is allowed freely to take that road which he thinks will lead him to heaven, just as the law permits every citizen to have the right of choosing his own government" (p. 436).

19 Lyndon B. Johnson, in U.S., *Congressional Record*, House, March 15, 1965, pp. 4924, 4926.

20 See Louis Hartz, "The Feudal Dream of the South," pt. 4, *The Liberal Tradition in America* (New York: Harcourt, Brace & Co., 1955).

21 Senator J. William Fullbright, speech of April 28, 1966, as reported in *The New York Times*, April 29, 1966.

22 Henry David Thoreau, In Yehoshua Arieli, *Individualism and Nationalism in American Ideology* (Cambridge, Mass.: Harvard Univ. Press, 1964), p. 274.

26 The Abominations of Leviticus

Mary Douglas

Mary Douglas (1921–2007), a British social anthropologist, was born in San Remo, Italy, and received her doctorate at Oxford. She conducted fieldwork among the Lele of the Belgian Congo (now the Democratic Republic of Congo) and taught at University College, London for about twenty-five years. Among her key contributions was the observation that schemes of classification within all cultures produce anomalies, which are accorded ambivalent values. She developed these ideas in her seminal book, *Purity and Danger* (1966), from which the selection that follows is taken. In "The Abominations of Leviticus," perhaps her best known piece, she applies her theory on anomalous entities to aspects of the code of laws found in the Hebrew Bible. Her other influential works include *Natural Symbols* (1970), in which she presented the concepts of "group and grid" as means of analyzing social structure and classifying cultures.

Defilement is never an isolated event. It cannot occur except in view of a systematic ordering of ideas. Hence any piecemeal interpretation of the pollution rules of another culture is bound to fail. For the only way in which pollution ideas make sense is in reference to a total structure of thought whose key-stone, boundaries, margins and internal lines are held in relation by rituals of separation.

To illustrate this I take a hoary old puzzle from biblical scholarship, the abominations of Leviticus, and particularly the dietary rules. Why should the camel, the hare and the rock badger be unclean? Why should some locusts, but not all, be unclean? Why should the frog be clean and the mouse and the hippopotamus unclean? What have chameleons, moles and crocodiles got in common that they should be listed together (Levi, xi, 27)?

To help follow the argument I first quote the relevant versions of Leviticus and Deuteronomy using the text of the New Revised Standard Translation.

Deut. xiv

3. You shall not eat any abominable things. 4. These are the animals you may eat: the ox, the sheep, the goat, 5. the hart, the gazelle, the roe-buck, the wild goat, the ibex, the antelope and the mountain-sheep. 6. Every animal that parts the hoof and has the hoof cloven in two, and chews the cud, among the animals you may eat. 7. Yet of those that chew the cud or have the hoof cloven you shall not eat these: The camel, the hare and the rock badger, because they chew the cud but do not part the hoof, are unclean for you. 8. And the swine, because it parts the hoof but does not chew the cud, is unclean for you. Their flesh you shall not eat, and their carcasses you shall not touch.

9. Of all that are in the waters you may eat these: whatever has fins and scales you may eat. 10. And whatever does not have fins and scales you shall not eat; it is unclean for you. 11. You may eat all clean birds. 12. But these are the ones which you shall not eat: the eagle, the vulture, the osprey. 13. the buzzard, the kite, after their kinds; 14. every raven after its kind; 15. the ostrich, the night hawk, the sea gull, the hawk, after their kinds; 16. the little owl and the great owl, the water hen 17, and the pelican, the carrion vulture and the cormorant, 18. the stork, the heron, after their kinds; the hoopoe and the bat. 19. And all winged insects are unclean for you; they shall not be eaten. 20. All clean winged things you may eat.

Lev. xi

2. These are the living things which you may eat among all the beasts that are on the earth. 3. Whatever parts the hoof and is cloven-footed and chews the cud, among the animals you may eat. 4. Nevertheless among those that chew the cud or part the hoof, you shall not eat these: The camel, because it chews the cud but does not part the hoof, is unclean to you. 5. And the rock badger, because it chews the cud but does not part the hoof, is unclean to you. 6. And the hare, because it chews the cud but does not part the hoof, is unclean to you. 7. And the swine, because it parts the hoof and is cloven-footed but does not chew the cud, is unclean to you. 8. Of their flesh you shall not eat, and their carcasses you shall not touch; they are unclean to you. 9. These you may eat of all that are in the waters. Everything in the waters that has fins and scales, whether in the seas or in the rivers, you may eat. 10. But anything in the seas or the rivers that has not fins and scales, of the swarming creatures in the waters and of the living creatures that are in the waters, is an abomination to you. 11. They shall remain an abomination to you; of their flesh you shall not eat, and their carcasses you shall have in abomination. 12. Everything in the waters that has not fins and scales is an abomination to you. 13. And these you shall have in abomination among the birds, they shall not be eaten, they are an abomination: the eagle, the ossifrage, the osprey, 14. the kite, the falcon according to its kind, 15. every raven according to its kind, 16. the ostrich and the night hawk, the sea gull, the hawk according to its kind, 17. the owl, the cormorant, the ibis, 18. the water hen, the pelican, the vulture, 19. the stork, the heron according to its kind, the hoopoe and the bat. 20. All winged insects that go upon all fours are an abomination to you. 21. Yet among the winged insects that go on all fours you may eat those which have legs above their feet, with which to leap upon the earth. 22. Of them you may eat: the locust according to its kind, the bald locust according to its kind, the cricket according to its kind, and the grasshopper according to its kind. 23. But all other winged insects which have four feet are an abomination to you. 24. And by these you shall become unclean; whoever touches their carcass shall be unclean until the evening, 25. and whoever carries any part of their carcass shall wash his clothes and be unclean until the evening. 26. Every animal which parts the hoof but is not cloven-footed or does not chew the cud is unclean to you: everyone who touches them shall be unclean. 27. And all that go on their paws, among the animals that go on all fours, are unclean to you; whoever touches their carcass shall be unclean until the evening, 28. and he who carries their carcass shall wash his clothes and be unclean until the evening; they are unclean to you. 29. And these are unclean to you among the swarming things that swarm upon the earth; the weasel, the mouse, the great lizard according to its kind, 30. the gecko, the land crocodile, the lizard, the sand lizard and

the chameleon. 31. These are unclean to you among all that swarm; whoever touches them when they are dead shall be unclean until the evening. 32. And anything upon which any of them falls when they are dead shall be unclean. 41. Every swarming thing that swarms upon the earth is an abomination; it shall not be eaten. 42. Whatever goes on its belly, and whatever goes on all fours, or whatever has many feet, all the swarming things that swarm upon the earth, you shall not eat; for they are an abomination.

All the interpretations given so far fall into one of two groups: either the rules are meaningless, arbitrary because their intent is disciplinary and not doctrinal, or they are allegories of virtues and vices. Adopting the view that religious prescriptions are largely devoid of symbolism, Maimonides said:

> The Law that sacrifices should be brought is evidently of great use ... but we cannot say why one offering should be a lamb whilst another is a ram, and why a fixed number of these should be brought. Those who trouble themselves to find a cause for any of these detailed rules are in my eyes devoid of sense. ...

As a mediaeval doctor of medicine, Maimonides was also disposed to believe that the dietary rules had a sound physiological basis, but we have already dismissed in the second chapter the medical approach to symbolism. For a modern version of the view that the dietary rules are not symbolic, but ethical, disciplinary, see Epstein's English notes to the Babylonian Talmud and also his popular history of Judaism (1959, p. 24):

> Both sets of laws have one common aim ... Holiness. While the positive precepts have been ordained for the cultivation of virtue, and for the promotion of those finer qualities which distinguish the truly religious and ethical being, the negative precepts are defined to combat vice and suppress other evil tendencies and instincts which stand athwart man's striving towards holiness. ... The negative religious laws are likewise assigned educational aims and purposes. Foremost among these is the prohibition of eating the flesh of certain animals classed as 'unclean'. This law has nothing totemic about it. It is expressly associated in Scripture with the ideal of holiness. Its real object is to train the Israelite in self-control as the indispensable first step for the attainment of holiness.

According to Professor Stein's *The Dietary Laws in Rabbinic and Patristic Literature*, the ethical interpretation goes back to the time of Alexander the Great and the Hellenic influence on Jewish culture. The first century A.D. letters of Aristeas teach that not only are the Mosaic rules a valuable discipline which 'prevents the Jews from thoughtless action and injustice', but they also coincide with what natural reason would dictate for achieving the good life. So the Hellenic influence allows the medical and ethical interpretations to run together. Philo held that Moses' principle of selection was precisely to choose the most delicious meats:

> The lawgiver sternly forbade all animals of land, sea or air whose flesh is the finest and fattest, like that of pigs and scale-less fish, knowing that they set a trap for the most slavish of senses, the taste, and that they produced gluttony,

(and here we are led straight into the medical interpretation)

> an evil dangerous to both soul and body, for gluttony begets indigestion, which is the source of all illnesses and infirmities.

In another stream of interpretation, following the tradition of Robertson Smith and Frazer, the Anglo-Saxon Old Testament scholars have tended to say simply that the rules are arbitrary because they are irrational. For example, Nathaniel Micklem says:

> Commentators used to give much space to a discussion of the question why such and such creatures, and such or such states and symptoms were unclean. Have we, for instance, primitive rules of hygiene? Or were certain creatures and states unclean because they represented or typified certain sins? It may be taken as certain that neither hygiene, nor any kind of typology, is the basis of uncleanness. These regulations are not by any means to be rationalised. Their origins may be diverse, and go back beyond history …

Compare also R. S. Driver (1895):

> The principle, however, determining the line of demarcation between clean animals and unclean, is not stated; and what it is has been much debated. No single principle, embracing all the cases, seems yet to have been found, and not improbably more principles than one co-operated. Some animals may have been prohibited on account of their repulsive appearance or uncleanly habits, others upon sanitary grounds; in other cases, again, the motive of the prohibition may very probably have been a religious one, particularly animals may have been supposed, like the serpent in Arabia, to be animated by superhuman or demoniac beings, or they may have had a sacramental significance in the heathen rites of other nations; and the prohibition may have been intended as a protest against these beliefs. …

P. P. Saydon takes the same line in the *Catholic Commentary on Holy Scripture* (1953), acknowledging his debt to Driver and to Robertson Smith. It would seem that when Robertson Smith applied the ideas of primitive, irrational and unexplainable to some parts of Hebrew religion they remained thus labeled and unexamined to this day.

Needless to say such interpretations are not interpretations at all, since they deny any significance to the rules. They express battlement in a learned way. Micklem says it more frankly when he says of Leviticus:

> Chapters xi to xv are perhaps the least attractive in the whole Bible. To the modern reader there is much in them that is meaningless or repulsive. They are concerned with ritual 'un-cleanness' in respect of animals (11) of childbirth (12), skin diseases and stained garments (13), of the rites for the purgation of skin diseases (14) of leprosy and of various issues or secretions of the human body (15). Of what interest can such subjects be except to the anthropologist? What can all this have to do with religion?

Pfeiffer's general position is to be critical of the priestly and legal elements in the life of Israel. So he too lends his authority to the view that the rules in the Priestly Code are largely arbitrary:

> Only priests who were lawyers could have conceived of religion as a theocracy regulated by a divine law fixing exactly, and therefore arbitrarily, the sacred obligations of the people to their God. They thus sanctified the external, obliterated from religion both the ethical ideals of Amos and the tender emotions of Hosea, and reduced the

> Universal Creator to the stature of an inflexible despot. ... From immemorial custom P
> derived the two fundamental notions which characterise its legislation: physical holiness
> and arbitrary enactment—archaic conceptions which the reforming prophets had
> discarded in favour of spiritual holiness and moral law.
>
> (p. 91)

It may be true that lawyers tend to think in precise and codified forms. But is it plausible to argue that they tend to codify sheer nonsense—arbitrary enactments? Pfeiffer tries to have it both ways, insisting on the legalistic rigidity of the priestly authors and pointing to the lack of order in the setting out of the chapter to justify his view that the rules are arbitrary. Arbitrariness is a decidedly unexpected quality to find in Leviticus, as the Rev. Prof. H. J. Richards has pointed out to me. For source criticism attributes Leviticus to the Priestly source, the dominant concern of whose authors was for order. So the weight of source criticism supports us in looking for another interpretation.

As for the idea that the rules are allegories of virtues and vices Professor Stein derives this vigorous tradition from the same early Alexandrian influence on Jewish thought (p. 145 seq.). Quoting the letter of Aristeas, he says that the High Priest, Eleazar:

> admits that most people find the biblical food restrictions not understandable. If God is the Creator of everything, why should His law be so severe as to exclude some animals even from touch (128 f)? His first answer still links the dietary restrictions with the danger of idolatry. ... The second answer attempts to refute specific charges by means of allegorical exegesis. Each law about forbidden foods has its deep reason. Moses did not enumerate the mouse or the weasel out of a special consideration for them (143 f). On the contrary, mice are particularly obnoxious because of their destructiveness, and weasels, the very symbol of malicious tale-bearing, conceive through the ear and give birth through the mouth (164 f). Rather have these holy laws been given for the sake of justice to awaken in us devout thoughts and to form our character (161–68). The birds, for instance, the Jews are allowed to eat are all tame and clean, as they live by corn only. Not so the wild and carnivorous birds who fall upon lambs and goats, and even human beings. Moses, by calling the latter unclean, admonished the faithful not to do violence to the weak and not to trust their own power (145–48). Cloven-hoofed animals which part their hooves symbolise that all our actions must betray proper ethical distinction and be directed towards righteousness. ... Chewing the cud, on the other hand stands for memory.

Professor Stein goes on to quote Philo's use of allegory to interpret the dietary rules:

> Fish with fins and scales, admitted by the law, symbolise endurance and self-control, whilst the forbidden ones are swept away by the current, unable to resist the force of the stream. Reptiles, wriggling along by trailing their belly, signify persons who devote themselves to their ever greedy desires and passions. Creeping things, however, which have legs above their feet, so that they can leap, are clean because they symbolise the success of moral efforts.

Christian teaching has readily followed the allegorising tradition. The first century epistle of Barnabus, written to convince the Jews that their law had found its fulfilment, took the clean and unclean animals to refer to various types of men, leprosy to mean sin, etc.

A more recent example of this tradition is in Bishop Challoner's notes on the Westminster Bible in the beginning of this century:

> Hoof divided and cheweth the cud. The dividing of the hoof and chewing of the cud signify discretion between good and evil, and meditating on the law of God; and where either of these is wanting, man is unclean. In like manner fishes were reputed unclean that had not fins and scales: that is souls that did not raise themselves up by prayer and cover themselves with the scales of virtue.
>
> Footnote verse 3.

These are not so much interpretations as pious commentaries. They fail as interpretations because they are neither consistent nor comprehensive. A different explanation has to be developed for each animal and there is no end to the number of possible explanations.

Another traditional approach, also dating back to the letter of Aristeas, is the view that what is forbidden to the Israelites is forbidden solely to protect them from foreign influence. For instance, Maimonides held that they were forbidden to seethe the kid in the milk of its dam because this was a cultic act in the religion of the Canaanites. This argument cannot be comprehensive, for it is not held that the Israelites consistently rejected all the elements of foreign religions and invented something entirely original for themselves. Maimonides accepted the view that some of the more mysterious commands of the law had as their object to make a sharp break with heathen practices. Thus the Israelites were forbidden to wear garments woven of linen and wool, to plant different trees together, to have sexual intercourse with animals, to cook meat with milk, simply because these acts figured in the rites of their heathen neighbours. So far, so good: the laws were enacted as barriers to the spread of heathen styles of ritual. But in that case why were some heathen practices allowed? And not only allowed—if sacrifice be taken as a practice common to heathens and Israelites—but given an absolutely central place in the religion. Maimonides' answer, at any rate in *The Guide to the Perplexed,* was to justify sacrifice as a transitional stage, regrettably heathen, but necessarily allowed because it would be impractical to wean the Israelites abruptly from their heathen past. This is an extraordinary statement to come from the pen of a rabbinical scholar, and indeed in his serious rabbinical writings Maimonides did not attempt to maintain the argument: on the contrary, he there counted sacrifice as the most important act of the Jewish religion.

At least Maimonides saw the inconsistency and was led by it into contradiction. But later scholars seem content to use the foreign influence argument one way or the other, according to the mood of the moment. Professor Hooke and his colleagues have clearly established that the Israelites took over some Canaanite styles of worship, and the Canaanites obviously had much in common with Mesopotamian culture (1933). But it is no explanation to represent Israel as a sponge at one moment and as a repellent the next, without explaining why it soaked up this foreign element but repelled that one. What is the value of saying that seething kids in milk and copulating with cows are forbidden in Leviticus because they are the fertility rites of foreign neighbours (1935), since Israelites took over other foreign rites? We are still perplexed to know when the sponge is the right or the wrong metaphor. The same argument is equally puzzling in Eichrodt (pp. 230–31). Of course no culture is created out of nothing. The Israelites absorbed freely from their neighbours, but not quite freely. Some elements of foreign culture were incompatible with the principles of patterning on which they were constructing their universe; others were compatible. For instance, Zaehner suggests that the Jewish abomination of creeping things may have been taken over from

Zoroastrianism (p. 162). Whatever the historical evidence for this adoption of a foreign element into Judaism, we shall see that there was in the patterning of their culture a preformed compatibility between this particular abomination and the general principles on which their universe was constructed.

Any interpretations will fail which take the Do-nots of the Old Testament in piecemeal fashion. The only sound approach is to forget hygiene, aesthetics, morals and instinctive revulsion, even to forget the Canaanites and the Zoroastrian Magi, and start with the texts. Since each of the injunctions is prefaced by the command to be holy, so they must be explained by that command. There must be contrariness between holiness and abomination which will make overall sense of all the particular restrictions.

Holiness is the attribute of Godhead. Its root means 'set apart'. What else does it mean? We should start any cosmological enquiry by seeking the principles of power and danger. In the Old Testament we find blessing as the source of all good things, and the withdrawal of blessing as the source of all dangers. The blessing of God makes the land possible for men to live in.

God's work through the blessing is essentially to create order, through which men's affairs prosper. Fertility of women, livestock and fields is promised as a result of the blessing and this is to be obtained by keeping covenant with God and observing all His precepts and ceremonies (Deut. xxviii, 1–14). Where the blessing is withdrawn and the power of the curse unleashed, there is barrenness, pestilence, confusion. For Moses said:

> But if you will not obey the voice of the Lord your God or be careful to do all his commandments and his statutes which I command you to this day, then all these curses shall come upon you and overtake you. Cursed shall you be in the city, and cursed shall you be in the field. Cursed shall be your basket and your kneading trough. Cursed shall be the fruit of your body, and the fruit of your ground, the increase of your cattle, and the young of your flock. Cursed shall you be when you come in and cursed shall you be when you go out. The Lord will send upon you curses, confusion, and frustration in all that you undertake to do, until you are destroyed and perish quickly on account of the evil of your doings, because you have forsaken me … The Lord will smite you with consumption, and with fever, inflammation, and fiery heat, and with drought, and with blasting and with mildew; they shall pursue you till you perish. And the heavens over your head shall be brass and the earth under you shall be iron. The Lord will make the rain of your land powder and dust; from heaven it shall come down upon you until you are destroyed.
>
> (Deut. xxviii, 15–24)

From this it is clear that the positive and negative precepts are held to be efficacious and not merely expressive: observing them draws down prosperity, infringing them brings danger. We are thus entitled to treat them in the same way as we treat primitive ritual avoidances whose breach unleashes danger to men. The precepts and ceremonies alike are focused on the idea of the holiness of God which men must create in their own lives. So this is a universe in which men prosper by conforming to holiness and perish when they deviate from it. If there were no other clues we should be able to find out the Hebrew idea of the holy by examining the precepts by which men conform to it. It is evidently not goodness in the sense of an all-embracing humane kindness. Justice and moral goodness may well illustrate holiness and form part of it, but holiness embraces other ideas as well.

Granted that its root means separateness, the next idea that emerges is of the Holy as wholeness and completeness. Much of Leviticus is taken up with stating the physical perfection that is required of things presented in the temple and of persons approaching it. The animals offered in sacrifice must be without blemish, women must be purified after childbirth, lepers should be separated and ritually cleansed before being allowed to approach it once they are cured. All bodily discharges are defiling and disqualify from approach to the temple. Priests may only come into contact with death when their own close kin die. But the high priest must never have contact with death.

Levit, xxi

17. Say to Aaron, None of your descendants throughout their generations who has a blemish may approach to offer the bread of his God. 18. For no one who has a blemish shall draw near, a man blind or lame, or one who has a mutilated face or a limb too long. 19. or a man who has an injured foot or an injured hand, 20. or a hunch-back, or a dwarf, or a man with a defect in his sight or an itching disease or scabs, or crushed testicles; 21. no man of the descendants of Aaron the priest who has a blemish shall come near to offer the Lord's offerings by fire; …

In other words, he must be perfect as a man, if he is to be a priest.

This much reiterated idea of physical completeness is also worked out in the social sphere and particularly in the warriors' camp. The culture of the Israelites was brought to the pitch of greatest intensity when they prayed and when they fought. The army could not win without the blessing and to keep the blessing in the camp they had to be specially holy. So the camp was to be preserved from defilement like the Temple. Here again all bodily discharges disqualified a man from entering the camp as they would disqualify a worshipper from approaching the altar. A warrior who had had an issue of the body in the night should keep outside the camp all day and only return after sunset, having washed. Natural functions producing bodily waste were to be performed outside the camp (Deut. xxiii, 10–15). In short the idea of holiness was given an external, physical expression in the wholeness of the body seen as a perfect container.

Wholeness is also extended to signify completeness in a social context. An important enterprise, once begun, must not be left incomplete. This way of lacking wholeness also disqualifies a man from fighting. Before a battle the captains shall proclaim:

Deut. Xx

5. What man is there that has built a new house and has not dedicated it? Let him go back to his house, lest he die in the battle and another man dedicate it. 6. What man is there that has planted a vineyard and has not enjoyed its fruit? Let him go back to his house, lest he die in the battle and another man enjoy its fruit. 7. And what man is there that hath betrothed a wife and has not taken her? Let him go back to his house, lest he die in the battle and another man take her.

Admittedly there is no suggestion that this rule implies defilement. It is not said that a man with a half-finished project on his hands is defiled in the same way that a leper is defiled. The next verse in fact goes on to say that fearful and faint-hearted men should go home lest they spread their fears. But there is a strong suggestion in other passages that a man should not put his hand to the plough and then turn back. Pedersen goes so far as to say that:

in all these cases a man has started a new important undertaking without having finished it yet … a new totality has come into existence. To make a breach in this prematurely i.e. before it has attained maturity or has been finished involves a serious risk of sin.

(Vol. III, p. 9)

If we follow Pedersen, then blessing and success in war required a man to be whole in body, whole-hearted and trailing no uncompleted schemes. There is an echo of this actual passage in the New Testament parable of the man who gave a great feast and whose invited guests incurred his anger by making excuses (Luke xiv, 6–24; Matt. xxii. See Black & Rowley 1962, p. 836). One of the guests had bought a new farm, one had bought ten oxen and had not yet tried them, and one had married a wife. If according to the old Law each could have validly justified his refusal by reference to Deut. xx, the parable supports Petersen's view that interruption of new projects was held to be bad in civil as well as military contexts.

Other precepts develop the idea of wholeness in another direction. The metaphors of the physical body and of the new undertaking relate to the perfection and completeness of the individual and his work. Other precepts extend holiness to species and categories. Hybrids and other confusions are abominated.

Lev. xviii

23. And you shall not lie with any beast and defile yourself with it, neither shall any woman give herself to a beast to lie with it: it is perversion.

The word 'perversion' is a significant mistranslation of the rare Hebrew word *tebhel*, which has as its meaning mixing or confusion. The same theme is taken up in Leviticus xix, 19.

You shall keep my statutes. You shall not let your cattle breed with a different kind; you shall not sow your field with two kinds of seed; nor shall there come upon you a garment of cloth made of two kinds of stuff.

All these injunctions are prefaced by the general command: 'Be holy, for I am holy.'

We can conclude that holiness is exemplified by completeness. Holiness requires that individuals shall conform to the class to which they belong. And holiness requires that different classes of things shall not be confused.

Another set of precepts refines on this last point. Holiness means keeping distinct the categories of creation. It therefore involves correct definition, discrimination and order. Under this head all the rules of sexual morality exemplify the holy. Incest and adultery (Lev. xviii, 6–20) are against holiness, in the simple sense of right order. Morality does not conflict with holiness, but holiness is more a matter of separating that which should be separated than of protecting the rights of husbands and brothers.

Then follows in chapter xix another list of actions which are contrary to holiness. Developing the idea of holiness as order, not confusion, this list upholds rectitude and straight-dealing as holy, and contradiction and double-dealing as against holiness. Theft, lying, false witness, cheating in weights and measures, all kinds of dissembling such as speaking ill of the deaf (and presumably smiling to their face), hating your brother in your heart (while presumably speaking kindly to him), these are clearly contradictions between what seems and what is. This chapter also says much about generosity and love, but these are positive commands, while I am concerned with negative rules.

We have now laid a good basis for approaching the laws about clean and unclean meats. To be holy is to be whole, to be one; holiness is unity, integrity, perfection of the individual and of the kind. The dietary rules merely develop the metaphor of holiness on the same lines.

First we should start with livestock, the herds of cattle, camels, sheep and goats which were the livelihood of the Israelites. These animals were clean inasmuch as contact with them did not require purification before approaching the Temple. Livestock, like the inhabited land, received the blessing of God. Both land and livestock were fertile by the blessing, both were drawn into the divine order. The farmer's duty was to preserve the blessing. For one thing, he had to preserve the order of creation. So no hybrids, as we have seen, either in the fields or in the herds or in the clothes made from wool or flax. To some extent men covenanted with their land and cattle in the same way as God covenanted with them. Men respected the first born of their cattle, obliged them to keep the Sabbath. Cattle were literally domesticated as slaves. They had to be brought into the social order in order to enjoy the blessing. The difference between cattle and the wild beasts is that the wild beasts have no covenant to protect them. It is possible that the Israelites were like other pastoralists who do not relish wild game. The Nuer of the South Sudan, for instance, apply a sanction of disapproval of a man who lives by hunting. To be driven to eating wild meat is the sign of a poor herdsman. So it would be probably wrong to think of the Israelites as longing for forbidden meats and finding the restrictions irksome. Driver is surely right in taking the rules as an *a posteriori* generalisation of their habits. Cloven-hoofed, cud-chewing ungulates are the model of the proper kind of food for a pastoralist. If they must eat wild game, they can eat wild game that shares these distinctive characters and is therefore of the same general species. This is a kind of casuistry which permits scope for hunting antelope and wild goats and wild sheep. Everything would be quite straightforward were it not that the legal mind has seen fit to give ruling on some borderline cases. Some animals seem to be ruminant, such as the hare and the hyrax (or rock badger), whose constant grinding of their teeth was held to be cud-chewing. But they are definitely not cloven-hoofed and so are excluded by name. Similarly for animals which are cloven-hoofed but are not ruminant, the pig and the camel. Note that this failure to conform to the two necessary criteria for defining cattle is the only reason given in the Old Testament for avoiding the pig; nothing whatever is said about its dirty scavenging habits. As the pig does not yield milk, hide nor wool, there is no other reason for keeping it except for its flesh. And if the Israelites did not keep pig they would not be familiar with its habits. I suggest that originally the sole reason for its being counted as unclean is its failure as a wild boar to get into the antelope class, and that in this it is on the same footing as the camel and the hyrax, exactly as is stated in the book.

After these borderline cases have been dismissed, the law goes on to deal with creatures according to how they live in the three elements, the water, the air and the earth. The principles here applied are rather different from those covering the camel, the pig, the hare and the hyrax. For the latter are excepted from clean food in having one but not both of the defining characters of livestock. Birds I can say nothing about, because, as I have said, they are named and not described and the translation of the name is open to doubt. But in general the underlying principle of cleanness in animals is that they shall conform fully to their class. Those species are unclean which are imperfect members of their class, or whose class itself confounds the general scheme of the world.

To grasp this scheme we need to go back to Genesis and the creation. Here a three-fold classification unfolds, divided between the earth, the waters and the firmament. Leviticus takes up this scheme and allots to each element its proper kind of animal life. In the firmament two-legged fowls fly with wings. In the water scaly fish swim with fins. On the earth four-legged animals hop, jump or walk. Any class of creatures which is not equipped for the right kind of locomotion in its element is contrary to holiness. Contact with it disqualifies a person from approaching the Temple. Thus anything in the water which has not fins and scales is unclean (xi, 10–12). Nothing is said about predatory habits or of scavenging. The only sure test for cleanness in a fish is its scales and its propulsion by means of fins.

Four-footed creatures which fly (xi, 20–26) are unclean. Any creature which has two legs and two hands and which goes on all fours like a quadruped is unclean (xi, 27). Then follows (v. 19) a much disputed list. On some translations, it would appear to consist precisely of creatures endowed with hands instead of front feet, which perversely use their hands for walking: the weasel, the mouse, the crocodile, the shrew, various kinds of lizards, the chameleon and mole (Danby, 1933), whose forefeet are uncannily hand-like. This feature of this list is lost in the New Revised Standard Translation which uses the word 'paws' instead of hands.

The last kind of unclean animal is that which creeps, crawls or swarms upon the earth. This form of movement is explicitly contrary to holiness (Levit. xi, 41–44). Driver and White use 'swarming' to translate the Hebrew *shérec*, which is applied to both those which teem in the waters and those which swarm on the ground. Whether we call it teeming, trailing, creeping, crawling or swarming, it is an indeterminate form of movement. Since the main animal categories are defined by their typical movement, 'swarming' which is not a mode of propulsion proper to any particular element, cuts across the basic classification. Swarming things are neither fish, flesh nor fowl. Eels and worms inhabit water, though not as fish; reptiles go on dry land, though not as quadrupeds; some insects fly, though not as birds. There is no order in them. Recall what the Prophecy of Habakkuk says about this form of life:

For thou makest men like the fish of the sea, like crawling things that have no ruler.

(1, v. 14)

The prototype and model of the swarming things is the worm. As fish belong in the sea so worms belong in the realm of the grave, with death and chaos.

The case of the locusts is interesting and consistent. The test of whether it is a clean and therefore edible kind is how it moves on the earth. If it crawls it is unclean. If it hops it is clean (xi, v. 21). In the Mishnah it is noted that a frog is not listed with creeping things and conveys no uncleanness (Danby, p. 722). I suggest that the frog's hop accounts for it not being listed. If penguins lived in the Near East I would expect them to be ruled unclean as wingless birds. If the list of unclean birds could be retranslated from this point of view, it might well turn out that they are anomalous because they swim and dive as well as they fly, or in some other way they are not fully birdlike.

Surely now it would be difficult to maintain that 'Be ye Holy' means no more than 'Be ye separate'. Moses wanted the children of Israel to keep the commands of God constantly before their minds:

Deut. Xi

18. You shall therefore lay up these words of mine in your heart and in your soul; and you shall bind them as a sign upon your hand, and they shall be as frontlets between

your eyes. 19. And you shall teach them to your children, talking of them when you are sitting in your house, and when you are walking by the way, and when you lie down and when you rise. 20. And you shall write them upon the doorposts of your house and upon your gates.

If the proposed interpretation of the forbidden animals is correct, the dietary laws would have been like signs which at every turn inspired meditation on the oneness, purity and completeness of God. By rules of avoidance holiness was given a physical expression in every encounter with the animal kingdom and at every meal. Observance of the dietary rules would thus have been a meaningful part of the great liturgical act of recognition and worship which culminated in the sacrifice in the Temple.

QUESTIONS FOR REVIEW AND DISCUSSION

1. What are some of the earlier interpretations of the laws of Leviticus that Douglas explores and dismisses? Do you find any of those interpretations convincing?
2. Why does Douglas choose "holiness" and "abomination" as the two primary structural categories for her analysis?
3. How does Douglas develop her arguments for what characterizes "holiness" in the first books of the Hebrew Bible, and what are these characteristics?
4. According to Douglas, why do some domesticated or wild animals fall outside the scheme as acceptable dietary items?
5. What are some of the other characteristics that would cause a creature to be regarded as unclean and unfit as food, according to Douglas's analysis?
6. What does Douglas conclude to be the overarching purpose of these dietary laws?
7. Douglas's analysis of the dietary laws in the book of Leviticus demonstrates a masterful blend of methodologies. What are some of the various methods that she uses to develop her theory? Is she engaged in anthropology or religious studies?

27 Beauty and the Drainpipe: Art and Symbolism in Religion

Sam Gill

Sam D. Gill (1943–) attained his doctorate at the University of Chicago and is Professor of Religious Studies at the University of Colorado, where he has taught for the last thirty years of his forty-year academic career. His nine books address various aspects of Native American religion and, to borrow the title of one of his many articles, "The Religions of Traditional Peoples" more generally. Gill's work emphasizes practice, ritual, performance, dance, play, and other active and embodied dimensions that have been underrepresented in scholarship. In addition to articles reflecting on the importance of these areas for the academic study of religion, Gill exemplifies a complementary approach between engaging these topics through scholarship, such as his 1987 book *Native American Religious Action: A Performance Approach to Religion*, and through his own practice of dance. His website http://sam-gill.com/ highlights the practice of dance in his teaching as well, such as the course, Dancing Culture Religion. In the article below, Gill challenges ideas about art, symbolism and religion through examples from nonliterate peoples that illustrate art as process and its inseparability from religion and cultural context.

The Song of the Forest: Ideas about Art and Religion

In the Ituri forest in Zaire, Colin Turnbull lived for a time with the Bambuti, who are Pygmy people. He shares his experience in a book, *The Forest People*. One of my favorite incidents in the book may help to introduce ideas about the nature of art and symbolism in the religions of nonliterate peoples.

The incident occurs in the context of a ceremonial which takes place over a period of several months. Each night the Pygmy men construct a special communal fire around which they gather to sing and to feast. Their songs are directed toward the forest, which they perceive as their provider, an entity or deity whose presence they feel especially on these occasions. The forest responds to them in beautiful song heard throughout the night from many different places in the forest surrounding the Pygmy camp. The song of the forest is made by the skillful playing of a trumpet. The ceremonial and the trumpet are called by the name *molimo*.

Turnbull had been made fully aware of the sacredness attributed to this nightly ceremony and had felt the Pygmy's reluctance to talk with him about the *molimo*. He had been carefully guarded from seeing the trumpet or knowing much about it.

One evening during the ceremony, Turnbull was happily surprised by an invitation to enter the forest with several young Pygmy men to retrieve the trumpet from its resting place. He was warned that he must keep up with the rapid pace the Pygmies set as they ran along small animal trails through the dense forest. After half an hour or so they came to a river, where they paused to wash and purify themselves before they neared the sacred *molimo* trumpet. As they entered a clearing a hush fell over them and several Pygmies went to retrieve the trumpet. Turnbull was filled with the anticipation of seeing what he expected to be an ornately carved bamboo trumpet, the most sacred object of the Pygmy. When the Pygmies returned Turnbull saw them carrying two lengths of drainpipe threaded at the ends, the sacred *molimo* trumpets. The longer, some fifteen feet, was slightly bent in the middle, accidentally caused, no doubt, by being bent around a tree during rapid transit through the forest. To top this, one of the Pygmies approached the trumpet and blew "a long, raucous raspberry." This gesture was received by the others with considerable side slapping and interminable laughter. Turnbull, shocked and disenchanted, asked if these drainpipes didn't constitute a gross sacrilege. But his concerns were met with a counter question: "What does it matter what the *molimo* is made of? This one makes a great sound, and, besides, it does not rot like wood. It is much trouble to make a wooden one, and then it rots away and you have to make another."[1]

Moreover, Amabosu, the great singer, soon appeared and demonstrated the potential of the instrument. "He gently filled the forest with strange sounds—the rumblings and growls of buffalo and leopards, the mighty call of the elephant, the plaintive cooing of the dove. Interspersed with snatches of song, transformed by the trumpet into a sound quite unlike the song of men—richer, softer, more distant and unapproachable."[2]

If we share Turnbull's shock and disappointment, it is perhaps based on certain ideas we have about the nature of religion and art. We expect that objects of religious importance should be objects of artistic value and should be approached with attitudes of reverence and respect. When confronted by the drainpipe trumpets and the raucous raspberries we find that the Pygmies do not meet our expectations, and we are inclined to dismiss them as a culture simply undeveloped in the areas of art and religion. Many have done so. But we must not dismiss the Pygmies and their *molimo* too quickly, for their response and actions may provide for us a glimpse into the profundity of their perspectives. There is a cluster of ideas suggested in this example. We will lift them up here and then turn to further illustration to develop them.

The event in our example is associated with the religious process in which the Pygmies communicate with the forest as an entity. In what they say and do they show that their religious and aesthetic values are placed on the song produced by the trumpet. They see the physical trumpet as only instrumental. As we would expect, the Pygmies' religious symbols, in this case borne in the form of song, are associated with aesthetic values, but they make it plain to Turnbull, whose attention seems riveted to the trumpets, that objects that are but instrumental in religious processes need not bear these values. The religious object must serve the religious intent unconstrained by aesthetic values. There is no regard for the objects as objects of art. They may be considered utterly commonplace and treated with disregard when out of the sacred context.

Overcoming our initial shock and accepting what the Pygmies say, we may shift our attention from the object to the true bearer of aesthetic and religious values, *sound*, the song of the trumpet. We have identified nonliteracy as a primary distinctive feature of the cultures with which we are concerned, that is, their use of oral and nonverbal rather than literary means by which to bear culture. It should not surprise us to find that sound is a primary medium of the arts and religions of nonliterate cultures.

The Pygmy people have a story about the importance of song. It is called "The Bird with the Most Beautiful Song." It tells of a boy who heard a very beautiful song in the forest. He caught the bird that was singing it and took it home with him. Annoyed at having to feed the bird, the boy's father charged him to get rid of his pet. With persistent pleading, the boy kept the bird for several days. But finally the father took the bird from the boy and dismissed him. "When his son had left, the father killed the Bird, the Bird with the Most Beautiful Song in the Forest, and with the Bird he killed the Song, and with the Song he killed himself and he dropped dead, completely dead, dead forever."[3]

The most beautiful song of the forest is identified with the forest and subsequently with all life within the forest. When the song ceases, the forest does not live. When the forest is dead, it cannot give life to those who live within it.

These Pygmy views may also suggest to us that art is inseparable from religious processes, but that these processes are creative in a sense that may depart from our usual understanding of creativity in art. In this example, the *molimo* trumpet is brought out only on life-threatening occasions. To sing to the forest awakens the forest so that it will maintain its responsibility to its children, the Pygmies. The *molimo* is an aesthetic and religious event which is creative in a primary sense. It creates life. The *molimo* is not a reflection upon the nature of life and reality, nor is it a symbolic statement about what life should be like to be used as a goal or idea. In either of these senses it would be creative in a secondary or simply artistic sense. For the Pygmy, as for many nonliterate people, many aesthetic acts are at once religious acts and must be so because life utterly depends upon them.

It follows that we may never appreciate some aspects of the art of nonliterate cultures without also appreciating the contexts in which art is produced, especially when our understanding of art is so heavily focused upon objects of art. These objects may be only the tools or the leftovers of a meaningful and creative event. If we do not know the event or its significance, we can scarcely understand the by-products we consider, perhaps in error from the point of view of their makers, as art objects. The Pygmy peoples are not typical of nonliterate cultures, and we need not hope to find their religious and aesthetic values universally held among these many diverse cultures. What we hope to achieve through the introduction of these ideas is a stance of sensitivity from which to approach more meaningfully the arts and religions of these cultures. Let us turn now to other examples.

Destructible and Disposable Art Objects

We commonly find observers of nonliterate peoples who are confounded by attitudes of apparent disregard for objects of art and religion. For example, in the late nineteenth century a man named Washington Matthews became acquainted with ritual sandpainting practiced by the Navajo in the American Southwest. He observed elaborate pictures constructed by sprinkling finely ground sands of various colors upon the floor of ceremonial houses. Deeply impressed with the beauty and complexity of these paintings, he was taken aback when he saw them being destroyed within a short time of their completion. He declared these pictures to be the most transient in the history of human art. But when we look at the art of Navajo sandpainting in its religious context, we find that this destruction of a sacred art object is no sacrilege nor violation of aesthetic values; quite the contrary. Sandpainting is performed in ceremonials to cure ailing persons by identifying them with the cosmic designs depicted in the paintings. The cosmic powers represented as humanlike beings are present in the sandpainting when properly prepared. The ailing person sits on the middle of the sandpainting and is physically identified with each element in it. Pinches of sand are placed on the body parts of the ailing person which were taken from the corresponding body parts of all the figures in the painting. It is through the use, and therefore also the destruction, of this object that a person is given life and health. The act, not the object, bears both the religious and aesthetic values. Navajos believe that sandpaintings must be destroyed by sundown on the day they are made, and no visual record is kept.

Many scholars have been confounded by the common incidence in prehistoric rock art wherein one scene is etched or painted directly over another. We may think of examples such as those at Camonica Valley in the Italian Alps. If we insist that the object produced by the graphic work must bear the aesthetic values, we can only conclude from what we observe that these values are confused. Yet, if we were to know the context, be it ceremonial or otherwise, we might find that the objects served the meaning of these events. This perspective would hold that these pictures are just the leftovers from some cultural event in the context of which they were meaningful. This view has not yet been taken by students of these works of art.

We can see another example in the *kiva* wall painting of the Pueblo peoples in North America. From prehistoric times murals have been painted on the walls of ceremonial chambers to present an environment or setting appropriate to ceremonial occasions. As the seasons pass and the ceremonial cycle advances, the old murals are whitewashed and new ones painted. We might be shocked by this act, especially seeing the beauty of the murals, but we must see that from the Pueblo perspective the art objects must serve the occasion and are of little significance apart from it.

African masks are commonly collected by Westerners as art objects, but this is not necessarily the view of Africans. To the people of Cameroun in Central Africa, for example, masks come to life only when worn by properly attired dancers performing to music. Apart from this context, the masks are little more than dead wood.

It seems that our perspective on art is inadequate to support an understanding of these objects from the perspective of the cultures which produce them. It forces us to look in the wrong places for art. It prevents us from recognizing that art and religion are inseparable from the human endeavor to participate in and maintain creative activities. On this point I am reminded of the essay written by Imamu Amiri Baraka (formerly LeRoi Jones) entitled "Hunting is Not Those Heads on the Wall." He criticizes the history of Western art for what he considers a worship of art objects. He feels that the price paid for this emphasis is the failure to appreciate the creative processes of art. In his view, art objects are what is left over from the art process, and they have no more to do with art than hunting trophies have to do with the hunt. Our examples show a kinship to this idea, but they differ in that at least certain art processes in nonliterate cultures cannot be separated from religious processes. We must appreciate the point of view found in nonliterate cultures that reverence for the artistic products or the tools of religion can become a kind of tyranny which stifles the full expression of ideas and the proper performance of religious acts. This is no small point since these acts are creative in a primary sense; they literally make life possible. There is an undeniable honesty and sensibility in this view.

Sound in Art and Religion

The symbolic medium most central to and most common among the many diverse nonliterate cultures is sound, especially as it is formed in song, prayer, story, and poetry. In other words, sound, as communicated via the human voice, is a predominant and distinctive feature of nonliterate cultures. As we saw in the Pygmy ritual, there is a close association between acts of speech and life itself. We often find that nonliterate peoples hold speech to be more highly sacred than they do objects of any kind. This belief suggests to us that the aesthetic and religious significance of sound in nonliterate cultures should be considered more closely. Eskimo culture provides illuminating examples.

In Eskimo language, the word meaning "to breathe" also means "to make poetry," and it is rooted in the word denoting the eternal life force. It is no surprise that priest and poet are one in Eskimo culture. Orpingalik, Netsilik Eskimo poet and shaman, was articulate about these matters in conversations he had with Knud Rasmussen, who led a major expedition among the Eskimo in the 1920s.

It became clear to Rasmussen that Orpingalik linked his power as hunter and shaman closely to his songs. As shaman, Orpingalik could communicate with spirits while in a trance, and he had his own guardian spirits whose strengths and abilities he could call upon by the use of their spirit songs. His source of strength and power was in his song and poetry. Through them he could gain the power to hunt successfully, to travel safely, to cure, and even to bring harm to his enemies. His poetry was his possession and others could not use it. Orpingalik went so far as to identify his very being with his songs. He said, "All my being is song and I sing as I draw breath."[4]

We may see here reflections of the Pygmies' drainpipe *molimo*. For the Eskimo, songs are not things to be sung simply for amusement or even for their beauty. They are life. They are breath.

For the Pygmy and the Eskimo, sound and the power of speech are identified with life. Speech is impossible without breath. The spoken word emerges from the breast, from the region of the heart and lungs, and is itself evidence of vitality, of life. The act of speech has a life of its own. As words or sounds are born from the mouth or musical instrument, they live and move, but their life is short and leaves no traces.

The vitality and dynamics, even the transient quality, of sound may affect the aesthetic values of plastic art. A look at Eskimo carving can demonstrate this factor.

Contemporary stone carvings of the Eskimo are well known, but this is a quite recent development arising to meet the economic needs of Eskimo peoples. I certainly do not wish to suggest anything negative about these very beautiful works of art, but simply to point out that they arise out of a situation heavily influenced by Eskimo contact with Western civilization and consequently bear many ideas related to Western art history. Still they stand in continuity with a long history of carving, which has been an Eskimo tradition for many centuries. It is upon the roots of the carving tradition that we must focus in order to most appreciate that which is indigenous to the Eskimo.

Edmund Carpenter, in his book, *Eskimo Realities*, has pointed out that Eskimo carvers use their knives like Eskimo poets use words. For the Eskimo the use of language is the way in which they reveal the forms that are in nature, but whose significance is otherwise hidden from them. Through language things take form; nature is revealed to be meaningful. So it is with Eskimo carvers. Taking a piece of ivory in their hands, they contemplate it, and speak to it, in order to perceive the form that it contains. They do not approach the material as raw or neutral with an intent to dominate it and make it subservient to their ideas. Rather, through their craftsmanship they permit the material to reveal its underlying or inner form. The carvers and their knives are only instruments in this process. This belief would make it difficult for an Eskimo to accept art commissions, for the material, not the patron, determines what will be carved. Art is a process in which the carver enters into a relationship with nature and perceives that process as life. Eskimo art, too, is not composed of things made but of relationships experienced, relationships critical to life. Art is dynamic, not static. It is process, not product.

Consequently, it is not surprising that the object carved is a thing to be held in the hand, not to be viewed on a shelf or in a glass case. No single visual perspective is dictated in the process, and often a range of interrelationships within a carving are revealed from various perspectives as the object is turned in the hand. The complexity of these relationships reflects essential aspects of Eskimo life.

Carpenter reports an interesting anecdote. A collector of traditional Eskimo art was faced with the difficulty of displaying his collection. Since the objects, carved to be held, often do not have flat bottoms, they tended to roll about when placed on the collector's shelf. The collector remedied the problem by filing flat bottoms. Ironically this destroyed something central to the aesthetic principles dynamically working even in the carved pieces themselves.

In considering Eskimo art, Carpenter concluded that:

> The concept "art" is alien to the Eskimo, but the thing itself, the act of art, is certainly there, carefully implemented as a dimension of culture. It is not, however, always easy to recognize. The Eskimo don't put art into their environment: they treat the environment itself as art form.
>
> Such art is invisible: it belongs to that all-pervasive environment that eludes perception. It serves as a means of merging the individual and his environment, not as a means of training his perception upon that environment.[5]

Art is a Process

Through these examples we can see more and more clearly that what we should consider as art is not limited to expressive functions; it quite often embraces relations of a life-giving character. Art is never static and cannot be confined to things. We might want to adopt the term *arting*, coined by Baraka in his previously mentioned article, to help us "remember that the art of nonliterate peoples is often a process of creating and maintaining life-giving relationships."

The appropriateness of the term *arting* is never more obvious than in the case of African art that is usually "danced." In recent decades the art of nonliterate peoples has received widespread attention in the Western art world, where it is always referred to as primitive art. African art has been in the limelight cast by admiring remarks by Western artists of such stature as Picasso and Matisse. Still, the overwhelming proportion of interest in this art has been confined to the art objects and almost invariably from a perspective completely ignorant of the cultures and cultural events in which these objects have meaning and life. Given the probability of misunderstanding, of misuse, and of error that such an approach brings to the art of nonliterate peoples, we may begin to appreciate another dimension of the wisdom in their common practice of discarding, destroying, or defacing the leftovers from arting. In one sense, the objects are no more art than are the sculptor's mallet and chisel or the painter's palette and brushes. Let us look at an example.

A revolution of sorts was begun in the understanding of African art when Robert Thompson published *African Art in Motion*. His insight into the nature of African art is apparent in the title and in Thompson's opening words:

> The Tiv people of Nigeria use a basic verb which means "to dance." The word, *vine*, unites the dance with further worlds of artistic happening. ... This broad conception of the dance is widely shared in subsaharan Africa, *viz.* that dance is not restricted to the

moving human body, but can combine in certain contexts with things and objects, granting them autonomy in art, intensifying the aliveness an image must embody to function as a work of art.[6]

Thus, Thompson introduces us to a history of what he calls *danced art*, turning our attention from the fascination of objects as displayed in our museum cases and galleries to the significance of a whole cultural complex in which movement and sculpture are blended in dance with a primary creative effect.

An impressive example of African sculpture which may illustrate this point is the Epa mask of the Yoruba of Nigeria. At the base of the mask is a Janus helmet (a helmet on which two faces are carved, one looking forward, the other backward) upon which is a representation of realistic figures sometimes supported by a tray. The masks are commonly three to four feet high and may weigh more than fifty pounds. To dance the masks requires someone of considerable physical strength, and this in itself is closely associated with the religious significance of the mask. As Thompson's findings show, Africans hold youthfulness and strength in such esteem that they have religious significance. It is appropriate that only a strong man can support the Epa mask, for the occasion of the dance is the transformation of young men into adults. The display of strength and youthfulness expressed in their masked dance is evidence of their capability to lead and protect their people. On these occasions dance and sculpture are joined through musical drama, not to artfully comment upon the nature of life, but rather to enact that art which is itself life.[7]

Conclusion

Since much of the religious belief and thought of nonliterate peoples are borne in physical objects and in the processes which produce these objects, several factors have been shown to be especially important if we are to understand and appreciate the religious significance of those objects of nonliterate cultures we usually identify by the term *art*. As we have shown, it does not always make sense to divide these art objects into religious and secular categories. The most utilitarian of objects, like a house or a bowl, may have high religious significance. Further, objects we find aesthetically attractive, like Navajo sand-paintings and African masks, may have, in isolation, little religious significance. They may even be viewed negatively from a religious perspective if they are retained as objects to be displayed for their beautiful appearance. We have shown that much of the significance of artifacts is inseparable from the context of the cultural and religious processes and associated beliefs and principles from which they rise. It is very rare that even a hint of this dimension is available in our museum displays and art collections because so often the display can contain only the leavings of a religiously meaningful process.

In these several examples, we have also discerned that nonliterate peoples commonly base their ideas of beauty on those human processes and actions by which they carry out their responsibility for maintaining the cosmos, that is, for keeping order and meaning in their world. Art and religion are here inseparable. By realizing this fact we can also gain a new appreciation about the kind of creativity in which nonliterate peoples may engage. By Western standards, we commonly evaluate their art as overly repetitive and lacking innovation; we place it in functional, decorative, or craft categories. Now we should see that commonly these objects come about as a result of human actions which are creative in the primary sense, that is, in the sense of bearing cosmic responsibilities, in the sense of making life possible.

QUESTIONS FOR REVIEW AND DISCUSSION

1. Why does Gill choose to start with the account of the *molimo* trumpet? What does this tell us about religion, art, and performance? What does it suggest about the expectations of students and scholars?
2. What are some of the lessons that Gill draws out of the Pygmies' perspectives on religious processes as well as religious and aesthetic values?
3. What are the roles and values of the forest and of sound in this account of the Pygmy people?
4. How does Gill support his assertion that "The *molimo* is an aesthetic and religious event which is creative in a primary sense"?
5. What are several of the illustrations provided by Gill for his section on "Destructible and Disposable Art Objects"? How do they differ? Why is the outside observer's dismay at the destruction of Navajo ritual sandpainting not shared by the Navajo?
6. What do you make of Gill's assessments that some pictures and objects revered by outsiders in our own time as art are in fact "just the leftovers from some cultural event in the context of which they were meaningful"?
7. What is the importance of sound, song, and poetry in the art and religion of nonliterate peoples?
8. Gill uses a number of examples to illustrate art as dynamic process rather than static object. What does he mean by "Eskimo art, too, is not composed of things made but of relationships experienced"? Does this observation hold for art in other examples in this essay?
9. Why does Gill indicate that Baraka's term "arting" may be useful? In this context, how does Gill contrast misconceptions arising from interest only in the art object with the richer understanding exemplified by what Thompson calls "danced art"?

Notes

1 Colin M. Turnbull, *The Forest People: A Study of the Pygmies of the Congo* (New York: Simon & Schuster, 1961), p. 76.
2 *Ibid*, p. 78.
3 *Ibid*, p. 83.
4 Knud Rasmussen, *Report of the Fifth Thule Expedition, 1921–1924*, Vol. 8, Nos. 1 & 2, *The Netsilik Eskimos—Social Life and Spiritual Cultures* (Copenhagen: Gyidendalske Boghandel, 1931), pp. 16, 321.
5 Edmund Carpenter, *Eskimo Realities* (New York: Holt, Rinehart & Winston, 1973), pp. 202–3.
6 Robert F. Thompson, *African Art in Motion: Icon and Art* (Los Angeles: University of California Press, 1974), p. xii.
7 *Ibid*, pp. 191–98.

28 The Principles and Meaning of the Study of Religion

Ninian Smart

Ninian Smart (1927–2001) was born in Cambridge, England, and studied languages, history, and philosophy of religion at the University of Oxford. He held professorships at various universities, including Birmingham, the University of California at Santa Barbara, and at Lancaster, where he established the first department of religious studies in Great Britain. He is regarded as a pioneer in the development of a secular approach to the study of religion, distinct from theology, and was president of the American Academy of Religions (AAR) at the time of his death. Among the over thirty books that he authored, his *The World's Religions* (1989) is a popular introductory university text. Although it was produced by the BBC in 1977, the television series entitled *The Long Search*, on which he served as editorial consultant, is still one of the best explorations of the beliefs and practices within the major religions of the world. The selection that follows presents one of his many articulations of the various dimensions that the secular study of religion should include, and has proven to be an influential guiding framework of principles for religious studies scholars. In later writings than this one, he added a material dimension to the list of six listed here. More significantly, in this article, Smart discusses approaches to the study of the various dimensions, and offers rationales for why these are indispensable.

It is time that thinking about religion in the context of higher and other forms of education was clarified and reformed. I shall concentrate here on the theoretical side of the subject, but I shall not attempt to delineate in detail the social confusions and anxieties which have tended to put a question-mark over many of the theological studies in our universities. There is much to commend in what goes on elsewhere, but the fundamental basis of the study of religion has scarcely been thought out. If someone complains that my theoretical approach is divorced from the practical applications of religion or atheism, my reply is that applications presuppose understanding and clarity of aim.

What kind of discipline is the study of religion? If it tenderly embraces such figureheads as Weber, Durkheim, Lévi-Strauss, Evans-Pritchard; Otto, Pettazzoni, Eliade, van der Leeuw, Zaehner; Feuerbach, Marx, Schweitzer, Barth, Buber, Bultmann, Gogarten, Ebeling, Karl Rahner; Sartre; Aquinas, Hume, Kant, Schleiermacher, Kierkegaard, William James, John Wisdom – not to mention Isaiah, Jesus, Paul, the Buddha, Nagarjuna, Ramanuja, Muhammad and Al-Ghazzali: if it involves the consideration of all these, what form and meaning can it have?

Religion is concretely manifested in a variety of traditions, social structures, forms. Just as there is no colour which is not one of the colours, so there is no religion which is not a particular religion. This multiplicity of form is highly important to the establishing of the foundations of the subject, as we shall see. But there is a further complexity which needs attention.

A religion is complex, organic and subject to change. By saying that it is complex, I mean that there are, so to speak, different dimensions of religion. Thus a religion typically incorporates doctrines, myths, ethical injunctions, rituals and styles of experience, and these are all embodied and manifested in social institutions. It has, in other words, a doctrinal, a mythic, an ethical, a ritual, an experiential and a social dimension. Perhaps the study of religion has too often been over-intellectualistic, and has concentrated too much upon the doctrinal dimension of religion, and the history of religious ideas. This can involve a distortion, precisely because religions are organic. By saying that they are organic, I mean that the different elements and dimensions interpenetrate one another. Thus the meaning of doctrinal concepts has to be understood in the milieu of such activities as worship and of such personal and communal experiences as give vitality to belief. One might in this sense say that religions are 'vertically organic'; but even within one of the dimensions which I have referred to, there is a kind of 'horizontal' organicness. For instance, within the doctrinal dimension, it is not possible to understand the concept of nirvana in Buddhism, without seeing the way in which it is embedded in a whole fabric of doctrines – about the self, about the impermanence of things, about the role of the Buddha, etc. Religious concepts typically come 'not in utter nakedness / But trailing clouds of doctrine do they come'. These concepts also in part gain their meaning from their 'vertical' relationship to practices such as meditation, institutions such as the Sangha, and so forth. In brief, a religion is both complex and organic. Understanding one feature of a religion involves looking more widely at the whole, just as the meaning of a particular patch of colour in a painting is seen by reference to the rest of the painting. The attempt to describe the inter-relationships between the elements in a faith may be called a 'structural description'.

But also a religion changes, and thus a central place in religious studies must always be given to history. Indeed, the historical descriptions of religious changes themselves generate historical explanations; and in understanding a religion from the structural point of view, one tends to be driven to consider the historical origins of particular features of a faith.

But it is necessary, in describing the past, to look at it both from an inward and from an outer perspective. By this I mean that one is not only concerned with the 'outer' fact that the Buddha preached at a certain time or that Paul went on a particular voyage. One is concerned too with the inner intentions and attitudes of the participants in historical events. We might call this *the principle of inwardness*.

This means that the study of religion has some of the properties of anthropology. The anthropologist can scarcely be a mere observer of externals. To understand the meaning of the belief-system of the people with whom he is concerned, he has to engage with them. He may not belong to the group that he studies, but the encounter with people and his own imaginative capacities can lift him from the condition of not belonging to a position of imaginative participation. At least this is required in the study of religion. Some people would go further, and say that there could be no proper structural description of a faith save by those who belong to it. The only description of a religion worth having is one that comes from within, it may be said. There is an important truth contained in this thesis, and I would not wish to under-estimate the problems of entering into other men's religious beliefs, feelings and experiences. Nevertheless, the need to believe in order to understand, in this sense, can be exaggerated. Indeed, if the thesis were taken rigorously, a whole number of important studies would collapse – history, for instance, would become trapped in insuperable problems if ever the historian were concerned with the impact of more than one religious faith on any given phase of human culture. Further, if we think that only a person of the same faith or the same community can understand that faith and that community, then we must ask: What counts as the *same faith* or the *same community?* For example, the modern Christian will regard himself as belonging to a community and faith line going back to New Testament times. But the early adherents of Christianity lived in a cultural milieu highly different from our own today. This, indeed, is a main reason for self-conscious contemporary attempts within Christianity to 'de-mythologise', namely to re-present the essential meaning of New Testament myths, but without using the New Testament cultural clothing. (When I speak of myths here, of course, I do not mean the word in the vulgar sense, to indicate stories which are false, but rather to mean a certain style of expressing beliefs.) In principle, even where a linear identity of community is claimed, the exercise of understanding early phases of the community's faith involves cross-cultural understanding. To put the point crudely: Is the contemporary Christian culturally not more different from the primitive Christian than he is from the present-day Jew?

Again, in regard to the problem of understanding a religion's inwardness, it should be noted that not only are there degrees of understanding, but there are relevant forms of understanding other than the understanding of inwardness. For instance, historical and structural explanations can be relevant to the way a person expresses his inner understanding of his own religion. Belonging to a faith is no guarantee of a *superior* understanding of the religion in question, though it *helps*. A danger of appealing to the principle of inwardness is that a handle is given to artificial restrictions upon the study of religion which are common in our culture.

To sum up so far: a religion is complex, organic, subject to change. It contains both an inward and an outer aspect. Because of its changing character, the history of religion is important. Because of its complex and organic nature, the structural study of religion is important. Because of its inward nature, both historical and structural studies require imaginative participation.

I have attempted to sketch what is meant by a structural description. To some extent the very achievement of a structural description of a religion forms a kind of explanation of its particular features, for the meaning of a given element is brought out by placing it in its living and complex milieu. For instance, to understand what some Christians mean by Real Presence, one has to place this idea in the context of a fabric of ideas and of a fabric of sacramental activities and worship. But in addition to this sort of explanation, which I shall call an internal explanation, there is another kind which ranges further afield. One might, for instance, consider Freud's theory of religion as an attempt at a structural rather than an historical explanation of certain kinds of religious ideas. It is true that Freud himself had a compulsion to back his structural theory by pseudo-historical explanations as well. The tendency in anthropological, psychological and sociological studies of religion is towards such structural explanations of religious phenomena. These, clearly, also become relevant to our treatment of history. If Freud were correct about religion, which I personally partly doubt, his theory would help to explain the appeal and therefore the spread of certain cults.

But this means that the study of religion must be comparative, for the nearest thing to experimentation as a test of structural theories is seeing how they work in relation to separate cultures and historical traditions. For instance Freudian theory of religion seems to break down in Rangoon and Kandy, where Father-figures in religion are notoriously absent. Again, considering the debate about religion between Marxists in China it is obvious that the Marxist classifications of religion which are used do not strictly apply to

Chinese religion, even if they may have applied in the West. Weber's account of Indian religion, in the attempt to establish experimentally his theory about religion and the rise of capitalism, is partly outmoded because the secondary sources have changed so much. The comparative study of religion, unfortunately, is not always geared to this task of the testing of theories, but it has nevertheless been vital to many studies of religion, and remains so. Consider the following quotation from Lévi-Strauss, which indicates also that some of the most exciting problems in the social sciences arise about religion. He writes:

> Of all the chapters of religious anthropology, probably none has tarried to the same extent as studies of mythology. From a theoretical point of view the situation remains very much the same as it was fifty years ago, namely chaotic. Myths are still widely interpreted in conflicting ways: as collective dreams, as the outcome of a kind of aesthetic play, or as the basis of ritual. Mythological figures are considered as personified abstractions, divinised heroes or fallen gods. Whatever the hypothesis, the choice amounts to reducing mythology either to idle play or to a crude kind of philosophic speculation.[1]

But if Lévi-Strauss' diagnosis is correct, think what it means for a whole range of inquiries – for anthropology itself, for biblical studies, for some aspects of the philosophy of religion, for some areas of literature, for some areas of history. If we have indeed failed to understand the nature of myth, these studies to that extent rest upon insecure foundations. Where such great problems exist, there is bound to be excitement and the promise of fruitful advances in understanding. Thus in the sphere of biblical studies, for various reasons, people want to penetrate to the real meaning of early Christian faith. But how can we do this without knowing what it is like to look at, say, the Ascension not from a modern perspective, as an apparently miraculous historical event, but from the perspective of mythic thinking, where *our* distinctions between history and interpretation are not made?

To sum up so far: the fact that the study of religion must be both historical and structural entails that it must also be comparative. Much is lost in understanding if the study of religion is confined simply to one line and one tradition.

I suggested earlier that *at least* what is required for the understanding of religion is a kind of imaginative participation. I say *at least*, but one might better say that actual participation itself is a form of imaginative participation. But clearly the imaginative entering in to other people's perspectives becomes vital and necessary if the study of religion is unavoidably in part comparative. But one needs to say more about this form of participation, which involves, as I said earlier, the encounter with people. To understand others one has to understand oneself. Some of the misinterpretations of religion in anthropology, for instance, have occurred because investigators and theorists have tended to adopt the rationalistic assumptions of their particular society. It is too easy to look upon myth-oriented rituals as simply irrational. If they are treated from such a modern, technological perspective, their real significance is lost, and one is liable to invent such theories as that of Lévy-Bruhl, where a pre-logical way of thinking is ascribed to 'primitives'. The way in which one's own cultural assumptions can distort is brought out in a nice comment by Franz Steiner:

> But we need not retain Lévy-Bruhl's independent category 'primitive punishment' as opposed to the *rational* concept of punishment – as if, since the beginning of the world, there had ever been a rational punishment![2]

In brief, the understanding of others, whether in the past of one's own tradition or in other cultures, requires self-understanding – the understanding of one's own milieu. The observer is not wholly detached: in encountering others and in participating imaginatively in their life, he as it were enters into the very field which he is contemplating. In entering into that field, he himself becomes a subject of his own investigation and he must question his own assumptions. I would therefore argue that historical studies themselves, in the case of religion, need to be coordinated to modern structural studies. There is a continuing dialectic between the ancient and the modern, and between our culture and others.

The combination of the need for imaginative participation and the fact that the study of religion is necessarily bound up with modern structural approaches entails another important side to the whole subject. I have referred to a certain assumption about rationality in Lévy-Bruhl. One can find similar assumptions elsewhere. Thus, in regard to the sociology of religion, Talcott Parsons remarks:

> Weber's theoretical analysis of the role of nonempirical ideas is in fact part of a much broader system of analytical social theory, the emergence of which can be traced in a number of sources quite independent of Weber.
>
> Moreover not only did Weber, Durkheim, and others converge on this particular part of a theoretical system, dealing mainly with religion, but as, among other things, very important parts of the work of both men show, this common scheme of the sociology of religion is in turn part of a broader theoretical system which *includes* the economic and technological analysis of the role of empirical knowledge in relation to rationality of action.[3]

It is clear here that a certain model of the relation between scientific and empirical ideas on the one hand and those of religion on the other is implied. But such a model is, in part at least, the consequence of a certain philosophical position. Many of the notorious problems in the sociology of knowledge and in the history of ideas arise from uncertainty about the interplay between the inner logic of a branch of inquiry and the structural and historical factors in society influencing its development. Consequently, it is not possible to avoid conceptual issues in structural and historical explanations in sociology of religion and elsewhere. The question of the relation between different styles of discourse and ways of thinking is a philosophical question. It follows, therefore, that the logic of the study of religion itself impels one towards taking the philosophy of religion seriously.

But how is the philosophy of religion seriously to be conducted? It should be firmly analytic, in the sense that we should take a careful look at the nature of religious concepts and their logical and other relationships to concepts in different spheres. Thus, for instance, much depends, if we are contemplating the relation between religious concepts and those of science, on conclusions about the real significance of seemingly cosmological statements in religion. Crudely, is *Genesis* playing in the same league as Fred Hoyle? This crude question, on examination, crumbles into many lesser questions about the proper way of analysing and interpreting mythic language, etc. So the philosophy of religion must at least be strongly conceptual and analytic in its concerns. But by the same token, philosophy of religion must be realistic about its subject matter. There is a danger that one may philosophise not about religious language as it actually is and has been, but about a reconstruction of religious language as it ought to be. Thus some supposed recent analyses of religious language turn out to be partly in the nature of apologetics – either in favour of Christianity, or some other religion, or in favour of an atheistic standpoint. If philosophy of religion is to be realistic, then it must be closely related to descriptive and comparative inquiries, and also must be sensitive to the ways in which the understanding of religion changes.

This last remark could be expressed in a different way. One important mode in which a religion may change is the continuing reinterpretation of its meaning in the light of cultural and other changes. It follows from an earlier point in my argument, the point namely that a single community or faith line stretches through a diversity of cultures, that even an appearance of being static involves a changed interpretation of meaning. For instance, the theology of St Thomas Aquinas as used by many Roman Catholic theologians since Leo XIII's Encyclical *Aeterni Patris* has quite a different flavour and significance in the context of these latter days from its flavour and significance in the time of Aquinas himself. To complicate matters, a religious tradition at a given time tends to be variegated, so that different positions are held within it. Sometimes an important point about these positions is that they themselves represent criticisms of current and older interpretations of faith. This is why we sometimes want to make a distinction between empirical Christianity, say, and 'true' or 'authentic' Christianity: one who speaks thus is implicitly criticising aspects of the tradition. Further, changes in the expression of a religion themselves may be a response to external criticisms. It is, for instance, difficult to understand the nineteenth- and twentieth-century developments in Christianity in the West without paying attention to atheistic and agnostic criticisms of Christianity. To some degree, the converse is also true.

In the light of such changes and critical positions, the engagement with religion which is necessary to the project of imaginative participation (including in this, as I said earlier, actual participation) must incorporate engagement with the changing ideas of the religion one is concerned with. Here the concern is not directly descriptive or explanatory, though it is very relevant to these concerns, since the latter themselves, as I have argued, drive one towards philosophical problems about religion, which themselves in turn drive one to a realistic evaluation of religious and atheistic positions. But in being engaged with these, one is placed in the same arena. One might call this engagement with ideas and positions the 'expressive-critical' side of the study of religion. One is liable to be expressing a position within the field, or criticising a position within the field. By the principle I enunciated earlier, namely that ancient studies should always be placed in relationship to modern ones, the most natural way of incorporating the expressive-critical side of the study of religion is by treating it in the modern and even strictly contemporary context. In any event, the only direct access which we have to the inwardness of religion is in the present.

It should be noted that the expressive-critical principle implies that religious studies must always have a penumbra. If we define religion in such a way that it does not include anti-religious atheism – and there seems to be a good reason for defining it in this way, or the atheist is deprived of his anti-religion – then the study of religion itself must always move out into the consideration of positions, such as atheism, which in some respects at least play in the same league.

To sum up this phase of the argument: the descriptive and explanatory aspects of the study of religion themselves raise conceptual issues, and therefore imply the necessity of the philosophy of religion. In turn, the philosophy of religion has to take account of the changing interpretations of religious traditions and in general needs to be realistic. By the principle of imaginative participation, and so engagement with the object, philosophy of religion is bound to take seriously the expressive-critical side. To put this in another way, theological and other expressions of the contemporary tradition, together with external criticisms of these expressions, have a necessary function in the study of religion.

Since concern with the expressive-critical side has sometimes been much abused in the shaping of religious studies, I would wish to insist that, however seriously positions within the field may be taken, the shape of religious studies must not be determined by a single position within the field. I believe that no field of inquiry should have its total shape determined by a position within it. The position within the field which has determined the shape of many university studies of theology has been this – that biblical and early Church ideas and realities are normative for Christian faith, and that the task of theology is some-how to study the latter. There are at least two ways of treating this task. One is to confine inquiries to the empirical level – to turn them into historical and to some extent structural inquiries, though restricting attention primarily to the early material. The other is to accept the logic of the term 'normative' and to use the material as a basis for *expressing* the Christian faith. The former way of approaching the study of religion is defective because of its con-finement to a small area of empirical data. If my argument hitherto has been persuasive, a very restricted understanding of religion, or of a particular phase of religion, is bound to accrue upon the ancient-history approach to Christianity. The second way of approaching the study of religion is at least more candid, but has a double defect: firstly it tends to be insulated from the wider understanding of religion which structural and comparative studies can bring[4] and secondly, by the very fact that it begins from an exclusive position within the expressive-critical field, it is liable to become inhibited and even secretive in the context of academic institutions devoted to an open and critical pursuit of truth. The logic of religious studies leads to a degree of pluralism, and it is in the pluralistic situation in any case that expressions and criticisms of religious faith can be candidly and excitingly made.

The danger of the dominance of a particular position in shaping the study of religion implies that a clearer pattern of studies will always emerge if one sees the expressive-critical side as following logically from the descriptive and explanatory sides, rather than con-versely. I would as a matter of fact argue that the converse logic works also. But it should not escape attention that the study of religion is so often treated by reference to a single tradition and on the basis of a particular position. Too often the deeper consideration of modern social anthropology, sociology, psychology, philosophy and history has been neglected, as though an elucidation of biblical and early Christian ideas were sufficient and as if interest in these other matters were an amateurish luxury. By the converse logic I would argue that in any event the elucidation of those early ideas requires a very ramified, modern and imaginative structure of inquiry.

I have attempted to formulate the principles for the study of religion. I have not been concerned with the application and usefulness of this study to society at large. The nerve of the argument can be summed up as follows. The study of religion must be in part historical and therefore descriptive. But the principle of inwardness must be employed, so that his-torical and other descriptions must incorporate descriptions of the perspectives of those who hold religious beliefs and participate in worship and other religious activities. In view of the complex and organic nature of religious belief-systems, inner description involves a form of structural description. Both historical accounts and structural descriptions in some measure function in an explanatory manner, and one is thus driven in the study of religion to wider forms of explanation, chiefly structural. These themselves need to be tested comparatively, and therefore the study of religion itself must involve some multiplicity. The principle of inwardness implies that the investigator himself must engage with the belief and positions that he seeks to understand. He thus enters the field of his own investigation, and thus must have an understanding of his own individual and cultural condition. This implies that there must always be a dialectic between ancient and modern studies and between one's own culture and others'. But also, attempts at explanation themselves generate conceptual issues, philosophical ones. This is a further reason for engagement with the expressive-critical side of religion, for philosophical approaches need to be living and realistic. Thus a necessary feature of the study of religion is the interplay from within it of expressive-critical positions, and it is in this sense that religious studies incorporate theology. But the shape of the field must not be determined from a position within it. Concretely it follows from all this that at least the following branches of study are necessary.

First, there must be history of religions, for without it there are no data for a testing of structural explanations. *Second*, there must be phenomenology of religion, in which a sound classification and understanding of elements of religion can be reached: without this the data supplied by the history of religions are unfruitful. *Third*, there must be sociology of religion and its kin, such as social anthropology and the psychology of religion; for without these our understanding of religious ideas and phenomena becomes unstructural, unself-critical and over-intellectualistic. *Fourth*, there must be philosophy of religion, for conceptual decisions are deeply embedded in structural explanations and descriptions within the social sciences. *Fifth*, there must be engagement with modern religious and atheistic thought, for without this philosophical and structural approaches to religion become insensitive to change and to one aspect of the inwardness of description; moreover they are necessary to self-understanding, without which the attempt to understand others by engagement and imaginative participation can be grossly distorted. *Sixth*, in our culture and because modern studies of religion have so far been primarily developed in the West, the engagement with modern religious thought most naturally is tied to an understanding of the Judaeo-Christian tradition, and part of the contemporary inwardness of this tradition is that it looks to origins. Hence, there is a strong argument for maintaining a dialectic between biblical studies and modern expressive-critical positions. It happens too that such studies raise actually the problems of anachronism that beset understanding. Thus the New Testament must be seen both historically and dialectically, where the dialectic is between ancient and modern, between the origins and their re-presentation.

There are other aspects of the study of religion which ought also to be developed, but these at least seem the most necessary.

The student of religion thus needs to have historical knowledge and expertise, sensitivity and imagination in crossing cultures and time, and analytical grasp. He has to be a latter-day Leonardo. This shows why Religious Studies is neither the Queen of the Sciences nor the Knave of Arts; but it is one of the foci of the humanities and social sciences. In it some of the most engaging and perplexing problems in these disciplines have a meeting point. For to tell the truth, we are all of us far from having anything but rather superficial grasp of the multiple structures of religious faith, myths and institutions.

QUESTIONS FOR REVIEW AND DISCUSSION

1. What are the various dimensions of religion that Smart discerns within the religions of the world? Which of these dimensions does he feel has received the most attention?
2. Does Smart see these dimensions as fundamentally distinct, or do they overlap with each other?
3. What does Smart mean by "imaginative participation," and why is it important? Do you agree?

4. Why does Smart recommend comparative study of religions to assess structural theories?
5. Why is a self-understanding of "one's own milieu" recommended as one attempts to understand the traditions of others? Do you agree?
6. What arguments does Smart offer to justify the importance of the philosophical study of religion? How does he characterize this approach, and what ought to be included within its scope?
7. What are some of the branches of study that Smart deems necessary for a holistic study of religion? He states that there are others that also ought to be developed. Could you propose a few additions?
8. What do you think are the strengths or limitations of how Smart formulates these principles for the study of religion?

Notes

1 *Structural Anthropology*, tr. Claire Jacobson and Brooke Grundfest Schoepf (1963), p. 207.
2 *Taboo* (1956), p. 113.
3 *Essays in Sociological Theory* (revised edition, 1954), p. 32.
4 For instance, Christian mysticism may be taken seriously, but the question of whether similar types of experience occur in, say, Buddhism is not raised.

29 Cognitive Science of Religion: What Is It and Why Is It?

Justin L. Barrett

Justin L. Barrett (1971–) studied psychology at Calvin College and received his PhD in experimental psychology with a cognitive and developmental focus from Cornell University. He has served on faculties at Calvin College, the University of Michigan, Ann Arbor, and the University of Oxford (where he was a senior researcher of the Centre for Anthropology and Mind and The Institute for Cognitive and Evolutionary Anthropology) before joining the Fuller Graduate School of Psychology as the Director of the Thrive Center for Human Development, Thrive Professor of Developmental Science, and Professor of Psychology. His interest in the cognitive study of culture is apparent in the *Journal of Cognition and Culture*, of which he is a founding editor. Barrett's books *Why Would Anyone Believe in God?* (2004); *Cognitive Science, Religion, and Theology: From Human Minds to Divine Minds* (2011); and *Born Believers: The Science of Children's Religious Belief* (2012) are geared to introducing a general audience to this relatively recent interdisciplinary area of the cognitive science of religion (CSR). The following 2007 article serves this same goal. Barrett suggests a "natural religion," into which everyone is born, that is shaped by human cognition with similarities across cultures. His 2011 book's inclusion in the Templeton Science and Religion Series suggests a view of cognitive science that is not antagonistic toward religious claims.

Abstract

Cognitive science of religion (CSR) brings theories from the cognitive sciences to bear on why religious thought and action is so common in humans and why religious phenomena take on the features that they do. The field is characterized by a piecemeal approach, explanatory non-exclusivism, and methodological pluralism. Topics receiving consideration include how ordinary cognitive structures inform and constrain the transmission of religious ideas, why people believe in gods, why religious rituals and prayers tend to have the forms that they do, why afterlife beliefs are so common, and how human memory systems influence socio-political features in religious systems. CSR is often associated with evolutionary science and anti-religious rhetoric but neither is intrinsic nor necessary to the field.

Fifteen years ago, there was no such thing as cognitive science of religion (CSR). Only a handful of scholars independently using insights from the cognitive sciences to study religion existed. Today CSR boasts dozens of authored and edited volumes, numerous academic units and centers prominently featuring its activities, and a scholarly association with more than 100 members (the International Association for the Cognitive Science of Religion). Findings from CSR have attracted the attention of the popular media as well, appearing in such places as the *New York Times Sunday Magazine* and *Atlantic Monthly*.[1] What accounts for all of the attention to this upstart area of scholarship?

On the substantive side, CSR as a field offers at least three attractive features for scholars interested in explaining religious phenomena. First, it avoids the age-old problem of defining 'religion'. Rather than specify what religion is and try to explain it in whole, scholars in this field have generally chosen to approach 'religion' in an incremental, piecemeal fashion, identifying human thought or behavioral patterns that might count as 'religious' and then trying to explain why those patterns are cross-culturally recurrent. If the explanations turn out to be part of a grander explanation of 'religion', so be it. If not, meaningful human phenomena have still been rigorously addressed.

This piecemeal approach makes the field complementary to the activities of other religion scholars from many disciplinary perspectives, a stance of explanatory non-exclusivity. CSR does not pretend to exhaustively explain everything that might be called 'religion' (provocative book titles aside). Rather, it seeks to detail the basic cognitive structure of thought and action that might be deemed religious and invites historians, anthropologists, sociologists, psychologists and other religion scholars to fill in the hows and whys of particular religious phenomena.

A third scholarly virtue that CSR presents is methodological pluralism. In seeking out what constitute cross-culturally and historically recurrent features of human religious cognition, scholars in this field have turned to whatever data collection and analysis methods that appear appropriate to the questions at hand including ethnographic,[2] interview,[3] historical,[4] archeological,[5] computer modeling,[6] and experimental, including cross-cultural and developmental techniques.[7]

In this essay, I illustrate the presence of these three scholarly virtues in CSR (a piecemeal approach, explanatory non-exclusivism, and methodological pluralism) through a brief summary of CSR's state of the art. Such a review is necessarily selective and so I apologize to my colleagues whose valuable contributions I have been unable to include.

Unifying Theoretical Commitments

What unifies the various projects in CSR is the commitment that human conceptual structures are not merely a product of cultural contingencies but that they inform and constrain cultural expression, including religious thought and action. That is, as demonstrated in numerous ways since the start of the cognitive revolution in psychology, human minds are not blank slates or undifferentiated all-purpose processing machines that are wholly socially constructed.[8] Rather, through the course of development in any cultural context, human minds/brains exhibit a number of functional regularities regarding how they process information. These functional regularities are also known as domain-specific inference systems or 'mental tools'.[9] For instance, one mental tool concerns language. Humans (especially pre-pubescent humans) readily acquire and use natural languages but are not facile with non-natural symbolic communication systems such as binary code. By better understanding how the particulars of our language-processing systems handle information, we have been able to better understand why human languages take the forms that they do. Cognition informs and constrains linguistic expression. Analogously, many different mental tools inform and constrain religious expression.

This theoretical commitment to the shaping power of naturally emerging mental tools is illustrated by two prominent findings of the field: theological correctness (TC) and the minimal counterintuitiveness (MCI) theory.

Theological Correctness

Through a series of experiments with religious believers and non-believers in the USA and in India, Barrett and colleagues demonstrated that adults' god concepts can function in markedly divergent ways depending on the conceptual demands of the context (Barrett 1998, 1999; Barrett & Keil 1996; Barrett & VanOrman 1996).

In the case of simply reporting one's theological beliefs, a so-called off-line task, adults in all samples claimed a theologically correct or TC understanding of the god in question. In contrast, however, during an on-line task in which adults had to use their god concepts to process information, their god concept looked far less TC and far more anthropomorphic.

The on-line task took advantage of previous cognitive psychological research demonstrating that people sometimes make intrusion errors when remembering stories. Their concepts fill in inferential gaps necessarily present in any narrative and so they can misremember the conceptual information as having been present in the original story (Bransford & McCarrell 1974). Barrett and colleagues' stories included God (or Shiva, Vishnu, Krishna, or Brahman) as a character but left gaps regarding God's physical and mental properties. Regularly adults who denied God as having a particular location in space reported that the stories told of God moving from one place to another or that God was walking on a road – information that was not included in the story nor even necessarily implied (as demonstrated by control experiments using novel characters in the place of God). Similarly, adults who claimed that God can listen to or attend to any number of things at once, misremembered stories as saying that God was unable to hear something because of a loud noise or had to answer one prayer before *going* and attending to another. Across a number of different physical and mental properties adults exhibited a gulf between their TC off-line concepts of God and their more anthropomorphic on-line concepts. It appears that the greater computational demands of the on-line task require adults to use concepts with which they have greater processing fluency; in this case, a human-like concept.

Minimal Counterintuitiveness

More follows from cognitive constraint on religious thought than an occasional and amusing tendency to think of gods as more human-like than we know we ought. As religious communication typically takes place in on-line contexts, the cognitive pressure for individuals to use computationally easy concepts creates a collective tendency to transmit successfully only concepts that largely satisfy the output assumptions of our mental tools. That is, during typical on-line communication, concepts may not be more than minimally counterintuitive if they are to be successfully communicated.

Dan Sperber has developed a strategy for studying culture that he has termed *epidemiology of representations* (Sperber 1996). We can explain why some ideas or practices are so widespread by considering how human minds might be more likely to generate and transmit some ideas over others. Our naturally developing mental tools readily generate certain kinds of ideas we call *intuitive* regardless of cultural context. For instance, our mental tool for understanding physical objects assumes that solid objects cannot pass through other solid objects.[10] If someone tells a story about someone being frustrated by a treasure being locked behind a closed door, all listeners understand the problem – the person cannot simply walk through the wall.

These rather pedestrian-sounding observations about communication and intuitive cognition come to explanatory life when applied to cultural concepts such as religious ideas. Pascal Boyer has offered a cognitive optimum theory, also known as the MCI theory of religious transmission.[11] Boyer suggested that though fully intuitive concepts are readily transmitted, concepts that slightly deviate from the intuitive expectations of our mental tools might be transmitted even more successfully (all else being equal). This advantage stems from minimally counterintuitive concepts avoiding overtaxing our conceptual systems (and hence being subject to distortion or confusion as in TC), but offering an idea just challenging enough to require additional attention.

Compare the idea of a barking dog that is brown on the other side of the fence to a barking dog that is able to pass through solid objects on the other side of the fence. The first dog is wholly intuitive and excites little interest. The second dog is slightly or minimally counterintuitive and is, consequently, more attention demanding but without overloading on-line conceptual systems. The idea of a dog that passes through solid objects, is made of metal parts, gives birth to chickens, experiences time backwards, can read minds, and vanishes whenever you look at it would amount to a massively counterintuitive concept – if it is a coherent concept at all. Boyer argues that it is the second dog and not the first or the third that will tend to be better remembered and more faithfully transmitted. Note that whether or not something is intuitive or counterintuitive in this technical sense is based on natural dispositions of mental tools and not on cultural particularities. Hence, Boyer's prediction is that the second dog would be best remembered and transmitted by people anywhere.

Research on MCI theory has been generally supportive. Lisdorf (2001) demonstrated that Roman prodigy lists from the first three centuries BC conform tightly to Boyer's predictions: a majority show counterintuitive features with 99% of these having only a single counterintuitive violation, 1% having two violations, and none of 354 having more than two. Barrett and Nyhof experimentally tested the claim that MCI concepts possess a transmission advantage over intuitive and culturally bizarre but not counterintuitive concepts. They used a story recall design and two transmission designs that involved the telling and re-telling of stories. Results supported Boyer's predictions, becoming even stronger after a 3-month delay before recall (Barrett & Nyhof 2001). Boyer and Ramble used a similar recall design and found in France, Gabon, and Nepal that MCI concepts were more faithfully remembered than intuitive or more than MCI concepts (Boyer & Ramble 2001). More recent studies have suggested that these effects may be modulated by the context of the transmission but appear to use some items that deviate from Boyer's strict sense of *counterintuitive*.[12]

Boyer argues that the religious concepts of ordinary laypeople the world over are not all that counterintuitive. Rather they tend to be MCI concepts, particularly minimally or modestly counterintuitive *agents* (Boyer 2001, 2003). Part of the reason they are such successful cultural concepts is that they do not overload our cognitive systems. Theological ideas that exceed this cognitive optimum would likely be distorted or ignored, a dynamic Boyer (2001) calls the 'tragedy of the theologian' and D. Jason Slone dubbed 'theological incorrectness' (Slone 2004). Agents gain additional reinforcement through some of the mechanisms described below.

Ordinary, naturally developing cognitive systems (mental tools) inform and constrain religious thought and action. This theme recurs in the many different problems CSR has addressed, and the field has emphasized the role of intuitive vs. explicit theology, though syntheses have been suggested.[13]

Cognition and Gods

A cognitive science perspective offers a theoretically motivated working definition for a *god:* a counterintuitive agent that motivates actions – provided its existence is believed in.[14] Gods, ghosts, ancestor spirits, devils, witches, and angels would all count as gods under such a definition but powerful human leaders, rock stars, and athletes would not – no matter how much they are worshipped, adored, used as role models, or inspire the formation of cohesive communities.

Perhaps the earliest cognitive treatment of a religious domain was anthropologist Stewart Guthrie's revival of the anthropomorphism theory of why belief in gods is so prevalent (Guthrie 1980, 1993). Guthrie argues that humans have a perceptual bias to attend to human-like forms or other information that might be caused by humans-like beings. He casts the argument in terms of an evolved tendency that produces false positives for the sake of survival. As humans and other agents (such as predatory mammals) represented our greatest threats and promises for survival and reproduction in our evolutionary environment, better to assume the rustling in the brush is an intentional agent than assume it is just the wind. To assume it is an agent and be wrong may carry some cost in terms of needless running away, but not nearly so much cost as missing a tiger and becoming lunch. Guthrie argues that we evolved a bias to over-detect evidence of human-like agency around us and so we attribute natural forces and events to human-like beings or gods.

This cognitive system responsible for detecting intentional agency is the hypersensitive agency detection device (HADD).[15] Although determining whether HADD delivers false positives in the case of detecting spirits, ghosts, and gods is to make metaphysical commitments, HADD certainly merits the 'hypersensitive' labeling at least because it does not require a human form or very much information for HADD to (at least temporarily) detect something as an agent. Experiments with infants suggest that HADD is active in the first 5 months of life and only requires self-propelled and purposeful-looking movement for it to identify colored disks as agents (Rochat, Morgan & Carpenter 1997).

The reflexive and easily overridden agency detection of HADD has led some scholars in the field to question its centrality in generating beliefs in gods (Atran 2002; Boyer 2001). Why do we sometimes think the bump in the night is just the wind and sometimes decide it is a ghost? Do people really often have experiences that they then take to be the direct presence or action of a god? Even though these concerns challenge the sufficiency of HADD for explaining why people believe in gods, undoubtedly HADD may play a role in encouraging the spread of ideas about or belief in gods (counterintuitive agents that motivate actions). As Guthrie suggests, a HADD experience of detecting agency may fail to be rejected as irrelevant and may motivate the postulation of a (MCI) god to account for the experience. This god belief may be entertained by others because of similar otherwise inexplicable HADD experiences and especially if the god concept candidate meets the cognitive optimum of being minimally counterintuitive. Alternatively, people already familiar with a god concept (but who do not necessarily believe) may have an HADD experience that either strengthens their belief or motivates them to transmit the concept. Either way, HADD experiences may add emotional motivation to aid the generation or transmission of god concepts, even if only rarely.

Psychosocial Reasoning

Religious concepts and particularly god concepts may be successful cultural ideas because they are minimally or modestly counterintuitive and because they receive an occasional boost in a population by their ability to make sense of HADD experiences. Additional motivation to talk about and believe in gods may come from their ability to account for striking events that otherwise have no intuitive explanation.[16] When our intuitive reasoning systems that find basic physical or biological causes for events fail to explain satisfactorily an emotionally salient event (e.g., a series of illnesses or a devastating natural disaster), we appear prone to turn to psychosocial explanations. As psychosocial agents that have different powers than people, gods may readily be incorporated into such reasoning. (The gods are angry with my cousin and so have afflicted him with illness.) If exercised repeatedly, such patterns of reasoning may gain cumulative plausibility and reinforce belief in and the transmission of god concepts (Barrett 2004b; Boyer 2001).

Born Believers

In addition to the numerous ways in which god concepts may enjoy horizontal transmission advantages within and between groups, research suggests that children's cognitive systems may be especially receptive to certain god concepts (Barrett & Richert 2003; Richert & Barrett 2006). Indeed, Deborah Kelemen has even suggested that children may be 'intuitive theists' (2004) and Paul Bloom has proclaimed that when considering the developmental evidence, 'Religion is natural' (2007).

As summarized by Kelemen (2004), evidence from British and American children demonstrates that children have a strong bias to see the natural world as purposeful even in ways that religiously committed adults would never (deliberately) teach their offspring. For instance, children are inclined to say rocks are 'pointy' not because of some physical processes but because being pointy keeps them from being sat upon. This 'promiscuous teleology' extends to living and non-living natural things (Kelemen 1999a,b,c,d, 2003). Recent research suggests that even 12-month-olds understand that only intentional beings create order from disorder (Newman et al. forthcoming). Not surprisingly, then, children have a strong bias to see the world as purposefully designed (DiYanni & Kelemen 2005; Kelemen & DiYanni 2005). But designed by whom?

Interviews with children conducted by Jean Piaget (1929) led him to conclude that children are 'artificialists', attributing natural entities such as lakes and mountains to human ingenuity. More recent and more tightly controlled research demonstrates that preschoolers regard gods and not people as the origin of natural design (Gelman & Kremer 1991; Petrovich 1997, 1999). No wonder then that Margaret Evans has documented that children, regardless of their parents' beliefs about the origins of animals, prefer creationist accounts to evolutionary ones until late childhood (2000, 2001).

Given these experimental findings, it would not be at all surprising that children would readily latch onto the notion of a creator god or gods. Children's preparedness to believe in gods does not, however, end with a god's creative power. Children also appear ready to believe in a super knowing and super perceiving God.

Barrett and colleagues demonstrated that children younger than 8 or 9 years need not strictly anthropomorphize God, a position advanced by many researchers in the Piagetian tradition (Elkind 1970; Goldman 1965). At least when it comes to mental properties such as perception and beliefs, children as young as 4 or 5 may hold markedly different expectations for God and people. Across a series of experiments, Barrett and his collaborators replicated a standard finding that children presume others' beliefs and perceptions are reliable reflections of what the child knows to be reality. If the 3-year-olds know that a cracker box contains rocks, so would his mother, a bear, God, or anyone else (Barrett,

Richert & Driesenga 2001). Hence, 3-year-olds answer correctly (theologically speaking) for God but incorrectly for mother. By age 5, children generally know that beliefs are fallible and, for instance, mother would likely believe a cracker box to contain crackers even if the child knows that there are rocks in the box. But children did not extend this fallibility to God. They continued to be theologically accurate. Knight et al. (2004) replicated this finding with Mayan children living in Mexico.

Barrett and colleagues also investigated children's understanding about who can know the meaning of a secret code or newly invented game (Barrett, Newman & Richert 2003), who would be able to see an object in the dark, hear a currently inaudible sound, or smell something not currently detected (Richert & Barrett 2005). Across these different problems a single developmental pattern emerged: 3-year-old children assume that all intentional agents have super knowledge or perception and as children mature they learn that people and some animals (but not necessarily God) have mental limitations. By age 5, children are capable of distinguishing God's super abilities from more mundane human ones, but it is human limitations that have to be learned (Barrett 2001a; Barrett & Richert 2003; Richert & Barrett 2006).

Children's early developing cognitive bias to see the natural world as purposefully designed by non-human agency makes God a natural idea for children to acquire. Children's default assumption that intentional agents are likewise super knowing and super perceiving means that acquiring the notion of an all-knowing, all-perceiving God likewise presents no special difficulties. That God is unseen is no particular problem to children either. Research on imaginary friends demonstrates that normal children readily reason about the mental and emotional states and actions of invisible beings (Taylor 1999); hence, God's invisibility is no obstacle to belief in young children.

Afterlife and Spirits

Arguably the oldest and most widespread form of god concepts is the ancestor spirit or ghost, a type of afterlife belief. At least three competing schools of thought regarding afterlife beliefs might be identified among cognitive scholars: those who regard belief in an afterlife as a counterintuitive idea that must be taught and encouraged much as beliefs in fairies or magic (Astuti & Harris forthcoming); those who see afterlife beliefs as slightly counterintuitive but supported as a unique by-product of the natural functioning of two sometimes contradicting domain-specific functional units of the human brain (Boyer 2001); and those who see afterlife beliefs as intuitive and almost inevitable because of selective pressure in their favor (Bering 2006).

Bering's controversial position might be called the simulation constraint theory, and has received the most empirical attention. He argues that belief in the afterlife is intuitive because of our inability to simulate or imagine what it would be like to no longer have thoughts, feelings, or awareness (Bering 2002; Bering & Bjorklund 2004). Consequently, all people from childhood, he suggests, are strongly biased to believe in an afterlife, a bias that those who deny an afterlife must struggle against. Counter to a simple learning model, Bering shows in one set of experiments that American children have stronger commitments to an afterlife earlier in childhood.[17] Bering further argues that such a strong predisposition to have afterlife beliefs was encouraged by evolutionary selective pressure because holding such a belief promotes reputation-enhancing behavior. If you believe ghosts or ancestor spirits might be around and watching, you are more inclined to behave in ways good for your social reputation. He supports this claim by experiments with adults and children that show that a suggested ghost or invisible observer deters cheating.[18]

Actions

CSR provides theoretical resources for partitioning religious actions not by way of their function or meaning but by virtue of how they are cognitively represented.[19] Still an understudied area in the field, below I offer sketches of three areas of religious action that have received attention.

Religious Ritual

E. Thomas Lawson and Robert McCauley's ritual form theory begins by circumscribing its focus as those actions that change the status of participants and represent culturally postulated superhuman agents in the action structure (Lawson & McCauley 1990; McCauley & Lawson 2002). Lawson and McCauley call these actions 'religious rituals'. They argue that as actions religious rituals are conceptualized using the same action representation system as is used for any other action. That is, they do not use culturally specific or specially acquired cognitive mechanisms for generating expectations, inferences, and explanations about religious rituals. Consequently, across religious traditions or cultures some commonalities in how religious rituals are understood would be expected. Specifically, Lawson and McCauley make a number of predictions about how the form of the ritual (e.g., where superhuman agency is represented in the action structure) would predict participant and observer judgements regarding aspects of the religious ritual performance. These predictions include whether a given religious ritual is ritually reversible or repeatable, the ritual is performed with high levels of sensory pageantry, substitutions of different elements are permissible, and the relative centrality of the religious ritual to the religious tradition. Capturing so many performance-related features of religious rituals without appeal to cultural particulars, theological meaning, or social function would be a major explanatory achievement. But is the ritual form theory correct? Additional empirical treatment is essential, but so far experimental and ethnographic results are generally consistent with the theory. Malley and Barrett report evidence from interviews that the ritual form theory's various predictions are largely consistent with intuitions regarding religious rituals in Hinduism, Judaism, and Islam.[20]

Prayer

In studies demonstrating how cognitive systems can inform religious practice where theology is silent, Barrett examined petitionary prayer among North American Protestants (Barrett 2001b, 2002a). Although Protestants are taught to make requests of God, they are not generally instructed regarding the mode of causation to ask God to operate through. When I lose my keys I could ask God to act on me psychologically (remind me where I left them or help me detect where they are in a cluttered house) or I could ask God to act physically (have them materialize in my pocket). Either course of action is possible for an all-powerful God, but the TC findings predict an intuitive preference to ask a psycho-social being to act psychologically or socially. How then do people tend to pray? Through analysis of prayer journals and through a questionnaire technique asking young adults to judge their most likely prayer strategy in a number of hypothetical situations, Barrett found a tendency for his young adult participants to pray for God to act through psychological or social causation more than through biological or physical causation. These findings suggest intuitive assumptions about agentive causation creep in when theology is silent.

Spirit Possession

A more common phenomenon than many Westerners realize, spirit possession prompts some profound cognitive challenges (Cohen 2007). The identity of a spirit or god must be understood by observers even when it clothes itself in the bodies of different people at different times. Furthermore, the actions and moral culpability of the actions of people must be distinguished from those of the possessing spirit. Given these difficulties, why is spirit possession cross-culturally pervasive in recognizably similar forms? Research in this area is still young, though Emma Cohen's cognitive engagement on the subject has already provided a promising-sounding hint: understanding spirit possession capitalizes on an already present conceptual arrangement that appears naturally as part of human development, an unconscious causal and representational distinction between minds and bodies, or 'intuitive dualism' (Bloom 2004). Through ethnographic and experimental work, Cohen has provided some preliminary evidence that even in the face of contrary theological teaching, spirit possession is most readily construed by observers and participants as a displacement of the mind from the body, and that a one-mind/one-body principle emerging from human cognitive architecture supports the ready understanding of spirit possession in this manner (Cohen 2007; Cohen & Barrett forthcoming).

Socio-Political Arrangements: Modes of Religiosity

Perhaps the most ambitious project in CSR is Harvey Whitehouse's modes of religiosity theory (1995, 1996a, 2000, 2004). Whitehouse tries to capture how cognitive dynamics in different types of collective religious events prompt the clustering into two distinct modes of religiosity of a number of social and political features.

In the imagistic mode, the transmission of central theological insights is through rarely performed but highly emotional events such as brutal initiation rites or rites of terror (Whitehouse 1996b). These events are cognitively conducive for creating emotion-laden memories of events and co-participants, generating individual exegetical rumination, and spurring feelings of relational connectedness with co-participants. Because of these psychological dynamics, religious systems in this mode will tend to have relatively local, egalitarian political structures, be light on orthodoxy controls, and slow at expanding membership.

In contrast, the doctrinal mode revolves around frequently performed, relatively low-arousal theological transmission events (e.g., modern Protestant Christianity). Such events are cognitively suitable for transmission of complex theological ideas by means of explicit instruction (e.g., in sermons and texts) and the storing of such ideas in semantic memory. Religions of the doctrinal mode tend to involve relatively hierarchical political structures for enforcing doctrinal orthodoxy, the potential for large imagined communities of fellow participants, and the potential for rapid expansion.

More thorough explanations of Whitehouse's theory and evidence and historical, archeological, and anthropological applications relevant to it may be found elsewhere (Barrett 2005; Whitehouse 2000, 2004; Whitehouse & Martin 2004).

Additional Areas of Promising Inquiry

Numerous other areas of research related to religion are also beginning to benefit from cognitive scientific perspectives. These include magic (Sørensen 2007), scripture as artifact and scripturalism (Malley 2004), miracles (Pyysiäinen 2004b, forthcoming), the nature of souls (Richert & Harris 2006), and atheism (Barrett, 2004b; Saler & Ziegler 2006). Engagement with prominent themes in psychology of religion such as religious experience, attachment, and god image research remains in need of greater development.[21]

Using evolutionary-adaptationist perspectives alongside cognitive ones is increasingly prevalent in contemporary natural scientific studies of religion.[22] For instance, the idea of religious rituals as a form of costly-signaling that facilitates reciprocal altruism and intra-group cooperation has been receiving considerable attention.[23] Perhaps, too, belief in gods gains selective reinforcement because of its tendency to produce reputation-enhancing or pro-social actions (Bering & Johnson 2005; Johnson 2005). Additionally, an account connecting an evolved hazard precaution system to why people engage in ritualized behaviors in religious and non-religious contexts has recently been developed (Boyer & Lienard 2006; Lienard & Boyer 2006). Perhaps a genuine cognition-evolution synthesis in which evolutionary accounts of subsystems that underlie religious thought and action and how particular religious thought and action might have adaptive value will increasingly characterize the field.

Clarifications and Conclusions

The summary above aims to demonstrate that CSR is characterized by three substantive tendencies that may contribute to its growing prominence: a piecemeal approach, explanatory non-exclusivism, and methodological pluralism. Joining these three substantive factors, however, are at least two rhetorical ones deserving mention and clarification. First, CSR is often associated with an anti-religious agenda (Henig 2007). For instance, books by Dennett (2006) and Dawkins (2006) parade findings from CSR as part of their quixotic quest of freeing the world from religious thought. By no means does the cognitive approach or findings necessarily entail such a perspective nor does it represent the personal position of many of those prominent in the field.[24] Nevertheless, strident, combative rhetoric – merited or not – attracts attention.

Similarly, CSR has become closely identified with evolutionary psychology and anthropology. Perhaps the ironic possibility of evolution not just competing with religion over 'human nature' but explaining religion as well tantalizes observers of the field and participants alike. The relationship between CSR and evolutionary science is, however, more opportunistic than necessary. That is, CSR could explore how natural human cognition informs and constrains religious expression without explaining why human cognition is how it is. Such an explanation, perhaps provided by evolutionary psychology, increases the depth of CSR's accounts,[25] but in fact amounts to a secondary project. To illustrate, specifying HADD's role in promoting belief in gods may help to explain the recurrence of theistic beliefs whether or not we know why humans have such a device. An evolutionary account of HADD amplifies the explanation but is peripheral. At its core CSR describes how human cognition is (not why it is) and how that explains religious expression.

To conclude, although a number of factors have undoubtedly sped the blossoming of CSR over the past 15 years, three scholarly, substantive factors (a piecemeal approach, explanatory non-exclusivism, and methodological pluralism) and two unnecessary rhetorical ones (anti-religious tone and connection with evolutionary sciences) may have contributed. More importantly, perhaps, CSR works. It does not merely offer useful analogies or interpretive frameworks or new tools for richer descriptions of religious phenomena. Rather CSR offers empirically testable, theoretically motivated scientific explanations for why religious thought and actions tend to develop and spread the way they do.

QUESTIONS FOR REVIEW AND DISCUSSION

1. How do Barrett's perspectives on the cognitive science of religion (CSR) contrast with Freud's early psychological perspectives on religion and with Dennett's contemporary cognitive studies views?

2. How is the cognitive science of religion (CSR) defined in this article? Is there a dominant method or approach?

3. CSR is a very new interdisciplinary field of study. What examples does Barrett provide as evidence for its rapid growth?

4. What does Barrett list as key attractions for scholars to engage with CSR? Which of these "three scholarly virtues" do you think might be most beneficial for the academic study of religion?

5. In your own words, paraphrase how "human conceptual structures ... inform and constrain cultural expression, including religious thought and action." What are some of the "mental tools" involved in this process?

6. What is minimal counterintuitiveness (MCI) theory? Can you give an example from a religious tradition that seems consistent with Pascal Boyer's cognitive optimum theory in which "concepts that slightly deviate from the intuitive expectations of our mental tools might be transmitted even more successfully"?

7. Barrett offers the following definition for a god from a cognitive science perspective: "definition for a *god:* a counterintuitive agent that motivates actions – provided its existence is believed in." What are the advantages or limitations to this definition?

8. What are some of the cognitive reasons given for why people believe in god(s)?

9. What are some of the findings that suggest children "may be especially receptive to certain god concepts"?

10. Describe Bering's position about belief in the afterlife and spirits. How does he relate this to the promotion of "reputation-enhancing behavior"? How does this theory differ from the other two theories in the "Afterlife and Spirits" section?

11. In his concluding section, Barrett asserts that CSR works and "offers empirically testable, theoretically motivated scientific explanations for why religious thought and actions tend to develop and spread the way they do." He also indicates some of the attention received by CSR might be related to the fact that "books by Dennett (2006) and Dawkins (2006) parade findings from CSR as part of their quixotic quest of freeing the world from religious thought." What is Barrett's position on the relationship between CSR and this "anti-religious tone", belief in god(s), and evolutionary science?

Notes

1 Henig, R, (2007), 'Darwin's God', *New York Times Sunday Magazine*, March 4, 2007; Bloom, P, (2005), 'Is God An Accident?' *Atlantic Monthly* (December 2005), pp. 1–8. The name 'Cognitive Science of Religion' appears to have been first used in print to refer to this field by Barrett (2000).

2 For example, Cohen (2007); Whitehouse & Laidlaw (2004). Pyysiäinen & Anttonen (2002) include examples of work from many different methodological and disciplinary perspectives.

3 Malley & Barrett (2003).

4 Lisdorf (2001); Luomanen, Pyysiäinen & Uro (2007); Pyysiäinen (2001); Whitehouse & Martin (2004).

5 Whitehouse & Martin (2004).

6 For example, Bainbridge (2006).
7 For example, Knight et al. (2004). See also Whitehouse & McCauley (2005) for examples.
8 For accessible overviews, see Pinker (1997); Thagard (1996).
9 For evidence of domain-specific systems, see Hirschfeld & Gelman (1994); Barrett (2004b) coined the term 'mental tools'.
10 Spelke & Kinzler (2007) succinctly review developmental experimental evidence.
11 Boyer developed the theory through a series of publications including Boyer (1993, 1994, 1995, 1996, 1998, 2000). Barrett (2000, 2004b) referred to these optimal concepts as 'minimally counterintuitive', because the optimal concepts appear to have typically only one counterintuitive feature in a single communicative episode.
12 Gonce et al. (2006), Norenzayan et al. (2006), Tweney et al. (2006), and Upal et al. (2007) offer mixed support for the theory but include as 'counterintuitive' some items that may not be represented as 'counterintuitive' by participants in Boyer's narrow sense.
13 For instance, see Pyysiäinen (2004a). Connecting explicit and implicit religious cognition is an important area for future research in this field and will help bridge cognitive science approaches with more traditional treatments of religion.
14 A fuller account of what it takes to be a god from a cognitive perspective may be found in Barrett forthcoming. Belief is discussed in Boyer (2001, Chapter 9, 2004b).
15 Barrett first used the acronym HADD in Barrett (2000), but there called it the 'hyperactive agent detection device'. Barrett (2004b) later renamed it 'hypersensitive agency detection device' to capture a broader range of inputs.
16 See Atran (2002); Barrett (2004b); Boyer (2001); Pyysiäinen (2004b); Slone (2004) for discussions.
17 Bering & Bjorklund (2004); Bering, Hernandez-Blasi & Bjorklund (2005); but see also Astuti & Harris (forthcoming).
18 Bering, McCleod & Shackelford (2005); Bering & Parker (2006); see also Shariff & Norenzayan (forthcoming).
19 Barrett & Malley (2007) offer a cognitive typology of counterintuitive events including religious events such as ceremonies, miracles, rituals, prayer, spirit possession, and magic.
20 Barrett (2004a) offers an analysis of empirical gaps. Barrett & Lawson (2001); Barrett (2002b); Malley & Barrett (2003), represent empirical treatments to date.
21 Andresen (2001) presents some considerations of religious experience. For some, examples of connecting CSR with topics in psychology of religion, see Gibson (2006); Gibson & Barrett (forthcoming); Kirkpatrick (2005).
22 For example, Alcorta & Sosis (2005); Bulbulia (2007); Bulbulia et al. (forthcoming).
23 For example, Atran (2002); Bulbulia (2004a,b); Ruffle & Sosis (2006, 2007); Sosis (2003, 2005); Sosis & Alcorta (2003).
24 Barrett (2007) discusses some potential arguments against theistic belief based on findings and theories from biological and cognitive treatments of religion but concludes that none of the arguments succeed. Barrett (2004b) suggests that the findings of the field are neutral with regard to whether one should believe in gods.
25 Tremlin (2006) provides an excellent introduction to the field with extensive evolutionary context.

Works Cited

Alcorta, C, & Sosis, R, 2005, 'Ritual, Emotion, and Sacred Symbols: The Evolution of Religion as an Adaptive Complex', *Human Nature*, vol. 16, no. 4, pp. 323–59.

Andresen, J, (ed.), 2001, *Religion in Mind: Cognitive Perspectives on Religious Belief, Ritual and Experience*, Cambridge University Press, Cambridge, UK.

Astuti, R, & Harris, PL, forthcoming, 'Understanding Mortality and the Life of the Ancestors in Rural Madagascar', *Cognitive Science*.

Atran, S, 2002, *In Gods We Trust: The Evolutionary Landscape of Religion*, Oxford University Press, Oxford, UK.

Bainbridge, WS, 2006, *God from the Machine: Artificial Intelligence Models of Religious Cognition*, AltaMira Press, Walnut Creek, CA.

Barrett, JL, 1998, 'Cognitive Constraints on Hindu Concepts of the Divine', *Journal for the Scientific Study of Religion*, vol. 37, no. 4, pp. 608–19.

——, 1999, 'Theological Correctness: Cognitive Constraint and the Study of Religion', *Method and Theory in the Study of Religion*, vol. 11, no. 4, pp. 325–39.

——, 2000, 'Exploring the Natural Foundations of Religion', *Trends in Cognitive Sciences*, vol. 4, no. 1, pp. 29–34.

——, 2001a, 'Do Children Experience God Like Adults? Retracing the Development of God Concepts', in J Andresen (ed.), *Keeping Religion in Mind: Cognitive Perspectives on Religious Experience*, Cambridge University Press, Cambridge, UK.

——, 2001b, 'How Ordinary Cognition Informs Petitionary Prayer', *Journal of Cognition and Culture*, vol. 1, no. 3, pp. 259–69.

——, 2002a, 'Dumb Gods, Petitionary Prayer, and the Cognitive Science of Religion', in I Pyysiäinen and V Anttonen (eds), *Current Approaches in the Cognitive Study of Religion*, pp. 93–109, Continuum, London.

——, 2002b, 'Smart Gods, Dumb Gods, and the Role of Social Cognition in Structuring Ritual Intuitions', *Journal of Cognition and Culture*, vol. 2, no. 4, pp. 183–94.

——, 2004a, 'Bringing Data to Mind: Empirical Claims of Lawson and McCauley's Theory of Religious Ritual', in BC Wilson and T Light (eds), *Religion As a Human Capacity: A Festschrift in Honor of E. Thomas Lawson*, pp. 265–88, Brill, Leiden, The Netherlands.

——, 2004b, *Why Would Anyone Believe in God?* AltaMira Press, Walnut Creek, CA.

——, 2005, 'In the Empirical Mode: Evidence Needed for the Modes of Religiosity Theory', in H Whitehouse and RN McCauley (eds), *Mind and Religion*, pp. 109–26, AltaMira Press, Walnut Creek, CA.

——, 2007, 'Is the Spell Really Broken? Bio-psychological Explanations of Religion and Theistic Belief', *Theology and Science*, vol. 5, no. 1, pp. 57–72.

——, forthcoming, 'Why Santa Claus Is Not a God', *Journal of Cognition and Culture*.

Barrett, JL, & Keil, FC, 1996, 'Anthropomorphism and God Concepts: Conceptualizing a Non-Natural Entity', *Cognitive Psychology*, vol. 31, no. 3, pp. 219–47.

Barrett, JL, & Lawson, ET, 2001, 'Ritual Intuitions: Cognitive Contributions to Judgments of Ritual Efficacy', *Journal of Cognition and Culture*, vol. 1, no. 2, pp. 183–201.

Barrett, JL, & Malley, B, 2007, 'A Cognitive Typology of Religious Actions', *Journal of Cognition and Culture*, vol. 7, no. 3–4, pp. 201–11.

Barrett, JL, Newman, RM, & Richert, RA, 2003, 'When Seeing Does Not Lead to Believing: Children's Understanding of the Importance of Background Knowledge for Interpreting Visual Displays', *Journal of Cognition and Culture*, vol. 3, no. 1, pp. 91–108.

Barrett, JL, & Nyhof, M, 2001, 'Spreading Non-Natural Concepts: The Role of Intuitive Conceptual Structures in Memory and Transmission of Cultural Materials', *Journal of Cognition & Culture*, vol. 1, no. 1, pp. 69–100.

Barrett, JL, & Richert, RA, 2003, 'Anthropomorphism or Preparedness? Exploring Children's God Concepts', *Review of Religious Research*, vol. 44, no. 3, pp. 300–312.

Barrett, JL, Richert, RA, & Driesenga, A, 2001, 'God's Beliefs Versus Mom's: The Development of Natural and Non-Natural Agent Concepts', *Child Development*, vol. 72, no. 1, pp. 50–65.

Barrett, JL, & VanOrman, B, 1996, 'The Effects of Image Use in Worship on God Concepts', *Journal of Psychology and Christianity*, vol. 15, no. 1, pp. 38–45.

Bering, JM, 2002, 'Intuitive Conceptions of Dead Agents Minds: The Natural Foundations of Afterlife Beliefs as Phenomenological Boundary', *Journal of Cognition and Culture*, vol. 2, no. 4, pp. 263–308.

——, 2006, 'The Folk Psychology of Souls', *Behavioral and Brain Sciences*, vol. 29, no. 5, pp. 453–62.

Bering, JM, & Bjorklund, DF, 2004, 'The Natural Emergence of Reasoning About the Afterlife as a Developmental Regularity', *Developmental Psychology*, vol. 40, no. 2, pp. 217–33.

Bering, JM, Hernandez-Blasi, C, & Bjorkland, DF, 2005, 'The Development of 'Afterlife' Beliefs in Secularly and Religiously Schooled Children', *British Journal of Developmental Psychology*, vol. 23, no. 4, pp. 587–607.

Bering, JM, & Johnson, DDP, 2005, '" O Lord … You Perceive My Thoughts from Afar": Recursiveness and the Evolution of Supernatural Agency', *Journal of Cognition and Culture*, vol. 5, no. 1, pp. 118–42.

Bering, JM, McLeod, K, & Shackelford, TK, 2005, 'Reasoning About Dead Agents Reveals Possible Adaptive Trends', *Human Nature*, vol. 16, no. 4, pp. 360–81.

Bering, JM, & Parker, BD, 2006, 'Children's Attributions of Intentions to an Invisible Agent', *Developmental Psychology*, vol. 42, no. 2, pp. 253–62.

Bloom, P, 2004, *Descartes' Baby: How Child Development Explains What Makes us Human*, William Heinemann, London.

——, 2005, 'Is God an Accident?' *Atlantic Monthly* December, pp. 1–8.

——, 2007, 'Religion is Natural', *Developmental Science*, vol. 10, no. 1, pp. 147–51.

Boyer, P, 1993, 'Cognitive Aspects of Religious Symbolism', in P Boyer (ed.), *Cognitive Aspects of Religious Symbolism*, pp. 4–47, Cambridge University Press, Cambridge, UK.

——, 1994, *The Naturalness of Religious Ideas. A Cognitive Theory of Religion*, University of California Press, Berkeley, CA.

——, 1995, 'Causal Understandings in Cultural Representations: Cognitive Constraints on Inferences From Cultural Input', in D Sperber, D Premack and AJ Premack (eds), *Causal Cognition: A Multidisciplinary Debate*, Clarendon Press, Oxford, UK.

——, 1996, 'What Makes Anthropomorphism Natural: Intuitive Ontology and Cultural Representations', *The Journal of the Royal Anthropological Institute (N.S.)*, vol. 2, pp. 83–97.

——, 1998, 'Cognitive Tracks of Cultural Inheritance: How Evolved Intuitive Ontology Governs Cultural Transmission', *American Anthropologist*, vol. 100, no. 4, pp. 876–89.

——, 2000, 'Evolution of a Modern Mind and the Origins of Culture: Religious Concepts as a Limiting Case', in P Carruthers and A Chamberlain (eds), *Evolution and the Human Mind: Modularity, Language and Meta-cognition*, Cambridge University Press, Cambridge, UK.

——, 2001, *Religion Explained: The Evolutionary Origins of Religious Thought*, Basic Books, New York, NY.

——, 2003, 'Religious Thought and Behavior as By-Products of Brain Function', *Trends in Cognitive Sciences*, vol. 7, no. 3, pp. 119–24.

Boyer, P, & Lienard, P, 2006, 'Why Ritualized Behavior? Precaution Systems and Action-Parsing in Developmental, Pathological, and Cultural Rituals', *Brain and Behavioral Sciences*, vol. 29, no. 6, pp. 595–613.

Boyer, P, & Ramble, C, 2001, 'Cognitive Templates for Religious Concepts: Cross-Cultural Evidence for Recall of Counter-Intuitive Representations', *Cognitive Science*, vol. 25, no. 4, pp. 535–64.

Bransford, JD, & McCarrell, NS, 1974, 'A Sketch of a Cognitive Approach to Comprehension: Some Thoughts About Understanding What It Means to Comprehend', in WB Weimer and DS Palermo (eds), *Cognition and the Symbolic Processes*, pp. 189–229, Lawrence Erlbaum, Hillsdale, NJ.

Bulbulia, J, 2004a, 'Religious Costs as Adaptations that Signal Altruistic Intention', *Evolution and Cognition*, vol. 10, no. 1, pp. 19–38.

——, 2004b, 'The Cognitive and Evolutionary Psychology of Religion', *Biology and Philosophy*, vol. 18, no. 1, pp. 19–42.

——, 2007, 'Evolution and Religion', in RI Dunbar and L Barrett (eds), *Oxford Handbook of Evolutionary Psychology*, Oxford University Press, New York, NY.

Bulbulia, J, Sosis, R, Genet, R, Harris, E, Wyman, K, & Genet, C, (eds), forthcoming, *The Evolution of Religion: Studies, Theories, and Critiques*, Collins Foundation Press, Santa Margarita, CA.

Cohen, E, 2007, *The Mind Possessed: The Cognition of Spirit Possession in An Afro-Brazilian Religious Tradition*, Oxford University Press, New York, NY.

Cohen, E, & Barrett, JL, forthcoming, 'When Minds Migrate: Conceptualising Spirit Possession', *Journal of Cognition and Culture*.

Dawkins, R, 2006, *The God Delusion*, Bantam Press, London.

Dennett, D, 2006, *Breaking the Spell: Religion as A Natural Phenomenon*, Viking, New York, NY.

DiYanni, C, & Kelemen, D, 2005, 'Time to Get A New Mountain? The Role of Function in Children's Conceptions of Natural Kinds', *Cognition*, vol. 97, no. 3, pp. 327–35.

Elkind, D, 1970, 'The Origins of Religion in the Child', *Review of Religious Research*, vol. 12, no. 1, pp. 35–42.

Evans, EM, 2000, 'The Emergence of Belief About the Origins of Species in School-Aged Children', *Merrill Palmer Quarterly*, vol. 46, no. 2, pp. 221–54.

——, 2001, 'Cognitive and Contextual Factors in the Emergence of Diverse Belief Systems: Creation Versus Evolution', *Cognitive Psychology*, vol. 42, no. 3, pp. 217–66.

Gelman, SA, & Kremer, KE, 1991, 'Understanding Natural Cause: Children's Explanations of How Objects and Their Properties Originate', *Child Development*, vol. 62, no. 2, pp. 396–414.

Gibson, NJS, 2006, *The Experimental Investigation of Religious Cognition*, Unpublished doctoral dissertation, University of Cambridge, UK.

Gibson, NJS, & Barrett, JL, forthcoming, 'On Psychology and Evolution of Religion: Five Types of Contribution Needed From Psychologists', in J Bulbulia, R Sosis, R Genet, E Harris, K Wyman, C Genet, (eds), *The Evolution of Religion: Studies, Theories, and Critiques*, Collins Foundation Press, Santa Margarita, CA.

Goldman, RG, 1965, *Readiness for Religion*, Routledge and Kegan Paul, London.

Gonce, LO, Upal, MA, Slone, DJ, & Tweney, RD, 2006, 'Role of Context in the Recall of Counterintuitive Concepts', *Journal of Cognition & Culture*, vol. 6, nos. 3 –4, pp. 521–47.

Guthrie, SE, 1980, 'A Cognitive Theory of Religion', *Current Anthropology*, vol. 21, no. 2, pp. 181-94.

——, 1993, *Faces in the Clouds: A New Theory of Religion*, Oxford University Press, New York, NY.

Henig, R, 2007, 'Darwin's God', *New York Times Sunday Magazine*, March 4, 2007.

Hirschfeld, LA, & Gelman, SA, (eds), 1994, *Mapping the Mind: Domain Specificity in Cognition and Culture*, Cambridge University Press, Cambridge, UK.

Johnson, DDP, 2005, 'God's Punishment and Public Goods: A Test of the Supernatural Punishment Hypothesis in 186 World Cultures', *Human Nature*, vol. 16, no. 4, pp. 410–46.

Kelemen, D, 1999a, 'The Scope of Teleological Thinking in Preschool Children', *Cognition*, vol. 70, no. 3, pp. 241–72.

——, 1999b, 'Why Are Rocks Pointy? Children's Preference for Teleological Explanations of the Natural World', *Developmental Psychology*, vol. 35, pp. 1440–53.

——, 1999c, 'Beliefs About Purpose: On the Origins of Teleological Thought', in M Corballis, and S Lea (eds), *The Descent of Mind: Psychological Perspectives on Hominid Evolution*, pp. 278–94, Oxford University Press, Oxford, UK.

——, 1999d, 'Functions, Goals, and Intentions: Children's Teleological Reasoning about Objects', *Trends in Cognitive Sciences*, vol. 3, no. 12, pp. 461–68.

——, 2003, 'British and American Children's Preferences for Teleo-Functional Explanations of The Natural World', *Cognition*, vol. 88, no. 2, pp. 201–21.

——, 2004, 'Are Children "Intuitive Theists"? Reasoning About Purpose and Design in Nature', *Psychological Science*, vol. 15, no. 5, pp. 295–301.

Kelemen, D, & DiYanni, C, 2005, 'Intuitions About Origins: Purpose and Intelligent Design in Children's Reasoning About Nature', *Journal of Cognition and Development*, vol. 6, no. 1, pp. 3–31.

Kirkpatrick, LA, 2005, *Attachment, Evolution, and the Psychology of Religion*, Guilford, New York, NY.

Knight, N, Sousa, P, Barrett, JL, & Atran, S, 2004, 'Children's Attributions of Beliefs to Humans and God: Cross-Cultural Evidence', *Cognitive Science*, vol. 28, no. 1, pp. 117–26.

Lawson, ET, & McCauley, RN, 1990, *Rethinking Religion: Connection Cognition and Culture*, Cambridge University Press, Cambridge, UK.

Lienard, P, & Boyer, P, 2006, 'Whence Collective Ritual? A Cultural Selection Model of Ritualized Behavior', *American Anthropologist*, vol. 108, no. 4, pp. 814–27.

Lisdorf, A, 2001, 'The Spread of Non-Natural Concepts', *Journal of Cognition & Culture*, vol. 4, no. 1, pp. 151–74.

Luomanen, P, Pyysiäinen, I, & Uro, R, (eds), 2007, *Explaining Christian Origins and Early Judaism: Contributions from Cognitive and Social Science. (Biblical Interpretation Series, 89)*, Brill, Leiden, The Netherlands.

Malley, B, 2004, *How the Bible Works: An Anthropological Study of Evangelical Biblicism*, AltaMiraPress, Walnut Creek, CA.

Malley, B, & Barrett, JL, 2003, 'Does Myth Inform Ritual? A Test of the Lawson-McCauley Hypothesis', *Journal of Ritual Studies*, vol. 17, no. 2, pp. 1–14.

McCauley, RN, & Lawson, ET, 2002, *Bringing Ritual to Mind: Psychological Foundations of Cultural Forms*. Cambridge University Press, Cambridge, UK.

Newman, GE, Keil, FC, Kuhlmeier, V, & Wynn, K, 2010, *Preverbal Infants Appreciate that Only Agents Can Create Order*. Proceedings of the National Academy of Sciences, 107, 17140–17145.

Norenzayan, A, Atran, S, Faulkner, J, & Schaller, M, 2006, 'Memory and Mystery: The Cultural Selection of Minimally Counterintuitive Narratives', *Cognitive Science*, vol. 30, no. 3, pp. 531–53.

Petrovich, O, 1997, 'Understanding of Non-Natural Causality in Children and Adults: A Case Against Artificialism', *Psyche and Geloof*, vol. 8, pp. 151–65.

——, 1999, 'Preschool Children's Understanding of the Dichotomy Between the Natural and the Artificial', *Psychological Reports*, vol. 84, no. 1, pp. 3–27.

Piaget, J, 1929, *The Child's Conception of the World*, Harcourt Brace, New York, NY.

Pinker, S, 1997, *How the Mind Works*, W. W. Norton & Company, New York, NY.

Pyysiäinen, I, 2001, *How Religion Works: Towards a New Cognitive Science of Religion, Cognition and Culture Book Series, 1*, Brill, Leiden, The Netherlands.

——, 2004a, 'Intuitive and Explicit in Religious Thought', *Journal of Cognition & Culture*, vol. 4, no. 1, pp. 123–50.

——, 2004b, *Magic, Miracles, and Religion: A Scientist's Perspective*, AltaMira Press, Walnut Creek, CA.

——, forthcoming, 'The enduring fascination of miracles,' in JH Ellens (ed.), *Miracles: God, Psychology, and Science in 'Inexplicable' Events*, Greenwood-Praeger, Westport, CT.

Pyysiäinen, I, & Anttonen, V, (eds), 2002, *Current Approaches in the Cognitive Science of Religion*, Continuum, London.

Richert, RA, & Barrett, JL, 2005, 'Do You See What I See? Young Children's Assumptions About God's Perceptual Abilities', *International Journal for the Psychology of Religion*, vol. 15, no. 4, pp. 283–95.

——, 2006, 'The Child's God and Cognitive Development', *The Encyclopaedia of Spiritual Development in Childhood and Adolescence*, Sage Publishing, Thousand Oaks, CA.

Richert, RA, & Harris, PL, 2006, 'The Ghost in My Body: Children's Developing Concept of the Soul', *Journal of Cognition and Culture*, vol. 6, nos. 3–4, pp. 409–27.

Rochat, P, Morgan, R, & Carpenter, M, 1997, 'Young Infants' Sensitivity to Movement Information Specifying Social Causality', *Cognitive Development*, vol. 12, no. 4, pp. 537–61.

Ruffle, B, & Sosis, R, 2006, 'Cooperation and the In-Group-Out-Group Bias: A Field Test on Israeli Kibbutz Members and City Residents', *Journal of Economic Behavior and Organization*, vol. 60, no. 2, pp. 147–63.

——, 2007, 'Does It Pay to Pray? Costly Ritual and Cooperation', *The B. E. Journal of Economic Analysis and Policy*, vol. 7, no. 1, pp. 1–35.

Saler, B, & Ziegler, CA, 2006, 'Atheism and Apotheosis of Agency', *Temenos*, vol. 42, no. 2, pp. 7–41.

Shariff, AF, & Norenzayan, A, forthcoming, 'God is Watching You: Supernatural Agent Concepts Increase Prosocial Behavior in an Anonymous Economic Game', *Psychological Science*.

Slone, DJ, 2004, *Theological Incorrectness: Why Religious People Believe What They Shouldn't*, Oxford University Press, New York, NY.

Sørensen, J, 2007, *A Cognitive Theory of Magic*, AltaMira Press, Walnut Creek, CA.

Sosis, R, 2003, 'Why Aren't We All Hutterites? Costly Signaling Theory and Religious Behavior', *Human Nature*, vol. 14, no. 2, pp. 91–127.

——, 2005, 'Does Religion Promote Trust? The Role of Signaling, Reputation, and Punishment', *Interdisciplinary Journal of Research on Religion*, vol. 1, pp. 1–30.

Sosis, R, & Alcorta, C, 2003, 'Signaling, Solidarity, and the Sacred: The Evolution of Religious Behavior', *Evolutionary Anthropology*, vol. 12, no. 6, pp. 264–74.

Spelke, ES, & Kinzler, KD, 2007, 'Core Knowledge', *Developmental Science*, vol. 10, no. 1, pp. 89–96.

Sperber, D, 1996, *Explaining Culture: A Naturalistic Approach*, Blackwell, Oxford, UK.

Taylor, M, 1999, *Imaginary Companions and the Children Who Create Them*, Oxford University Press, New York, NY.

Thagard, P, 1996, *Mind: Introduction to Cognitive Science*, MIT Press, Cambridge, MA.

Tremlin, T, 2006, *Minds and Gods: The Cognitive Foundations of Religion*, Oxford University Press, New York, NY.

Tweney, RD, Upal, MA, Gonce, LO, Slone, DJ, & Edwards, K, 2006, 'The Creative Structuring of Counterintuitive Worlds', *Journal of Cognition & Culture*, vol. 6, nos. 3–4, pp. 483–98.

Upal, MA, Owsianiecki, L, Slone, DJ, & Tweney, R, 2007, 'Contextualizing Counterintuitiveness: How Context Affects Comprehension and Memorability of Counterintuitive Concepts', *Cognitive Science*, vol. 31, no. 3, pp. 1–25.

Whitehouse, H, 1995, *Inside the Cult: Religious Innovation and Transmission in Papua New Guinea*, Clarendon Press, Oxford, UK.

——, 1996a, 'Apparitions, Orations, and Rings: Experience of Spirits in Dadul', in J Mageo and A Howard (eds), *Spirits in Culture, History, and Mind*, Routledge, New York, NY.

——, 1996b, 'Rites of Terror: Emotion, Metaphor, and Memory in Melanesian Initiation Cults', *Journal of the Royal Anthropological Institute*, vol. 2, no. 4, pp. 703–15.

——, 2000, *Arguments and Icons: Divergent Modes of Religiosity*, Oxford University Press, Oxford, UK.

——, 2004, *Modes of Religiosity: A Cognitive Theory of Religious Transmission*, AltaMira Press, Walnut Creek, CA.

Whitehouse, H, & Laidlaw, JA, (eds), 2004, *Ritual and Memory: Towards a Comparative Anthropology of Religion*, AltaMira Press, Walnut Creek, CA.

Whitehouse, H, & Martin, LH, (eds), 2004, *Theorizing Religions Past: Archaeology, History, and Cognition*, AltaMira Press, Walnut Creek, CA.

Whitehouse, H, & McCauley, RN, (eds), 2005, *Mind and Religion: Psychological and Cognitive Foundations of Religiosity*, AltaMira Press, Walnut Creek, CA.

PART 4

The Discipline: Contemporary Practices and Positions

30 *Breaking the Spell: Religion as a Natural Phenomenon*

Daniel Dennett

Daniel Dennett (1942–) was born in Boston and received his doctorate in philosophy from the University of Oxford. A professor of philosophy at Tufts University, he is also the co-director of the Center for Cognitive Studies located there. Although his career work has been wide ranging, he is centrally concerned with developing a philosophy of mind and consciousness. He has written on evolutionary theory, phenomenology, and cognitive psychology, and has been effective in transmitting the theories and findings of the behavioral sciences to the public at large. Dennett, a confirmed atheist, or a "bright" (a term he explains in the following selection), has his commentaries on religion often grouped with other contemporary figures in the new atheist movement, such as Richard Dawkins and Christopher Hitchens. The selection that follows is an opening chapter to Dennett's book *Breaking the Spell: Religion as a Natural Phenomenon*, in which he analyzes religion and related phenomena through an application of the theories and findings of cognitive psychology.

CHAPTER ONE: BREAKING WHICH SPELL?

1. What's going on?

> *And he spake many things unto them in parables, saying, Behold, a sower went forth to sow; And when he sowed, some seeds fell by the way side, and the fowls came and devoured them up.*
>
> Matthew 13:3–4

> *If "survival of the fittest" has any validity as a slogan, then the Bible seems a fair candidate for the accolade of the fittest of texts.*
>
> Hugh Pyper, "The Selfish Text: The Bible and Memetics"

You watch an ant in a meadow, laboriously climbing up a blade of grass, higher and higher until it falls, then climbs again, and again, like Sisyphus rolling his rock, always striving to reach the top. Why is the ant doing this? What benefit is it seeking for itself in this strenuous and unlikely activity? Wrong question, as it turns out. No biological benefit accrues to the ant. It is not trying to get a better view of the territory or seeking food or showing off to a potential mate, for instance. Its brain has been commandeered by a tiny parasite, a lancet fluke *(Dicrocelium dendriticum),* that needs to get itself into the stomach of a sheep or a cow in order to complete its reproductive cycle. This little brain worm is driving the ant into position to benefit *its* progeny, not the ant's. This is not an isolated phenomenon. Similarly manipulative parasites infect fish, and mice, among other species. These hitchhikers cause their hosts to behave in unlikely—even suicidal—ways, all for the benefit of the guest, not the host.[1]

Does anything like this ever happen with human beings? Yes indeed. We often find human beings setting aside their personal interests, their health, their chances to have children, and devoting their entire lives to furthering the interests of an *idea* that has lodged in their brains. The Arabic word *islam* means "submission," and every good Muslim bears witness, prays five times a day, gives alms, fasts during Ramadan, and tries to make the pilgrimage, or *hajj*, to Mecca, all on behalf of the idea of Allah, and Muhammad, the messenger of Allah. Christians and Jews do likewise, of course, devoting their lives to spreading the Word, making huge sacrifices, suffering bravely, risking their lives for an idea. So do Sikhs and Hindus and Buddhists. And don't forget the many thousands of secular humanists who have given their lives for Democracy, or Justice, or just plain Truth. There are many ideas to die for.

Our ability to devote our lives to something we deem more important than our own personal welfare—or our own biological imperative to have offspring—is one of the things that set us aside from the rest of the animal world. A mother bear will bravely defend a food patch, and ferociously protect her cub, or even her empty den, but probably more people have died in the valiant attempt to protect sacred places and texts than in the attempt to protect food stores or their own children and homes. Like other animals, we have built-in desires to reproduce and to do pretty much whatever it takes to achieve this goal, but we also have creeds, and the ability to transcend our genetic imperatives. This fact does make us different, but it is itself a biological fact, visible to natural science, and something that requires an explanation from natural science. How did just one species, *Homo sapiens*, come to have these extraordinary perspectives on their own lives?

Hardly anybody would say that the most important thing in life is having more grandchildren than one's rivals do, but this is the default *summum bonum* of every wild animal. They don't know any better. They can't. They're just animals. There is one interesting exception, it seems: the dog. Can't "man's best friend" exhibit devotion that rivals that of a human friend? Won't a dog even die if need be to protect its master? Yes, and it is no coincidence that this admirable trait is found in a domesticated species. The dogs of today are the offspring of the dogs our ancestors most loved and admired in the past; without even trying to breed for loyalty, they managed to do so, bringing out the best (by their lights, by our lights) in our companion animals.[2] Did we unconsciously model this devotion to a master on our own devotion to God? Were we shaping dogs in our own image? Perhaps, but then where did we get our devotion to God?

The comparison with which I began, between a parasitic worm invading an ant's brain and an idea invading a human brain, probably seems both far-fetched and outrageous. Unlike worms, ideas aren't alive, and don't invade brains; they are created by minds. True on both counts, but these are not as telling objections as they first appear. Ideas aren't alive; they can't see where they're going and have no limbs with which to steer a host brain even if they could see. True, but a lancet fluke isn't exactly a rocket scientist either; it's no more intelligent than a carrot, really; it doesn't even have a brain. What it has is just the good fortune of being endowed with features that affect ant brains in this useful way whenever it comes in contact with them. (These features are like the eye spots on butterfly wings that sometimes fool predatory birds into thinking some big animal is looking at them. The birds are scared away and the butterflies are the beneficiaries, but are none the wiser for it.) An inert idea, if it were designed just right, might have a beneficial effect on a brain without having to know it was doing so! And if it did, it might prosper because it had that design.

The comparison of the Word of God to a lancet fluke is unsettling, but the idea of comparing an idea to a living thing is not new. I have a page of music, written on parchment in the mid-sixteenth century, which I found half a century ago in a Paris bookstall. The text (in Latin) recounts the moral of the parable of the Sower (Matthew 13): *Semen est verbum Dei; sator autem Christus.* The Word of God is a seed, and the sower of the seed is Christ. These seeds take root in individual human beings, it seems, and get those human beings to spread them, far and wide (and in return, the human hosts get eternal life—*eum qui audit manebit in eternum*).

How are ideas created by minds? It might be by miraculous inspiration, or it might be by more natural means, as ideas are spread from mind to mind, surviving translation between different languages, hitchhiking on songs and icons and statues and rituals, coming together in unlikely combinations in particular people's heads, where they give rise to yet further new "creations," bearing family resemblances to the ideas that inspired them but adding new features, new powers as they go. And perhaps some of the "wild" ideas that first invaded our minds have yielded offspring that have been domesticated and tamed, as we have attempted to become their masters or at least their stewards, their shepherds. What are the ancestors of the domesticated ideas that spread today? Where did they originate and why? And once our ancestors took on the goal of spreading these ideas, not just harboring them but cherishing them, how did this *belief in belief* transform the ideas being spread?

The great ideas of religion have been holding us human beings enthralled for thousands of years, longer than recorded history but still just a brief moment in biological time. If we want to understand the nature of religion today, as a natural phenomenon, we have to look not just at what it is today, but at what it used to be. An account of the origins of religion, in the next seven chapters, will provide us with a new perspective from which to look, in the last three chapters, at what religion is today, why it means so much to so many people, and what they might be right and wrong about in their self-understanding as religious people. Then we can see better where religion might be heading in the near future, our future on this planet. I can think of no more important topic to investigate.

2. A working definition of religion

> *Philosophers stretch the meaning of words until they retain scarcely anything of their original sense; by calling "God" some vague abstraction which they have created for themselves, they pose as deists, as believers, before the world; they may even pride themselves on having attained a higher and purer idea of God, although their God is nothing but an insubstantial shadow and no longer the mighty personality of religious doctrine.*
>
> Sigmund Freud, *The Future of an Illusion*

How do I define religion? It doesn't matter *just* how I define it, since I plan to examine and discuss the neighboring phenomena that (probably) aren't religions—spirituality, commitment to secular organizations, fanatical devotion to ethnic groups (or sports teams), superstition. So, wherever I "draw the line," I'll be going over the line in any case. As you will see, what we usually call religions are composed of a variety of quite different phenomena, arising from different circumstances and having different implications, forming a loose family of phenomena, not a "natural kind" like a chemical element or a species.

What is the essence of religion? This question should be considered askance. Even if there is a deep and important affinity between many or even most of the world's religions, there are sure to be variants that share some typical features while lacking one or another "essential" feature. As evolutionary biology advanced during the last century, we gradually came to appreciate the deep reasons for grouping living things the way we do—sponges are animals, and birds are more closely related to dinosaurs than frogs are—and new surprises are still being discovered every year. So we should expect—and tolerate—some difficulty in arriving at a counterexample-proof definition of something as diverse and complex as religion. Sharks and dolphins look very much alike and behave in many similar ways, but they are not the same sort of thing at all. *Perhaps*, once we understand the whole field better, we will see that Buddhism and Islam, for all their similarities, deserve to be considered two entirely different species of cultural phenomenon. We can start with common sense and tradition and consider them both to be religions, but we shouldn't blind ourselves to the prospect that our initial sorting may have to be adjusted as we learn more. Why is *suckling one's young* more fundamental than *living in the ocean?* Why is *having a backbone* more fundamental than *having wings?* It may be obvious now, but it wasn't obvious at the dawn of biology.

In the United Kingdom, the law regarding cruelty to animals draws an important moral line at whether the animal is a vertebrate: as far as the law is concerned, you may do what you like to a live worm or fly or shrimp, but not to a live bird or frog or mouse. It's a pretty good place to draw the line, but laws can be amended, and this one was. Cephalopods—octopus, squid, cuttlefish—were recently made *honorary vertebrates*, in effect, because they, unlike their close mollusc cousins the clams and oysters, have such strikingly sophisticated nervous systems. This seems to me a wise political adjustment, since the similarities that mattered to the law and morality didn't line up perfectly with the deep principles of biology.

We may find that drawing a boundary between *religion* and its nearest neighbors among cultural phenomena is beset with similar, but more vexing, problems. For instance, since the law (in the United States, at least) singles out religions for special status, declaring something that has been regarded as a religion to be really something else is bound to be of more than academic interest to those involved. Wicca (witchcraft) and other New Age phenomena have been championed as religions by their adherents precisely in order to elevate them to the legal and social status that religions have traditionally enjoyed. And, coming from the other direction, there are those who have claimed that evolutionary biology is really "just another religion," and hence its doctrines have no place in the public-school curriculum. Legal protection, honor, prestige, and a *traditional exemption from certain sorts of analysis and criticism*—a great deal hinges on how we define religion. How should I handle this delicate issue?

Tentatively, I propose to define religions as *social systems whose participants avow belief in a supernatural agent or agents whose approval is to be sought.* This is, of course, a circuitous way of articulating the idea that a religion without *God* or *gods* is like a vertebrate without a backbone.[3] Some of the reasons for this roundabout language are fairly obvious; others will emerge over time—and the definition is subject to revision, a place to start, not something carved in stone to be defended to the death. According to this definition, a devout Elvis Presley fan club is not a religion, because, although the members may, in a fairly obvious sense, *worship* Elvis, he is not deemed by them to be literally supernatural, but just to have been a particularly superb human being. (And if some fan clubs decide that Elvis is truly immortal and divine, then they are indeed on the way to starting a new religion.) A supernatural agent need not be very *anthropomorphic.* The Old Testament Jehovah is definitely a sort of divine man (not a woman), who sees with eyes and hears with ears—and talks and acts in real time. (God *waited* to *see* what Job would do, and *then* he *spoke* to him.) Many contemporary Christians, Jews, and Muslims insist that God, or Allah, being omniscient, has no need for anything like sense organs, and, being eternal, does not act in real time.

This is puzzling, since many of them continue to pray to God, to hope that God *will* answer their prayers tomorrow, to express gratitude to God for *creating* the universe, and to use such locutions as "what God intends us to do" and "God have mercy," acts that *seem* to be in flat contradiction to their insistence that their God is not at all anthropomorphic. According to a long-standing tradition, this tension between God as agent and God as eternal and immutable Being is one of those things that are simply beyond human comprehension, and it would be foolish and arrogant to try to understand it. That is as it may be, and this topic will be carefully treated later in the book, but we cannot proceed with my definition of religion (or any other definition, really) until we (tentatively, pending further illumination) get a *little* clearer about the spectrum of views that are discernible through this pious fog of modest incomprehension. We need to seek further interpretation before we can decide how to classify the doctrines these people espouse.

For some people, prayer is not literally *talking to God* but, rather, a "symbolic" activity, a way of talking *to oneself* about one's deepest concerns, expressed metaphorically. It is rather like beginning a diary entry with "Dear Diary." If what they call God is really *not* an agent in their eyes, a being that can *answer* prayers, *approve* and *disapprove, receive* sacrifices, and *mete out* punishment or forgiveness, then, although they may call this Being God, and stand in awe of *it* (not *Him*), their creed, whatever it is, is not really a religion according to my definition. It is, perhaps, a wonderful (or terrible) surrogate for religion, or a *former* religion, an offspring of a genuine religion that bears many family resemblances to religion, but it is another species altogether.[4] In order to get clear about what religions *are*, we will have to allow that some religions may have turned into things that aren't religions any more. This has certainly happened to particular practices and traditions that used to be parts of genuine religions. The rituals of Halloween are no longer religious rituals, at least in America. The people who go to great effort and expense to participate in them are not, thereby, practicing religion, even though their activities can be placed in a clear line of descent from religious practices. Belief in Santa Claus has also lost its status as a religious belief.

For others, prayer really is talking to God, who (not *which*) really does listen, and forgive. Their creed *is* a religion, according to my definition, provided that they are part of a larger social system or community, not a congregation of one. In this regard, my definition is profoundly at odds with that of William James, who defined religion as "the feelings, acts, and experiences of individual men in their solitude, so far as they apprehend themselves to stand in relation to whatever they may consider the divine" (1902, p. 31). He would have no difficulty identifying a lone believer as a person with a religion; he himself was apparently such a one. This concentration on individual, private religious *experience* was a tactical choice for James; he thought that the creeds, rituals, trappings, and political hierarchies of "organized" religion were a distraction from the root phenomenon, and his tactical path bore wonderful fruit, but he could hardly deny that those social and cultural factors hugely affect the content and structure of the individual's experience. Today, there are reasons for trading in James's psychological microscope for a wide-angle biological and social telescope, looking at the factors, over large expanses of both space and time, that shape the experiences and actions of individual religious people.

But just as James could hardly deny the social and cultural factors, I could hardly deny the existence of individuals who very sincerely and devoutly take themselves to be the lone communicants of what we might call private religions. Typically these people have had considerable experience with one or more world religions and have chosen not to be joiners. Not wanting to ignore them, but needing to distinguish them from the much, much more typical religious people who identify themselves with a particular creed or church that has many other members, I shall call them *spiritual* people, but not *religious*. They are, if you like, honorary vertebrates.

There are many other variants to be considered in due course—for instance, people who pray, and believe in the efficacy of prayer, but don't believe that this efficacy is channeled through an agent God who literally hears the prayer. I want to postpone consideration of all these issues until we have a clearer sense of where these doctrines sprang from. The core phenomenon of religion, I am proposing, invokes gods who are effective agents in real time, and who play a central role in the way the participants think about what they ought to do. I use the evasive word "invokes" here because, as we shall see in a later chapter, the standard word "belief" tends to distort and camouflage some of the most interesting features of religion. To put it provocatively, religious belief isn't always *belief*. And why is the approval of the supernatural agent or agents to be sought? That clause is included to distinguish religion from "black magic" of various sorts. There are people—very few, actually, although juicy urban legends about "satanic cults" would have us think otherwise—who take themselves to be able to command demons with whom they form some sort of unholy alliance. These (barely existent) social systems are on the boundary with religion, but I think it is appropriate to leave them out, since our intuitions recoil at the idea that people who engage in this kind of tripe deserve the special status of the devout. What apparently grounds the widespread respect in which religions of all kinds are held is the sense that those who are religious are well intentioned, trying to lead morally good lives, earnest in their desire not to do evil, and to make amends for their transgressions. Somebody who is both so selfish and so gullible as to try to make a pact with evil supernatural agents in order to get his way in the world lives in a comic-book world of superstition and deserves no such respect.[5]

3. To break or not to break

> *Science is like a blabbermouth who ruins a movie by telling you how it ends.*
> Ned Flanders (fictional character in *The Simpsons*)

You're at a concert, awestruck and breathless, listening to your favorite musicians on their farewell tour, and the sweet music is lifting you, carrying you away to another place … and then somebody's cell phone starts ringing! Breaking the spell. Hateful, vile, inexcusable. This inconsiderate jerk has ruined the concert for you, stolen a precious moment that can never be recovered. How evil it is to break somebody's spell! I don't want to be that person with the cell phone, and I am well aware that I will seem to many people to be courting just that fate by embarking on this book.

The problem is that there are good spells and then there are bad spells. If only some timely phone call could have interrupted the proceedings at Jonestown in Guyana in 1978, when the lunatic Jim Jones was ordering his hundreds of spellbound followers to commit suicide! If only we could have broken the spell that enticed the Japanese cult Aum Shinrikyo to release sarin gas in a Tokyo subway, killing a dozen people and injuring thousands more! If only we could figure out some way today to break the spell that lures thousands of poor young Muslim boys into fanatical madrassahs where they are prepared for a life of murderous martyrdom instead of being taught about the modern world, about democracy and history and science! If only we could break the spell that convinces some of our fellow citizens that they are commanded by God to bomb abortion clinics!

Religious cults and political fanatics are not the only casters of evil spells today. Think of the people who are addicted to drugs, or gambling, or alcohol, or child pornography. They need all the help they can get, and I doubt if anybody is inclined to throw a protective mantle around these entranced ones and admonish, "Shhh! Don't break the spell!" And it may be that the best way to break these bad spells is to introduce the spellbound to a good spell, a god spell, a gospel. It may be, and it may not. We should try to find out. Perhaps, while we're at it, we should inquire whether the world would be a better place if we could snap our fingers and cure the workaholics, too—but now I'm entering controversial waters. Many workaholics would claim that theirs is a benign addiction, useful to society and to their loved ones, and, besides, they would insist, it is their right, in a free society, to follow their hearts wherever they lead, so long as no harm comes to anyone else. The principle is unassailable; we others have no right to intrude on their private practices so *long as we can be quite sure that they are not injuring others*. But it is getting harder and harder to be sure about when this is the case.

People make themselves dependent on many things. Some think they cannot live without daily newspapers and a free press, whereas others think they cannot live without cigarettes. Some think a life without music would not be worth living, and others think a life without religion would not be worth living. Are these addictions? Or are these genuine needs that we should strive to preserve, at almost any cost?

Eventually, we must arrive at questions about ultimate values, and no factual investigation could answer them. Instead, we can do no better than to sit down and reason together, a political process of mutual persuasion and education that we can try to conduct in good faith. But in order to do that we have to know what we are choosing between, and we need to have a clear account of the reasons that can be offered for and against the different visions of the participants. Those who refuse to participate (because they already *know* the answers in their hearts) are, from the point of view of the rest of us, part of the problem. Instead of being participants in our democratic effort to find agreement among our fellow human beings, they place themselves in the inventory of obstacles to be dealt with, one way or another. As with El Niño and global warming, there is no point in trying to argue with them, but every reason to study them assiduously, whether they like it or not. They may change their minds and rejoin our political congregation, and assist us in the exploration of the grounds for their attitudes and practices, but whether or not they do, it behooves the rest of us to learn everything we can about them, for they put at risk what *we* hold dear.

It is high time that we subject religion as a global phenomenon to the most intensive multidisciplinary research we can muster, calling on the best minds on the planet. Why? Because religion is too important for us to remain ignorant about. It affects not just our social, political, and economic conflicts, but the very meanings we find in our lives. For many people, probably a majority of the people on Earth, nothing matters more than religion. For this very reason, it is imperative that we learn as much as we can about it. That, in a nutshell, is the argument of this book.

Wouldn't such an exhaustive and invasive examination damage the phenomenon itself? Mightn't it *break the spell?* That is a good question, and I don't know the answer. *Nobody knows the answer.* That is why I raise the question, to explore it carefully now, so that we (1) don't rush headlong into inquiries we would all be much better off not undertaking, and yet (2) don't hide facts from ourselves that could guide us to better lives for all. The people on this planet confront a terrible array of problems—poverty, hunger, disease, oppression, the violence of war and crime, and many more—and in the twenty-first century we have unparalleled powers for doing something about all these problems. But what shall we do?

Good intentions are not enough. If we learned anything in the twentieth century, we learned this, for we made some colossal mistakes with the best of intentions. In the early decades of the century, communism seemed to many millions of thoughtful, well-intentioned people to be a beautiful and even obvious solution to the terrible unfairness that all can see, but they were wrong. An obscenely costly mistake. Prohibition also seemed like a good idea at the time, not just to power-hungry prudes intent on imposing their taste on their fellow citizens, but to many decent people who could see the terrible toll of alcoholism and figured that nothing short of a total ban would suffice. They were proven wrong, and we still haven't recovered from all the bad effects that well-intentioned policy set in motion. There was a time, not so long ago, when the idea of keeping blacks and whites in separate communities, with separate facilities, seemed to many sincere people to be a reasonable solution to pressing problems of interracial strife. It took the civil-rights movement in the United States, and the painful and humiliating experience of Apartheid and its eventual dismantling in South Africa, to show how wrong those well-intentioned people were to have ever believed this. Shame on them, you may say. They should have known better. That is my point. We *can* come to know better if we try our best to find out, and we have no excuse for not trying. Or do we? Are some topics off limits, no matter what the consequences?

Today, billions of people pray for peace, and I wouldn't be surprised if most of them believe with all their hearts that the best path to follow to peace throughout the world is a path that runs through their particular religious institution, whether it is Christianity, Judaism, Islam, Hinduism, Buddhism, or any of hundreds of other systems of religion. Indeed, many people think that the best hope for humankind is that we can bring together all of the religions of the world in a mutually respectful conversation and ultimate agreement on how to treat one another. They may be right, but *they don't know*. The fervor of their belief is no substitute for good hard evidence, and the evidence in favor of this beautiful hope is hardly overwhelming. In fact, it is not persuasive at all, since just as many people, apparently, sincerely believe that world peace is less important, in both the short run and the long, than the global triumph of their particular religion over its competition. Some see religion as the best hope for peace, a lifeboat we dare not rock lest we overturn it and all of us perish, and others see religious self-identification as the main source of conflict and violence in the world, and believe just as fervently that religious conviction is a terrible substitute for calm, informed reasoning. Good intentions pave both roads.

Who is right? I don't know. Neither do the billions of people with their passionate religious convictions. Neither do those atheists who are sure the world would be a much better place if all religion went extinct. There is an asymmetry: atheists in general welcome the most intensive and objective examination of their views, practices, and reasons. (In fact, their incessant demand for self-examination can become quite tedious.) The religious, in contrast, often bristle at the impertinence, the lack of respect, the *sacrilege*, implied by anybody who wants to investigate their views. I respectfully demur: there is indeed an ancient tradition to which they are appealing here, but it is mistaken and should not be permitted to continue. *This* spell must be broken, and broken now. Those who are religious and believe religion to be the best hope of humankind cannot reasonably expect those of us who are skeptical to refrain from expressing our doubts if they themselves are unwilling to put their convictions under the microscope. If they are right—especially if they are obviously right, on further reflection—we skeptics will not only concede this but enthusiastically join the cause. We want what they (mostly) say they want: a world at peace, with as little suffering as we can manage, with freedom and justice and well-being and meaning for all. If the case for their path cannot be made, *this is something that they themselves should want to know*. It is as simple as that. They claim the moral high ground; maybe they deserve it and maybe they don't. Let's find out.

4. Peering into the abyss

Philosophy is questions that may never be answered. Religion is answers that may never be questioned.

Anonymous

The spell that I say *must* be broken is the taboo against a forthright, scientific, no-holds-barred investigation of religion as one natural phenomenon among many. But certainly one of the most pressing and plausible reasons for resisting this claim is the fear that if that spell is broken—if religion is put under the bright lights and the microscope—there is a serious risk of breaking a different and much more important spell: the life-enriching enchantment of religion itself. If interference caused by scientific investigation somehow disabled people, rendering them incapable of states of mind that are the springboards for religious experience or religious conviction, this *could* be a terrible calamity. You can only lose your virginity once, and some are afraid that imposing too much knowledge on some topics could rob people of their innocence, crippling their hearts in the guise of expanding their minds. To see the problem, one has only to reflect on the recent global onslaught of secular Western technology and culture, sweeping hundreds of languages and cultures to extinction in a few generations. Couldn't the same thing happen to your religion? Shouldn't we leave well enough alone, just in case? What arrogant nonsense, others will scoff. The Word of God is invulnerable to the puny forays of meddling scientists. The presumption that curious infidels need to tiptoe around to avoid disturbing the faithful is laughable, they say. But in that case, there would be no harm in looking, would there? And we might learn something important.

The first spell—the taboo—and the second spell—religion itself—are bound together in a curious embrace. *Part* of the strength of the second may be—may be—the protection it receives from the first. But who knows? If we are enjoined by the first spell not to investigate this possible causal link, then the second spell has a handy shield, whether it needs it or not. The relationship between these two spells is vividly illustrated in Hans Christian Andersen's charming fable "The Emperor's New Clothes." Sometimes falsehoods and myths that are "common wisdom" can survive indefinitely simply because the prospect of exposing them is itself rendered daunting or awkward by a taboo. An indefensible mutual presumption can be kept aloft for years or even centuries because each person assumes that *somebody else* has some very good reasons for maintaining it, and nobody dares to challenge it.

Up to now, there has been a largely unexamined mutual agreement that scientists and other researchers will leave religion alone, or restrict themselves to a few sidelong glances, since people get so upset at the mere thought of a more intensive inquiry. I propose to disrupt this presumption, and examine it. If we shouldn't study all the ins and outs of religion, I want to know why, and I want to see good, factually supported reasons, not just an appeal to the tradition I am rejecting. If the traditional cloak of privacy or "sanctuary" is to be left in place, we should know why we're doing this, since a compelling case can be made that we're paying a terrible price for our ignorance. This sets the order of business: First, we must look at the issue of *whether* the first spell—the taboo—should be broken. Of course, by writing and publishing this book I am jumping the gun, leaping in and *trying* to break the first spell, but one has to start somewhere. Before continuing further, then, and possibly making matters worse, I am going to pause to defend my decision to try to break that spell. Then, having mounted my defense for *starting* the project, I am going to start the project! Not by answering the big questions that motivate the whole enterprise but by asking them, as carefully as I can, and pointing out what we already know about how to answer them, and showing why we need to answer them.

I am a philosopher, not a biologist or an anthropologist or a sociologist or historian or theologian. We philosophers are better at asking questions than at answering them, and this may strike some people as a comical admission of futility—"He says his specialty is just *asking* questions, not answering them. What a puny job! And they pay him for this?" But anybody who has ever tackled a truly tough problem knows that one of the most difficult tasks is finding the right questions to ask and the right order to ask them in. You have to figure out not only what you don't know, but what you *need* to know and *don't* need to know, and what you need to know in order to *figure out* what you need to know, and so forth. The form our questions take opens up some avenues and closes off others, and we don't want to waste time and energy barking up the wrong trees. Philosophers can sometimes help in this endeavor, but of course they have often gotten in the way, too. Then some other philosopher has to come in and try to clean up the mess. I have always liked the way John Locke put it, in the "Epistle to the Reader" at the beginning of his *Essay Concerning Human Understanding* (1690):

> ... it is ambition enough to be employed as an under-labourer in clearing the ground a little, and removing some of the rubbish that lies in the way to knowledge;—which certainly had been very much more advanced in the world, if the endeavours of ingenious and industrious men had not been much cumbered with the learned but frivolous use of uncouth, affected, or unintelligible terms, introduced into the sciences, and there made an art of, to that degree that Philosophy, which is nothing but the true knowledge of things, was thought unfit or incapable to be brought into well-bred company and polite conversation.

Another of my philosophical heroes, William James, recognized as well as any philosopher ever has the importance of enriching your philosophical diet of abstractions and logical arguments with large helpings of hard-won fact, and just about a hundred years ago, he published his classic investigation, *The Varieties of Religious Experience*. It will be cited often in this book, for it is a treasure trove of insights and arguments, too often overlooked in recent times, and I will begin by putting an old tale he recounts to a new use:

> A story which revivalist preachers often tell is that of a man who found himself at night slipping down the side of a precipice. At last he caught a branch which stopped his fall, and remained clinging to it in misery for hours. But finally his fingers had to loose their hold, and with a despairing farewell to life, he let himself drop. He fell just six inches. If he had given up the struggle earlier, his agony would have been spared.
>
> [James, 1902, p. III]

Like the revivalist preacher, I say unto you, O religious folks who fear to break the taboo: Let go! Let go! You'll hardly notice the drop! The sooner we set about studying religion scientifically, the sooner your deepest fears will be allayed. But that is just a plea, not an argument, so I must persist with my case. I ask just that you try to keep an open mind and refrain from prejudging what I say because I am a godless philosopher, while I similarly do my best to understand you. (I am a *bright*. My essay "The Bright Stuff," in the *New York Times*, July 12, 2003, drew attention to the efforts of some agnostics, atheists, and other adherents of naturalism to coin a new term for us nonbelievers, and the large positive response to that essay helped persuade me to write this book. There was also a negative response, largely objecting to the term that had been chosen [not by me]: *bright*, which seemed to imply that others were dim or stupid. But the term, modeled on the highly successful hijacking of the ordinary word "gay" by homosexuals, does not have to have that implication. Those who are not gays are not necessarily glum; they're *straight*. Those who are not brights are not necessarily dim. They might like to choose a name for themselves. Since, unlike us brights, they believe in the supernatural, perhaps they would like to call themselves *supers*. It's a nice word with positive connotations, like *gay* and *bright* and *straight*. Some people would not willingly associate with somebody who was openly gay, and others would not willingly read a book by somebody who was openly bright. But there is a first time for everything. Try it. You can always back out later if it becomes too offensive.)

As you can already see, this is going to be something of a roller-coaster ride for both of us. I have interviewed many deeply religious people in the last few years, and most of these volunteers had never conversed with anybody like me about such topics (and I had certainly never before attempted to broach such delicate topics with people so unlike myself), so there were more than a few awkward surprises and embarrassing miscommunications. I learned a lot, but in spite of my best efforts I will no doubt outrage some readers, and display my ignorance of matters they consider of the greatest importance. This will give them a handy reason to discard my book without considering just which points in it they disagree with and why. I ask that they resist hiding behind this excuse and soldier on. They will learn something, and then they may be able to teach us all something.

Some people think it is deeply immoral even to *consider* reading such a book as this! For them, *wondering whether* they should read it would be as shameful as wondering whether to watch a pornographic videotape. The psychologist Philip Tetlock (1999, 2003, 2004) identifies values as *sacred* when they are so important to those who hold them that the very act of considering them is offensive. The comedian Jack Benny was famously stingy—or so he presented himself on radio and television—and one of his best bits was the skit in which a mugger puts a gun in his back and barks, "Your money or your life!" Benny just stands there silently. "Your money or your life!" repeats the mugger, with mounting impatience. "I'm thinking, I'm thinking," Benny replies. This is funny because most of us—religious or not—think that nobody should even think about such a trade-off. Nobody should *have to* think about such a trade-off. It should be unthinkable, a "no-brainer." Life is sacred, and no amount of money would be a fair exchange for a life, *and if you don't already know that, what's wrong with you?* "To transgress this boundary, to attach a monetary value to one's friendships, children, or loyalty to one's country, is to disqualify oneself from the accompanying social roles" (Tetlock et al., 2004, p. 5). That is what makes life a sacred value.

Tetlock and his colleagues have conducted ingenious (and sometimes troubling) experiments in which subjects are obliged to consider "taboo trade-offs," such as whether or not to purchase live human body parts for some worthy end, or whether or not to pay somebody to have a baby that you then raise, or pay somebody to perform your military service. As their model predicts, many subjects exhibit a strong "mere contemplation effect": they feel guilty and sometimes get angry about being lured into even thinking about such dire choices, even when they make all the right choices. When given the opportunity by the experimenters to engage in "moral cleansing" (by volunteering for some relevant community service, for instance), subjects who have had to think about taboo trade-offs are significantly more likely than control subjects to volunteer—for real—for such good deeds. (Control subjects had been asked to think about purely secular trade-offs, such as whether to hire a housecleaner or buy food instead of something else.) So this book may do *some* good by just increasing the level of charity in *those* who feel guilty reading it! If you feel yourself contaminated by reading this book, you will perhaps feel resentful, but also more eager than you otherwise would be to work off that resentment by engaging in some moral cleansing. I hope so, and you needn't thank me for inspiring you.

In spite of the religious connotations of the term, even atheists and agnostics can have sacred values, values that are simply not up for evaluation at all. I have sacred values—in the sense that I feel vaguely guilty even thinking about whether they are defensible and would *never* consider abandoning them (I like to think!) in the pursuit of solving a moral dilemma. My sacred values are obvious and quite ecumenical: democracy, justice, life, love, and truth (in alphabetical order). But since I'm a philosopher, I've learned how to set aside the vertigo and embarrassment and ask myself what in the end supports even them, what should give when they conflict, as they often tragically do, and whether there are better alternatives. It is this traditional philosophers' open-mindedness to *every* idea that some people find immoral in itself. They think that they *should* be closed-minded when it comes to certain topics. They know that they share the planet with others who disagree with them, but they *don't* want to enter into dialogue with those others. They want to discredit, suppress, or even kill those others. While I recognize that many religious people could never bring themselves to read a book like this—that is part of the problem the book is meant to illuminate—I intend to reach as wide an audience of believers as possible. Other authors have recently written excellent books and articles on the scientific analysis of religion that are directed primarily to their fellow academics. My goal here is to play the role of ambassador, introducing (and distinguishing, criticizing, and defending) the main ideas of that literature. This puts my sacred values to work: I want the resolution to the world's problems to be as *democratic* and *just* as possible, and both democracy and justice depend on getting on the table for all to see as much of the *truth* as possible, bearing in mind that sometimes the truth hurts, and hence should sometimes be left concealed, out of *love* for those who would suffer were it revealed. But I'm prepared to consider alternative values and reconsider the priorities I find among my own.

5 Religion as a natural phenomenon

> As every enquiry which regards religion is of the utmost importance, there are two questions in particular which challenge our attention, to wit, that concerning its foundation in reason, and that concerning its origin in human nature.
>
> David Hume, *The Natural History Of Religion*

What do I mean when I speak of religion as a natural phenomenon? I might mean that it's like natural food—not just tasty but healthy, unadulterated, "organic." (That, at any rate, is the myth.) So do I mean: "Religion is *healthy;* it's good for you!"? This might be true, but it is not what I mean.

I might mean that religion is not an artifact, not a product of human intellectual activity. Sneezing and belching are natural, reciting sonnets is not; going naked—*au naturel*—is natural; wearing clothes is not. But it is obviously false that religion is natural in this sense. Religions are transmitted culturally, through language and symbolism, not through the genes. You may get your father's nose and your mother's musical ability through your genes, but if you get your religion from your parents, you get it the way you get your language, through upbringing. So of course that is not what I mean by *natural.*

With a slightly different emphasis, I might mean that religion is *doing what comes naturally,* not an acquired taste, or an artificially groomed or educated taste. In this sense, speaking is natural but writing is not; drinking milk is natural but drinking a dry martini is not;

listening to tonal music is natural but listening to atonal music is not; gazing at sunsets is natural but gazing at late Picasso paintings is not. There is some truth to this: religion is not an unnatural act, and this will be a topic explored in this book. But it is not what I mean.

I might mean that religion is natural as opposed to *supernatural*, that it is a human phenomenon composed of events, organisms, objects, structures, patterns, and the like that all obey the laws of physics or biology, and hence do not involve miracles. And that *is* what I mean. Notice that it could be true that God exists, that God is indeed the intelligent, conscious, loving creator of us all, and yet *still* religion itself, as a complex set of phenomena, is a perfectly natural phenomenon. Nobody would think it was presupposing atheism to write a book subtitled *Sports as a Natural Phenomenon* or *Cancer as a Natural Phenomenon*. Both sports and cancer are widely recognized as natural phenomena, not supernatural, in spite of the well-known exaggerations of various promoters. (I'm thinking, for instance, of two famous touchdown passes known respectively as the Hail Mary and the Immaculate Reception, to say nothing of the weekly trumpetings by researchers and clinics around the world of one "miraculous" cancer cure or another.)

Sports and cancer are the subject of intense scientific scrutiny by searchers working in many disciplines and holding many different religious views. They all assume, tentatively and for the sake of science, that the phenomena they are studying are natural phenomena. This doesn't prejudge the verdict that they are. Perhaps there *are* sports miracles that actually defy the laws of nature; perhaps some cancer cures *are* miracles. If so, the only hope of ever demonstrating this to a doubting world would be by adopting the scientific method, with its assumption of no miracles, and showing that science was utterly unable to account for the phenomena. Miracle-hunters must be scrupulous scientists or else they are wasting their time—a point long recognized by the Roman Catholic Church, which at least goes through the motions of subjecting the claims of miracles made on behalf of candidates for sainthood to objective scientific investigation. So no deeply religious person should object to the scientific study of religion with the presumption that it is an entirely natural phenomenon. If it isn't entirely natural, if there really are miracles involved, the best way—indeed, the only way—to show that to doubters would be to demonstrate it scientifically. Refusing to play by these rules only creates the suspicion that one doesn't really believe that religion is supernatural after all.

In assuming that religion is a natural phenomenon, I am not prejudging its value to human life, one way or the other. Religion, like love and music, is natural. But so are smoking, war, and death. In this sense of *natural*, everything artificial is natural! The Aswan Dam is no less natural than a beaver's dam, and the beauty of a skyscraper is no less natural than the beauty of a sunset. The natural sciences take everything in Nature as their topic, and that includes both jungles and cities, both birds and airplanes, the good, the bad, the ugly, the insignificant, and the all-important as well.

Over two hundred years ago, David Hume wrote two books on religion. One was about religion as a natural phenomenon, and its opening sentence is the epigraph of this section. The other was about the "foundation in reason" of religion, his famous *Dialogues Concerning Natural Religion* (1779). Hume wanted to consider whether there was any good reason—any *scientific* reason, we might say—for believing in God. *Natural* religion, for Hume, would be a creed that was as well supported by evidence and argument as Newton's theory of gravitation, or plane geometry. He contrasted it with *revealed* religion, which depended on the revelations of mystical experience or other extra-scientific paths to conviction. I gave Hume's *Dialogues* a place of honor in my 1995 book, *Darwin's Dangerous Idea*—Hume is yet another of my heroes—so you might think that I intend to pursue this issue still further in this book, but that is not in fact my intention. This time I am pursuing Hume's other path. Philosophers have spent two millennia and more concocting and criticizing arguments for the existence of God, such as the Argument from Design and the Ontological Argument, and arguments against the existence of God, such as the Argument from Evil. Many of us brights have devoted considerable time and energy at "Some point in our lives to looking at the arguments for and against the existence of God, and many brights continue to pursue these issues, hacking away vigorously at the arguments of the believers as if they were trying to refute a rival scientific theory. But not I. I decided some time ago that diminishing returns had set in on the arguments about God's existence, and I doubt that any breakthroughs are in the offing, from either side. Besides, many deeply religious people insist that all those arguments—on both sides—simply miss the whole point of religion, and their demonstrated lack of interest in the arguments persuades me of their sincerity. Fine. So what, then, *is* the point of religion?

What is this phenomenon or set of phenomena that means so much to so many people, and why—and how—does it command allegiance and shape so many lives so strongly? That is the main question I will address here, and once we have sorted out and clarified (not settled) some of the conflicting answers to this question, it will give us a novel perspective from which to look, briefly, at the traditional philosophical issue that some people insist is the *only i*ssue: whether or not there are good reasons for believing in God. Those who insist that they *know* that God exists and can prove it will have their day in court.[6]

Chapter [recap] Religions are among the most powerful natural phenomena on the planet, and we need to understand them better if we are to make informed and just political decisions. Although there are risks and discomforts involved, we should brace ourselves and set aside our traditional reluctance to investigate religious phenomena scientifically, so that we can come to understand how and why religions inspire such devotion, and figure out how we should deal with them all in the twenty-first century.

QUESTIONS FOR REVIEW AND DISCUSSION

1. What is Dennett's intent when he uses the analogy of a lancet fluke in an ant's brain to religious ideas in the minds of believers? What does Dennett hope to present in this book?
2. What are some of the complexities that Dennett identifies as a preamble to his definition of religion?
3. What is the definition that he proposes for the purpose of his study? What does he include in the notion of a "supernatural agent"?
4. What is the distinction that Dennett makes between "religious" and "spiritual"? How does he distinguish religion from magic? Do you find his distinctions reasonable or problematic?
5. What does Dennett mean by "breaking the spell"? Which two spells does Dennett intend to investigate in his book? Is what he is proposing, regarding the "exhaustive and invasive examination" of religion, similar to or different from the discipline of religious studies?
6. Where does Dennett situate himself within the parameters of the investigation? Is he a relatively objective observer and inquirer, or does he take a particular stance in his investigation?

7. Dennett hopes to "reach as wide an audience of believers as possible" through this study. What features in his approach might be regarded as enabling him to achieve his objective? What aspects might work to undermine his efforts?

8. What does Dennett mean by "religion as a natural phenomenon"? Do you think that religion is a natural phenomenon of the sort defined by Dennett? If not, how is it different?

Notes

1 I discussed the example of *Dicrocelium dendriticum* in Dennett, 2003; for more on its fascinating life cycle, see Ridley, 1995, and Sober and Wilson, 1998. For a striking case of a fish parasite, see LoBue and Bell (1993). A parasite of mice, *Toxoplasma gondii*, will be discussed in more detail in chapter 3. The epigram from Hugh Pyper is found in Blackmore (1999), as well as in Pyper (1998). All references can be found in the bibliography at the end of the book, and in general will be inserted in the text, not footnoted. Notes such as this will be used to expand on the points in the text in ways that may be of interest only to specialists.

2 Why the potential for breeding loyalty was present in dogs but not in cats is itself an interesting chapter of biology, but it would take us far afield. For more on the limits of domestication, see Diamont, 1997.

3 Here are two of the best-known definitions of religion with which to compare mine:

> ... a unified system of beliefs and practices relative to sacred things, that is to say, things set apart and forbidden—beliefs and practices which unite into one single moral community called a Church. [Emile Durkheim, *The Elementary Forms of Religious Life*]

> (1) A system of symbols which acts to (2) establish powerful, pervasive, and long-lasting moods and motivations in men by (3) formulating conceptions of a general order of existence and (4) clothing these conceptions with such an aura of factuality that (5) the moods and motivations seem uniquely realistic. [Clifford Geertz, *The Interpretation of Culture*]

4 These transformations typically happen gradually. Doesn't there have to have been a Prime Mammal, the first mammal whose mother was not a mammal? Not really. There doesn't have to be a principled way of drawing the boundary between the therapsids, those descendants of reptiles whose descendants include all the mammals, and the mammals (for a discussion of this perennially puzzling point, see Dennett, *Freedom Evolves*, 2003, pp. 126–28). A religion of long standing could turn into a former religion gradually, as its participants gradually shed the doctrines and practices that mark the genuine article. No value judgment is implied by such a description; mammals are former therapsids and birds are former dinosaurs, and none the worse for it. Of course the *legal* implications of whether or not the boundary had been crossed would have to be settled, but this is a political issue, like the moral status of the octopus, not a theoretical issue.

5 May the Force Be With You! Is Luke Skywalker religious? Think how differently we would react to this incantation if the Force were presented by George Lucas as satanic. The recent popularity of cinematic sagas with fictional religions—*The Lord of the Rings* and *The Matrix* offer two other examples—is an interesting phenomenon in its own right. It is hard to imagine such delicate topics being tolerated in earlier times. Our growing self-consciousness about religion and religions is a good thing, I think, for all its excesses. Like science fiction generally, it can open our eyes to other possibilities, and put the actual world in better perspective.

6 During the 1950s and 1960s, when Freudian psychoanalysis was riding high, critics who tried to point out to its devotees the many weaknesses and mistakes of Freud's theory were typically stymied by an infuriatingly bland wall of psychoanalytic deflection, along the lines of "Let's see if we can figure out why you're so *hostile* to psychoanalysis, and why you feel this emotional need to 'refute' its claims. Why don't you start by telling us about your relations with your mother." This was question-begging, or circular reasoning, even when it was sincerely meant, and it was often

simply dishonest. I recognize that my *postponement* of consideration of the issue of whether God exists may be seen by those who are armed with arguments as a similarly unprincipled evasion of intellectual responsibility. But if I began this book with their issue, framed as it traditionally is, it would take hundreds of pages of plowing over familiar terrain before I could ever get to a novel contribution. Bear with me, please. I will not forget my obligation to treat this topic!

Works cited

Dennett, Daniel. 1995. *Darwin's Dangerous Idea: Evolution and the Meanings of Life.* NY: Simon & Schuster.

———. 2003. *Freedom Evolves.* New York: Viking Penguin.

Diamond, Jared. 1997. *Guns, Germs, and Steel: The Fates of Human Societies.* NY: W. W. Norton & Co.

Durkheim, Émile. 1912. *The Elementary Forms of Religious Life.* Trans. Karen Fields. New York: The Free Press, 1995.

Freud, Sigmund. 1927. *The Future of an Illusion.* Trans. James Strachey. New York: W. W. Norton, 1961.

Hume, David. 1757. "The Natural History of Religion." In *Dialogues and Natural History of Religion,* edited by J.A.C. Gaskin. Oxford & New York: Oxford University Press, 1993.

———. 1779. *Dialogues Concerning Natural Religion.* Edited and introduced by Martin Bell. London: Penguin, 1990.

James, Williams. 1902. *The Varieties of Religious Experience.* Ed. Martin Marty. NY: Penguin, 1982.

LoBue, C. P. and M. A. Bell. 1993. "Phenotypic manipulation by the cestode parasite *Schistocephalus solidus* of its intermediate host, *Gasterosteus aculeatus,* the threespine stickleback" *American Naturalist* 142:725–735.

Locke, John. 1690. "Epistle to the Reader" at the beginning of his *Essay Concerning Human Understanding.*

Pyper, Hugh S. 1998. "The Selfish Text: The Bible and Memetics." In *Biblical Studies/Cultural Studies; the Third Sheffield Colloquium [April 1997].* Ed. by J. Cheryl Exum and Stephen D. Moore. Sheffield: Sheffield Academic Press, 70–90.

Ridley, Mark, 1995, *Animal Behaviour* (2nd edn), Boston: Blackwell Science.

Sober, Elliott and Wilson, David Sloan. 1998. *Unto Others: The Evolution of Unselfish Behavior,* Harvard University Press.

Tetlock, Philip. 2003. "Thinking the Unthinkable: Sacred Values and Taboo Cognitions." *Trends in Cognitive Science* 7(7): 320–324.

31 Introduction: Secularists and the Not Godless World

Jacques Berlinerblau

Jacques Berlinerblau holds a doctorate in Sociology from The New School for Social Research, as well as in Ancient Near Eastern Languages and Literatures from New York University. He directs the Program for Jewish Civilization at Georgetown University. His research includes work on the Hebrew Bible, religion in American politics, and heresy. His most recent book, entitled *How to be Secular* (2012), argues for a reappraisal of the values of secularism, and the crucial role it plays in defending religious freedom. The selection that follows is the Introduction to *The Secular Bible: Why Nonbelievers Must Take Religion Seriously* (Cambridge University Press, 2005). It is a call for a secular reading and interpretation of the Bible, and by extension, all religious scripture, because understanding should be a starting point in the development of an informed intellectual secularism.

> Question: What is the opposite of faith?
> Not disbelief. Too final, certain, closed. Itself a kind of belief.
> Doubt.
>
> Salman Rushdie, *The Satanic Verses*

Nonbelievers, the Bible, and Religion

In all but exceptional cases, today's secularists are biblically illiterate. Truth be told, their repertoire of knowledge about religion in general leaves much to be desired. It might consist of prurient jokes about the clergy, the citation (or miscitation) of a few noxious verses from Scripture, and maybe a Bertrand Russell quote thrown in for good measure. Secularists are free, of course, to disregard issues pertaining to religious belief. They do not need to pay attention to the actual words of the Hebrew Bible/Old Testament or to those of the New Testament and the Qur'ān. Nor do they need to think about the countless ways in which such words have been interpreted. These interpretations, incidentally, inspire those manifestations of piety that so puzzle nonbelievers: the fasting and the frenzy; the pilgrims on bloodied knees; the athletic feats of sexual repression; the acts of utterly selfless grace, and the wearing of turbans, *Yarmulkes*, veils, and other forms of sacred headgear, to name but a few. Secularists are free to remain oblivious to all this.

But perhaps now is not the best time to exercise this freedom. Contrary to what so many nineteenth- and twentieth-century social theorists believed (and hoped for), the species has not abandoned its faith in the divine. Karl Marx's optimism about the impending abolishment of religion was unfounded. The masses have not turned away from their beliefs "with the fatal inevitability of a process of growth," as Sigmund Freud predicted. And no, the gods are not "growing old or dying" – to invoke Émile Durkheim's famous words. Presently, a situation prevails that few of those thinkers could have ever imagined possible: in most countries, the irreligious and areligious comprise a small minority, an exception to the rule of God. They live in a world abounding in ancient creedal antagonisms (and modern weapons). In Pakistan and India, and in Palestine and Israel, not to mention in regions where other segments of the Islamic world clash with the predominantly Christian United States, the old faiths seem to be engaging in an apocalyptic staring contest. One flinch and secularists everywhere may have the opportunity to experience the end of days right along with the euphoric faithful.[1]

This book starts from the premise that indifference to all things religious is no longer a viable option for secularists. The word "secular," after all, derives from the Latin term *saeculum*, which refers to "living in the world" or "being of the age." In light of a revitalized and often repolarized religious scene, it would seem prudent for nonbelievers to take stock of the not Godless world and age in which they live. They will need to understand how ancient sacred texts impact the lives of citizens in modern nation-states. They will need to make sense of those interfaith and intrafaith conflicts that will affect their lives for years to come. And although it may drive them to distraction, nonbelievers will need to confront religion's durability, its pervasiveness, and perhaps even its inescapability in the domain of thought and social action.

If nonbelievers were to actually think about such issues, perhaps they would eventually ponder something that is rarely discussed: the anomalous and, in some places, precarious status of secularism itself. Although statistically small in number, secularists in many nations exert cultural, intellectual, and political influence disproportionate to their size. Or, as T. N. Madan describes it, "Secularism is the dream of a minority that wishes to shape the majority in its own image, that wishes to impose its will upon history but lacks the power to do so under a democratically organized polity." To the Jewish, Christian, and Muslim fundamentalist, secularism is no dream. It is a globally hegemonic culture – the culture of (nondivinely authorized) Sex, Sex, Sex!, the culture of depravity that invokes the flood and the blinding light. It is the culture that has *temporarily* perverted the rightful order of things.[2]

It is no surprise, then, that in societies or groups where religious extremists govern or are demographically numerous, free thinkers do not fare particularly well. The indignities suffered by the novelist Salman Rushdie are instructive in this regard. The book burnings, the threats, the murders, the contempt for the mischievous sovereignty of the imagination – this is what the empowered and undersecularized in any religion have in store for critical thinkers. While we are on the topic, let it be noted that it was not a secular militia that liberated the author of *The Satanic Verses*. A telethon hosted by a tuxedoed atheist did not precipitate his eventual release. There was no walkathon in which 1 million non-believers raised funds for his security detail by traipsing down Fifth Avenue holding placards, wearing fanny packs, and drinking lots of bottled water. Rather, it was the largesse of various Western democracies, Anglican Britain in particular, that saw him through the whole nasty episode. These are not Godless states. They consist of a religiously moderate majority that has made its peace with secularism. It is because these moderates tolerate secularism (and are to varying degrees secularized themselves) that nonbelievers are able to persevere and prosper. The mainstream religions of the Occident are the pontoons of secularism. Only by virtue of their tacit consent can this minority remain buoyant in the arts, letters, mass media, and so on.[3]

"Secular versus religious" is a convenient dichotomy, but it is one that misrepresents a complex reality. As the presence of the tolerant religious mainstream should indicate, the lines of demarcation are quite blurry. This is partly because the centuries-long process of secularization has had great success in "taking the edge off" of most extreme forms of religious devotion in the West. As the theologian Harvey Cox once phrased it, secularization "has convinced the believer that he *could* be wrong, and persuaded the devotee that there are more important things than dying for the faith." It has also created a large class of believers who share considerable common ground with nonbelievers. We might refer to them as the "secularly religious." Think of the Jewish man who pops up every year at Yom Kippur services with his Zoroastrian wife; the Muslim woman who regularly goes drinking with her friends in a sleeveless blouse after a prayerless day at work; or the gay Christian who is deacon of his church.[4]

These examples are, admittedly, generic. Yet, they point to a substantial number of the faithful who demonstrate a self-conscious willingness to live in tension with more orthodox incarnations of their own religious traditions. The secularly religious do not have a major gripe with modernity. Old creedal antagonisms do not inflame their passions, and the burning of books is not their cup of tea. In fact, they are often friends, patrons, and even producers of the arts. Village atheists – who tend to associate all religion with religious extremism – need to ask themselves what it means to share so many similarities with those who are supposed to be their antithesis.

The Current Crisis of Secular Intellectual Culture

The secularist's lack of familiarity with the Hebrew Bible/Old Testament and religion in general, we have just suggested, constitutes a looming political liability. But not everything is politics. This disregard of religion also points to a crisis and paradox of secular identity. Members of the overlapping secular sectaries (e.g., "secularists," "secular humanists," "free thinkers," "atheists," "agnostics," "brights," "universists") define themselves in opposition to religions, albeit religions about which they know very little. Above all, the secularist is *not a* Jew, *not a* Christian, *not a* Muslim, even though certain contingencies may have once imposed such a designation on him or her. To construct one's self against something that one does not understand, or care much about, does not make for a very coherent, compelling, or durable self.

It does not make for an influential or rich culture of ideas either. Presently, one would be hard pressed to identify more than a few recognizable intellectuals in the English-speaking sector who speak knowledgeably about religion *qua* secularists. Informed perspectives about the post–September 11 world, Church and State relations, fundamentalisms, and so on are almost nonexistent. A secular viewpoint, or something approximating it, is most likely to be articulated by a liberal or lapsed Jewish or Christian theologian. What ever happened to secular intellectual culture? It is a culture not lacking in historical import or integrity, or in heroisms or good works on behalf of the species. Yet, it is currently experiencing something of an existential crisis. If it moves forward, it does so only by grace of inertia – momentum gathered in a prepostmodern golden age of science and reason. It is a trust fund baby, living off of the intellectual capital of Karl Marx, Friedrich Nietzsche, Émile Durkheim, Max Weber, Bertrand Russell, Sigmund Freud, and Jean-Paul Sartre – to name just a few members of the pantheon.[5]

Believing intellectuals, in contrast, are thriving once again. The enlightenment critique of religion that came to maturity in the nineteenth century did not strike the fatal blow, the "kill shot." Although staggered, theological modes of reasoning arose, dusted themselves off, focused, amended, and absorbed. From this experience, religious thinkers emerged craftier than ever. They now draw skillfully on the full range of sciences, social sciences, and humanities. In so doing, their proofs for the existence of God and the importance of belief, ritual, communities of the faithful, and so on have become increasingly rigorous and coherent. To the atheist or agnostic who wants to *rationally* justify his or her own nonbelief, we say, *"Come prepared. Come armed with erudition. Shuck the Bertrand Russell quotes, for the love of God! Your opponents have regrouped. Do not take them lightly."*

The retreat of secular intellectuals from the domain of religious questions is most visible in the realm of contemporary higher education. For how often does a village atheist teach a course on Scripture, sacred languages, hermeneutics, or church history? How often does such a person actually have any accurate and detailed knowledge of such things? As a result, many of the West's most and least distinguished universities simply outsource their instruction of religious studies to the nearest seminary. Less promisingly, classes are sometimes taught by university chaplains or itinerant clergy. Often, one's religious studies instructor is (or was) qualified to preside over a marriage, perform a circumcision, or administer last rites. This comprises one of those exquisite ironies of the Occidental research university – a bastion of irreligious thought if there ever was one. The militantly secular academy does not sponsor the explicitly secular study of any religious issue, nor has it ever denied employment to legions of theist intellectuals (under the condition that they refrain from all manner of proselytizing activities). Although this may illustrate the university's enlightened tolerance of dissenting viewpoints, we suspect that it says more about its complete lack of interest in this subject, if not its fiscal priorities.[6]

Secular intellectual culture, we have claimed, is undergoing a crisis. This crisis is aggravated by the absence of nonbelieving scholars who can speak coherently about religion. The situation in Old (and New) Testament studies illustrates this perfectly. This discipline, whose roots burrow deep into biblical antiquity, has always been dominated by *homines religiosi*. Professional biblicists, even those teaching at secular institutions, are usually trained in theological seminaries. The field is staffed almost exclusively by those who read the Witness incessantly and piously during their youth (although as we will see, many have become secularized themselves). Blasphemers, the morally incorrigible, and cultured despisers of religion – the types of characters who appear en masse in sociology, anthropology, and English departments – rarely venture into Old Testament scholarship. We cite an observation made by M. H. Goshen-Gottstein nearly 30 years ago, one that still rings true today: "practically all academic students of the Bible remain heavily indebted to their own tradition and upbringing ... However we try to ignore it – practically all of us are in it because we are either Christians or Jews." As the exegete David Clines lamented, "it's a bit of a scandal really that in the academic context it is religious believers who are setting the tone for the study of the Bible."[7]

This is not to deny that, here and there, a few isolated New Secularists (i.e., refugees from a religious past) or Heritage Secularists (i.e., ethnic, life-long secularists) have labored in the guild of biblical studies. Yet, they have seldom scrutinized the Old Testament from a self-consciously nontheist perspective. Although they may occasionally grumble – and with good reason – about the overwhelmingly theological cast of the discipline, they have proffered few alternatives. They have not posed the really interesting questions, which go something like this: insofar as the Hebrew Bible/Old Testament has been studied in near exclusivity by Christians and Jews from antiquity to postmodernity, how would and how *should* scholars who bracket the existence of God make sense of sacred Scripture? What would their nontheist alternative look like? In what ways, if any, would it differ from traditional modes of scriptural analysis? The answers to be proposed here do not represent a privileged or authoritative perspective. They represent *one* type of perspective – albeit one that deserves far greater representation in secular universities.[8]

"Secularism" Redefined

But we are getting ahead of ourselves. A more fundamental question must be addressed, namely, what do we mean by "secularism"? Our understanding is somewhat idiosyncratic. As we see it, secularism cannot be reduced to a political platform insisting on the categorical separation of Church and State. It need not apotheosize humanity and its capacity to reason. No particular emphasis is placed on the importance of living exclusively in the "here and now." Nor are we seduced by the lure of hyperscientific rationality and its ability to power our triumphant march through history. Secularism, at its essence and at its absolute best, comprises an unrelenting commitment to judicious and self-correcting critique. Historically, it emerged in antagonistic dialectic with the most potent and intractable of human collective representations, that which is commonly referred to as religion. In confronting such a formidable adversary, secular thinkers forged a critical tradition of world historical significance, albeit one currently mired in a slump. Secularism's "job" consists of criticizing *all* collective representations. Its analytical energies should be inflicted on any type of mass belief or empowered orthodoxy, whether it is religious, political, scientific, aesthetic, and so on. Voltaire's Candide was certainly on to something when he declared, "isn't their pleasure in criticizing everything, in seeing faults where other people think they see beauties?" Secularism, as we envision it, is elitist and heretical by nature. When it aspires to become a popular movement, an orthodoxy, or the predicate of a nation-state, it betrays itself and is not likely to succeed.[9]

This means that the secular study of the Hebrew Bible (or any sacred text) is animated by a spirit of critique. The motto of our enterprise might just as well be *"criticize and be damned!"* We are bound by honor to cast aspersions on the integrity and historical reliability of holy documents. A secular exegete reads such works in heckle mode. He or she cannot accept that the Bible is the infallible word of God (as fundamentalists are wont to argue), nor the word of God as mediated by mortals (as the secularly religious and most biblical scholars often contend), nor the distortion of the word of God by prejudiced humans (as some radical theologians have charged). The objective existence of God – as opposed to the subjective perception of Him – is not a legitimate variable in scholarly analysis. The Hebrew Bible/Old Testament is a human product *tout court*.

Our next assumption marks a sharp break with existing secularism. Traditional approaches have always been predicated on a misty-eyed, person-centered humanism. The individual is seen as autonomous. Not under God. He or she is capable of comprehending and changing the world. Perfectible. *"You go girl!"* the secularist seems to exhort to all mankind. All this positive thinking is somewhat out of place. After all, nonbelievers categorically reject what most other humans believe to be true about the universe. Secularists are wont to think of religious beliefs as illusions, wish fulfillments, infantile projections, phantasmagoria, and so on. A wincing frustration with humanity, as opposed to an unqualified enthusiasm for its potential, would seem to be a more appropriate position for the secularist. The French novelist Michel Houellebecq recently eulogized the species in a manner more acceptable to the nonbeliever: "vile, unhappy race, barely different from the apes, which nevertheless carried within it such noble aspirations. Tortured, contradictory, individualistic, quarrelsome, and infinitely selfish, it was sometimes capable of extraordinary explosions of violence, but never quite abandoned its belief in love." That's better. That's the secular spirit.[10]

We want, then, to detach secularism from its incongruously philanthropic moorings. Following one of the grandest (and presently least appreciated) strands in social theory, we advance a less sanguine assessment of humans. They are seen as virtuosi of self-delusion. We concentrate on their vulnerability to causal factors beyond their comprehension and control. The assumptions that they always accurately understand why they do what they do, or the consequences of their actions, are contested. Not everything happens because of conscious deliberation, not everything results from an act of will. In the same vein, we assert that history is inherently ironic; the least expected (and desired) outcomes are often the ones that come to pass. These are themes that will be visited repeatedly in our discussions of the Bible.

This skeptical appraisal of human agency, incidentally, has a lengthy intellectual genealogy. Disquisitions on our capacity for self-deception and mass deception appear in works as varied as Michel de Montaigne's essay "On the Power of the Imagination" and Freud's *The Future of an Illusion*. Marx, for his part, spoke of illusions that bind and blind entire epochs. In his youth, he exhorted humanity to awaken from the dream it was having about itself. Following Auguste Comte, Émile Durkheim referred to the "anthropocentric postulate" – that is, the misconception that societies progress because of conscious human planning. Max Weber made much of "the ironic relationship between human intentions and their historical consequences." In short, among some of the Church Fathers of secular intellectual culture, a deep skepticism concerning the divine has often been paired with *a corresponding skepticism concerning the human*. This is the omnicritical tradition we want to revive in the study of religious phenomena and is more in line with the curmudgeonly spirit of secularism.[11]

Conclusion: The Challenge for Secular Intellectuals

It has been insisted that secularists should get to know the Hebrew Bible/Old Testament. Maybe we should also suggest, politely, that Christian and Jewish laypersons should get to know the Bible *differently*. Even within their own traditions, they will find alternatives to the simplistic readings and conceptions of Scripture to which they so often cling. College Bible professors – who are excellently positioned to make such observations – routinely express dismay at the immense bathetic gap that exists between the most sublime fruits of religious thought and the naive dogmas advocated by freshmen who have endured a basic religious education. Among many of our students, one notices a tangible poverty of knowledge concerning what their own storied intellectuals believed about the Hebrew Bible/Old Testament. They attribute to the Good Book a transparency and intelligibility that some of the most venerated thinkers in the Judaeo-Christian tradition did not believe was there.

In an effort to transcend the parallel caricatures of the Hebrew Bible that predominate in both religious and irreligious lay cultures, we propose a counterorientation called "secular hermeneutics." Aspiring to be unapologetic, it consciously performs an act of discursive aggression on Scripture and, by extension, those who hold it dear. It is a form of analysis performed in bad faith, invariably yielding un-Christian and un-Jewish readings. For these reasons, this study will be taken by some as a polemic. This charge is unavoidable and, to a certain extent, warranted. *The Secular Bible* does promote ways of thinking about Scripture that could, conceivably, neutralize claims made on behalf of sacred texts by extremists (or just about anyone else). It is virtually guaranteed to displease certain Jews, Christians, and Muslims.

But this book is not necessarily intended for secular activists. It does not seek to equip nonbelievers with refutations that will definitively trump self-righteous men and women of God. Such refutations do not exist; it is the astonishing complexity of the Old Testament that always trumps any self-righteous claim made on its behalf. Besides, the secularist fulminating about all that is irrational in religion is a doleful cliché – about as enlightening and spontaneous as a member of the Soviet Politburo flogging the Italian fashion industry in the year 1972. Mustiness, blockheadishness, and predictability have come to characterize contemporary secular writings on religion; a book-length, antireligious screed would be redundant.

Our goal, then, is *not* to cast the spotlight of enlightenment reason on the dumb show of religious belief. In truth, we can only express appreciation for accomplishments made by religious students of Scripture. The scholarly bibliography on the Bible produced by nonbelievers is negligible, but the amount of research produced by Old Testament exegetes is so immense that it defies quantification. Under no circumstances can it be written off as uninteresting or uncritical. As a body of scholarship, it rivals in ingenuity and scruple anything produced within the comity of secular university disciplines. No dumb show there.

The problem with modern biblical research is that it has not gone far enough. Too often, it has deferred to tradition, censured itself, and refused to pursue the delectably blasphemous implications of its own discoveries. Even at its most critical, Old Testament scholarship is the theological equivalent of the Loyal Opposition. For these reasons, we feel obligated to draw out or amplify certain heretical leads that have been alluded to by otherwise pious scholars. Ideally, secular hermeneutics provides new theories and methods for the study of sacred texts. But often it simply reads established theories and methods through the optic of a new, highly critical orientation. We really like the theologian John Macquarrie's description of secularism as "an attitude, a mood, a point of view, a way of noticing and (equally) of failing to notice." It is this secular way of noticing that redirects or unleashes the energy of our discipline in more critical directions. This attitude of radical doubt frees us, or perhaps forces us, to speak the unspeakable truth, truths, and truthlessness of the Hebrew Bible.[12]

Part I of *The Secular Bible* is devoted to the issue of how the Hebrew Bible was composed. With more than a few winks and nods, we pose some of the most commonly asked questions about this document's origins. Who wrote it? Who do Jews and Christians think wrote it? To whom do modern scholars attribute its authorship? What does it mean? What is its enduring message to humanity? Why is it so difficult to understand?

The crucial distinction between the Bible's contents and *interpretations* of its contents tends be lost on many laypersons, whether they are secular or religious. For these reasons, we devote Part II to the problem of how Scripture is read. Of interest to us here are queries such as why is the Hebrew Bible/Old Testament so widely interpreted? What is the nature of the relation between religious intellectuals and their beloved Scriptures? Why does the text exert the history-altering effects that it does? Why is there so little agreement as to what it says? What role do readers play in constructing the Bible's "meaning?" Much attention is devoted to professional interpreters, otherwise known as biblical scholars. The reader is forewarned that we are positively obsessed with them. Exegetes are the central protagonists of the opera whose stage notes you are now reading. We have cast them in every imaginable role. They are our betrayed Madama Butterfly, our unconscionable Pinkerton, soothing Suzuki, ambivalent Sharpless, and crazy Uncle Bonze too.

This, then, is a book about the Hebrew Bible's composition and its interpreters. It is also a meditation on the predicament of secularism in a world where sacred texts are not the irrelevant artifacts that nonbelievers once thought they would be. Part III – the Judaism-Christianity-Islam component of our curriculum – provides concrete illustrations of the theories and methods discussed in Parts I and II. These chapters on intermarriage (in Judaism) and same-sex eroticism (in Christianity) examine how the Bible is dragooned into debates that affect citizens of contemporary democracies. The difficulty, if not the utter absurdity, of invoking this text in the sphere of politics is explored. Indeed, one of our central claims is that the peculiar way in which the Bible was composed in antiquity makes it far too contradictory and incoherent a source for public policy decisions in modernity. Chapter Eight compares the role of interpreters in Judaism and Christianity on one side, and Islam on the other. Here, we explore the obstacles that confront Muslim scholars who want to liberalize prevailing interpretations of the Qur'an.

The Secular Bible is intended for scholars and cultivated laypersons. We remind our nonspecialist readers of a few rudimentary terms and concepts. "Hebrew Bible" refers to a collection of ancient documents written in Hebrew and, to a much lesser extent, Aramaic. Those documents were assembled into a fairly stable canon by Jews somewhere between the second century BCE and the first century AD. Christians generally refer to what is *roughly* the same body of texts as the "Old Testament" (although many official Christian Old Testaments are translations from Hebrew into languages such as Greek and Latin). More than 2,000 years ago Jews, and later Christians, began feverishly interpreting their Hebrew Bibles and Old Testaments. We use the phrases "Rabbinic/Talmudic literature" and "writings of the Church Fathers/patristic literature" to designate two of the most influential bodies of scriptural interpretation ever produced. The reader, ideally, will have a more nuanced understanding of these concepts by the end of this book.[13]

It is hoped that this inquiry will serve as a prototype for examinations of other foundational religious writings. In the monotheistic sphere, we envision works with titles such as *The Secular New Testament, The Secular Talmud, The Secular Church Fathers, The Secular Qur'an,* and *The Secular Hadith.* The goal is not to establish a chain of academic franchises, but rather to outline a coherent nontheological, nonapologetic paradigm for the study of sacred Scriptures. To speak of the awesome complexity of religion critically, judiciously, and with clarity – this is the challenge and responsibility of secular intellectuals in a not Godless world.

Suggestions for Further Reading

Discussions of the current plight of secularism are appearing with increasing frequency. An excellent start would be the pitch-perfect essay of Wilfred McClay, entitled "Two Concepts of Secularism," in *Religion Returns to the Public Square: Faith and Policy in America.* Eds. Hugh Heclo and Wilfred McClay. Baltimore: The Johns Hopkins University Press, 2003, pp. 31–61. Many Indian scholars have explored secularism and its discontents in their own country. Their debates are wide ranging and entertaining, and raise issues of interest to polities far and wide. We would recommend Brenda Cossman and Ratna Kapur's *Secularism's Last Sigh? Hindutva and the (Mis)Rule of Law.* Delhi: Oxford University Press, 1999, pp. 81–135, as well as the balanced collection of essays edited by Rajeev Bhargava, *Secularism and Its Critics.* Delhi: Oxford, 1998. Of special interest is the critique of secularism in the previously mentioned volume advanced by T. N. Madan. Studies of the demise of "secularization hypothesis" (which, as we note in the Conclusion, is not the same thing as secularism) are too plentiful to be mentioned here. Rodney Stark's "Secularization, R.I.P.," *Sociology of Religion* 60 (1999) 249–73, provides a good, if somewhat strident, overview. The complex question of the absence of secularists in fields that study religion, most notably biblical scholarship, is explored in our own, "'Poor Bird, Not Knowing Which Way to Fly': Biblical Scholarship's Marginality, Secular Humanism, and the Laudable Occident," *Biblical Interpretation* 10 (2002) 267–304. One of the few works of biblical scholarship working from an explicitly non-confessional angle is Philip Davies' *Whose Bible Is It Anyway?* Sheffield: Sheffield Academic Press, 1995. A handy and reader-friendly reference guide for those who want to familiarize themselves with basic concepts involving the Bible as a text is Paul Wegner's *The Journey from Texts to Translations: The Origin and Development of the Bible*. Grand Rapids, MI: Baker Books, 1999. Finally, a wonderful, critical, "big picture" study of the Bible can be found in Robert Carroll's *Wolf in the Sheepfold: The Bible as a Problem for Christianity*. London: SPCK, 1991.

QUESTIONS FOR REVIEW AND DISCUSSION

1. What is the traditional meaning of secularism? How similar are such non-believers to those whom Berlinerblau calls the "secularly religious"?

2. What does Berlinerblau mean by secular intellectual culture? Why, in his opinion, is it undergoing a crisis?

3. For the purposes of this study, how does Berlinerblau re-define secularism? What sorts of skepticism does it embody?

4. What does Berlinerblau mean by "secular hermeneutics"? What attitude should it take towards the reading of scripture? Why does he recommend such a stance?

5. Why does Berlinerblau call for secular intellectuals to become knowledgeable about scripture? Do you agree?

6. Do you think that secular interpretations of scripture, as proposed by Berlinerblau, would provide valuable insights into humanity's religious propensities? Why or why not? Would secular interpretations produce "more" or "less" correct understandings of scripture?

7. What impacts could the secular interpretative approach to scripture have on societies in which the majority are "not Godless"?

8. Would you characterize Berlinerblau's approach as consistent with that endorsed by the discipline of religious studies, or do you regard it as imbalanced in any way? Explain your appraisal.

Notes

1 On the abolishment of religion and the necessity of human emancipation, see Karl Marx, "The Jewish Question," in *The Marx-Engels Reader*, 2nd ed. Ed. Robert Tucker. New York: W. W. Norton, 1978, pp. 26–52. Sigmund Freud, *The Future of an Illusion*, Trans. James Strachey. New York: W. W. Norton, 1961, p. 55. Émile Durkheim, *The Elementary Forms of Religious Life*. Trans. Karen Fields. New York: The Free Press, 1995, p. 429. In a more recent article, a sociologist of knowledge declared, "once and for all, let us declare an end to social-scientific faith in the theory of secularization, recognizing that it was the product of wishful thinking." Rodney Stark, "Secularization, R.I.P.," *Sociology of Religion* 60 (1999) 249–73. See his remarks on the small demographic presence of atheists (p. 266). Also of interest is Jeffrey Hadden's "Desacralizing Secularization Theory," in *Secularization and Fundamentalism Reconsidered: Religion and the Political Order*, Volume III. Eds Jeffrey Hadden and Anson Shupe. New York: Paragon House, 1989, pp. 3–26. More cautious assessments of the demise of secularization hypothesis can be found in José Casanova's

thoughtful *Public Religions in the Modern World*. Chicago: University of Chicago Press, 1994, and N. J. Demerath III, "Secularization," in *Encyclopedia of Sociology: Volume 4*, 2nd ed. Ed. Edgar Borgatta. New York: Macmillan, 2000, pp. 2482–91. The Gallup Poll's 1999 survey revealed that 96 percent of Americans believed in God. George Gallup, Jr. and D. Michael Lindsay, *Surveying the Religious Landscape: Trends in U.S. Beliefs*. Harrisburg, PA: Morehouse Publishing, 1999, p. 2. A great amount of demographic research on religious belief and unbelief in the United States is available for analysis on the Lilly Endowment's American Religion Data Archive (www.thearda.com). See Jane Lampman, "Charting America's Religious Landscape," *Christian Science Monitor* (October 10, 2002) 12, for a review of data indicating that 81 percent of Americans expressed a religious preference.

2 As defined, for example, in the *Oxford English Dictionary*. On the etymological possibilities of the term "secular," see Casanova, *Public Religions*, pp. 12–13. See T. N. Madan's discussion in *Modern Myths, Locked Minds: Secularism and Fundamentalism in India*. Delhi: Oxford, 1997, pp. 3–16. The quote about the "dream" of the secular minority can be found in T. N. Madan, "Secularism in Its Place," in *Secularism and Its Critics*. Ed. Rajeev Bhargava. Delhi: Oxford, 1998, p. 298 (297–315). For a discussion of secularists as members of a globalized elite culture, see Peter Berger, "Secularism in Retreat" in *Islam and Secularism in the Middle East*, edited by John L. Esposito and Azzam Tamimi. New York: New York University Press, 2000, pp. 38–51.

3 A readable account can be found in Daniel Pipes' *The Rushdie Affair: The Novel, The Ayatollah, and the West*. New York: Birch Lane Press, 1990. On a statement made by the twelve foreign ministers of the European Common Market opposing the fatwa, see pp. 30–31. Also of interest is Malise Ruthven, *A Satanic Affair: Salman Rushdie and the Rage of Islam*. London: Chatto and Windus, 1990. A collective 1993 volume, *Pour Rushdie: Cent intellectuels arabes et musulmans pour la liberté d'expression*. Paris: La découverte/Carrefour des littératures/Colibri, 1993, is a document of great import. For an informative summary of the basic tenets of the fundamentalist movement in the United States, see Wade Clark Roof, "The New Fundamentalism: Rebirth of Political Religion in America," in *Prophetic Religions and Politics: Religion and the Political Order*, Volume One. Eds Jeffrey Hadden and Anson Shupe. New York: Paragon House, 1986, pp. 18–34. The increasingly hostile relation of fundamentalists to secularism and modernity is charted in Gabriel Almond, R. Scott Appleby, and Emmanuel Sivan, *Strong Religion: The Rise of Fundamentalisms Around the World*. Chicago: University of Chicago Press, 2003. Also of use in understanding the attitude of fundamentalists to secularists is Carol Flake, *Redemptorama: Culture, Politics, and the New Evangelicalism*. Garden City, NJ: Anchor Press, 1984.

4 Harvey Cox, *The Secular City: Secularization and Urbanization in Theological Perspective*. New York: Macmillan, 1965, p. 2.

5 For an insightful and balanced discussion of the troubles that afflict secularism, as well as an assessment of its possibilities, see Brenda Cossman and Ratna Kapur, *Secularism's Last Sigh? Hindutva and the (Mis)Rule of Law*. Delhi: Oxford University Press, 1999, pp. 81–135. An equally insightful analysis is offered by Wilfred McClay, "Two Concepts of Secularism," in *Religion Returns to the Public Square: Faith and Policy in America*. Eds Hugh Heclo and Wilfrid McClay. Baltimore: The Johns Hopkins University Press, 2003, pp. 31–61. McClay writes about the demise of secularism and its inability to respond to "a growing, intellectually sophisticated … conservative religious counterculture." p. 38.

6 Remarks on the relation between secularism, religion, and the university can be found in Cox, *The Secular City*, p. 217ff. Also see George Marsden, *The Soul of the American University: From Protestant Establishment to Established Nonbelief*. New York: Oxford, 1994; George Marsden and Bradley Longfield (Eds). *The Secularization of the Academy*. New York: Oxford, 1992; David Gill (Ed.). *Should God Get Tenure?: Essays on Religion and Higher Education*. Grand Rapids, MI: Eerdmans, 1997. The concerns of Christian scholars are expressed in William Marty, "Christians in the Academy: Overcoming the Silence," *Journal of Interdisciplinary Studies* 10 (1998) 1–16. Also see Christian Smith, "Introduction: Rethinking the Secularization of American Public Life," in *The Secular Revolution: Power, Interests and Conflict in the Secularization of American Public Life*. Ed. Christian Smith. Berkeley: University of California Press, 2003, pp. 2–3, 32–33.

7 M. H. Goshen-Gottstein, "Christianity, Judaism and Modern Bible Study," *Supplements to Vetus Testamentum* 28 (1975) 83 (68–88). Goshen-Gottstein returns to these themes in "Modern Jewish Bible Research: Aspects of Integration," in *Proceedings of the Eighth World Congress of Jewish Studies*, Jerusalem, August 16–21, 1981. Jerusalem: World Union of Jewish Studies, 1983, pp. 1–18. David

Clines, *The Bible and the Modern World*. Sheffield: Sheffield Academic Press, 1997, p. 17. John Barton writes, "The vast majority of biblical interpreters until very recently have been religious believers." "Historical-Critical Approaches," in *The Cambridge Companion to Biblical Interpretation*. Ed. John Barton. Cambridge: Cambridge University Press, 1998, p. 15 (9–20). The memorable remarks of Morton Smith should be mentioned, "The Present State of Old Testament Studies," *JBL* 88 (1969) 19–35. The widespread suggestion that a secularizing current has infiltrated biblical scholarship is contested in Jacques Berlinerblau, "'Poor Bird, Not Knowing Which Way to Fly': Biblical Scholarship's Marginality, Secular Humanism, and the Laudable Occident," *Biblical Interpretation* 10 (2002) 267–304.

8 On the difference between atheists who are refugees from a Christian past and those that never believed in God in the first place (a difference that approximates our distinction between New and Heritage Secularists), see Alasdair MacIntyre and Paul Ricoeur, *The Religious Significance of Atheism*. New York: Columbia University Press, 1969, p. 15. Perceptive criticisms of biblical scholarship have been advanced. Yet, in terms of articulating the basic assumptions of nonconfessional biblical scholarship, little work has been done. For examples of such critical work, see Philip Davies, *Whose Bible Is It Anyway?* Sheffield: Sheffield Academic Press, 1995, and Robert Oden, *The Bible Without Theology: The Theological Tradition and Alternatives to It*. San Francisco: Harper & Row, 1987. The absence of secularistic interpretation is briefly discussed by James Barr, *The Scope and Authority of the Bible*. Philadelphia: Westminster Press, 1980, p. 21. In addition to these works, one can point to other studies that lean in a secular or at least sufficiently critical direction. Most are written by secularly religious intellectuals. See, for example, André Paul. *Et l'homme créa la Bible: d'Hérodote à Flavius Josèphe*. Paris: Bayard, 2000. The French house of Bayard has published a Bible translation that has been accused of being unduly secular. *La Bible: Nouvelle traduction*. Paris: Bayard, 2001. Other works of interest include Zvi Adar, *Humanistic Values in the Bible*. New York: Reconstructionist Press, 1967. There is also a "how to resist the Bible" manual by Jim Hill and Rand Cheadle, *The Bible Tells Me So: Uses and Abuses of Holy Scripture*. New York: Anchor Books, 1996. For an early science-loving, religion-debunking assault, see Joseph Lewis, *The Bible Unmasked*. New York: Freethought Publishing, 1926. An attempt at a somewhat secular reading of the Bible was advanced in the work of Louis Wallis, *The Bible Is Human: A Study in Secular History*. New York: Columbia University Press, 1942. One can also consult Erich Fromm, *You Shall Be as Gods: A Radical Interpretation of the Old Testament and Its Tradition*. New York: Holt, Rinehart and Winston, 1966, which features a good example of the species-loving secular humanism mentioned previously. A more recent submission is that of Tal Ilan, "A Secular, Jewish, Feminist Look at the Bible," in *Feminist Interpretation of the Bible and the Hermeneutics of Liberation*. Eds Silvia Schroer and Sophia Bistenhard. Sheffield: Sheffield Academic Press, 2003, pp. 94–102. Also see Dennis McKinsey, *Encyclopedia of Biblical Errancy*. Buffalo, NY: Prometheus Books, 1995. An early classic of the genre is William Henry Burr, *Self-Contradictions of the Bible*. Buffalo, NY: Prometheus Books. 1987.

9 For a treatment of Durkheim's notion of the "collective representation," see the articles in W. S. F. Pickering (Ed.). *Durkheim and Representations*. London: Routledge, 2000, and Stjepan Meštrović, *Emile Durkheim and the Reformation of Sociology*. Lanham, MD: Rowman & Littlefield, 1993. Also see Jacques Berlinerblau, "Durkheim's Theory of Misrecognition: In Praise of Arrogant Social Theory," in *Teaching Durkheim*. Ed. T. Godlove. New York: Oxford University Press, 2005, pp. 213–33. Also, see Jacques Berlinerblau, "Free Will and Determinism in First Isaiah: Secular Hermeneutics, the Poetics of Contingency, and Émile Durkheim's *Homo Duplex*," *JAAR* 71 (2003) 767–91. Voltaire, *Candide*. Trans. and Ed. Robert Adams. New York: W. W. Norton, 1966, p. 65.

10 The species-positive ethos surfaces in, for example, James Hitchcock, *What Is Secular Humanism? Why Humanism Became Secular and How It is Changing Our World*. Ann Arbor, MI: Servant Books, 1982, pp. 7–17. On the notion of secularism and the perfectibility of human kind, see Madan, *Modern Myths*, pp. 5–25; Michel Houellebecq, *The Elementary Particles*. Trans. Frank Wynne. New York: Vintage International, 2000, pp. 263–65.

11 We have referred to views such as those advocated by our secular "Church Fathers" as "misrecognition theory." In fact, we have elsewhere identified an early variant of this view in parts of the Hebrew Bible. Jacques Berlinerblau, "Free Will," and Jacques Berlinerblau, "Toward a Sociology of Heresy, Orthodoxy, and Doxa," *History of Religions* 40 (2001) 327–51, and Jacques Berlinerblau, "Ideology, Pierre Bourdieu's Doxa, and the Hebrew Bible," *Semeia* 87 (1999) 193–214. Michel de Montaigne, "On the Power of the Imagination," in *Essays*. Trans.

J. M. Cohen. New York: Penguin, 1958, pp. 36–48. For discussions of Marx's tendency to see humans as deluded, see Berlinerblau, "Ideology." Marx's well-known dream remark can be found in Karl Marx, "For a Ruthless Criticism of Everything Existing," in *The Marx-Engels Reader*, 2nd ed. Ed. Robert Tucker. New York: W. W. Norton, 1978, p. 15. Durkheim speaks of the "anthropocentric postulate" in *The Rules of Sociological Method and Selected Texts on Sociology and Its Method*. Ed. Steven Lukes. Trans. W. D. Halls. New York: The Free Press, 1982, p. 46. On Durkheim's thinking about illusions and its relation to Comte, see Berlinerblau, "Durkheim's Theory of Misrecognition." Peter Berger is responsible for the quote that summarizes Weber's understanding of history. *The Sacred Canopy: Elements of a Sociological Theory of Religion*. Garden City, NJ: Doubleday, 1969, p. 200, fn. 6.

12 John Macquarrie, *God and Secularity: New Directions in Theology Today*, Volume Three. Philadelphia: Westminster Press, 1969, pp. 43–44.

13 For a discussion of the problems involved in dating the Rabbinic period (which we place between the first and sixth centuries AD), see Isaiah Gafni, "The Historical Background," in *The Literature of the Sages: First Part: Oral Tora, Halakha, Mishna, Tosefta, Talmud, External Tractates*. Ed. Shmeul Safrai. Fortress Press: Philadelphia, 1987, pp. 1–34. More detailed discussions concerning debates about when canonization occurred are found throughout this book.

32 Who's Right about Reality: Traditionalists, Modernists, or the Postmoderns?

Huston Smith

Huston Smith (1919—), a son of Methodist missionaries, was born and lived in China for the first seventeen years of his life. He received his doctorate from the University of Chicago and was professor of philosophy at the Massachusetts Institute of Technology prior to holding positions in religious studies at Syracuse University and the University of California at Berkeley. Smith's *The Religions of Man* (1958) (later renamed *The World's Religions*), having sold some two and a half million copies worldwide, is arguably the most widely read survey presentation of the major religious traditions of the world. Often used as an introductory textbook in university classes, its distinction lies in its pioneer efforts to portray religions with accuracy, but also with a sympathy derived from Smith's participant encounters with aspects of many of them. Smith's engagement with Tibetan Buddhism, for instance, later led him to the discovery of Tibetan multiphonic chanting. In his work and personal orientation, he shares certain convictions with others, such as Aldous Huxley, in what is often termed the "perennial philosophy." Perennialist philosophers hold that there is a universal truth that is the foundation for the various teachings – particularly the mystical dimensions – of many of the world's religious traditions. This truth is perennially rediscovered or revived by sages, mystics, and others, but framed by the particular cultural or historical contexts in which it is articulated. The selection that follows derives from *Why Religion Matters* (2001), which won the Wilbur Award for the best book on religion in that year. It offers an example of writings with popular appeal that attempt to present religion in a positive light.

Wherever people live, whenever they live, they find themselves faced with three inescapable problems: how to win food and shelter from their natural environment (the problem nature poses), how to get along with one another (the social problem), and how to relate themselves to the total scheme of things (the religious problem). If this third issue seems less important than the other two, we should remind ourselves that religious artifacts are the oldest that archeologists have discovered.

The three problems are obvious, but they become interesting when we align them with the three major periods in human history: the traditional period (which extended from human beginnings up to the rise of modern science), the modern period (which took over from there and continued through the first half of the twentieth century), and post-modernism (which Nietzsche anticipated, but which waited for the second half of the twentieth century to take hold).

Each of these periods poured more of its energies into, and did better by, one of life's inescapable problems than did the other two. Specifically, modernity gave us our view of *nature*—it continues to be refined, but because modernity laid the foundations for the scientific understanding of it, it deserves credit for the discovery. Postmodernism is tackling *social injustices* more resolutely than people previously did. This leaves *worldviews*—metaphysics as distinct from cosmology, which restricts itself to the empirical universe—for our ancestors, whose accomplishments on that front have not been improved upon.

The just-entered distinction between cosmology and metaphysics is important for this book, so I shall expand it slightly. *Cosmology* is the study of the physical universe—or the world of nature as science conceives of it—and is the domain of science. *Metaphysics*, on the other hand, deals with all there is. (The terms *worldview* and *Big Picture* are used interchangeably with *metaphysics* in this book.) In the worldview that holds that nature is all there is, metaphysics coincides with cosmology. That metaphysics is named *naturalism*.

Such is the historical framework in which this book is set, and the object of this chapter is to spell out that framework. Because I want to proceed topically—from nature, through society, to the Big Picture, tying each topic to the period that did best by it—this introduction shuffles the historical sequence of the periods. I take up modernity first, then postmodernity, leaving the traditional period for last.

Modernity's Cosmological Achievement

In the sixteenth and seventeenth centuries Europe stumbled on a new way of knowing that we refer to as the *scientific method*. It centers in the controlled experiment and has given us modern science. Generic science (which consists of careful attention to nature and its regularities) is as old as the hills—at least as old as art and religion. What the controlled experiment adds to generic science is proof. True hypotheses can be separated from false ones, and brick by brick an edifice has been erected from those proven truths. We commonly call that edifice the *scientific worldview*, but *scientific cosmology* is more precise because of the ambiguity of the word *world*. The scientific edifice is a *worldview* only for those who assume that science can in principle take in all that exists.

The scientific cosmology is so much a part of the air we breathe that it is hardly necessary to describe it, but I will give it a paragraph to provide a reference point for what we are talking about. Some fifteen billion years ago an incredibly compact pellet of matter exploded to launch its components on a voyage that still continues. Differentiation set in as hydrogen proliferated into the periodic table. Atoms gathered into gaseous clouds. Stars condensed from whirling filaments of flame, and planets spun off from those to become molten drops that pulsated and grew rock-encrusted. Narrowing our gaze to the planet that was to become our home, we watch it grow, ocean-filmed and swathed in atmosphere. Some three and a half billion years ago shallow waters began to ferment with life, which could maintain its inner milieu through homeostasis and could reproduce itself. Life spread from oceans across continents, and intelligence appeared. Several million years ago our ancestors arrived. It is difficult to say exactly when, for every few years paleontologists announce discoveries that "set the human race back another million years or so," as press reports like to break the news.

Taught from primary schools onward, this story is so familiar that further details would only clutter things.

Tradition's Cosmological Shortcomings

That this scientific cosmology retires traditional ones with their six days of creation and the like goes without saying. Who can possibly question that when the scientific cosmology has landed people on the moon? Our ancestors were impressive astronomers, and we can honor them unreservedly for how much they learned about nature with only their unaided senses to work with. And there is another point. There is a naturalism in Taoism, Zen Buddhism, and tribal outlooks that in its own way rivals science's calculative cosmology, but that is the naturalism of the artist, the poet, and the nature lover—of Li Po, Wordsworth, and Thoreau, not that of Galileo and Bacon. For present purposes, aesthetics is irrelevant. Modern cosmology derives from laboratory experiments, not landscape paintings.

Postmodernism's Cosmological Shortcomings

With traditional cosmology out of the running, the question turns to postmodernism. Because science is cumulative, it follows as a matter of course that the cosmology we have in the twenty-first century is an improvement over what we had in the middle of the twentieth, which on my timeline is when modernity phased into postmodernity. But the refinements that postmodern scientists have achieved have not affected life to anything like the degree that postmodern social thrusts have, so the social Oscar is the one postmodernists are most entitled to.

The next section of this chapter will discuss postmodernism achievements on the social front, but before turning to those I need to support my contention that postmodern science (it is well to say postmodern *physics* here) does not measure up to modern physics in the scope of its discoveries. It says nothing against the brilliance of Stephen Hawking, Fred Hoyle, John Wheeler, Freeman Dyson, Steven Weinberg, and their likes to add that they have discovered nothing about nature that compares with the discoveries of Copernicus, Newton, Maxwell, Planck, Einstein, Heisenberg, Bohr, Schrodinger, and Born. In molecular chemistry things are different. DNA is a staggering discovery, but, extending back only millions of years compared with the astrophysicists' billion, it is not in nature's foundations. The fact that no new abstract idea in physics has emerged for seventy years may suggest that nothing more remains to be discovered about nature's foundations. Be that as it may, postmodernism's discoveries (unlike modern discoveries in physics—the laws of gravity, thermodynamics, electromagnetism, relativity theory, and quantum mechanics, which continue to be used to make space shuttles fly and to help us understand how hot electrons behave in semiconductors) have concerned details and exotica. The billions of dollars that have been spent since the middle of the twentieth century (and the millions of papers that have been written on theories that change back and forth) have produced no discoveries that impact human beings in important ways. All are in the domain of the meta-sciences of high-energy particle physics and astronomy, whose findings—what is supposed to have happened in the first 10–42 seconds of the universe's life, and the like—while headlined by the media have no conceivable connection to human life and can be neither falsified nor checked in normal ways. This allows the building blocks of nature—particles, strings, or whatever—to keep changing, and the age of the universe to be halved or doubled every now and then. Roughly 99.999 percent of science (scientist Rustum Roy's estimate) is unaffected by these flickering hypotheses, and the public does not much care about their fate.

Outranking the foregoing reason for not giving the cosmological Oscar to postmodernism is the fact that the noisiest postmodernists have called into question the very notion of truth by turning claims to truth into little more than power plays. According to this reading of the matter, when people claim that what they say is true, all they are really doing is claiming status for beliefs that advance their own social standing. This relativizes science's assertions radically and rules out even the possibility of its closing in on the nature of nature. The most widely used textbook on college campuses for the past thirty years has been Thomas Kuhn's *The Structure of Scientific Revolutions*, and its thesis—that facts derive their meaning from the paradigms that set them in place—has shifted attention from scientific facts to scientific paradigms. As there are no neutral standards by which to judge these paradigms, Kuhn's thesis (if unnuanced) leads to a relativism among paradigms that places Hottentot science on a par with Newton's. Kuhn himself phrased his thesis carefully enough to parry such relativism, but even taken at its best, it provides no way that science could get to the bottom of things. This demotes the enterprise, and in doing so provides a strong supporting reason for not giving postmodernism the cosmological prize. It does better with social issues, to which I now turn.

Postmodernism's Fairness Revolution

The magic word of postmodernism is *society*. This is not surprising. With the belief that there is nothing beyond our present world, nature and society are all that remain, and of the two nature has become the province of specialists. We seldom confront it directly any-more; mostly it comes to us via supermarkets and cushioned by air-conditioning and central heating. This leaves society as the domain that presses on us directly and the one in which there is some prospect of our making a difference.

And changes are occurring. Post colonial guilt may play a part here, and so much remains to be done that self-congratulation is premature. Still, a quick rehearsal of some changes that have occurred in a single lifetime makes it clear that social injustices are being recognized and addressed more earnestly today than they were by our ancestors:

In 1919 the Brooklyn Zoo exhibited an African American caged alongside chimpanzees and gorillas. Today such an act would be met with outrage anywhere in the world.

The civil rights movement of the 1960s accomplished its major objectives. In the United States and even in South Africa today, people of different races mix where they never could before—on beaches, in airline cabin crews, everywhere.

In the 1930s, if a streetcar in San Francisco approached a stop where only Chinese Americans were waiting to board, it would routinely pass them by. By contrast, when (fifty years later) I retired from teaching at the University of California, Berkeley, my highly respected chancellor was a Chinese American who spoke English with a Chinese accent.

No war has ever been as vigorously protested as was the war in Vietnam by United States citizens. When things were going so badly that military leaders advised President Nixon to use nuclear weapons, he declined because (as he said) if he did that, he would face a nation that had taken to the streets.

The women's movement is only a blink in the eyes of history, but it has already scored impressive victories. Until long after the Civil War, American women really had no civil rights, no legal rights, and no property rights. Not until 1918 did Texas alter its law that everyone had the right to vote except "idiots, imbeciles, aliens, the insane, and women."

Arguably, the most important theological development of the latter twentieth century was the emergence of the theology of liberation, with its Latin American and feminist versions in the vanguard.

In an unprecedented move, in March 2000 the pope prayed to God to forgive the sins his church had committed against the people of Israel, against love, peace, and respect for cultures and religions, against the dignity of women and the unity of the human race, and against the fundamental rights of persons. Two months later, two hundred thousand

Australians marched across Sydney Harbor Bridge to apologize for their treatment of the aborigines while the skywritten word SORRY floated above the Sydney Opera House.

Tradition's Social Shortcomings

These signs of progress acquire additional life when they are set against the unconcern of earlier times regarding such matters. There is no reason to think that traditional peoples were more callous than we are, but on the whole they saw their obligations as extending no further than to members of their primary communities: Buddhism's *dana* (gifts), Jesus' "cup of water given in my name," and their likes. Encountered face-to-face, the hungry were fed, the naked were clothed, and widows and orphans were provided for as means allowed, but there human obligations ended. Injustices that were built into institutions (if such injustices were even recognized) were not human beings' responsibility, for those institutions were considered to be God-given and unalterable. People regarded them in the way we regard laws of nature—as givens to be worked with, not criticized.

Modernity changed this attitude. Accelerating travel and trade brought encounters between peoples whose societal structures were very different from one another, and these differences showed that such institutions were not like natural laws after all; they were humanly devised and could therefore be critiqued. The French Revolution put this prospect to a historic test; scrapping the divine right of kings, it set out to create a society built on liberty, equality, and fraternity. The experiment failed and the backlash was immediate, but its premise—that societies are malleable—survived.

Modernity's Social Shortcomings

Modernity deserves credit for that discovery, and (if we wished) we might excuse it for its poor handling of its discovery on grounds that it was working with a new idea. The record itself, however, is by postmodern standards, deplorable. Under the pretext of shouldering "the white man's burden" to minister to "lesser breeds without the law," it ensconced colonialism, which raped Asia and Africa, hit its nadir in the Opium Wars of 1841–42, and ended by subjecting the entire civilized world to Western domination. David Hume is commonly credited with having the clearest head of all the great philosophers, but I read that somewhere in his correspondence (I have not been able to find the passage) he wrote that the worst white man is better than the best black man. What I can report firsthand is signs posted in parks of the international settlements in Shanghai, where I attended high school, that read, "No dogs or Chinese allowed." With a virgin continent to rape, the United States did not need colonies, but this did not keep it from hunting down the Native Americans, continuing the institution of slavery, annexing Puerto Rico and Hawaii, and establishing "protectorates" in the Philippines and several other places.

Having dealt with nature and society, I turn now to the third inescapable issue that human beings must face: the Big Picture.

The Traditional Worldview

Modernity's Metaphysical Shortcomings

Modernity was metaphysically sloppy. Ravished by science's accomplishments, it elevated the scientific method to "our sacral mode of knowing" (Alex Comfort), and because that mode registers nothing that is without a material component, immaterial realities at first dropped from view and then (as the position hardened) were denied existence. In the distinction registered earlier in this chapter, this was metaphysics reduced to cosmology. When Carl Sagan opened his television series, *Cosmos*, by announcing that "the Cosmos is all that is or ever was or ever will be," he presented that unargued assumption as if it were a scientific fact. Modernity's Big Picture is materialism or (in its more plausible version) naturalism, which acknowledges that there *are* immaterial things—thoughts and feelings, for example—while insisting that those things are totally dependent on matter. Both versions are stunted when compared with the traditional outlook. It is important to understand that neither materialism nor naturalism is required by anything science has discovered in the way of actual facts. We have slid into this smallest of metaphysical positions for psychological, not logical, reasons.

Postmodernity's Metaphyscial Shortcomings

As for postmodernity, it sets itself against the very idea of such a thing as the Big Picture. It got off on the right foot by critiquing the truncated worldview of the Enlightenment, but from that reasonable beginning it plunged on to argue unreasonably that worldviews (often derisively referred to as *grand narratives*) are misguided in principle. In *The Postmodern Condition*, Jean François Lyotard goes so far as to *define* postmodernism as "incredulity toward meta-narratives," a synonym for metaphysics.

The incredulity takes three forms that grow increasingly shrill as they proceed. Postmodern *minimalism* contents itself with pointing out that we have no consensual worldview today; "we have no maps and don't know how to make them." *Mainline* postmodernism adds, "and never again will we have a consensual worldview, such as prevailed in the Middle Ages, Elizabethan England, or seventeenth-century New England; we now know too well how little the human mind can know." *Hardcore* postmodernism carries this trajectory to its logical limit by adding, "good riddance!" Stated in the in-house idiom postmodernists are fond of, worldviews "totalize" by "marginalizing" minority viewpoints. They are oppressive in principle and should be resolutely resisted.

If hardcore postmodernism were accurate in this charge it would stop this book in its tracks, but it has not proved that it is accurate—it merely *assumes* that it is accurate and rests its case on examples of oppression that, of course, are not lacking. What has not been demonstrated is the impossibility of a worldview that builds the rights of minorities into its foundations as an essential building block. There is irony here, for the very postmodernism that is dismissing the possibility of a comprehensive humane outlook is working toward the creation of such through its fairness revolution—its insistence that everybody be given an equal chance at the goods of life. The deeper fact, however, is that to have or not have a worldview is not an option, for peripheral vision always conditions what we are attending to focally, and in conceptual "seeing" the periphery has no cutoff. The only choice we have is to be consciously aware of our worldviews and criticize them where they need criticizing, or let them work on us unnoticed and acquiesce to living unexamined lives.

To say as I have that neither modernism nor postmodernism handled the metaphysical problem well is, of course, no proof that traditionalists handled it better. If this chapter were a self-contained unit, I would need to complete it by describing the traditional worldview and defending its merits. That, however, comes so close to being the object of this entire book that I will not try to compress it into a page or two here. Moreover, the traditional worldview is so out of favor today that the only possible way to gain a hearing for it is to ease into it, so to speak, by suggesting plausibilities wherever openings for them appear.

That leaves this present chapter open ended, but even so these early pages have accomplished two things. The first of these is descriptive: this chapter has placed the present in its historical setting. The second is prescriptive, for an obvious moral emerges from what has been said. We should enter our new millennium by running a strainer through our past to lift from each of its three periods the gold it contains and let its dross sink back into the sands of history. Modernity's gold—i.e., science—is certain to figure importantly in the third millennium, and postmodernity's focus on justice likewise stands a good chance of continuing. It is the traditional worldview that is in jeopardy and must be rehabilitated if it is to survive.

QUESTIONS FOR REVIEW AND DISCUSSION

1. What are the three historical periods that Smith defines and how do these relate to the three fundamental human problems that he observes?
2. How does he distinguish metaphysics from cosmology? When do they align?
3. What does Smith mean by the cosmological achievements of modernity, and how do they surpass the shortcomings of traditional cosmological achievements?
4. What is Smith's argument for the shortcomings of postmodern science when compared to the achievements of modern science?
5. Why does Smith feel that postmodernism's greatest successes have been in tackling issues of social injustice? What does he discern to have been among the shortcomings of modernity in this area?
6. What, according to Smith, are modernity's shortcomings with regards to metaphysics? Do you agree with his assessment?
7. What in Smith's opinion are the shortcomings of postmodernity's assessment of what he calls "the Big Picture"? Do you concur with his assessment?
8. Does Smith argue that traditionalists have handled the Big Picture better than modernism or postmodernism? What does he prescribe for the future in terms of learning from the contributions of each of the three historical periods?
9. Would you regard Smith's chapter as an example of religious studies scholarship? If not, how would you characterize it?

33 Who is a Buddhist? Night-Stand Buddhists and Other Creatures

Thomas A. Tweed

Thomas A. Tweed (1954–) received his doctorate in Religious Studies from Stanford University with a specialization in Religion in North America. His publications indicate the diversity of his interests within this specialization: from Asian religions in the United States (*Asian Religions in America: A Documentary History* [Oxford, 1999] and *The American Encounter with Buddhism, 1844–1912: Victorian Culture and the Limits of Dissent* [Indiana, 1992; UNC, 2000]) and Catholicism in America (*Our Lady of the Exile: Diasporic Religion at a Cuban Catholic Shrine in Miami* [Oxford, 1997] and *America's Church: The National Shrine and Catholic Presence in the Nation's Capital* [Oxford, 2011]) to religion and geography as well as method and theory in the study of religion (*Crossing and Dwelling: A Theory of Religion* [Harvard, 2006]). After teaching at the University of Miami, the University of North Carolina at Chapel Hill, and the University of Texas at Austin, Tweed moved to the University of Notre Dame in 2013 as the Harold and Martha Welch Endowed Chair in American Studies. His award-winning publications, active role at the American Academy of Religions (AAR), training of graduate students, and engagement with print and broadcast media have brought more nuanced attention and creative conceptualization to the complexity of religious identity.

An American Catholic bishop once confided to me with dismay that the Vietnamese who attend mass in his archdiocese are "not really Catholic." Initially I was perplexed by this claim. Did he mean that they had not been baptized in their homeland? Something else? "They're still too Buddhist," he explained. He meant that the Buddhist influence was great among Vietnamese Catholics and that they carried that hybrid tradition with them to the United States when they fled after the fall of Saigon in 1975. I thought of that conversation as I read a newspaper article that called attention to hundreds of thousands of Americans who practice Buddhist meditation but do not affiliate with any Buddhist temple or center. What do these examples—Vietnamese Catholics and Buddhist meditators—have in common? They raise central questions in the study of religion. How do we define religious identity? (Who is Catholic? Who is Buddhist?) And how do we view those who have interest in a religion but do not affiliate? In this essay, I focus on the issue of religious identity as it confronts scholars who investigate the history of Buddhism in the West, especially the United States. First, I propose a strategy for establishing religious identity. Second, I suggest that we add another category—*sympathizer*—to those we use to interpret religious life.[1]

Adherents: Complicating Religious Identity

Even though many monographs have described peoples with Creole practices that have changed in interaction with other traditions—as in the religious histories of Cuba and Haiti, Thailand and China—most Western scholars of religion still have assumed that religious identity is singular and fixed, and that the subjects of studies fall into two categories: adherents and non-adherents. Further, identifying adherents seems straightforward. An adherent can be defined as one who accepts certain defining beliefs and practices, a strategy I call an *essentialist* or *normative approach*. For others, an adherent is one who joins a religious organization or participates in its ritual life. But these three standard strategies for defining religious identity—applying norms, counting members, or observing attendance—introduce conceptual confusions and overlook important characters. The normative approach might suggest, for example, that a Buddhist is one who has formally taken refuge in the Three Jewels (the Dharma, the Buddha, and the Sangha), practiced prescribed rituals at a Buddhist temple (chanting), or affirmed defining beliefs (the Four Noble Truths). But this constructs an essentialized notion of the tradition, imagining the religion as static, isolated, and unified. It fails to acknowledge that traditions change, that they have contacts and exchanges with other traditions, and that hybrid traditions with diverse expressions emerge and claim authenticity. Any normative definition of a religion, therefore, excludes many who might want to count themselves as followers. The other two strategies for establishing religious identity—membership and attendance—invite fewer conceptual difficulties, because they do not imagine a defining core, but they fail to account for those who have little or no relation with a Buddhist institution yet still understand the world in Buddhist terms, engage in Buddhist practices, or (at least) view themselves as Buddhists. In short, the usual ways of deciding who is Buddhist—or Christian, Hindu, or Muslim—fail to take seriously enough the complexity of religious identity.[2]

And, as some studies have shown, religious identity can be complex in several ways. First, as in Japan, religions can be functionally compartmentalized: you might be married in one tradition (Shinto) and memorialized in another (Buddhism). Second, especially in diverse cultural contexts where religious identity does *not* carry harsh political or economic consequences, some religious women and men self-consciously and unapologetically draw on varied practices from multiple traditions. In some periods and regions in China, for instance, men and women have turned to Buddhist bodhisattvas, Confucian sages, and Taoist immortals—along with a host of other human or suprahuman exemplars who have emerged from vernacular religious traditions. In seventeenth-century America, many Massachusetts Puritans combined occult practices, like astrology, with their Protestant piety, just as some who attended Spiritualist séances in the 1850s identified themselves as Episcopalians. Today, some who turn to the healing powers of crystals during the weekday sing hymns at a United Methodist Church on Sunday.[3]

Third, even in cultural contexts where admitting that you incorporate practices or beliefs from multiple traditions can get you sanctioned by religious leaders, relegated to menial labor, or sentenced to prison, religious identity can be multiple or ambivalent. There can be ism-crossing—a combining in practice of more than one tradition (often less self-conscious), as in the influence of Santeria on Cuban Catholicism or the impact of Shinto on Japanese Buddhism. In fact, these sorts of religious combinations are so common that if we ignore those who affiliate with hybrid traditions, engage in Creole practices, or express ambivalent identities, there would be no one left to study. Most of the religions I know emerged in contact and exchange with other traditions, and they continued to change over time—always in interaction. Scholars cannot locate a pristine beginning or pre-contact essence to use as a norm to define orthodoxy or orthopraxis. There is hybridity all the way down. In this sense, religious identity is usually complex. Ambivalence is the norm.[4]

Finally, religious identity also can be complex for converts. Conversion involves a more or less (often less) complete shift of beliefs and practices. The old tradition never fades completely; the new one never shapes exclusively. This was true of Christian converts in colonial Africa, Asia, and North and South America, where indigenous practices colored the religious life of many native "converts." It remains true of self-identified Buddhist converts in modern industrialized nations with legislated religious freedom. Conversion also has its social costs and payments, and these affect the character of religious belief and practice. In some colonized nations in nineteenth-century Africa, for example, conversion to Christianity could slightly raise one's social status. On the other hand, in nineteenth-century Britain, conversion to Vedanta Hinduism might prompt derision. In periods and places where conversion has high social *value*, the number of self-announced converts might multiply, even though their spiritual practice might retain many elements of the denounced tradition. Where conversion has high social *costs*, many of the converted who have found their frameworks of meaning and habits of practice profoundly altered by a realignment with another tradition might do all they can to hide that from public view. Some celebrate conversion; others conceal it. Either way, the converts' self-understanding and everyday practice are complex.[5]

If religious identity is as complex as I have suggested, then this has implications for the study of Buddhist adherents in the West. Those adherents include convert Buddhists; followers of European and African descent who chose the faith for themselves; and several types of so-called cradle Buddhists who were born into the tradition—"oldline" Buddhists who are the descendants of the earliest Asian migrants; immigrants and refugees who have arrived since 1965; and converts' children, who—if Western-convert Buddhism manages to flourish—will be a more visible presence in the next twenty-five years. And as we study these adherents we must note the complexities of religious identity. For example, as we study the recently arrived cradle Buddhists we should be alert to the ways that their religious practice has been hybrid and their religious identity ambivalent—in the homeland, in transit, and in the new land. As we study converts, we should attend carefully to the evidence in language, artifact, and gesture that their religious life reveals influences from multiple sources, including the tradition they rejected when they joined the Buddhist Sangha.[6]

Sympathizers and the Story of Western Buddhism

So far I have discussed only adherents: cradle Buddhists who inherited the faith and converts who chose it, those followers who might meet the standard criteria for defining Buddhist identity. But placing the focus there excludes a great deal. It overlooks those who have not offered full or formal allegiance to the tradition.

Many in the West fit that profile. Fifteen percent of the French express "an interest" in Buddhism and two million describe it as "the religion they like best," according to one report. Of the six hundred thousand Buddhists in France, less than one hundred thousand are "full-blown Buddhists." But, the report continued, "many millions are said to be influenced by Buddhism." The recent article about meditators that I mentioned at the start of this essay made a similar point about the United States. One scholar quoted in that story suggested—correctly, I think—that we do not know how many Americans use Buddhist meditation practices. But, she estimated, "the number is large, probably in the many hundreds of thousands, possibly more." In that same article, Helen Tworkov, the editor of the popular Buddhist quarterly *Tricycle*, estimated that half of the publication's sixty thousand subscribers do not describe themselves as Buddhists. I call those thirty thousand *Tricycle* subscribers and the hundreds of thousands of unaffiliated meditators *sympathizers*, or, in a flashier but less precise and inclusive phrase, *night-stand Buddhists*.[7]

What, then, is a sympathizer or night-stand Buddhist? It might be useful to clarify first what it is *not*. *Sympathizer* does not refer to men and women who identify with a tradition self-consciously but fail to practice it vigorously or regularly. Lukewarm adherents deserve scholarly attention, but they are not night-stand Buddhists. The term *sympathizer* does not signal the level of commitment among those who self-identify with a tradition.[8]

Rather, it points to those who have some sympathy for a religion but do not embrace it exclusively or fully. When asked, these people would *not* identify themselves as Buddhists. They would say they are Methodist, or Jewish, or unaffiliated. If we could talk with them long enough—or, better yet, visit their homes and observe their daily routines—we would notice signs of interest in Buddhism. They might practice zazen, subscribe to a Buddhist periodical, or read books about the tradition. They might attend lectures at the local university. They might visit a Buddhist center's web page or participate in an online Buddhist discussion group. They might self-consciously decorate their homes with Buddhist artifacts. Night-stand Buddhists, then, are those who might place a how-to book on Buddhist meditation on the night-stand—say, Philip Kapleau's *The Three Pillars of Zen*—and read it before they fall to sleep, and then rise the next morning to practice, however imperfectly or ambivalently, what they learned the night before. If I am right, these sympathizers have been an important part of the story of Buddhism in North America and the West since the 1880s—from philosopher Paul Carus and businessman Andrew Carnegie to composer John Cage and painter William Wiley and, more important, the many ordinary sympathizers whose names have been lost to us.[9]

These Western sympathizers have encountered Buddhism in different social sites—in other words, several cultural practices have created and sustained their interest in the tradition. Those include reading texts, viewing artifacts, and performing rituals. We could consider artifacts (including domestic furnishings and landscape architecture, as well as paintings and computers) or analyze ritual practices (including meditation, chanting, and the medical uses of mindfulness practice). But consider just one example: contemporary American sympathizers' engagement with Buddhism through reading. In recent decades, the number of books with Buddhist themes has multiplied many times. For example, in 2000, *Books in Print* listed 218 titles that begin with *Zen*. The list includes, by my count, 70 how-to books that apply Zen to one or another aspect of life, from the silly to the sophisticated, including Zen *and Creative Management*, Zen *and the Art of Kicking Butts: The Ultimate Guide for Quitting Smoking Forever*, Zen *in the Art of Golf*, Zen *and the Art of the Internet*, and Zen *and the Art of Changing Diapers*. However we might assess these popular prescriptive texts, which sometimes have little to do with Zen as most scholars and practitioners understand it, they clearly show the breadth of Buddhist sympathy in the culture.[10]

The list of recent titles on Buddhism also includes fine translations of sacred texts, informed advice about practice, and reflections by Western or Asian teachers. Among the latter, Thich Nhat Hanh's *The Miracle of Mindfulness* (1975) is a good example. Beacon Press reports that the book has sold "about 125,000" copies. If we added the publication figures for Nhat Hanh's other English-language books, from Riverhead Press and Parallax Press, his influence seems indisputable. (For example, his recent text, *Living Buddha, Living Christ*, has sold 80,000 copies for Riverhead Press.) As with all texts, it is impossible to count the proportion of sympathizers included among Nhat Hanh's readers (or to determine how readers interpret the books). It seems clear, however, that many of his readers do not belong to Buddhist groups or identify themselves with Buddhism.[11]

The Meaning of Adherent in the Scholarship

Some readers might object at this point. They would say, "But we know this. You have built a monument to the obvious. We know that religious identity is hybrid and that there are Buddhist dabblers." And it is true that some of the best writing about Buddhism in North America acknowledges the problem of determining identity. In his important 1979 study, *American Buddhism*, Charles Prebish takes on the issue in a two-page section titled "What Constitutes a Buddhist?" Prebish acknowledges that "it has become difficult to know what constitutes a Buddhist today." He points to the varying ways in which Buddhist institutions count members. Does membership refer to those who donate, attend, or join? Emma McCloy Layman, in *Buddhism in America*, a study published three years earlier, also noticed the problem as she tried to count American Buddhists. "There are several reasons for the difficulty in estimating the number of Buddhists in America," Layman proposed. Among the four she listed were these: that most "nominal Buddhists" had failed to ritually accept the tradition, while other "self-styled Buddhists" had not joined any Buddhist institution.[12]

Other more recent reflections on Asian-immigrant Buddhists acknowledge a related difficulty in defining Buddhists, making the point I emphasize here: religious belief and practice, in the homeland and the new land, have been hybrid. In his study of the Vietnamese in the United States, the anthropologist Paul James Rutledge noticed:

> The religious thought of many Vietnamese has been a *blending* of a number of systems, choosing not to claim one and denounce the others but rather to *mix* the teachings of various faiths in order to meet the particular needs of their community or family. This *syncretistic* practice is deeply rooted in the practice of religion by Vietnamese people. ... Although most Vietnamese are Buddhist, either by practice or claim, Vietnamese refugees in America also ascribe [to] Confucianism, Taoism, Roman Catholicism and a variety of Eastern religions less known in the West.[13]

Penny Van Esterik, an anthropologist who specializes in Southeast Asia, makes a similar point in *Taking Refuge*, her book-length study of Lao Buddhists in Toronto. She notes that Lao religion combines both "spirit worship" and Theravada Buddhism. The vernacular tradition of venerating spirits has been strong in Laos, as strong as anywhere in Asia, and for Van Esterik that indigenous tradition has become part of Laotian Buddhism. "Ghosts and spirits," she suggests, "are interacted with as part of the Buddhist world order." For that reason, "understanding Lao religion in the past and the present requires close attention to obeisance owed to the spirit world as well as the system of Theravada Buddhism. The relation between these two systems provides the unique characteristics of Lao religion." Van Esterik essentializes and isolates the two religious "systems" a bit too much for me—interpreting them as if they were two originally distinct and self-contained cultural forms that then came into contact with each other—but still she recognizes the hybrid character of Buddhist identity.[14]

Other scholars have noticed how cradle and convert Buddhists have had complex and ambivalent relationships with Western cultural and religious values and practices. Even if he offers an interpretation that is not sympathetic enough to Henry Steel Olcott's self-understanding as a Buddhist, Stephen Prothero's sophisticated book, *The White Buddhist*, centers on the issue of religious identity. In an imaginative use of linguistic theory, Prothero argues that Olcott's was a "creole" faith, combining a Buddhist "lexicon," a Theosophical "accent," and a liberal Protestant "grammar." Olcott, according to Prothero, accepted and promoted a Protestantized and Americanized Buddhism. In his study of Americanization in two Theravada Buddhist temples in Los Angeles and Chicago, Paul Numrich noticed that in Los Angeles temples hold summer camps, and in Chicago monks wear overcoats. In other words, Asian-American Buddhists have accommodated themselves to American culture, as well as resisted it, and complex forms of the tradition have emerged in this cultural context, where Buddhists meet not only Christians, Jews, and Muslims, but a wider variety of Buddhists than anywhere in Asia. Many scholars and Buddhists, and some Buddhist scholars, have considered the problems of adapting this Asian tradition to a Western culture. One scholar, writing for an issue of *Amerasia Journal*, exhorted Asians not to be afraid of "religious symbiosis" as the younger generations seek to revitalize "Asian American religious identities." Some Buddhist leaders in the United States have made similar suggestions, while others have held a more traditional line. Either way, observers have noticed cultural exchanges and new forms of Buddhism as practitioners make their way in America, as they meditate in chairs, sing Buddhist hymns, bite into burgers, and gather on Sundays.[15]

If some scholars have acknowledged the hybrid character of Buddhist identity, others have not; but even those who note its complexity have not usually explored that fully in their writings. Let's return to one of the first and best books on the subject, Prebish's *American Buddhism*. Prebish acknowledges the problem of defining Buddhist identity in two pages, as I have noted. He then writes as if that were not very complicated, as he surveys the Buddhist scene in the 1970s. He considers in turn, the various Buddhist traditions and groups: Buddhist Churches of America, San Francisco Zen Center, Buddhist Vihara Society, Tibetan Nyingma Meditation Center, and so on. Rick Fields, in his lively and important historical narrative of Buddhism in the United States, also shows that he knows that Buddhism has been creole, assuming varied forms in Asian cultures and encountering great diversity in America. He repeats, for example, the common wisdom about Chinese religious blending in China and America: "The Chinese temples reflected popular Chinese religion, which was a *mixture* of Taoism, Confucianism, and Buddhism." Still, most of his story overlooks or underemphasizes the hybrid character of Buddhism in the United States, especially among Asian immigrants. My point here—and I want to be clear—is not that these writers, and the rest of us, too, have failed to notice the complexity of Buddhist identity. Most of us have. Rather, we have not taken that insight seriously enough. Those of us working in this subfield have not always systematically or fully applied our best insights about the hybrid character of Buddhist identity in our studies.[16]

To shift the focus slightly—and approach the center of my interest in this topic—I think that part of the problem in the study of Western Buddhism, and in religious studies more broadly, is that we continue to draw on essentialist-normative definitions of religious identity, those that construct a core or essence of right practice or belief and measure all historical expressions against it. Fields, for instance, suggests that "Buddhist history is the record of lineage—of who gave what to whom. ... " To, apply this standard means that those who have teachers and who affiliate with institutions are authentic Buddhists; others are suspect, and (mostly) excluded from our stories about Western Buddhist history. In order to avoid the theoretical problems of essentialist definitions and allow more characters into our historical narratives, I suggest that we use self-identification as one helpful standard for identifying Buddhists. Of course, we will use other standards too, and we want to know who takes the precepts, who studies with a teacher, and who chants at a temple. That information tells us important things. But we cannot exclude from our analysis those who don't meet the traditional standards but still claim Buddhist identity for themselves. For our purposes as scholars, Buddhists are those who say they are.[17]

Some readers might object that this position is too uncritical, that it allows a flood of Buddhist pretenders through the scholarly gates. That concerns Philip C. Almond, the author of a fine study of Buddhism in Britain, and he worries most about occult Buddhists, those connected with the Theosophical Society. His solution: ignore them, even though esoteric Buddhists far outnumbered all other self-identified Caucasian Buddhists in Europe and America during the late nineteenth century. He explains his stance in a footnote: "I have not dealt with the Esoteric Buddhism of Madame Blavatsky and her English disciple, Alfred Sinnett. Esoteric, it may have been. Buddhism it certainly was not. ... " Fields never responds directly to this issue, but he, too, implicitly rejects self-identification as a standard when he emphasizes the importance of lineages and institutions. In his *American Buddhism*, Prebish follows Holmes Welch, the accomplished scholar of Chinese Buddhism, in arguing that "it is insufficient to simply ask 'Are you a Buddhist?'" Because of the interpenetration of religious traditions, in China, and the concomitant overlapping of religious identities, the respondent might say that, yes, he is a Buddhist. In the next minute, however, he might also admit to being a Taoist or a Confucian. Prebish proposes another strategy for settling Buddhist identity: "A more appropriate question might be (as Professor Welch suggests): 'Have you taken the Three Refuges?' Further, 'Do you practice the five layman's vows?'" Prebish then complicates the issue further by pointing out that he has ignored "a consideration of the *quality* of membership and *commitment* to the tradition." And here enters a misleading essentialist-normative definition of Buddhist identity. In this view, which I think remains common among scholars and almost universal among practitioners, a Buddhist is someone who meets certain standards of orthodoxy or orthopraxis. She is a Buddhist if she takes refuge in the Three Jewels, accepts the doctrine of no-self, or chants regularly. But Prebish worried that some readers might misinterpret him: "It might be inferred my sympathies rest with the older, traditional forms of Buddhism; that I assume the only valid form of a religious tradition is its pristine expression. Each claim, however, would simply be ungrounded." Still, though Prebish tried to clear a middle path by acknowledging the need for accommodation to the host culture, there are limits on what he (and most scholars and practitioners) will accept as Buddhist: "Of course there is no Ur-Buddhism, but we must ask at what point the 'aloha-amigo' amalgam becomes so strange and fantastic that it ceases to be *Buddhist, American,* or a *meaningful combination of the two*." I see his point, of course: some claims to Buddhist identity seem very odd when measured against the history of the tradition in Asia, or even the West. Still, I stand by my proposal—that attending carefully to self-identification can be very useful.[18]

Let me support that claim with two U.S. examples, one from the turn of the twentieth century and the other from the contemporary period. F. Graeme Davis, a self-proclaimed Buddhist from Vermillion, South Dakota, is one of the characters in the story of Buddhism in America whom we might exclude if we use the usual standards for settling religious identity. Graeme, one of the most memorable figures in the Victorian American encounter with Buddhism, saw himself as a Buddhist. He subscribed to a Buddhist magazine, *The Light of Dharma,* and even corresponded with the Japanese priests at the Jōdo Shinshū Buddhist mission in San Francisco. "My sympathies are altogether with you and your work," Graeme wrote to the Reverend Nishijima in San Francisco in 1901, "[and] it is my hope that I may sometime be able and worthy to aid in working for the same cause, for I believe Buddhism to be the religion of humanity." But I have been unable to find evidence that he ever joined, or even attended, a Buddhist institution or ritually proclaimed his allegiance by taking refuge in the Buddha, Dharma, and Sangha. He tried his best to live the Buddha's teachings. He even organized a group, with three other students at the University of South Dakota, which met every Friday evening "for the purpose of studying Buddhism." Not enough historical evidence survives to offer a textured interpretation of the meaning of Buddhism for Graeme and his three friends—wouldn't you love to sit in that dorm room in 1901 and hear his study group's conversations about Buddhism?—but he is an important character in the story of American Buddhism, even if essentialist or institution-focused standards for deciding religious identity would lead us to ignore him.[19]

A second example of a self-proclaimed Buddhist who might be excluded if we use other criteria for deciding identity, is, I hope, familiar to you. Margaret—let's give her a pseudonym to protect her—is a middle-aged woman from a suburb just outside a major northern city. When we inquire about her life, we find that she practices zazen intermittently, dangles a crystal from her rearview mirror, watches television programs on yoga, and reads books on Zen and Tibetan Buddhism. At home she is (mostly) vegetarian and, on the mornings when she can find the time, she practices t'ai ch'i. On some Saturday afternoons, after she finishes with the soccer carpool and before preparing dinner, Margaret visits the local bookstore, lingering around the "New Age" section, and usually leaves with a book on past lives or healthy relationships. On most Sundays, she attends St. Mark's Episcopal Church. Margaret has never attended or joined a Buddhist group. She has not taken refuge in the Three Jewels. Nor does she seem to meet most formal criteria for Buddhist identity. Still, when we ask her, Margaret insists that she is a Buddhist. Now, why would we want to take her claim seriously? In short, because of what it reveals about her and the culture. It helps us attend to someone—and a wider cultural pattern—that we otherwise might have missed. It is important to know that in American culture at this particular moment, or at least in that middle-class (mostly white) suburban subculture, some folks want to claim Buddhist identity. Then we can begin to ask a series of questions, beginning with the most basic: why does she say she is Buddhist? We might learn that it is fashionable in her circle to be Buddhist or that she wants to signal, to anyone who will listen, her dissent from the Christian church she visits on Sunday, a church she attends mostly because she feels compelled to raise her children in some faith and the local Buddhist center has no religious education (and joining there would invite too much ridicule from her extended family). There are other reasons she identifies with Buddhism, ones that we cannot fully or confidently recover. In any case, my point is that a normative definition of Buddhism excludes Margaret, and Graeme, from the historical narrative, and thereby overlooks important characters and significant trends.

These examples, and many others, indicate that there might be reasons to widen our definition of *Buddhist* to include these self-identified followers. I realize that some readers still might have other grounds for rejecting the strategy I propose, since personal religious commitments and role-specific obligations can shape our responses on this issue. For practitioners, and especially for religious leaders, it might make sense to draw boundaries, to set limits on acceptable belief and practice. In one sense, religious leaders have a role-specific obligation to disallow certain practices and contest certain beliefs. Some followers might insist, for example, that *authentic* Buddhists do not condone violence or affirm theism. Yet scholars, and practitioners who are working as scholars, do not have the same obligations to establish right practice or right belief. Scholars' duty, I suggest, is to understand as much as possible about religion and culture. For that reason, self-identification is a useful standard for defining religious identity, and not only because it avoids the theoretical problems of essentialist approaches and includes the greatest range of characters. It also uncovers much about the status and meaning of the religion at a given historical moment and in a given cultural setting.

The Significance of Sympathizers

Whether or not scholars have used self-identification as one important standard for locating Buddhists (and most have not), some have acknowledged the hybrid character of religious identity, even if they have not always emphasized this awareness in their work. Fewer interpreters, however, have taken seriously the many Westerners who have had sympathy for Buddhism but have not self-identified with the tradition.[20]

Among those who have written about Western Buddhism, Emma Layman did seriously consider sympathizers. She called them, alternately, *inquirers* or *Dharma-hoppers*, and discussed each briefly. By *inquirers*, she meant those "who are transients at the temple or meditation center, as well as non-Buddhist scholars and Christian clergymen who may be on several Buddhist mailing lists." *Dharma-hoppers*, in her usage, are "shopping around for a magic key to happiness and peace of mind, then dropping out." "Many have tried several Buddhist sects," Layman continues, "some have tried several Christian denominations before becoming Buddhists, and some played around with Yoga, Krishna Murti, or Sufi *[sic]*". It is not clear that Layman's Dharma-hoppers are actually sympathizers in my terminology, since some (or many) might identify themselves as Buddhists at some point along their religious journey. Still, Layman recognizes that among non-Asians there have been many seekers who have been interested in Buddhism, and have had some ambivalent entanglement with the tradition, even if these "hoppers" never self-identify or formally affiliate.[21]

But *sympathizer* is not an interpretive category for most scholars of religion, or students of Western Buddhism in particular, and so these so-called inquirers and Dharma-hoppers are not among the characters in our narratives about the history of Buddhism in the West.

Conclusion: Including Diverse Characters in the Story

I have argued, first, that religious identity is hybrid (which scholars have sometimes acknowledged but rarely emphasized) and that using self-identification to locate Buddhists helps us account for this religious hybridity. Second, I have argued that scholars have attended even less carefully to those who have sympathy for Buddhism but do not fully or formally embrace it, and that these sympathizers enrich the narrative of Buddhist history, revealing a great deal about the beliefs and practices of Western cultures.

A wide assortment of characters have played their roles in the story of Buddhism in the West, and we should find a place in the scholarly narratives for them all. Of course, we need to consider both *cradle Buddhists*, those born into the faith, and *convert Buddhists*, those who choose it, as we highlight the creole character of their religious life—for example, Asian immigrants who unselfconsciously blend Laotian spirit-religion with Theravādin practices, or Euro-American converts who unwittingly combine Protestant principles and Vajrayāna values. But there are also *not-just-Buddhists*, who (if asked) might acknowledge dual or multiple religious identities: the Vietnamese refugee who says she is Confucian and Buddhist, the Zen convert who claims to be both a practicing Buddhist and a religious Jew. We also should remember *lukewarm Buddhists*, who practice more at some times of the year than others, or, even though they join a temple or center, practice less vigorously than most religious leaders would prescribe. *Dharma-hoppers*, to use Emma Layman's term, move from one group to another in their spiritual journey, and some claim Buddhist identity while others, distancing themselves from all institutional piety, prefer the *seeker* label. Some other non-Buddhists, whom I have not discussed here, also play an important role in the story: *Buddhist opponents*, such as evangelical Protestants who dismiss Buddhism as a dangerous "cult" or try to convert followers in Asia; and *Buddhist interpreters*, journalists, filmmakers, scholars, poets, painters, and novelists who represent the tradition for Western audiences. And, as I have tried to suggest, we should remember the many *night-stand Buddhists*, who have found themselves drawn to Buddhism, even if they never have gone farther in their practice than sitting almost cross-legged on two folded pillows, imitating an illustration in Kapleau's *The Three Pillars of Zen*, silently facing a bedroom wall.[22]

QUESTIONS FOR REVIEW AND DISCUSSION

1. How would you characterize Tweed's strategy for establishing religious identity? In your assessment, is this useful for the study of religion in general or do you find that the insights and prescriptions are primarily restricted to the analysis of Buddhism in the West?
2. Describe some of the factors that complicate religious identity. What limitations arise when scholars focus on two categories, such as adherents and non-adherents?
3. What is Tweed's position on an "essentialist or normative approach" for determining who should count as an adherent to a tradition?
4. What does Tweed have to say about the variety of ways that religious identity can be complex? List some of the examples drawn from diverse religious traditions.
5. What does Tweed present as the benefits that attend adding "sympathizer" into this already complex mix of interpretive categories? Do you agree?
6. *Night-stand Buddhists* is one of the terms introduced by Tweed. What does it signify?
7. Tweed notes the vast number of non-academic book titles that make reference to Zen or Buddhism more generally. Does he indicate that scholars should pay attention to these? Why?
8. How does Tweed define this new category of "sympathizer" and how does he differentiate it from other categories, such as "lukewarm adherents" or "Dharma-hoppers"?
9. Tweed indicates that although other scholars have noticed the complexity of Buddhist identity, they "have not taken that insight seriously enough. Those of us working in this subfield have not always systematically or fully applied our best insights about the hybrid character of Buddhist identity in our studies." Discuss this claim in connection both to Tweed's critique of where other scholars have stopped short and to Tweed's own examples and recommendations of how to better pursue the full range of complex identity.

Notes

1 This essay is a revised version of Thomas A. Tweed, "Night-Stand Buddhists and Other Creatures: Sympathizers, Adherents, and the Study of Religion," in *American Buddhism: Methods and Findings in Recent Scholarship*, edited by Duncan Ryūken Williams and Christopher S. Queen

(Richmond, U.K.: Curzon Press, 1999), 71–90. The initial comments come from a personal interview with The Most Reverend Agustín A. Román, 9 June 1994, Archdiocese of Miami Pastoral Center, Miami Springs, Florida. See also Ira Rifkin, "The Accidental Buddhist," *News and Observer* (Raleigh), 7 February 1997, 1E, 4E. For a review of literature on Buddhism in the West see Martin Baumann, "The Dharma Has Come West: A Survey of Recent Studies and Sources," *Journal of Buddhist Ethics* 4 (1997), 194–211, http://jbe.la.psu.edU/4/baum2.html [1 Feb. 2002]. For a hard copy of that review, see *Critical Review of Books in Religion* 10 (1997), 1–14. See also Peter N. Gregory, "Describing the Elephant: Buddhism in America," *Religion in American Culture* 11, no. 2 (Summer 2001), 233–63, and Martin Baumann, "American Buddhism: A Bibliography on Buddhist Traditions and Schools in the U.S.A. and Canada," www-user.uni-bremen.de/~religion/bau mann/bib-ambu.htm [1 Feb. 2002].

2 Most students of Buddhist history know well that religion is hybrid. It is not only classic studies of Chinese or Thai religion that teach us that; see, for instance, Erik Zürcher's *The Buddhist Conquest of China* (Leiden: Brill, 1959) and Stanley J. Tambiah's *Buddhism and the Spirit Cults in Northeast Thailand* (Cambridge: Cambridge University Press, 1970). Throughout Asia, Buddhist religious belief and practice changed as they encountered new cultures and other traditions—for example, Buddhist ideas combined with vernacular spirit religions, blended with Confucianism, mixed with Shinto, and incorporated Taoism. In a similar way, students of Christian history have emphasized the Hellenization, and later Germanization, of Christianity as it moved throughout the Mediterranean and Europe. On the latter see, for example, James C. Russell, *The Germanization of Early Medieval Christianity* (New York: Oxford University Press, 1994). Contact and exchange among indigenous, African, and European religions is especially clear in the Caribbean and Latin America. Consider, for example, the studies of religious life in Cuba and Haiti in Leslie G. Desmangles, *The Faces of the Gods: Vodou and Roman Catholicism in Haiti* (Chapel Hill: University of North Carolina Press, 1992), and George Brandon, *Santeria from Africa to the New World: The Dead Sell Memories* (Bloomington: Indiana University Press, 1993). See also Anthony M. Stevens-Arroyo and Andres I. Pérez y Mena (eds), *Enigmatic Powers: Syncretism with African and Indigenous Peoples' Religions among Latinos*, Program for the Analysis of Religion among Latinos Series, no. 3 (New York: Bildner Center for Western Hemisphere Studies, 1994). Many other historical and ethnographic monographs document religious hybridity, while many theorists in cultural studies have emphasized hybridity in other areas of culture. For example, Homi K. Bhabha takes "the cultural and historical hybridity of the postcolonial world" as his "point of departure" in *The Location of Culture* (London: Routledge, 1994), 21.

3 Howard Kerr and Charles L. Crow (eds), *The Occult in America: New Historical Perspectives* (Urbana: University of Illinois Press, 1983); David D. Hall, *Worlds of Wonder, Days of Judgment: Popular Religious Belief in Early New England* (Cambridge: Harvard University Press, 1990); R. Laurence Moore, *In Search of White Crows: Spiritualism, Parapsychology, and American Culture* (New York: Oxford University Press, 1977); James R. Lewis and J. Gordon Melton (eds), *Perspectives on the New Age* (Albany: State University of New York Press, 1992).

4 I have made a similar point in my analysis of Cuban religion in "Identity and Authority at a Cuban Shrine in Miami: Santeria, Catholicism, and Struggles for Religious Identity," *Journal of Hispanic/Latino Theology* 4 (August 1996), 27–48, and in *Our Lady of the Exile: Diasporic Religion at a Cuban Catholic Shrine in Miami* (New York: Oxford University Press, 1997), 43–55.

5 My view of religious transformation is shaped by many studies in the sociology of conversion, including David Snow and Richard Machalek, "The Convert as a Social Type," in *Sociological Theory*, edited by R. Collins (San Francisco: Jossey-Bass, 1983); David Snow and Richard Machalek, "The Sociology of Conversion," *Annual Review of Sociology* 10 (1984), 167–90; Clifford L. Staples and Armand L. Mauss, "Conversion or Commitment? A Reassessment of the Snow and Machalek Approach to the Study of Conversion," *Journal for the Scientific Study of Religion* 26 (1987), 133–47; John Lofland, "'Becoming a World-Saver' Revisited," *American Behavioral Scientist* 20 (July/ August 1977), 805–18; and Lorne Dawson, "Self-Affirmation, Freedom, and Rationality: Theoretically Elaborating 'Active' Conversions," *Journal for the Scientific Study of Religion* 29 (June 1990), 141–63. The anthropological literature on conversion is helpful, too, because it is even more sensitive to the wielding of power and the persistence of hybridity. For example, see John L. Comaroff and Jean Comaroff, *Of Revelation and Revolution: Christianity, Colonialism, and Coercion in South Africa* (Chicago: University of Chicago Press, 1991); Elizabeth Colson, "Converts and Tradition: The Impact of Christianity on Valley Tonga Religion," *Southwestern Journal of Anthropology* 26 (1970),

143–56; Cornelia Kammerer, "Customs and Christian Conversion among Akha Highlanders of Burma," *American Ethnologist* 17 (1990), 277–91.

6 *Oldline Buddhists* is Richard Hughes Seager's term, from *Buddhism in America* (New York: Columbia University Press, 1999), 10. Other scholars have considered the types of Buddhists in the West, especially the United States. See Charles S. Prebish, "Two Buddhisms Reconsidered," *Buddhist Studies Review* 10 (1993), 187–206; bell hooks, "Waking Up to Racism," *Tricycle: The Buddhist Review*, no. 13 (Fall 1994), 42–45; Jan Nattier, "Buddhism Comes to Main Street," *Wilson Quarterly* 21 (Spring 1997), 72–80; Jan Nattier, "Who Is a Buddhist? Charting the Landscape of Buddhist America," in *The Faces of Buddhism in America*, edited by Charles S. Prebish and Kenneth K. Tanaka (Berkeley: University of California Press, 1998), 183–95; and Gregory, "Describing the Elephant: Buddhism in America."

7 "Buddhist Revival French-Style," *Religion Watch* 12 (December 1996), 7. This piece originally appeared in the *National Catholic Register* for November 1996, 17–23. See also Rifkin, "The Accidental Buddhist," 1E, 4E. I used the term *sympathizers* in *The American Encounter with Buddhism, 1844–1912: Victorian Culture and the Limits of Dissent*, rev. ed. (Chapel Hill: University of North Carolina Press, 2000; original publication, 1992). I introduced the phrase *night-stand Buddhists* in "Asian Religions in America: Reflections on an Emerging Subfield," in *Religious Diversity and American Religious History: Studies in Traditions and Cultures*, edited by Walter Conser and Sumner Twiss (Athens: University of Georgia Press, 1998).

8 For a Christian example, see David Hall's discussion of "horse-shed Christians" in Hall, *Worlds of Wonder*, 15. Hall borrowed the term *horse-shed Christians* from the psychologist G. Stanley Hall, who used it to describe his own male relatives in his memoirs, *Life and Confessions of a Psychologist* (New York: D. Appleton, 1923), 58.

9 Rōshi Philip Kapleau, *The Three Pillars of Zen: Teaching, Practice, and Enlightenment, Twenty-Fifth Anniversary Edition* (New York: Anchor, 1989). This book, which originally appeared in 1965, has been popular. It had four hardcover printings by Weatherhill (the first publisher) and Harper and Row (the second publisher), as well as fourteen printings in paperback by Beacon Press. In 1989, Anchor Books issued a twenty-fifth-anniversary paperback edition. In the contemporary period, other media—videocassette and computer—can function in similar ways for sympathizers. For example, Zen Mountain Monastery in Mount Tremper, New York, under the leadership of Abbot John Daido Loori, has distributed a how-to video on zazen, *Introduction to Zen Meditation*, produced by John Daido Loori and Dharma Communications (54 min., 1991, videocassette). That Buddhist community also has an elaborate web page, sells recordings of Dharma discourses, and maintains an online Zen-practice training advisor via electronic mail, called *cyber-monk* (cybermonk@mhv. net), where would-be meditators or longtime practitioners can get advice. Paul Carus wrote many works on Buddhism, even if he never embraced the tradition exclusively or fully, but he expressed his personal religious views (and sympathy for Buddhism) most clearly in his voluminous correspondence in the Open Court Publishing Company Papers, Morris Library, Southern Illinois University, Carbondale, Illinois. On Andrew Carnegie's affection for Buddhism, and Edwin Arnold's poetic life of the Buddha in particular, see Andrew Carnegie, *Autobiography of Andrew Carnegie* (Boston: Houghton Mifflin, 1920); 207. I offer overviews of Carus's and Carnegie's sympathy for Buddhism in *The American Encounter with Buddhism*, 65–67 (Carus) and 44–45 (Carnegie). For evidence of Buddhism's influence on Cage's work, see John Cage, *Silence: Lectures and Writings* (Middletown, Connecticut: Wesleyan University Press, 1973). For a helpful autobiographical fragment concerning his relation to Buddhism, see "Where I'm Now," in *Beneath a Single Moon: Buddhism and Contemporary American Poetry*, edited by Kent Johnson and Craig Paulenich (Boston: Shambhala, 1991), 43–44. An exhibition catalog helpfully discusses the painter William Wiley's sympathy for Buddhism, and the tradition's influence on his art. It is Gail Gelburd and Geri De Paoli, *The Transparent Thread: Asian Philosophy in Recent American Art* (Philadelphia: University of Pennsylvania Press, 1990), 112–15.

10 *Books in Print, 1999–2000: Subjects* (New Providence, New Jersey: R.R. Bowker, 2000); Albert Low, *Zen and the Art of Creative Management* (Rutland, Vermont: Charles E. Tuttle, 1993); Dennis G. Marthaler, *Zen and the Art of Kicking Butts: The Ultimate Guide for Quitting Smoking Forever* (Duluth, Minnesota: Dennis G. Marthaler, 1995); Joseph D. McLaughlin, *Zen in the Art of Golf* (Atlanta: Humanics Trade, 1997); Brendan P. Kehoe, *Zen and the Art of the Internet: A Beginners Guide* (Englewood Cliffs, New Jersey: Prentice-Hall, 1993); Sarah Arsone, *Zen and the Art of Changing Diapers* (Ventura, California: Printwheel, 1991). Of course, the number of books on Zen is much larger

still. On 3 September 2000, the online catalog of the Library of Congress listed 4,208 books under the keyword *Zen*. Of those, 1,472 were in English.

11 Thich Nhat Hanh, *The Miracle of Mindfulness: A Manual on Meditation*, translated by Mobi Ho, rev. ed. (Boston: Beacon Press, 1987). The sales figures for *Miracle of Mindfulness* and *Living Buddha* were provided by Beacon Press in communication with the author, by Susan G. Worst, editor, Beacon Press, electronic mail, 14 March 1997.

12 Charles S. Prebish, *American Buddhism* (North Scituate, Massachusetts: Duxbury Press, 1979), 42–43; Emma McCloy Layman, *Buddhism in America* (Chicago: Nelson-Hall, 1976), xiv–xv. Although he does not emphasize hybridity or sympathy, Richard Seager also raises the question, "Who are American Buddhists?" See Seager, *Buddhism in America*, 9–10.

13 Paul James Rutledge, *The Vietnamese Experience in America* (Bloomington: Indiana University Press, 1992), 47. Italics mine.

14 Penny Van Esterik, *Taking Refuge: Lao Buddhists in North America* (Tempe, Arizona: Program for Southeast Asian Studies, Arizona State University, 1992), 41.

15 Stephen Prothero, *The White Buddhist: The Asian Odyssey of Henry Steel Olcott* (Bloomington: Indiana University Press, 1996); Paul David Numrich, *Old Wisdom in the New World: Americanization in Two Immigrant Theravada Buddhist Temples* (Knoxville: University of Tennessee Press, 1996); Rudy V. Busto, "Response: Asian American Religious Identities, Building Spiritual Homes on Gold Mountain," *Amerasia Journal* 22, no. 1 (1996), 189.

16 Rick Fields, *How the Swans Came to the Lake: A Narrative History of Buddhism in America*, 2nd ed. (Boston: Shambhala, 1986), 74.

17 Fields, *How the Swans Came to the Lake*, xiii. The position I argue here on religious identity, and the role of self-identification, has been revised somewhat. I am grateful to those who read my work and discussed these issues with me at the Workshop in Buddhist Studies at Princeton University on 3 March 2000 – especially Jacqueline Stone, R. Marie Griffith, and Stephen F. Teiser, of Princeton, and Donald Swearer of Swarthmore. I have softened my insistence on self-identification as the sole criterion, though I continue to hold that we should attend closely to those who claim Buddhist identity, whether or not they meet long-established standards for determining affiliation among Buddhists.

18 Philip C. Almond, *The British Discovery of Buddhism* (Cambridge: Cambridge University Press, 1988), 147, n. 10, and Prebish, *American Buddhism*, 43–44. Although Richard Seager does not highlight the issue, he seems to presuppose self-identification as the primary criterion for determining Buddhist identity when he addresses the diversity of Western Buddhists: "At the outset, it should be assumed that there are many different kinds of Americans who, in one way or another, identify themselves as Buddhist" (Seager, *Buddhism in America*, 9).

19 F. Graeme Davis to Rev. Nishijima, 27 April 1901, reprinted in *Light of* Dharma 1 (June 1901J, 28–29). On F. Graeme Davis, see Tweed, *American Encounter with Buddhism*, 44.

20 Prebish's *American* Buddhism did not consider those who did not affiliate formally with Buddhism. Only a handful of sympathizers find their way into Fields's long narrative, *How the Swans Came to the Lake*, 153–54, 164. In his *Buddhism in America*, Seager mentions only a few figures I would identify as sympathizers as he discusses the 1960s history of U.S. Buddhism (34–44).

21 Layman, *Buddhism in America*, xiv, 203. For an analysis of one Dharma-hopper—or, in my terms, religious seeker—who actually did ritually align herself with Buddhism in a public ceremony, only to later practice Baha'i and Vedanta Hinduism, see Thomas A. Tweed, "Inclusivism and the Spiritual Journey of Marie de Souza Canavarro (1849–1933)," *Religion* 24 (1994), 43–58.

22 For a contemporary evangelical Protestant interpretation of Buddhism as a dangerous or misguided "cult," see Walter Martin, *Kingdom of the Cults* (Minneapolis, Minnesota: Bethany House Publishers, 1985), 261–69. Other evangelical handbooks and pamphlets do not classify Buddhism as a cult but still dismiss it, refuting its major claims and challenging its practices, often as a means of preparing Christians to evangelize. For example, see Fritz Ridenour, *So What's the Difference?* (Ventura, California: Regal Books, 1979), 83–92. That evangelical description and assessment of the world's religions has been popular among conservative Christians: more than 615,000 copies of the first edition were in print when the second edition appeared in 1979. The publisher now claims "more than 800,000" copies have been sold. Buddhist opponents, then, are an important part of the story. Our imaginary meditator might consult chapter 9 of Kapleau's *Three Pillars of Zen*, called "Postures," which includes fifteen drawings of meditators in various positions, from the full lotus to the Burmese posture, on zafus, benches, and chairs (327–53).

34 Rationality

Rodney Stark

Rodney Stark (1934–) was raised in Jamestown, North Dakota and received his doctorate from the University of California, Berkeley. A specialist in the sociological study of religion, Stark is particularly well known for *A Theory of Religion* (1987), which he co-authored with William Bainbridge. In it, Stark and Bainbridge attempt to construct a theory of religion through a series of definitions and propositions. However, Stark's prolific contributions have been more wide-ranging, including examinations of church–sect relationships, secularization and cult formation, and historical examinations of religion in America. He has also made notable propositions about the nature of early Christianity. The 2000 selection that follows is an example of Stark's application of rational choice theory as a means of understanding the human religious impulse. The theory essentially posits that religion is not the result of irrational human behavior, but derives from a rational response to particular human needs, such as for meaning in life.

An immense intellectual shift is taking place in the social-scientific study of religion. During the past few years many of its most venerated theoretical positions—faithfully passed down from the famous founders of the field—have been overturned. The changes have become so dramatic and far-reaching that R. Stephen Warner identified them "as a paradigm shift in progress" (1993: 1044)—an assessment that since then "has been spectacularly fulfilled," according to Andrew Greeley (1996).

As is typical in science, the emergence of a new paradigm rests both on an empirical and a theoretical basis. During the past several decades there was a resurgence in research on religious topics and a substantial number of well-established facts were accumulated. The bulk of these turned out to be inconsistent with the old paradigm. Soon, in response to the growing incompatibility between fact and traditional theory, new theories were constructed to interpret the empirical literature. These incorporate new insights, some of them imported from other branches of social science.

Since I have played an active part in empirical studies of religious phenomena and have led the way in developing these new theories, it seems appropriate for me briefly to summarize and contrast key elements of the new and old paradigms. Fuller treatment will appear in a forthcoming book (Stark and Finke).

Elements of the Old Paradigm

In the beginning, religion was a central concern of social scientists. Thomas Hobbes, Adam Smith, David Hume, Auguste Comte, Karl Marx, Friedrich Engels, Herbert Spencer,

Edward Tyler, Max Weber, Ernst Troeltsch, Émile Durkheim, William James, Lucien Lévy-Bruhl, Carl Jung and Sigmund Freud each wrote extensively about religious phenomena—a corpus of "theorizing" that was for generations the received wisdom on the subject. Indeed, although these founders of social science disagreed about many things, with the exception of Adam Smith and, to a lesser extent, Max Weber, there was remarkable consensus among them on key issues concerning religion.

Religion is False and Harmful

It is claimed that religion harms the *individual* because it impedes rational thought. As Sigmund Freud explained on *one* page of his famous book on the subject (1927: 88; cf. 1989: 54–56), religion is an "illusion," a "sweet—or bittersweet—poison," a "neurosis," an "intoxicant" and "childishness to be overcome." Moreover, Freud's views were not particularly extreme; similar claims abound in the writings of early social scientists. For example, nearly three centuries before Freud, Hobbes (1956 [1651]: 1.98) dismissed all religion as "credulity," "ignorance," and "lies" in one paragraph of his enormously influential book *Leviathan*; on the next page he explained that the gods exist only in the minds of believers, being but "creatures of their own fancy," and hence humans "stand in awe of their own imaginations." A century later, David Hume attributed religious enthusiasm to "blind and terrified credulity" and to "weakness, fear, melancholy, together with ignorance" (1882 [1741]: 144), while across the channel in France, Jean Meslier (circa 1733) explained that "Our nurses are our first theologians; they talk to children about God as they talk to them of werewolves" (in Durant and Durant, 1965: 613–14). And Auguste Comte, who coined the term "sociology," dismissed religion as "hallucinations" resulting from the triumph of "the passions over reason" (1896 [1830–42]: 11.548).

In similar fashion, the traditional view is that religion harms *society* because it sanctifies tyrants and justifies exploitation of the masses. According to Marx and Engels, religion "is a great retarding force, is the *vis inertiae* of history" (1955: 18) and "the parson has ever gone hand in hand with the landlord" (1955: 15). Given the general acceptance of such views, it has been a virtual article of social-scientific faith that religious movements typically are reactionary responses against enlightenment and progress. Thus, the recent growth of evangelical Protestant groups is dismissed by the contemporary heirs of the received wisdom as a "flight from modernity" (Bruce 1992; Hunter 1983)—that is, people who feel threatened by the erosion of traditional morality are flocking into religious havens. Thus did Peter Berger describe evangelical Protestant churches: "They are like besieged fortresses, and their mood tends toward a militancy that only superficially covers an underlying sense of panic" (1969: 11).

A corollary of this line of analysis is that, in addition to being harmful, religion serves as a *pain-killer* for frustration, deprivation and suffering. The influential German sociologist Georg Simmel pronounced that religion is "a sedative for the turbulence of the soul" (1959 [1906]: 32). As Kingsley Davis (1949: 352) explained,

> the ego can stand only a certain amount of frustration ... The culture that drives him to seek goals that he cannot reach also, for the sake of sanity, provides him with goals that anybody can reach. These are goals that transcend the world of actual experience, with the consequence that no evidence to attain them can be conclusive. If the individual believes he has gained them, that is sufficient. All he needs is sufficient faith, and

faith feeds on subjective need. The greater his disappointment in this life, the greater his faith in the next.

Marx, of course, put it rather more succinctly, identifying religion as opium, a view that prompted his collaborator Friedrich Engels to claim that early Christianity "first appeared as a religion of slaves and emancipated slaves, of poor people deprived of all rights, of peoples subjugated and dispersed by Rome" (Marx and Engels 1955: 316). Hence, the received wisdom: *religion appeals most strongly to the lower classes.*

Religion is Doomed

As the social sciences emerged in the wake of the "Enlightenment," the leading figures eagerly proclaimed the demise of religion. Alexis de Tocqueville wrote in his famous early nineteenth-century study, *Democracy in America:* "The philosophers of the eighteenth century explained in a very simple manner the gradual decay of religious faith. Religious zeal, said they, must necessarily fail the more generally liberty is established and knowledge diffused" (1956 [1840]: 11.319). This came to be known as the *secularization thesis:* that in response to modernization, "religious institutions, actions, and consciousness, [will] lose their social significance" (B. R. Wilson 1982: 149). Tocqueville, as we shall see, was virtually alone in his rejection of the secularization thesis—perhaps no other social-scientific prediction enjoyed such nearly universal acceptance for so long. Thus, the very prominent anthropologist Anthony F. C. Wallace (1966: 265) wrote in an undergraduate textbook:

> The evolutionary future of religion is extinction. Belief in supernatural beings and supernatural forces that affect nature without obeying nature's laws will erode and become only an interesting historical memory ... Belief in supernatural powers is doomed to die out, all over the world, as the result of the increasing adequacy and diffusion of scientific knowledge.

A third basis of consensus among the founders is that *religion is an epiphenomenon.* Despite imputing so many harmful effects to religion, the founders clung to the claim that religion was not real—that it was but a reflection of more fundamental social phenomena. As Marx and Engels explained, "All religion ... is nothing but the fantastic reflection in men's minds of those external forces which control their daily lives" (1955: 16). In Marxist analysis, these external forces are variously the mode of production, nature, and "the forces of history." In similar fashion, in his famous study of suicide, although the topic of religion takes up a substantial portion of the book, Durkheim (1951 [1897]) did not treat religion as something in itself, but only as an elaborate reflection of the more basic reality: one's degree of social integration (Stark and Bainbridge 1997).

Over the decades, this tendency of social scientists always to seek more "fundamental"— that is, material and secular—causes of all things religious has become such a basic assumption that it is routinely invoked by the news media. Thus, for example, the reasons offered for the growth of evangelical Protestant groups and the decline of the liberal denominations are always secular and usually discreditable. Among the more common suggestions about why the evangelicals grow are repressed sexuality, urbanization, racism, sexism, status anxieties and rapid social change. Never do proponents of the old paradigm even explore possible *religious* explanations: for example, that people are drawn to the evangelical churches by a superior religious product. From their viewpoint, since all religions are false and all gods are imaginary, there can be no point in examining whether some religions are more plausible and satisfying than others. One surely need not be a believer to see the absurdity of this position—imagine applying it to science fiction novels or to horror movies.

Religion is a Psychological Phenomenon

Fourth, proponents of the old paradigm *rarely examine religion as a social phenomenon, as a property of groups or collectivities*, but instead treat it as fundamentally *psychological*.

They often talk about religion in collective terms, but in the end they reduce it to mental states and do not use aggregate or group units of analysis. Discussions of sects, for example, typically devolve to studies of sectarian attitudes rather than comparisons of religious groups. Even when the object of study is a group (a specific sect, for example), the usual result is a case study utterly lacking in systematic comparisons with other groups. Rarely did any of the founders (nor do their heirs) examine such things as the interplay among religious groups or variations in religious social structures across societies. Even the "obvious" exceptions to this claim turn out not to be very exceptional. Thus, when Durkheim devoted a book (1912; English trans. 1995) to the thesis that religion is, in effect, society worshiping itself, his research focused on the inner life of Australian aborigines and his conclusions about such things as totemism would not have survived even rudimentary cross-cultural comparisons (Goldenweiser 1915; Runciman 1969; Evans-Pritchard 1981). Or, even when Max Weber attempted to trace the rise of capitalism to the "Protestant Ethic," for the most part he conceived of the ethic as a psychological property of the individual (Hamilton 1996)—although, quite unlike most of his peers, he did attempt to contrast several societies in terms of the presence or absence of this property. Marx's and Engels' writings on religion also are overwhelmingly psychological, despite their mandatory mentions of modes of production and social evolution. The complete version of Marx's most famous quotation on this subject is typical: "Religion is the sigh of the oppressed creature, the heart of a heartless world, just as it is the spirit of a spiritless situation. It is the *opium* of the people" (1955: 11).

This tendency continues in that the overwhelming preponderance of contemporary research is based on individuals rather than on groups. But, no amount of surveys of individual opinions will reveal answers to questions such as why some new religions succeed while most fail, or why rates of religious participation are so much higher in some societies than in others. These are not questions primarily about individuals; they can be answered adequately only by reference to attributes of *groups*—in these instances, to attributes of new religions or of societies.

The Threat of Religious Pluralism

Finally, to the extent that the founders did take any interest in religion as part of a social system (rather than of the individual consciousness), their primary concern was to condemn the *harmful effects of religious pluralism and to stress the superiority of monopoly faiths*. Only monopolies, it was asserted, can sustain the unchallenged authority on which all religions depend. In contrast, as Durkheim explained, where multiple religious groups compete, religion becomes open to question, dispute and doubt, and thereby "the less it dominates lives" (1951 [1897]: 159). Even with the contrary American example staring them in the face, those committed to the old paradigm continue to express their faith in this doctrine. Thus Steve Bruce (1992: 170):

pluralism threatens the plausibility of religious belief systems by exposing their human origins. By forcing people to do religion as a matter of personal choice rather than as fate, pluralism universalizes "heresy." A chosen religion is weaker than a religion of fate because we are aware that we chose the gods rather than the gods choosing us.

Notice too that Bruce, like Durkheim, conforms to the practice of reducing a social phenomenon—competing religious groups—to its presumed psychological effects.

The Emergence of the New Paradigm

The immense amount of attention given to religion in the formative days of the social sciences was motivated primarily by atheism (Evans-Pritchard 1965: 15). In addition, as Jeffrey Hadden reminded us, the social sciences emerged as part of a new political "order that was at war with the old order" (1987: 590). This new order aimed to overthrow the traditional European ruling elites and repressive political and economic structures, a battle in which the churches, Protestant as well as Catholic, often gave vigorous support to the old order. In response, social scientists declared themselves against religion as well as against the state. And, although most probably were not prepared to follow Denis Diderot's proposal, "Let us strangle the last king with the guts of the last priest," most found the pairing apt and the end result desirable.

However, in the early part of the twentieth century, as the center of gravity of the social sciences shifted from Europe to America, the image of religion as a political enemy waned and anti-religious antagonisms were muted. Lacking a compelling motive to attack religion, but also tending to be personally irreligious (Leuba 1921), American social scientists mostly ignored religion altogether. Like insects embedded in amber, the views of the founders were dutifully displayed to generations of students, but the social-scientific study of religion was far more of a museum than an area of research—"It was as if the founders had said it all" (Hammond 1985: 2).

No one has summed up the period as well as Gordon W. Allport in his major psychological study of religion, published in 1950:

> Among modern intellectuals—especially in the universities—the subject of religion seems to have gone into hiding ... Whatever the reason may be, the persistence of religion in the modern world appears an embarrassment to the scholars of today. Even psychologists, to whom presumably nothing of human concern is alien, are likely to retire into themselves when the subject is broached.
>
> During the past fifty years religion and sex seemed to have reversed their positions ... Today, psychologists write with ... frankness on the sexual passions of mankind, but blush and grow silent when the religious passions come into view. Scarcely any modern textbook writers in psychology devote as much as two shamefaced pages to the subject—even though religion, like sex, is an almost universal interest of the human race.
>
> (1950: 1–2)

Following World War II, a rapidly increasing number of American social scientists—Allport among them—began to do research on religious phenomena. Their interest was stimulated by the vigor of American religion, which not only refused to conform to the secularization doctrine, but seemed to grow in popularity. Indeed, during the 1940s and the 1950s a substantial religious revival appeared to be taking place in the United States. This probably was primarily a media event sustained by the proliferation of church construction projects which were necessitated by the rapid growth of new suburbs. Nonetheless, it stimulated a great deal of research and legitimated support for such research by major granting agencies. Research on religion also was stimulated at this time by the repeated encounter with stubborn religious "effects" by those working in other areas—for example, religion has a substantial independent impact on marriage, divorce, fertility, educational attainment, infidelity, crime, drug and alcohol consumption, to name but a few (Wuthnow 1979; Stark and Bainbridge 1997; Beit-Hallahmi and Argyle 1997).

The first stirring of renewed academic interest in religion among American social scientists took the form of a regular faculty seminar on the sociology of religion which began at Harvard during the 1940s. This seminar led directly in 1949 to the organization of the Committee for the Scientific Study of Religion which in 1956 was renamed the Society for the Scientific Study of Religion (SSSR). In 1961 the SSSR first published the *Journal for the Scientific Study of Religion*. In response to the journal, membership in SSSR leaped from around 200 in 1960 to more than 800 by 1962 (Newman 1974). Meanwhile, the growth of denominational research departments prompted the organization of the Religious Research Association (RRA) in 1951, thus giving formal status to an informal "committee" that had begun to meet in 1944 (Hadden 1974). In 1959 the RRA began to publish the *Review of Religious Research*. A decade later the American Catholic Sociological Society changed its name to the Association for the Sociology of Religion and dedicated its journal, *Sociological Analysis*, entirely to social-scientific research and theorizing on religion. (In 1993 the journal was renamed *Sociology of Religion*.)

These journals were founded to provide an outlet for articles reporting social-scientific research on religion, which the existing journals too often rejected for reasons rooted in the old paradigm—that these were merely studies of a dying and objectionable phenomenon (Beckford 1985; K. Thompson 1990). The existence of these new journals stimulated a considerable increase in the number of social scientists working in the area. By 1973 the SSSR had become an international organization with 1,468 members. Consequently, a body of new, competent studies (by now numbering in the thousands) soon began to pile up—"a vast, rapidly growing literature," as Warner put it (1993: 1044). Moreover, this was not primarily a literature of polemics or of speculation. Rather, as Bryan Wilson remarked, "sociological interest in religion has found increasingly empirical expression" (1982: 11). For all that, much of it seems dull, even pedestrian, most of the new literature deals in *fact* (Argyle 1959; Argyle and Beit-Hallahmi 1975; Beit-Hallahmi and Argyle 1997). And, from the beginning, many of the facts were inconsistent with the old paradigm; indeed, researchers often expected to find the precise opposite of what they did find. For example, study after study attempted to identify religiousness as a cause or consequence of neurosis and psycho-pathology, but again and again the results were to the contrary (Stark and Bainbridge 1997). And any number of studies sought in vain for evidence in support of secularization (Hadden 1987; Warner 1993; Stark, in press).

In short, this has always been a literature of *discovery* and therefore quite ill-suited to a museum environment. As early as 1973 Charles Y. Glock and Phillip E. Hammond recognized that the strain between the received theoretical wisdom and the expanding corpus of research findings necessitated a new paradigm, although they were rather pessimistic that one soon would be forthcoming. However, slightly more than a decade later, in his introduction to an edited volume of essays attempting to explain the failure of the secularization thesis, Hammond (1985: 3) recognized that the first fragments of "a new paradigm" already were in view. He concluded:

Findings may seem scattered, therefore, and theories fragmented, though this is only because the master schemes—the eventual replacements of the secularization model— have not yet come into focus. Obviously, the successor volume to this one is waiting to be born.

The new paradigm arrived as predicted, as I shall summarize below.

Elements of the New Paradigm

The new paradigm not only rejects each of the elements of the old paradigm outlined above, but it proposes the precise opposite of each. As to the claim that religion is harmful at the individual level, the new paradigm cites a huge and growing literature that finds religion to be a reliable source of better mental and even physical health. Indeed, the new paradigm directly contradicts the postulate that religion is rooted in irrationality, and the research literature is far more consistent with the new paradigm than with the old on this point. This leads to discussion of the most basic premise of the new paradigm.

On Rationality

All of the leading approaches to social theory share a common first premise or proposition. It has been stated in a great many ways, but each variant asserts the same insight: that when faced with choices, humans try to select the most rational or reasonable option. Some advocates of "rational choice theory," especially economists, limit their definition of rationality to the elegantly simple proposition: *humans attempt to maximize*—to gain the most at the least cost (Becker 1976, 1996; Iannaccone 1995). One of the greatest virtues of this version is that it lends itself so well to inclusion in mathematical models. This virtue may also be its primary shortcoming—in their daily lives humans tend to fall well short of its fulfillment.

Consequently, I prefer a formulation of the rationality axiom that softens and expands the maximization assumption. Just as those working in the area of artificial intelligence have turned to models based on what they call "fuzzy logic" (Kosko 1992), I acknowledge that human reasoning often is somewhat unsystematic and "intuitive," and that maximization is often only partial and somewhat half-hearted. Indeed, aspects of laziness probably ought to be considered in the calculation of maximization. In any event, I use the more subjective and bounded conception of rationality, the one John Ferejohn (1991) identified as the "thick" model which has sustained a substantial sociological theoretical literature going back at least as far as Max Weber (Simon 1957; March 1978; Boudon 1993; Hechter and Kanazawa 1997). It seems worthwhile to consider some of the virtues of this approach.

First, this conception of rationality recognizes that humans pursue a variety of rewards or goals and confront an array of potential costs. It is obvious that many of the things humans seek tend to be somewhat mutually exclusive, and consequently "maximization" must consist of the best fit among these conflicting ends. For example, some people's best fit would be partial maximizations of the satisfactions of parenting and those of career achievement. It was mainly to deal with the complexities of the pursuit of multiple and somewhat conflicting goals that Herbert Simon (1957) coined the word "satisficing" as a substitute for "maximizing." That is, Simon combined the words "satisfy" and "suffice" to identify the tendency of humans to settle for a sufficient level of satisfaction. In addition to facing conflicting goals, humans also must function within limits, often quite severe, on their information and their available options. Consequently, I feel it excessive to use the maximizing proposition. But, being equally reluctant to resort to a neologism such as "satisficing," I adopt Simon's (1982) later formulation of *subjective rationality*. As summed up by Raymond Boudon, subjective rationality applies to all human actions that are based on what appear to the actor to be "good reasons," reasons being "good" to the extent to which they "rest upon plausible conjectures" (1993: 10). But, whatever the good reasons for making choices, the imputation of rationality always assumes *the presence of subjective efforts to weigh the anticipated rewards against the anticipated costs*, although these efforts usually are inexact and somewhat casual.

The subjective approach to rationality is entirely consistent with the axiom of symbolic interactionism in that in order to understand behavior we must know how an actor defines the situation (G. H. Mead 1934; Blumer 1969), for only from "inside" can we assess the rationality—that is, the reasonableness—of a choice. As James S. Coleman put it: "much of what is ordinarily described as nonrational or irrational is merely so because observers have not discovered the point of view of the actor, from which the action *is* rational" (1990: 18).

These considerations lead me to this formulation of the principle of human rationality: *Within the limits of their information and understanding, restricted by available options, guided by their preferences and tastes, humans attempt to make rational choices.*

Let us analyze this sentence to see precisely what it does and does not mean. The first part of the sentence—*within the limits of their information*—recognizes that we cannot select choices if we do not know about them nor can we select the most beneficial choice if we have incorrect knowledge about the relative benefits of choices. The second part of the phrase—*within the limits of their ... understanding*—acknowledges that people must make choices based on the set of principles, beliefs or theories they hold about how things work. These may, of course, be false, as the history of science demonstrates, but the rational person utilizes his or her principles about the world, because these are, for the moment, the most "plausible conjectures." Finally, it is self-evident that people may only select from among *available options*, although the full range of choices actually available may not be evident to them.

However, if humans all attempt to make rational choices, why is it that they do not always act alike? Why do people reared in the same culture not all seek the same rewards? Because their choices are *guided by their preferences and tastes*. Preferences and tastes define what it is that the individual finds rewarding or unrewarding. Consequently, people may differ in what they want and how much they want it (Hechter 1994). This not only helps us understand why people do not all act alike, but why it is possible for them to engage in exchanges: to swap one reward for another.

Of course, not all preferences and tastes are variable; clearly, there are some things that virtually everyone values, regardless of their culture: food, shelter, security and affection are among them (Aberele et al. 1950). Obviously, too, culture in general, and socialization in particular, will have a substantial impact on preferences and tastes. It is neither random nor a matter of purely personal taste whether someone prays to Allah or Shiva, or indeed, whether one prays at all. Still, the fact remains that even within any culture there is substantial variation across individuals in their preferences and tastes. Some of this variation is also at least partly the result of socialization differences—for example, we probably learn as children our preferences concerning highly liturgical services. But, a great deal of variation is so idiosyncratic that people have no idea how they came to like certain things. It's as the old adage says "There's no accounting for taste." As noted above, that people differ greatly in terms of tastes and preferences facilitates exchanges. But it also explains what often are rather remarkable differences in behavior, as will be seen.

Finally, as already mentioned, the phrase that "humans attempt to make rational choices" means that *they will attempt to follow the dictates of reason in an effort to satisfy their desired goals.* Within the limits noted, this will involve some effort to maximize the net of rewards over costs. The word "attempt" is included to note that people do not *always* act in entirely rational ways. Sometimes we act impulsively—in haste, passion, boredom or anger ("I really didn't stop to think about what I was doing"). But, most of the time normal human beings will choose what they *perceive* to be the more reasonable option, and whenever they do so, their behavior is fully rational even if they are mistaken. For example, people buy stocks hoping to profit. If their stocks decline in value that does not mean they acted irrationally, only that they were wrong about which stocks to buy.

This formulation also leaves explicit leeway for people to act in ways others would define as "unselfish" choices, but it leaves no leeway for *altruism*, if that term is defined as intentionally selecting a negative cost / benefit ratio purely for the benefit of others. Such a claim usually produces tales of heroism—a soldier who held out to the end, a parent who rushed into a burning building to save a child. Or, you may wonder, what about people like Mother Teresa who forego a comfortable life to aid the sick and the poor? How are such people acting reasonably, let alone to maximize their personal rewards and minimize their personal costs? Or, as the British sociologist Anthony Heath put it: "The people who act out of a sense of duty or friendship, it is said, cannot be accounted rational and cannot be brought within the scope of [the] rational choice [proposition]" (1976: 79). But, Heath went on:

> Of all the fallacies [about rationality], this is the least excusable. Rationality has nothing to do with the *goals* which [people] pursue but only with the *means* they use to achieve them. When we ask whether someone is behaving rationally we ... are not asking whether he [or she] is choosing the "right" goal.
>
> (1976: 79)

As Heath implies, social scientists are fully aware of people such as Mother Teresa. But, we also recognize that their behavior violates the principle of rationality *only* if we adopt a very narrow, materialistic and entirely egocentric *definition of rewards*, and if we ignore the immense variety of preferences and tastes. Human life and culture are so rich because of the incredible variety of our preferences and tastes, of things we perceive as rewarding. There is no need to suggest that a parent has acted against self-interest by rushing into a burning building. Rather, let us recognize that the ability of humans to regard the survival of a child as more rewarding than their own survival is a credit to the human spirit and to our capacity to love. To call that altruism and place it in opposition to the rationality premise is to reduce noble behavior to crazy and irrational action. In fact, the "selfish" premise of rationality is humanistic in the fullest sense. It acknowledges our capacity to find rewards in our dreams, hopes, loves and ideals.

It is all the more amazing that social scientists have refused to extend the rationality axiom to religion in light of the fact that religious teachers always have stressed maximizing behavior as the justification for faith—that belief is the most rewarding (hence most *reasonable*) option. Blaise Pascal's "wager" is a very well-known example (Durkin and Greeley 1991), but in his 148th *Pensée* he asserts the maximizing axiom with an enthusiasm that not even an economist would dare:

> All men seek happiness. There are no exceptions. However different the means they employ, they all strive towards this goal ... This is the motive of every act of every man, including those who go and hang themselves.
>
> (1966 [1670]: 45)

Indeed, most of the world's religious scriptures abound in the language of exchange. For example:

> O Indra ... may plentiful libations of the people, and singing sages' holy prayers rejoice thee ... thus may we be made partakers of the new favours that shall bring us profit.
>
> *(Rig Veda* 10:89)

> Make for Me an altar of earth and sacrifice on it your burnt offerings and your sacrifices of well-being, your sheep and your oxen; in every place where I cause My name to be mentioned I will come to you and bless you.
>
> (Exodus 21:21)

> But to those men who honour me, concentrating on me alone, who are constantly disciplined, I bring gain and security.
>
> (Bhagavad Gita 9:22)

> He that believeth and is baptised shall be saved.
>
> (Mark 16:16)

> And give glad tidings, O Muhammad, unto those who believe and do good works; that theirs are Gardens underneath which rivers flow.
>
> (Qur'an, surah 2:25)

Thus, I stand with Max Weber when he wrote:

> religiously or magically motivated behavior is relatively rational behavior ... It follows rules of experience ... Thus, religious and magical behavior or thinking must not be set apart from the range of everyday purposive conduct.
>
> (1963: 1)

Recognize, too, that the rationality proposition is *only the starting assumption* of most modern social science. Thus, while of immense importance, it offers very little in the way of theory. To say, for example, that people try to be rational even when making religious choices is little more than a slogan when we confront the real explanatory tasks. Suppose we wish to explain why people select one church over another, or why they drop out of a religious movement following an initial period of enthusiasm. The rationality premise tells us to look for variations in payoffs or satisfactions, but no more than that, leaving the social scientist in the same position as a detective seeking motives in a murder case. The real work is yet to be accomplished.

The Opiate Thesis

That religion is harmful at the level of society is a political, not a scientific claim. While the old paradigm was content to identify religion as the opium of the people, the new paradigm notes that religion also often is the "amphetamines" of the people in that it was religion that animated many medieval peasant and artisan rebellions (N. R. C. Cohn 1961), generated repeated uprisings among the native peoples of Africa and North America against

European encroachment (Wilson 1973), and recently served as a major centre of mobilization against the tyrants of Eastern Europe (Echikson 1990). Indeed, the whole notion that religion primarily serves to compensate the deprived and dispossessed has become untenable. The consensus among scholars rejects as "imaginary history" Engels' notion that the early Christian movement was rooted in proletarian suffering. The facts force the conclusion that Christianity's greatest early appeal was to the privileged classes (Judge 1960; Scroggs 1980; Stark 1996). In similar fashion, since the early 1940s many researchers have attempted to connect religiousness to social class, but their findings have been weak and inconsistent. Consequently, the need for new theorizing on the role of religion in the political affairs of nations has been recognized and efforts in that direction can be found in Stark and Bainbridge (1985, 1996) and I particularly refer the reader to the recent work of Anthony J. Gill (1998).

Against the Secularization Thesis

I have devoted an entire recent essay to entombing the secularization thesis beneath a mountain of contrary fact (Stark, forthcoming). The facts are these. First, there is no consistent relationship between religious participation and modernization. Indeed, the very few significant, long-term declines in religious participation to be seen anywhere in the world are greatly outnumbered by remarkable increases. What it needed is not a simple-minded theory of inevitable religious decline, but a theory to explain variation. Second, even in nations such as those in Europe, where religious participation has *always* been quite low, the overwhelming majority express firm belief in basic religious tenets and describe themselves as religious. It is perverse to describe a nation as highly secularized (as many do) when two-thirds or more say they are "a religious person," and fewer than five percent say they are atheists. Third, the spread of science cannot result in secularization, because science and religion are unrelated: overall, scientists are as religious as anyone else and the more scientific their field, the more religious they are (Stark, Iannaccone and Finke 1996, forthcoming).

Seeking Religious Causes of Religious Phenomena

Despite their frequent claims that religion is an epiphenomenon, the founders often postulated religious effects, not all of them bad. For example, theorists as diverse as Karl Marx and Herbert Spencer took it for granted that religion reinforced the moral order, and if this placed it in league with the ruling classes, religion also was thought to sustain honesty, charity and temperance. The new paradigm is entirely compatible with the premise that religion has many effects and, indeed, a huge empirical literature finds religious people more likely to observe laws and norms and, consequently, that cities having higher rates of religious participation have lower rates of deviant and criminal behavior (Stark and Bainbridge 1997). Where the old and new paradigms part company is over the causes of religion.

The old paradigm directs social scientists to dig as deeply as necessary in order to uncover the "real" causes of religious phenomena. For example, a wave of public religious enthusiasm took place in various American cities between 1739 and 1741. In each city, "huge crowds of crying, sobbing people [gathered], thousands upon thousands of desperate souls, asking what they must do to be saved" (Wood 1993: 20). Then, at the start of the nineteenth century came widespread reports of similar activities going on in rural areas along the western frontier as again crowds gathered and people moaned and groaned for divine forgiveness. These events came to be known as the first and second "Great

Awakenings" and social scientists have devoted a great deal of effort to explaining why each took place when and where it did.

Proponents of the old paradigm invariably begin their explanations by postulating a *sudden*, generalized *need* for more intense religion. Thus, William G. McLoughlin, regarded by many as the leading authority on awakenings, attributed them to sudden periods of "grave personal stress" (1978: 2). Such stress, in turn, has been traced to such "underlying causes" as floods, epidemics, crop failures, business failures, financial panics, financial booms, the incursions of a market economy, industrialization, rapid immigration and so on (Barkun 1986; Gordon-McCutchan 1983; G. M. Thomas 1989). But, a far more plausible interpretation of these "awakenings" makes no mention of any intensifications of religious needs or of the impact of social or natural crises (Jon Butler 1982, 1990; Finke and Stark 1992; T. L. Smith 1983). Instead, these scholars trace the revivals in question to organized *religious* innovations and actions. Specifically, proponents of the new paradigm note that religious organizations led by George Whitefield in the eighteenth century and Charles Finney in the nineteenth used vigorous and effective marketing techniques to sustain revival campaigns, which later historians have classified as "awakenings." In contrast to scholars who explain that because of various crises "the times" were right for huge crowds to "materialize" to hear Whitefield, for example, the new interpretation stresses that:

> Whitefield was a master of advance publicity who sent out a constant stream of press releases, extolling the successes of his revivals elsewhere, to cities he intended to visit. These advance campaigns often began two years ahead of time. In addition, Whitefield had thousands of copies of his sermons printed and distributed to stir up interest. He even ran newspaper advertisements announcing his impending arrival … It was from these efforts that crowds "materialized."
>
> (Finke and Stark 1992: 88–89)

What Whitefield accomplished was not to exploit new religious needs, but to appeal successfully to needs going essentially unserved by the lax, state-supported churches in the American colonies at this time—something which Whitefield fully recognized, remarking during his visit to Boston in 1740, "I am persuaded, the generality of preachers [in New England] talk of an unknown and unfelt Christ. The reason why congregations have been so dead, is because they have had dead men preach to them" (Whitefield 1969 [1747]: 471).

An equally huge literature attributes the "explosive growth" of new religious movements in the United States in the late 1960s and early 1970s to profound social causes. Particular attention has been given to uncovering the secular causes of the special appeal of Eastern faiths for Americans during this period. Thus, Harvey Cox blamed the whole thing on capitalism, charging that converts to Eastern faiths had "been maddened by consumer culture" (1983: 42). Not only the sensational media, but "serious" journals abounded with equally hysterical theories. As Thomas Robbins summarized, each of these identified one or more "acute and distinctively modern dislocation which is said to be producing some mode of alienation, anomie or deprivation to which Americans are responding" (1988: 60). With her usual grasp of the essentials, Eileen Barker commented, "those who have read some of the sociological literature could well be at a loss to understand why *all* young adults are not members [of new religious movements], so all-encompassing are some of the explanations" (1986: 338).

In fact, there was *no growth*, explosive or otherwise, of new religious movements in this era (Finke and Stark 1992); the rate of new movement formation was constant from 1950 to

1990. As for the brief increase in the proportion of Eastern faiths among new American movements, capitalism had nothing to do with it. Rather, in 1965 the elimination of exclusionary rules against Asian immigration made it possible for the first time for authentic Eastern and Indian religious leaders directly to seek American followers. Consequently, there was an increase in the number of Eastern religious organizations, but the number of actual converts was minuscule. Even so, growth was the result of *religious* efforts—of face-to-face recruitment activities.

Explosive growth by new religions did in fact occur in Japan following World War II—so many new groups appeared that observers spoke of "the rush hour of the gods" (McFarland 1967). It has been assumed that the cause of this religious fervor was the devastation and suffering produced by the war. But, no similar religious activity took place in post-war Germany or in the Soviet Union, where devastation and suffering surely equaled that of Japan. On the other hand, there also was a religious "rush hour" in South Korea which was hardly touched by the war, at the end of which it was liberated from Japanese rule. The common element is religious liberty. The German state church tradition was not challenged by the occupying governments, except in the Eastern Zone where the Soviets repressed all religion. As I have demonstrated elsewhere (Stark and Iannaccone 1994; Stark 1998), state churches suppress religious competition and thus new religious groups could not prosper in either part of Germany. But, in Japan, the "MacArthur" constitution inaugurated complete religious freedom in a nation where the government previously had strictly repressed all but a few traditional religions. In South Korea, too, a policy of religious liberty replaced the prior Japanese religious repression. In both nations the emergence of new religions took place almost at once. However, the end of Japanese rule brought no similar eruption of new religions in Taiwan (Formosa) because its new Nationalist Chinese rulers did not condone religious freedom.

The notion that the war caused Japan's "rush hour" is further refuted by the fact that nearly all of what became the leading new religious movements in the post-war period originated *prior* to the war—sometimes long before. Konkō-kyō was founded in 1885, Reiyukai Kyōdan in 1925, the immensely successful Sōka Gakkai movement was organized in 1930, as were PL Kyodan and Seichō no Ie, and Risshō Kōsei-kai began in 1938 (McFarland 1967; Moroto 1976). But, government repression was sufficient to limit them to a small group of followers, often restricted to a single village or neighborhood. Thus, Neill McFarland described them as "innumerable captive and incipient religious movements" and noted that the new constitution allowed "their voice to be heard" (1967: 4). As Aiko Moroto noted, these groups originated in pre-war Japan, and what was new after the war was that "these groups came out into the open and flourished" (1976: 1). Harry Thomsen pointed out that what was new about these religions was that their new freedom allowed them to utilize "new methods of evangelism" (1963: 17). Hence, the primary "secular" cause of the proliferation of new religions in Japan and Korea was merely the legal right to function, and the rest of the story involves actions by religious organizations based on religious motives.

Therefore, while the new paradigm accepts that secular crises often do have religious consequences, it denies that secular social factors *must* underlie religious phenomena. Nor need religious causes (or secular ones for that matter) be "material" as opposed to ideas and beliefs. Proponents of the new paradigm accept that religious doctrines *per se* often have consequences. For example, the "root causes" of efforts by the early Christians to nurse the sick during the great plagues that periodically swept the Roman Empire, in contrast with their pagan neighbors who shunned and abandoned stricken family members, were doctrinal: belief that death was not final and in the obligation to be one another's keepers (Stark 1996a).

Equally obvious contemporary instances of doctrinal causation can be seen by comparing various religious movements on the basis of their capacity to sustain leaders with sufficient authority. There are many bases for legitimate authority within organizations. However, when organizations stress doctrine, as all religious movements do, these doctrines must define the basis of leadership. Who may lead and how is leadership obtained? What powers are granted to leaders? What sanctions may leaders impose? These are vital matters, brought into clear relief by the many examples of groups that failed (or are failing) for lack of doctrines defining a legitimate basis for effective leadership.

That doctrines can directly cause ineffective leadership is widely evident in contemporary New Age and "metaphysical" groups. If everyone is a "student," and everyone's ideas and insights are equally valid, then no one can say what must be done or who is to do what, when. The result is the existence of virtual non-organizations—mere affinity or discussion groups incapable of action. In similar fashion, some of the early Christian gnostic groups could not sustain effective organizations because their fundamental doctrines prevented them from ever being anything more than a loose network of individual adepts, each pursuing secret knowledge through private, personal means (Pagels 1979; M. A. Williams 1996). In contrast, from the start Christianity had doctrines appropriate for an effective structure of authority since Christ himself was believed to have selected his successors as head of the church.

Thus can one utilize religious doctrine as a causal factor vis-à-vis other religious phenomena, both individual and organizational. It is, of course, logically possible to raise the issue of from whence particular doctrines came and why these, rather than some other doctrines, were adopted. We may grant the legitimacy of such questions without promoting infinite regress or admitting that all fundamental causes are secular.

Finally, to grant causal status to doctrines forces recognition that the most fundamental aspect of any religion is its *conception of the supernatural*. Many religious doctrines and related practices presuppose supernatural beings having certain characteristics, among them consciousness and virtue. For example, it would seem unavailing to appeal to an impersonal higher power such as the Tao, and quite risky to do so to the undependable and often wicked gods of the Greek pantheon.

Many of the most interesting and pressing questions facing the social-scientific study of religion require that religion be conceived of as social rather than as psychological, as a property of groups or even of whole societies. It is this emphasis on the social as against the psychological that is the most important feature of the new paradigm. To see more fully what is at issue here, consider the following questions, none of which can be reduced to psychology alone:

Why is religious participation so low in most European nations and so high in the United States?

Why are some Roman Catholic religious orders growing while others decline?

Why are strict churches so much stronger than those that ask less of their members?

Why do most sect movements fail?

Why do cult movements thrive on the West Coasts of Canada and the United States and why are they even more successful in Europe?

I have attempted answers to these and other such questions in many recent publications which will be synthesized in a forthcoming book (Stark and Finke). In doing so I have, of course, utilized psychological assumptions and data as appropriate—I do not think psychological states are unimportant or that data on individuals (such as survey studies) are useless. Rather, my concern is to not *inappropriately* reduce group phenomena to individual traits, or to mistake attitudes for collective activity.

If stressing the social aspect of religion is a hallmark of the new paradigm, its most innovative theoretical feature is to identify religion as a subsystem within the social system: a *religious economy* (Stark 1985).

The Religious Economy

Religious organizations do not exist in a vacuum and therefore cannot be studied in isolation from their socio-cultural environments. Moreover, most of the time for most religious organizations a crucial aspect of that environment is *religious*—aspects of other religious organizations (including their doctrines), and aspects of the rules and norms governing religious activities. To facilitate analysis at this level of abstraction, my colleagues and I examine the religious life of societies within an overall conceptual and theoretical model: the *religious economy*. A religious economy is *a subsystem of all social systems* (Parsons 1951). It encompasses *all of the religious activity going on in any society*.

I use the term "economy" in order to clarify that, in terms of certain key elements, the religious subsystem of any society is entirely parallel to the subsystem involved with the secular (or commercial) economy: both involve the interplay of supply and demand for valued products. Religious economies consist of a market of current and potential followers (demand), a set of organizations (suppliers) seeking to serve that market, and the religious doctrines and practices (products) offered by the various organizations. My application of economic language to things often regarded as "sacred" is meant neither to offend nor as mere metaphor. Rather, my purpose is to facilitate immense explanatory power that can be gained by applying elementary principles of economics to religious phenomena at the group or social level—an application pioneered by Adam Smith more than two centuries ago.

As Smith recognized, and as I have demonstrated at length (Stark and Iannaccone 1994; Stark 1998), the most significant single feature of a religious economy is the degree to which it is unregulated and therefore market-driven, as opposed to being regulated by the state in favor of monopoly. Herein lies the key to explaining variations in the "religiousness" of societies, for the founders were entirely wrong about the harmful effects of pluralism and religious competition. Rather than eroding the plausibility of all faiths, competition results in eager and efficient suppliers of religion just as it does among suppliers of secular commodities, and with the same results: far higher levels of overall "consumption."

These, then, are the elements of the new paradigm. In this rapidly growing new literature, many different scholars pursue these fundamental assumptions to a great variety of conclusions, many of them not at all obvious. I am under no illusions that my colleagues and I have everything right; there undoubtedly will be many revisions and a great many extensions to come. But, there is nothing illusory about a basic paradigm shift in the social-scientific study of religion. A mountain of fact bars any return to the simple certitudes of the past.

QUESTIONS FOR REVIEW AND DISCUSSION

1. What does Stark submit were some key shared perspectives about the nature of religion among many early theorists? How does he support this analysis?

2. Explain what Stark means when he says that theorists (both early and contemporary) tend to treat religion as a psychological rather than a sociological phenomenon.

3. Outline the rise in academic interest in religion among American social scientists since the 1940s as presented by Stark.

4. What are the features of the new paradigm concerning religion, as presented by Stark?

5. What is meant by subjective rationality?

6. Does Stark feel that religion is a purely sociological phenomenon?

7. What does he mean by religious economy? How does this concept mesh with his arguments about the relationship between religion and rationality?

8. Stark asserts that "the most significant single feature of a religious economy is the degree to which it is unregulated and therefore market-driven, as opposed to being regulated by the state in favor of monopoly." What do you think of this insight? How might you design research projects to test or to take advantage of this observation?

Bibliography

Aberele, David F., Albert K. Cohen, Arthur K. Davis et al. (1950) "The Functional Prerequisites of a Society." *Ethics* 60:100–111.

Allport, Gordon W. (1950) *The Individual and His Religion: A Psychological Interpretation.* New York: Macmillan.

Argyle, Michael (1959) *Religious Behavior.* Glencoe, IL: Free Press.

Arygle, Michael and Benjamin Beit-Hallahmi (1975) *The Social Psychology of Religion.* London: Routledge and Kegan Paul.

Barker, Eileen (1986) "Religious Movement: Cult and Anti-Cult Since Jonestown." *Annual Review of Sociology* 12:329–346.

Barkun, Michael (1986) *Crucible of the Millennium: The Burned-Over District of New York in the 1840s.* Syracuse, NY: Syracuse University Press.

Becker, Gary S. (1976) *The Economic Approach to Human Behavior.* Chicago: University of Chicago Press.

——. (1996) *Accounting for Tastes.* Cambridge, MA: Harvard University Press.

Beckford, James A. (1985) "The Insulation and Isolation of the Sociology of Religion." *Social Analysis* 46:347–354.

Beit-Hallahmi, Benjamin and Michael Argyle (1997) *The Psychology of Religious Behaviour, Belief and Experience.* London: Routledge.

Berger, Peter (1969) *The Sacred Canopy: Elements of a Sociological Theory of Religion.* Garden City, NY: Doubleday.

Blumer, Herbert (1969) *Symbolic Interactionism: Perspective and Method.* Englewood Cliffs, NJ: Prentice-Hall.

Boudon, Raymond (1993) "Toward a Synthetic Theory of Rationality." *International Studies in the Philosophy of Science* 7:5–19.

Bruce, Steve (ed.) (1992) *Religion and Modernization: Sociologists and Historians Debate the Secularization Thesis.* Oxford: Clarendon.

Butler, Jon (1982) "Enthusiasm Described and Decried: The Great Awakenings as Interpretive Fiction." *Journal of American History* 69:305–325.

——. (1990) *Awash in a Sea of Faith: Christianizing the American People.* Studies in Cultural History. Cambridge, MA: Harvard University Press.

Cohn, Norman R. C. (1961) *The Pursuit of the Millennium.* New York: Harper & Row.

Coleman, James S. (1973) *The Mathematics of Collective Action. Methodological Perspectives*. Chicago: Aldine.

——. (1990) *Foundations of Social Theory*. Cambridge, MA: Harvard University Press.

Comte, Auguste (1896) *Cours de philosophie positive*. Paris: Bachelier, 1830–42; *The Positive Philosophy*, Harriet Martineau (trans. and ed.). New York: C. Blanchard, 1955.

Cox, Harvey (1983) "Interview." In Steven J. Gelberg (ed.), *Hare Krishna, Hare Krishna*. New York: Grove.

Davis, Kingsley (1949) *Human Society*. New York: Macmillan.

Durant, Will and Ariel Durant (1965) *The Age of Voltaire*. New York: Simon and Schuster.

Durkheim, Émile (1951) *Suicide: A Study in Sociology*, John A. Spaulding and George Simpson (trans.). George Simpson (ed.). Glencoe, IL: Free Press; original French edn, 1897.

Durkin, John, Jr. and Andrew M. Greeley (1991) "A Model of Religious Choice Under Uncertainty: On Responding Rationally to the Nonrational." *Rationality and Society* 3:178–196.

Echikson, William (1990) *Lighting the Night: Revolution in Eastern Europe*. London: Sidgwick & Jackson; New York: William Morrow.

Evans-Pritchard, E. E. (1965) *Theories of Primitive Religion*. Oxford: Clarendon.

——. (1981) *A History of Anthropological Thought*. New York: Basic.

Ferejohn, John (1991) "Rationality and Interpretation: Parliamentary Elections in Early Stuart England," pp. 279–305 in Kristen Renwick Monroe (ed.), *The Economic Approach to Politics: A Critical Reassessment of the Theory of Rational Action*. New York: HarperCollins.

Finke, Roger and Rodney Stark (1992) *The Churching of America, 1776–1990: Winners and Losers in Our Religious Economy*. New Brunswick, NJ: Rutgers University Press.

Freud, Sigmund (1927) *Die Zukunft einer Illusion*. Leipzig: Internationaler psychoanalytischer Verlag.

——. (1989) *The Future of an Illusion*, With a biographical Introduction by Peter Gay, James Strachey (ed. and trans.). New York: Norton; original German edn, 1927.

Gill, Anthony J. (1998) *Rendering Unto Caesar: The Roman Catholic Church and the State in Latin America*. Chicago: University of Chicago Press.

Goldenweiser, Alexander A. (1915) "A Review of *Les Formes*." *American Anthropologist* 17:719–735.

Gordon-McCutchan, R. C. (1983) "Great Awakenings" *Social Analysis* 44:83–95.

Greeley, Andrew (1996) "The New American Paradigm: A Modest Critique." Paper, German Sociological Association Annual Meetings, Cologne, Germany.

Hadden, Jeffrey (1974) "A Brief Social History of the Religious Research Association." *Review of Religious Research* 15:128–136.

——. (1987) "Toward Desacralizing Secularization Theory." *Social Forces* 65:587–611.

Hamilton, Richard F. (1996) *The Social Misconstruction of Reality: Validity and Verification in the Scholarly Community*. New Haven: Yale University Press.

Hammond, Phillip E. (Ed.) (1985) *The Sacred in a Secular Age: Toward Revision in the Scientific Study of Religion*. Berkeley: University of California Press.

Heath, Anthony (1976) *Rational Choice and Social Exchange: A Critique of Exchange Theory. Themes in the Social Sciences*. Cambridge: Cambridge University Press.

Hechter, Michael (1994) "The Role of Values in Rational Choice Theory." *Rationality and Society* 6:318–333.

Hechter, Michael and Satoshi Kanazawa (1997) "Sociological Rational Choice Theory." *Annual Review of Sociology* 23:191–214.

Hobbes, Thomas (1839) *The English Works of Thomas Hobbes of Malmesbury; Now First Collected and Edited by Sir William Molesworth, Bart*, vol. 1. London: John Bohn.

Hume, David (1882) *Essays: Moral, Political and Literary*. London: Longmans, Green & Co.; original edn, 1741.

Hunter, James Davison (1983) *American Evangelicalism: Conservative Religion and the Quandary of Modernity*. New Brunswick, NJ: Rutgers University Press.

Iannaccone, Laurence R. (1995) "Voodoo Economics? Review the Rational Choice Approach to Religion." *Journal for the Scientific Study of Religion* 34:76–89.

Judge, E. A. (1960) *The Social Patterns of Christian Groups in the First Century*. London: Tyndale.

Kosko, Bart (1992) *Neural Networks and Fuzzy Systems: A Dynamical Systems Approach to Machine Intelligence*. Englewood Cliffs, NJ: Prentice-Hall.

Leuba, James H. (1921) *The Belief in God and Immortality: A Psychological, Anthropological and Statistical Study*. Chicago: Open Court; original edn, 1916.

March, James G. (1978) "Bounded Rationality, Ambiguity, and the Engineering of Choice." *Bell Journal of Economics* 9:587–607.

Marx, Karl and Friedrich Engels (1955) *On Religion*. Moscow: Foreign Language Publishing House.

McFarland, H. Neill (1967) *Rush Hour of the Gods: A Study of New Religious Movements in Japan*. New York: Macmillan.

McLoughlin, William G. (1978) *Revivals, Awakenings, and Reform: An Essay on Religion and Social Change in America, 1609–1977*. Chicago: University of Chicago Press.

Mead, George Herbert (1934) *Mind, Self, and Society: From the Standpoint of a Social Behaviorist*. Chicago: University of Chicago Press.

Moroto, Aiko (1976) "Conditions for Accepting a New Religious Belief: A Case Study of Myochikai Members in Japan." Unpublished MA Thesis, University of Washington, Seattle.

Newman, William M. (1974) "The Society for the Scientific Study of Religion: The Development of an Academic Society." *Review of Religious Research* 15:137–151.

Pagels, Elaine (1979) *The Gnostic Gospels*. New York: Random House.

Parsons, Talcott (1951) *The Social System*. Glencoe, IL: Free Press.

Pascal, Blaise (1966) *Pensées*, A. J. Krailsheimer (trans.) Harmondsworth: Penguin Classics; original French edn, 1670.

Robbins, Thomas (1988) *Cults, Converts, and Charisma: The Sociology of New Religious Movements*. London: Sage.

Runciman, W. G. (1969) "The Sociological Explanation of 'Religious' Beliefs." *Archives européennes de sociologie* 10:149–191.

Scroggs, Robin (1980) "The Sociological Interpretation of the New Testament: The Present State of Research." *New Testament Studies* 26:164–179.

Simmel, Georg (1959) *Sociology of Religion*, Curt Rosenthal (trans.). New York: Philosophical Library; original German edn, 1906.

Simon, Herbert A. (1957) *Models of Man: Social and Rational*. New York: John Wiley & Sons.

——. (1982) *Models of Bounded Rationality*. Cambridge, MA: MIT Press.

Smith, Timothy L. (1983) "My Rejection of the Cyclical View of 'Great Awakenings' in American Religious History." *Social Analysis* 44:97–101.

Stark, Rodney (1985) "From Church-Sect to Religious Economies," pp. 139–149 in Phillip E. Hammond (ed.), *The Sacred in a Secular Age: Toward Revision in the Scientific Study of Religion*. Berkeley: University of California Press.

——. (1996) *The Rise of Christianity: A Sociologist Reconsiders History*. Princeton: Princeton University Press.

—— (1998) "Explaining International Variations in Religiousness: The Market Model." *Polis*, Special Issue: *Recerche e studi su società e politica in Italia*.

Stark, Rodney and Lawrence R. Iannaccone (1994) "A Supply-Side Reinterpretaion of the 'Secularization' of Europe." *Journal for the Scientific Study of Religion* 33:230–252.

Stark, Rodney and William Sims Bainbridge (1985) *The Future of Religion: Secularization, Revival, and Cult Formation*. Berkeley: University of California Press.

——. (1996) *A Theory of Religion*. New Brunswick, NJ: Rutgers University Press.

——. (1997) *Religion, Deviance, and Social Control*. New York: Routledge.

Thomas, George M. (1989) *Revivalism and Cultural Change: Christianity, Nation Building, and the Market in the Nineteenth Century United States*. Chicago: University of Chicago Press.

Thompson, Kenneth (1990) "Religion: The British Contribution." *British Journal of Sociology* 41:531–535.

Thomsen, Harry (1963) *The New Religions of Japan*. Rutland, VT: Charles E. Tuttle.

Tocqueville, Alexis de (1956) *Democracy in America*, 2 vols., Henry Reeve (trans.). New York: Vintage; original French edn, 1835–40.

Wallace, Anthony F. C. (1966) *Religion: An Anthropological View*. New York: Random House.

Warner, R. Stephen (1993) "Work in Progress Towards a New Paradigm for the Sociological Study of Religion in the United States." *American Journal of Sociology* 98:1044–1093.

Weber, Max (1963) *The Sociology of Religion*, Introduction by Talcott Parsons, Ephraim Fischoff (trans.) Boston: Beacon; original German edn, 1922.

Whitefield, George (1969) *George Whitefield's Journals*. Gainsville, FL: Scholars' Facsimiles and Reprints; original edn, 1747.

Williams, Michael Allen (1996) *Rethinking "Gnosticism": An Argument for Dismantling a Dubious Category*. Princeton: Princeton University Press.

Wilson, Bryan R. (1973) *Magic and the Millennium: A Sociological Study of Religious Movement of Protest Among Tribal and Third-World Peoples*. London: Heinemann.

——. (1982) *Religion in Sociological Perspective*. Oxford: Oxford University Press.

Wood, Gordon S. (1993) "Founding a Nation, 986–1787." In Arthur M. Schlesinger, Jr. (ed.) *The Almanac of American History*. New York: Barnes and Noble.

Wuthnow, Robert (Ed.) (1979) *The Religious Dimension: New Directions in Quantitative Research*. New York: Academic Press.

35 World

William E. Paden

William E. Paden (1939—) studied philosophy at Occidental College and received his MA and PhD in comparative religion from Claremont Graduate University. He served as Chair for more than twenty of his forty-four years as a member of the Department of Religion at the University of Vermont before retiring in 2009. His expertise in cross-cultural patterns of religious behavior informs his books and many articles, which contribute both to insights about the nature of religion and reflection on theory and method in the study of religion. Some of Paden's more recent articles connect these cross-cultural patterns to processes of human evolution. Both *Religious Worlds: The Comparative Study of Religion* (1988) and *Interpreting the Sacred: Ways of Viewing Religion* (1992) are in their second editions and have been translated into numerous foreign languages. Religious worlds are the central theme of his 1988 book, but the selection on "World" below comes instead from Paden's chapter in the 2000 *Guide to the Study of Religion* edited by Willi Braun and Russell T. McCutcheon.

The concept of world provides a tool for understanding and analyzing the plurality, contextuality and self-positing nature of religious cultures. Thus, rather than viewing religions in terms of a given standard—whether religious or nonreligious—of what "the" world is and then seeing how they, the religions, represent "it," here the assumption is that religious systems themselves create their own versions of world. Religions are one of culture's primary systems of world definition, constructing universes of language, behavior and identity with their own particular organizing categories.

The concept world in some ways overlaps with the notions of system, belief system and world-view, but has more textured, contextualistic and behavioral reference. World encompasses all forms of habitation, action and language, and not just viewpoints, ideas or self-conscious doctrines and philosophies. Like the notion "environment," a world suggests operating life space, actively selected and negotiated. Any organism that attends to a particular environmental context has formed a version of world. In human cultures, there are multiple, alternating genres of worlds, for example, those of the military, business, arts, courtship, mathematics and sport.

World is then a systematic indicator of domain difference and specificity. The etymological meaning of the Germanic / English word "world" is "the age or life of man," (from *wer-*, "man," and *ald-*, "age"), as distinguished from the "age" or domain of the gods. In Christian cultures, where the gospels had already introduced phrases like "my kingdom is not of this world (Greek, *kosmos*)" it became conventional to distinguish "this world" of human life in contrast to "the next." As the long entry in the *Oxford English Dictionary* (1989) shows, the term world eventually invited extended uses to denote any sphere or realm, as in "the Old World and the New World," "the world of plants," "one's own world," "the world of the honeybee," "the world of the Cistercian monk." Now we have "the world of teenage romance" or "the cyberworld." What is common here is the notion of a frame of reference or domain that constitutes the horizon of certain kinds of behaviors, objects, persons or communities and thus differentiates those horizons from others so that their particular contextualities and schemas can come into focus.

Applied to human life systems, then, a world is not just a matter of conceptual representation, but also a specific form of habitation and practice—the structure of meaningful relationships in which a person exists and participates. More fully put, it is *the operating environment of linguistic and behavioral options which persons or communities presuppose, posit and inhabit at any given point in time and from which they choose courses of action.* Religious worlds, in particular, are cultural systems that organize language and behavior around engagement with postulated superhuman agencies. A person is "in" a religious world just as one can be "in" the army, "in" a game or "in" a relationship.

As an analytical concept in religious studies, "world" is most definitely not just a term for "the totality of things" in general, but rather for the particular ways totalities are constructed in any particular environment. On the one hand, the idea directs attention to the lived context, categories and realities of "insiders." In the study of religion this is critical for the goal of "understanding the other," for ideally it checks the blatant imposition of foreign classifications onto other people's self-representations. Yet, on the other hand, to label the insiders' systems "worlds" is not to simply validate them, admire them, or give them voice. Rather, the analytic purpose is to be able to identify the internal relationships and functions of objects and categories within a given domain, as compared with the arrangements of other life-systems. Historians of religion investigate what beliefs and actions refer to as real in the classificatory perspectives of the adherents—while also asking what they refer to within their own very different and broader horizon of explanation.

The notion of world, then, helps clarify the difference of insider and outsider points of view. Much confusion has resulted from scholars attributing their version of what religion signifies to that of the adherents themselves. What things "mean" in the world of the observer does not have to correspond to what things mean in the world of the insider. In anthropological terminology, emic categories represent terms entirely specific to a culture and its insiders. Etic categories, in contrast, represent the scholar's own concepts that have been formed by generalization and comparative analysis (for analysis and debate about these concepts in anthropology, see Headland 1990; as applied to the study of religion, see McCutcheon 1998). The notion of world is itself an etic category—designed partly to direct attention to its emic versions.

The concept of world therefore includes not only a descriptive function, but also a redescriptive one (McCutcheon 1997). That is, it not only is used to attend to the categories of the insider's life-world, but also to account for them within the broader conceptual resources of the outside scholar. The analyst or comparativist brings a general understanding of world formation and its shaping factors to the interpretation of any single world. In this sense, the notion of world includes and employs much of the theoretical capital of other concepts described in this *Guide*, such as culture, discourse, ideology, cognition, structure, myth, gender and classification—all of these being dimensional components, or factors of world construction and lenses to analyze it. Any human world involves the variables of physical geography, language, social class, historical change, economics and even individuality; any world is an open-ended, interactive process, filled with various and complex sensory and cognitive domains, encompassing both representation and practice, both imaginal objects and bodies-in-performance. As a concept, world provides something of an integrative matrix in which the particular, faceted contributions of various disciplines can find their places.

Background of the Concept

More than a loose figure of speech, world is a concept that has undergone specialized development as a tool of the philosophic, human sciences. For example, the common-sense, descriptive move to unpack world into different domains may be accompanied by the epistemologically radical conclusion that no single one of them constitutes an absolute standard for describing the others; that the "universe" is always a product of a manner of description rather than an objectively determined referent; or that the concept of world does not assume a single, *a priori* system of knowledge in terms of which all human experience should be described.

The idea that world is not just a common, ready-made entity that humans passively receive or discover, but rather something humans also produce, has a conceptual genealogy with many branches. In each, we find concepts that "the world" is a product of the instrumentations and modes through which it is apprehended and inhabited, and that world describes versions of life-space without reducing those versions to an independent norm. These traditions include but are not limited to Kantian philosophy, phenomenology, sociology of knowledge, social anthropology and the history of religions model of Mircea Eliade.

In the first lineage, the philosopher Immanuel Kant (1724–1804) described how the mind and its categories are factors that structure reality and that without these structures there is no access to reality "in itself." From this, others developed the idea that concepts and symbol systems of all kinds become the different frames through which different kinds of "reality" take place. Ernst Cassirer (1874–1945), for example, in his "Philosophy of Symbolic Forms" [*Die Philosophie der symbolischen Formen*, 1923–29], showed how disparate forms of cultural languages like art, myth and science organize distinctive kinds of reality (Cassirer 1955). Nelson Goodman developed a radical form of relativism, summarized in his *Ways of Worldmaking* (1978), showing how the world only comes in "versions": "None of them," he writes, "tells us *the* way the world is, but each of them tells us *a* way the world is" (N. Goodman 1972: 31). A musical score, a painting or a scientific theory each compose one of these worlds, each realm with its own "schemes" (N. Goodman and Elgin 1988: 7). These are not versions of one and the same neutral, underlying world, for no version is the primordial descriptor of reality and each world version has an independence. Thus, seemingly conflicting assertions like "the sun always moves," and "the sun never moves," while at odds on the surface, need to be read within their own systems of description as statements that are true in different worlds. Truth is then a function of system genre, some truths requiring denotational, empirical criteria, and others, such as various forms of aesthetic truth, inviting "rightness" and consistency internal to the requirements of the logic of their own domain.

The second tradition is that of phenomenology, launched systematically with Edmund Husserl (1859–1938). Husserl developed the concept of a "life-world" (*Lebenswelt*), or the world as immediately experienced by subjects, as distinguished from the objectivizing conceptual world of science without human subjects in it. He focused on describing "the structures of experience" as they occur in consciousness and as they are "lived"—for example, to consciousness, time is not quantitative or homogeneous, but heterogeneous and qualitative. Martin Heidegger (1889–1976) produced an extensive, original analysis of the human situation as characterized by one's "being-in-the-world." Again, this existential focus on the structure of "habitative" existence was an alternative to philosophies that pictured consciousness, mind or subjectivity as independent of environments, and that had isolated subjects from their world fields. In the terms of existential phenomenology, what humans "are" is what they do as agents in their worlds, a world being here a mutually constitutive relation of subject and objects. Arguably in the phenomenological spirit, even the American philosopher William James (1842–1910) had analyzed seven genres of "sub-worlds"— namely, the worlds of the senses, science, abstract truths, collective prejudices, individual opinion, religion and myth, and madness (1890: 291–95), noting that "each world *whilst it is attended to* is real after its own fashion; only the reality lapses with the attention" (1890: 293).

Peter Berger's and Thomas Luckmann's *The Social Construction of Reality* (1967) and Berger's *The Sacred Canopy* (1969)—which gave particular semantic currency to the terminology of "world-construction"—encapsulated another trajectory of the category of world, the so-called "sociology of knowledge," drawing on the work of Karl Marx (1818–83), Emile Durkheim (1858–1917), Max Weber (1864–1920) and Alfred Schütz (1899–1959). Marx and Durkheim had already developed the radical claims that the entire world of thought and knowledge, including "religion," was a social creation. These creations are nevertheless very real in their effects. This approach went much further than just observing that thought and world views are "influenced" by social norms. Rather, it attested that knowledge is itself a *product* of human, cultural activity.

Berger and Luckmann described a basic sociological dialectic in three processes. In the first, society externalizes itself, putting its categories—like language and institutions—out onto the world; in the second, such externalization then assumes the features and "facticity" of objective reality, and this is the "objectivation" process; and in the third, that reality is then internalized as normative by society's individual members. Language, social roles and identities, which are initially our products, thus take on the aura of factuality. "[T]he fundamental coerciveness of society lies not in its machineries of social control," Berger writes, "but in its power to constitute and to impose itself as reality" (1969: 12). Society is here a world-building enterprise that must always maintain and "legitimize" its own meaningful order, or *nomos* (Greek "law") (1969: 19). Separation from the social world, in turn, constitutes *anomy*—essentially worldlessness (1969: 22). Social institutions are endowed with an ontological status "to the point where to deny them is to deny being itself—the being of the universal order of things and, consequently, one's own being in this order" (1969: 25); nomos and cosmos then become "co-extensive" (1969: 25). Religion, in Berger's view, is what "cosmizes" and sacralizes this nomos. In the face of chaos, religions ground nomic institutions in a trans-humanly legitimated realm.

A fourth trajectory is that of social anthropology *per se*, which has emphasized the culture-specific construction of world, the autonomy of "collective representations," worlds as cultural languages and mappings, and communities as systems. Representative are Robert Redfield on the notion of communities as "wholes" (1955), Mary Douglas on the boundaried character of social orders (1989 [1966]), and Clifford Geertz (1973) on the context-specific nature of cultural categories. Others, like Pierre Bourdieu (1977) and Talal Asad (1993), have drawn particular, nuanced attention to the role of "practice" in the "negotiation" of worlds. Michael Kearney's *World View* (1984) is a notable systematic analysis of cross-culturally universal categories of world-view formation, for example, the distinction of self and others, causality, classification, and notions of space and time.

Finally, and particularly influential in the vocabulary of comparative religion, has been the work of Mircea Eliade (1907–86). Eliade made programmatic use of the concept of world, applying it as a tool of the history and phenomenology of religion. Where sociologists and anthropologists established the role of social norms in the formation of worlds, Eliade attempted to show the specific role of religious myth and ritual. Religious and nonreligious people, he posited, represent different modes of "being in the world" (1959b: 14–16), different "existential situations." Thus, for *homo religiosus* (the "religious person") the universe is constituted by "sacred histories," and sacred times and places that make the mythic realities present. What is taken as sacred becomes "the real"—it "ontologically founds the world" (Eliade 1959b: 21). To Eliade, religious world creation with its distinctive mythic style, parallels the imaginal, creative systems of novelists and artists.

In the Eliadean approach, religious worlds are those which interpret space, time, nature and human existence in terms of trans-human meanings. Thus, traditional religious cultures oriented their worlds around certain fixed, sacred points—either natural sites such as mountains or caves, or constructions such as temples or shrines, or even portable sacred objects—in the midst of otherwise homogeneous space. These "centers of the world" also function as "openings" or points of communication with the trans-human agencies which underlie existence. Where the symbolism is vertical, these points comprise an *axis mundi* (world axis), linking the world above with that below. The fundamental distinction of "our world" versus foreign, chaotic space, reflects the opposition between organized and unknown territory. Eliade calls it a traditional "system of the world" (1959b: 37) where one's own world is at the center, is believed to be founded by the gods, and involves points of communication with the gods by certain breaks in the homogeneity of space.

A second Eliadean category of religious world-making is the construction of time and history through mythic classifications. For a traditional religious world, time has a reversible quality. Religious actors orient themselves toward and define themselves in terms of the eternal "time" of the myth—the time of the great events recounted in one's sacred histories. Ritual gives access to these realities. Eliade offers the example of cultures for whom the word for world is also the word for year, indicating that the annual time of the New Year festival is also literally the time when "the world" is reborn anew through the reempowerment of the mythic forces of creation (1959b: 73).

Traditional *homo religiosus* also experiences nature as a manifestation of divine activity, so that sacrality is revealed "through the very structures of the world" (1959b: 117). This is to say that the system of nature and its features, such as the transcendence and infinity of the sky, the life-death cycle of the earth, and the dissolving but creative nature of water, all are experienced as having a trans-human, cosmic value and signification.

Finally, for Eliade, religious worlds are apt to locate all human activities, such as eating, work, art and marital life, within a cosmic or mythic framework of significance. It is the nature of the lens of mythic thinking to find its categories and archetypes manifest or divined in and through the ordinary world of objects. Transitions and events such as birth, puberty / adulthood, marriage and death, are always ritually placed within an encompassing, sacred world-view.

Besides these five approaches to world building, recent scientific models may also hold promise for religious studies, including "systems" analysis and complexity theory (Malley 1995), and biological concepts of "self-organizing systems" (Jantsch 1980). Varela, Thompson and Rosch present a cognitive science model—influenced by phenomenology and Madhyamika Buddhist dialectics—which develops the idea that mind and world arise together in an "enactive" manner (Varela et al. 1991). Some cognitivists would maintain that the human mind is engaged in a "co-evolutionary relationship" with religious systems (Malley 1995: 7). Generally, renewed interest in the application of bio-anthropology to religious behavior (Burkert 1996), in "human universals" (D. E. Brown 1991), and the cognitive basis of religious ideas (Boyer 1994; Malley 1995) may add significant conceptual resources to the notion of world-building.

Religious Worlds: Features and Dynamics

Religious systems are topographies of language and practice in which humans construe the world as a place of engagement with superhuman beings and become actors in that culturally generated system. These same religious people may also, simultaneously, live within several other organizational and behavioral systems and roles that have no trans-human reference points, for example physical, social and geographical worlds. Where a religious world version is in effect, though, one finds the language of superhuman agency, sacred, focal objects, notions of an inviolable world order, and the process of periodic, ritual world renewal.

Religion as World Script

A religious world is a particular way of seeing the world and acting in it through the matrix of languages that involve trans-human agency. Religious language names the empowering forces of the world as gods, spirits or god-like beings, evoking their presence, authority and communicative possibilities. These beings also form the ingredients of cosmologies, mythologies and sacred "histories"—which constitute a kind of semantic, categorial membrane around "one's world," explaining its origin and course, and why things are as they are. Such constructions of world and knowledge, believed to signify the realities behind appearances, create domains of experience within which human actors and religious objects evolve their interactive life. These mental mappings have been endlessly imaginative. They produce other worlds, future worlds, higher worlds, parallel spirit universes, heavens and hells, the worlds of gods and worlds produced by gods. The ordinary world, in juxtaposition with these others, accordingly may come to be seen as a place of illusion, a playground of the gods, a prison house requiring a savior, an exact mirror duplicate of "the world above" or a laborious stage in an evolutionary series.

Religious language, and thus its accompanying world version, is participatory and self-involving, unlike the language of scientific objectivity. It is itself a form of practice, involving various reciprocities of giving and receiving in relation to its postulated sacred objects; and a form of communication and performance—in some ways, a form of competency. In this sense, religious accounts of the creation and generation of the world are not just hypotheses about what happened in the past, but foundational charters and indices for how to behave in the present.

Empowered Sacred Objects

Religious worlds form around particular objects believed to be sacred. The objects come in various genres—not only as names of gods, but as the manifestations of superhuman power or authority in places and times, endowed authorities, sacraments and rites, icons and symbols, scriptures and mythic words, teachings and precepts. Sacred objects may be tangible or mental, spatial or linguistic, but they will tend to have a centripetal, centering function, serving as openings to a nonmaterial zone. They thereby become forms of bonding and reciprocal empowerment. Around them, with all their mystery, charisma, inviolateness and attention-demanding obligations, religious worlds and the logic of religious behaviors arise.

None of this indicates that a religious world is not at the same time a social world. Religious objects receive their sacrality from the collectivities they belong to. They are marks of membership or social identity. The Pope, the Ganges river, the mandalas of Soka Gakkai Buddhism, the Qur'an are holy only within their own world frames, and not in others. The absolutes, the cosmic maps, the reigning authorities, and the holy of holies of one group are irrelevant or nonexistent in other systems. Thus, thousands of "Centers of the World" sit side by side. Each group or sub-group elevates and absolutizes its own authoritative objects.

Sacred Order

Religious worlds are not just about relations with objects but also posit normative, moral orders taken to be the cosmic order itself, and these determine proper and improper behavior. Such orders draw lines forming distinctions of good and evil, right and wrong, pure and impure, and endow these boundaries with the sanctity of superhuman legitimation. Not only domains for the experience of "the other," religions are systems which monitor their own integrity by purging what is offensive, often through acts of purification. Sacred order is then not just a template for world design or a passive, aesthetic arrangement, but a process of self-maintenance in the face of wrongness and violation. The world must be kept "right," and if something is wrong with the world, it must be made right—the polarity and procedure being relative to each system. Religion is here one of the more far-reaching forms of world stability in the face of an otherwise chaotic cosmos. Religious worlds, moreover, are highly defined and developed versions of the tendency of all human worlds to seek self-preservation against threats of violation. The need to defend territory, honor, tradition, membership and collective loyalties is intimately linked with the inviolability of religious order (Paden 1996b).

Religions themselves have their own terms for world-order, such as the Hindu idea of dharma. Dharma, from a root meaning "to uphold," signifies the eternal, divinely endowed moral order, and can be synonymous with the concepts of law, duty, righteousness, religion. Chinese religions have the category of T'ien, or the "order of Heaven," reflected in all social relationships, and even Tao, the natural "way" of things; and monotheistic traditions hold conceptions of the revealed, normative Word of God manifest in scriptures such as the Qur'an, the Torah or the Bible. Religious order tends to become the guideline for all other forms of order, whether dietary, legal or political.

World Renewal

Worlds not only need to be defended but also renewed. Where the religious world is not kept up, the authority of the gods is diminished. Thus, periodic religious observances and festivals have become not only the shapers of time and calendars, but also acts that give continuing "life" to the superhuman powers. Ritual observance, then, becomes the matrix of world renewal, as Durkheim (1995 [1912]: 330–54) and later Eliade (1959b: 68–113) emphasized. Through regular acts of memorializing sacred objects and transmitting ritual behaviors, the social and mythic reality of religion are maintained as plausible and unchanging. Daily prayer for Muslims or puja for Hindus build the category of divinity into the heart of the day; Judeo-Christian Sabbath and Sunday observances return time to God on a regular weekly cycle; great annual festivals like Ramadan, the Jewish New Year or Easter, regenerate the cosmos on a pervasive, large scale. All major passages and events in life are given religious context. Thus, religious worlds are sustained and refounded periodically through commemorative and ritual practices that construct a kind of temporal geography. Without these normative, shaping intersections that mark and punctuate time, religious worlds would scarcely survive.

Varieties and Dynamics of Religious Worlds

Worlds transform, re-form, expand and extend. Buddhism completely reinterpreted what had previously been a Hindu cosmos, as Christianity did with Judaism, as Islam did with its Judeo-Christian predecessors and as Protestantism did with Catholicism. Any religion gets reshaped by new environments. Religions grow, transmute, combine, sub-divide, accommodate, migrate, die off. They are fashioned out of the stuff of endless cultural locations and genres: Where culture is territorial, so is religion; where culture is individualistic, religion reflects it; where culture is hierarchic, religion follows suit; where cultures combine, religion becomes syncretic; where culture is revolutionary, so are the gods. Likewise, religions themselves reshape cultures. They are not only reflections of social systems, but also create and recreate them, and they do this because they are themselves a form of social life.

New religious movements, numbering in the thousands when looked at globally, show how the language of spirituality constantly recreates itself to address the needs of emerging cultural identities. The enormous variety of these innovative systems shows the naturalness of religious world building, each group reconstituting a cosmology, manufacturing a revised version of history, offering a new set of ontological markers and new interactive objects of authority and communication. They do this as naturally and inevitably as any species will form a habitat.

Each purposive zone of culture, whether religious, medical, musical, commercial or political, will have its "life"—its structures, styles of productivity, goals and flow of activity. Any of them or any combination of them has a self-organizing course of its own, following the logic and strategies of its own subject matter, availability of resources, opportunities, conflict and competition, and creative leadership. Each generates its own classifications of relevant knowledge, its own lenses for construing experience. In religious terms, one who devotes his or her life "to God" comes to encounter a range of significations, processes and new experiences along the way, just as the same could be said for those who pursue other cultural genres, such as fashion designers, culinary experts or tennis players.

Religions have a tendency to spread their effects through an entire world system, and thus to totalize and universalize their influence. This drive toward extension may either take the form of so-called "world" religions which set out to win the allegiance of all cultures and thus fill the planet with their globalizing norms, or in the form of any religion that extends its influence to the entirety of educational, political and even aesthetic systems within its own cultural world. It is part of the power of "the sacred"—for example, a god—to make or authorize a world. There may also be an element of compelling, colonizing authority that attends dedication to "supreme" gods or religious founders. The public is familiar with the way fundamentalist thinking about creationism tries to take on ownership of the entirety of world-description even in the face of challenges by evolutionary science, or the way some sectarian religious groups will opt out of the secular system altogether and construct their own internally consistent and self-verifying cultures.

Comparativism and Religious Worlds

The notion of world formation supplies a basis for comparative analysis because it constitutes a common, human activity against which differences may also be discerned. The world-making model identifies both common *forms* of world-fashioning behaviors and historically different socio-cultural *contents* of world expressions.

If all religious worlds create and transmit sacred pasts, construct sacred objects, absolutize or cosmicize their moral orders and forms of authority, and periodically renew their commitments to sacred objects with calendrical and passage rites, these features are also but mythically explicit versions of themes that appear in the world making of any social group. Memory-construction, the absolutizing of values and objects, and renewal practices can be identified as comparative themes pervading the general human condition. Behaviors that otherwise might appear distant, primitive or odd, here take on a context of intelligibility as instances of common, familiar human activities.

Yet in their content, worlds are different. If all have "pasts," every past is a different genealogy than any other, even within a so-called common tradition: Pentecostalists and Catholics construct different Christian lineages, Shia and Sunni Muslims have incompatible readings of the succession of Islamic authority, Buddhist denominations affiliate with disparate genealogies of teaching authority. Indeed, every traditional village, town and city, like every family, is apt to have its own salient, chronicled memories (Braun 1999). And if all cultures have annual renewal festivals, nevertheless the content of those rites is not the same but rather a reflector of very different value orientations—such as hierarchic family relationships, moral conscientiousness, economic bonding or male prowess. If all religions draw lines distinguishing behavior that is right or pure from that which is transgressive or impure, nevertheless what it is that is pure or impure is not the same. Identifying patterns of world orientation, therefore, can actually enhance or highlight differences relative to that pattern, showing what makes a world its own and not another.

Issues and Evaluation

The notion of world is open to various forms of problematizing and debate, which may be briefly summarized:

1. It may be argued that the concept of world puts an artificial circumscription on an area that exists only in the mind of the interpreter, and thus gives a false sense of order or totality, imposing an intelligibility on things that is in fact not there. It could be said that every event is really a fluid, interdependent mixture of many networks, so complex as to be impossible to distinguish in any but an arbitrary way, and that humans essentially live in this chaos rather than in any bounded system. As anthropologist Renato Rosaldo points out, "order vs. chaos" is not the whole story of culture—there is an important, even less explored realm of behavior marked by "improvisation, muddling through, and contingent events" (Rosaldo 1989: 103).

    In response, one could show that the notion of world does not necessarily imply a fixed, boundaried system. A world can be a process of change, a form of interaction, even a momentary staging, as well as a durable institution, a long-range commitment or a changeless structure. One can be "in" a process as well as "in" a fixed order. Insofar as a world is a product of language and consciousness, it can be switched on or off in the blink of an eye. Many worlds lie both close at hand and overlapping.

2. It has been argued that "religion" is not itself a viable analytical category but only a convention, and that religious life lacks cultural autonomy (Fitzgerald 1997).

   Every analytic concept, including that of "religious worlds," has aspects of arbitrariness. But concepts may also direct attention to what otherwise would not be noticed. The notion of world points to the prospect of locating and sorting out the diversity of rule-based, purposive systems of behaviors. A religious version of world is at least potentially such an identifiable, intentional sphere or program of cultural experience.

3. Another issue, alluded to earlier, is: *Whose* religious world is being described, that of the insider or that of the interpreter? In the analogy from psychotherapy, the patient's self-description may be altogether at variance from the therapist's explanation. For the latter, the patient's world may exhibit self-deception, mental illness, social dysfunction, paranoia. No Marxist would accept a religion's description of its own world as a real account of that world.

   The two horizons of description are indeed discrepant. The study of religion is not limited to simple reiteration of the religious insider's self-description, but also involves a representation of that world, or aspects of it, within a broader repertoire of conceptual, comparative and analytical resources (Paden 1992, 1994). At the same time, if one cannot identify how objects and relationships are constituted within the experience of the insider, one lacks the basic data that is the subject matter for explanation.

4. Is the notion of world reductionistic? Does the category of world construction take away the elements of "otherness" in experience, as Paul Ricoeur worries (1980: 116)? Is world more than a construct?

   Certainly the concept of world is not reducible to the metaphor of building and fabrication. Worlds are not just built, as with hammer and nails. They are environments acted upon, responded to, engaged with, practiced, performed—environments to which one "attends" (Ingold 1996: 112–17). As Ricoeur puts it, humans "render" a world, like an artist (1980: 116–20). It is the nature of religious worlds, in particular, to provide contexts in which persons may pursue various forms of engagement with "the other," with gods, with transcendence. "World" is then an open-ended affair that includes any imaginable content of experience. It gives itself through the matrices of its own designs and structures and through the receiving and configuring acts of the subject (Paden 1992: 110–35).

   At the same time, the notion of world provides a referent for the analysis of religion that in some ways replaces the classical theological referents of "the Holy" or "the Divine." Thus, instead of worlds being "about" the Holy, holiness is here a feature of ways certain object-relationships drive certain kinds of behaviors in certain kinds of worlds.

5. Finally, there is the issue of whether the reference to multiple worlds ignores the reality of a *common* world. Does the world just melt down into world-versions? Is there no world in which all these other worlds subsist?

   The answer must be that there is, but our understanding of it as a totality will itself still only be a world-version. The study of hundreds of religious worlds certainly leads to a larger sense of the kind of world in which these many worlds take place, and of the kinds of recurrent structures and environmental differences that condition the existence of multiple worlds. This common world then becomes the world of the interpreter, just as a physicist may form a world model that attempts to accommodate all the known data of the physical universe.

   The notion of world provides an integrative matrix for linking concepts, insights and explanatory frames from the work of humanistic, social and even biological sciences. It has the versatility to distinguish large-scale or small-scale regions of kinds of activity, and it can help demarcate insiders' and outsiders' frames of reference. It differentiates domains of behavior that have an element of self-organizing purpose.

In these ways, the concept of world may be productive when applied to religion, just as religion also becomes a productive subject matter for identifying the thematics of world building as a universal human activity.

QUESTIONS FOR REVIEW AND DISCUSSION

1. How is the concept of "world" useful in understanding religious culture? What does this concept encompass?
2. Does world refer to "the totality of things"? How does this concept "clarify the difference of insider and outsider points of view"?
3. Paden introduces at least five major trajectories or traditions for making sense and use of this concept of worlds. Which of the five (Kantian philosophy, phenomenology, sociology of knowledge, social anthropology and the history of religions model of Mircea Eliade) do you find most useful for understanding religious worlds? Why?
4. How are the concepts of "world" and "world-making" used by Eliade? How do they relate to concepts of the sacred, time, place, and *homo religiosus* (the "religious person")?
5. In addition to the five approaches listed in question three, Paden briefly addresses recent trends in scientific models, such as cognitive studies. Does he see these as promising for understanding religious worlds? Do you agree?
6. Do religious people simultaneously inhabit additional non-religious worlds or are they bound exclusively to the religious system they inhabit?
7. Paden provides a helpful definition of religious systems as "topographies of language and practice in which humans construe the world as a place of engagement with superhuman beings and become actors in that culturally generated system." What are key features and dynamics of language and practice that shape and respond to these systems?
8. What does Paden mean when he writes that religious language is a form of practice? Do you agree?
9. How does Paden relate religious notions of a sacred order to world stability and to all other forms of order (e.g. legal or political)?
10. Provide examples of whether dynamic change or static continuity is more characteristic of religious worlds?
11. What can comparative analysis of religious worlds offer?
12. Select one of Paden's five points of debate in the final section on "Issues and Evaluation". What do you think about this issue and how does it relate to other selections in this Reader?

Suggested Readings

Asad, Talal. 1993 *Genealogies of Religion: Discipline and Reasons of Power in Christianity and Islam*. Baltimore: Johns Hopkins University Press.

Berger, Peter. 1969 *The Sacred Canopy: Elements of a Sociological Theory of Religion.* Garden City, NY: Doubleday. Chs. 1 and 2.

Bourdieu, Pierre. 1977 *Outline of a Theory of Practice,* Richard Nice (trans.) Cambridge Studies in Social Anthropology, vol. 16. Cambridge: Cambridge University Press; original French edn, 1972.

Boyer, Pascal. 1994 *The Naturalness of Religious Ideas: A Cognitive Theory of Religion.* Berkeley: University of California Press.

Braun, Willi. 1999 "Amnesia in the Production of (Christian) History." *Bulletin of the Council of Societies for the Study of Religion* 28 (1) 3–8.

Burkert, Walter. 1996 *Creation of the Sacred: Tracks of Biology in Early Religions.* Cambridge, MA: Harvard University Press.

Douglas, Mary. 1989 *Purity and Danger: An Analysis of the Concepts of Pollution and Taboo.* London: Ark Paperbacks; original edn, London: Routledge & Kegan Paul, 1966; reprinted London: Routledge, 1994.

Durkheim, Émile. 1995 *The Elementary Forms of the Religious Life,* Karen E. Fields (trans.) with an Introduction. New York: Free Press; original French edn, 1912.

Eliade, Mircea. 1959a "Methodological Remarks on the Study of Religious Symbolism," pp. 86–107 in Mircea Eliade and Joseph M. Kitagawa (eds.), *The History of Religions: Essays in Methodology,* With a preface by Jerald C. Brauer. Chicago: University of Chicago Press.

——. 1959b *The Sacred and Profane: The Nature of Religion.* Willard R. Trask (trans.). New York: Harcourt, Brace Jovanovich.

Fitzgerald, Timothy. 1997 "A Critique of 'Religion' as a Cross-Cultural Category." *Method and Theory in the Study of Religion* 9(2):91–110.

Geertz, Clifford. 1973 *The Interpretations of Cultures: Selected Essays.* New York: Basic.

——. 1983 *Local Knowledge: Further Essays in Interpretive Anthropology.* New York: Basic. Ch. 3.

Goodman, Nelson. 1978 *Ways of Worldmaking.* Indianapolis: Hackett. Ch. 1.

Goodman, Nelson and Catherine Z. Elgin. 1988 *Reconceptions in Philosophy and Other Arts and Sciences.* Indianapolis: Hackett.

Headland, Thomas N., Kenneth L. Pike and Marvin Harris (Eds.). 1990 *Emics and Etics: The Insider/Outsider Debate.* Newbury Park, CA: Sage.

Ingold, Tim, editor. 1996 "1990 Debate: Human Worlds Are Culturally Constructed," pp. 99–146 in Tim Ingold (ed.), *Key Debates in Anthropology.* London: Routledge.

James, William. 1890 *The Principles of Psychology.* New York: Henry Holt.

Jantsch, Erich. 1980 *The Self-Organizing Universe: Scientific and Human Implications of the Emerging Paradigm of Evolution.* Pergamon International Library of Science, Technology, Engineering and Social Studies. Oxford: Pergamon.

Kearney, Michael. 1984 *World View.* Novato, CA: Chandler & Sharp.

Malley, Brian E. 1995 "Explaining Order in Religious Systems." *Method and Theory in the Study of Religion* 7:5–22.

McCutcheon, Russell T. 1997 "A Default of Critical Intelligence? The Scholar of Religion as Public Intellectual." *Journal of the American Academy of Religion* 65:443–468.

——. 1998 "Redescribing 'Religion' as Social Formation: Toward a social Theory of Religion," pp. 51–71 in Thomas A. Idinopulos and Brian C. Wilson (eds.), *What is Religion? Origins, Definitions, and Explanations.* Studies in the History of Religions, vol. 81. Leiden: E. J. Brill.

Paden, William E. (1992) *Interpreting the Sacred: Ways of Viewing Religion.* Boston: Beacon.

——. 1994 *Religious Worlds: The Comparative Study of Religion.* 2nd edn. Boston: Beacon.

——. 1996a "Elements of a New Comparativism." *Method and Theory in the Study of Religion* 8:5–14.

——. 1996b "Sacrality as Integrity: 'Sacred Order' as a Model for Describing Religious Worlds." pp. 3–18 in Thomas A. Idinopulos and Edward A Yonan (eds.), *The Sacred and Its Scholars: Comparative Methodologies for the Study of Primary Religious Data.* Studies in the History of Religions, vol. 73. Leiden: E. J. Brill.

Redfield, Robert. 1955 *The Little Community: Viewpoints for the Study of the Human Whole.* Chicago: University of Chicago Press.

Ricoeur, Paul. 1980 "Review of Goodman's *Ways of Worldmaking.*" *Philosophy and Literature* 4:107–120.

Rosaldo, Renato. 1989 *Culture and Truth: The Remaking of Social Analysis.* Boston: Beacon.

Tambiah, Stanley J. 1990 *Magic, Science, Religion, and the Scope of Rationality.* Lewis Henry Morgan Lectures, 1984. Cambridge: Cambridge University Press. Ch. 5.

Varela, Francisco J., Evan Thompson and Eleanor Rosch. 1998 *The Embodied Mind: Cognitive Science and Human Experience.* Cambridge, MA: Massachusetts Institute of Technology Press.

36 *Women and Gender in Islam: Historical Roots of a Modern Debate*

Leila Ahmed

Leila Ahmed (1940–) was born in Cairo, and received her doctorate from the University of Cambridge. She directed the Near Eastern Studies program at the University of Massachusetts prior to taking an appointment in women's studies in religion at Harvard Divinity School, where she currently teaches. Her work includes the historical study of the roots of contemporary attitudes to Islam by Western thinkers, and the examination, within Islam, of issues such as Arab nationalism and attitudes towards women. Her most influential book, *Women and Gender in Islam* (1992), highlights the contrasts between the ethical, egalitarian teachings of Islam, and the historical processes through which Islamic societies developed doctrines and practices that are unfavorable to women. The selection that follows is the concluding chapter of that study.

CONCLUSION

In the discourses of geopolitics the reemergent veil is an emblem of many things, prominent among which is its meaning as the rejection of the West. But when one considers why the veil has this meaning in the late twentieth century, it becomes obvious that, ironically, it was the discourses of the West, and specifically the discourse of colonial domination, that in the first place determined the meaning of the veil in geopolitical discourses and thereby set the terms for its emergence as a symbol of resistance. In other words, the reemergent veil attests, by virtue of its very power as a symbol of resistance, to the uncontested hegemonic diffusion of the discourses of the West in our age. And it attests to the fact that, at least as regards the Islamic world, the discourses of resistance and rejection are inextricably informed by the languages and ideas developed and disseminated by the West to no less a degree than are the languages of those openly advocating emulation of the West or those who, like Frantz Fanon or Nawal El-Saadawi, are critical of the West but nonetheless ground themselves in intellectual assumptions and political ideas, including a belief in the rights of the individual, formulated by Western bourgeois capitalism and spread over the globe as a result of Western hegemony.

Islamic reformers such as al-Afghani and Abdu and the militant Islamists of today; intellectuals radically critical of the West, including Marxists such as Fanon, Samir Amin, and El-Saadawi; and liberal intellectuals wholeheartedly embracing the colonial thesis of Western superiority and advocating the importance of emulating the West all differ fundamentally in their political stance, but they do not differ in the extent to which, whether they acknowledge it or not, they draw on Western thought and Western political and intellectual languages. The revitalized, reimagined Islam put forward by the Islamic militants or by

Abdu and his contemporaries is an Islam redefining itself against the assaults of the West but also an Islam revitalized and reimagined as a result of its fertilization by and its appropriation of the languages and ideas given currency by the discourses of the West. In the discourses of the Arab world comprehensively, then, whether they are discourses of collaboration or resistance, the goals and ideals they articulate and even the rejection of and often-legitimate anger at the West that they give voice to are formulated in terms of the dominant discourse—Western in origin—of our global society.

This is of particular relevance to Islamist positions. Marxists, secularists, and feminists generally concede, tacitly if not overtly, their grounding in Western thought, but Islamists, arguing for what they claim to be a restoration of an "original" Islam and an "authentic" indigenous culture, make their case, and conduct the assault on secularism, Marxism, or feminism on the grounds that these represent alien Western importations whereas Islamism intends the restoration of an indigenous tradition. But today, willy-nilly, as the Indian psychologist and critic Ashis Nandy has remarked, the West is everywhere, "in structures and in minds," and Western political ideas, technologies, and intellectual systems comprehensively permeate all societies.[1] There is no extricating them, no return to a past of unadulterated cultural purity—even if in this ancient and anciently multicultural part of the world such a project had ever been other than chimerical.

The Islamist position regarding women is also problematic in that, essentially reactive in nature, it traps the issue of women with the struggle over culture—just as the initiating colonial discourse had done. Typically, women—and the reaffirmation of indigenous customs relating to women and the restoration of the customs and laws of past Islamic societies with respect to women—are the centerpiece of the agenda of political Islamists. They are the centerpiece of the Islamist agenda at least in part because they were posed as central in the colonial discursive assault on Islam and Arab culture. I described in an earlier chapter how in the late nineteenth century the discourses of colonial domination coopted the language of feminism in attacking Muslim societies. Male imperialists known in their home societies for their intransigent opposition to feminism led the attack abroad against the "degradation" of women in Muslim societies and were the foremost champions of unveiling. The custom of veiling and the position of women in Muslim societies became, in their rhetoric, the proof of the inferiority of Islam and the justification of their efforts to undermine Muslim religion and society. This thesis and the societal goal of unveiling were, in addition, adopted and promoted (as I also described earlier) by the upper classes in Arab societies whose interests lay with the colonial powers; and they were opposed and the terms of the thesis inverted (and the importance of veiling and other indigenous practices insisted on) in the discourse of resistance.

The notion of returning to or holding on to an "original" Islam and an "authentic" indigenous culture is itself, then, a response to the discourses of colonialism and the colonial attempt to undermine Islam and Arab culture and replace them with Western practices and beliefs. But what is needed now is not a response to the colonial and postcolonial assault on non-Western cultures, which merely inverts the terms of the colonial thesis to affirm the opposite, but a move beyond confinement within those terms altogether and a rejection or incorporation of Western, non-Western, and indigenous inventions, ideas, and institutions on the basis of their merit, not their tribe of origin. After all and in sober truth, what thriving civilization or cultural heritage today, Western or non-Western, is not critically indebted to the inventions or traditions of thought of other peoples in other lands? And why should any human being be asked to do without some useful invention, political, technological, or of any kind, because it originated among some other tribe or, conversely, be compelled to practice a custom that has nothing to recommend it or even much against it for no better reason than that it is indigenous?

Rejection of things Western and rage at the Western world—an attitude that noticeably does not include the refusal of military equipment or technology—is understandable. Arabs have suffered and continue to suffer injustices and exploitation at the hands of colonial and postcolonial Western governments. But neither rage as a politics nor the self-deception and doublethink involved in relying on Western technologies—and indeed drawing on the intellectual and technical paraphernalia of the Western world in all aspects of contemporary life while claiming to be intent on returning to a culturally pure heritage—and in selectively choosing which aspects of the past will be preserved (for example, the laws controlling women) are persuasive as policies capable of leading the Arab world from entrapment in powerlessness and economic dependence.

Similarly, with respect to the more distant past and the proclaimed intention of restoring "original," "authentic" Islamic ways for women, the Islamist position is again problematic. It assumes, first, that the meaning of gender inhering in the initiatory Islamic society and in Muhammad's acts and sayings is essentially unambiguous and ascertainable in some precise and absolute sense and that the understanding of gender articulated in the written corpus of establishment Islam represents the only possible and uncontested understanding of the meaning of gender in Islam. The evidence reviewed in the preceding pages lends support to neither assumption, however. The meaning and social articulation of gender informing the first Islamic society in Arabia differed significantly from those informing the immediately succeeding Muslim societies, including most particularly those of the society that contributed centrally to the articulation of the founding institutional, legal, and scriptural discourses of dominant Islam—Abbasid Iraq. The meanings of gender specific to Abbasid society and the distinctive meaning that the notion "woman" acquired in that society (a society in which the traditions of a number of religions and cultures, including the Judaic, Christian, and Iranian, blended inextricably and were absorbed into Islamic thought) were inscribed into the literary, legal, and institutional productions of the age—productions that today constitute the founding and authoritative corpus of establishment Muslim thought. The androcentric and misogynist biases of this society affected in particular the different weight given to the two divergent tendencies within the Islamic message. As I argued earlier, even as Islam instituted, in the initiatory society, a hierarchical structure as the basis of relations between men and women, it also preached, in its ethical voice (and this is the case with Christianity and Judaism as well), the moral and spiritual equality of all human beings. Arguably, therefore, even as it instituted a sexual hierarchy, it laid the ground, in its ethical voice, for the subversion of the hierarchy. In the Abbasid context, the regulations instituting a sexual hierarchy were given central emphasis while the ethical message stressing the equality of all human beings and the importance of justice went largely unheeded and remained, with respect to women, essentially unarticulated in the laws and institutions that were now formulated.

Unheeded by the dominant classes and by the creators of establishment Islam, that ethical voice was, in contrast, emphasized by some often-marginal or lower-class groups who challenged the dominant political order and its interpretation of Islam, including its conception of the meaning of gender and the arrangements regarding women. From the start, the interpretation of the meaning of gender in the dominant society and other key issues, such as the proper political and social organization of Muslim societies, were contested. Establishment Islam's version of the Islamic message survived as the sole legitimate interpretation not because it was the only possible interpretation but because it was the interpretation of the politically dominant—those who had the power to outlaw and eradicate other readings as "heretical."

It is this technical, legalistic establishment version of Islam, a version that largely bypasses the ethical elements in the Islamic message, that continues to be politically powerful today. But for the lay Muslim it is not this legalistic voice but rather the ethical, egalitarian voice of Islam that speaks most clearly and insistently. It is because Muslim women hear this egalitarian voice that they often declare (generally to the astonishment of non-Muslims) that Islam is nonsexist. Only within the politically powerful version of Islam (and in its reflection in Western Orientalist literature)—a version with no greater claim to being regarded as the only possible interpretation of Islam than Papal Christianity has to being regarded as the only possible interpretation of Christianity—is women's position immutably fixed as subordinate. Just as with other monotheistic (and indeed non-monotheistic) religions, what the import of Islam was and what its significance for human societies might be are subjects that yielded varieties of interpretations in past societies and that again today are open to a range of interpretations, including feminist interpretations.[2]

Thus, the Islamist position with respect to the distant past is flawed in assuming that the meaning of gender informing the first Islamic society is reducible to a single, simple, unconnected meaning that is ascertainable in some precise and absolute sense, as well as in assuming that the legacy was open to only one interpretation on matters of gender and that the correct interpretation was the one captured and preserved in the corpus of Muslim thought and writing and constituting the heritage of establishment Islam, created decades and indeed centuries after Muhammad, in the societies of the Middle East. In making these assumptions Islamists overlook the complexity of a gender system diversely and comprehensively articulated in social mores, verbal prescriptions, and the interplay between these, on the one hand, and the critical role of interpretation, on the other. Underlying the above assumptions—and in particular the belief that the laws developed in Abbasid and other societies of early Islam merely preserved and precisely elaborated the pristine originary meaning of Islam—is the notion that ideas, systems of meaning, and conceptions of gender traveled to and were transmitted by other societies without being blurred or colored by the mores, culture, and gender systems of the societies through which they passed. In a similarly literalist approach, Islamists assume that identifying the rulings regarding gender current in the first Muslim society—rulings presumed to be ascertainable in some categorical fashion—and transposing and applying them to modern Muslim societies would result in the reconstitution of the meaning of gender inhering and articulated in that first society. Such an assumption fails to recognize that a society's rulings in matters of gender form part of a comprehensive and integral system, part of a society's variously articulated (socially, legally, psychically) discourse on gender, and thus that the transposition of a segment of the Arabian Muslim society's discourse (even if this were absolutely ascertainable) to the fundamentally different Muslim societies of the modern world is likely to result not in the reconstitution of the first Arabian Muslim understanding of gender but rather in its travesty.

The meaning of gender as elaborated by establishment Islam remained the controlling discourse in the Muslim Middle East until about the beginning of the nineteenth century. Unambiguously and on all levels—cultural, legal, social, and institutional—the social system it devised and informed was one that controlled and subordinated women, marginalized them economically, and, arguably, conceptualized them as human beings inferior to men. So negatively were women viewed within this system that even women of the spiritual stature of Rabi'a al-'Adawiyya still could be deemed inferior to the least spiritually developed man in the eyes of an establishment spokesman like the theologian al-Ghazali. Evidently, dissent from this dominant view existed and found formal expression in the thought of such groups as the Sufis and the Qarmatians and in the thought of a rare philosopher, like Ibn al-'Arabi. Evidently, too, informal resistance to the dominant culture was to be found within families and among individuals. That families economically in a position to contractually impose monogamy on their daughter's spouse or otherwise protect her interests in marriage sometimes did impose such terms is one indication of familial and personal resistance to the view of the dominant culture on the place and rights of women. Similarly, that some families educated their daughters despite the lack of any formal avenue for the education of women not merely to the point of literacy but to the point where they could become distinguished scholars and eminent women of learning is another kind of evidence of resistance among people to the prescriptions and dicta of the dominant view of women.

The unraveling of this system began to occur with European economic encroachment in about the early nineteenth century. From that point forward, the consonance that had thitherto pertained in the Muslim Middle East between the discourse on gender espoused by establishment Islam and the social and institutional articulation of that discourse began to be steadily eroded. That erosion, leading to the gradual foundering of the old order and institutions, continues into our own day.

Muslim women have no cause to regret the passing of the customs and formulas of earlier Muslim societies or the foundering of the old order and its controlling and excluding institutions. In the course of the last century or so women in a significant number of Arab countries have attained civil and political rights and virtually equal access to education, at least insofar as public policies are concerned; cultural prejudices, however (as in other parts of the world, Western and non-Western), and inadequate resources continue to hold back women's education in some areas. Again, in a significant number of Arab countries women have gained or are gaining entry into virtually all the professions, from teaching and nursing to medicine, law, and engineering. Developments in these matters have occurred at slightly different rates in different countries, but broadly speaking, most Middle Eastern nations have moved or are moving toward adopting the Western political language of human and political rights and toward according these rights to women as well as to men.

There are two kinds of exceptions to this tendency. One is an exception with regard to a geographic region. The societies in the Arabian Peninsula, the area in the Middle East least subject to European economic, cultural, or political domination and least open generally to other cultures and ideas, continue to resist the current of change. Moreover, in response to increasing exposure to global influences in recent decades, the societies in the region, particularly Saudi Arabia, have attempted to erect yet-more-impregnable cultural and ideological walls. Although the peninsular countries have opened up education to women, in most other ways the old strictures remain firmly in place, and modern ideas about rights such as the right to vote, constituting part of contemporary political thought, have made no inroads. (Kuwait, however, prior to its invasion by Iraq, was beginning to move toward important changes for women.)

The other exception to the trend toward amelioration and extension of rights to women in Middle Eastern countries other than those of the Arabian Peninsula is with respect to Islamic family law—the laws governing men's and women's rights in marriage, divorce, and child custody. These laws have remained profoundly resistant to change. Even though for a good part of this century liberals and feminists in many Muslim societies have persistently mounted attempts to introduce reforms, the laws developed in highly misogynist societies in the first three or four centuries of Islam continue to govern the relations between men and women. Only a few countries—Iraq, Syria, and Tunisia—have introduced modifications in their laws that improve on the laws of establishment Islam in varying degrees.

Family law is the cornerstone of the system of male privilege set up by establishment Islam. That it is still preserved almost intact signals the existence of enormously powerful forces within Middle Eastern societies determined to uphold male privilege and male control over women. Among political Islamist movements such forces are gaining ground. Where Islamist movements have led to the institution of "Islam" as the formal basis of political power—Iran, Pakistan under Zia ul-Huq—the governments have proceeded to transform the countries, as well as women's homes, into prison houses for women, where the confinement of women, their exclusion from many fields of work, and their unjust and inhumane treatment are the proclaimed laws of the land. In addition, the misogynist rhetoric they let loose into the social system implicitly sanctions male violence toward women and sets up women—rather than the corruptions and bankruptcies of the government—as targets of male frustration at poverty and powerlessness. Besides the costs to women themselves, limiting their access to remunerative work deprives their societies of the creativity and productivity that women throughout the world have proven themselves to be capable of.

Clearly, the Islam such governments set up bears no relation to an Islam reinterpreted to give precedence to the ethical voice of Islam. With respect at any rate to women, it is the technical, legalistic legacy of establishment Islam that political Islamism institutes once it gains power. There is one difference between these modern enforcers of technical Islam and their predecessors who developed the laws being reinstituted today. The encoders of the earlier Islamic period, hostage to societies in which misogyny and androcentrism were the uncontested and invisible norms, strove to the best of their abilities to render Islamic precepts into laws that expressed justice according to the available measures of their times. In contrast, their descendants, today reinstituting the laws devised in other ages and other societies, are choosing to eschew, when it comes to women, contemporary understandings of the meanings of justice and human rights, even as they adopt modern technologies and languages in every other domain of life.

Deferring justice to women until rights and prosperity have been won for all men, perpetuating and reinstituting systems immoral by contemporary standards in order to pander to male frustrations—these are sterile and destructive to no less an extent than the politics of rage and the disingenuous rhetoric of rejecting the West in favor of a return to indigenous culture while allowing the mental and technological appurtenances of the West to permeate society without barrier.

Just as the discourses within Arab societies are enmeshed in the discourses of the West and thoroughly implicated, in particular, in the history of colonialism and the discourses of domination that colonialism unleashed upon the Muslim Middle East, so too, is the study of Muslim Arab women as it is pursued today in the West so enmeshed and implicated. As I described in an earlier chapter, the discourse of patriarchal colonialism captured the language of feminism and used the issue of women's position in Islamic societies as the spearhead of the colonial attack on those societies. Imperialist men who were the enemies of feminism in their own societies, abroad espoused a rhetoric of feminism attacking the practices of Other men and their "degradation" of women, and they used the argument that the cultures of the colonized peoples degraded women in order to legitimize Western domination and justify colonial policies of actively trying to subvert the cultures and religions of the colonized peoples. That posture was perfectly exemplified by Lord Cromer. Famous in England for his opposition to feminism, in Egypt, where he was British consul general, Cromer was a principal advocate of the need to end Islamic degradation of women and a declared champion of the importance of unveiling. It was the practice of veiling and the Islamic degradation of women that stood in the way, according to the imperialist thesis, of the "progress" and "civilization" of Muslim societies and of their populaces being "persuaded or forced" into imbibing "the true spirit of Western civilization."

That thesis was accepted and promoted not only by chauvinist male servants of empire but generally by members of Western civilization and also by natives of the upper and upper-middle classes inducted into the ideas of Western culture. European feminists critical of the practices and beliefs of the men of their societies with respect to themselves acquiesced in and indeed promoted the European male's representations of Other men and the cultures of Other men and joined, in the name of feminism, in the attack on the veil and the practices generally of Muslim societies. Whether the attack on Muslim customs and societies, and especially on their practices, regarding women, was made by imperialist men who were supporters of male dominance, by missionaries, or by feminists and whether it was made in the name of "civilizing" the natives, or Christianizing them, or of rescuing women from the religion and culture in which they had the misfortune to find themselves, invoking the issue of women served to license, and to impart an aura of moral legitimacy to, denouncing and attacking the customs of the dominated society and insisting that it change its ways and adopt the superior ways of the Europeans.

It was in this discourse of colonial "feminism" that the notion that an intrinsic connection existed between the issues of culture and the status of women, and in particular that progress for women could be achieved only through abandoning the native culture, first made its appearance. The idea was the product of a particular historical moment and was constructed by the discourses of patriarchal colonialism in the service of particular political ends. As the history of Western women makes clear, there is no validity to the notion that progress for women can be achieved only by abandoning the ways of a native androcentric culture in favor of those of another culture. It was never argued, for instance, even by the most ardent nineteenth-century feminists, that European women could liberate themselves from the oppressiveness of Victorian dress (designed to compel the female figure to the ideal of frailty and helplessness by means of suffocating, rib-cracking stays, it must surely rank among the more constrictive fashions of relatively recent times) only by adopting the dress of some other culture. Nor has it ever been argued, whether in Mary Wollstonecraft's day, when European women had no rights, or in our own day and even by the most radical feminists, that because male domination and injustice to women have existed throughout the West's recorded history, the only recourse for Western women is to abandon Western culture and find themselves some other culture. The idea seems absurd, and yet this is routinely how the matter of improving the status of women is posed with respect to women in Arab and other non-Western societies. Whether those societies did or did not, will or will not, abandon the ways of one culture in favor of those of another is commonly presented in Western-based literature as the crux of the matter of progress for women. To this day, the struggle against the veil and toward westernization and the abandoning of backward and oppressive Arab Muslim ways (the agenda propounded by Cromer and his like as the agenda to be pursued for Muslim women) is still commonly the framestory within which Western-based studies of Arab women, including feminist studies, are presented.

The presumption underlying these ideas is that Western women may pursue feminist goals by engaging critically with and challenging and redefining their cultural heritage, but Muslim women can pursue such goals only by setting aside the ways of their culture for the nonandrocentric, nonmisogynist ways (such is the implication) of the West. And the presumption is, too, that Islamic cultures and religion are fundamentally inimical to women in a way that Western cultures and religions are not, whereas (as I have argued) Islam and Arabic cultures, no less than the religions and cultures of the West, are open to reinterpretation and change. Moreover, the different histories of feminism in the Western world and in the Middle East suggest that the significant factors in Western societies that permitted the emergence of feminist voices and political action in those societies somewhat before their emergence in the Middle East were not that Western cultures were necessarily less androcentric or less misogynist than other societies but that women in Western societies were able to draw on the political vocabularies and systems generated by ideas of democracy and the rights of the individual, vocabularies and political systems developed by white male middle classes to safeguard their interests and not intended to be applicable to women. That women in Western societies are the beneficiaries of the political languages and institutions of democracy and the rights of the individual is commonly assumed to be proof that Western cultures are less androcentric or misogynist than other cultures, but political vocabularies and political and civil rights are quite distinct from the cultural and psychological messages, and the structures of psychological control, permeating a society. The notion that non-Western women will improve their status by adopting the culture, ways of dress, and so on of the West is based on a confusion between these different spheres. Of course, Arab Muslim women need to reject, just as Western women are trying to reject, the androcentrism of whatever culture or tradition in which they find themselves, but that is quite different from saying they need to adopt Western customs, goals, and life-styles.

The study of Muslim women in the West is heir to this history and to these discourses and to the ideas and assumptions they purveyed: it is heir to colonialism, to colonialism's discourses of domination, and to its cooperation of the ideas of feminism to further Western imperialism. Research on Middle Eastern women thus occurs in a field already marked with the designs and biases written into it by colonialism. Consequently, awareness of this legacy, and of the political ends silently being served by the assumptions, the narratives, and the versions of history and culture with which the Western discourse on Arab women is already inscribed, needs itself to be the starting point of any such investigation. At least, such awareness is essential if we are to avoid complicity in the reinscription of the Western discourse of domination and if the study of women and the ideas of feminism are to be prevented from functioning yet again as a tool serving the political ends of Western domination. Of course we must also be wary of reinscribing the contentions of the Arabic narrative of resistance, which entails the wholesale affirmation of indigenous culture and with it the acceptability of injustice to women because indigenous. But few investigators working in the West are in danger of this latter possibility. The discourse of Islamic resistance, although a discourse of power within the Middle East, commands little authority here: a point that underscores the fact that discourses of power nest one within the other, the dominant discourse in the Middle East nesting within—indeed a dependent discourse of—the globally dominant discourse of the West.

The success of Western feminism, or at any rate its success in gaining legitimacy in the academy (what practical gains it has made particularly for women of the more economically deprived classes and for women of color is a more problematic matter), has meant that scholarship on women that is produced within a Western framework is itself now to some extent a discourse of authority in relation to other societies.[3] It would be a pity if this very success should lead, as Western-based feminists direct their gaze toward other women, to the elaboration of a literature rearticulating the old formulas in new guise and reinscribing the old story of the inferiority of Arabs and Muslims, supported now with the apparatus of scholarship. It would be a pity if instead of striving to disengage itself from such designs, feminism should fall once more to inadvertently serving the political ends of the Western political order and of Western-style male dominance. At the very least, perpetuating this approach would lead to the alienation of a younger generation of Arab women and men from feminism. The designs and manipulations of Western discourses, and the political ends being served by the deployment of feminism against other cultures, are today no longer hidden and invisible: on the contrary, to many non-Western people they are transparently obvious.

There can be few people of Arab or Muslim background (including, and perhaps even particularly, the feminists among them) who have not noticed and been disheartened by the way in which Arab and Muslim "oppression" of women is invoked in Western media and sometimes in scholarship in order to justify and even insidiously promote hostility toward Arabs and Muslims. It is disheartening, too, that some feminist scholarly work continues to uncritically reinscribe the old story. Whole books are unfortunately still being published in which the history of Arab women is told within the framework of the paradigm that Cromer put forward—that the measure of whether Muslim women were liberated or not lay in whether they veiled and whether the particular society had become "progressive" and westernized or insisted on clinging to Arab and Islamic ways. In its contemporary version this essentially still-colonial (or colonial and classist) feminism is only slightly more subtle than the old version. It may be cast, for example, in the form of praising heroic Arab feminist women for resisting the appalling oppressions of Arab culture and Islam. Whereas this is its stated message, the unstated message when the inherited constructs of Western discourse are reproduced unexamined is often, just as in colonial days, that Arab men, Arab culture, and Islam are incurably backward and that Arab and Islamic societies indeed deserve to be dominated, undermined, or worse.

In the context of the contemporary structure of global power, then, we need a feminism that is vigilantly self-critical and aware of its historical and political situatedness if we are to avoid becoming unwitting collaborators in racist ideologies whose costs to humanity have been no less brutal than those of sexism. It may be, moreover, that in the context of Western global domination, the posture of some kinds of feminism—poised to identify, deplore, and denounce oppression—must unavoidably lend support to Western domination when it looks steadfastly past the injustice to which women are subject in Western societies and the exploitation of women perpetrated abroad by Western capitalism only to fix upon the oppressions of women perpetrated by Other men in Other societies.

In its analyses of Western societies, feminism, or rather the many feminisms that there now are, has moved far beyond the somewhat simplistic approach of deploring and denouncing. Feminist analysis of Western societies now comprehends a variety of subtle and complicated analytical perspectives and positions. Among the most illuminating is the critique of the way in which feminism is implicated in the dominant political languages of Western societies and its inadvertent complicity in the ideologies and social systems that it explicitly criticizes; also illuminating is the critical analysis of the erosions and costs for women wrought by advanced capitalism. Elizabeth Fox-Genovese, for instance, writing of U.S. society, observes that the history of the twentieth century "confirms that sexism, instead of receding with the triumph of modernity, has probably become more general and more difficult, to locate in any single institution. If the so-called sexual revolution has loosened the grip of the nuclear family on female sexuality, it has not indisputably weakened sexism or acceptance of conventional gender roles." Late capitalist society, she notes, "has contributed a bitter twist to the centuries of female oppression. Consumerism, suburban residence patterns, declining family size, increased male occupational mobility, increased female education, declining parental control over children … rising divorce rates, and a host of other changes have been interwoven in a dense network of isolation and anxiety." Fox-Genovese fears that feminism itself, in its uncritical adoption of the ideals of individualism, may come one day to be seen as having "done the dirty work of capitalism—of having eroded the older communities and bourgeois institutions that blocked the way to a sinister new despotism."[4]

Research on Arab women is a much younger field. Analysis of this complexity is rare in work on Arab women, in which it is often assumed that modernity and "progress" and westernization are incontestably good and that the values of individualism are always unambiguously beneficial. The sum of what is currently known about women and gender in Arab societies—the many and different Arab societies and cultures that there are—is minuscule. The areas of women's lives and the informal structures they inhabit that are still unexplored are vast. And perhaps the posture of studying other cultures in order to identify their worst practices is not after all likely to be the best way to further our understanding of human societies. The noted Indian anthropologist T. N. Madan, reflecting on the ambiguous legacy of anthropology and the contribution the discipline might nevertheless make to a common human enterprise, rather than serving Western interests, suggests that a productive starting point could be looking to other cultures in an attitude of respect and in acknowledgment of their affording opportunities for critiquing and enhancing awareness of the investigator's culture. The study of anthropology "should not merely tell us how others live their lives: it should rather tell us how we may live our lives better," and ideally it should be grounded in the affirmation "that every culture needs others as critics so that the best in it may be highlighted and held out as being cross-culturally desirable."[5] Perhaps feminism could formulate some such set of criteria for exploring issues of women in other cultures, including Islamic societies—criteria that would undercut even inadvertent complicity in serving Western interests but that, at the same time, would neither set limits on the freedom to question and explore nor in any way compromise feminism's passionate commitment to the realization of societies that enable women to pursue without impediment the full development of their capacities and to contribute to their societies in all domains.

QUESTIONS FOR REVIEW AND DISCUSSION

1. What is Ahmed's point about the pervasive influence of Western cultural colonialism, even within the discourse of Islamism that seeks to return to a pure, indigenous state? Do you agree with her appraisal?

2. Explain Ahmed's observation that certain critiques of Muslim practice (such as the "degradation" of women) espoused by Westerners and the acceptance or resistance of these critiques still represent an effect of colonialism. Can you think of other examples of such colonial legacies?

3. How, according to Ahmed, is the Abbasid period in Islamic history responsible for shaping the dominant ongoing interpretations in Islam of the meaning of gender and its relationship to women?

4. What are Ahmed's critiques of the notion by certain Islamist groups that a return to the values and attitudes (regarding gender, for instance) of early Muslim societies (i.e., "establishment Islam") is desirable?

5. What are some of the examples offered by Ahmed of groups that resisted the dominant discourse of "establishment Islam's" views about the status of women? What does Ahmed see as the difference between the misogyny of the earlier Islamic legalists and those of today?

6. How, according to Ahmed, do attitudes to the veil reveal the relationship between "colonial feminism" and the anti-westernism reactions it provokes? Can you think of other instances of such processes?

7. How is the critique of Islamic misogynism conflated with the call to reject one's culture and embrace Western cultural customs and life-styles? What problems does Ahmed see in this? What does she note as problematic about the return to indigenous culture?

8. What are some of the cautionary remarks offered by Ahmed on the trajectory of modern feminism? Do you agree? What are some orientations to feminist analysis of other cultures prescribed by Ahmed?

9. Is Ahmed's work within the purview of the discipline of religious studies, or does it fall outside the discipline's preferential parameters? Is it sound scholarship? Is it objective? Neutral? Agenda driven? What is its theoretical orientation? What is its methodology? Apply these questions to other articles in this anthology.

10. If one were to apply the categories offered by Rita Gross in her article in this volume, would Ahmed's piece fall under "women's studies of religion," or "feminism"?

Notes

1 Ashis Nandy, *Intimate Enemy: Loss and Recovery of Self under Colonialism* (Delhi: Oxford University Press, 1983), xi.

2 I just referred to Orientalism's reproducing—and thereby also endorsing, even if inadvertently, in its own account of Islam—dominant Islam's view of itself as the sole possible and only legitimate version of Islam. Orientalism is most familiar as the West's mode of representing, and misrepresenting, the Islamic world as a domain of otherness and inferiority; it is also familiar as a field of domination. But it should be noted that the discourses of Orientalism and those of establishment Islam are androcentric discourses of domination and that consequently in some ways they complement or endorse each other, even as in other ways they are at war.

3 For critiques of the politics of Western or white feminism and women of the non-Western world and women of color see Gayatri Chakrovorty Spivak, *In Other Worlds: Essays in Cultural Politics* (New York: Methuen, 1987); and bell hooks, *Feminist Theory: From Margin to Center* (Boston: South End Press, 1984).

4 Elizabeth Fox-Genovese, *Feminism without Illusions: A Critique of Individualism* (Chapel Hill: University of North Carolina Press, 1991), 137–38, 14, 31.

5 T. N. Madan, "Anthropology as Cultural Reaffirmation" (The first of three papers delivered as the William Allan Neilson Lectures at Smith College, Northampton, Mass., October 1990), 5–6.

37 Defining Feminism, Religion, and the Study of Religion

Rita Gross

Rita M. Gross (1943?—) was born in Rhinelander, Wisconsin, and received her doctorate from the University of Chicago. She taught at the University of Wisconsin Eau Claire. Initially her research was focused on Judaism, but she eventually developed a deep interest in Vajrayana Buddhism. She has been well-known for her work on feminism in the study of religion since the publication of *Buddhism After Patriarchy* (1993), a book which examines women's historical roles in Buddhism. She also imaginatively reconstructs how the Buddhist tradition might appear if the sexist attitudes that are socially and historically widespread in it and other world religions were to end and the egalitarian attitudes to women that it espouses were to flourish. In the following selection, taken from *Feminism and Religion: An Introduction* (1996), Gross offers many general guidelines for a holistic approach to religious studies, which overcomes the shortcomings of preceding scholarship in the discipline that had marginalized women.

Religion was the last of the controversial, passion-inspiring human pursuits—such as politics, economics, and ethics—to be accorded its own academic discipline in the neutral setting of research, debate, and free thinking that characterizes the university. As an undergraduate, I could not major in religious studies because the state university system in which I was educated did not believe it was possible for a public institution to teach religion without violating the separation of church and state. Eight years later, I returned to that same system to teach religious studies to undergraduates. What had changed in education philosophy in the intervening years?

The single greatest change that enabled religious studies to emerge as an academic discipline was the recognition that one could *understand* a religious position without *adhering* to it. I believe that this recognition was made possible by the study of non-Western religions; more removed from sectarian battles within culturally familiar religious settings, scholars realized that they could understand and appreciate, with great empathy, a point of view that they did not share. Therefore, such understanding could also be taught to others, without the rancor, dogmatism, competitiveness, hostility, and suasion that typically characterize sectarian religious education. Knowing about and understanding a religion is quite different from believing in it. The academic study of religion depends on that distinction.

Another major factor in the development of religious studies was the recognition that since religion has been a major mover and motivator in human culture from time immemorial to the present, it is impossible to understand human history and culture while ignoring religion. Only an extremely artificial division of human life and culture could tolerate the teaching of history, art, or social custom without understanding their connection with religion. Those trained in these disciplines are not fully prepared to explicate the religious beliefs that inform their subject matter; scholars formally trained in religious studies could contribute greatly to the overall environment of inquiry and learning that characterize a university.

Finally, the new imperative to understand divergent cultures, worldviews, and value systems in our complex world has brought religious studies to the fore. Except for anthropology, no academic discipline is so thoroughly imbued with the mandate to study its matter cross-culturally as is religious studies. In fact this characteristic of religious studies was essential to its development; to justify themselves as practitioners of a genuine academic discipline rather than a sectarian recruiting exercise, professors of religious studies encouraged a cross-cultural, comparative dimension in the field from the beginning. "To know one religion is to know none" paraphrases a famous and widely circulated statement made by Max Müller (1823–1900),[1] often credited as the founder of comparative studies in religion.

What is the academic study of religion? At the most basic level it is a descriptive discipline that gathers and disseminates accurate information about the variety of religious beliefs and practices people have entertained and engaged in throughout time and space. The academic study of religion, I often say on the first day of class, takes controversial material about which people care deeply and places it in the neutral setting of the academic classroom, so that we can examine it and learn about it. Personal agreement or disagreement with the symbols, rituals, and beliefs about which we are learning is largely irrelevant at this stage. Scholars may debate alternative hypotheses about the information being studied, but debating the truth or falsity of the religious ideas is irrelevant to the academic study of religion as a descriptive discipline. If one truly understands what the academic study of religion is about, it will not be problematic or stressful to learn that Hinduism and Christianity have very different ideas about deity, and to learn both sets of ideas. And it will not be too tempting to argue that the Christian, Hindu, or some other view of deity is "correct." ...

Though professionals in the study of religion do not agree on a single definition of religion, it is clear that a nonethnocentric definition of religion would not focus on the *content* of belief systems. There are no universally held religious beliefs of symbols. But the various beliefs and symbols found in the world's religions do share a similar *function* in human life. Religious beliefs and behaviors typically answer people's questions regarding matters of significant, overriding importance to them. Thus, many widely used definitions of religion in the academic study of religion talk of religion as one's "ultimate concern" or what one regards as sacred. Central to any particular religion is its worldview, the basic, often unconscious presuppositions its followers hold about the nature of reality.

By this definition any belief that functions as the most significant arbiter for decisions and actions and any behaviors whose value is unlimited to the actor are religious beliefs and behaviors, whatever their content. This definition is both broad enough to avoid ethnocentrism and specific enough to distinguish religious phenomena from nonreligious phenomena. Things of limited importance or significance are not religious. This definition also allows one to study the "religious" dimensions of phenomena not usually classified as religion, such as political allegiance and deeply held psychological orientations. This working definition of religion is especially helpful when considering the impact of feminism on religious studies.

Religion and Religious Studies

When discussing controversial subjects about which people already have strong opinions, employing empathy is the only pedagogically appropriate method. Without empathy, we cannot attain the accuracy that is so central to academic teaching and learning.

How does empathy work in the academic study of religions? I define empathy as a two-step process. First, it involves temporarily dropping, or "bracketing," one's own worldview, values, and preconceptions as much as possible while engaged in study. The subject matter should be approached with an open mind, which includes the possibility of leaving the learning situation changed by new knowledge. Second, empathy involves imaginatively entering into the milieu of the phenomenon being studied. One cannot *become* an insider, contrary to the expectations of some who want to appropriate completely the perceptions and views of the insider. But one can and should understand and appreciate why insiders feel compelled by their views and behaviors. Scholars of religion try to speak as if they participate in the point of view under discussion, though they well may not. For example, one of my all-time favorite teaching evaluations, meant as a criticism but taken as a compliment, read, "The problem with her is that she teaches all those religions as if they were true!"

To continue the example introduced earlier, the academic study of religion may seek to impart accurate information about Christian and Hindu concepts of deity, which are quite different from each other. Those involved in the learning enterprise should be able to explain and *understand* why a Hindu finds a plurality of divine images cogent with the same facility that they can explain and understand why a Christian finds monotheism compelling. Without such empathy, one can be neither accurate nor informed about religion, nor can one acquire what limited objectivity is possible in the study of religion. More dangerous, without such empathy, the acquisition of information may increase ethnocentrism, intolerance, and chauvinism. Someone who learns that Hinduism encourages multiple images of the divine and that such images are often venerated in their painted or sculpted forms, without learning to understand why such concepts and practices make sense to the Hindu, has not been helped by the academic study of religion. She may, in fact, be more dangerously ill informed than before, precisely because she has more facts at her disposal, but does not understand them accurately and empathically.

Thus, as empathic scholars, we come to the issue of the relationship between religious studies as a discipline and the personal practice of religion, an issue which should be faced head-on rather than skirted. Although religious studies is not instruction about what one should believe religiously, learning information about religious views and behaviors other than one's own can still be unnerving. Truly understanding religious data requires empathy, but empathy often changes the way we think about the world and our place in it. This is not to say that our religious affiliation will change when we study religion academically and empathically, but our *attitudes* about religion may well change. Some attitudes we had previously rejected may become more appealing, whereas others that had seemed obviously correct may become less tenable. Such changes are especially likely when studying feminism and religion together. To expect or advocate otherwise is to promote academic learning in the worst sense of the term *academic*: a collection of irrelevant information that does not affect its bearer in any way.

If the practice of empathy is so important to the academic study of religion, does that mean that one can never evaluate the religious beliefs and behaviors being studied? This question is quite important in the study of feminism and religion, since most feminists criticize religious patriarchy. The practice of empathy does not mean that one must agree with or approve of the point of view being studied; although empathy involves appreciatively entering into the spirit of that which is being studied, one could not agree with all the positions one understands empathically because many are mutually exclusive.

Some kinds of evaluations are not incompatible with empathic understanding, if a few basic ground rules are observed. First, an empathic understanding of the religion must *precede* evaluation. Before formulating suggestions or critiques, it is important to have some idea of the justifications for current beliefs and behaviors put forth by those who adhere to them. Otherwise the evaluation is likely to be extremely ethnocentric, a problem to which feminism is not immune. Second, the same evaluative standards must be applied to all traditions, whether familiar or foreign, whether one's own or that of another.

Most scholars of religious studies talk more about the importance of neutrality and objectivity than they do about empathy, and indeed certain commonsense meanings of neutrality and objectivity are appropriate for the academic study of religion. The academy is not the place for proselytizing for any specific religion or religious position. Full and fair presentation of the strengths and weaknesses of all positions studied can and should be expected. However, although students and teachers should exhibit neutrality concerning interreligious competition and rivalry, a completely value-free position is impossible. Being objective and neutral when discussing controversial issues does not mean being value-free. On closer inspection, "objectivity" often turns out to be nothing more than advocacy of the current conventions and not a neutral position at all. Some perceive feminist scholarship as adversarial because it challenges such conventions; still, feminist scholarship can claim to be more "objective" than male-centered scholarship, because it is more inclusive and therefore more accurate.

Looking more deeply into neutrality and objectivity as they pertain to the academic study of religion helps to fully clarify the relationship between religious studies and religion. Students of religion sometimes expect or even hope that academic neutrality means that what they learn about the variety of religious phenomena will not affect their beliefs in any way. But simply because the academic study of religion is neutral vis-à-vis competing religions' claims does not mean that it is value-free. The study of religion can never be value-free because the very existence of the discipline depends on this value: the development of a worldview that cherishes a neutral position vis-à-vis the various religions as well as an ability to see the internal coherence and logic that empowers each of them. This value is emphatically rejected by at least some segments of all major religions.

In other words, living with religious diversity and regarding it as an interesting resource, rather than an undesirable deviation from truth, are the values that dominate the academic study of religion. Information about unfamiliar perspectives on religion is meant to challenge monolithic or universalistic presuppositions about the world. One *should* feel that sexist, racist, ethnocentric, and religious chauvinisms, if present, are being threatened by the academic study of religion. Even neutral and objective information, if absorbed rather than merely memorized, can change the one who assimilates that information. It is rarely possible to conclude one's studies carrying the same opinions regarding religious, ethnic, class, gender, and cultural diversity with which one began.

The academic study of religion is radically deabsolutizing because accurate information about and empathy for the other is radically deabsolutizing. Once one really understands the point of view of "the other" or the foreign, claims that one's belief is the only truth are no longer as attractive or compelling. This is the most significant point of contact between the academic study of religion and the way in which religion is sometimes practiced as a personal faith perspective. If religion necessarily involves war among absolute truth claims, its subject matter would be too disruptive and counterproductive to the rational and dispassionate discourse favored in the academy. But the empathic understanding required in the academic of religion encourages one to separate the absolutism some religions claim for themselves from information about their beliefs and practices, resulting in deabsolutized understanding of all religions and deabsolutized appreciation of religious pluralism and diversity.

For some, the appreciation of religious diversity is difficult because it contradicts religious instruction they have received. It may be helpful for people experiencing this difficulty to realize that it is quite possible to appreciate one's own perspective without believing that all people everywhere should adopt it. Such appreciation is a *different*, not a *lesser*, valuing of one's own particularity. This distinction is often difficult to appreciate at first, but I believe that no other alternative is possible in the global village in which we live. No lesson learned from the academic study of religion could be more valuable.

Like neutrality, objectivity in the study of religion is more complex than it appears. Because religion is so controversial and engenders such passion, calls for objectivity—approaching the subject without a point of view—are frequent. But all scholars speak and write from a particular point of view whether or not they claim objectivity for themselves. Once scholars agree upon methodological rules that determine what data are relevant and what techniques of interpretation are standard, scholarship can, in fact, be relatively "objective" within the limits of that system. For example, male-centered scholarship agreed upon the rule that data about women did not need to be included. Scholars abiding by that rule can do "objective" scholarship that is not gender inclusive. But when other scholars challenge that rule by demonstrating that one should also include data about women, it becomes clear that male-centered scholarship was objective only in a limited sense.

Because academic fashions can become relatively entrenched and long lasting, methodologically less reflective scholars sometimes think that their work is genuinely objective. Nevertheless, their work does not transcend the worldview and the methodology within which they record and interpret. It is not objective in the sense of having no perspective or reflecting no interests and values. Claims of objectivity from a scholar who is relatively unaware of his biases and perspectives do not obviate or negate his actual standpoint.

This issue is especially important for feminist studies in religion, since feminist scholarship is often thought to be "biased" because it self-consciously and deliberately includes information about women, whereas conventional androcentric scholarship is not similarly regarded as biased because it includes more information about men. For example, some believe courses on women and religion or gender-balanced mainstream courses on religion to be biased because they present more information about women than other courses do. But these kinds of claims only mask a desire to hear familiar perspectives and emphases, a wish that assumptions that have been taken for granted should not be challenged. This mistaken perception of bias is intensified because feminist scholars usually make their methodological values explicit, whereas conventional androcentric scholars usually do not, thereby fostering the illusion that they are without any specific agenda. But first-generation feminist scholars such as myself, who were reared to regard the generic masculine as genuinely generic and inclusive but could not find ourselves and our sisters in the data we studied, will never again be naïve enough to think scholarship can be value-free.

Instead, scholars need to practice intense methodological self-awareness and introspection, combined with honest self-disclosure. Once one recognizes one's own standpoint, one can then argue on its behalf, making the case openly that this specific standpoint is more adequate than the alternatives. For example, when teaching my course on world religions, I always explain that I teach from a perspective that values diversity because only that approach promotes harmony and well-being in the global village. I also explain that the course will be gender balanced, which, to those used to androcentrism, may give the false impression that the course focuses on women. Likewise, in my course on feminist theology, I explain that, by definition, this course is quite critical of conventional religious points of view. Furthermore, in a course on feminist theology, neutrality involves presenting the various options within feminist theology but does not include antifeminist arguments or conventional theology in addition.

I also state openly that in my *viewpoint*, scholarship that values pluralism and diversity is more moral and humane than scholarship that longs for universal agreement and unity, and that in my viewpoint, gender-balanced and gender-inclusive scholarship is far more objective than androcentric scholarship, simply because it is more complete. Having stated the values that guide my scholarship and teaching, I have achieved the level of objectivity that is possible. Everyone, including me, knows *why* I include the data that I include and why I prefer the interpretations that I prefer. I can argue cogently for those preferences. Other scholars may offer other points of view, but not greater objectivity.

Feminism as Academic Method and as Social Vision

Learning feminist perspectives is more likely to change one's personal point of view than the academic study of religion. But popular perceptions of feminism, many of which are negative, have little to do with feminism as it intersects with the academic study of religion. Because such different impressions of feminism are found in our culture, it is important to clarify what is meant by feminism in this book.

The most basic definition of *feminism* is the conviction that women really do inhabit the human realm and are not "other," not a separate species. Sometimes I wear a T-shirt that proclaims: "Feminism is the radical proposition that women are human beings." This proclamation seems so simple and obvious, but its implications are profound and radical because neither conventional scholarship nor lifestyles really take the humanity of women seriously. Fully internalizing that statement involves a subtle and profound change of consciousness for both men and women. Living it out definitely involves a change in lifestyle for most people.

This definition of *feminism* has implications for both the academic study of religion and for the personal practice of religion because feminism can be understood as both an academic method and as a social vision. Although these two forms of feminism are interdependent because both grow out of the paradigm shift that occurs with the realization that women are human beings, they are more easily understood if they are initially separated. I prefer to call feminism as academic method *women studies*, to highlight the fact that it has no political implications, or agenda (even though it arose out of one) and to differentiate women studies from *feminism*, by which I mean a critical and reconstructive stance vis-à-vis the institutions and values of one's own culture, religion, and academic environments.

Women Studies: Feminism as Academic Method

One can use feminism as an academic method without embracing feminism as a social vision. Scholars who are reluctant to change their lifestyle to transcend gender roles and stereotypes and otherwise accommodate the full humanity of women nevertheless should recognize the need to study women as thoroughly, as critically, and as empathically as men. To do less is to fail to understand the human. Women studies has irrevocably changed our information-gathering habits, so that we can never again be content to know only what men did or thought, or to have a reading list that includes only male authors (unless men are the subject of the study). Every course in the religious studies curriculum would change if those who taught it and took it understood that women are human beings whose lives are not adequately covered and included by the "generic masculine."

The first challenge of women studies is to expose and critique the androcentrism that underlies most traditional scholarship. I will offer a simple example of this androcentrism in lieu of a definition. I have often heard or read the equivalent of the following statement: "The Egyptians allow (or don't allow) women to. … " The structure is so commonplace that even today many do not see what is wrong with it. But for both those who make such statements and for those who hear them without wincing, real Egyptians are men. Egyptian women are objects acted upon by real Egyptians, but are not themselves full Egyptians. What, in more analytical terms, is behind this long-standing habitual pattern of speech? The androcentric model of humanity has three central characteristics that, when stated bluntly, suffice to demonstrate both the nature and the inadequacy of androcentrism.

First, the male norm and the human norm are collapsed and seen as identical. … Thus in androcentric thinking, any awareness of a distinction between maleness and humanity is clouded over, and femaleness is viewed as an exception to the norm.

The second characteristic of androcentrism follows directly from the first. When I first questioned the completeness of androcentric accounts of religion, my mentors told me that the generic masculine includes the feminine, making it unnecessary to study women specifically. This is a logical implication of collapsing maleness with humanity, but the result is that research about religion actually deals mainly with the lives and thinking of males, whereas women's religious lives are treated much more peripherally as a footnote or a short chapter toward the end of the book. The habit of thinking and doing research in the genetic masculine is so ingrained that many scholars are genuinely unaware that the religious lives and thoughts of men are only part of a religious situation.

The third and most problematic aspect of androcentrism is its attempt to deal with the fact that, since men and women are taught to be different in all cultures, the generic masculine simply does not cover the feminine. The generic masculine would work only in religions or cultures that had no sex roles, but no such culture exists. Therefore, women must sometimes be mentioned in accounts of religion. At this point, adherents of the androcentric model of humanity reach a logical impasse. Their solution to this impasse is the most devastating component of the androcentric outlook. Because women inevitably deviate from male norms, androcentric thinking deals with them only as objects exterior to "mankind," needing to be explained and fitted in somewhere, having the same epistemological and ontological status as trees, unicorns, deities, and other objects that must be discussed to make experience intelligible. Therefore, in most accounts of religion, although males are presented as religious subjects and as namers of reality, females are presented only in relation to the males being studied, only as objects being named by the males being studied, only as they appear to the males being studied.

Nothing less than a paradigm shift in our model of humanity will remedy these problems. Instead of the current androcentric, "one-sexed" model of humanity, we need an androgynous, "two-sexed" or bisexual model of humanity. A more accurate model of humanity would compel recognition that humans come in two sexes and that both sexes are human. It would also recognize that in virtually every religion, culture, or society, gender roles and stereotypes intensify biological sexual differences. As a result, men's and women's lives are more separate and different from each other's than is biologically dictated. An accurate model of humanity would also forbid placing one gender in the center and the other on the periphery. Androgyny as a two-sex model of humanity, as the conviction that despite gender and sexual differences, women and men are equally human, meets those requirements; both traditional androcentrism, which objecti[fies] women, and a sex-neutral model of humanity, which ignores the reality of culture-based gender roles, do not. …

When this model of humanity and these methodological guidelines are applied to virtually any subject in the humanities or social sciences, massive changes in scholarship result, affecting what one studies, how one studies it, what conclusions one draws from research data, the analyses one finds cogent, and the overarching theories that one accepts as good basic tools with which to understand the world. Furthermore, internalizing this model of humanity often results in a transformation of consciousness so profound that one's everyday habits of language and perception change as well. Once one makes the change from an androcentric to an androgynous model of humanity, other models seem completely inadequate.

It is important to recognize that feminist scholarship does not inherently make judgments about what women's position in society should be. It only entails a requirement to study women thoroughly and completely. To construct a feminist vision of society is a different task. Therefore, feminism, at least in the academic context, is first and foremost an academic method, not a socio-political perspective. The key issue is including information about women in all studies about any human phenomenon. The scholar's personal views are irrelevant to whether he has an academic obligation to teach a gender-balanced course: Even nonfeminists must include information about women in their scholarship if they want to claim that their scholarship is accurate.

Feminism as Social Vision

My claim that feminism is, *first*, an academic method is controversial because the emergence of the feminist method was inextricably linked with a movement of social protest and dissatisfaction. Indeed, the methodological demand to gather and include information about women could not have emerged and flourished apart from feminism as an alternative social vision, for it was protest against women's limited options in American society that first impelled feminist scholars to notice and name androcentricism and to create women studies methodology.

Feminism as social vision deals with views about ideal social arrangements and interactions between women and men. Therefore, almost by definition, all feminist perspectives are radically critical of current conventional norms and expectations and advocate some degree of change in social, academic, political, religious, and economic institutions to foster greater equity between men and women. Just as feminist scholarship finds androcentrism to be the basic problem with previous scholarship, so feminist social philosophy has focused on patriarchy as the fundamental obstacle to human well-being for women, as well as for men, to a lesser extent. Just as androcentrism regards men as normal and women as exceptions to the norm, so patriarchy regards men as rightful leaders and holders of all positions that society values, whereas women should be subservient and help men maintain their status. As such, the word *patriarchy* has become feminist shorthand for the anti-vision of female subservience and irrelevance that fueled much of society and religion for the past several thousand years and led to the mind-set in which the androcentric model of humanity not only found acceptance, but reigned without conceptual alternatives.

For more than twenty years, feminists have discussed the creation, outlines, and inadequacies of patriarchy and have formulated visions of a postpatriarchal world. Because women in a number of religious traditions are feminist and use feminist ideals to critique and reenvision their traditions, feminism as a social vision, although different from women studies, does in fact intersect with the academic study of religion. Feminists' use of feminism as a social vision in their reflections on their religions has become data for the academic study of religion. Therefore, the ways in which feminism as a social philosophy has affected, criticized, and changed the world's religions must be included in academic study of contemporary religion.

Feminism as social vision relies upon the results of feminist scholarship in history, sociology, and psychology, as well as religion. The most important conclusion of feminist scholarship is that patriarchy is the cultural creation of a certain epoch in human history, not an inevitable necessity of human biology.[2] The importance of this claim is that whatever is created within time is subject to decay and dissolution—a point commonplace in Buddhism among other major religions. This realization overcomes the advice given to generations of rebellious daughters: "You can't do anything about *that*." One *can* do something about patriarchy, though the task is immense.

...

What about patriarchy makes it such an offensive system to its critics? The literal meaning of patriarchy—"rule by fathers"—provides two clues. First, patriarchy is a system, in which ruler-ship, "power over," is quite central; second, by definition, men have power over women. The extent of men's power over women was the first element of the complex to be thoroughly recognized and described. Men monopolize or dominate all the roles and pursuits that society most values and rewards, such as religious leadership or economic power. Therefore, inequality became one of the first patriarchal demons to be named. Furthermore, men literally ruled over women, setting the rules and limits by which and within which they were expected to operate. Women who did not conform, and many who did, could be subjected to another form of male dominance—physical violence.

...

My claim that the problem of patriarchy is the very existence of gender roles and that postpatriarchy is freedom from gender roles is both radical and controversial. Some may well feel that a world without gender roles is even more unlikely to develop than a world without relationships of domination and submission. Some may think that feminists' goal should be finding and institutionalizing more equitable and just gender roles, rather than abolishing them. It is clear, however, that virtually every feminist critique of patriarchy and every feminist agenda for the future really derives from an unstated assumption that sex is not a relevant criterion for awarding roles or value. Furthermore, any set of gender roles whatsoever will be a prison for those who do not readily fit them. Because the prison of gender roles has been one of the greatest sources of suffering in my life, I am reluctant to make any place for them in a visionary postpatriarchal future.

...

Conclusion

It is important to note what links these two arenas of feminist thought. Feminism as scholarly method is critical of the androcentric mind-set. Feminism as social vision is critical of patriarchal culture. Androcentrism and patriarchy share the same attitude toward women. In both cases, women are objectified as nonhuman, are spoken about as if they were objects but not subjects, and are manipulated by others. In both cases, the end result is silence about women and the silencing of women. Androcentric scholarship proceeds as if women do not exist, or as if they are objects rather than subjects. Patriarchal culture discourages women from naming reality, and patriarchal scholarship then ignores the naming of reality that women create nevertheless. But women studies scholarship takes seriously women's naming of reality, even in patriarchal contexts, and feminism as social philosophy encourages women's authentic, empowered naming of reality and demands that these namings be taken seriously by the whole society.

QUESTIONS FOR REVIEW AND DISCUSSION

1. What, according to Gross, are some of the factors that led to the rise of the discipline of religious studies within an academic setting? What does Gross propose as a working definition of religion? Is this adequate for the purposes of her essay?

2. What reasons does Gross provide for encouraging the use of empathy in the study of religion? Do you agree? What does Gross mean by empathy? Is it the same as agreement? How is it different from neutrality and objectivity?

3. What does Gross perceive as a potential pitfall of neutrality? Is neutrality value-free? According to Gross, what sorts of values are embedded in the religious studies approach? Is this problematic? What does Gross mean by the "deabsolutizing" quality of academic study of religion?

4. What are some of the limitations of objective scholarship, according to Gross? From Gross's perspective, in what way does feminist scholarship appear to be "biased," despite similar biases embedded in non-feminist (i.e., androcentric) scholarship? Do you agree?

5. What is Gross's definition of feminism? Is it adequate for the purposes of her essay? In what ways does it (as women's studies) function as an academic method? How is it (as feminism) a social vision? How does Gross perceive the first function as different from the second? Do you agree?

6. What are some of the characteristics of androcentrism in religious studies, according to Gross? How do both traditional androcentrism and a sex-neutral model of humanity tend to marginalize women?

7. What is the relationship between the women's studies academic approach and the feminist social vision? In what ways might they affect each other?

Notes

1 William E. Paden, *Religious Worlds: The Comparative Study of Religion* (Boston: Beacon Press, 1988), p. 38.
2 Gerda Lerner, *The Creation of Patriarchy* (New York: Oxford University Press, 1986).

PART 5

Religious Studies: Prescriptions and Prospects

A. Disciplinary Boundaries

B. Religious Studies in the Academy

38 The Failure of Nerve in the Academic Study of Religion[1]

Donald Wiebe

Donald Wiebe (1943−) was born in Niagara Falls, Ontario, and received his doctorate from Lancaster University. His expertise includes philosophy of religion and philosophical theology, but he is probably most widely known for his contributions in the areas of method and theory in the study of religion. Wiebe has served as president of the North American Association for the Study of Religion, which he cofounded. His books include *The Irony of Theology and the Nature of Religious Thought* (1991), and *The Politics of Religious Studies: The Continuing Conflict with Theology in the Academy* (1999). A professor in the theological department of Trinity College at the University of Toronto, Wiebe has closely studied the historical interplay between theology and religious studies. In the selection that follows he argues that the major professional academic institutions, arguably created for furthering the secular, academic study of religion have not been able to free themselves from their origins in theological studies, but that they should continue to strive to do so.

My concern in this essay is with the relationship of theology to the study of religion, and, more particularly, to the "academic study of religion." I shall not, however, focus attention here on how theology has received the results of academic research on religion[2]—its concerns may be legitimate—nor on historical and institutional questions about the two communities of scholars,[3] or even on the notion that theology as an element of religion overall constitutes a focus of interest and concern to the academic student of religion.[4] My interest here is in the methodological problems implicit in that relationship—even though the matter thus expressed hardly reveals the depth of the issue. Briefly put, the question of theology's methodological relationship to the academic study of religion jeopardizes the existence of such an academic study, for it re-opens the debate about who controls the agenda for such study—is it the scholar-scientist or the scholar-devotee, the academy or the Church, scientific procedure or transcendent subject-matter, and so on.

As I shall show here, it was in the precise act of distinguishing itself from theology that the study of religion gained a political identity within the academic community. I shall also show that there is currently an argument being made for an explicit role for theology in Religious Studies in the "interpenetration" of the two.[5] And I shall argue that, even though under constant pressure from a hidden (if unconscious) theological agenda of many of its practitioners, the re-establishment of such an explicit role for theology constitutes a rejection of scientific, academic goals and, therefore, amounts to a "failure of nerve" by the academic community in Religious Studies.[6]

Some clarification of the term "theology" must precede the argument of this paper—both to counter criticism of my "ambiguous" use of the term in earlier discussions,[7] and to correct misinterpretations of my position which would place me within the "theological camp."[8] Moreover, I would like to pre-empt, if possible, an attack on my perception of historical fact, as might be attempted by those who, like Charles Davis, see the conflict between theology and religious studies as due to a failure of the antagonists to recognize a radical shift of meaning in the use of the concept from medieval to modern times.[9]

In trying to account for the history of "God-talk" ("god-talk") and talk about God (the gods, or any other functionally equivalent Ultimate) I find it helpful to distinguish "confessional theology" from "non-confessional theology." The basis of the distinction is essentially pre-suppositional. Confessional theologies presume the existence of some kind of Ultimate Transmundane Reality, whereas non-confessional theologies recognize only the cultural reality of "the gods" (that is, of some transcendent reality) and attempt to account for it rationally but without subscribing to the supposition that the Ultimate exists.[10] Such a "theoretical theology"—or theology proper—in attempting to provide a rational account of the reality of the gods, leaves open the possibility for a reductionistic account.[11] For as a truly scientific enterprise, theology must hold God (the Ultimate) as problematic, as I shall argue below.[12]

I point out, furthermore, that not all confessional theologies are of the same order. For example, I distinguish "small-c" *confessional theology* from "capital-c" *confessional theology*—the latter being commonly used to refer to (exclusivist) theologies of particular creeds and confessions in the history of Western religious thought.[13] "Small-c" confessional theology, however, is used to cover even the more general acknowledgement of the ontological reality (existence) of the "Focus" of religion—that is, the independent existence of some Ultimate or other to which religious discourse points.

Such distinctions, I suggest, will help students of religion recognize the radical difference between those persons who acknowledge the claim of a transcendent and sacred reality on their lives and those who do not—even when that claim is not tied to a particular historical and exclusivist understanding of some form of divine revelation. Such a non-exclusivistic "confession" I nonetheless take here to be "confession" despite its lack of specificity.

To clarify further the notion of theology as it is used in this essay, I shall respond briefly to Charles Davis' claim that a properly critical theology, which emerged with medieval Christendom, is wholly compatible with Religious Studies. Even for Davis there is a form of theology from which the academic study of religion should be separated, namely, the theology which is nothing more than an elaboration of a particular religious tradition or faith and which, therefore, merely presupposes and reconfirms that tradition. This corresponds to what I have referred to above as capital-c confessional theology, and is rejected by Davis in favor of a critical or theoretical theology. The distinction between such a confessional (or naive in Davis's terms) and critical theology is not, however, clearly drawn; his conception of critical or theoretical theology will be seen to differ vastly from mine and to reveal in fact the character of the "small-c" confessional theology described above.

Confusion is generated in Davis's discussion of this matter by several apparent contradictions in his use of theological terminology. This occurs, for example, when he compares and contrasts concepts of "theology as a whole," with "the properly theological," and with the various theologies—historical, systematic, theoretical, foundational, confessional, etc. And at one point Davis insists that capital-c confessional theology is not really theology at all (1975: 221). Furthermore, his claim that systematic theology is concerned essentially with the ordered exposition of the doctrines of a particular tradition which rests on revelation and authority (212) is contradicted by his further claim that the science of religion is simply a more advanced stage of systematic theology rather than something essentially different

(219), though he still maintains that he has kept the term "theology" simply to refer to "reflection" upon religion as opposed to the process of expression and communication proper to religion as such (220).

His claim to be using "theology" in a non-partisan, critical fashion is undermined in the underlying assumption of his work that "the religious"—whether it be experience, expression, or activity—is sufficiently different from other social phenomena for it to become the object of a distinct and special science.[14] The assumption excludes reductionistic explanations of religion for the rather circularly-argued reason that "[r]eligious phenomena [...] call for a direct [special] investigation to analyze their common elements ... " (1975: 214). This specious and ultimately tautological argument reappears later in the essay in the claim that "the science of religion is an empirical enquiry distinguished from sociology and psychology by its primary concern with religious data as religious" (219). All of this amounts, of course, to the patent non-sequitur that since theology, as "rational discourse about God," exists, then God too must exist; and this effective "presumption of theism"[15] I would argue, makes of Davis a "small-c" confessional theologian.[16] To conclude: I do not take issue here with theology of the theoretical kind which recognizes the Ultimate as problematic; for such a theology leaves open the possibility of a reductionistic account of it. All uncritical thinking about God or the gods which relies on revelation or on the presumption of theism"— therefore, refusing to countenance the possible non-existence of the divine—is "confessional theology." Such theology constitutes a species of what I call "religious thought," operating within the framework of general religious assumptions or traditions and is therefore incompatible with what will be referred to below as the basic minimum presuppositions for the academic study of religion.

The study of religion as a scholarly exercise has a very long history;[17] antedating by far the institutionalized, academically-legitimated study of religion which emerged in the late nineteenth century.[18] And it is important to see that its acceptance in the academic domain was not occasioned by a natural, spontaneous recognition either of its academic style or methodological significance. Rather, it came about as a result of a quest for such recognition that required establishing the scientific objectivity of religious studies—a quest which, as has often been pointed out, is the product of the Enlightenment. This in turn required giving up the theological interests and confessional stance so characteristic of that study in the past.[19] Indeed, in some countries—France being a case in point[20]—the teachers of the new discipline replaced the Theological Faculty altogether. In this sense Jacob Neusner is right to suggest that the new academic student of religion attempted to overcome an unwanted past, although I think he exaggerates when he claims that the attempt was successful (1977b). Similarly Joachim Wach (1951, 1958) and Joseph Kitagawa (1958) speak of the study of religion as being emancipated from a theological agenda, and Robert W. Friedrichs (1974) talks of the "detheologizing" of the subject. The study of religion, they assert, was becoming more neutral, objective, and scientific. This meant adopting a notion of a universally applicable mode of inquiry, implying that religions could be studied in exactly the same way as any other social phenomenon. The scholar *qua* scholar, therefore, was to eliminate religious commitments from all scholarly analysis. The several concerns of the "new" discipline included: (1) morphology of religion, involving primarily a description of rites, rituals, beliefs, practices, art, architecture, and so on of the various historical religions; (2) stages of religious development; (3) parallels among the various traditions; and, later, (4) the phenomenology of religious meaning and the structure of religions. The discipline, then, was primarily empirical, heavily centered on philological and historical concerns, and resulted in the production of scholarly monographs and interpretive studies.

The institutionalization of this new discipline was not only to be found in universities; an international association (The International Association for the History of Religions [IAHR]) was eventually formed in the 1950s although International Congresses had been held from 1900 on, and under the pressure of various religious sentiments—especially as the Association expanded membership to include religion "scholars" from the Far East[21]—theological and religious matters began to appear on the agenda of its Congresses. This unforeseen regression led to a stricter formulation of the scientific goals and intentions of the new discipline *(Religionswissenschaft)* by R. J. Zwi Werblowsky. His five-point enunciation of the "basic minimum presuppositions" for the pursuit of historical and comparative studies of religion was reproduced in *Numen*, the official publication of the IAHR (Schimmel, 1960).[22] A summary of that statement here will provide a kind of benchmark for the "retreat to theology" I shall attempt to document below:[23]

"Comparative religion" or *Religionswissenschaft* is a scientific discipline;

Religionswissenschaft is a branch of the humanities, and as such it is an anthropological discipline, studying the religious phenomenon as a creation, feature and aspect of human culture. The common ground on which students of religion, *qua* students of religion, meet is the realization that the awareness of the numinous or the experience of transcendence (where these happen to exist in religions) are, whatever else they may be, undoubtedly empirical facts of human existence and history, to be studied like all human facts by appropriate method;

Religionswissenschaft rejects the claim that religion is a *sui generis* phenomenon that can only be understood if ultimately seen to be a realization of transcendent truth;

Although the study of religion may arise from non-academic motivation, it needs no such external justification (and ought not to rely on one);

The IAHR must keep itself free from all ideological commitments.[24]

Some critics have seen this program as Comtean *ersatz* religion.[25] But Werblowsky's review of Wach's "theological" approach to the study of religion counters that: "Of course historical analysis can never yield the norms without which life is not worth living … but, then, nobody ever supposed historical analysis to do just that. There is, after all, a world of difference between study and living, between studying history and making it" (Werblowsky, 1959: 354).

Religious Studies did in fact gain the academic legitimation it sought. But it failed to live up to the commitments it had given the academic community to pursue its agenda in a religiously non-partisan fashion. E. J. Sharpe (1986, chapter 6) points out, for example, that in the early days of the "discipline,"[26] Religious Studies was still considered by many to be religious instruction even if not on the confessional scale found in theological faculties—an impression bolstered by the close association of some of its leading practitioners (such as F. M. Müller) with movements such as the World's Parliament of Religions held in Chicago in 1893. Kitagawa has noted, in a review of the subject as taught in the United States, that although its early formation followed European scientific lines, it eventually submitted to the pressures of conservatism and orthodoxy (1959, 1983). This seems less surprising when one considers that the majority of those in the field hail from a religious background and likely entered the discipline with theological baggage if not an agenda.[27] The situation is further compounded by the connected complaint—voiced by C. J. Bleeker (1961, 1975) and still heard today—that the IAHR has not been able to attract social scientists interested in the study of religious phenomena. As Oxtoby put it, Religious Studies was simply "not scientific enough" (1968: 591).

I do not mean to suggest here, however, that scholars were being duplicitous—in fact, they made the conscious effort to "bracket" their own beliefs and made this "bracketing" a requirement of the discipline. In so doing there emerged a general methodological agreement that the truth-question not be raised in Religious Studies—that is, that the academic study of religion forego the philosophical-metaphysical justification of the various historical religious traditions which had thus far been such an unsuccessful and divisive exercise. So it is not that those who adopted the bracket—*epoché*—denigrated that metaphysical exercise or denied its value in other contexts but just that, for the sake of achieving a convergence—however short-range—of scholarly opinion on general religious issues from a wide range of competing theological frameworks, they restricted their concerns to less speculative, more positive matters where all could agree on the criteria for assessing claims.

The *epoché* (or bracketing) freed the student and the study of religion from ecclesiastical domination, although there was still a certain amount of theological suspicion attached to those so engaged (Oxtoby, 1968: 591). However, there are methodological corollaries implied in the *epoché* to suggest that such a study of religion, even though free from a certain ecclesiastical—and therefore capital-c confessional—domination, is nonetheless influenced by religious or theological commitment. The most damning corollary, as I have indicated elsewhere, is the "descriptivist doctrine"—whereby the substance of the Science of Religion is reduced to phenomenological description—especially when connected with the widely-held belief that such a study constitutes a new discipline (namely, the "Science of Religion.")[28] The corollary requires that the study of religion remain free from theory and forego explaining religious phenomena. For to explain is to grant that the phenomenon is some-how illusory or veridical—in other words, to invoke the very category of truth which the *epoché* banished in its attempt to achieve academic neutrality. However, the enterprise, if it is to be scientific, must necessarily move beyond mere ideographic description to a more nomothetic explanation and theory.[29] This can be done without entering the metaphysical or theological fray—and so, without contravening the conventionally adopted stratagem of the *epoché*—by means of analysis of the cognitive components of the religious tradition concerned compared with the cognitive universe of the investigator. If the cognitive "worlds" clash, the student of religion then proceeds to consider alternative accounts of the religious phenomenon by regarding factors or aspects of human existence not in themselves religious. It is this potentially reductionist accounting for religion that the "descriptivist doctrine" is meant to preclude. For descriptionists, "to explain" is "to explain away" and that, it appears, must be avoided at all costs. But to avoid that possibility altogether is to assume that it can never be "explained away." That assumption, however, indicates a religious or theological bias, for it grants an ontological reality to religion which the latter may not really possess.

The first corollary—the descriptivist doctrine—is complemented by the doctrine of "the autonomy of religion." The obviously circular argument is given that since the discipline of Religious Studies exists, it must have a peculiar subject-matter inviting an equally peculiar method of analysis. Religion being a *sui generis* phenomenon, it is to be treated "on its own terms." Ultimately, to see it as anything other than "religious" is not to take religion "seriously."[30]

To reiterate, the *epoché* and its corollaries, taken together, imply that Religious Studies is a science with a methodology peculiar to itself, distinct from theology-religion on the one hand and the physical and social sciences on the other. I have shown elsewhere, however, that this argument is flawed because it is based on mutually exclusive sets of assumptions and because it fails to delineate clearly the methodology assumed peculiar to itself (Wiebe, 1978).

My arguments on this issue have been criticized as distortions of the original intent of the founders of this "new" science as well as of their successors (Widengren, 1983). It has been claimed that the science is not restricted to the descriptive or ideographic level but rather that it extends to "understanding." Widengren chooses as illustrative of such an approach the work of C. J. Bleeker, who goes beyond mere "fact gathering" in his study of religion to phenomenological understanding (Bleeker, 1954, 1971). I do not deny that Bleeker wishes to go beyond the fact-gathering stage—as do most of his colleagues—but I must point to the problems inherent in that exercise. The "understanding" Bleeker seeks quite obviously presumes the validity of the devotee's position, for the bracketing is still very much in effect in this exercise. The devotee's self-understanding in effect provides the point of departure for this task. This principle was accepted early on in "Science of Religion" circles which we see in F. M. Müller's adoption of "Comparative Theology" as an element of that science. The student, he insists, must deal with the facts as discovered, so that "if people regard their religion as revealed, it is to them a revealed religion and has to be treated as such by every impartial historian" (Müller, 1893: 74).[31]

There is no doubt that the understanding sought by phenomenology "goes beyond" descriptive, historical and philological fact-gathering. The question which needs raising, however, is whether that "understanding" is still description (perhaps at a deeper level), or whether in fact it goes beyond that ideographic to a truly nomothetic grasp of religious phenomena. And if the latter, its *epoché* in fact amounts to an *a priori* acceptance of an ontological reality although it refuses to commit publicly—or even privately—to that reality. Therefore, it is assumed that reductionist accounts are unable to provide an understanding of religion; and that means, conversely, that religion necessarily involves persons with what is ultimately "real," and "good." *Understanding*, then, would by definition preclude causal explanation; because the latter, where applicable, is of limited value, for this kind of understanding is broader than explanation.[32] Such an "understanding," to conclude, amounts to a non-specific theology, for it assumes the ontological reality of the religious phenomenon without consciously espousing any particular historical religious tradition's view of that reality.[33] It rests uncritically on the assumption of the metaphysical validity of "religion in general."[34]

What I hope to show in this section of the paper is the hidden theological agenda of Religious Studies.[35] Neusner's relatively recent suggestion (1977b) that the academic study of religion in the United States and Canada has developed a set of norms which exclude religiosity from the classroom, and that there has developed a consequently detached and objective approach to the study seems a fairy tale, which ignores the significance of the literature produced, as the discussion to follow should demonstrate. Furthermore, with respect to "what goes on" in our Departments of Religious Studies and in our other academic institutions, the evidence simply does not support his claim, but documentation of this will have to be left for another paper.[36]

Space does not permit a detailed analysis of all the positions and arguments against what amounts to a "detheologized" academic study of religion; nevertheless I shall attempt to delineate here the major stances taken. I am not sure that the two major arguments (and their subdivisions) I shall deal with are clearly distinguishable from each other—nor are they set out by their authors in a pure and pristine form. However, the typology I shall offer should be of some use in assessing what has grown to be a large body of literature; and the overview provided should at least indicate a trend in Religious Studies which threatens to jettison the gains it has made since the Enlightenment.

The most common type of argument to be found in this literature might best be designated the "complementarity thesis." The claim usually put forward in this case is not that Religious Studies is of no use to our search for understanding religious phenomena but simply that it is inadequate. The "heart of religion," that is, cannot be perceived if the subject is approached "in purely informative, descriptive, scientific terms" (Kegley, 1978: 280). According to Mostert: "One must go beyond the historical and socio-scientific approach that adheres simply to empirical methods of data collection and description or even explanation" (1976: 8–9); or as Ladner puts it, the proper study of religion "entails more than employing the intellectual instruments of criticism and analysis to investigate various forms of faith and belief" (1972: 216)—something which has been neglected recently in the shallowness fostered by an expansion of Religious Studies, while it blindly vaunts "that we are finally getting our intellectual foot in the academic door of secular education … " (Ladner, 1972: 216).

In an early essay in this genre, Bernard E. Meland raises questions about the assumption that the student of religion need only be concerned with "objective methods" (1961). According to Meland, the student of religion must be distinct from the regular historian or the run-of-the-mill social scientist. The student of religion "is not *just* a historian or a scientist in the sense that defines the anthropologist or social scientist. He is a student of religions in a specific and specialized sense" (269–70, emphasis added), involving "deeper" dimensions of religion. And Kees Bolle, while admitting that the study of religion—historically at least—is an enterprise in its own right, and that emphasis on such study in the early days assisted the establishment of Religious Studies in university centers and departments, denies that it alone will "make our field acceptable in a modern academic framework" (1967: 98). Indeed, he predicts that, without complement, the pure academic approach would bring the discipline to an end: "Religious phenomena are never just intellectual propositions or just individual affairs. Hence neither can the manner in which religious phenomena are approached have its centre in logical investigation and a resulting synthesis of general laws *alone*, even if the individual following this method is a master in the fields of logic and anthropology" (100).

Such complementarity might best be characterized as "incremental," the academic study of religion being supplemented by theology as, say, physics is "exceeded" by chemistry. Theology, that is, is an entirely different way of knowing" than the "knowing" of science which increases our information. As Kegley expresses it, the student of religion cannot remain detached in an information-gathering exercise but rather must share in the religious experience of the devotee. And, he maintains, "this […] is not a call for indoctrination but for the wooing of the spirit" (1978: 280).[37] Kegley, however, does not see the complementarity as unilinear but rather as a "mutual benefiting" of Theology and Religious Studies: "Theology without serious religious studies tends to pious arrogance; religious studies without theology tends to parasitical aloofness. In a dialectical encounter, both may thrive" (1978: 282).

A similar "mutual complementarity" thesis is to be found in the work of R. H. Drummond: "If theologians need the history of religions to give full-bodiedness and contemporary relevance to their own work, the historians of religion need theology in order to come to grips with that which they are really supposed to deal—the central elements of the religious life of humankind" (1975: 403). J. P. Mostert insists "it rests with theology to illuminate [religion's] ultimate depth dimension" (1976: 12); as do Meland and Bolle (among others), although Bolle at least calls for a "deprovincializing of Christian theology" in the process (1967: 116).[38]

"Incremental complementarity," however, is not the only response to the issue of the relationship of Theology to Religious Studies; there is an alternative, which I will refer to as "incorporative complementarity." It is a position halfway between the simple "complementarity thesis" and the "identity thesis" (to be discussed below), which does not fully insist on the distinction between Religious Studies and Theology but instead points to the subordination of the former by the latter. The position seems well expressed by A. Jeffner in the conclusion to his paper on "Religion and Understanding":

> [R]eligion can be seen as a kind of understanding and explanation of a part of reality. Such religious understanding is parallel to other kinds of understanding, e.g., the scientific one. But religious understanding aims at an understanding of our total situation, in other words an all-inclusive understanding. The religious all-inclusive understanding need not be opposed to a scientific understanding of a part of reality, but it is opposed to a scientific world view and a scientific all-inclusive understanding.
>
> (1981: 225)

Science, then, has a place, but it is secondary; it can only make its contribution within a wider frame of reference. Theologians taking up this stance effectively "hybridize" disciplines, tending to talk of "religio-sociology," or "religio-ecology," or "religio-history," and so on.[39] As J. Kitagawa (himself a proponent in this category) puts it with regard to J. Wach's work, there is an attempt to "combine the insights and methods of *Religionswissenschaft*, philosophy of religion, and theology" (1958: xxxviii). As one sees in Wach's writings and activities, this implies that although as a student of religion one does not wish to give up the ideal of objectivity, one comes to recognize that such objectivity falls short of the broader vision in which neutrality is precluded. "What is required," he writes, "is not indifference, as positivism in its heyday believed [...] but rather engagement of feeling, interest, *metexis*, or participation" (Wach, 1958: 12). And to settle for less is to adopt a form of scientism.[40] Kitagawa echoes Wach in this matter, advocating the exploiting of such "new" disciplines as religio-sociology and religio-science to show the possible "syntheses" and "interpenetration" of disciplines sought by Wach.[41]

But Wach and Kitagawa are not the only scholars to hold this position. Indeed, as Kitagawa points out, the line of thought goes back to Wach's Marburg teachers, including F. Heiler and Rudolph Otto (Kitagawa, 1971: 49). What Wach envisages in his redefinition of Religious Studies, according to Kitagawa "is the interpenetration between constructive theology, which is informed and purified by careful studies of history of religions, and history of religions, itself liberated from the 'narrowly defined' scientific approach to the study of religion" (1971: 52). Other scholars in this tradition include Paul Tillich,[42] Mircea Eliade,[43] and Eliade's many followers.[44] What all have in common is what Kitagawa found essential to Wach's attempt at a deep penetration into the nature of religion—namely, "the recognition of the objective character of ultimate reality" (1971: 46). In other words, what is implied (if not sought) is a concept of "meaning" as a "transcendent something" unaffected by the dictates of science.[45] The sciences (including the scientific study of religion) are thus in effect contaminated by the religious vision. Science, it appears, cannot ultimately comprehend religion; the latter remains, in Wach's words, "one of the inexplicable mysteries which have accompanied the ascent of man ... " (1944: 307).

This mysteriousness, I maintain, is essentially a religious attribute—and proof of a confessional stance. And I would argue that such a pronouncement reveals a similar approach wielded by all those methods for the study of religion which subordinate the detached, scientific "outsider" approach to religion to the confessional "insider" approach.[46]

The last type of argument for a re-theologized Religious Studies mentioned above as the "identity thesis," amounts to a variation of the preceding forms. Its claim is that following analysis of the nature and task of Theology and Religious Studies the two will in fact be pronounced essentially the same enterprise. This position has been set out elaborately by W. Pannenberg (1976) within the framework of a defense of theology as a science (and therefore as an academic discipline). He allows that theology can be described as the "science of Christianity," but if Christianity is seen as only one religion among many others in the context of the history of religions, it should rather be placed under the general heading of the Science of Religion (1976: 256). The kind of unity which "reduces" theology to a sub-discipline, however, he rejects, arguing that theology does justice to Christianity only as a science of God," where "God" stands for "reality-as-a-whole" while admitting that an "anthropological turn" has taken place in theology to make both the concept and theology itself problematic. He then goes on to ground such a hypothetical theology in the Science of Religion (346), theology's concern being, as he puts it, "the communication of divine reality experienced in [religions ...]" (365). This amounts to a critical theology of religions "in virtue of its attempt to examine the specifically religious theme of religious traditions and ways of life, the divine reality which appeared in them, and not some other psychological or sociological aspect" (365–66). Theology, therefore, he equates with the Science of Religion when that task is being properly carried out. In an earlier essay Pannenberg describes an identical characterization of Theology and the Science of Religion, but there he admits that the exercise is not simply historical but rather a kind of "religious-historical" research and therefore a religious exercise. Such an admission unwittingly supports the thesis that academic and religious pursuits are mutually exclusive (1971: 116).

Pannenberg's kind of stance is taken up by a number of other scholars as well. A similar but much briefer statement is presented, for example, by B. Hebblethwaite (1980). Carl-Martin Edsman contends that Religious Studies, when placed in Faculties of Theology as it has often been, has not fared badly; and he maintains that those who call for a separation of the two disciplines are propagandists ignorant of the strictly scientific scholarship of both fields (1974: 70). A. D. Galloway maintains that it is in the human quest for truth that we see "the unity and integrity of our discipline" (1975: 165). And Paul Wiebe, while disclaiming any connection with the systematic theologies taught at seminaries, maintains that Religious Studies is a constructive science, not merely self-reflective and historical, and therefore indistinguishable from theology (1975: 18, 23). He states his position: "the creation of norms is the final good of religious studies. This is to say that the real impetus behind the investigation of religion is not a mere intellectual or aesthetic curiosity, but is a desire for existential truth" (23). This of course makes it obvious that the so-called academic discipline is at the same time a religious activity. And it is certainly reminiscent of Paul Tillich's nebulous view of the History of Religion's being merely a form of theology in the process of transformation into "the religion of the concrete spirit" (1963: 87). Charles Davis similarly maintains that once one recognizes theoretical theology for what it really is—and has been since at least the Middle Ages—the modern development of the science of religion will be seen to be in continuity with that medieval progression (1975: 207).[47] On one level he insists that to study religion is not in itself a religious exercise (207), but on another he maintains that theology cannot simply be seen as a datum on a different level from the science of religion (208). Consequently he advocates a convergence of the two disciplines, with each having as its primary concern religious data *qua* religious (219), even though this seems to contradict his earlier disclaimer about the religiosity of that study. In conclusion he states "the science of religion is [...] a more advanced stage of systematic theology, [and] not an essentially different enterprise (219).

A twist on the identity thesis is often found in the literature as well. It is often claimed, that is, that the so-called academic study of religion is itself a religion and therefore simply rivals religious faith of the established traditions. This was the thrust, for example, of W. C. Smith's 1984 presidential address to the American Academy of Religion (1963).[48] The most vocal exponent of this thesis, in my opinion, however, is R. N. Bellah. He readily admits that he has no anxiety about blurring the boundary line between religion and the teaching of religion—of infecting the study, so to speak, with its own subject matter (1970c: 4). Indeed, boundaries cannot be erected since "whatever fundamental stance one takes in teaching about religion is in itself a religious position" (4), though he does elsewhere refer to it as implicitly religious (1970a: 95).[49] In the latter article he refers to his position as one of "symbolic realism" which is both academically sound, according to him, and self-consciously religious. Indeed, he maintains that it "is the *only* adequate basis for the social scientific study of religion" (1970a: 93, my emphasis).[50]

Paul Ingram captures the sentiments of Bellah well in his methodological statement against the "cartesian methodology" that is "basically a technology for manipulating 'religious data' into precise intelligible patterns that can be understood by anyone who followed the same technical procedures" (1976: 392). Rather than attempting to seize the truth about religion the students must be seized by truth and insight in spite of the methodologies they may hold (1975: 394). And Walter Capps also talks about the need to fight against "the monopolizing compact between the Enlightenment and religious studies ... " (1978: 104). Religious studies, that is, must involve itself, as does theology, in the process of the formation of the truth (1978: 105). This, then, is the dominant story one hears from an ever-expanding circle of spokespersons for Religious Studies.

Although rather lengthy, this review does not at all exhaust the bewildering variety of arguments calling for a return to Theology in Religious Studies—calls to turn to religion and the Supermundane, to Ultimate Reality and the Truth. There is, however, sufficient documentation here to support the claim that the objective, detached, and scientific study of religion, so eagerly sought in the heady days of the late nineteenth century, is no longer a major factor in the study of religion in our universities. We have now a return to religion under the apparent pressure of a breakdown of our culture,[51] but to believe that we are returning to our "origins" is sheer illusion. The "limitations" of the classroom in our attempt to understand religion[52] have not so much led to a misunderstanding of religion, I would suggest, as they have fostered the creation of what R. Michaelson calls "classroom religion."[53] Bellah's symbolic realism is an example of precisely that, but it is arguable as to whether—with respect to the religious traditions originally studied by the academic community—such an interpretation is not itself reductionistic.[54]

Before leaving this matter I should like to focus special attention on my own academic community in Canada which I think is aptly described as having "lost its nerve" in this enterprise—if it ever had it—as evinced in the work of Davis discussed above. In a more recent essay on theology and religious studies Davis categorically insists that a scientific study of religion cannot operate devoid of religious faith (1981: 13). That view, moreover, presents itself in a more general fashion in Davis's work as editor of the Canadian journal *Studies in Religion (SR)*. The conclusion drawn by P. B. Riley after close analysis of the journal's content over the first ten years of its existence is that the journal has been devoted to (quoting Davis) "collaboration between theologians and religionists" (1984: 427). Indeed, he correctly suggests that this is the distinctive contribution of the journal and, I would maintain with only slight qualification, that the groups for whom the journal serves as official organ are quite happy with the ideological direction it has taken.

The editorial policy of Davis, moreover, perpetuates a long tradition. In this regard it is interesting to note that, in some sense, *SR* is a continuation of the old *Canadian Journal of Theology*. That journal, experiencing financial difficulties and being unable to secure Canada Council funding because of its "religious character," signed away its existence to the new religious studies periodical able to secure such financial support. In return, however, the *Canadian Journal of Theology* received assurance from W. Nicholls, the first editor of *SR*, that the new journal would not abandon its theological readership. That promise has been kept (Riley, 1984: 444).[55]

This is not, of course, the only indication of the state of Religious Studies in Canada. The influence of Wilfred Cantwell Smith on the Canadian scene is almost all-pervasive, and it most certainly influences the "re-theologizing" of Religious Studies. Riley, in his look at *SR* claims that Smith's "work and influence perhaps more than that of any individual, permeates the pages of *SR*"[56] and the claim applies, I think, to his general influence on Religious Studies elsewhere as well,[57] although space does not permit substantiating that claim here. Finally, other events in the emergence and operation of departments for the study of religion in Canada could be cited to support the claim.[58]

It was with some surprise that I found myself taken to be an exponent of the very position I have argued against here and elsewhere.[59] It is true that in my discussion of the possibility of a Science of Religion I admitted that Religious Studies might well contain theological elements (Wiebe, 1978). But the theology I had in mind was of a scientific nature, capable of accepting the demands of intellectual honesty to the point of abandoning any absolute or ultimate commitments, and leaving itself open to radical change (1978: 125).[60] In this sense, which I may not have explained clearly enough, theology (philosophical, theoretical, or scientific) as "the rationale of God or the gods" permits the possibility of reductionism, although, quite obviously, it does not necessitate it. It is for this reason that I found it justifiable to talk of the possibility of the study of religion as proceeding from the point of view of the "critical participant" (or "detached devotee") while refusing to recognize an "autonomous discipline" presupposing an independent subject matter—that is, God, the gods, the Transcendent, Ultimate Reality, and so on. For the *a priori* acceptance of the reality and existence of the Ultimate is a species of religious thinking and, if it is to be called theology at all, ought to be referred to as "confessional theology." And it is this kind of theologizing which I argue is incompatible with Religious Studies since it in fact constitutes the subject matter of that study. As I have pointed out in my discussion of Davis and others above, to accept without question (as a condition of the study) the existence of an Ultimate Reality is to espouse confessional theology, even if it is of a more "ecumenical" variety than in the past. So, to avoid any further ambiguity, I reiterate here: theology, when it commits itself to the existence of the Ultimate, constitutes a form of religious thought which cannot complement the academic study of religion but can only "infect" it.[61]

Imprecision on this matter may unfortunately have been fostered by my failure to point out clearly there that the "critical insider" and "sympathetic outsider" converge—and ought to do so—on the descriptive level only and not necessarily on the explanatory and theoretical level.[62] The confusion is due, it appears to me now, to my earlier, predominant apologetic concerns. In my work on the role of explanation in the study of religion (Wiebe, 1975), however, even though showing some sympathy for the argument of the "insiders," I expressed nagging doubts about the matter but did not pursue the issue at that time.

In this paper I have taken up a matter which has challenged me over many years, and I think I have assessed it here a little more clearly. I have shown that the explicit agenda adopted by the founders of Religious Studies as an academic (university) concern committed the enterprise to a detached, scientific understanding of religion wholly uninfected by any sentiment of religiosity. I have also pointed out that the study was—and still is—dominated by a hidden theological agenda, but that the *epoché* invoked by its practitioners had nevertheless provided the ground for beginning a new tradition of thought on matters religious. Finally, I have shown that the crypto-theological agenda informing that study is becoming more overt, actually being touted as the only proper method for the study of religion. This last step, I argue here, dismisses the tentative move toward the development of a scientific study of religion that was heralded by the first generation of *Religionswissenschaftler* and, therefore, constitutes a failure of nerve in the academic study of religion.

QUESTIONS FOR REVIEW AND DISCUSSION

1. What does Wiebe intend to argue when he speaks of a "failure of nerve by the academic community in Religious Studies"?
2. What is the distinction that Wiebe draws between "confessional" and "non-confessional" theology? Between "small-c" and "capital-c" confessional theology?
3. On what grounds does Wiebe critique Davis's distinction between theology and religious studies? Do you find Wiebe's appraisal reasonable that Davis's position would suggest that Davis is a "small-c" confessional theologian?
4. What does Wiebe discern as some of the defining characteristics of the "new" discipline of religious studies when it emerged? What were the five "basic minimum presuppositions" formulated by R. J. Zwi Werblowsky for the pursuit of studies in religion?
5. What does Wiebe mean by *epoché* or the practice of "bracketing" one's religious beliefs when engaged in religious studies? How is it a useful stance when engaged in the discipline?
6. What problems does Wiebe see inherent in the purely "descriptivist" approach to the study of religion? Do you agree with his observations? What problems does Wiebe discern in the notion of the "autonomy of religion"? Do you agree with his observations?
7. What does Wiebe mean when he notes that the scholar's acknowledgement of some mysterious transcendent reality is essentially indicative of a confessional theological stance? Do you agree with his position?
8. What does Wiebe mean by the "identity thesis"? Is religious studies a subcategory of theology or vice versa? If not, how ought they to be distinguished from each other?
9. Do you think that Wiebe is realistic or pessimistic in his argument that the "crypto-theological agenda" frequently found within the practice of religious studies is becoming more overt, and demonstrates a failure in the academic study of religion to stand up for its foundational non-theologically oriented principles?

Notes

1 This essay is a revised version of a paper prepared for the Eastern International Regional Meeting of the AAR held at McMaster University in the spring of 1984. I wish to thank the participants

(especially Lorne Dawson for helpful comments and criticisms). I am also grateful to Peter Slater, whose criticisms of an early draft of this paper were also of assistance.

2 See R. H. Drummond, "Christian Theology and the History of Religion" (1975); A. R. Gualtieri, "Confessional Theology in the Context of the History of Religions" (1972); and D. Wiebe, "Is a Science of Religion Possible?" (1978).

3 See Carl-Marrin Edsman, "Theology or Religious Studies?" (1974); W. Panenberg, *Theology and the Philosophy of Science* (1976); Eric J. Sharpe, *Comparative Religion: A History* (1975) and *Understanding Religion* (1983); and B. Hebblethwaite, "Theology and Comparative Religion" (1980).

4 See N. Smart, "Resolving the Tensions between Religion and the Science of Religion" in *The Phenomenon of Religion* (1973); R. J. Zwi Werblosky, "The Comparative Study of Religions: A Review Essay" (1959), and "On Studying Comparative Religion" (1975).

5 For examples of such imagery see Drummond, "Christian Theology" (1975); and J. M. Kitagawa, "*Verstehen und Erlösung*: Some Remarks on Joachim Wach's Work" (1971).

6 The phrase "failure of nerve" is borrowed from G. Murray (*Five Stages of Greek Religion* [1955]). For Murray, a "failure of nerve" characterized the shift from confidence in human effort and the enlightened mind from the presocratics to the rise of asceticism and mysticism after Plato and Aristotle. See also S. Hook, *The Quest for Being* (1961). Other scholars have used the phrase in quite a different way, even to the point of reversing its original intent. See, for example, Carl A. Raschke, "The Future of Religious Studies: Moving Beyond the Mandate of the 1960s (1983); Eric J. Sharpe, "Some Problems of Method in the Study of Religion" (1971); and, especially, J. C. McLelland, "Alice in Academia: Religious Studies in an Academic Setting." The Enlightenment, as I point out below, constitutes the source from which the academic study of religion emerged. If Peter Gay's (1966) interpretation of that period as the re-establishing of the derailed presocratic Enlightenment is anywhere near the truth, then Murray's "failure of nerve" concept applies particularly well to the subject of my essay.

7 See J. P. Mostert, "Complementary Approaches in the Study of Religion." In the hope of avoiding confusion I use the concept "theology" in a less specific sense than do theologians, so that its rejection as a part of Religious Studies ought not to be taken as an argument for the rejection of theology *per se*. As used here—and in general methodological literature pertaining to Religious Studies—"theology" denotes religious thought, whether carried out by the naïve devotee or by the systematically reflective, intellectually sophisticated devotee. The term "theoretical theology" will be used to refer to a "religiously neutral" discipline—although, as will become clear, there is question as to whether that constitutes a discipline—a distinct mode of thought—as its supposed task is indistinguishable from that of the philosophy of religion.

8 See especially Phillip B. Riley, "Theology and/or Religious Studies: A Case Study *Studies in Religion/ Sciences Religieues* 1971–81" (originally presented at the 1983 meeting of the Canadian Society for the Study of Religion). A version of the paper that revises his 1983 judgment somewhat appears in *Studies in Religion*.

9 Charles Davis, "The Reconvergence of Theology and Religious Studies" (1975). If space permitted, I would dispute this claim. I agree with Davis that theoretical theology emerges in the Middle Ages, but I would argue that he does not adequately grasp the import of that development. Bernard of Clairvaux did see the significance of the "new theology" of Peter Abelard (and others) more clearly than Davis. A descriptive account of this state of affairs can be found in J. Leclercq, *The Love of Learning and the Desire for God* (1961), and a persuasive alternative interpretation of the Bernard-Abelard conflict can be found in B. Nelson, *On the Roads to Modernity: Conscience, Science and Civilization* (1981). The tension separating "new" and "old" theology, I would maintain, resembles that found between religious and scientific communities of recent Western history. I have addressed this problem more comprehensively in a monograph, *The Irony of Theology and the Nature of Religious Thought* (1991a).

10 On the distinction between the reality and existence of the Focus of the devotee's attention see N. Smart, *The Phenomenon of Religion* (1973).

11 The kind of theology I have in mind here is to be found, for example, in the work of L. Feuerbach or, more recently, in the Christian atheism of the 1960s.

12 Such a scientific theology is undertaken, for example, by W. Pannenberg in his *Theology and the Philosophy of Science* (1976).

13 It might be argued that a further distinction within "capital-c" confessional theology is also necessary in order to account for the differences between the main confessional churches of the

Reformation and the left-wing or more extreme groups who explicitly distinguished themselves from the mainstream and did not consider themselves confessional in that sense. This is not, however, a problem to be settled here. (I wish to thank Thomas Yoder Neufeld for drawing this point to my attention.)

14 Similar arguments are to be found in E. J. Streng, "The Objective Study of Religion and the Unique Quality of Religiousness" (1970), and K. K. Klostermaier, "From Phenomenology to Metascience: Reflections on the Study of Religion" (1977).

15 For a philosophical discussion of this matter, see A. Flew, "The Presumption of Atheism" (1972).

16 Davis's argument here might on first sight seem to find support in the attempt by R. Morgan and Michael Pye to recall the argument of Ernst Troeltsch. Troeltsch maintained that the positivist or materialist method of study was unacceptable in this field because, in an *a priori* fashion, it precludes the possibility that religion is veridical rather than illusory. A closer reading of Troeltsch, and of the commentaries by Morgan and Pye, however, reveal Troeltsch's methodological idealism to be guilty of a similar *a priori*. Unfortunately, space does not permit elaboration of that critique here. See the essays by Troeltsch and the Morgan and Pye commentaries in *Ernst Troeltsch: Writings on Theology and Religion* (1977).

17 The scholarly study of world religions has, for many, been a religious exercise. On this point see K. K. Klostermaier's "The Religion of Study" (1978). On the suggestion that the academic study of religion should substitute as a religious exercise, see. E. R. Goodenough, *"Religionwissenschaft"* (1959).

18 Likely the best source for details on this development is E. J. Sharpe, *Comparative Religion: A History* (1975), See also J. Jastrow, Jr., *The Study of Religion* (1981), and J. de Vries, *The Study of Religion: A Historical Approach* (1967).

19 See C. Dawson, "Natural Theology and the Scientific Study of Religion" in *Religion and Culture* (1948); also S. M. Ogden, "Theology and Religious Studies: Their Difference and the Difference It Makes" (1978). Some may argue that the early practitioners of the new style of Religious Studies wished to liberate that study from direct ecclesiastical control and therefore were ready to "give up" only "capital-c" confessional theology while seeking to integrate the new study with their "small-c" confessional stances. Yet even a superficial reading of the methodological literature of the period shows that the rejection of confessional theology was much more radical in intent. For it was to allow students of religion to avoid having to settle the apparently unresolvable ontological and metaphysical questions that preclude "convergence of opinion (belief)" even on the level of "small-c" confessional theology. Nevertheless, as I point out below, it is true that much of the work of the early practitioners in this field could appropriately be described as a species of confessional theology.

20 See Sharpe, *Comparative Religion* (1975).

21 See Sharpe, *Comparative Religion* (1975), ch. 6.

22 Many influential members of the IAHR signed the document. It is important to note that Eliade and Kitagawa did sign this positivist-sounding statement despite their sympathies lying elsewhere, as I point out below.

23 My use of this phrase recalls William Warren Bartley's "retreat to commitment" in *Retreat to Commitment* (1962).

24 These sentiments are also expressed in the following essays by R. J. Zwi Werblowsky: "Revelation, Natural Theology and Comparative Religion" (1956); "The Comparative Study of Religions: A Review Essay" (1959); "Marburg and After" (1960); and "On Studying Comparative Religion" (1975).

25 See, for example, C. Davis, "Theology and Religious Studies," *Scottish Journal of Religious Studies* 2 (1981): 11–20.

26 I apply quotation marks to the word "discipline" to show that it is being used for convenience—I am reluctant to call the academic study of religion a discipline in the formal sense. See my essay "Is a Science of Religion Possible?" (1978) and *Religion and Truth: Towards an Alternative Paradigm for the Study of Religion* (1981).

27 See, for example, W. C. Oxtoby, *"Religionswissenschaft* Revisited" (1968); and U. Drobin, "Psychology, Philosophy, Theology, Epistemology—Some Reflections" (1982).

28 See D. Wiebe, "Is a Science of Religion Possible?" (1978).

29 See D. Wiebe, "Explanation and the Scientific Study of Religion" (1975), and "Theory in the Study of Religion" (1983).

30 On this see especially C. J. Blecker, "The Relation of the History of Religions to Kindred Religious Sciences, Particularly Theology, Sociology of Religion, Psychology of Religion and Phenomenology of Religion" (1954); "Comparing the Religio-Historical and the Theological Method" (1971); and "The Phenomenological Method" (1963).

31 See also Bleeker (1974), W. B. Kristensen, *The Meaning of Religion* (1960), W. C. Smith, "Comparative Religion: Whither and Why?" or *The Meaning and End of Religion* (1963); or "The Modern West in the History of Religions" (1984).

32 The concept of "understanding" used in this fashion has an existentialist, religious connotation, for it suggests that "understanding" constitutes not simply knowledge about religion but perception of a reality that surpasses knowledge or, succinctly put, that constitutes a special kind of knowledge beyond ordinary knowledge. This state of affairs certainly demands further analysis—unfortunately not a task that can be taken up here. On this matter consult J. Waardenburg, "Introduction: A View of a Hundred years of Religion" (1973).

33 See Oxtoby, "*Religionswissenschaft* Revisited" (1968).

34 This constitutes, I think, a kind of "theology of humanism" and, therefore, an implicit religion. It is clearly on display in, for example, D. R. Blumental, "Judaic Studies: An Exercise in the Humanities" (1977).

35 I do not wish here to assess why the agenda is becoming apparent—nor what is behind these attacks on the scientific study of religion. Some discussion of these issues can be found in C. W. Kegley, "Theology and Religious Studies: Friends or Enemies?" (1978); or G. D. Kaufman, "Nuclear Eschatology and the Study of Religion" (1983). The image of an "attack" on the scientific study of religion is appropriate given the level of hostility evident in the work of a number of authors. Much of this approaches invective and is thus not worth analysis, but it does display the vehement reaction to what I have referred to as a "failure of nerve," as well as a fear (initially generated by the Enlightenment) that academic life might transcend, and thereby threaten the "intellectual" and the faithful. Among others see M. Marty, "Seminary/Academy: Beyond the Tensions" (1983); M. Novak, *Ascent of the Mountain, Flight of the Dove: An Introduction to Religious Studies* (1972); and "The Identity Crisis of Us All: Response to Professor Crouter" (1972); and "B. Ladner, "Religious Studies in the University: A Critical Reappraisal" (1972); and David Burrell, "Faith and Religious Convictions: Studies in Comparative Epistemology" (1983). Other offenders, such as R. Bellah and W. C. Smith, are discussed below.

36 I have in mind here the example of the development in Canadian universities of rather close, official ties to church-related colleges characterized predominantly by their "advocacy-learning" environment. See R. W. Neufeldt, *Religious Studies in Alberta: A State-of-the-Art Review* (1983). It is also important to note that some Canadian universities have funded appointment financed by religious groups in the community, since such a procedure contributes to a blurring of the distinction between religion and the study of religion. This type of funding activity has received some attention with respect to "study conferences" underwritten by the Unification Church in a recent "Symposium on Scholarship and Sponsorship" involving I. L. Horowitz, B. R. Wilson, J. A. Beckford, E. Barker, T. Robbins, and R. Wallis.

37 See also R. Holley, *Religious Education and Religious Understanding* (1978).

38 Bolle in effect is asking that "capital-c" confessional theology be replaced by "small-c" confessional theology.

39 On this subject see my "Theory in the Study of Religion" (1983).

40 See as well Wach's "General Revelation and the Religions of the World" (1954): 83–93, and "Introduction: The Meaning and task of the History of Religion" (1967).

41 See especially J. Kitagawa, "Theology and the Science of Religion" (1975), and "*Verstehen und Erlösung*" (1971).

42 Paul Tillich, *Christianity and the Encounter of World Religions* (1963), and "The Significance of the History of Religions for the Systematic Theologian" (1966). See also Howard R. Burkle, "Tillich's 'Dynamic-Typological' Approach to the History of Religions" (1981).

43 See, for example, the essays in M. Eliade's *The Quest: History and Meaning of Religion* (1969).

44 See, for example, *Imagination and Meaning: The Scholarly and Literary Worlds of Mircea Eliade* edited by N. J. Girador and M. L. Ricketts.

45 The concept of "meaning" is complete and ambiguous, requiring a good deal of clarification if it is to be of use to the student of religion. Minimal bibliographical orientation would take more space than is available at present and must, therefore, be left for another essay.

46 The literature, I suggest, shows an increasing number of the latter, which, however, neither time nor space allow for analysis here. See, among others, F. Streng, "Objective Study of Religion" and his "Religious Studies: Processes of Transformation" (1974); N. Ross Reat, "Insiders and Outsiders in the Study of Religious Traditions" (1983); C. Vernoff, "Naming the Game—A Question of the Field" (1963); J. Arthur Martin, "What Do We Do When We Study Religion?" (1975); and Blumental, "Judaic Studies" (1977). There are several essays by J. Neusner which seem to support this kind of position—but they do so ambiguously. For this reason I reserve discussion of his position for another context. The *Journal of the American Academy of Religion*, I understand, is soon to publish papers on this topic by J. Neusner, W. May, J. Cahill, W. Capps, and L. O'Connell. (See L. O'Connell, "Religious Studies, Theology, and the Undergraduate Curriculum" [1984].) O'Connell's article appeared after this paper was written and so no account of it has been taken into consideration here, although the paper is wholly in "the failure of nerve" stream as I have developed it above. O'Connell does, however, refer to the forthcoming articles that he prepared for publication (146). These papers were published in that journal as what Strenski calls "The Report of the Saint Louis Project" (see I. Strenski, "Our Very Own 'Contras': A Response to the 'St. Louis Project' Report"). W. Nicholl's recent paper to the Canadian Society for the Study of Religion annual meeting in Guelph (1983), entitled "Spirituality and Criticism in the Hermeneutics of Religion" and J. Wiggins' paper on "Theology and Religious Studies," read to the Eastern International Regional Meeting of the American Academy of Religion at McMaster University (1983), are also likely to see publication in the near future (to my knowledge, neither paper has appeared in print).

47 See also G. Baum *et al.*, "Responses to Charles Davis" (1975).

48 It is, in fact, the bulk of Smith's methodological message to the community of academic students of religion. Since I have discussed his position on a variety of occasions I shall say no more here; see especially my essays "The Role of Belief in the Study of Religion: A Response to W. C. Smith" (1979), and "Three Responses to *Faith and Belief*: A Review Article" (1981).

49 See also the response by James Tunstead Burtchaell to this paper and Bellah's reply in the *Journal for the Scientific Study of Religion* 9 (1970: 97–115).

50 For similar statements see also his "Religion in the University: Changing Consciousness, Changing Structures" (1972), and "Religious Studies as New Religion," (1978).

51 See, for example, T. J. J. Altizer, *Oriental Mysticism and Biblical Eschatology* (1961): 161, 172–74.

52 See Neusner, "Being Jewish" (1977).

53 See R. Michaelson, "The Engaged Observer: Portrait of a Professor of Religion" (1972). A slightly different view can be found in J. C. McLelland, "The Teacher of Religion: Professor or Guru?" (1972).

54 Bellah's attempt to salvage religion from the students of religion, I am afraid, is about as effective as Durkheim's attempt to rescue the reality of religion from its "demise" at the hands of the intellectualist (largely British) anthropologists. But this argument cannot be taken up here. See, however, R. Aron's parallel critique of Durkheim (Aron, 1967: 56).

55 In fairness, it must be noted that clarification of this whole matter is needed as Professor Nicholls recently informed me that the "theological turn" taken by *Studies in Religion* was not an intentional policy of his nor the result of any promise freely given by him. Whether or not his disappointment and mine with that "theological turn" converge is something we need not explain further here.

56 The sentence appears on page 13 of a draft of the essay distributed by Riley at a 1983 meeting of the Canadian Society for the Study of Religion. For some reason, it was deleted from the published version.

57 In support of this claim see, for example, A. R. Gualtieri, "Faith, Tradition and Transcendence: A Study of Wilfred Cantwell Smith" (1969), and "'Faith, Belief and Transcendence' According to Wilfred Cantwell Smith" (1981). Gualtieri's work itself provides a good example of the results of the influence, see, for instance, his "Descriptive and Evaluative Formulae for Comparative Religion" (1968); "Confessional Theology in the Context of the History of Religions" (1972) and "Normative and Descriptive in the Study of Religion" (1979). There are a number of other prominent Canadian scholars whose thought shows a like influence and even others who argue a similar case quite independently of Smith. I regret to say that these scholars appear jointly to dominant the Canadian scene.

58 See note 36 above.

59 See note 8 above.

60 I expressed that understanding of theology earlier in my essay "'Comprehensively Critical Rationalism' and Commitment" (1973).

61 W. Burkert expresses this conflict between religion and the study of religion most succinctly in his *Homo Necans: The Anthropology of Ancient Greek: Sacrificial Ritual and Myth* (1983), which is worth citing here: "The language that has proved the most generally understood and cross-cultural is that of secularized scholarship. Its practice today is determined by science in its broadest sense, its system of rules by the laws of logic. It may, of course, seem the most questionable endeavour of all to try to translate religious phenomena into this language: by its self-conception, a religion must deny that such explanations are possible. However, scholarship is free to study even the injection of knowledge and repudiation of independent thought, for scholarship, in attempting to understand the world, has the broader perspective here and cannot abstain from analyzing the worldwide fact of religion. This is not a hopeless undertaking. *However, a discussion of religion must then be anything but religious*" (xxi; my emphasis).

62 This was the primary focus of my doctoral work at the University of Lancaster (1974). My early views and subsequent re-evaluation of them are to be found in the volume entitled *Beyond Legitimation: Essays in the Problem of Religious Knowledge* (1994e).

Works cited

Bleeker, C. J. 1954. "The Relation of the History of Religions to Kindred Religious Sciences, Particularly Theology, Sociology of Religion, Psychology of Religion and Phenomenology of Religion." *Numen*. 1: 142–152.

——. 1961. "The Future of the History of Religions," in G. Schroder, ed., *X. Internationaler Kongress fur Religionsgeschicte*. Marburg: N. G. Elwert, 229–240.

——. 1963. "The Phenomenological Method," in C. J. Bleeker, ed., *The Sacred Bridge*. Leiden: E.J. Brill 1–15.

——. 1975. *The History of Religions: 1950–1975. The Organized Study of the History of Religions During a Quarter of a Century*. Lancaster: University of Lancaster Press.

Bolle, K. W. 1967. "History of Religions with a Hermeneutic Oriented toward Christian Theology?" in Mircea Eliade, Joseph Kitagawa and Charles Long, eds., *The History of Religions: Essays on the Problem of Understanding*. Chicago: University of Chicago Press, 89–118.

Capps, W. H. 1978. "The Interpenetration of New Religions and Religious Studies," in J. Needleman and G. Baker (eds.), *Understanding the New Religions*. New York: Seabury Press, 104.

Davis, Charles. 1975. "The Reconvergence of Theology and Religious Studies." *Studies in Religion*. 4: 205–221.

——. 1981. "Theology and Religious Studies." *Scottish Journal of Religious Studies*. 2: 11–20.

Drummond, R. H. 1975. "Christian Theology and the History of Religion." *Journal of Ecumenical Studies*. 12: 389–405.

Edsman, Carl-Martin. 1974. "Theology or Religious Studies?" *Religion*. 4: 59–74.

Friedrichs, Robert W. 1974. "Social Research and Theology: End of Detente?" *Review of Religious Research*. 15: 113–127.

Galloway, A. D. 1975. "Theology and Religious Studies–The Unity of our Discipline." *Religious Studies*. 11: 157–65.

Jeffner, A. 1981. "Religion and Understanding." *Religious Studies*. 17: 217–225.

Kegley, C. W. 1978. "Theology and Religious Studies: Friends or Enemies?" *Theology Today*. 35: 273–284.

Kitagawa, Joseph M. 1958. "The Life and Thought of Joachim Wach," in Joachim Wach, *The Comparative Study of Religion*. New York: Columbia University Press, xiii–xlvii.

——. 1959. "The History of Religions in America," in M. Eliade and J. M. Kitagawa, eds., *The History of Religions: Essays in Methodology*. Chicago: University of Chicago Press: 1–30.

——. 1971. "*Verstehen und Erlösung*: Some Remarks on Joachim Wach's Work." *History of Religions*. 11: 31–53.

——. 1983. "Humanistic and Theological History of Religions with Special Reference to the North American Scene," in Peter Slater and Donald Wiebe, eds., *Traditions in Contact and Change*. Waterloo: Wilfrid Laurier University Press: 553–563.

Ladner, Benjamin. 1972. "Religious Studies in the University: A Critical Reappraisal." *Journal of the American Academy of Religion.* 40: 207–218.

Meland, Bernard E. 1961. "Theology and the Historian of Religion." *The Journal of Religion.* 41: 263–276.

Mostert, J.P. 1976. "Complementary Approaches in the Study of Religion." Inaugural Lecture at University of Zululand, June, 1976.

Neusner, Jacob. 1977a. "Being Jewish and Studying About Judaism." *Address at the Inauguration of the Jay and Leslie Cohen Chair of Judaic Studies.* Atlanta: Emory University Press, 1–22.

——. 1977b. "Religious Studies: The Next Vocation." *Bulletin of the Council of Societies for the Study of Religion.* 8: 117–120.

Oxtoby, Williard. 1968. "*Religionswissenschaft* Revisited," in J. Neusner, ed., *Studies in the History of Relgions: Religions in Antiquity.* Leiden: E. J. Brill, 590–608.

Pannenberg, W. 1971. "Toward a Theology of the History of Religions," in W. Pannenbert, *Basic Questions in Theology.* London: SCM, Vol 2, 65–118.

——. 1976. *Theology and the Philosophy of Science.* Trans. Francis McDonagh. London: Darton, Longman and Todd.

Riley, Phillip B. 1984. "Theology and/or Religious Studies: A Case Study of *Studies in Religion/Sciences religieuses*, 1971–1981." *Studies in Religion.* 13: 423–444 (originally presented at the 1983 meeting of the Canadian Society for the Study of Religion).

Schimmel, Annemarie. 1960. "Summary of the Discussion." *Numen.* 7: 235–239.

Sharpe, Eric J. 1986. *Comparative Religion: A History* [1975]. London: Duckworth.

Tillich, Paul. 1963. *Christianity and the Encounter of World Religions.* New York: Columbia University Press.

Wach, J. 1944. *Sociology of Religion.* Chicago: University of Chicago Press.

——. 1951. *Types of Religious Experience, Christian and Non-Christian.* Chicago: University of Chicago Press.

——. 1958. *The Comparative Study of Religion.* New York: Columbia University Press.

Werblowsky, R. J. Zwi. 1959. "The Comparative Study of Religions: A Review Essay." *Judaism.* 8: 352–360.

Wiebe, Donald. 1975. "Explanation and the Scientific Study of Religion." *Religion.* 5: 33–52.

——. 1978. "Is a Science of Religion Possible?" *Studies in Religion.* 7: 5–17.

39 'Religion' and 'Religious Studies': No Difference at All

Jonathan Z. Smith

Jonathan Z. Smith (1938–) was raised in Manhattan, attended Haverford for his BA and received his PhD in the history of religions from Yale. He has spent more than forty years of his distinguished career at the University of Chicago. His influence on religious studies exceeds his published works on Frazer, the theory of ritual, religions of late antiquity, early Christianity, Maori cults, and the Jonestown massacre. His teaching, training of scholars, and various books and essays relate a distinctive and incisive voice that has been central to theoretical reflection about religion, its study, methods, and the role of scholars in creating this category, determining appropriate data, and engaging in classification, definition, and comparison. In this essay Smith clarifies long-standing problems for religious studies within a larger context of the academy while also challenging scholars to own up to and move beyond self-created obstacles as well as to participate more fully in larger intellectual fields of inquiry. Other influential publications include *Map is not Territory: Studies in the History of Religions* (1978), *Imagining Religion: From Babylon to Jonestown* (1982), *To Take Place: Toward Theory in Ritual* (1987), *Drudgery Divine: On the Comparison of Early Christianities and the Religions of Late Antiquity* (1990), and *Relating Religion: Essays in the Study of Religion* (2004) – all from the University of Chicago Press.

***

This paper was prepared by J. Z. Smith for a colloquium "The Santa Barbara Colloquy: Religion within the limits of Reason Alone." Although Smith is responding to "the Conference Document"—G. J. Larson's "Revising Graduate Education"—his analysis and insights within that context speak to larger and enduring issues of religious studies and intellectual pursuits in the academy that are not neatly contained by boundaries often used to carve up academic territory. Larson's conference document was included as an appendix in the same issue of *Soundings: An Interdisciplinary Journal* where this essay was published (LXXI: 2–3, Summer/Fall 1988).

From one perspective, if I take seriously the title for this session which has embedded within it the question we are to discuss, it will not take me very long to transact my part of the business. "What is the difference between religion and religious studies?" Either every difference or no difference at all. "What is the difference between religious studies and other humanistic and social scientific fields?" In principle, none.

I have given two opposing answers to the first question—that of the difference between religion and religious studies—because I know what is usually meant by such a question (for which, the approved answer would be, "every difference") and I know how I would like to take the question (under this guise, the answer I have proposed elsewhere would be, "no difference at all").

As usually understood, the distinction between religion and religious studies reduces to some version of the duality between 'being religious' or 'doing religion' and the study of the same. This sort of distinction is expressed in our conference document by the disclaimer, "the academic study of religion is clearly not itself religious." It is a preeminently political contrast, one of value in carving out a place for the study of religion within the university, but of dubious value beyond. It is, quite frankly, a ploy. We signal this political ancestry by using as contrast terms, 'seminary,' or 'theological' or by adopting the valorizing terminology of the academy: first, *history (Geschichte)* or *science (Wissenschaft)*, more recently, and happily free from Teutonic pedigree, *studies*. The elaboration of the distinction has set the political (and secondarily, the intellectual) agenda of religious studies in the last century as signaled in your conference document with the phrase, "it was clearly recognized at Santa Barbara that the task was to develop the academic study of religion in a manner appropriate to the letters and science mission of a modern, secular state university." Note which party conforms "in a manner appropriate" to whom. The political distinction was, at heart, a counsel to passivity and integration, not to interesting thought.

As a sheerly political move, analogous to other self-justifications from other fields who sought recognition and legitimation from centers of articulate power, the distinction can be applauded. Raised to the level of theory, it has proved mischievous, especially when confused with other sorts of distinctions such as those between the "insider" and the "outsider"—the "emic" and the "etic" in contemporary jargon. Its most current formulation is that between the normative and the descriptive.

While I recognize the value of this distinction in some analytic contexts, as used in religious studies it appears all too often to be a continuation of the old political jargon (after many of the battles have been long settled). It does not yield the same sort of theoretical clarification that analogous distinctions provide: for example, as between the formal and the empirical, the monothetic and the polythetic, definition and classification. It continues to serve the old tactical ends of establishing legitimacy by lay, juridical language rather than theoretical discourse. It is but a more elegant form of the sort of language employed by the French Ministry of Education in 1885 (as Eric Sharpe reminds us) when it closed down the Catholic Theological Faculties and established the Fifth Section of Religious Sciences: "we do not wish to see the cultivation of polemics but of critical research, we wish to see the examination of texts and not the discussion of dogmas."[1] This language was continued by the United States Supreme Court in School District of Abington vs. Schempp, when Mr. Justice Goldberg declared, in what was to be the "Magna Carta" for religious studies within state universities: "It seems clear to me … that the Court would recognize the propriety of … the teaching about religion as distinguished from the teaching of religion in the public schools."[2]

Not only is the putative distinction naive and political, it is also anachronistic. It speaks out of a period when the norms of theological inquiry (as experienced in the west) were largely governed by an intact canon, when the ideology of the human sciences were chiefly governed by the goal of achieving "objectivity" or "value-free" knowledge. The most superficial reading of much contemporary theological discourse will reveal that the notion of an intact canon has largely been abandoned or has been perceived as problematic. An equally superficial reading of the current literature of human sciences will reveal that the subjectivity of the individual researcher now stands at the very center of the critical enterprise. Kant, Marx, Freud, *et al.* have won over both sides. Within the academy, neither can escape the discourse of modernity.

Allow me to introduce a revision of the question by taking a bit of a detour, a set of reflections first stimulated by a project undertaken by Walter Capps at UCSB at least a decade ago. He convened a conference to study the "the undeniable fact that religious studies may have created a phenomenon against which it has been judiciously trying to distinguish itself. Religious studies, in effect, has stimulated religion." But, what a religion! For it has been, more often than not, one shorn of most if not all communal and consensual sanctions. We have seen the emergence, within the academy, of a highly personalist religiosity in which each individual constitutes his or her own ad hoc canon in the name of generic religion. (In Burkhardt's sense of the term, what we have seen is the emergence of a kind of religious "barbarism.") This generic term 'religion' requires further attention.

I take it we can agree that the term "religion" is not an empirical category. It is a second-order abstraction. This changes our previous mode of discourse. While it is possible to speak of theorizing about religion in general, it is impossible to "do it" or "believe it" or be normative or descriptive with respect to it. Ways of meaningful speaking of first order phenomena have become impossibly conjoined to a second order abstraction resulting, at the very least, in misplaced concreteness. What meaning, then, can the word "religion" have in such a situation?

College catalogues and college-level textbooks display two chief understandings. The first employs the language of *religion* and postulates some essence of religion (usually vaguely defined in terms of ultimacy or transcendence) which becomes manifest in particular historical or geographical traditions or artifacts. However, the mechanism of the 'manifestation' is rarely exhibited, and the ubiquity of the alleged essence is not much insisted on after the opening chapter or first lecture in the introductory course.

The second employs the language of the *religious*. It appears to make the claim that there is a religious aspect, approach, perspective, or dimension to some subject or area of human experience which has non-religious dimensions as well. As in the first case, the definition of the "religious" in such formulations is vague. The "religious" most frequently appears to function as a sort of extra-plus (the "most integrative" is quite common), Here the "religious" has come to mean some loosely characterized quality of life or experience.

It is we, that is to say, the academy, who fill these definitions with content or meaning, who give them status, who employ them as part of our language. It is we in the academy who imagine kingdoms, phyla, classes, orders, families and genera—life, after all, is lived only at the level of species or individuals. As Herb Fingarette wrote on another topic some years ago: "Home is always home for someone. ... There is no absolute home in general."[3] *Mutatis mutandis* religion in general.

This has led me to the relatively simple proposition that it is the study of religion that created the category, it is the study of religion that invented "religion." As I have written elsewhere:

> If we have correctly understood the archeological and textual record, man has had his entire history in which to imagine deities and modes of interaction with them. But man, more precisely western man, has had only the last few centuries in which to imagine religion. It is this act of second order, reflexive imagination which must be the central preoccupation of any student of religion. That is to say, while there is a

staggering amount of data, of phenomena, of human experiences and expressions that might be characterized in one culture or another, by one criterion or another as religious—there is no data for religion. Religion is solely the creation of the scholar's study. It is created for the scholar's analytic purposes by his imaginative acts of comparison and generalization. Religion has no independent existence apart from the academy.[4]

This is to say, the concept "religion" functions as a category formation for religious studies as its close analogue "culture" functions for anthropology or "language" functions for general linguistics. Like them, it is to be judged solely by its theoretical utility.

As an aside I may add that there is no more pathetic spectacle in all of academia than the endless citation of the little list of fifty odd definitions of religion from James Leuba's *Psychology of Religion*, in introductory textbooks as proof that religion is beyond definition, that it is fundamentally a *mysterium*. Nonsense! We created it and, following the Frankenstein-ethos, we must take responsibility for it.[5]

I doubt, factually, that religious studies constitutes a "coherent disciplinary matrix in and of itself." I equally doubt that we should attempt to make the claim. It is, once again, an enterprise that served well the politics of establishing departments by some principle of intellectual economy. It is an enterprise that characterized nineteenth-century encyclopedia and philosophical classifications of the sciences,[6] but I know of no other field preoccupied with making such claims at the present time. The question of distinction between fields of study in the academy has largely yielded to the complex question of the classification of objects of study within broad domains of inquiry. There is, most certainly, no "unique idiom or language of religious studies" … not even a dialect, at best, only a mongrel, polyglot jargon, again quite typical of the present academy. We are, at our firmest, what Steven Toulmin has termed a "would-be discipline," and we must be content, for the present, that that be the case. After all, the same characterization applies to the vast majority of our conversation partners within the academy in both the humanities and the social sciences.

Allow me to cite two descriptions of the characteristics of "would-be disciplines." I would hope not only that we would recognize ourselves in these descriptions, but also that they might suggest some curricular implications. The first is from Steyen Toulmin's *Human Understanding*, which remains the most searching discussion of intellectual disciplines and professions that I know.

Toulmin writes:

> [Those] attempting to co-operate in launching a new science (say) may not merely disagree about their particular observations and interpretations, concepts and hypotheses: they may even lack common standards for deciding what constitutes a genuine problem, a valid explanation, or a sound theory. … the various practitioners of a scientific 'would-be discipline' can presuppose no agreed aims, ideals, or standards. The immediate result of this lack is that theoretical debate in the field concerned becomes largely—and unintentionally—methodological or philosophical; inevitably, it is directed less at interpreting particular empirical findings than at debating the general acceptability (or unacceptability) of rival approaches, patterns of explanation, and standards of judgement. [Within a 'would-be discipline'] the theoretical debate can—at best—concentrate on the acknowledged methodological failings of the subject in the attempt to analyze, and see the relations between, the alternative intellectual goals which it might be pursuing.[7]

The second quotation is from the initial pages of Thomas Kuhn's opening chapter, "The Route to Normal Knowledge," in *The Structure of Scientific Revolutions*:

> In the absence of a paradigm or some candidate for paradigm, all of the facts that could possibly pertain to the development of a given science are likely to seem equally relevant. As a result, early fact gathering is a far more random activity than the one that subsequent scientific development makes familiar. Furthermore, in the absence of a reason for seeking some particular form of more recondite information, early fact-gathering is restricted to the wealth of data that lie ready to hand. ... This is the situation that creates the schools characteristic of the early stages of a science's development. No natural history can be interpreted in the absence of at least some implicit body of intertwined theoretical and methodological belief that permits selection, evaluation and criticism. [Lacking internal paradigm] it must be externally supplied, perhaps by a current metaphysic, by another science, or by personal or historical accident. No wonder that in the early stages of development of any science different men confronting the same range of phenomena, but not usually all the same particular phenomena, describe and interpret them in different ways.[8]

In the absence of that corporate consciousness which constitutes an intact discipline, the present task for the student of religion is a kind of "damage control," taking up the various sorts of issues signaled by Toulmin and Kuhn and substituting individual self-consciousness for collective agreement (or stipulation) by making plain that one is engaged in matters of choice rather than happenstance (or, for that matter, revelation). This consciousness must be demanded and trained for at both the levels of data (i.e. examples accepted for purposes of an argument) and of interpretative frameworks. With respect to the one I have argued:

> For the self-conscious student of religion, no datum possesses intrinsic interest. It is of value only insofar as it can serve as an exemplum of some fundamental issue in the imagination of religion. The student of religion must be able to articulate clearly why 'this' rather than 'that' was chosen as an exemplum. His primary skill is concentrated in this choice. This effort at articulate choice is all the more difficult, hence all the more necessary, for the student of religion who accepts neither the boundaries of canon nor of community as constituting his intellectual domain, in providing his range of exempla. Implicit in this effort at articulate choice are three conditions. First, that the exemplum has been well and fully understood. This requires the mastery of both the relevant primary material and the history and tradition of its interpretation. Second, that the exemplum be displayed in the service of some important theory, some paradigm, some fundamental question, some central element in the academic imagination of religion. Third, that there be some method for explicitly relating the exemplum to the theory, paradigm or question and some stipulated method for evaluating each in terms of the other.[9]

With respect to the other, I have argued, with particular reference to graduate studies, that:

> Whatever else they learn, graduate students should be exposed to their field's past in such a way as to learn the art of critical evaluation and to gain the ability to account for this past in terms of a broadly based historical consciousness. They must learn the context of their second-order tradition as well as they have mastered the primary texts,

and the difficult art of evaluating each in terms of the other as well as in terms of historical perspectives and intellectual principles. They should learn, through explicit attention to rules and by the careful study of examples, the crafts of argument and dialectics, the art of making things count and of determining what counts, as well as more philosophic issues relative to the types and status of definitions, taxonomies and explanations. They should be capable of stipulating why their chosen data are exemplary in terms of clearly stated, well formulated issues central to their academic field, and they should be taught ways of 'cost accounting' for the decisions of choice and interpretation that they make. Such concerns (and there are others which might have equal claim to attention) are not the domain of any particular discipline or field of study. They are what constitutes an endeavor as academic. As such, they form the elements of a general education at the graduate level.[10]

This last begins to hint at my reasons for responding to the second question before us, "What is the difference between religious studies and other humanistic and social scientific fields?" with the blunt answer: "In principle, none." That is to say, to the degree that we are citizens of the academy, sharing common presuppositions as to "what is the case" (e.g. the appeal in the conference document to the widely held notion of *homo symbolicus*), our commonalities, qua the academy, far outweigh what I would understand to be differences of economic efficiency that separate the currently mapped fields within the human sciences. From this point of view, I am more than content to hold the position, critically described in Larson's paper that "the distinction between religious studies and other humanistic disciplines is largely heuristic" and that "religious studies is simply one more functional way of cutting up the pie in the modern university." Nor am I aware of other "would-be disciplines" making stronger claims. The internal differences within one field are often sharper than the extramural differences between one field and another, or, to personalize this, each of us frequently finds closer conversation partners with some representative of "other" fields than we do with the majority of members of our own putative area. What is more, Toulmin, in the passage I quoted, gives us good reason why this is bound to be the case.

I am not in the least persuaded by the conference document's attempt to describe a "second level," in particular, I am made uneasy by its appeal to "the apprehension or experience of transcendence" as the differentiating principle. Beyond some doubt that a "discipline" is usefully described in terms of subject matter rather than in terms of methods, conventions, and intellectual tasks, there are profound and well-known problems with the formulation which may be expressed briefly in two parallel forms. (1) As I have already indicated, I find the language of transcendence distressingly vague. A field in quest of an undefined (or, is it held to be undefinable?) *sine qua non* is no field at all. (2) Despite its Geertzian flavor, this revision of an essentially Tillichian proposal does not escape the dual problems of pansymbolism and monopolarity which were thoroughly exposed by Charles Hartshorne and taken up by W.M. Urban, W.P. Alston, and H.H. Penner, among others.[11]

Even more troublesome is the derivative proposition in the conference document that religious studies be understood as an "inquiry into the human need for symbolizing transcendence." Unless this be radically reformulated as "an inquiry into the human response to the transcendent"—a move that the document appears properly to eschew—what prevents this statement of "need" from being subsumed by some form of biological, social, or psychological functionalism, with all of the latter's well-known problems, thus collapsing the grounds for the proposed disciplinary distinction? If one rewrites the definition in the conference statement in a manner formally congruent with that by a sophisticated functionalist such as Melford Spiro, the problem for its proposers becomes clear: "Religion is a network of culturally patterned symbols of and interactions with culturally posited modes of transcendence."[12]

I fear such arguments concerning the putative autonomy of religious studies will not rapidly disappear. I must insist that, when not sheerly political, they are not designed to serve an academic end, but to protect the object of religion (the sacred, transcendent, what have you) from the academy by declaring its autonomy—that is to say, a weak return to the old enterprise of Otto. While there have been a few elegant and instructive recent examples of the discourse of autonomy (recall Kurt Rudolph versus Alfred Rupp),[13] most such endeavors have yielded sterile, inedible fruit.

For these and other reasons, I doubt the success of the fissive enterprise, let alone its legitimacy. However, there are other sorts of reasons for abstention from such differentiations which are for me far more provocative.

The first is the sense that we have reached a point in the academy where many of the fields within the human sciences are debating the same issues from quite similar perspectives. What appears to have emerged is a broad agreement upon a number of co-equal possibilities which, while surely characteristic of particular scholars or scholarly styles, cannot be used to identify one field over against another. Each alternative represents a potentially responsible choice for scholarship. Each has advantages and disadvantages, but in theoretical and methodological discourse, it is often the set of problems one is willing to live with that finally determines the stance. Students need to be exposed to exemplars of these wider universes of choice and to the consequences entailed by their acceptance—whether the examples be found within or without the area-code assigned to religious studies.

Time prevents more than a telegraphic citation of some of these issues. Each deserves long and careful study. To allude to just two: one of the issues that has exercised the AAR of late concerns the issues of privilege with respect to the interpretative enterprise. Is the interpreter privileged with respect to the native or to that which is being interpreted? Is the native, or the indigenous exegetical tradition, privileged with respect to the interpreter? Such issues are at least as old as Kant,[14] and while they have been raised recently within religious studies, they are also being hotly debated in most of the fields within the human sciences—especially within literary studies and anthropology.[15] Is the controlling metaphor for relating and understanding an "other" that of photograph, text or dialogue? These questions are generic to the human sciences and encourage wide, corporate discussion and debate among our varied conversation partners.

Quite similar is that issue which is signaled by the shorthand term, "reductionism" over which much ink has been spilled. On examination this turns out to be a pseudo-issue. It is not that there are reductive disciplines as opposed to non-reductive ones ("we're O.K. … but take care, the next tribe over is cannibalistic"), even supposing that we could agree on an adequate definition of "reductionism." A far broader issue appears to be at stake. For example, in *Ideology and Utopia*, Karl Mannheim distinguishes between "right wing" and "left wing" methodologies of the human sciences. The "right wing," he argues:

> tend to use morphological categories which do not break up the concrete totality of the data of experience, but seek rather to preserve it in all its uniqueness. As opposed to this morphological approach [characteristic of the "right"], the analytical approach characteristic of the parties of the left, broke down every concrete totality in order to arrive at smaller, more general units which might then be recombined (in thought).[16]

Redescribing the matter in this fashion, in terms of conservative and radical, eliminates the usual discourse in which the parties of the "right" tend to be all too readily identified with the non-reductive, and smokes out the other sorts of ideological assumptions involved in this seemingly intuitively correct approach: no more good guys and bad guys. Parties of the "left" and "right," "lumpers" and "splitters," "hedgehogs" and "foxes," the "hermeneutics of recovery" and the "hermeneutics of suspicion"—these are coeval and coequal possibilities which can be entertained responsibly by scholars within each of the human sciences. I do not mean to suggest the absence of difference, only to insist that real intellectual differences may well need to be reconfigured in other than traditional disciplinary modes (*scilicet*, departments) around issues basic to all of the human sciences.

This leads to my final point. There is a growing recognition that there may no longer be a set of clear and interesting distinctions between the humanities (broadly conceived) and the social sciences (equally broadly understood). It is a view which, rhetorically, is best expressed in Geertz's classic 1980 essay, "Blurred Genres," in which the interpretive turn ascendent in both the humanities and the social sciences ...

> is a phenomenon general enough and distinctive enough to suggest that what we are seeing is not just another redrawing of the cultural map—the moving of a few disputed borders ... —but an alternation of the principles of mapping. Something is happening to the way in which we think about the way we think ... [it is] a culture shift ... [a] refiguration of social thought ... It is not an interdisciplinary brotherhood that is needed nor even less highbrow eclecticism. It is recognition on all sides that the lines grouping scholars together into intellectual communities, or (what is the same thing) sorting them out into different ones, are these days running at some highly eccentric angles.[17]

It is a view proposed in operational terms by the University of Chicago's 1982 *Report of the Commission on Graduate Education*, which argued:

> There seems to be a growing sense among humanists and social scientists that the customary disciplinary divisions are collapsing. New forms of intellectual discourse are appearing that are erasing the conventional lines of demarcation between the humanities and the social sciences, on the one hand, while realigning their component disciplines on the other. ... We may well be experiencing a sea-change in the human sciences, a transformation of intellectual boundaries and a reorientation of intellectual interests comparable to that which created the principle disciplines as we know them scarcely a century ago.[18]

In its early discussions, members of the Commission argued for removing Ph.D. granting powers from individual departments in the humanities and social sciences and vesting them in an Institute for the Human Sciences with the notion that students would do some significant fraction of their work in courses within the Institute and would constitute their dissertation committees from its members. In its published Report, the Commission kept the intellectual notion but bowed to political realism. It recommended the establishment of an Institute for research in the human sciences (or, that failing, two institutes, one in the humanities, one in the social sciences) as the locus of "research and writing leading to the dissertation," but now under departmental supervision. Furthermore, a series of standing seminars and workshops, with faculty and graduate student membership, were to be located in these institutes "to investigate fundamental problems. ... without limitation by departmental or divisional boundaries."[19] (These have been established under an administrative committee without adopting the institute[s] recommendation.) Furthermore, the Commission recommended the creation of a parallel series of "wide" Ph.D. programs "in the humanities [or the social sciences] or possibly in the humanities and social sciences, which would educate graduate students, or some of them, more liberally and less narrowly than we have done so far."[20]

From such a point of view, the second pedagogical and programmatic question: "To what extent should graduate training in religious studies be intradepartmental and to what extent interdepartmental?" becomes moot. For educational purposes (not to speak of intellectual ends), departments ought to be considered invisible.

To pick up an analogy from the conference document, our present, time-bound topography of fields of study may be seen, at best, as dialects within a far broader language system which has priority of claim upon both the students' and the scholars' attention. That old Latin tag from Terence, revived with such force in those Renaissance and Enlightenment academies that gave rise to the study of religion—"Nothing human is foreign to me"—might now be revised: "Nothing in the human sciences is foreign to me."

QUESTIONS FOR REVIEW AND DISCUSSION

1. Smith indicates that common distinctions made between religion and religious studies can be understood as political exercises to carve out a space for religious studies scholars. Even the claim that "the academic study of religion is clearly not itself religious" is characterized as a ploy. Explain Smith's claim in your own words. How does this emphasis on the political nature of the contrast between religion and its study fit with the history of religious studies? How does it fit with other selections in this volume?

2. How does Smith support the apparently contradictory answers that he provides to his own question, "What is the difference between religion and religious studies?" He gives one answer in the subtitle of this article. What is the thrust of his argument in favor of "no difference at all"?

3. Smith also argues for a lack of difference "between religious studies and other humanistic and social scientific fields." Do you agree? How would advocates for religious studies being uniquely different from these other fields argue their point? On what grounds would Smith object?

4. Smith characterizes the US Supreme Court ruling that distinguishes between "teaching about religion" as opposed to "the teaching of religion in the public schools" as naïve, political, and anachronistic. Paraphrase Smith's position. Do you agree?

5. What characteristics does Smith offer to describe the religion that religious studies has created (in keeping with Walter Capps' quotation to this end)?

6. Smith describes two primary understandings of religion or religious in university textbooks. What are these? Can you identify selections in this Reader that fit (or resist) one or the other understanding?

7. One of the thought-provoking assertions in this article is the role of scholars and the academy in creating the categories we study and filling "these definitions with content or meaning." What are some of the implications for Religious Studies that follow from this assertion? Do you agree? What arguments, examples, and analogies do you find most clear or convincing?

8. Just before Smith's extended quotation about what graduate students should learn in terms of general education, he indicates that "self-conscious" students of religion should be able to articulate the value of the data they select with three conditions in mind. What are the three? Can you come up with an example (from studies in this volume or elsewhere) that satisfies all three?

9. Explain Smith's statement that arguments concerning the autonomy of religious studies—"when not sheerly political"—represent "a weak return to the old enterprise of Otto"?

10. What is Smith's view of critiques that level the charge of "reductionism" against some disciplines?

Notes

1 Quoted in Eric Sharpe, *Comparative Religion: A History* (London: Duckworth Press; 1975) 122.
2 It would be a worthwhile project to collect legal definitions of 'religion.' 'Religion' was a juridical term long before it became an academic one.
3 Herbert J. Fingarette, *The Self in Transformation* (New York: Harper & Row, 1963) 237.
4 Jonathan Z. Smith, *Imagining Religion* (Chicago: University of Chicago Press, 1982) xi [slightly revised].
5 See R.G.A. Dolby, "Classification of the Sciences: The Nineteenth Century Tradition," in Roy F. Ellen and David Reason, *Classifications in their Social Context*: (London: Academic Press, 1979) 167–93.
6 See, for example, the following statement by H. Perkin, Director of the Center for Social History, University of Lancaster: "History is the maverick among disciplines, the misfit, the bull in the china shop. Since everything has a history and history, potentially at least, deals with everything that has ever happened in human society, the historian is a kind of licensed rustler who wanders at will across his scholarly neighbors' fields, poaching their stock and purloining their crops and breaking down their hedges. In a very real sense it is not a discipline at all. … The historian can never say, like the physicist or the economist or the theologian, 'That is not my subject' … It may best be described as a concern with change and stability." H. Perkin, "The Historical Perspective," in B.R. Clark, *Perspectives on Higher Education: Eight Disciplinary and Comparative Views* (Berkeley: University of California Press, 1984) 17–18.
7 Steven Toulmin, *Human Understanding*, vol. 1, *The Collective Use and Evolution of Concepts* (Princeton: Princeton University Press, 1972) 380–81.
8 Thomas S. Kuhn, *The Structure of Scientific Revolutions*, 2nd ed. (Chicago: University of Chicago Press, 1970) 15–17.
9 Smith, xi–xii [slightly revised].
10 Jonathan Z. Smith, "Here and Now: Prospects for Graduate Education," in J. Neusner, ed., *New Humanities and Academic Disciplines* (Madison: University of Wisconsin Press, 1984) 36–37 [slightly revised].
11 Charles Hartshorne and William L. Reese, *Philosophers Speak of God* (Chicago: University of Chicago Press, 1963) 1–25. See the other literature cited in Hans H. Penner, "Bedeutung und Probleme der religiösen Symbolik bei Tillich und *Eliadea" Antaios* 9 (1967): 127–43.
12 I toy here with Melford E. Spiro, "Religion: Problems of Definition and Explanation," in Michael Banton, ed. *Anthropological Approaches to the Study of Religion* (London: Tavistock Publications, 1966) 96.
13 Alfred Rupp, *Phänomenon und Geschichte: Prolegomena zur Methdologie der Religionsgeschichte* (Saarbrucken, 1978) and the review of K. Rudolph, *Numen* 27(198): 180–85.
14 Immanuel Kant, *Critique of Pure Reason*, trans. Norman K. Smith, (London: Macmillan & Co., 1956) 310 (B 370). See further the discussion of Hans-Georg Gadamer, *Truth and Method* (New York: Crossroad Press, 1975) 170–71 for a brief history of the notion.
15 See among others, George E. Marcus and Michael M.J. Fischer, *Anthropology as Cultural Critique: An Experimental Moment in the Human Sciences* (Chicago: University of Chicago Press, 1986).

16 Karl Mannheim, *Ideology and Utopia* (New York: Harcourt Brace and Co., 1936) 274.

17 Clifford Geertz, "Blurred Genres," reprinted in Geertz, *Local Knowledge* (New York: Basic Books, 1983) 19–35. I have taken the passage quotes from pages 20, 19, 23–4.

18 "Report of the Commission on Graduate Education," *The University of Chicago Record* 16.2 (1982): 169.

19 "Report" 171–72.

20 "Report" 159.

40 Teaching Buddhism in the Postmodern University: Understanding, Critique, Evaluation

Frank E. Reynolds

Frank E. Reynolds (1930—) received his BD from Yale Divinity School in 1955 and served at the Student Christian Center in Bangkok, Thailand for several years as program director before studying the History of Religions at the University of Chicago. His work with Buddhists and Muslims in Thailand (as well as Christians) prompted him to pursue non-sectarian and empirically oriented study of religion. Not only did he receive his PhD at the University of Chicago, he also became part of the "Chicago School" in 1967 as a professor of history of religions and Buddhist studies in the Divinity School and the Department of South Asian Languages and Civilizations. His 2005 "Distinction in Theological Education" alumni award from the Yale Divinity School notes that "Throughout Reynolds's career at Chicago, he has fostered – through his writing, his teaching, and the research projects he has directed – the establishment and development of religious studies as an independent discipline that utilizes and creatively adapts approaches employed in other areas of the humanities and social sciences." These contributions are evident in the selection below, which stems from a keynote address at a McGill University conference on teaching Buddhsim and serves as the opening essay to the related volume, *Teaching Buddhism in the West: From the Wheel to the Web*, edited by Victor Sōgen Hori, Richard P. Hayes, and James Mark Shields.

It is very propitious that the Faculty of Religious Studies at McGill has chosen to celebrate the establishment of its recent Numata endowment by sponsoring an international conference that focuses attention on the teaching of Buddhism. Over the years I have been involved in many excellent Buddhist Studies activities devoted to the exploration of particular textual and historical issues; I have participated in a good number of very useful meetings and publications that have had as their focus the historical development, the present state, and/ or the future direction of Buddhist Studies research; and I have participated in several events that have had the essentially apologetic purpose of communicating a Buddhist message to active or potential Buddhist practitioners. However the McGill Conference on Teaching Buddhism: The State of the Art (and this correlated collection of essays) is the first major Buddhist Studies project that I am aware of that has had, as its primary focus, the teaching of Buddhism to undergraduate students. It is hard to imagine a more timely topic for Buddhist Studies scholars to consider.[1]

In what follows, I would like to sketch out an overall orientation to the topic of teaching Buddhism to undergraduate students. My hope is that this general orientation will have sufficient substance that it can be supported, extended or challenged by other contributors to this volume.

The basic claim that undergirds the approach that I will take is that, in the under-graduate context, the primary purpose of teaching Buddhism is to contribute to the liberal education of students. At first glance this basic claim may seem rather obvious and innocuous. However I will try to make the case that a serious exploration of the issues that this claim raises can generate an overall perspective within which and against which relevant delib-erations can creatively proceed. I will begin with a discussion of three different ways of understanding liberal education, including a newly emerging perspective that takes our postmodern intellectual and social situation seriously into account. As my exposition proceeds, I will at various points suggest particular ways in which teaching in Buddhist Studies can contribute to the process.

How, then, can we identify the kind of approach to liberal education—particularly liberal education in the humanities and social sciences—that will be truly viable as we enter into the twenty-first century?[2] Certainly it will not be the Renaissance-oriented humanistic ideal of engaging a culturally prescribed canon of texts drawn from the so-called classical tradi-tion of the West. To be sure, this view has had a number of very influential supporters in recent years, but I am quite certain that for most contemporary scholars (including virtually everyone who is involved in Buddhist Studies) it has long since lost its power to convince.

Serious and well meaning attempts have been made to update this classics-oriented approach by including, within the canon of privileged texts, items written by women, members of minority groups, and representatives of non-Western traditions—including in some cases representatives of various Buddhist traditions. But unfortunately, despite a number of attempts, no one has yet been able to provide convincing intellectual criteria for making the innumerable choices that must be made in order to responsibly implement this kind of reform. James Foard, one of the very few Buddhist Studies scholars who has given serious thought to issues of liberal education, has put the point very precisely. If we proceed in this way, he writes, "we justify adding things *ad infinitum* … *and* inevitably advocate the absurdity of unlimited limits. Our opponents know this," he continues, "and we should concede the point."[3] This certainly does not mean, either for Foard or for me, that we should avoid the teaching of texts that have been labeled as classics. Quite to the contrary. But it does mean that we cannot responsibly accept a vision of liberal education that depends on the identification of a canon of privileged texts, no matter how multicultural and forward looking that canon may seem to be.

The other really major ideal of liberal education that we have inherited from our Euro-American past is what I label the modernist ideal. This modernist ideal had its origins in the Enlightenment and is characterized by the assertion of the pre-eminence and hegemony of an Enlightenment-generated understanding of Reason (Reason with a capital "R"). In its heyday in the late nineteenth and early twentieth century this modernist approach was sometimes advocated in direct opposition to the emphasis on a canon of classical texts; on the other hand it was sometimes yoked in an uneasy alliance with it. Either way, it was an approach that dominated the intellectual scene in North America.

According to the proponents of this Enlightenment-oriented approach, the kind of Reason that was constructed and deployed by Enlightenment thinkers had thoroughly unmasked and discredited other more traditional ways of apprehending and engaging rea-lity. These Enlightenment enthusiasts were also convinced that this kind of Reason could be utilized to generate truly objective knowledge of the one empirically accessible world in which all human beings supposedly live. The direct pedagogical corollary of this modernist understanding of Reason was the notion that liberal education should be constituted by an initiation into the various positivist sciences that were specifically developed in order to pursue this reputedly objective form of knowledge. These positivist sciences included, among others, historical sciences, social and cultural sciences, and psychological sciences.

In recent years, as the hegemony of the Enlightenment notion of Reason has been increasingly challenged by a variety of late modern and postmodern critiques, the modernist ideal of liberal education has, like the classics-oriented ideal, become thoroughly untenable. Unfortunately the ghosts of the hegemony of the Enlightenment notion of Reason still haunt some areas of contemporary scholarship and teaching, including some contemporary scholarship and teaching within Buddhist Studies. However, a serious intellectual defense of the modernist ideal is no longer possible.

Given the demise of these two major notions of liberal education that we have inherited from our past—i.e., the classics-oriented view and the modernist view—those of us who continue to believe that some coherent and convincing approach to liberal education is an intellectual and social necessity face a very serious challenge. Is it really possible to develop a fully up-to-date approach to liberal education that takes adequate account of the new realities of globalization and pluralism on the one hand, and the consequences of the postmodern dethronement of the Enlightenment notion of Reason on the other? This is certainly neither the time nor the place to attempt to provide a definitive answer to this vexing question. However, a few positive suggestions may provide a useful orientation as we strive to identify and explore the issues that will be basic to the teaching of Buddhism in colleges and universities in the years that lie ahead. (To avoid misunderstanding I should indicate at the outset that in the discussion that follows I am using a rather conservative notion of postmodernity. It is a view of the postmodern situation that recognizes that the hegemony of the Enlightenment notion of Reason has been definitively undercut. But it is at the same time a view that resists the tendency of many postmodern scholars to throw out the Enlightenment baby with the Enlightenment bath water.)

The most basic characteristics of the view of liberal education that I want to affirm are the following. First, this view of liberal education presumes that human beings (including ourselves, the students we teach and the people we study) create, discover, think within and live within a variety of different and often competing worlds, all of which are historically situated and engaged. Second, it affirms that a liberal education in the postmodern era should involve the exploration of a variety of very different humanly constituted worlds. (Here I quite intentionally leave open the question of whether such worlds are "constructed" or "discovered.") These humanly constituted worlds should include some that are assumed to be familiar, and others that are quite unfamiliar. They should also include some that are "life worlds" and some that are constituted or projected in texts of various sorts. Finally, it is my contention that an appropriate and up-to-date liberal education must also include the cultivation of well-disciplined interpretive skills and strategies through which significant worlds and their interactions with one another can be rationally and imaginatively engaged.[4]

The pedagogical implications of this kind of view of liberal education for the teaching of Buddhism are legion. At the most fundamental level they include the need to justify the Buddhist Studies courses that we choose to teach in at least two distinct ways. The specific courses that we teach need to be justified in terms of the intrinsic significance of the world or worlds that are taken as the object(s) of study. At the same time these courses also need to be justified in terms of the interpretive skills and strategies that the teacher deploys and that the students are encouraged to engage and to cultivate. In what remains I will provide three specific examples of the kind of Buddhist Studies courses that seem to me to focus on topics and materials that meet the criteria of postmodern relevance and interest.

I will then turn to a more detailed discussion of the kind of interpretive skills and strategies that need to be identified and cultivated.

In choosing Buddhist worlds that are appropriate for exploration in a postmodern liberal arts curriculum, the teacher's own areas of specialized interest and expertise necessarily play a very crucial role. Thus I am well aware that the examples that I will provide inevitably embody components that arise out of my own personal interests and my own areas of competence. Nonetheless it will be useful to put forward, at least as illustrations, three specific possibilities that highlight, in very concrete ways, the kinds of topics and data that I have in mind.

Most college or university teachers will probably agree that the hardest course to teach well in any area of scholarship is the introductory course. (Which is, of course, the reason that in most departments this responsibility is foisted off on the youngest and most vulnerable member!) At the same time, the introductory course is the most important course in any given area of study, both because it generally involves the greatest number of students and because it provides an ideal context for the recruitment of students into courses that are more advanced and more specialized.

Over the past two decades I have given a great deal of thought to ways of teaching an introductory course in Buddhist Studies, primarily in the context of teaching graduate students and preparing and evaluating textbooks. As the years have gone by, I have become increasingly uncomfortable with the kind of introduction that I have myself taught and that has for many decades dominated the scene. I mean, of course, the kind of survey course that begins with what (in our most optimistic moods) we think that Buddhist Studies may have learned about the historical life and teachings of Gautama Buddha. It moves through a rapid-fire treatment of some 2500 years of Buddhist intellectual and social history. And it finally concludes with an equally rapid-fire survey of contemporary Buddhism in various countries around the world. Whatever usefulness that kind of pseudo-historical approach to the introductory course may have had in the past, it is my conviction that it has very little to commend it in the present or in the future.

The question that arises for those of us who have come to this kind of conclusion is whether or not it is possible to develop an alternative approach that will be appropriate and effective within a postmodern liberal arts curriculum. I believe that the answer is "yes." And I have invested a great deal of effort over the past two years in the preparation of a textbook that will—if it is successful—help to confirm my optimism. The book, which is entitled *The Life of Buddhism*, includes short introductions written by myself and my co-editor that provide crucial historical background and introduce a basic technical vocabulary. But the main body of the text is constituted by fifteen different accounts of the religious context, the religious practices and the lived experiences of a wide variety of twentieth-century Buddhist communities and practitioners situated throughout many diverse areas of Asia and North America. These essays, which have been written by a wide array of Buddhist Studies scholars from various disciplines, are divided into four segments. The first segment focuses on "Temples, Sacred Objects and Associated Rituals," the second deals with "Monastic Practices," and the third looks at "Lay Practices." The final segment is constituted by a single essay that describes the practices of an American Zen community located in Rochester, New York.[5]

The topic-oriented, data-oriented goal of a course using this kind of textbook would be to introduce students to a broadly representative variety of the real worlds of real Buddhists who are involved in real Buddhist practices that generate real Buddhist experiences. The course would be designed to convey to a wide range of students a kind of collage of vivid impressions and insights. Assuming that the essays have been well chosen and that the course is well taught, these impressions and insights should constitute a responsible and compelling introduction to significant commonalities, differences and conflicts that are characteristic of various Buddhist traditions. Hopefully, for some students, this kind of introductory course will also generate the motivation to seek out more advanced courses in the Buddhist Studies area.

But what about Buddhist Studies courses that are appropriate at the more advanced levels of the curriculum? The challenge is to select topics and bodies of data that are in tune with the topics and bodies of data characteristic of the very best courses being offered by other religious studies teachers and the kind being offered in other related humanistic and social science disciplines. Or, if the courses are not so tuned, the instructor should be prepared to make a convincing argument that the criteria of selection being used represent the exploration of a new frontier rather than the last vestige of a rearguard resistance to change.

Given the kind of practice-oriented introductory course that I have suggested, I will use as my second example a course that deals with a so-called "canonical" text. The basic assumption underlying the kind of text course that I have in mind is that it is necessary to give serious attention not only to the text itself (whatever that might mean), but also to the way in which the text in question has been appropriated and used within the Buddhist tradition. The best example that I can provide, given my own interests and expertise, is a course focused on a rather short text that has been preserved in the Pali canon under the title of *Mangala Sutta* (the Discourse of Blessings). This is a *sutta* that contains thirty-eight distinct, ethically oriented segments. Over the centuries it has been one of the most important and popular texts in the Theravāda tradition that presently holds sway in Sri Lanka and mainland Southeast Asia.

The course that I have in mind would begin with a relatively concise consideration of sub-topics that have in the past tended to occupy the total attention of most scholars and teachers who have focused on this kind of text. These sub-topics would include text-critical issues of authorship, manner of composition or compilation, and questions of canonical status. They would also include a basically literary overview of the form of the text and the content of the message or teaching that it contains. In this kind of course, however, such text-critical and literary matters, though they would be addressed, would certainly not be dominant. On the contrary, they would provide a launching pad for subsequent segments of the course that would focus on different ways in which the text has been received and put to use in the tradition that it has helped to constitute. In the case of the *Mangala Sutta* one segment of the course could focus on its incorporation into an ancient source book for ritual chants that has been used throughout Theravada history to exorcise evil spirits and evil influences. Another segment could trace the interpretation of the text generated in the traditional commentaries that have been written over the centuries by Theravada monastic scholars. A final segment could conclude the course by focusing on the way in which the *Mangala Sutta* is presently being employed in the on-going ideological struggle between the military rulers in Myanmar (Burma) and the democratic resistance led by Aung San Su Kyi.[6]

A third, very different kind of course that would be important to include in the Buddhist Studies component of an up-to-date liberal arts curriculum is one that would deal with the nineteenth and twentieth-century impact and establishment of Buddhism in the Western world, particularly in North America. This is a fascinating story within which many of the basic issues of modernity and postmodernity could be explored in a direct and immediate way. For example, one segment of the course could cover the development of Buddhist Studies in the United States and Canada; another could deal with the impact of Buddhism on the literary and artistic culture of the North American elite; another could highlight and analyze the fascinating representations of Buddhism in films and the media; another could focus on the establishment and development of Buddhist immigrant communities; and still another could consider the establishment and development of various indigenous Buddhist communities. One primary question that could be posed is why, in the nineteenth and twentieth centuries, the United States and Canada have provided such extremely fertile ground for the reception of Buddhist approaches to life. An intriguing and appropriate counterpoint question would be how Buddhism has been adapted and transformed as it has become engaged with the modern and postmodern environments that these North American countries have provided.

Since other papers in this volume will suggest other possible topics and correlated sets of data, I will turn now to the second major component that in my judgement needs to be present in really useful and up-to-date Buddhist Studies courses. This second major component, which is seldom discussed in Buddhist Studies circles, is the very explicit display of well honed interpretive skills by the teacher, and the closely correlated formation and cultivation of those skills in the students. As Mark Taylor has written in his "Introduction" to a collection of essays recently published under the title *Critical Terms for Religious Studies*, "it is no longer sufficient to think about different religions; now [and Taylor is quite explicitly taking account of the present postmodern context] it is necessary to consider how one thinks about these religions."[7] As the title of my paper suggests, the three very basic kinds of interpretive skills that I believe it is important to highlight are the skills of sympathetic understanding, the skills of critical analysis, and the skills of personal evaluation or judgement.[8]

Though in the actual process of interpretation sympathetic understanding, critical analysis and personal evaluation are intimately interrelated and interdependent, there is an obvious heuristic value in beginning with sympathetic understanding. What I really want to emphasize here is that those of us who teach Buddhist Studies courses cannot be satisfied with simply presenting some aspect of Buddhism in a sympathetic and appealing way. We do need to do that, but in addition we need to be very explicit about the theories and methods that scholars have used in generating this kind of understanding; we need to be very explicit about the problems and possibilities that are associated with the application of these theories and methods; and we need to be very explicit about the way in which these ways of proceeding can be justified in contemporary intellectual terms.

Obviously this kind of epistemological self-consciousness becomes more feasible and more necessary as one moves from entry level courses to courses designed for more advanced students. However, at all levels, from the most elementary to the most sophisticated, students should come away from Buddhist Studies courses having acquired a sympathetic understanding of some interesting and important aspect of Buddhism. At least equally important, they should also have learned something important about the skills of understanding that they will be able to utilize in many other contexts, both within and beyond the walls of the academy.

Sympathetic understanding is a primary aspect of the interpretive process. But (and I am convinced that this is an absolutely crucial point that is missed by many Buddhist Studies teachers) it is by no means sufficient. In the academic context sympathetic understanding needs to be complemented and supplemented by critical analysis. There are various relevant forms of critical analysis that have been developed. Some have been generated within the Buddhist tradition itself. (One of the most interesting is being propounded by a highly respected group of contemporary Japanese Buddhist scholars who are putting forth the explicitly normative claim that "Buddhism is criticism.")[9] There are also the quite different modes of critical analysis that are being developed and widely deployed in the postmodern academy. These include post-positivist modes of critical analysis that are central to historical, social, cultural and psychological sciences. They also include the newer forms of so-called critical theory that focus on the dynamics of power, particularly as these dynamics of power are played out in the hierarchies of ethnicity, class and gender.

It is obvious that in different Buddhist Studies courses the extent of the critical component will vary and the modes of critical analysis that are deployed will differ. However, I am convinced that in virtually all Buddhist Studies courses some emphasis on the cultivation of critical skills is crucial. In each case students should at least be introduced to the relevant critical scholarship that is being carried forward within contemporary Buddhist communities. In each case students should also be exposed to the relevant critical scholarship that is being generated within the secular academy. Hopefully, as students proceed through the various segments of the liberal arts curriculum, they will gradually acquire for themselves the kinds of intellectual and imaginative expertise that various forms of critical analysis require.

Thus both sympathetic understanding and critical analysis are necessary components within the interpretive process that teachers in the liberal arts should seek to encourage in their students. However, even taken together, they are not sufficient. The third component that must be added to the mix is the cultivation of well-disciplined judgements and evaluations. So far as I am aware, the best exposition of the importance of this third component of the interpretive process, and of the best means for cultivating it in students, appeared recently in a multi-authored essay entitled "Rhetoric, Pedagogy and the Study of Religions," published in the *Journal of the American Academy of Religion*. In this article the authors propose what they call a "rhetorical paradigm." Within this paradigm the chief goal of undergraduate teaching, particularly but not exclusively in the Religious Studies area, is "neither to improve technique nor to make students more knowledgeable, but to empower individual voices and to provide a space for practicing critical skills and reflective inquiry about matters of personal and public importance."[10]

The key point that I want to emphasize here is that within this rhetorical model the formation and cultivation of well-disciplined judgements and evaluations becomes an integral and culminating segment within the interpretive process itself. The role of the teacher is certainly not to convince students to adopt his or her position on the issues that may arise. On the contrary, the art of teaching within this paradigm consists in helping students to develop, alongside the skills of sympathetic understanding and the skills of critical analysis, the rhetorical skills of articulation and argumentation that facilitate the cultivation and expression of their own personal commitments. These are, it is important to add, the very same skills that will ultimately facilitate an effective engagement in the kind of serious and rational public dialogue that is absolutely essential for the future health of a democratic society.[11]

It is quite evident that up-to-date, well taught courses in Buddhist Studies will raise issues that are of serious personal and social importance. Therefore these courses provide one of the very best contexts within which to help students cultivate the skills that are involved in generating and expressing well disciplined, rationally formed evaluations and judgements.

By way of conclusion let me simply reiterate the basic normative claim that I made at the very outset—namely the claim that the primary purpose of teaching Buddhism to undergraduates in North American colleges and universities should be to facilitate and implement the process of liberal education. I am convinced that if this purpose is taken seriously, and if textbooks, courses and classroom teaching methods are self-consciously oriented toward that goal, the results will be very positive. On the one hand, liberal education will benefit from a distinctive Buddhist Studies contribution. On the other, Buddhist Studies will be able to secure and expand its still very tenuous presence within the North American academy.

QUESTIONS FOR REVIEW AND DISCUSSION

1. Reynolds indicates that "the McGill Conference on Teaching Buddhism: The State of the Art … is the first major Buddhist Studies project that I am aware of that has had, as its primary focus, the teaching of Buddhism to undergraduate students." What are the more typical emphases of conferences related to Buddhism according to Reynolds. Why does he think this focus is valuable?

2. What does Reynolds indicate is "the primary purpose of teaching Buddhism" to undergraduates? Would this be the case for teaching other religious traditions as well?

3. What suggestions does Reynolds make for liberal education in the twenty-first century? Is there still a place for classics? What additions might you suggest?

4. Reynolds discusses the modernist ideal of the Enlightenment notion of Reason. Explain this ideal in your own words. Does Reynolds think that the dominance of this notion of Reason is intellectually defensible? Why? Do you concur?

5. Reynolds "affirms that a liberal education in the postmodern era should involve the exploration of a variety of very different humanly constituted worlds"— including some worlds that are quite unfamiliar. How does his description of these worlds fit with those by Paden earlier in this volume? Do you agree that exposure to unfamiliar worlds, such as Buddhism for many undergraduates, is beneficial to a liberal arts education? Why?

6. What kinds of Buddhist studies courses meet Reynolds' criteria?

7. How does Reynolds describe introductory courses at university in general? How does he characterize the typical introductory to Buddhism course? What does he suggest as an alternative? What advantages does he claim such an approach would hold? Do you agree?

8. What are some of the potential advantages that accompany offering a course on Buddhism in the West? What primary questions does he say such courses could address?

9. Reynolds advocates cultivating interpretive skills, namely: skills of sympathetic understanding, the skills of critical analysis, and the skills of personal evaluation or judgement. Describe what he means by each of these. Is there any interpretive skill you would add to this list or substitute in place of one of these three?

Notes

1 The timeliness of the topic is directly related to recent very rapid developments in Buddhist Studies research. For a review of the research situation in North America see Reynolds 1999 and an unpublished paper by Bruce Matthews entitled "Buddhist Studies in Canada: 1970–1998."

2 I am keenly aware that any full understanding of liberal arts education must include a strong natural science component. However, given the concerns of this conference, I will focus my attention on issues that arise in the humanities / social science context.

3 Foard 1990a, 170.

4 My reflections on this topic began to develop in a serious way in the context of a project sponsored by the U.S. National Endowment for the Humanities in the late 1980s. The book that was generated by that project—*Beyond the Classics? Essays in Religious Studies and Liberal Education*—contains a number of essays that are still useful for those interested in pursuing the topic further. The most relevant are the following: Judith Berling, "Religious Studies and Exposure to Multiple Worlds"; Sheryl Burkhalter, "Four Modes of Discourse: Blurred Genres in the Study of Religion"; James Foard, "Beyond Ours and Theirs: The Global Character of Religious Studies"; Robin W. Lovin, "Confidence and Criticism: Religious Studies and the Public Purpose of Liberal Education"; Frank Reynolds "Reconstructing Liberal Education: A Religious Studies Perspective"; and Lawrence Sullivan, "'Seeking an End to the Primary Text' or 'Putting an End to the Text as Primary'."

5 This book, which I have co-edited with Jason Carbine (an advanced graduate student specializing in Buddhist Studies within the History of Religions program at Chicago) will be published by the University of California Press in the fall of 2000.

6 The kind of Buddhist Studies research that is correlated with this kind of course development was the topic of a conference on "Pali Texts in New Contexts" held at the University of Chicago Divinity School in May 1998. For two superb and highly relevant papers presented at that conference see Walters 1999 and Blackburn 1999.

7 Taylor 1998, 12.

8 In the discussion that follows I am self-consciously referring to the cultivation of interpretive skills that presume that students have already acquired basic college-level abilities in reading, writing, conceptualization and argumentation. For a suggestion for a very basic introductory course that focuses on the cultivation of the really primary skills that many students have not yet acquired, see James Foard's superb essay entitled "Writing Across the Curriculum: a Religious Studies Contribution" (Foard 1990b). Though the specific course that Foard describes deals with "Religions of the World," the pedagogical strategies that he sets forth could easily be adapted to a course focused on Buddhism.

9 See Hubbard and Swanson 1997.

10 Milter, Patton and Webb 1995, 820.

11 For an earlier presentation of this same kind of view see Lovin 1990.

References

Blackburn, Anne. 1999. "Magic in the Monastery: Textual Practice and Monastic Identity in Sri Lanka." *History of Religions* 36 (4): 354–72.

Burkhalter, Sheryl, and Frank Reynolds, eds. 1990. *Beyond the Classics? Essays in Religious Studies and Liberal Education*. Atlanta: Scholars Press.

Foard, James. 1990a. "Beyond Ours and Theirs: The Global Character of Religious Studies." In *Beyond the Classics? Essays on Religious Studies and Liberal Education*, edited by Sheryl Burkhalter and Frank Reynolds. Atlanta: Scholars Press.

——. 1990b. "Writing Across the Curriculum: A Religious Studies Contribution." In *Beyond the Classics? Essays on Religious Studies and Liberal Education*, edited by Sheryl Burkhalter and Frank Reynolds. Atlanta: Scholars Press.

Hubbard, Jamie, and Paul L. Swanson, eds. 1997. *Pruning the Bodhi Tree: The Storm Over Critical Buddhism*. Honolulu: University of Hawaii Press.

Lovin, Robin W. 1990. "Confidence and Criticism: Religious Studies and the Public Purposes of Liberal Education." In *Beyond the Classics? Essays en Religious Studies and Liberal Education*, edited by Sheryl Burkhalter and Frank Reynolds. Atlanta: Scholars Press.

Milter, Richard B, Laurie L. Patton and Stephen H. Webb. 1995. "Rhetoric, Pedagogy and the Study of *Religions.*" *Journal of the American Academy of Religion* 62 (3): 819–50.

Reynolds, Frank. 1999. "Coming of Age: Buddhist Studies in the United States 1972–98." *Journal of the International Association of Buddhist Studies* (fall).

Taylor, Mark, ed. 1998. *Critical Terms for Religious Studies*. Chicago: University of Chicago Press.

Walters, Jonathan. 1999. "Suttas as History; Four Approaches to the Sermon on the Noble Quest." *History of Religions* 38 (3): 247–84.

41 Toward a Global Vision of Religious Studies

Gregory D. Alles

Gregory D. Alles received a BA degree from Valparaiso University (Indiana), a MDiv from Lutheran School of Theology, Chicago, and MA and PhD degrees from the University of Chicago. He is Professor and Chair of the Department of Philosophy and Religious Studies, McDaniel College, Maryland. As with other scholars in this volume who did graduate work at the University of Chicago, he is engaged with issues of theory and method in the study of religion in addition to his regional specialization in religions of south Asia. His work on theory of religion and the study of religion worldwide is apparent not only in his books and articles, but also in his roles such as past president of the North American Association for the Study of Religion and co-editor of the journal *Numen* as well as editorial board member of the journals *Religion, Method and Theory in the Study of Religion, Studies in Religion/ Sciences religieuses*, and the *Moscow e-Journal of Religion*. The selection below serves as the afterword to his edited volume *Religious Studies: A Global View* (2008).

The preceding chapters [in Alles, ed., *Religious Studies: A Global View*, Routledge, 2008] do not yet provide a global vision of religious studies. They provide satellite images, as it were, of the study of religion in different parts of the globe. To have a global vision, these images need to be stitched together. Placing them between the covers of a book goes part of the way to doing that. It is like spreading satellite images out next to one another on a large table-top. But it is not yet the composite image that one finds, for example, when images are combined seamlessly.

In this Afterword, almost a chapter in itself more than a typical Afterword, I want to try to stitch the images together a little. That is because a collection of region by region views amplifies regional identities and commonalties, but tends to neglect transregional connections and global movements. As a result, it seems useful to transgress the normal, behind-the-scenes role that editing entails and assume a voice. So in this Afterword I stitch the pieces together. The composite image that results will not be seamless, and it will not have a very high resolution. But perhaps it can contribute to developing a global vision of religious studies.[1]

In a sense, such a vision is not new. Each of the scholars whom as a student I came to regard as the leading figures in the field had a global vision of religious studies. I suspect that the same is true of leading scholars in other parts of the world, too. I have already mentioned Wilfred Cantwell Smith's vision of interreligious dialogue in the introduction. Mircea Eliade's vision may have been more limited, but I still remember reading as an undergraduate many years ago a sentence that may have been the ultimate inspiration for this book:

> When, in one or two generations, perhaps even earlier, we have historians of religions who are descended from Australian, African, or Melanesian tribal societies, I do not doubt that, among other things, they will reproach Western scholars for their indifference to the scale of values indigenous to these societies.
>
> (Eliade 1969: 75)

By the 1990s Ninian Smart was envisioning a global context for all kinds of reflection having to do with worldviews, including not only the study of religion but also philosophy (Smart 1999: 261–372) and Christian theology (Smart 1996). Part of that vision was his proposal for a World Academy of Religion, which would "not [be] tied to the rightly and strictly scholarly and scientific stance of the IAHR" and so would "embrace all kinds of committed and non-committed scholarly organisations" (Smart 1990: 305).

Smith's, Eliade's, and Smart's visions mostly assumed the form of dreams. They referred to what will or might occur. Today we should talk about what is. What can we say about this activity of human beings all over the planet that we call the study of religion? To avoid misunderstanding, I should emphasize that a global vision is never, in Thomas Nagel's (1986) still useful phrase, a view from nowhere. In the realm of vision, the constraints of geometry make a seamless view of the globe impossible. Our eyes cannot simultaneously detect, nor can our minds simultaneously represent, every spot on the surface of a sphere without making tears someplace. The same is true here. What follows inevitably reflects my own complex and in some ways idiosyncratic locations, probably in many ways that I do not even recognize. No one should expect a global vision to escape the limitations of its author's embeddedness in space, time, cultures, politics, economics, and so on. The most one can hope for is a vision whose subjective horizons, like its objective ones, are not too narrow, whose analytical constructs are not simplistic, and whose ambitions respect basic human rights, including the right of others to self-determination.

Structures and Networks

One way to formulate a global vision of religious studies is in terms of global structures and institutions. Very few, if any, institutions or structures within the study of religions are *not* represented in the preceding chapters. In other words, very few institutions or structures in the study of religions are truly global. Almost all are limited by national, linguistic, and regional boundaries.

Perhaps the leading candidate for a global institution is the International Association for the History of Religions (founded 1950) along with its flagship journal, *Numen*, and the *Numen* book series. But despite the early participation of some Japanese scholars, the IAHR was at first "international" not in the sense that it was global but primarily in the sense that it transcended national boundaries in Europe. Already in 1960 R. J. Zwi Werblowsky was commenting on the growing internationalization—today we might call it globalization—of the Association. By the end of 2006 the IAHR recognized local and regional affiliates on every continent except Antarctica and, because of a complicated mutual history, Australia. It has held five of its international Congresses, including the last four, outside of Europe and North America (Tokyo 1958 and 2005, Sydney 1985, Mexico City 1990, and Durban 2000). In addition, its leadership base has broadened since its founding. Since 1960 the IAHR's vice presidents have included, in addition to Europeans and North Americans, four scholars from Japan, Teruji Ishizu (1960–65), Ichiro Hon (1965–70), Masao Abe (1975–80), and Akio Tsukimoto (2005–present; I count Joseph Kitagawa, vice president 1975–85, as a

North American), and one from Mexico, Yólotl Gonzáles Torres (1995–2000). Under the leadership of Michael Pye (general secretary 1985–95, president 1995–2000) the IAHR made a concerted effort to include members from outside Europe and North America on the executive committee. The current deputy treasurer, Pratap Kumar (2005–present), is from South Africa, a current member-at-large of the executive board, Alef Theria Wasim (2000–present), is from Indonesia, and a current editor of *Numen*, Gustavo Benavides, is from Peru, although he was in part educated and is now working in the United States. The offices of president, general secretary, deputy general secretary, and treasurer, however, have all been filled exclusively by Europeans and, more recently, North Americans.

Another way to formulate a global vision of religious studies, probably a better way, is to examine not institutions and structures but webs of scholarly networks. At least for the moment, the actual study of such networks is beyond both my capabilities and resources. There might be several places to start mapping such networks: the production and distribution of translations, posts on email discussion lists, such as those administered by the European Association for the Study of Religion, or participation in the new IAHR network of women scholars. I suspect that the result of such mapping might resemble a composite photograph of the globe at night or, perhaps better, a map of routes serviced by a major airline. In terms of the first metaphor, some places on the globe would be "brighter"—have more scholarly activity and denser networks—than others. In terms of the second, certain regions would emerge as hubs—or nodes or major contact points—for global scholarly exchange. Given the preceding chapters, I suspect that quite a few places around the globe would light up brightly. I also suspect that the largest hubs for scholarly exchange are still in Western Europe and North America, and that there are few non-stop flights—few direct connections—between scholars working in, let us say, China and Brazil or Nigeria and Indonesia. I also suspect that there are many one-way flights or, to change the metaphor, that much scholarship is exported from North America and Western Europe to other regions without scholarship being imported in reverse. Seen from a global perspective the study of religions suffers from a serious imbalance of trade.

There is yet a third way to formulate a global vision of religious studies. That is to identify the common threads and distinct patterns in the chapters that form the heart of this book. I limit myself to three major topics, discussed very broadly: history; institutionalization; and objects, methods, and theories.

History

One feature of the history of religious studies that emerges from these chapters is striking—and often understated. The 1950s and especially the 1960s were a formative period for the study of religion almost everywhere in the world. During this period, with some regional variation—for Australia and New Zealand the 1970s were formative—Africans, Australians, East Asians, North Americans, and South and Southeast Asians incorporated the study of religions in earnest into university programs, while Western Europeans greatly expanded existing programs and founded new ones. Much of Latin America, North Africa, and West Asia seem to have remained somewhat removed from this development, but there were notable exceptions, such as Israel. Scholarship in Eastern Europe went in a different direction.

In a climate such as ours, in which the approach to intellectual history is so heavily endebted to Michel Foucault, it is inevitable that we look to politics to explain these changes. Political factors do seem to carry explanatory power, in part because of the large role governments play in funding and administering universities and research institutes worldwide.

For example, under the aegis of Communism scholars were often expected to attack religion, at least in those parts of their writings that state authorities might actually read. As He Guanghu notes, under Mao a critical approach to religions meant "absolute negation, severe attack, complete suppression, and an utter clearing away". Institutional organization followed suit. For example, the government of the German Democratic Republic (East Germany) attempted to transform the Institute for the Study of Religion at Leipzig into an Institute for the Study and Promotion of Atheism (Rudolph 1992: 337–39).

In the "free world" scholars took a much different attitude. After all, at the height of the Cold War the United States both proclaimed itself to be a nation "under God" (1954) and funded research in the study of religions (McCutcheon 2004). Michael Stausberg has highlighted the degree to which conservative political loyalties characterized many, although not all, post-World War II Western European scholars of religions. He Guanghu points out that scholarship favorable to religion—indeed, that tried to appropriate the benefits of religion—emerged in China with the end of the Cultural Revolution in 1976 and then grew tremendously. Scholars in South Korea seem to have steered a course that in many respects closely mirrored developments within the United States. Within a European community living side-by-side with an appreciable number of Muslim "migrants" and "guest-workers", Islam became an object of increased attention, as it did in the United States after September 11, 2001. When Romania hosted the European Association for the Study of Religion in Bucharest in September 2006, a political edge was unmistakable. Writing in the official conference booklet, the Minister of Foreign Affairs welcomed participants with the thought that, after so many years of Communist repression, it was now "payback time" (Ungureanu 2006).

It is certainly tempting to attribute the widespread blossoming of the study of religion that took place during the 1950s and 1960s to a rejection of anti-religious Communism by pro-religious—or at least anti-anti-religious—Capitalists. But that is probably not a full explanation. The blossoming also occurred in regions such as Sub-Saharan Africa and South and Southeast Asia, where the most important political events were not connected with the Cold War but with de-colonization. When the European colonial tapestry began to unravel with Indian and Pakistani independence on August 15, 1947, that event ushered in a time of great expectations for the newly established nations. In order to establish their national dignity they often founded universities (see Brodeur and Chitando in this volume), and when people in these universities studied religions, they tended to study the religions of their own regions, not someone else's. That certainly suggests that their studies were informed by an underlying nationalistic purpose, or at least a deep-rooted nationalistic interest. But the degree to which the desire to establish a post-colonial identity motivated and shaped the study of religion in these regions demands further study.

Thus, political factors would seem to provide a rich account of the motivation for and direction of the study of religions that emerged almost globally after World War II, but they are probably not the whole story. None of the factors mentioned above provides any real justification for the emergence of religious studies. Just as the political goals of Communists could be met by a dogmatic attack upon religion, so the political goals of anti-Communists and emergent nationalists could have been met by simply embracing religion—but they were not. The popularity of political explanations should not blind us to other forces that may also have been at work, some of them global in scale. Nor should we consider the study of religions only in isolation.

In the period following World War II, several factors interacted to produce a tremendous increase in the number of tertiary educational institutions worldwide. It is common to mention the desire of new nations to establish independent universities, a shift from elite to mass education, and a post-war increase in population (but cf. Schofer and Meyer 2005 on demonstrable causal factors). As John W. Meyer (2006: x) has observed:

> [A]lmost 20 percent of a cohort of young people in the world is now found in an institution of higher education—fifty years ago [in the mid 1950s], it might have been 2 percent, and fifty years before that it might have been a fraction of 1 percent. ... A country like Kazakhstan, for instance, might have as many higher education students as the whole world had in 1900.

Less impressionistically, Evan Schofer and Meyer (2005: 898) note that in 1900 there were about 500,000 higher education students worldwide; in 2000 there were about 100,000,000—20,000 percent more. The vast majority of this growth has occurred since 1960. With such a large increase in academic activity worldwide, a global increase in the number of people studying religions will have an impact on scholarly production, but it is hardly newsworthy.

Other developments may be newsworthy. In one of the very few careful studies devoted to the university worldwide, David John Frank and Jay Gabler (2006) examine the ways in which universities throughout the world changed during the twentieth century. They acknowledge the role of political and economic factors, but they see those factors as too variable to account for global patterns. Adopting a neo-institutional perspective, they explain changes in university structure in terms of "changing assumptions about reality, written into the cultural and organizational foundations of world society" (p. 114). In very broad terms, they postulate a global shift in what counts as universal, objective knowledge (citing Bourdieu 1988: xii) from an embrace of spiritual forces, both religious and "idealistic" (e.g. art as revelatory, the poet as "genius"), hierarchical organization, and categorical structures to naturalistic-materialistic explanation, horizontal organization, and dynamic networks. Among other things, their model predicts a decrease in what was earlier an important facet of the university, designated "theology". The data, however, reveal something different. In the period 1915–35, theology claimed about 4.5 percent of the faculty in universities worldwide. (Frank and Gabler speculate that earlier the percentage was higher.) In fine with their model, by 1955–75 theology had lost almost two-thirds of its faculty share. But then something unexpected happened. The percentage of "theology" faculty began to rise (p. 110).

This pattern interests us because in their tabulation Frank and Gabler did not distinguish between theology and religious studies. They themselves (personal communication) are inclined to attribute the faculty share gained by "theology" to the emergence of a manner of studying religions more in accord with the new patterns defining universal, objective knowledge, what we have been calling the study of religion or religious studies. That inclination is at least consistent with the inverse relationship Stausberg observes in Western Europe between the decline in institutional Christendom and the rise of religious studies, but much more work needs to be done. For one thing, it is not actually known what part religious studies played in reversing the decline in "theology" worldwide. For another, the rest of the world has not undergone the secularization that Europe has. Perhaps the political emergence of very strong religious commitments, often called fundamentalisms, in places as diverse as the United States, West Asia, and India during the 1970s contributed to the observed average rise in the weight of theology worldwide—or perhaps not. Universities may adhere to different standards of knowledge from those that prevail in the broader population. Think of tensions between Indian academics and Hindu nationalists, or between university biologists in the US state of Kansas and advocates of intelligent design.

If further research does bear out that it was the emergence of religious studies that led to greater weight for "theology" in universities worldwide, a further question arises: did the relative distance of Latin America and North Africa-West Asia from the development of religious studies result from the prevalence in those regions of a different set of cultural assumptions about what makes for universal, objective knowledge? In discussing the neo-liberal assumptions that often accompany the study of religion, Brodeur's account of North Africa and West Asia suggests that this may indeed be the case. But Brodeur also emphasizes the political dimension, namely, a link between the study of religions and democratic institutions. That postulated link is attractive, but it is also complicated both by the attraction that fascism and Nazism exercised on earlier European exemplars of the study and by the flourishing of the study of religion in the People's Republic of China today.

Other, complementary global factors may also be responsible for the rise of religious studies worldwide in the 1950s and 1960s. One is what we might call the "World War II effect". Such an effect is discernible in the constellation of knowledge in both the natural and social sciences. To quote Frank and Gabler (2006: 67) again: "The war stigmatized ethnic nationalisms and other exclusive corporate groupings and on the flipside gave rise to expressions of encompassing humanity (e.g. in the Universal Declaration of Human Rights, adopted in 1948)." One supposes that one kind of "exclusive corporate grouping" that the war may have helped stigmatize, especially given the long history of Christian involvement with European if not Nazi anti-Semitism, was the kind of privileged epistemic community that religious claims presuppose. We should also not overlook other, basic global factors in the post-World War II environment that may have helped undercut claims specific to isolated religious corporate groupings, at least among people with sufficient resources: the emergence of commercial television and commercial jet air travel. (Presumably, these effects would only be amplified by more recent developments such as videoconferencing, the Internet, and email. One should note, however, that the use of these technologies is hardly incompatible with strongly held, exclusive religious convictions.)

Besides the global and political factors already mentioned, a finely grained history of the study of religions in any locality will need, no doubt, to take into account local factors as well (cf. Borgeaud 1999, cited by Stausberg). It seems likely that the changing demographic patterns which resulted when the empire not only "wrote back" (Rushdie 1982; cf. Ashcroft, Giffiths, and Tiffin 1989) but also settled in the land of the former colonizers significantly shaped the development of religious studies in the UK. In the US, a series of decisions by the Supreme Court, starting with *McCollum v. Board of Education*, 333 US 203 (1948), applied First Amendment protections against religious establishment to state and local governments, including school districts, resulting in a body of law that proscribed the teaching *of* religion in public institutions but allowed and even encouraged teaching *about* it (*School District of Abington v. Schempp* 374 US 225 [1963]). In sub-Saharan Africa, according to Ezra Chitando, the different colonial policies of the British, the French, the Portuguese, and the Belgians are responsible for the significantly different trajectories of the study of religion in different regions. In China after the Cultural Revolution scholars came to terms with Marx's views through an "Opium War", a term with unique cultural resonances in China. In Latin America, very real limitations posed by the demands of politicians, together with a complicated story of relations between church and state, have obliged scholars to work within parameters that have been in some respects unique to the region.

There is rich potential for exploring these developments. But most work done to date, including what I have written above, remains impressionistic and anecdotal. We need hard, quantified evidence. Once gathered, the difficulty, as always, will be to distinguish actual causes from non-causal correlations. To take an example outside of religious studies that many people should be able to appreciate: it is often possible to demonstrate a clear, direct correlation between ice-cream consumption and crime, but that does not mean that eating ice cream causes crime, or vice versa. Both go up with an increase in temperature.

Institutionalization

In her chapter, Satoko Fujiwara notes that although the study of religions has a relatively long history in Japan, it occupies a rather marginal place in Japanese universities. That lament is something of a refrain among scholars of religion worldwide. What can we say about this marginality?

The vast expansion of the university that has taken place since World War II has meant that, in terms of absolute numbers, every component of the educational core at tertiary institutions now has more faculty and students worldwide than it did fifty years ago (Drori and Moon 2006: 163). But some components have done better than others. According to UNESCO's International Standard Classification of Education (1976, revised 1997) "religion and theology" belong to the core area of the university that has fared the worst, the humanities (class 22).[2] According to a study by Gili Drori and Hyeyoung Moon (2006: 164), in the thirty years from 1965 to 1995 the percentage of students enrolling in the humanities dropped by about 40 percent (see Table 1). The loss of faculty share was similar (see Table 2; I omit "Humanities Applied", basically the study of law.) Drori and Moon (2006) do not distinguish subfields within the humanities, so without significantly more

Table 1   Worldwide share of student enrollments by division (after Drori and Moon 2006: 164, numbers approximate)

	1965 (%)	*1995 (%)*
Humanities	20	12
Social Sciences	15	30

Table 2   Worldwide share of faculty at tertiary institutions (after Frank and Gabler 2006: 68, 133)

	1915–1935 (%)	*1975–1995 (%)*
Humanities (basic)	27.4	15.6
Classics and archaeology	4.5	0.6
History	3.5	3.0
Non-Western languages and literatures	2.3	2.0
Philosophy	2.8	0.8
RELIGION AND THEOLOGY	**4.3**	**1.7**
Social Sciences (total)	9.3	30.0
Social Sciences (basic)	3.8	12.4
Social Sciences (applied)	5.5	17.6
Anthropology	0.2	0.4
Economics	1.7	3.8
Geography	0.4	2.9
Political Science	0.8	2.0
Psychology	0.7	0.8
Sociology	0.1	2.2

research it is not possible to say more precisely where the decline in humanities students took place, but in examining faculty share Frank and Gabler (2006) do distinguish subfields. According to their results, the loss in "religion and theology" (to use UNESCO terminology) was among the worst: down 60 percent from 1915–35 to 1975–95. But philosophy's loss was even worse (71 percent), and the loss in classics and archaeology was worst of all (87 percent). Note that these are fields with which religious studies has historical and institutional affinities. Similarly, a social science that is close to religious studies, anthropology, was also precarious. Frank and Gabler (2006: 136) write, "Anthropology ... remained marginal in the university throughout the twentieth century". Its faculty share did double, but the overall absolute numbers are very small. In addition, less than a third of the universities that Frank and Gabler (2006) sampled for 1986–95 taught anthropology. That is worse than either philosophy, represented in half of the universities sampled, and even classics and archaeology, represented in slightly more than a third. Compared with all of these fields, a 1.7 percent faculty share for religion and theology and representation in 60 percent of the universities sampled looks rather good.

Despite the poor showing of anthropology, the social sciences were the core area of the university that grew the most during the twentieth century. From 1965 to 1995, the share of students enrolled in the social sciences doubled worldwide (Drori and Moon 2006:164). From 1915–35 to 1975–95, the share of faculty in the social sciences more than tripled in both the basic and applied fields (Frank and Gabler 2006: 68). The gains were smallest in psychology, where the faculty share grew only slightly. In four other fields the gains were much larger, economics, geography, political science, and sociology, but of these four, only sociology continued to grow after 1975 (Frank and Gabler 2006: 138–39). It is also worth noting that some areas of the humanities with affinities to religious studies suffered losses that were relatively modest. History lost only about 14 percent of its faculty share, non-Western languages and literatures only 13 percent (Frank and Gabler 2006: 105).

What do all of these figures say about the position of religion and theology in the contemporary university? More than being marginalized, they occupy a place of tension—probably healthy and creative tension. To the extent that they steer toward anthropology, philosophy, and the study of antiquity, they would seem to face dwindling interest and support. To the extent that they steer toward sociology, geography, "non-Western" studies, history, and in some parts of the world, psychology, they rub shoulders with social sciences that have received increasing attention or with humanities that have resisted the general decline. Perhaps this tension, as well as disagreement over how religious the study of religion should be, is responsible for another distinctive feature of religion and theology. From a global perspective, universities moved over the course of the twentieth century to structural isomorphism in most areas, but not all. The area where structural divergence increased the most was religion and theology (Frank and Gabler 2006: 80). As the twentieth century proceeded, universities worldwide came increasingly to disagree about how—and whether—to incorporate religious studies and theology.

These observations need refinement. It would be desirable to have data that distinguished, to the extent that it is possible to do so, between religious studies and theology. It is also important to note that studies of faculty and student share do not address global variation in research and publication. They also undercount activity in religious studies. That is because they concentrate upon religious studies as a separate academic domain, located in an academic unit of its own. This observation touches upon a second issue of institutionalization that emerges from the chapters in this volume. Although some agreement has emerged on where to locate the study of religion, there is no unanimity.

The authors of most of the chapters in this volume concentrated on work within academic units devoted specifically to the study of religion. Most pointedly, Rowena Robinson did not, and for good reason. The study of religion in South Asia is not organized the way it is in many other regions. (But India is not alone; consider Argentina, but also Australia, New Zealand, and Eastern Europe, among other places.) Article 28 of the Indian Constitution prohibits religious instruction at state-funded universities (it allows such instruction at private ones), but as interpreted by several government commissions—the Radhakrishnan Commission (1948–49), the Secondary Education Commission (1952–53), the Sri Prakasa Committee (1959–60), and the Kothari Commission (1964–66)—that prohibition does not ban teaching about religions. Indeed, the commissions found such education desirable as a way to promote morality (Khan 2005; Llewellyn 2005). Furthermore, some activity in India has treated the study of religion as a separate academic domain. In 1967, a consultation on the study of religion took place in Bangalore involving Indian academics and professors from Harvard University (Khan 2005). Several decades later, two IAHR-related conferences took place in Delhi, "Religions in the Indic Civilization" (December 18–21, 2003) and "The Culture and Religious Mosaic of South and Southeast Asia: Conflict and Consensus through the Ages" (January 27–30, 2005). Nevertheless, in South Asia specific departments of religious studies are extremely rare. The only such department in India may be the Guru Gobindh Singh Department of Religious Studies at Punjabi University, Patiala, founded in 1967 following a recommendation of Wilfred Cantwell Smith (Llewellyn unpublished; Khan 2005: 8790). In a survey of the *Commonwealth Universities Handbook* J. E. Llewellyn (unpublished) found that only 5 percent of graduate institutions in India offer anything that might at all be associated with the study of religions. Using the same source, Abrahim Khan (2005) found that only thirteen institutions throughout the whole of South Asia "offer one or more courses on the study of religion as a subject either at the undergraduate or at the postgraduate level", among them the department of world religions at the University of Dhaka, Bangladesh, founded as a department of comparative religion in 1999 and renamed the next year (Khan 2005: 8791).

As Robinson's chapter makes clear, however, anyone who concluded from the preceding paragraph that religion was little studied in South Asia would be seriously mistaken. Scholars in South Asia study religion to a considerable degree. They simply do not institutionalize such studies in a distinct academic unit. In this respect India presents an alternative model to the trend, prevalent over the last fifty years, of establishing distinct programs, departments, and institutes in religious studies. On that alternative model, academics with an interest in religion would be dispersed throughout the university.

In accounting for a lack of religious studies in India, Abrahim Khan (2005: 8791) notes that in that part of the world religion—in Hindi, *dharm*—is conceived of differently than it is in Europe, North America, and Australia; it does not make a distinction between the sacred and the secular. Indeed, it is often observed that the category "religion" is an odd one. In this volume Satoko Fujiwara notes that the Japanese use of *shūkyō* has not been informed by the same concerns for essence as European uses of "religion" have been, although she also points out that the term "culture", popular with some critics of "religion", is actually the more problematical term in the Japanese context. He Guanghu, Chung Chin-hong, and Lee Chang-yick all remark upon how odd the term originally seemed in Chinese and Korean. Ezra Chitando expresses concerns about whether "religion" accurately reflects practice in sub-Saharan African. Patrice Brodeur notes that it has been common in Islamic universities to study not religion *(dīn)* or theology *(lāhūt)* but *sharī'ah*. Michael Stausberg and Gustavo Benavides mention several studies critical of the term. Yet as Stausberg observes for Western Europe, and as Chung and Lee underscore for Korea, few people actually seem willing to abandon "religion". For all its faults, people still find the term useful.

One question these observations provoke is the following: does religious studies require a concept of "religion" that is universal and unambiguous in order to be academically viable worldwide? An affirmative answer may seem self-evident, but it is not. On the one hand, the study of religion in South Asia is hardly the only case of institutional exceptionalism. In terms of faculty share, one of the most successful social sciences over the course of the twentieth century was geography, but not in the United States, where the field is very poorly represented. Is that exceptionalism due to a peculiarly US American conception of earth, planet, or land? On the other hand, some fields organized around categories with much firmer boundaries and presumably universal recognition prior to European colonialism have done considerably worse than religious studies. A good example is botany, which has lost a much larger proportion of faculty share than most other natural sciences and is represented at fewer universities in the Frank and Gabler sample than religion and theology (Frank and Gabler 2006: 160,164). A field in even worse shape is astronomy, whose boundaries would seem to be sharply and unexceptionally defined as the science that deals with anything that is not on the planet earth. Always marginal, it lost 89 percent of its faculty share over the course of the twentieth century—more than even classics and archaeology—and it is almost entirely absent in the Frank and Gabler sample of universities worldwide (Frank and Gabler 2006: 160, 164). Combine these examples with the moderate growth in faculty share in religion and theology since World War II, and there is room to doubt whether departments of religious studies really need an unambiguous, universal category "religion" to be academically viable. Indeed, there is reason to doubt the need for unambiguous highest-order structuring categories for any academic unit, from art and music to biology and chemistry. In the long run, what may be more important are categorical and methodological flexibility, a sense among other scholars that materials captured by the delimiter "religion" are unusual enough to require more than passing attention, and a consensus that those materials are sufficiently significant socially to merit academic investigation. There may, however, be other good reasons *not* to institutionalize religious studies in a separate academic unit. Consider discussions in Southeast Asia summarized at the end of Vineeta Sinha's contribution.

Space allows me to do no more than enumerate several other important issues concerning the institutionalization of religious studies. (1) Can and should the study of religion take place in other locations besides the university? In the United States, at least, a full 50 percent of basic research in the natural sciences is done outside of universities (Drori and Moon 2006: 160). (2) Chitando, Franzmann, and Stausberg note a connection between the study of religions at the tertiary level and primary and secondary education, including the training of teachers. Should the promotion of primary and secondary education in religious studies be a goal for scholars of religion worldwide? (3) In North America, Europe, and perhaps elsewhere, scholars of religion have been active as media, legal, and policy consultants. Is this an emerging activity worldwide? Especially in what has come to be known as a post-9/11 world, in which concerns for national security seem unavoidably to touch upon religions and religious identities, it certainly seems desirable for national leaders to understand religions better than they sometimes do today. (4) Inasmuch as the WTO's General Agreement on Trade in Services governs education, for example distance learning, to what extent will that agreement have an impact, beneficial or detrimental, on the study of religion, especially in poorer countries? (5) Several authors note changing demands placed upon researchers by the societies in which they live and work, as, for example, in Japan's Twenty-first Century Center of Excellence initiative. How should scholars of religions conduct themselves in a world which increasingly demands that scholarship should have social relevance and a potential for marketability?

Objects, Methods, and Theories

Gili Drori and Hyeyoung Moon (2006: 178) write, "To a certain degree … all educational activities worldwide are glocalized [sic] forms of science, presenting the adaptation of modern Western science into a local mold." The chapters in this book raise many issues about the objects scholars of religion study, the methods they employ, and the theories they develop. Here I address only one, an issue that cuts through objects, methods, and theories, all three. To what extent is the study of religion a form of Western science imposed on the rest of the world?

One difficulty concerns the language in which to frame this question. It is probably unhelpful to speak of a clash of civilizations in which the study of religion fights as a foot-soldier in a global campaign to spread Western civilization—terminology that would have the opposite effect from what someone like Samuel Huntington (1996) would desire. It is also probably unhelpful to see the study of religion as a representative of McWorld, one that some people will inevitably resist through *jihad* (cf. Barber 1995). Such language may capture something about the historical origin and expansion of the study of religion, but it hardly does justice to the careful scholarly work being done by people of non-European ancestry that is detailed in many chapters of this book. Language that plays on emotional loyalties and large-scale identities is more useful for rallying troops, figuratively or literally, than for careful analysis.

In dealing with the complexity of global influence and local agency, some globalization theorists have coined stranger and stranger words. As George Ritzer (2003, 2004; cf. 1996; Ritzer [ed.] 2002) of "McDonaldization" fame tells the story, a previously dominant account of globalization talked of Western modernization overwhelming and obliterating traditional cultures. Many theorists, among them Arjun Appadurai, Roland Robertson, and John Tomlinson, found this account unsatisfactory, because it ignored local agency in shaping the adoption of Western elements. In response, Robertson developed the notion of "glocalization". As Ritzer (2003: 193–94) explains it:

> *Glocalization* [sic] can be defined as the interpenetration of the global and the local, resulting in unique outcomes in different geographic areas. This view emphasizes global heterogeneity and tends to reject the idea that forces emanating from the West in general and the United States in particular … are leading to economic, political, institutional, and—most importantly—cultural homogeneity.

But according to Ritzer, glocalization itself encapsulates an incomplete analysis, because it fails to recognize the ways in which "nations, corporations, organizations, and other entities … desire—indeed … need—to impose themselves on various geographic areas" (Ritzer 2003: 194). The point is well taken, but to address it Ritzer coined the word "grobalization", which refers to "the proliferation of nothing" (Ritzer 2003: 194). Neither the term nor its reference is immediately intelligible. To emphasize this point, I have left them unglossed. Moreover, the apparently sweeping reach of "the proliferation of nothing" simply invites forceful rebuttals of the sort that James Watson and his collaborators offered in examining the positive contributions of McDonald's to East Asia (Watson [ed.] 1997).

Are such neologisms at all helpful in negotiating global hegemony and local agency in the study of religion? It is doubtful that the academic study of religion is in the business of proliferating "nothing", by which Ritzer (2003:195) means "a social form that is generally centrally conceived, controlled, and comparatively devoid of distinctive substantive content". This "nothing" may call to mind real issues in religious studies and other academic fields, such as the disproportionate weight given elsewhere to publishing in journals or with presses located in Europe or North America (Sinha 2003: 16–17), but is centralized control a sufficiently subtle term for issues of this sort? Nor does the study of religion seem particularly characterized by what Ritzer (1996) calls "McDonaldization", that is, "the process by which the principles of the fast-food restaurant are coming to dominate more and more sectors of American society as well as of the rest of the world" (Ritzer, 1996: 1). These principles—efficiency, calculability, predictability, and control through non-human technology—may indeed be shaping the manner in which research is conducted and supported and education delivered worldwide, but to the extent that they are doing so, and to the extent that the results are negative, scholars of religions in Europe, North America, Australia, and New Zealand would seem to be victims of these processes just as much as scholars elsewhere. Consider the conclusion to Stausberg's chapter and the kinds of stringent budgetary pressures that Franzmann identifies.

Rather than searching the literature for more adequate terms than globalization, glocalization, and grobalization, I want simply to reflect on the study of religions. I begin rather slowly with an observation that, I hope, is not controversial: there are ways of treating other people's knowledge, including religious knowledge, that are clearly unacceptable. Here are two current examples. Legality aside, it is immoral for a pharmaceutical company to patent traditional medical knowledge that it has learned for free from other people, especially when those other people have meager access to economic resources and may as a result be denied access to the benefits of their own traditional knowledge, now supposedly the possession of someone else (cf. Mgbeoji 2006). It is also immoral for people to establish exclusive legal ownership of religious practices that they have not themselves created. According to *Foreign Policy* (Gajilan 2006), by mid 2006 the United States government had granted "at least 137 patents and 1,098 trademarks and copyrights relating to yoga". To prevent the further patenting of its people's traditional knowledge, the government of India has established a massive Traditional Knowledge Digital Library.

Theft is clearly wrong, but most scholars of religions are not thieves. They do not copyright other people's knowledge in the hopes of making a fortune.[3] But do they destroy other people's knowledge? This is somewhat trickier. To reply that the study of religions, like anthropology, has actually helped to preserve religious knowledge is to miss the point. To reply that science is science, it is what the university does, come what may, is to beg the question. Does the study of religion impose one manner of thinking about religions and destroy others? Consider the opposition that has erupted in India over representations of the Harappans and the alleged Aryan invasion or migration by what a prominent Hindu-nationalist archaeologist has labeled "Marxists in India … Muslim fundamentalists and Neo-Imperialists in England and America" (Gupta 2001: 58). Recently, some have taken to calling the destruction of traditional knowledge, especially in colonial situations, "epistemicide" (e.g. Moosa 2006).

There are legitimate concerns about the creation and advancement of knowledge in situations characterized by inequality in power and access to resources—situations epitomized by colonialism—but it should also be easy to see problems with a simplistic invocation of "epistemicide". Like invocations of "perspectivalism", "incommensurability", or "imperialism", the specter of epistemicide may lead to an argument that all local knowledges are equally true. We all know that knowledge is always contextually embedded and that we see the world from different perspectives. Nevertheless, it is impermissible—by virtue of the genetic fallacy—to accept or reject claims to knowledge on the basis of such embeddedness, as if British chemists two centuries ago were entitled either to deny the existence of oxygen or to insist upon their right to hold the phlogiston theory because the oxygen theory was French knowledge threatening British knowledge with epistemicide. (The word "oxygen" was coined by the French chemist Lavoisier.) Scholars, including scholars of religion, do not set out to destroy knowledge; they aim to create it. But they do set out to assess claims to knowledge as critically as possible and to reject those claims that cannot withstand testing. Without such an attitude, one can hardly pursue knowledge seriously.

That is not to deny that the study of religion faces issues concerning objects, methods, and theories that are global in scope, even if those issues have been mis-stated or over-stated, sometimes ludicrously so. A claim to be heard is not a claim to have one's views accepted but a claim not to be excluded from the common pursuit of knowledge for arbitrary reasons. If this volume demonstrates nothing else, it should demonstrate that there are scholars of religions around the world whose thinking deserves attention by virtue of its quality. As Vineeta Sinha has noted, along with many others, that is not always the norm. To risk excessive generalization: keynote speakers at conferences in Southeast Asia—and I suspect elsewhere—tend to be Western Europeans and North Americans. Keynote speakers at conferences in Europe and North America tend to be—Western Europeans and North Americans (Sinha 2003: 15). When scholars in, for example, Africa, South Asia, or Latin America examine persons, events, and things in their localities or areas of interest, their results tend to be taken as having local significance. When scholars in Europe, North America, and to some extent Australia and New Zealand examine persons, events, and things in their own localities or areas of interest, they have a greater chance of "having" universal significance (Sinha 2003: 16). Theories that claim wide attention generally originate in Europe and North America. Scholars elsewhere tend to apply those theories more than develop their own. To the extent that they do develop theories, the impact of their theories tends to remain local (Sinha 2003: 10–11).

As in the case of androcentrism, which Sinha also addresses, these observations have a political edge—in her words, they issue a call to "open the social sciences" (Gulbenkian Commission 1996)—but they do so only because they point to violations of the ideals of universality and equality implicit in global standards of knowledge and scholarship. The same is true of the widespread efforts to deconstruct inherited terminology. Statements such as "religion is a Western construction and therefore inapplicable elsewhere" are simply examples of poor reasoning. But it is not poor reasoning to ask about each of our categories, including "religion", what Vineeta Sinha (2006) has asked about "folk Hinduism": "Given that the category was generated in a particular sociocultural, historical context in relation to a specific research agenda, what is its relevance in analysing phenomena in vastly different circumstances?" Posing that question is nothing more than standard scholarly practice in every field, provided one does not prejudge the answer. For "religion", at least, the current consensus seems to favor keeping it.

Where some see difficulties, others see opportunities. Some opportunities for a global study of religion are institutional: the opportunity to include representatives from various parts of the world on governing bodies; the opportunity to design conferences with keynote speakers who do not originate from or work in Europe or North America, as when, at the nineteenth Congress of the IAHR (Tokyo, 2005) scholars from China (Zhuo Xinping) and Japan (Shizuteru Ueda) as well as from Europe and North America gave plenary addresses. Other opportunities are intellectual. People recite their pasts in part to say who they are today. Scholars of religions who simply trace the study of religions to the arrival of

Europeans or European thought in their regions overlook opportunities to explore earlier traditions of thought. For example, prior to European colonialism West Africans produced a rich literature in Arabic on religions, along with many other topics. The first Ming emperor, Ming Taizu (1328–98), wrote a treatise on religion (Pye 2004: 91). In this volume Patrice Brodeur provides a rich account of the "proto-history" of the study of religion in North Africa and West Asia, including the work of al-Shahrastānī (1076–1153), who, according to some, wrote the world's first history of religions. Exploring such predecessors may in turn open up opportunities to explore distinctive objects, methods, and theories.

The success with which scholars worldwide make use of opportunities for a global study of religion depends in part upon the seriousness with which we recognize challenges within them. One significant challenge is the unequal distribution of wealth and power throughout the world, a point that Ezra Chitando emphasizes. On the whole, scholars from poorer nations find it more costly in terms of percentage of income and wealth, and therefore more difficult, to participate in international activities than scholars from richer nations do. Without significant support, these scholars will inevitably have limited voice. Poorer regions also face challenges in terms of human capital. One such challenge arises when a relatively large number of high-profile scholars understandably take advantage of opportunities to work in richer countries. Another simply comes from not being able to afford the social or monetary costs of higher education. Over the last fifty years, an increasing number of people throughout the world have pursued tertiary education, but while in the year 2000 all other regions of the globe averaged more than 200 students in tertiary education for every 10,000 persons, that number for sub-Sarahan Africa was less than fifty (Schofer and Meyer 2005: 908). A related problem, which emerges not only from Chitando's chapter but also from the contributions by Eugen Ciurtin, He Guanghu, and Patrice Brodeur, is political. We should be wary, however, of attributing political problems exclusively to the world outside Europe, North America, Australia, and New Zealand. For example, along with others I argued, as president of the North American Association for the Study of Religion, against proposing to host the next IAHR Congress in the United States because of potential difficulties participants might face in gaining entrance to the country. (The 2010 Congress will be held in Toronto.)

Another significant challenge that a global study of religions faces is the challenge to avoid trivialization.[4] We trivialize when we reduce epistemological issues to slogans such as "epistemicide" or "neo-liberal imperialism". We trivialize when we ignore the complexity of people who inhabit our world, as in speaking about "the Other", which excuses us from engaging with other people, including colleagues, and allows us to trade instead in nothing more than Hegelianesque antitheses to whatever it is "we" happen to think—or more likely, whatever arguably prevalent views we happen to dislike. We also trivialize when we make, as I sometimes see happen in North America, the issue of studying versus practicing religion an issue of "the West versus the rest". On the one hand, interreligious dialogue is just as much a European and North American program as is the academic study of religion. Compare the distinction that Fujiwara notes (citing Tsuneya Wakimoto) between "Japanese pluralism" and "Western tolerance and dialogue"; note, too, that at Bangalore in 1967 Cantwell Smith tried to sell interreligious dialogue to Indian academics (Khan 2005: 8790). On the other hand, such an approach ignores the complex levels on which intellectual activity takes place in all parts of the world and risks confining scholars outside of Europe, North America, Australia, and New Zealand to the role of ethnographic object, nothing more. (Ezra Chitando reminds us how wrong it is simply to assume that prior to European colonization "everyone" in sub-Saharan Africa was religious.) We trivialize when we speak today of the "Western" university. The contemporary university is a distinctively global institution that arose after World War II. It is informed by European and North American predecessors, it is true; but it also differs from them, just as it differs from more distant predecessors in North Africa and West Asia and from the even earlier Buddhist universities of northeast India. Similarly, we trivialize when we speak of "Western science". Science is a global undertaking. It must be. A science that is geographically limited—one that sees the oxygen theory of combustion as fit for one group of people, but the phlogiston theory as fit for another—is no science at all. (That different groups of people may actually hold different theories is beside the point.)

Finally, a global study of religion may face a practical challenge that characterizes all human intellectual activity, but one that particularly characterizes the study of religion. If Robert McCauley is right, the human brain finds religion easy but science considerably more difficult. In addition, I suspect that the study of religion tends to draw people who find religious thinking personally attractive. That is probably especially true where, as in much of the world, the study of religion is localized in its own academic unit. Given both neurobiological and social dynamics, scholars of religion will probably always face the challenge of distinguishing religious from scientifically demonstrable claims. Among other things, that means that the study of religion as imaged in this book will never encompass all human discourse about religion.

QUESTIONS FOR REVIEW AND DISCUSSION

1. What does Alles indicate is the purpose of this Afterword? What are the limitations of presenting different "images" of the study of religion in various regions without stitching these images together?

2. In note 1, Alles clarifies that he intends "to provide a 'vision of' religious studies, not a 'vision for' religious studies." What does he mean by this distinction. What chapters in this Reader could be characterized as intending to set a "vision for religious studies"?

3. Alles mentions a sentence by Eliade "that may have been the ultimate inspiration for this book." What is Eliade's point? Does this selection advance the vision for religious studies indicated by Eliade in that sentence?

4. What is Alles indicating when he writes "No one should expect a global vision to escape the limitations of its author's embeddedness in space, time, cultures, politics, economics, and so on"? Do you concur? What might be some of the limitations to Alles' global vision?

5. Does Alles indicate whether most religious studies institutions are global? Why? Which institutions qualify as most global?

6. In terms of evaluating the degree to which something is truly global, how would efforts to map scholarly networks compare to examining institutions? Why?

7. Alles identifies themes in the book *Religious Studies: A Global View*. Discuss a few key points about each of the major topics: history; institutionalization; and objects, methods, and theories. Which of these three is most helpful for formulating a global vision of religious studies.

8. What are some of the "complementary global factors" that Alles indicates "may also be responsible for the rise of religious studies worldwide in the 1950s and 1960s"?

9. Where Alles indicates the need to move beyond "impressionistic and anecdotal" accounts of religion in favor of "hard, quantified evidence," he indicates that the primary difficulty "will be to distinguish actual causes from non-causal correlations"? What does this mean? Do you concur?

10. What are the implications for religious studies of the rapid rise in university enrolments in the social sciences during the last third of the twentieth century?

11. Alles asks and responds to the question "does religious studies require a concept of 'religion' that is universal and unambiguous in order to be academically viable worldwide?" What is his response? Do you agree?

12. What does Alles suggest is the outlook for the global study of religions? What are the most significant challenges?

Notes

1 To avoid possible ambiguity, let me say that—along the lines of Clifford Geertz's distinction between symbols of and symbols for—my intention is to provide a "vision of" religious studies, not a "vision for" religious studies, in the sense of setting a global agenda.

2 The classification appears in other languages as follows:

Arabic: *al-dīn* and *al-lāhūt* belong to *al-dirasāt al-insānīya;*
Chinese: *(zong jiao)* and *(shen xue)* belong to *(ren wen xue ke);*
French: *Religion* and *théologie* belong to *Lettres;*
Russian: *(religiya)* and *(teologiya)* belong to *(gumanitarnye nauki);*
Spanish: *Religión* and *teología* belong to *Humanidades.*

3 Some do, of course, set themselves up as gurus. I leave to one side the question of whether large academic salaries in rich countries are justified by the value added to material from religious traditions during the course of research. I also recognize intellectual property issues concerning royalties from publishing primary sources, such as traditional oral stories.

4 Discussing the Eurocentrism of the social sciences, Vineeta Sinha (2003: 12) warns against three dangers: trivializing the issue, rationalizing it, or incorporating it into one's considerations superficially.

REFERENCES

Ashcroft, Bill, Griffiths, Gareth and Tiffin, Helen 1989, *The Empire Writes Back: Theory and Practice in Post-Colonial Literature*, London: Routledge.

Barber, Benjamin R. 1995, *Jihad vs. McWorld*, New York: Times Books.

Borgeaud, Philippe 1999, "Qu'est-ce que l'histoire des religions?" *Equinoxe: Revue des sciences humaines*, vol. 21, pp. 67–83.

Bourdieu, Pierre 1988, *Homo academicus*, Stanford, CA: Stanford University Press.

Drori, Gili S., and Moon, Hyeyoung 2006, "The changing nature of tertiary education: Neo-institutional perspectives on cross-national trends in disciplinary enrollment, 1965–95", in Baker, David and Wiseman, Alexander W. (eds), *The Impact of Comparative Education Research on Institutional Theory*, Boston: Elsevier JAI pp. 157–85.

Eliade, Mircea 1969, *The Quest: History and Meaning in Religion*, Chicago: University of Chicago Press.

Frank, David John, and Gabler, Jay 2006, *Reconstructing the University: Worldwide Shifts in Academia in the 20th Century*, Stanford, CA: Stanford University Press.

Gajilan, Arlyn Tobias 2006, "Posing for Profit", *Foreign Policy*, vol. 154 (May–June), p. 18.

Gulbenkian Commission on the Restructuring of the Social Sciences 1996, *Open the Social Sciences: Report of the Gulbenkian Commission on the Restructuring of the Social Sciences*, Stanford, CA: Stanford University Press.

Gupta, S. P. 2001, "The myth of the saffronisation of Indian history", *History Today* [India], vol. 2, pp. 56–59.

Huntington, Samuel P. 1996, *The Clash of Civilizations and the Remaking of World Order*, New York: Simon & Schuster.

Khan, Abrahim H. 2005, "Study of religion: The academic study of religion in South Asia", in Jones, Lindsay (ed.), *The Encyclopedia of Religion*, 2nd edn, Detroit: Macmillan, pp. 8789–92.

Llewellyn, J. E. 2005, "The 'universal religion of human values': Teaching (about) religion in the US and India", Paper delivered at the 19th International Congress of the IAHR, Tokyo.

——unpublished, The Guru Gobind Singh Department of Religious Studies (cited by permission).

McCauley, Robert N. 2000, "The naturalness of religion and the unnaturalness of science", in Keil, Frank C., and Wilson, Robert A. (eds), *Explanation and Cognition*, Cambridge, MA: MIT Press, pp. 68–85.

McCutcheon, Russell T. 2004, "'Just follow the money': The Cold War, the humanistic study of religion, and the fallacy of insufficient cynicism", *Culture and Religion*, vol. 5, no 1, pp. 41–69.

Meyer, John W. 2006, "Foreword: Remaking the university", in Frank, David John, and Gabler, Jay 2006, pp. ix-xvii.

Mgbeoji, Dcechi 2006, *Global Biopiracy: Patents, Plants, and Indigenous Knowledge*, Ithaca, NY: Cornell University Press.

Moosa, Ebrahim 2006, "Contrapuntal readings in Muslim thought: Translations and transitions", *Journal of the American Academy of Religion*, March 2006, vol. 74, no. 1 (March), pp. 107–18.

Nagel, Thomas 1986, *The View from Nowhere*, New York: Oxford University Press.

Pye, Michael 2004, "Difference and coherence in the worldwide study of religions", in Jakelic, Slavica, and Pearson, Lori (eds), *The Future of the Study of Religion: Proceedings of Congress 2000*, Leiden: Brill, pp. 77–95.

Ritzer, George 1996, *The McDonaldization of Society: An Investigation into the Changing Character of Contemporary Social Life*, Thousand Oaks, CA: Pine Forge Press.

——2003, "Rethinking globalization: Glocalization/grobalization and something/nothing", *Sociological Theory*, vol. 21, no. 3 (September): 193–209.

——2004, *The Globalization of Nothing*, Thousand Oaks, CA: Pine Forge Press.

Ritzer, George (ed.) 2002, *McDonaldization: The Reader*, Thousand Oaks, CA: Pine Forge Press.

Rudolph, Kurt 1992, "Leipzig und die Religionswissenschaft", in Rudolph, Kurt 1992, *Geschichte und Probleme der Religionswissenschaft*, Leiden: Brill, pp. 323–39.

Rushdie, Salman 1982, "The Empire writes back with a vengeance", *The Times* (London), July 3, p. 8.

Schofer, Evan, and Meyer, John W. 2005, "The worldwide expansion of higher education in the twentieth century", *American Sociological Review*, vol. 70, no. 6 (December): 898–920.

Sinha, Vineeta 2003, "Decentring social sciences in practice through individual acts and choices", *Current Sociology* 51, no. 1 (January): 7–26.

——2006, "Problematizing received categories: Revisiting 'Folk Hinduism' and Sanskritization", *Current Sociology*, vol. 54, no. 1 (January): 98–111.

Smart, Ninian 1990, "Concluding reflections: Religious studies in global perspective", in King, Ursula (ed.), *Turning Points in Religious Studies: Essays in Honour of Geoffrey Parrinder*, Edinburgh: T. & T. Clark, pp. 299–306.

——1996, "Global Christian theology and education", in Astley, Jeff, and Francis, Leslie J. (eds), *Christian Theology and Religious Education: Connections and Contradictions*, London: SPCK, pp. 7–15.

——1999, *World Philosophies*, London: Routledge.

Ungureanu, Mihai Razvan 2006, Welcoming statement, Conference booklet, "Religious history of Europe and Asia/Histoire religieuse de l'Europe et de l'Asie, Bucharest, 20–23 September 2006", inside front cover.

Watson, James L. (ed.) 1997, *Golden Arches East: McDonald's in East Asia*, 2nd ed, Stanford, CA: Stanford University Press.

Werblowsky, R. J. Zwi 1960, "Marburg: And after?" *Numen*, vol. 7, no. 2. (December), pp. 215–20.

Index

References to end notes are given by the page number, followed by *n* and the number of the note, e.g. 157*n*6